Stephen Chambers

1982

8

GREECE
AND
ROME
AT
WAR

GREECE AND ROME AT WAR

Peter Connolly

Macdonald

© Macdonald Phoebus Ltd 1981

First published 1981
Macdonald Phoebus Ltd
Holywell House
Worship Street
London EC2A 2EN

Printed in Hong Kong

ISBN 0 356 06798 X

Contents

Peter Connolly has published three books on classical armies and armour which have made a lively contribution to a currently popular subject and have greatly helped in the wider diffusion of interest in it. This is due in part to his deep knowledge of ancient weaponry and the tactical problems of its manufacture and use, combined with great artistic skill and controlled imagination in presenting his material to his readers. He has now had the excellent idea of recasting and expanding this material in one larger volume. He provides a general sketch of the historical background from early Greek times to the fall of the Roman empire, which he expands in places to recount the course of some individual battles or campaigns in considerable detail. Here, despite the scale of his work, he has naturally had to be severely restrictive: thus in contrast to the relatively brief references to the campaigns of Alexander the Great, Julius Caesar or Pompey, the battles of the Greeks and Persians in 480–79 BC, and of Hannibal in the second Punic war, are treated very fully with discussion of some of the more detailed problems involved. Here Connolly's knowledge of the terrain and topography stand him in good stead, since he has tramped over a great number of ancient battlefields. The choice of these two wars, however, not only coincides with the author's own interests; they are also highly significant in their impact on world history. If the Persians had defeated the Greeks, would there have been a Periclean age of art and culture at Athens? Or if Hannibal had defeated the Romans, would most of western Europe now be speaking languages derived from Latin? Furthermore, the diagrammatic analyses of the organisation of the armies of, for example, Sparta or the Roman republic are helpful, while the dramatic reconstructions of a Macedonian phalanx or a Roman legion are most impressive and enable the reader to understand better the confession of Aemilius Paullus that he had never faced anything more terrifying than the advance of the Macedonian phalanx at the battle of Pydna.

Many works on the Roman army concentrate on the late republic and empire and skip lightly over the army that conquered Italy. Here not only is that army given due treatment, but also and equally important, its enemies are not forgotten. We are shown the fighting equipment of Etruscans, Aequi, Volsci, Samnites, Campanians,

Lucanians, Apulians, Celts and Carthaginians. Other topics are expounded in the same lucid manner: they include siege warfare and sieges (at considerable length), naval warfare and ship construction (here we may note the description of the ships recently found off the western coast of Sicily and the excavations that have revealed the history of the naval harbour at Carthage). Finally, Dr Brian Dobson and Dr Roger Tomlin have contributed very useful sections respectively on the organisation of the Roman imperial army and its later history.

It is perhaps in his treatment of arms and armour that Peter Connolly makes his greatest contribution. Thus in copying and testing a superb hoplite shield in the Vatican Museum (hitherto, I believe, unpublished) he discovered some of the ancient armourer's problems and the advantage of the sharp curve backwards on the inside edge of the wooden rim. Experiments also revealed both the problems faced by a Roman legionary when carrying the haft of his heavy *pilum* inside his shield, and also suggested possible solutions. An old problem is that of the so-called Boeotian shield with semi-circular slots in each side. It is depicted in paintings and on coins, but no examples survive: hence some believe that it is merely an artistic convention for a 'heroic' shield. Connolly, however, believes that the Thebans adopted a two-handed pike, but he found by experiment that it was physically impossible to grasp this with the left hand while holding an ordinary hoplite shield; this however could be done if the shield rim was notched as in the Boeotian shield. Thus whether he is right on this point or that, the reader is in the hands of a man who has a wide knowledge of the surviving physical remains of ancient weaponry, together with the technical problems of manufacture and subsequent use in the field. In the scholarly debate that surrounds so many battles, Peter Connolly stoutly maintains a position of his own, with full appreciation of the physical features involved (as for instance the ancient level of Lake Trasimene or the course of the river Ofanto at Cannae, or the site of Gerunium, which he 'sherded' to test the views of J. Kromayer). He has thus produced a splendid book which should appeal to a wide range of readers.

H. H. Scullard

The City States 800–360 BC

THRACE

MACEDONIA

•THERMA

SAMOTHRACE

HELLESPONT

VERGINA •

•POTIDAEA

•TROY

ASIA MINOR

MT OLYMPUS

TEMPE GORGE

THESSALY

CYME •
PHOCAEA •
SARDIS •

•SKIATHOS

•ARTEMISIUM

•AMBRACIA

TRACHIS • •THERMOPYLAE

LOCRIS   EUBOEA

IONIA

PHOCIS   ORCHOMENUS • •CHALCIS

DELPHI • •ANTICYRA   EURIPUS •ERETRIA

BOEOTIA   •THEBES

THESPIAE •   •TANAGRA

LEUKTRA • •PLATAEA

ATTICA •STYRA
•MARATHON

•ELEUSIS

SICYON •   •ATHENS

•CORINTH SALAMIS •PHALERUM

PHLIUS •   COLIAS PR •

AEGINA

SAMOS

MILETUS •

•MYCENAE
•ARGOS •EPIDAURUS

•OLYMPIA

MANTINAEA • •TROEZEN

ARCADIA

DELOS

LEPREUM •   •TEGEA   •HERMIONE

MESSENIA   LACONIA

•SPARTA

CRETE

Introduction

Soon after 1200 BC the great Bronze-Age civilisation which had flourished in Greece for several centuries went into a rapid decline and finally collapsed. Barbarous tribes poured southwards obliterating the last remnants of the Mycenaean culture, and a dark age descended on Greece. This book is a survey of the military systems that emerged from this dark age. An attempt is made to trace the development of military organisation, tactics and armament in Greece and Italy from the 8th century BC, when civilisation once more began to emerge in Greece, until the onset of the second dark age when the Roman empire in the West collapsed.

Both Greece and Rome had to face the supreme test. With Greece it was when the Persians invaded at the beginning of the 5th century, while Rome faced a similar crucial situation when the greatest of the ancient generals, Hannibal, invaded Italy 260 years later. Both these wars are examined in considerable detail to show how the two military systems rose to the situation. Most of Rome's organisation and equipment was borrowed from the nations with whom she came into conflict: the Etruscans, Samnites, Celts, Carthaginians and, of course, the Greeks. The contributions of each of these states will be examined in turn.

Already by the late Mycenaean period in the 13th and 12th centuries BC central European influences were being felt in the Aegean world. This continued in the succeeding centuries and, by the time that Homer's epic poems of the Mycenaean era, the *Iliad* and the *Odyssey*, were committed to writing, practically nothing of the ancient weaponry survived. For this reason, unless there is a clear derivation from the earlier period, the Bronze Age will be ignored. Our knowledge of the 8th and 7th centuries is very sparse but, by the 6th, we have a continuous written history.

The history of the 6th and 5th centuries is dominated first by the rise of Persia and later by the bitter war between Sparta and Athens. The period is very well documented by two great writers—Herodotus, who was alive at the time of the Persian invasion of Greece, and Thucydides, the greatest of the ancient historians, who was actually involved in the war between Sparta and Athens. To these one must add Xenophon, who wrote around the beginning of the 4th century BC. Xenophon's writings are not in the same class as Herodotus or Thucydides but he was a soldier and served for many years with the Spartans. He is thus an incomparable source of information about the Spartan military system.

These literary sources are supplemented by a mass of archaeological evidence. After a battle it was customary for the victor to dedicate some armour in a sanctuary such as Olympia. In time these shrines became so cluttered with armour that it became necessary to throw out the older pieces. At Olympia some were dumped in the streams and disused wells, whilst other pieces were used to reinforce the banks of the stadium. In recent years some of this armour has been recovered during excavations.

The States at War

When the Mycenaean states fell soon after 1200 BC, hordes of savage tribesmen, Greek speaking but from the mountainous north-western region, moved down into southern Greece. The most formidable of these invaders were the Dorians. Many of the original inhabitants fled from Greece and settled along the west coast of Asia Minor (Turkey) in the area that became known as Ionia.

The invasions and subsequent migrations came to an end about 1000 BC. This was followed by a period of settlement. Finally, order began to return. The little states which emerged consisted of several villages with their land under the control of a hereditary warlord. These gradually consolidated until, by the 8th century, a political structure which was to characterise Greece began to emerge. This was the *polis* or city state where the government of an area settled on a single town. Gradually powerful cities began to absorb their neighbours; the foremost of these were Sparta and Athens. In Athens, the king was subsequently ousted and supplanted by the nobility. In time they, too, were thrown out and control taken over by a demagogic dictator, or tyrant. Finally the tyrant was overthrown and democracy established. This last step was only achieved on the eve of the Persian wars.

Athens gained control of the whole of Attica during this period, and, by 500 BC, she was becoming the cultural centre of the Hellenic world and the most powerful state in central Greece.

Sparta, on the other hand, had a very different development. The Spartans were descended from the Dorian invaders who had conquered Laconia. They had enslaved part of the native population and subjected the rest. The enslaved population were called *helots*. They were tied to the land and compelled to work the state-owned farms which provided the Spartans with their livelihood. The subject peoples, called *perioeci*, were allowed a measure of independence but were compelled to provide soldiers to fight on the Spartan side. The Spartans were commanded in battle by two hereditary kings. By the end of the 7th century Sparta had overcome Messenia to the west and gained control of the whole of the southern Peloponnesus. Over the next 100 years, either by coercion or persuasion, she managed to unite the states of the Peloponnesus into a league known to the ancients as 'the Lacedaemonians and their allies', but called today simply the Peloponnesian League.

In the middle of the 6th century, the tyrant Peisistratus seized power at Athens, which he, and later his son Hippias, governed intermittently for half a century until deposed by the Spartan king Cleomenes when he invaded Attica in 511 BC. In the wake of the tyrants civil strife broke out as democrat and oligarch struggled for power. When the oligarch Isagoras was thrown out, he appealed to his personal friend Cleomenes for assistance. Cleomenes, with a small body of retainers, again invaded Attica, and so great was the aura of Sparta that he took the city without a blow and garrisoned the Acropolis.

When the Athenians discovered the paltry size of Cleomenes' party, they besieged the Acropolis and Cleomenes, in the face of starvation, was forced to surrender. Fearing reprisals, the Athenians felt obliged to release the king and his retainers. Enraged at his humiliation Cleomenes returned to Sparta and mobilised the entire Peloponnesian League against Athens. Accompanied by the other king Demaratus, he led his army towards the borders of Attica. In the north Thebes and Chalcis, Athens' commercial rival, seized the opportunity to strike at their enemy and also mobilised, but before the assault could be launched dissension broke out in the Peloponnesian ranks. Many of the allied states refused to fight Cleomenes' personal wars for him. Demaratus took their side and the army broke up. The Athenians could hardly have believed their good fortune and had the presence of mind to capitalise on the situation. They marched north and in the same day defeated both the Thebans and the Chalcidians, reducing the latter to the status of a colony. Thebes continued the war and was later joined by another of Athens' commercial rivals, the island of Aegina. It was during this war that Athens emerged as a military power. Her struggle with Aegina forced her to build a navy which, in a few short years, was to become the strongest in Greece.

The rise of Persia
Meanwhile, events in Asia were beginning to have an effect on Greece. At the end of the 7th century BC the great empire of Assyria had fallen and, by the middle of the succeeding century, a new giant had arisen which was to absorb all the previous empires. This was Persia. In 546 the Lydian empire fell and the Great King Darius overran Asia Minor (Turkey). One by one the Greek cities along the coast fell to the Persians. Some, in desperation, took to the sea. The Phocaeans, like the legendary Aeneas, crossed the Aegean and the Adriatic and finally settled at the colony of Alalia in Corsica. However they were moved on by the Etruscans in 535 and ultimately joined the colony of Massilia (Marseilles) on the southern coast of France.

In 510, when all the islands along the coast of Asia Minor were in Persian hands, Darius invaded Europe. Pushing up the west coast of the Black Sea, he crossed the Danube and invaded Scythia. Next Thrace was overrun and Macedonia forced to submit. Only Thessaly now stood between the Greek states and Persia. In 500 the Greek states in Asia Minor, led by Miletus, revolted and looked for help from the west. Athens and Eretria on the west coast of Euboea sent expeditionary

forces to Ionia which resulted in the sacking and burning of Sardis, capital of the Persian satrapy.

The Persians ruthlessly put down the revolt. Miletus was overthrown and its population sold into slavery. By 494 the revolt was over and the Persians prepared for a punitive expedition against Greece.

An embassy was sent to Greece demanding earth and water, the traditional symbols of submission. Although practically all the Greek states refused, Aegina, which had trading links with the east, submitted. Aegina lies in the Saronic gulf only ten kilometres off the Attic coast and controls access to Athens' harbours. With the island under Persian control Athens would be strangled. Aegina was a member of the Peloponnesian League and Athens appealed to her old enemy Cleomenes. The Spartan king took up the Athenian cause but once again he came into conflict with his colleague Demaratus. The enmity which had smouldered between the two since the abortive attempt to invade Attica some 17 years before now burst into flame. Cleomenes laid charges of illegitimacy against his colleague and Demaratus was deposed. The former king fled Greece and took refuge with the Persians. Cleomenes, freed of his partner, forcibly returned Aegina to its former loyalties and patched up an alliance with Athens against the threatened invasion. The Persians obviously intended only a limited punitive operation against Athens and Eretria which had aided the Ionian revolt.

In 490 the Persians launched a seaborne attack. Eretria was sacked and the fleet moved down to the bay of Marathon ready for the strike against Athens. The Athenians sent a runner to Sparta and marched out to meet the invaders. What happened at Marathon is confused and the truth will probably never be known. The Spartans delayed their march because they were celebrating a festival and arrived too late for the battle. To their astonishment they discovered that the Athenians had decisively defeated the Persians and driven them out of Attica.

The defeat at Marathon served only to irritate the Persians. All knew that the matter was unsettled, but it was ten years before a second attempt was made. In

the meantime Athens was able to build up her fleet until it was equal to the combined fleets of all the other Greek states.

When it became obvious that the Persian invasion was imminent, a congress was assembled at the isthmus of Corinth to try to settle the internal differences of the Greek states so that they could present a united front.

In the spring of 480 BC the Persian king Xerxes, accompanied by Demaratus, the deposed king of Sparta, crossed the Hellespont. His vast army advanced on Greece with the fleet following along the coast. The army forced its way through Thrace and down into Macedonia, building up the road as it advanced. Herodotus says that the Thracians were so overawed that even in his own day they would not dig or sow the area through which the army passed.

The Persian army
The ancient Greeks believed that Xerxes' army numbered three million plus camp followers—Herodotus gives the total as five and a quarter million, but he is clearly a little sceptical about how such an army could be fed. At the end of the 1920s, General Sir Frederick Maurice made a detailed study of Xerxes' route from the Hellespont, examining in particular the problem of water supply, and concluded that the Persian army could not have numbered more than 210,000 men plus 75,000 animals. It seems probable that the rainfall at this time was considerably higher than today (see p. 157), therefore these figures could be increased slightly. Even so, the figure could hardly have been over 250,000. Of this number about three-quarters would have been combatants.

The Persian army was a polyglot affair drawn from all quarters of a vast empire. Like the Romans, the Persians demanded troops from their subject races. The vast majority of the Persian army were light-armed skirmishers, either archers from central Asia or javelineers from the eastern Mediterranean. The Persians and Medes who formed the nucleus of the army wore loose caps, multicoloured, long-sleeved tunics (beneath which was a scale shirt) and breeches. They carried wicker shields, probably covered with hide, which were

somewhat similar in appearance to the Boeotian shields; this was a central-handgrip type on to which was stitched a metal boss. Their weapons consisted of a short spear about 2m in length, a long composite bow with bronze-tipped reed arrows and a dagger which hung on the right side.

The élite of the Persian army were the king's personal bodyguard, the 10,000 Immortals, so called because their strength was always kept up to this number. Their equipment differed from other Persians only in the richness of its accoutrements. The Persian cavalry was armed in the same fashion as the infantry except that some wore metal helmets. Herodotus claims that the Persian cavalry numbered 80,000, but 8,000 may be a more reasonable estimate.

Herodotus gives the size of the Persian fleet as 1,207 triremes, including 300 Phoenician vessels, 200 Egyptian and 290 Ionian Greek. It seems probable that the historian is here recording the paper strength of the Persian Mediterranean fleet and not the operational number, as it is clear from the later engagements that the Persians did not have a massive numerical superiority.

The principal vessel of the day was the trireme. This was a galley propelled by about 170 oars at three different levels. At the front of the ship, at water level, was a bronze-plated beak which was used to hole and sink enemy ships. This type of ship, varying only superficially, was used by all the Mediterranean fleets of the time. All these galleys carried a complement of marines whose job it was to try to board and capture the enemy ships. Greek ships carried ten hoplites and four archers, whereas the Ionian ships each carried 30 to 40 marines. These marines were armed mainly with spears, javelins and poleaxes.

The defence of Greece

Faced with invasion, Athens and Sparta had buried their differences. Athens had even gone so far as to place her entire military strength, ships as well as men, under Spartan command. It was decided to stop the Persian army at the Tempe Gorge, a narrow defile at the south end of Mount Olympus. A force of 10,000 hoplites was despatched and in position before the Persians had even crossed the Hellespont. These forces could have held the narrow passes to the south and west of Mount Olympus indefinitely. But, for some reason—perhaps because the troops did not like fighting so far from home—this forward position was abandoned. Herodotus suggests that the army withdrew because the Persian fifth column was already operating in the area and the southern Greeks felt they could not trust their northern allies. Herodotus also mentions the fear that the Persian fleet might outflank them and land troops further down the coast. In the unrestricted area along the coast the Greek fleet could not guarantee to stop the Persians doing this and it was probably the main reason for the withdrawal.

Thessaly was abandoned. This had serious repercussions among the allies. Many of the northern towns believed that Sparta only intended to make her real stand at the isthmus of Corinth, and in fact many of the Peloponnesians openly advocated this line. As a result many of the northern towns decided to submit. In order to halt this defection it was finally decided to make a stand at Thermopylae, a place whose name has become a byword for heroism.

Top
A Persian spearman/archer. This probably represents an 'Immortal', one of the 10,000 élite personal bodyguards of the Persian king. From Susa, 5th century BC. Now in the Louvre, Paris.

Above
1, 2, 3. Two arrow heads and a sling shot from Marathon. British Museum. **4** Arrow head from the 'last stand' hillock at Thermopylae. National Archaeological Museum, Athens. **5** Persian shield boss from Samos.

Above
Eastern helmet, possibly Phoenician, found at Olympia. Probably from the battle of Marathon. The dedication reads: 'To Zeus the Athenians dedicate these spoils from the Medes'. Archaeological Museum, Olympia.

At Thermopylae the mountains come in close to the sea, leaving only two possible routes south—one along the coast and the other a very difficult route over the mountains. Today there is a marshy plain between the hills and the sea, brought about by the silting of the river Spercheius; in the 5th century BC there was only a narrow passage between the hills and the sea. These hills, the Callidromus range, stretch in an east-west direction down the coast and at three points they come very close to the sea. The first of these (the west gate) is at the very beginning of the pass. Herodotus describes this as so narrow that there was only room for a single cartway. Here the hills are not very high and could easily be crossed. Beyond the west gate the pass widens. Here was situated the ancient village of Anthela. Two and a half kilometres beyond the west gate lay the village of Thermopylae, named after the hot springs which still rise there today. The calcium carbonate in these thermal springs gives the landscape the appearance of crusty grey rock. A great cliff, known as Zastano, towers nearly 1,000m above Thermopylae.

This cliff is the key to the pass. A short distance beyond the cliff a spur juts out towards the sea (this is the middle pass). Along this spur the people of Phocis had constructed a wall stretching out into the marshes to stop the Malians invading their country. Anyone wishing to bypass this point would have to negotiate the Zastano cliff. About three kilometres farther along the pass is a third narrow point (the east gate) with the ancient village of Alpeni built on a spur jutting out into the marshes. Here the hills are low and easy to cross.

As mentioned before, there was another steep and difficult route into central Greece at the west end of the range. This route follows the valley of the Asopus, which passes through a precipitous gorge. Today the railway and road both follow this route, the former passing through a tunnel on the west side of the gorge, whilst the latter climbs up the hillside on the east of the ravine and then runs over the hills above the gorge. This route was guarded by the ancient citadel of Trachis built on top of the steep cliffs overlooking the west side of the gorge. No commander would attempt to force a passage at this point in the face of determined and well-organised opposition.

A short distance off the coast lies the long island of Euboea, which stretches for 175km in a south-easterly direction, leaving only a narrow channel between the island and the mainland. Here, unlike the original position at Tempe, it was possible for the Greek fleet to prevent the Persian navy bypassing the Greek army on the mainland. This, then, was the area where the Greeks elected to halt the Persian advance.

An advance guard was immediately sent out to man the pass until the rest of the army could be brought up. Cleomenes had met a violent end seven years earlier and had been succeeded by his younger brother Leonidas. It was this new Spartan king who marched north with his bodyguard of 300, the *hippeis*, to hold the pass.

Below
A model of the pass at Thermopylae as it probably appeared c.500 BC. The Persians were encamped in the plain on the left. The Phocian wall is (**A**) and the hillock where the Spartans made their last stand (**B**).

With the Spartans were 2,800 other Peloponnesians. The war memorial seen by Herodotus at Thermopylae records 4,000 Peloponnesians—900 more than he lists; this may include the *helots* who accompanied every Spartan army.

As they advanced northward they were joined by 700 Thespians and 400 Thebans. This army was finally swelled by 1,000 Phocians and the complete army of the Locrians. Each group served under its own *strategos*, or general.

The Greek hoplite used a spear about 2.5m long, giving him the advantage in reach over his Persian opponent. He was heavily armed with a round shield 80–90cm in diameter, a cuirass, helmet and greaves (leg guards). He also carried a sword which he would only use if his spear broke. He fought in phalanx, or formation, about eight ranks deep. This phalanx was probably organised in units of 100 (*lochoi*) which were subdivided into four smaller units, each of three files of eight plus a rear-rank officer. The officer commanding each file fought in the front rank. This system may have varied slightly from state to state, and the Spartans seem to have confused the issue by applying the name of *lochos* to the five major divisions of their army (see p. 41).

The soldiers who joined Leonidas at Thermopylae were told that they were only the advance guard for the rest of the army. When they reached the pass they established a supply base in the village of Alpeni at the east gate and took up their position at the middle gate. They then set about repairing the wall which the Phocians had built. This wall was excavated just before the Second World War; remains were discovered only on the top of the ridge. The wall started with a tower and then zigzagged down the hill. It must have continued across the level ground and probably finished with another tower in the marshes. There is a narrow gateway next to the tower on the ridge, and Herodotus claims there were several more. The 1,000 Phocians were placed on top of the mountain to counter any Persian attempt to turn the Spartan position by forcing their way up the Asopus valley.

The combined Greek fleet, consisting of 271 triremes, took up position at Artemisium at the north end of Euboea. Of these 127 were from Athens. This was not the total muster—later, a further 80 ships were sent to Artemisium, of which 53 were Athenian. They had been held back in case the Persian fleet tried to sail round Euboea. This number was swelled by volunteers from Greek cities in Italy and desertions from Greek islands held by the Persians to bring the total up to 368, of which almost half were Athenian.

The Greek fleet, like the army, was under the overall command of a Spartan, Eurybiadas, whilst each of the squadrons from the various cities was under the command of its own admiral. The Athenian fleet was commanded by the wily Themistocles, who had played such an important part in building up the Athenian navy.

The Greek fleet, as it could travel faster, may have taken up its position at

Below
The pass of Thermopylae seen from the 'last stand' hillock. The cliffs of Zastano, towering nearly 1,000m over Thermopylae, rise on the left. The ancient coastline would have been just to the right of the modern road.

TEMPE GORGE

C PORI

THESSALY

MAGNESIAN PR

SKIATHOS

CAPE ARTEMISION
•ARTEMISIUM

R. Spercheius
MALIAN GULF
ASOPUS
TRACHIS• •THERMOPYLAE
MT. CALLIDROMUS **LOCRIS**
MT. OETA

EUBOEA

PHOCIS

•DELPHI

•CHALCIS
ERETRIA

BOEOTIA
•THEBES TANAGRA
•THESPIAE SCOLUS
LEUCTRA• •ERYTHRAE
HYSIAE
PLATAEA MT. PASTRA
MT. CITHAERON GYPHTOCASTRO MT. PARNES
•MARATHON

ELEUSIS

MEGARA **ATTICA**
PIRAEUS •ATHENS
SALAMIS •PHALERUM
•CORINTH

AEGINA

PELOPONNESUS
C. SUNIUM

•TROEZEN

Artemisium shortly before the land force reached Thermopylae. The site of the temple of Artemis, from which Artemisium got its name, has now been established with reasonable certainty. Its position is marked by the chapel of Agios Georgios on the hills between Asmini and Kurbatsi. The Greek anchorage can therefore be identified as the broad, open beach at Pevki Bay, which is ideally suited for the purpose. West of Pevki the beaches stretch out in an almost unbroken line along the north coast of Euboea, and the Greek ships would have had ample space to beach in a single line. Lookout posts were established on the hills. One of these must certainly have been placed above Cape Artemision, ten kilometres east of Pevki Bay. Another was posted on the island of Skiathos, which lies four kilometres off the headland of Magnesia. As the Persian fleet sailed south it would have to pass between Skiathos and the mainland in order to enter the Euboean channel. When the Persians were sighted, the lookouts on Skiathos would signal with beacons and the observation post above Cape Artemision would relay the message to the fleet at Pevki. Three ships were also posted at Skiathos to keep watch in case conditions were unsuitable for signalling.

Two light galleys, one stationed at Pevki and the other at Thermopylae, were used to maintain communications between the land and sea forces. Having established their positions the Greeks settled down to await the arrival of the Persians.

Xerxes advances into Greece

Xerxes, meanwhile, was at Therma (modern Saloniki) with both the fleet and the army. When he advanced into Thessaly the two arms of his force would be separated and would only be able to rejoin at the Euboean channel. At Therma the final plans for the invasion of the peninsula would have been worked out. As the army moved more slowly, it set out 11 days before the fleet. The two forces probably agreed to meet

in the Malian gulf on the fourteenth day, after the army had secured anchorages there for the fleet.

Xerxes already knew that the passes into Thessaly were not occupied and he entered the plain without opposition. As he advanced south his scouts informed him that the Spartans were holding the pass at Thermopylae. Herodotus records the story that the Great King sent out a horseman to reconnoitre the Greek position. This scout advanced to a position from which he could see the wall across the middle gate but was unable to see into the Greek camp. It was the Spartan day for duty. The Lacedaemonians had piled their arms outside the wall and were either stripped off exercising or combing their long hair. When Xerxes heard this he called Demaratus to ask him what it meant. The exiled king explained that it was the Spartan custom to comb their hair before putting their lives at risk. This story is probably apocryphal, but it illustrates the awe in which the Spartans were held by their fellow Greeks.

Xerxes reached the plain of Lamia 14 days after leaving Therma. He had covered the 280km at the rate of 20km a day. The army camped in front of Trachis and waited for the fleet to join them.

The Persian navy had sent out ten fast galleys to reconnoitre the coast. These advanced as far as Skiathos unnoticed and pounced on the three Greek galleys posted there to keep watch. When the lookouts on the island signalled to the fleet at Pevki, Herodotus claims that the Greeks panicked and withdrew down the channel to Chalcis, leaving the Spartan flank uncovered. Before rejecting this out of hand, it must be remembered that fire signalling at this time could only convey a single message (see p. 275) and the Greeks may have thought the dreaded Persians were upon them. The main Persian fleet sailed from Therma on the twelfth day after the army had left. It reached the area of Keramidhi just north of Cape Pori and stopped for the night. Here the beaches are very sparse and only the first arrivals could be pulled clear of the water, the rest having to ride at anchor eight deep. It was a clear, calm night but at dawn a storm got up and many of the ships were dashed on the rocky

coast. The storm lasted for three days, but on the fourth the fleet was able to set out again, round the promontory of Magnesia and beach at Aphetae. On the second day of the storm the watchers on the heights of Euboea had informed the Greek fleet of the shipwreck of the Persian fleet. Encouraged by this news the Greek ships returned to their original station at Artemisium.

This passage has been called into question by historians, and with some justification. It is possible that the lookouts on Skiathos, if they were still there after the capture of the three ships, might have seen a wreck or two. However, even on the clearest of days it would have been impossible to see a wrecked galley from a distance of about ten kilometres, let alone in a storm. They could therefore have had no idea of the extent of the damage. This part of the story is probably an attempt to account for the Greek fleet being back at Artemisium when the Persians reached Aphetae. The retreat to Chalcis is probably a complete fiction. Herodotus has also probably exaggerated the effect of the storm; the Persian fleet was probably never as big as he claimed. He knew that the fleet at Aphetae did not greatly outnumber the Greeks, so he has tried to reduce it to a more realistic size by wrecking a large part of it in the storm. He calmly wrecks another 200 galleys only a couple of days later.

The battle for Thermopylae

It was well into August when Xerxes reached the plain of Lamia. He hoped that when his army was assembled, its sheer size would cause the Greeks in the pass to lose heart and desert their posts. The Great King waited for four days, probably anticipating the arrival of the fleet. When they did not show up, and the Greeks remained obstinately lodged in the pass, he rather flamboyantly ordered forward his Medes and Cissians (who were similarly armed, but the latter wore turbans), with orders to 'bring them back alive'.

The Medes launched a series of charges which failed to make any impression on the Greeks. When Xerxes saw that the Greeks were holding firm, he sounded the recall and sent forward his personal bodyguard, the Immortals, led by their commander Hydarnes. Ten thousand crack troops of the greatest army that the world had ever seen marched out to do their king's bidding. To those who watched from the Persian camp as they moved forward, it must have seemed impossible that they could fail.

As the Immortals advanced, the Spartans passed through the wall to meet them. For all the aura that surrounded the Immortals, they could achieve nothing against the heavily armed Spartans. In the confined space of the pass their numbers were of no advantage and, because their spears were shorter than those of the Greeks, they were unable to engage them at close quarters. Herodotus here records the favourite Spartan trick of pretending to run away and then turning and catching the pursuing enemy unawares, but it seems most unlikely that this manoeuvre could have been carried out in these conditions and in such a cramped space. Also, as the Greeks were fighting a defensive action, it was essential that they kept their formation; any breaking of ranks would have presented the Persians with their chance.

On the following day the Persians attacked. Each Greek contingent fought them in turn. Although a few Greeks had been killed, at the end of the day the Persians were no nearer their objective.

The Persian fleet arrives

The Persian fleet arrived at Aphetae 16 days after the army had left Therma. The site where the fleet beached is uncertain; Herodotus says that it was about 80 *stades* (15km) from Artemisium and had a good supply of water. About 80 *stades* must be interpreted as between 70 and 90 *stades* (13–17km). This limits the site to Olizon or Platania Bay. W. K. Pritchett, who has spent many years tramping over Greek battlefields, convincingly argues in favour of the Platania site because of its larger water supply. Platania Bay consists of a series of small beaches separated by rocky promontories. The largest of these beaches is only about 450m long. This beach, which is just west of Platania, has a spring. Platania itself has a small stream. Since it was essential for the Persians to beach their galleys if they were not to lose any more to the weather, they would have needed a considerable

space to accommodate the whole fleet. None of the beaches at Platania is deep enough for more than one line of ships. If the fleet were only 450 strong, allowing a minimum of 7m per ship the line would stretch for more than three kilometres.

Platania Bay itself could only hold about 80 galleys, and the bay to the west about 65. This means that the rest of the fleet must have been beached, probably squadron by squadron, along the tiny beaches to the west of Platania stretching down as far as Olizon Bay six kilometres west of Platania. These beaches are very narrow and it would only have been possible to pull the stern of the ship clear of the water. The beaches slope quite steeply at the water's edge, which would mean that the prows of the galleys would have been completely afloat. This was probably normal practice when battle was imminent, allowing the ships to be launched easily and quickly. The supply ships were probably moored just offshore.

The Greeks on the south side of the channel had one great advantage over their adversaries on the north. For most of the day the haze makes it impossible to see across the channel from the north, whereas one gets a perfect view from the south side. So the Greeks could observe the Persian movements without being seen themselves, and they used this to

great effect.

The Persians feared that, if they attacked, the Greeks would withdraw into the narrows of the Euboean channel some 20km to the east. Here, where the narrows are only three kilometres wide, they could either stand and fight or slip away. The Greeks had chosen their position well, for this escape route was always open to them. The Persians could hardly sail down the channel before they had destroyed the Greek force, as the Greeks could then attack the rear half of the fleet when the front half was already in the channel. The Persians therefore decided to try to turn the Greek position by sending a force around Euboea to occupy the channel. On the afternoon of their arrival they despatched 200 ships to cruise off the island of Skiathos, apparently guarding the channel for the stragglers who were still coming in. (The figure of 200 should be treated with caution.) These then sailed round behind the island and, keeping sufficiently far out to sea to remain out of sight of the watchpost above Cape Artemision, set off down the east coast of Euboea. The Greek lookout post on Skiathos had

Below
Map showing the relative positions of the various forces during the battle for Thermopylae. **A** Leonidas; **B** Xerxes; **C** Greek fleet; **D** Persian fleet. The Spartan stand at Thermopylae has become a byword for heroism.

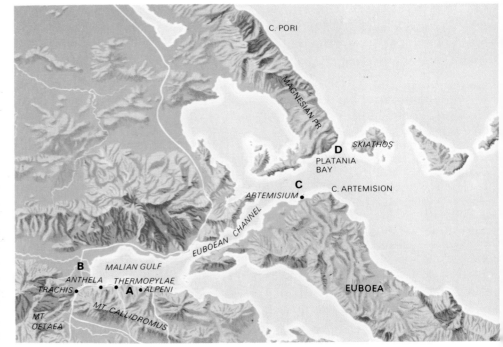

obviously been abandoned as the Greeks only learned what had happened from a deserter. This post had probably been withdrawn after the three watch ships at the island had been captured.

The deserter who informed the Greeks was a man called Scyllias, the greatest diver of his day. He had escaped by swimming the Euboean channel. The Greeks immediately sent a fast ship down through the Euripus to inform the 53 Athenian ships which had been held back in anticipation of the Persian move.

Fifteen Persian ships had been delayed at their anchorage farther up the coast and did not set out to join the main fleet at Aphetae until long after the other ships had left. These latecomers did not reach the channel between Skiathos and the mainland until late in the afternoon, when their view west was blinded by the glare of the setting sun. They failed to see their companions in the shadows at Platania Bay but did see the Greek vessels shining in the evening sun to the south-west. Mistaking them for the Persian navy, they held their course and sailed straight into the arms of the Greeks. This is interesting as it limits

the extent of the Persian anchorage to the east. If there had been any ships east of Platania they were bound to be seen, whereas the anchorage at Platania was shielded by a promontory at the east end.

Unfortunately, Herodotus' parallel diaries for the fleet and army break down at this point and he appears to lose two days. The fleet arrived at Aphetae on the sixteenth day after the army set out from Therma. The events of this and the succeeding three days seem to have been condensed into two days. A. R. Burn in his book *Persia and the Greeks* has made a detailed examination of these events and suggested a reconstruction which has generally been followed here.

The next day (the seventeenth) the Persians, who were waiting for their detachment to round Euboea, made no attempt to attack the Greek fleet. Late in the afternoon the Greeks launched their ships and rowed out into the channel, planning on a limited engagement to test the enemy's mettle and get some experience of their tactics.

When the Persians saw the Greek fleet approaching, they put to sea. The

Greeks had probably been rowing in a diamond formation. The enemy ships, putting out from their various anchorages, tried to use their superior numbers and greater manoeuvrability to surround them. As the enemy ships approached, the Greek ships, acting on a signal from Eurybiadas' flagship, turned their prows outwards, at the same time drawing their sterns together to form a circle. Then, on a second signal, they charged the lighter Persian ships head on. The Persians, who had expected an easy victory, had walked straight into the trap. Having moved right in close on the Greek ships, they were now unable to manoeuvre and use their superior seamanship; they were forced to fight on the Greek terms. When, shortly afterwards, darkness began to descend the battle was broken off. The Greeks rowed back to Artemisium elated with their success—they had captured 30

Below
The site of the Persian anchorage at Platania Bay at the southern tip of the Magnesian promontory. About 80 galleys were beached here. The remainder were strung out along smaller bays to the west as far as Olizon Bay.

enemy vessels and damaged or sunk several more. Herodotus does not state the Greek losses but several of their ships must have been sunk.

That night a violent sou'wester sprang up accompanied by torrential rain. The wind blew the wreckage from the battle into the Persian anchorages and it became entangled in the ships which were only half beached.

Although the fleet at Aphetae suffered considerably, their troubles were as nothing compared with the plight of their companions trying to round the southern end of Euboea. They were caught by the full force of the storm and dashed on to the rocky coast at the south end of the island.

Herodotus states that the following morning the 53 Athenian ships which had been left to watch the southern end of Euboea sailed into Artemisium bringing the news of the total destruction of the Persian detachment. This is impossible and clearly a day has been lost. In all likelihood nothing happened on this day as both sides repaired their storm damage. It would be the following morning, the nineteenth, that the

Athenian ships arrived bringing the news of the shipwreck.

Late that afternoon the reinforced Greek fleet once more rowed out into the channel. This time, probably because of the haze, they managed to cross the channel unobserved and swooped upon the Cilician galleys which were still at their moorings, destroyed some of the ships and then withdrew into the dusk. It is possible that the Cilician squadron was moored in Olizon Bay and that the Greek fleet was able to sail unobserved past Cape Griba, round the western headland and into the bay to attack the Cilician squadron before it could be manned. This is feasible as they would have been approaching out of the setting sun.

The end of Thermopylae
Meanwhile, at Thermopylae the second day's fighting had come to an end. Day after day Leonidas had sent messengers south pleading for reinforcements but it was now clear that none were coming. The Spartans were on their own and their code of honour expressly forbade them to desert their posts. Xerxes and

his advisers had probably been aware since soon after their arrival that there was a route over the mountain which could be used to outflank the Spartans in the pass. The Callidromus mountain is laced with paths varying from steep and narrow goat tracks to fairly wide paths. The trouble was that the mountain was densely forested and it would be impossible to find one's way across without a guide. Today, when a great deal of deforestation has taken place, it is still easy to lose one's way up there, even in daylight.

At last the Persians found a local peasant named Ephialtes who informed them that there was indeed a route known as the Anopaea path, and that for a price he would lead them across.

That night, as soon as it was dark, Hydarnes led the Immortals out of camp and, with Ephialtes showing the way, began the ascent of the mountain.

Below
The view across the Euboean channel from the Athenian position at Pevki Bay. The Persian anchorage to the right of centre on the opposite side of the strait is as clearly visible as it was to the Greeks.

All night long the Persians toiled up the winding path until, at last, as the sky began to grey in the east, the ground levelled off and they entered a small plain. They were plodding along beneath oak trees. Last year's leaves lay thick on the ground and rustled beneath their feet. Ahead of them there was a movement and voices broke the silence; then they saw Greek hoplites hastily donning their armour. Hydarnes asked who these men were, adding in consternation, 'Are they Spartans?' These were in fact the 1,000 Phocians whom Leonidas had detailed to cover the mountain path. Having established their identity, Hydarnes arrayed his men for battle and showered the Phocians with arrows.

The Phocians, forgetting their mission, became convinced that they were the Immortals' prime target, withdrew to the top of the hill and there prepared to sell their lives dearly. With the route clear the Persians ignored the Phocians on the hill and pushed on over the mountain.

The route taken by the Immortals has provoked a great deal of debate. In recent years Pritchett has made a very detailed study of the site and has suggested a route which seems to satisfy most of the criteria. Herodotus claims that Hydarnes took with him the men he commanded, i.e. the 10,000 Immortals. There seems no reason to doubt this. If the route were a narrow goat track where the men could only march in single file, then the column would have stretched out for ten kilometres or more. This is unacceptable, and Pritchett concludes that one must be looking for a broad path where the soldiers could march three or four abreast.

There is one point in Herodotus' topography which is easy to identify: 'It begins at the river Asopus which flows through the ravine.' The site of the Asopus gorge can hardly be in question. He continues that the Persians crossed the Asopus before starting the ascent. This conclusively places them on the east side of the gorge. There is a very easy route up the hillside about one kilometre east of the Asopus gorge. This is both the shortest and the easiest route up the mountainside from the Lamian plain. It leads by way of the Chalkomata spring to the village of Eleutherochori, where there are the remains of an ancient fort covering the beginning of the route. This proves that the path was in use in ancient times.

Herodotus describes the Persians as marching all night with the mountains of the Oetaeans on the right and those of the Trachinians on their left. On the face of it this is impossible to reconcile with any of the suggested routes over the mountains, particularly if the Persians crossed the Asopus before they started the ascent, for Trachis and Mount Oeta are both west of the Asopus gorge. However, since Thermopylae itself was in the territory of Trachis and Mount Oeta must surely be included amongst the mountains of the Oetaeans, one must conclude that the mountains of Trachis included the northern part of the Callidromus range. This is admittedly clumsy but there seems to be no other explanation, especially as Herodotus says the Persians marched 'all night' between these mountains. If this is the right explanation, then the march would be in a southerly direction along the west side of Mount Callidromus.

Herodotus also describes the route as passing along the backbone of the mountain. This is an accurate description of the route from Eleutherochori across the Nevropolis plain to the pass between the Liathitsa and Callidromus peaks. This route follows the plateau just below the ridge of the mountain on the south side. The Phocians, according to Herodotus, were stationed in a position from which they could defend the route over the mountains and the route to their own country. This can be no other place than the Nevropolis plain, which lies about two kilometres from the summit of the pass. Here there is a small lake which today dries out in the summer but may not have in ancient times. There is also a spring which would give an ample supply of drinking water for the 1,000 hoplites. The path from Phocis joins the Anopaea route at this point; if the Phocians had taken up their positions any nearer the pass, they would have

Left
The plain of Nevropolis just to the south of the Liathitsa-Callidromus pass. Its position at the junction of the route to the pass and the route to Phocis make it the most likely site for the Phocian position.

been cut off from the route to Phocis. Furthermore, any route over the Liathitsa-Callidromus pass would have to go this way. Both Burn and Pritchett are agreed that the Phocians took up their 'do or die' position on Mount Liathitsa to the north of the path, and this would certainly fit Herodotus' description.

The Persians would have reached the top of the pass about three-quarters of an hour later—about half past six in the morning.

Leonidas received the news that the Immortals were crossing the mountains first from deserters, who came in during the night, and then from lookouts posted on the heights who ran down to inform him just after dawn. The Greek commanders immediately held a council. Most were for withdrawing while they still had a chance. Leonidas, when he saw that their hearts were not in it, sent them on their way. As a Spartan, he

Left

The last day at Thermopylae. Leonidas and the remnants of his tiny army advance into the open ground ahead of the wall determined to sell their lives dearly. A desperate struggle raged over Leonidas' body after he fell.

Below

The site of the Spartan last stand. The hillock, a small mound rising some 15m above the battleground, was identified for certain just before the Second World War, when it was excavated and hundreds of Persian arrow heads discovered.

could never desert his post. The 700 Thespians and 400 Thebans remained with him. Herodotus suggests that Leonidas forced the Thebans to stay with him and adds that they deserted before the final battle.

As they ate their last meal together, Leonidas is supposed to have said, 'Have a good breakfast, lads; we shall dine in Hades'. It would take the Immortals several hours to get down from the heights and the Spartans intended to make the Persians pay dearly before they died.

Having gained the top of the mountain the Persians started the descent. Herodotus says that the Anopaea path came down into the pass at Alpeni. The site of this town has been established with some degree of certainty on a ridge jutting out into the marshes about three kilometres east of the Phocian wall at the site of the east gate. There is an easy descent to Alpeni going over the back of Zastano and on down through Drakospilia. It is about 12km long and probably took the Persians three to four hours to negotiate.

Xerxes held back his attack until midmorning. When his troops entered the pass the Spartans no longer tried to defend the wall but advanced along the pass to its widest point and here drew up in normal phalanx with the lighter-armed *helots* covering the wings. Here

they fought with reckless frenzy. The Persians, we are told, had to be driven on with scourges and clambered over the piles of their dead to get at the Greeks. Soon most of the Greek spears were broken and the hoplites drew their swords and moved in closer, hacking at the sea of faces before them. Here Leonidas fell and the battle raged over his corpse as Greek and Persian struggled for possession of the body. Four times the Persians captured it and four times the Greeks dragged it back again. So the struggle persisted until lookouts brought the news that the Immortals had reached the bottom of the path. The Greeks closed ranks and retreated towards the wall. They passed through the gates and withdrew to a small hillock rising about 15m above the marshy ground where they formed a circle and prepared to die. The Persians swarmed through the wall and tried to clamber up the hillside but they were driven back. At first the Greeks defended themselves with their swords, but when these broke they attacked their assailants with their fists and teeth. They fought on until they were overwhelmed by the hail of missiles. By midday all was still.

Herodotus records a story of two Spartans who at the time of the last stand were lying ill with ophthalmia at Alpeni. The first, named Eurytus, on learning that the Persians had crossed

the mountains, called for his armour and, though he could not see, ordered his *helot* to lead him into the thick of the battle. The second, Aristodemus, lost his courage and slipped away with the other escaping allies. When he returned to Sparta he was disgraced and was only able to redeem himself by his extraordinary courage at the battle of Plataea the following year.

As for Ephialtes, a price was put on his head. He fled into Thessaly, fearing that the Spartans would hunt him down. Years later he returned to his home at Anticyra, where he was killed by a man who had a private grudge against him but who nevertheless claimed the reward.

At about the same time as the last of the Spartans died in the pass, the Persian fleet, stung by the attack of the previous evening, put to sea and crossed the channel in force. The Greeks, who were determined to maintain close contact with their camp, lined up for battle in the shallows just off the beach. The Persian ships formed a half circle and tried to engulf the smaller Greek fleet. Once again the Greeks charged head on, crashing into the bows of the lighter Persian vessels. In the engagement the Greeks were roughly handled and lost several ships, but they also inflicted severe casualties on their enemies. When the Persians found that they were achieving little they withdrew. Although neither side could claim a victory, the Greeks had been severely mauled. About 90 Athenian ships had suffered damage.

Soon after the battle the 30-oared gal-ley which had been acting as a liaison ship between the force in the pass and the fleet came in bringing the tragic news from Thermopylae.

When the sailors heard of the death of Leonidas their hearts sank. They knew that there was no point in staying. They hauled in their anchors and set off down the channel towards the Euripus. They sailed in their appointed order, with the Corinthians making up the vanguard and the Athenians bringing up the rear.

The battered Greek fleet limped southward, passing through the Euripus, down past the site of the great Athenian victory at Marathon, around Cape Sunium and up to Athens. The Persians had not seen the Greek fleet slip away—once again the haze had covered the Athenian movements. They did not learn of the fleet's departure until early the following morning.

The fall of Athens

The disaster at Thermopylae, and especially the failure to relieve the troops in the pass, had a serious effect on the morale of Sparta's allies. The ancient accounts imply that there were serious defections amongst the north-western Peloponnesians. Western Arcadia had supplied a quarter of the Peloponnesian troops in Leonidas' army, but the following year when the call for troops went out to the whole of the Peloponnesian League, not a single unit was sent.

On the third day after taking the pass the Persian army set out again. The baggage train, especially the heavy wagons, must have gone by the coast road, but now that all opposition had been crushed, part of the army pushed through the mountains and invaded Phocis. They sacked every village, looting and burning the temples as they went. The inhabitants fled west and south to the mountains out of reach of the pillaging soldiers. Those that were caught were shown no mercy. Phocis was to be made an example for the rest of Greece to see and weigh carefully before they decided to continue the unequal contest.

The demonstration was not wasted. The towns of Boeotia offered earth and water, the token of submission, and they were spared but they were compelled, in accordance with the normal Persian custom, to send contingents to fight on the Persian side. Herodotus' claim that the Thebans surrendered at Thermopylae may be true, as only the towns of Thespiae and Plataea were listed for destruction: the Thespians for the part they played at Thermopylae, and the Plataeans for fighting on the Athenian side at Marathon and for serving with the Athenian fleet at Artemisium.

These Plataean sailors had disembarked at Chalcis when the fleet was passing through the Euripus and made their way home so that they could help in the evacuation of the town. Both the Plataeans and the Thespians were evacuated to the Peloponnesus.

Below
Model showing the position of Salamis in relation to Athens. The Greek fleet was beached in the narrowest part of the channel on the east (right) side of the island, and the Persian fleet was beached in Phalerum Bay.

ELEUSIS

MEGARA

AGIOS GIORGIOS

MT. AEGALEOS

ATHENS

SALAMIS

LIPSOKOUTALI

PIRAEUS

PHALERUM

PR. OF COLIAS

The Persian army pressed on south-eastwards and entered Attica. Athens was a scene of feverish activity as the population tried to evacuate the city. Most of the women and children were ferried across the Saronic Gulf to Troezen on the north-east corner of the Peloponnesus. Some were sent to the island of Aegina and the remainder, with all the able-bodied men, were removed to the island of Salamis in the bay of Eleusis only just over a kilometre from the Athenian coast. The evacuation was carried out in such a panic that many of the old and helpless were left to their fate. A few 'zealots' stayed behind and barricaded themselves in the temples.

Earlier, when the Athenians had sent to the oracle at Delphi to ask for its advice, they had received a reply which contained the sentence: 'Zeus of the broad heavens grants to the Triton born a wooden wall alone to remain unsacked, that shall help thee and thy children'. This was interpreted by Themistocles to mean that they should take to their wooden ships. Most Athenians accepted this interpretation, but a dissenting minority built a palisade around the top of the Acropolis and there awaited the Persians.

Meanwhile the Spartans had at last mobilised their army and assembled at Corinth under the command of the surviving king Cleombrotus. They broke up the coast road along the isthmus and threw up a rampart across its narrowest part near where the Corinth ship canal now runs.

The Persian army continued its thrust southwards, laying waste the countryside whilst the fleet sailed down the coast burning the seaside villages. They occupied Athens and captured the Acropolis, but only after a dogged resistance by its defenders. They then looted and burned the temples and all the other buildings on the ancient citadel. On the island of Salamis the Athenians must have been able to see the column of smoke that marked the end of their city. The Persian fleet moved up the Attic coast and beached at the old open harbour of Phalerum.

The Greek fleet was beached on the east side of Salamis. There was a furore on the island as the admirals of the various fleets argued about what to do. The squadrons from the Peloponnesus wanted to quit their position at Salamis and join up with the army at Corinth, whereas the Athenians quite understandably refused to abandon their families on the island.

Themistocles, in spite of opposition from the Corinthians, managed to convince Eurybiadas, the Spartan admiral, that if he left Salamis the fleet would disintegrate as each squadron looked to the defence of its own territory.

The battle of Salamis
As Pritchett remarked when he published his second article on the battle of Salamis in 1965, there have probably been more articles published on this battle than any other in world history—Herodotus devoted the equivalent of a book to it and Aeschylus wrote a play about it. It is also dealt with by Plutarch in two of his lives and Diodorus Siculus, who also gives an account of the battle.

Amongst the modern commentators, N. G. L. Hammond gives the most complete survey in which he includes some very important observations. He is quite right in insisting that Aeschylus should be used as, although the evidence comes from his play, *The Persians*, and he has used considerable 'poetic licence' in his presentation of the material, he fought in the battle and therefore must be treated as an eyewitness.

While Xerxes had been putting down the resistance at Athens the two fleets lay at anchor, each waiting for the other to make the first move. The main Persian fleet was beached in the bay of Phalerum just south of Athens, while detachments were anchored at the entrance to the Salamis strait. Herodotus later mentions detachments at Ceos and Cynosura. Ceos is impossible to identify but it may be one of the two small islands off Lipsokoutali. Cynosura (the dog's tail), however, is easy to identify as the long, narrow promontory projecting eastwards from Salamis island.

This places the Greek anchorage farther up the channel, probably divided into three parts: one in the bay of Ambelaki in front of the ancient town of Salamis; another in the bay of Paloukia; and a third in the bay of Arapis. Herodotus gives the number of ships in the Greek fleet as 380. Of this number 89 came from the Peloponnesus (this includes 40 from Corinth) and 180 from Athens. Among the minor contingents the largest numbers were from Aegina (30), Chalcis (20) and Megara (20). The subsequent battle formation implies that the Athenians occupied the bay of Paloukia, the Peloponnesians the northern bay of Arapis, and the others the southern bay of Ambelaki, for this is how they formed up in battle line.

Aeschylus in his play *The Persians* gives the Greek numbers as 310, but he has probably reduced the number for effect, just as he has surely grossly exaggerated the Persian numbers. 'How great was the number of the Greek ships that dared with their rams to engage the Persian host?' The answer—310 Greek against 1,207 Persian. The Persian figure is obviously not meant to be taken seriously as this is the number of ships given by Herodotus for the beginning of the campaign and, even if the original figure were to be accepted, it makes no allowance for the hundreds of ships lost in the storms along the east coast. To suggest that the fleet was brought up to exactly the same strength by reinforcements is quite absurd.

The strength of the Persian fleet may be guessed by examining the Persian strategy. Again and again Herodotus stresses the superiority of the Persian ships and seamen, so it is clear that Xerxes did not need to outnumber the Greeks to expect to win. Why then did Xerxes not blockade the Greek fleet in the Salamis channel with half his fleet and then launch a two-pronged attack on the Peloponnesus, by land along the isthmus and by sea with the remainder of the fleet?

The attraction of this course of action is enormous. Cut off by land and sea, the great number of Athenians on Salamis would soon have exhausted their meagre supplies. In a very short time they would have been starved into submission. Xerxes was unable to adopt these tactics for one simple reason—he had neither enough ships nor soldiers to accomplish the task. It is likely that the Persian fleet now numbered no more than 500 vessels.

Once again the Persians appear to have waited several days to see if the Greek fleet would abandon its position. Xerxes must have known that, as usual, the Greeks were at loggerheads. The story that it was Themistocles who brought on the battle by sending a messenger to Xerxes to tell him that the Greek fleet intended to escape is probably untrue. Autumn was drawing on and Xerxes almost certainly had only planned on a one-season campaign. Once the fleet was destroyed nothing could stop him invading the Peloponnesus. So he decided to take the initiative and bring on the battle.

Having decided to force a confrontation within the straits on the following morning, the Persians set about preparing the proposed battle area. The main fleet put out from Phalerum and began to move up towards the channel.

Soon after dusk the Persians moved as many soldiers as they could across to the island of Psyttalea, which lay between Salamis and the mainland. This island lay in the path of the projected battle area and many of the wrecks from the battle would be washed up there. Here the soldiers could slay the Greeks and offer succour to their shipwrecked friends. The identification of this island is hotly disputed. Hammond claims that it must be the island of Agios Georgios opposite Perama in the middle of the strait, whilst Pritchett contends that it must be the island of Lipsokoutali at the entrance to the channel. Hammond would appear to put too must trust in the accounts of ancient authors such as Strabo who had probably never visited the area. Drawing conclusions from their descriptions would appear to be very hazardous. If the Persians occupied Agios Georgios, which lies directly in front of the Greek anchorage only about 400m from the shore, the Greeks would certainly have seen them at first light. There would have been little that the Persians could have done to prevent their instant dislodgement. Moreover, the island of Lipsokoutali controls the entrance to the strait, and it would have been vital for the Persians to secure it before moving into the channel itself. It must be added that the wrecks did drift southwards after the battle.

After occupying the island the Persians despatched the Egyptians, who made up the western wing of the fleet, to blockade the western end of the Salamis channel. Then at midnight the rest of the fleet, including the detachments at Cynosura and Ceos, moved into the entrance of the strait, occupying the area from Salamis to Munychia.

News that the Persian fleet had moved up into the entrance to the strait was received in the Greek camp during the night. It was said to have been brought in by Aristides, the Athenian exile, who managed to get through the Persian lines from Aegina so that he could fight for his city in its hour of peril. The lookouts on Salamis, however, must have got some idea of what was happening. The Greeks now knew that they had to fight. Everything was to their advantage. In the narrow straits the Phoenicians would be unable to use their superior seamanship.

Just before first light the Greeks dragged their galleys down to the water, boarded, ran out their oars and waited for the signal. The trumpets sounded and the flutes struck up their tune. Then, to the rhythmic chant of their

Below
The site of the decisive battle of Salamis. The long promontory (Cynosura) is in the centre and the site of the ancient town of Salamis on the right. Part of the island of Lipsokoutali can be clearly seen on the left.

war song, they pulled at their oars and the galleys began to move out into the channel.

Xerxes had taken up his position on Mount Aegaleos overlooking the strait. Here a throne had been erected for him so that he could watch the battle.

The Persian seamen strained at their oars and pulled towards the Greek lines.

As the two fleets closed, the Greeks in the centre backed water so that their line bowed. Seeing the Greeks backing the Persian sailors were convinced that they were going to break in flight and, raising their war cry, they charged into the salient—and still the centre backed water. According to Plutarch they were waiting for something that they knew must happen. Suddenly the Persian fleet lurched as the swell came up the channel. The wave caught the Persian ships from behind. Some of them were knocked out of line, veering broadside on to the Greeks. The Greek sailors raised a great shout—'On you sons of Greece! Free your native land, free your children, your wives, the fanes of your fathers' Gods, and the tombs of your ancestors. Now you battle for your all'.

Then they charged; their bronze-plated rams darting through the foam crashed through the banks of oars and ripped into the bows of the Persian ships.

It is rather difficult to understand Herodotus' description of the battle formation: 'The Phoenicians (for they had the western wing, towards Eleusis) were arrayed opposite to the Athenians, and to the Lacedaemonians the Ionians, on the eastern wing, nearest the Piraeus'. It would only be possible to use the terms east and west wing if he is describing the position of the fleet before it entered the channel, and from thereon continuing to use this description for the Ionian and Phoenician fleets. (It is interesting that he does not use these terms for the Greek fleet.) If this were the case, then the description of the west wing as being towards Eleusis is a little strange. However, it would be impossible to use the terms east and west when the fleet is drawn up in a north to south line and advancing directly westwards.

It seems certain that the ships from Aegina were stationed in the bay of Ambelaki as this is the only point from

which they could have launched a flank attack on the withdrawing Persians. It was also they who came to the support of an Athenian ship that was in trouble. It follows that the Athenians must have held position next to the Aeginetans, i.e. the centre and right, and therefore the Peloponnesians held the left wing.

It seems to be agreed that there has been a general rise in the sea level in the area around Athens. Pritchett quotes many examples of places that were above the water level in classical times and are now below it. Several ancient quarries have been discovered submerged beneath two to three metres of water. The same feature was observed when the ship sheds at Zea were excavated. A classical shrine at the village of Agios Cosmas was also found below the water level.

There is a small reef 350m off the Attic coast opposite Perama; in classical

Below
The battle of Salamis. The Greeks withdrew the centre of their line, luring the Persian fleet further and further into the narrow straits, where the superior Phoenician seamanship was of no advantage.

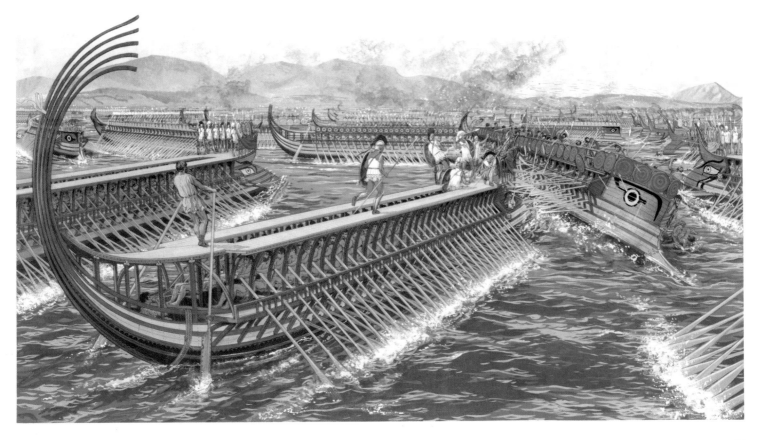

times this must have been an island. Between this island and the mainland there would have been a shallow channel where the water was not deep enough for galleys to navigate. This small island would have made an excellent point on to which the Greeks could lock their left wing without fear of missile attack from the Persian infantry on the mainland or of being outflanked. Their inferiority in numbers made it all the more important for the Greeks to avoid being outflanked. For this reason the Corinthian fleet of 40 ships was despatched to prevent the Egyptians entering the west end of the channel. There can be no truth in Herodotus' statement—almost certainly taken from a biased Athenian source—that the Corinthians fled before the battle.

This also undermines the arguments of those who would place the battle area farther up the channel in front of the island of Agios Georgios with no locking point for the right wing. This would have allowed the Persian ships to break through the right wing at will. The Greek fleet would have been drawn up in front of their anchorages with the

Peloponnesian fleet of 49 ships occupying the left wing and resting on the islet. It is also inconsistent to attempt to reconcile Aeschylus' figure of 310 for the Greek fleet with Herodotus' 380 by suggesting that the missing 70 ships formed the Corinthian squadron which left before the battle. This would have left only 19 Peloponnesian ships to form the left wing.

The Athenian fleet of 180 ships covered the centre with its right wing resting on the tip of the Kamatero promontory, whilst the other 111 ships, including the 30 ships from Aegina, occupied the bay of Ambelaki. The distance from the islet to the tip of the Kamatero promontory is about 1,050m. Allowing a minimum of 20m per galley the ships would have to be drawn up in four to five lines.

According to Aeschylus, as the Persians entered the straits they first heard the Greek fleet singing their battle hymn and only later saw them. This has been used to support the view that the Greek fleet was drawn up in the channel to the north of Kamatero, shielded from the Persian view by Mount Aegaleos. How-

ever, although Burn and Hammond both make this point, neither actually show the Greek fleet in this position. Both show it pivoted on the Kamatero promontory in full view of the Persian fleet. If Aeschylus is to be interpreted this way, then the battle would have to be fought between Arapis and Cape Filatouri. A more likely explanation is that there might have been a slight haze or it was still dark. Alternatively, the Persians may have heard the Greek singing before they actually entered the straits. Herodotus later mentions a west wind which blew the wreckage down the coast. This could have carried the sound of the Greek singing the three to four kilometres to the Persian fleet.

The battle was on. Caught in the narrow channel there was no room to manoeuvre. It was ship against ship. The Greeks managed to retain their formation but, for the Persians, this was impossible. The mass of the Persian ships were jostled in the centre of the channel, caught in the devastating pincer movement as the wings charged. The Persians tried desperately to turn about while at the same time trying to avoid ramming each other. The Greeks were able to pick off the enemy ships on the outside of the mass at will.

The Persian sailors fought bravely before the gaze of their king. The javelineers swept the decks of the Greek galleys as they tried to ram them. Just off the promontory of Kamatero an Ionian ship from Samothrace charged out from the mass of Persians and ripped into the hull of an Athenian galley, but before it could free itself from the wreckage a trireme from Aegina rounded the promontory and caught the Ionian ship amidships. While the Ionian ship was sinking, her complement of javelineers swept the Greek marines off the deck, boarded and captured the trireme, much to the delight of Xerxes.

Despite these isolated successes, the

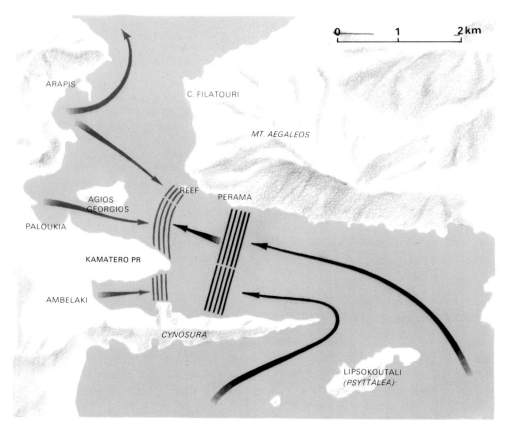

Left
The Persian fleet entered the strait with the Phoenicians sailing in column to the east of Lipsokoutali (nearest the Piraeus) and the Ionians to the west of the islet. They would have deployed into line in the strait. The Peloponnesians formed up opposite the Phoenicians and the Athenians opposite the Ionians whilst the rest (c.110 ships) lay in wait in the bay of Ambelaki, from which they attacked the retreating Persian ships.

Persian fleet, crammed helplessly in the channel, was in a desperate position. The battered fleet tried to disengage. As they withdrew from the narrows, the ships from Aegina lay waiting for them in the bay of Ambelaki and, as they passed, caught them in a devastating flank attack. The Athenians too, following up the retreat, played havoc amongst the fleeing ships.

The victorious Greek sailors showed no mercy to their shipwrecked enemies. Grabbing oars or any other weapon that came to hand, they clubbed to death or drowned the enemy sailors as they struggled helplessly in the water.

Meanwhile, Aristides, the Athenian exile, gathered together many of the hoplites who were on the shore watching the sea battle, and with these managed to capture the island of Psyttalea and slaughter the Persian garrison there, thus cutting off the last resort for the wrecked Persian ships. Those wrecks that did not drift ashore on the island floated down the coast and came ashore on the promontory of Colias about four kilometres south of Phalerum.

Although the Persian fleet was far from being destroyed and still probably outnumbered the Greeks, Xerxes now realised that his hopes of a quick campaign were gone. He handed over command of the bulk of his army—possibly 150,000 men—to Mardonius and returned to Asia. Mardonius withdrew into Thessaly and there went into winter quarters. For a few months at least southern Greece had a breathing space.

Xerxes feared that the defeat at Salamis might encourage the Ionians to revolt, so he withdrew the fleet to Cyme and the following spring stationed it at Samos.

The Spartans mobilise
In the following spring Aristides and Xanthippus, another exile who had returned to defend his country, were elected generals at Athens.

Mardonius now tried by diplomacy to separate Athens from her alliance with the Peloponnesians, offering her very handsome terms. But Athens was full of bitterness over what had happened and, although under normal circumstances she, like all the other Greek states, would not shy away from betraying a cause in the preference of self

interest, she now rejected the Persian proposals out of hand. However, she did use them to try, without success, to force Sparta into promising more aid.

Summer had arrived when Mardonius moved south again. Waiting until the crops were ripening, he advanced once more on Athens and once again occupied it unopposed. And once again Sparta failed to come to the aid of her ally. At Salamis Athens had risked all and in so doing saved Sparta. She had also refused to betray the Greek cause but this had little effect on the Spartans. The only thing that held the Greeks together was a foreign enemy, not any love for each other. The Greek resistance to Persia from Marathon onwards is a catalogue of bad planning, gross inefficiency and selfishness punctuated with occasional acts of brilliance and heroism. It is incredible that they could possibly have won. The Persians, on the other hand, displayed excellent strategy, a great deal of energy and considerable bravery but suffered from appalling back luck. In the final campaign they completely outmanoeuvred the Greeks, and then made one miscalculation which cost them the war.

With the reoccupation of Athens the citizens again crossed over to Salamis. Mardonius once more tried to come to terms with those on the island. The Athenians sent an embassy to Sparta to beg them to come to their aid but, as at Marathon and Thermopylae, they were keeping a religious festival and refused to move. In the meantime they were feverishly heightening the wall across the isthmus, making it clear to all that this was where they intended to fight. Day after day they temporised, each day putting off their decision until the next; this went on for ten days. It was not until the Athenians threatened to accept Mardonius' terms, which would place the Athenian navy under Persian control, thus laying the Peloponnesus wide open to attack and rendering the isthmus defences obsolete, that Sparta acted.

Once the decision was made Sparta acted with great energy. The entire Greek forces were placed under the command of Pausanias, son of king Cleombrotus (as Leonidas' son Pleistarchus was still a minor) and Euryanax, the son of Doreius whom Cleombrotus had co-opted as his colleague.

Five thousand Spartans, nearly two-thirds of the total Spartan levy, plus 35,000 *helots*, immediately set out northwards. On the way they were joined by 17,000 hoplites from the north-eastern Peloponnesus.

Mardonius immediately evacuated Athens, destroying what remained of the city before he left. Eleusis was also put to the flame. He now withdrew to Bocotia where the country was much more open and suitable for his cavalry.

As Mardonius started northward he heard that an advance guard of 1,000 Spartans had already reached Megara, only 45km from Athens. Mardonius turned and, sending his cavalry ahead, made a lightning strike against Megara, but when he failed to take the town and heard that the Greek army was gathering at the isthmus, he called off his troops and retired into Boeotia. He passed to the east of Mount Parnes, crossed the Asopus river (this is not the same as the river at Thermopylae) and ascended its north bank past Tanagra to Scolus in the territory of Thebes. Here he established a fortified camp which Herodotus describes as about 10 *stades* square (about 1,800m²), which is just over five times the size of the Roman camp described by Polybius which held 20,000 infantry and 2,500 cavalry. This suggests that Mardonius' army might not be much more than 120,000 men including cavalry.

Herodotus says that the Persian troops were ranged along the river from Erythrae to past Hysiae as far as the lands of Plataea. It is unfortunate that only the site of Plataea can be identified with certainty; the sites of Scolus, Hysiae and Erythrae are uncertain.

Over several years Pritchett has done a tremendous amount of groundwork on the battlefield of Plataea. He has walked scores of miles across the fields and hillsides that make up the battlefield search for traces of ancient habitation. The method he has used is called sherding—searching the ground, preferably immediately after ploughing, for fragments of ancient tiles and pots. Where these are found in large numbers over a wide area, one can postulate an ancient town or village. The results of his findings have been published in two articles. The first appeared in the *American Journal of Archaeology* in 1957. The second, in which he modified some of his views, appeared in a work entitled 'Studies in Ancient Greek Topography' published eight years later. Using this method of sherding he has identified three sites to the west of Plataea. Two of these are on the northern slopes of Mount Pastra which, with Mount Cithaeron, limits the southern side of the battlefield, and a third is on the river Asopus. Using the ancient sources, the two sites on the slopes of Mount Pastra can be identified with Hysiae (about 1.5km east of modern Erythrai) and ancient Erythrae (about one kilometre west of modern Daphne).

The third site on the Asopus was found while expressly looking for Scolus, which Pausanias describes as about 40 *stades* (eight kilometres) downstream from the Plataea to Thebes road. At a point exactly 40 *stades* downstream from the crossing, Pritchett found ample remains of a classical settlement. Subsequently, Burn has suggested that it should be located on the south side of the river but accepts in the main Pritchett's identification of the three towns. The remains that Pritchett found were in the area marked on the general staff maps from the last war as Paliomiloi. The lack of adequate Greek maps makes the study of topography in that country particularly difficult.

So the Persian army was ranged along the north bank of the river Asopus from opposite Erythrae to almost opposite Plataea for a distance of about 12km. The site of the Persian camp was probably on the high ground above Scolus; this would cover the main road from Athens to Thebes and secure the Asopus bridge. The Asopus itself in this area is a fairly insignificant stream which can be crossed easily.

Meanwhile the Peloponnesian army had moved along the isthmus to Eleusis, where they were joined by the Athenians who crossed over from Salamis. From here they headed north and followed the Persian army into Boeotia. Once past Mount Parnes they turned west along the south side of the Asopus. Herodotus tells us that the Greek army reached Erythrae where they learned of the Persian positions. Accordingly they took up their positions along the foothills of the mountain. Pritchett, in his original article on Plataea, made a detailed study

of the routes over the mountains into the valley of the Asopus. He concluded that there were only two routes: one followed roughly the route of the modern Athens–Thebes road which, for convenience, is termed the Gyphtocastro road, and the other, which was traced by Hammond, crossed a slightly higher pass about two kilometres farther west. This would have been the route to Megara and will be so called. In his later article he rejected the first route, claiming that only the Megara route was practicable. I must conclude from this that he meant for a baggage train of wheeled vehicles, as the existence of an Athenian fort at Gyphtocastro at the south end of the pass proves conclusively that it was in use in the 4th century BC. Both passes were occupied by the Athenian general Chabrias in 379. He himself occupied the Gyphtocastro pass but the Spartans forced their way over the route through Plataea, i.e. Hammond's Megara road.

If Pritchett is correct in his identification of ancient Erythrae, just west of Daphne, then the Greeks would have 'learned' of the Persian positions first hand, for from here one gets a panoramic view of the whole Persian line. In fact this view can be seen from any point along the base of the hills all the way to Plataea 12km farther west. The implication of Herodotus' remark is that it was from Erythrae that the Greeks first saw the Persian positions, which precludes any possibility that they entered the valley by either the Megara or Gyphtocastro passes about eight to ten kilometres farther west. Even if Herodotus' statement is disregarded, there can be no strategic justification for the Greek army moving eight to ten kilometres eastwards along the foot of the mountain, leaving their supply lines wide open to a flank attack, especially as they then proceeded to move westwards again. One must therefore conclude that they marched up the valley from the east.

Mardonius had skilfully chosen the site on which he wished to fight. He had fallen back on his own supply lines and at the same time placed a range of mountains between the Greeks and their source of supplies, which would have to come from the Peloponnesus as Attica had been systematically ravaged during

two successive years. With his cavalry he could wreak havoc on the Greeks' supply route.

When Mardonius saw that the Greek army planned to hold the high ground and did not intend to come down into the plain, he despatched Masistius with his cavalry. The horsemen crossed the river and charged up the hillside in squadrons, showering the hoplites with arrows.

The Greek army, which according to Herodotus consisted of 38,700 hoplites and about 70,000 light-armed troops, was stretched out in battle order along the foot of the hills with their backs to the cliffs. Allowing for a depth of eight, the hoplites alone would have stretched for about five kilometres. The light-armed troops would probably have been strategically placed on the wings and along the various spurs that jutted out into the plain. The obvious site for the right wing, made up of the Spartans, would be two kilometres west of modern Daphne with their 35,000 *helots* covering the supply route to the east. The rest of the hoplites would have been stretched out past ancient Erythrae as far as the long ridge that juts out into the plain two and a half kilometres west of Daphne, with a strong contingent of light-armed troops on the long ridge giving a fairly strong cover to the left wing. Although the light-armed troops on the spurs would have been able to give fairly good cover to the hoplites, there was one very weak spot just west of ancient Erythrae where the ground is open. Here the 3,000 hoplites from Megara were taking a terrible beating from Masistius' cavalry. The Megarians sent a herald to the generals begging for help. In response 300 Athenian hoplites with a contingent of archers volunteered to take up a position in front of the Megarians and break the force of the cavalry charges. Again and again the squadrons of Persian cavalry charged in upon the 300 Athenians, showering them with missiles. Masistius himself, clothed in a purple tunic, led the charges riding his richly caparisoned Nesaean horse with its golden bit. In the thick of the battle his horse was caught in the side by a stray arrow. The animal reared in pain, throwing the Persian general. Before he could get to his feet the Athenians were upon him. While some grabbed his horse, others thrust at him with their spears only to discover that beneath his purple tunic he was wearing a cuirass of gilded scales. Finding that they could not get to his body, one of the Athenians stabbed him through the eye and so despatched him.

It was some time before the Persian cavalry realised what had happened. When they saw the Athenians crowded round the corpse in their usual style, however, for everybody wanted to get a look, they rode back in mass and tried to recover the body. The Athenians yelled to the Megarians to come down and help them. A violent struggle raged over the body and the Athenians were almost driven from their prey but, when contingents from the rest of the army began to arrive and the Persian losses mounted, the latter drew back and halted about 400m away. Then, seeing that there was nothing they could do, they returned to their camp to report to Mardonius. The loss of their popular cavalry commander caused much distress in the Persian camp.

However, amongst the Greeks, there was great rejoicing. The body was placed on a cart and drawn along the ranks so that all might see it. Many of the hoplites broke ranks to come forward and gaze in awe on the body.

The Greek generals decided to take advantage of the disturbance in the Persian camp and move their position. They marched down to Plataea in the plain about 12km farther west. Herodotus says that the ground was fitter there in all ways, but chiefly because there was an abundant supply of water from a fountain called Gargaphia. Where they were it was impossible to get sufficient water as there were only tiny streams and the Persian archers prevented them watering at the Asopus. Herodotus does not mention one very important factor: supplies were having to be brought up either by the road around the east side of Mount Parnes or by a very hazardous route between Mount Parnes and Mount Pastra. If they moved across to Plataea they would be able to receive supplies direct from the Peloponnesus over the Megara pass.

The site of the new water source, the Gargaphia fountain, is uncertain but it is generally believed to have been one of the springs just south of the Agios Ioannis hill about three kilometres north-north-east of modern Erythrai. Pritchett convincingly identifies it with the Retsi spring, which he says is the most abundant in the area. Agios Ioannis hill is one of several small hillocks at the north end of a flat ridge of higher ground about three kilometres wide jutting out towards the Asopus between Mount Cithaeron and Mount Pastra; this is known as the Asopus ridge.

The Greeks gathered up their equipment and marched down past Hysiae to the lands of Plataea where they encamped 'nation by nation near the Gargaphia fountain and the precinct of the hero Androcrates among the low hills and in a level country'.

Unfortunately one can only guess at the position of the precinct of the hero Androcrates. Thucydides mentions it being on the right (east) side of the road

Below
The view from the first Greek position near modern Daphne. It was from here that the Greeks got their first view of the Persian positions in the distance. From here there is a panoramic view of the Persian line.

from Plataea to Thebes. This means that it, too, was in the area of the Agios Ioannis hill—possibly on it. Different religions have a habit of building shrines on the same spot, and many a Greek Orthodox chapel overlies a pagan shrine.

'Among low hills and in level country' would well describe a line stretching for some six kilometres over the several hillocks on the Asopus ridge and across the plain in front of Plataea, with its left wing locked on the Pyrgos hill. The Spartans, holding the right wing on the Asopus ridge, covered the water supply. None would dare challenge the Spartan right to the position of honour on the right wing, but the claim to the second most honourable position on the left wing was hotly disputed in true Greek fashion between the Athenians and the Tegeans (who always served on the left in the Spartan army). It could hardly be doubted that Athens would win but it shows an interesting sidelight on the ancient Greeks who, even in the face of a most formidable enemy where their very existence was at stake, were prepared to squabble about honour.

In the final line-up the right wing was held by the 5,000 Spartans and the 5,000 other Lacedaemonians under Pausanias, who was commander-in-chief. The 1,500 Tegeans were drawn up on their left. The left wing, on the Pyrgos hills, was held by Athenians commanded by

Aristides with their faithful allies the Plataeans, who supplied 600 hoplites, next to them. Between the two wings the levies from the other states were drawn up, with the Peloponnesians on the right next to the Spartans and the others next to the Athenians. The largest of these units was from Corinth, which supplied 5,000 men. The smallest contingents were from Lepreon in Triphylia and Pale in Cephallenia, which sent 200 men each. Mycenae and Tiryns, so famous in the Bronze Age, could muster only 400 between them. The 35,000 *helots* served on the right wing with the Spartans; the remaining 34,500 light-armed troops probably served on the other wing. Their role was to keep the Persian cavalry away from the flanks as this was the weakest point of a hoplite army.

When the Persians had finished mourning the death of Masistius, they too moved up the river until they were opposite the new Greek position. Here Mardonius deployed his troops along the north bank. He posted his crack Persian troops opposite the Lacedaemonians. His weaker Persians were placed opposite the Tegeans next in line. The Spartans probably fought four deep and the Tegeans and other Lacedaemonians possibly did the same. A deep formation was unnecessary against light-armed troops, and the longer the

line was the less likely they were to be outflanked. Allowing a little less than a metre per man, these 13,000 hoplites probably stretched out for about three kilometres. Next to the Persians Mardonius placed his Medes. Since these were opposite the contingents from Corinth, Potidaea, Orchomenus and Sicyon, consisting of 8,900 hoplites who, being less confident than the Spartans, were probably drawn up eight deep, the Medes would have stretched for a little over a kilometre. Likewise the Bactrians covered the men from Epidaurus, Troezen, Lepreum, Mycenae, Tiryns and Phlius, who were 3,400 strong with a front of about 400m. Next to the Bactrians Mardonius placed the Indians facing the contingents from Hermione, Eretria, Styra and Chalcis— 1,300 hoplites with a front of about 150m. Next to the Indians he drew up the last of his Asian units, the Scythians. These faced the 2,000 hoplites from Ambracia, Leucas, Anactorium, Pale and Aegina, covering a little over 200m. Opposite the 11,600 Megarians, Plataeans and Athenians on his right wing, with a front of about 1,250m, he placed

Below
Model of the upper Asopus valley looking south. The Greeks probably entered the plain from the east (left) and first saw the Persian positions as they approached Erythrae. Here the Persians launched their first attack on them.

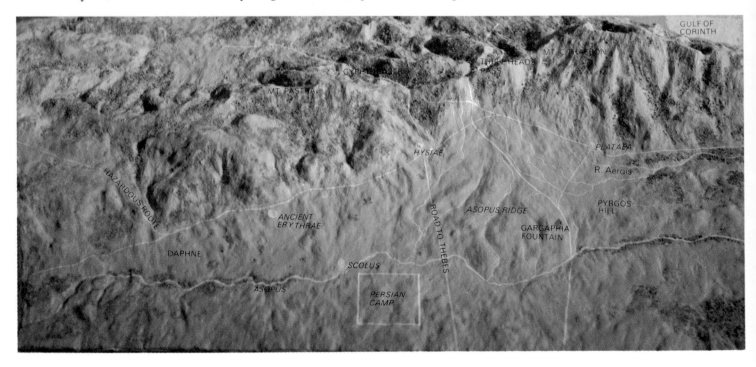

his northern Greek allies, the Boeotians, Locrians, Malians, Thessalians and Macedonians, plus 1,000 Phocians from those Phocian towns that had defected. Herodotus adds to this list the minor contingents from Phrygia, Thrace, Mysia, Paeonia, Ethiopia and Egypt. So, excluding cavalry and light-armed troops, the whole line covered about six kilometres.

The cavalry were drawn up separately, almost certainly on the wings opposite the Greek light-armed troops.

After drawing up their armies, both sides started offering sacrifices hoping for a favourable response from the Gods.

The final battle
For eight days the two armies sat eyeing each other across the valley whilst the diviners tried to produce favourable omens for an attack. This delay was of greater benefit to the Greeks than the Persians as supplies and reinforcements were now pouring into the Greek camps by way of the Megara pass. This pass, which the Boeotians called Treis Cephalae, 'the three heads', can be identified with the pass of the Megara route which runs between three peaks at the east side of Mount Cithaeron, Loukisthi, Fikhthi and Karoumsala, and from which it must derive its name.

On the eighth day Mardonius despatched part of his cavalry who rode round the right wing of the Greek army and occupied the entrance to the pass, capturing 500 baggage animals plus several wagons with their drivers and cutting the Greek supply line. Why the Greeks had not placed a strong holding force in the mouth of the pass defies understanding, but this sort of negligence is typical of the Greek city states.

For three days more neither army moved, although by now the Persian cavalry were constantly harassing the Greek lines. At first light on the eleventh day after they had taken up their new position, for some unfathomable reason the Athenians and Spartans decided to exchange positions. The reason given by Herodotus, that the Spartans were scared of the Persians on their wing, is so obviously an Athenian brag that it has to be ignored. The true reason is possibly just the opposite: the right wing on the hills in front of modern Erythrai was much the stronger position

and the Athenians on the left were finding it much more difficult to withstand the constant attacks of the Persian cavalry. So the Spartans may have offered to take over that position.

Mardonius responded by moving his crack Persian troops on to this wing as well, making the situation on the left wing around Pyrgos hill that much worse. So the Spartans moved back again to draw the Persians with them. Another possible reason, but this is highly unlikely as the Spartans were not prone to brilliant tactical moves, is that the Spartans intended to launch a surprise attack on Persia's Greek allies hoping to knock them out before the main battle. It is more than likely that the whole episode is untrue and anyway, by the end of the day, everybody was back to square one. Mardonius now launched a full-scale cavalry attack across the river. The Persian horsemen rode down the Greek lines showering them with arrows whilst some of their compatriots forced their way up on to the Asopus ridge and fouled the Gargaphia fountain which, as usual, the Spartans had failed to guard. The Greeks were now in serious trouble: they were unable to water at the narrow Asopus river for fear of the Persian archers on the opposite bank and they were also cut off from their supply lines —they had been completely outgeneralled by Mardonius.

At a war council the Greek generals decided that the only thing that they could do was to withdraw to the foot of the hills where they could reopen and cover their supply route. Here also, at a place called 'the Island', there was a plentiful supply of water.

The problem of the position of 'the Island' seems insoluble. Herodotus says that it was ten *stades* from the Asopus and the Gargaphian fountain and in front of the town of Plataea. It was an island formed by a stream called the Oëroë which divides in two and then rejoins 3 *stades* further on to form an island. Here they would have plenty of water and would not be harmed by the Persian horsemen. Such a site does not exist today nor anything like it in the whole battle area. The only other abundant spring in the area is the Vergutiani spring which rises just west of the church of Agia Anna two kilometres west of

modern Erythrai. In front of this there is a ridge of slightly higher ground that stretches out past Plataea on its eastern side. This is flanked on either side by tributaries of the Aerois, which may in ancient times have been much fuller. (The summertime water supply available today would be quite insufficient to satisfy the needs of a 100,000-strong army.)

It was decided to pull back as soon as it was dark. There is evidence that there were three roads running northwards from the foot of Mount Cithaeron towards Thebes. One, which descended from the Gyphtocastro pass, coincided roughly with the modern Athens–Thebes highway except that it would have run more directly north from the pass, whereas the modern road zigzags down the hillside and passes through Erythrai. The second road crossed the 'three heads' pass and then forked, with one branch going to Plataea and the other branch heading northwards across the Asopus ridge. West of Agios Ioannis hillock it was joined by the third road coming from Plataea. It then crossed the river and headed for Thebes. The plan was obviously for the Athenians on the left wing to withdraw on Plataea, for the centre to use the 'three heads' road, and for the Spartans on the right wing to withdraw along the Gyphtocastro road. Characteristically, the plan was bungled.

When darkness fell the centre, which being in the plain had been so badly mauled by the Persian cavalry during the day, withdrew in great haste and either intentionally or by accident took the wrong fork and finished up at Plataea. They piled up their arms by the Temple of Hera outside the walls of the town and camped there.

Pausanias, hearing what had happened, gave orders for the right wing to withdraw. However one *lochagos* named Amompharetus, who had not been consulted when it was decided to withdraw, now, in true Spartan fashion, refused to desert his post in the face of the enemy. The term *lochagos* here must mean a regimental commander and not a commander of a 100-strong *lochos* (see p. 41). Pausanias and Euryanax, his colleague, were in a quandary; they could hardly remain when the rest of the army were withdrawing but, on the other hand, they were loathe to abandon Amom-

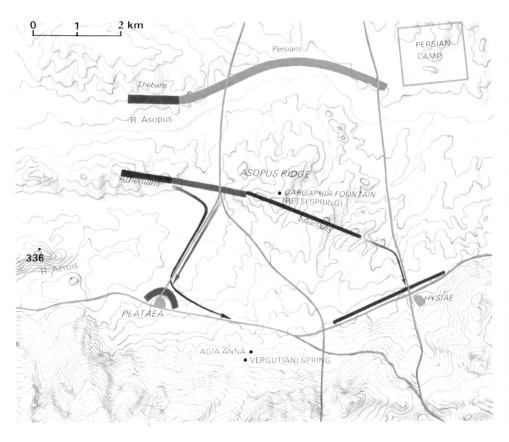

Left
The withdrawal of the Greeks from the Asopus ridge. The Lacedaemonians occupied the right wing on the Asopus ridge whilst the Athenians occupied the left and the other Greeks the centre. It was probably planned for the Athenians to withdraw by the road to Plataea, the Spartans by the road to Hysiae and the other Greeks in the centre by the route to the 'three heads' pass. The centre withdrew first and in the darkness took the wrong fork, finishing up at Plataea. When dawn came the Athenians, who had waited all night for the Spartans to move in spite of the fact that they were furthest away, had to try to fill the gap between the Spartans and the other Greeks at Plataea.

Below
The battlefield of Plataea seen from the north side of the Asopus looking south-east. Modern Plataea can be seen at the foot of Mount Cithaeron on the right. Ancient Plataea would have been just in front of it. Modern Erythrae is in the centre with the Gyphtocastro pass behind and the 'three heads' pass a little to the right. Daphne can just be seen on the left-hand side. This was the first Greek position. The ridge in front of Plataea is the Pyrgos hill.

pharetus and his regiment. So the Spartan army remained where it was while the generals tried to persuade Amompharetus to move. Meanwhile, on the left wing, the Athenians who had begun to fall back heard that there was trouble on the right wing and sent a mounted herald to Pausanias to ask him what they should do.

As the herald rode up the dispute was still raging, with Pausanias and Euryanax pleading with Amompharetus and, when this failed, losing their tempers and shouting at him. Amompharetus, on the other hand, was insisting that he should have been consulted before the decision was reached.

Herodotus says that Amompharetus commanded the *lochos* of Pitana, but does not explain what it was. Thucydides, on the other hand, whilst still not explaining what it was supposed to be, insists that there was not and never had been such a unit. All that we can conclude is that Amompharetus commanded a special regiment and that he would have been present at the normal Spartan war council just as the *primus pilus* was later in the Roman army. Probably he had been excluded as the council would have been restricted to the *strategoi* of the various Greek contingents, otherwise it would have got entirely out of hand with the commanders of every regiment and battalion wanting to be present. When voting took place in the council pebbles were cast into two piles —for or against an action. Now Amompharetus picked up a large stone with both hands and cast it down at Pausanias' feet, crying, 'There's my pebble and I vote for not fleeing from the foreigners'.

Pausanias shouted back calling him a lunatic and out of his mind. When the Athenian herald asked him for his instructions, Pausanias asked them to hold on and follow whatever the Spartans did.

When dawn broke the argument was still raging. Pausanias now did what he should have done all along and began to withdraw, leaving Amompharetus where he was. The column formed up with the Spartans at the front and the Tegeans at the rear. They withdrew along the Gyphtocastro road, marching between the hillocks and keeping to the broken ground.

The Athenians, on the other hand, withdrew across the plain towards Plataea. As expected Amompharetus, who had never believed that the rest of the army would desert him, now that he found himself alone, ordered his regiment to take up their equipment and followed.

When the lookouts in the Persian camp pointed out to Mardonius what was happening he could hardly have believed his eyes. The Greek positions were deserted. Part of the Greek army was visible, lounging around in front of Plataea; the Athenians had disappeared as they were screened from him by the Asopus ridge; and the Spartans were strung out along the Asopus ridge with Amompharetus and his regiment straggling behind as if in full flight.

When the Spartans saw that Amompharetus was following them two kilometres behind, they called a halt to wait for him. Herodotus says that they halted by a stream called the Moloïs at a place known as Argiopium where there is a shrine to the Eleusian Demeter. This shrine has to be at the foot of the hills just west of ancient Hysiae. In the fields just below the Pandanassa ridge, on which Hysiae probably stood, Pritchett found cut blocks of stone which had been turned up by a tractor-drawn plough. He suggests convincingly that this was the site of the shrine of Demeter.

Mardonius was quick to take advantage of the situation. He ordered out his cavalry and followed up with the whole of his infantry leading his Persians against the Spartan column, knowing that if he could knock out the Spartans the war would be over. The rest of the army he despatched against the Greeks near Plataea.

Amompharetus refused to run and continued to march in an orderly fashion. No sooner had he joined the main column than the Persian cavalry were upon them. Pausanias hastily deployed his hoplites along the foot of the mountain. Spartan discipline and training would have enabled them to form up in phalanx even under the hail of arrows from the Persian cavalry.

The Spartans were pinned down where they were and it was now impossible for them to move. Pausanias sent heralds to the Athenians begging

them to come to his assistance and, if possible, to close the gap in the line which had been left when the centre retreated to Plataea. It remained for the Athenians to make the necessary manoeuvres. In response the Athenians began to move eastwards along the foot of the hills towards the Spartan position. Meanwhile the Persian infantry had moved out of camp and crossed the river. The Persian camp was about six kilometres from the Spartan position and it must have taken them at least an hour and a half to come up, especially as the great mass of them would have had to advance across the open fields.

Gradually the Persian infantry began to move in, setting up their shields like a fence a short distance from the Spartan line. From here they kept up a constant barrage of missiles. The Lacedaemonians and Tegeans crouched down behind their shields to shelter from the arrows and waited for the order to charge. Pausanias, meanwhile, had climbed up the hillside and began frantically offering sacrifices, not daring to give the order to charge before the omens were favourable.

Meanwhile, on the left wing, the Athenian march had been halted as the rest of the Persian army closed in on them. On the hillside Pausanias lifted up his eyes towards the temple of Hera six kilometres away to the west beneath the walls of Plataea, beseeching the goddess to grant him the omens he needed but still without avail.

Below him the hoplites gradually began to fall out of line as the Persian arrows found their mark, and all the time more and more Persians were coming up. In the end the 1,500 Tegeans, whose discipline was never as good as the Spartans, could stand it no longer. Screaming their war cry they rose up and charged. On the hillside Pausanias knew that he had to act quickly. He ran down, took up his position in the front rank on the right wing and gave the order to advance. No doubt in order to avoid the charge of sacrilege, he declared that the omens were favourable, and Herodotus does not dispute this.

The Spartans rose as a man and, raising their spears, charged the mass of the Persians. Seeing them coming the Persians discarded their bows and took up their spears. At first they fought over the fence of Persian shields but soon the Spartans had trampled this down and they were in amongst the Persians thrusting their long spears into the lightly armed foreigners. The Persians fought bravely, grappling with their opponents, grabbing at their long spears and breaking them off. They were, however, no real match for the heavily armed Spartans. Gradually they fell and the Spartans clambered over their bodies to get at the rest.

Mardonius himself, riding a white horse, was in the thick of the battle urging on his men. He was surrounded by 1,000 picked men, the flower of the Persian army. These men fought valiantly charging the Lacedaemonians and many a Spartan fell before them. But the tide of the battle was inexorable. Gradually the Spartan hoplites cut their way through the 1,000. Finally Mardonius himself was struck from his horse. So long as he was alive the Persians stood their ground, but when the news spread through the ranks that Mardonius was dead and the majority of his bodyguard with him, the army began to falter and give ground. Soon their line broke and they turned in flight, rushing headlong for their camp with its wooden walls across the river.

When they saw the Persians fleeing the other Asians also took to their heels. Only the Boeotians, perhaps because of their age-old enmity with Athens, continued the fight. They showed great bravery and all 300 of their Sacred Band fell in the battle, but at last they too broke and fled across the river to Thebes. The Persian retreat was covered by the cavalry who kept between them and the advancing Greeks. This is a remarkable tribute to their training, discipline and devotion, as in most ancient battles the horsemen were the first to flee. Even so, many of the fleeing Persians were cut down by the light-armed *helots* who would now have rushed out ahead of the advancing phalanx.

The Spartans, being the nearest, were the first to reach the Persian camp but they found it impossible to approach the palisade. Later the Athenians arrived and the struggle grew hotter. For a long time the Persians fought them off but finally the wall was breached. The Tegeans were the first into the stockade and they were the ones who plundered Mardonius' tent. Once the Greeks were into the camp the Persians put up no great resistance and were slaughtered by the vengeful Greeks. The number of the Persian dead, just as the number of their army, is obviously grossly exaggerated. Herodotus says that only 3,000 of those who fled to the camp survived. He also talks of 40,000 who managed to get away from the battlefield under Artabazus. The Greek losses were small. The Lacedaemonians lost 91, the Tegeans 17 and the Athenians 52. These figures are probably true as it is in flight that most casualties are sustained.

Such was the result of the battle of Plataea. The Spartans had avenged the death of Leonidas and showed themselves, individually, as perhaps the greatest soldiers in history. Persia never again attempted to invade Greece and was herself overcome by the Greeks of Alexander the Great 150 years later.

Athens against Sparta

After the defeat of the Persians both Athens and Sparta were free to pursue their empire building which the Persians had so rudely interrupted. Although both states followed an anti-Persian policy and openly supported any anti-Persian activities in the eastern Mediterranean, it was only a matter of time before once more they were at each other's throats.

For half a century an intermittent peace existed between the two states. In order to fight the Persians at sea the Athenians formed a league of the maritime states; this was known as the Confederacy of Delos. By exercising more and more control over her fellow members in this league, Athens managed to convert a partnership into an empire. With the money appropriated from her allies she built a great fleet and the city that was the wonder of the world.

In 431 BC the long-expected war with Sparta broke out. At first it seemed that neither side could possibly win, for Athens controlled the sea and Sparta the land. Sparta could lay siege to Athens but could not stop supplies coming in from the sea. On the other hand, Athens could launch seaborne attacks on southern Greece but could not defeat the Spartan army. It became a war of sieges with practically no full-scale battles.

After the retreat of the Persians, the Athenians had massively strengthened the defences of their city and constructed long walls stretching from the city to the harbour at Piraeus. Provided that these long walls remained intact and food could be brought in by sea, it was impossible for Sparta to overcome her opponent.

From the beginning, however, Athens suffered from bad luck. When the Spartans laid siege to the city, food was brought in from Egypt. These same ships, however, also brought the plague. In the crowded conditions of the siege Athens was devastated by the disease. The irony was that, because Athens was operating a blockade against Sparta, the Spartans themselves never contracted the disease. For three long years the plague raged and carried off about a quarter of the population. Both sides were exhausted and in 421 BC a peace treaty was signed which left Athens hardly worse off than when she had started.

In 416, still lusting for empire, Athens embarked on the most disastrous blunder in Greek history—she decided to invade Sicily. This culminated in the siege of Syracuse. It should have been easily accomplished but, owing to the incompetence and indecision of the general, Nicias, it turned into an unmitigated disaster. The entire expeditionary force was captured, the generals were executed and the rest of the army sold into slavery. Worse still, during the expedition, Sparta had reopened the war in Greece to take the pressure off Syracuse. Now, in spite of her staggering loss of an entire army and 175 ships, Athens was compelled to take on her old enemy. She held out for another nine years. In the end the rest of her fleet was captured, Athens itself was besieged and, in the face of starvation, surrendered. But Sparta was exhausted and her domination was brought to an end at Leuctra in 371 by two Theban generals Epaminondas and Pelopidas. Their revolutionary theory of hoplite tactics enabled Thebes to invade southern Greece and defeat Sparta decisively at Mantinea in 362.

These ideas were taken up by Philip of Macedon, who as a youth had gone to Thebes as a hostage. On his accession he began to build a mighty army.

The Phalanx

During the 8th century BC there was a revolution in the Greek mode of warfare. The 'free for all' fighting of the heroic age was abandoned and a far more disciplined system introduced. This was the phalanx—an orderly battle line several ranks deep with the men in the second and succeeding ranks covering the men in the front rank, so that the phalanx was divided into files of men, one behind another. The phalanx was, in fact, composed of many short files and not of a few long ranks. Each file was a unit and when a man in the front rank fell, his place was taken by the man in the rank behind—the next man in his file.

The phalanx could be drawn up in open order with two paces per man or doubled up to form close order. The new formation was strengthened by the introduction of the Argive shield probably early in the 7th century. This was a round buckler which did away with the age-old central handgrip and was fastened to the left forearm; it was held across the chest covering the warrior from chin to knees. In close order, which was usual in battle, the shield was wide enough to offer protection to the unguarded side of the man on the left.

The development of the phalanx was a gradual process and in its early years must have gone through many changes. The new warrior was called a hoplite or armoured man. On the Chigi vase from the middle of the 7th century he is shown still carrying two Homeric throwable spears, but the vase shows that the traditional armour of helmet, cuirass and greaves, all made of bronze, had already been adopted. Gradually the weaponry and armour were improved. By the time of the Persian invasion the bronze cuirass had been replaced by a linen one which gave better protection and was a lot cheaper to produce. The throwable spears were replaced by a long thrusting spear and a short sword. With these weapons the hoplites could keep a tight formation.

Right
The 'archaic *lochos*', the hypothetical original unit of the phalanx from which all the others evolved. It was made up of four *enomotiai*, each of which was composed of three files of eight men and a rear ranker (*ouragos*);
O = *ouragos*.

The 'archaic lochos'

The difficulty of trying to understand the development of the phalanx is that our detailed knowledge of it comes almost entirely from the beginning of the 4th century, some 400 years after its conception. By using the scraps of information given by the earlier writers it is possible to reconstruct a hypothetical prototype phalanx. This will help considerably in the understanding of its later developments.

Since this proto-phalanx is reconstructed in retrospect, I shall not bother to retrace the steps leading to it as these should become obvious when we trace its later development. The 4th century Spartan army contained units called *pentekostyes* or 'fifties'. Two of these made up the standard unit of the phalanx called a *lochos*. By the 4th century, however, these *pentekostyes* were not 50 strong. The theory put forward

here presupposes that at some earlier period, possibly around 800 BC, there was a unit of 50 men. Despite the terminology, however, it will be presumed for the purpose of this reconstruction that there was a *lochos* consisting of 100 men which will henceforth be called the 'archaic *lochos*'. This *lochos* was composed of two *pentekostyes* which were in turn divided into two *enomotiai*. Each *enomotia* consisted of 23 hoplites, a veteran rear-rank officer (*ouragos* or *tergiductor*) and a commanding officer (*enomotarch*). In battle the *enomotia* would usually be drawn up in three files each of eight men, with the rear-rank officer standing clear at the back to make sure that the rear ranks did their job. The *enomotarch*, like all the officers of the phalanx, fought at the front of the right-hand file of his unit. When drawn up eight deep, the whole *lochos* would consist of 12 files. It was commanded by

a *lochagos* who fought at the front of the right-hand file. The left half of the *lochos* was commanded by a *pentekonter*, similarly fighting at the front of the right-hand file of his unit. So we have a 100-strong *lochos* with its officers fighting in the front rank and its rear-rank officers standing proud at the back. This isolated position of the rear-rank officers is illustrated by Xenophon at the fictional battle of Thymbrara, where the light-armed troops are placed behind the phalanx and the 'rear rankers' drawn up behind them to keep them in order.

The new formation was adopted by all the city states and, although details varied from state to state, the basic organisation always remained the same.

The Athenian army

At Athens, which was the largest of the city states, all Athenian citizens between the ages of 17 and 59 were liable for military service. During the 5th century Athens was able to field about 30,000 hoplites of whom nearly half were campaign soldiers. The remainder, those under 19 and the veterans, performed garrison duties. These hoplites were drawn from the wealthier classes as each man had to supply his own equipment which only the well-off could afford. However, a soldier whose father had been killed in battle was armed at public expense.

As far as can be seen, the Athenians retained the basic 'archaic *lochos*' and generally fought eight deep. The army consisted of ten divisions (*taxeis*), each commanded by a *taxiarch*. One division was drawn from each of the ten Athenian

tribes. Each of these *taxeis* was subdivided into *lochoi*, but we know of no intermediate division between the *taxis* and the *lochos*.

At Athens, as in all the democratic states, the general (*strategos*) was elected. At Athens ten were chosen annually—one for each tribe. In practice, usually only three went with the army, in which case either one was made commander-in-chief or each commanded in rotation on separate days. The officers seem to have served in the front rank and even the general, after giving his orders, took up his position, usually at the right end of the phalanx.

Sparta—a military state

There was one state that must be separated from the others as it deviated from the patterns along which the others evolved. This was Sparta—the most feared state in Greece. It was accepted that one Spartan was worth several men of any other state, and none of the other states, unless forced, would dare oppose Sparta on the battlefield.

The Spartans themselves were known as Spartiates. They formed the core of the army. The Spartan army was reinforced by levies from the subject *perioeci*. By the beginning of the 5th century *helots* were also serving with the army as light-armed skirmishers. The combined army of the Spartiates and *perioeci* is referred to as Lacedaemonian.

The Spartans had a strange constitution. Although they were commanded in battle by two hereditary kings who could be, and often were, removed if the people did not like them, they were

governed by five magistrates (*ephors*) who were elected annually. The kings must originally have had political power but, by the 5th century BC, the *ephors* were the true power in the state and were answerable only to their successors. Each king had a bodyguard of 300 hoplites who, in spite of their name, *hippeis*, were infantry, not cavalry. Originally both kings went on campaign but, shortly before the Persian wars, it was restricted to one.

If our knowledge of the Athenian military system is sparse, the absolute reverse is true of Sparta. The Athenian soldier and writer Xenophon spent many years with the Spartans and served on campaign with them. He had a great admiration for the Spartan military system and his writings bristle with details of their military practices. From his writings one can build up a very full picture of the Spartan army at the end of the 5th century BC. Sparta was a very conservative state and the vast majority of his description must hold good for the beginning of the century too.

Everything at Sparta was regulated by the state. All Spartans were soldiers. All other professions were forbidden to them. Spartan land was divided up into state-owned farms operated by *helots*. Each Spartan was assigned one of these farms from which he drew his sustenance, which left him free to devote his whole life to military prowess. The Spartan system was self-perpetuating; it was because they were warriors that they overcame and enslaved the *helots*, who greatly outnumbered them, and in order to maintain this status quo every

Spartan had to devote his life to soldiering so that he could keep the *helots* down.

The training of a Spartan boy
The state regulated everything in life. Expectant mothers had to perform strenuous exercises to ensure their children were strong; imperfect babies were put down.

At the age of seven boys were taken from their mothers, their hair was cut short and they were formed into classes where they all lived, ate and slept together, so that all were governed by the same discipline.

The Spartans did not entrust the education of their children to hired teachers; they nominated a mature and experienced citizen to perform this task. Academic education was minimal. Emphasis was always on discipline and exercise. Children for the most part went barefoot and naked. Their food was simple and scant to encourage them to steal. Although they were punished when caught, the punishment was for being caught, not for stealing, so that later a soldier might be able to endure famine and be a good forager.

At the age of 12 the discipline became much harsher. It was recognised that boys of this age could be very unruly, so they loaded them with hard work and constant exercises. The hardy routine of early childhood was continued: underclothes were forbidden, and one tunic had to serve for both winter and summer.

Fighting was encouraged among both adults and children, but never in anger. A fight had to break up when ordered by another citizen. This is illustrated by the young boy who was thrashed by his father, not because he had been fighting but because he complained that another boy had hit him.

Bravery was considered the ultimate virtue and cowardice the greatest vice. After a battle the dead were carried home on their shields. On the other hand, when running away from a battlefield, the first thing a hoplite discarded was his cumbersome shield, so a Spartan mother told her son to return from battle either carrying his shield or on it.

A boy reached manhood in his twentieth year, when he became liable for military service. The fittest youths were taken into the army. Those who were rejected were graded as inferiors; these may have formed a pool of replacements. Since the Spartan army was organised by age groups, the young men continued to live and exercise together; even when married a Spartan man lived and ate in the barracks without his wife. This separation of men from their wives encouraged homosexuality.

The Spartan army
Xenophon, in his *Constitution of the Lacedaemonians*, gives a very full account of the organisation of the Spartan army in his own time around the beginning of the 4th century BC. It is unfortunate that an account given by Thucydides when he is describing the first battle of Mantinea is somewhat different. Thucydides freely admits that he had great difficulty in obtaining information about the Spartan army and may have tried to reconstruct their

Above
The picture of hoplites going into battle (top) is taken from a 7th-century Corinthian vase found at Chigi in Etruria. The figure shows a reconstruction of a hoplite from about 600 BC based on the archaeological evidence.

organisation from a mixture of contemporary and earlier information. Xenophon's account is first hand and must be preferred.

All men between the ages of 20 and 60 were liable for military service. Spartan hoplites were armed in the same fashion as the other Greeks, but were easily recognisable by their uniform scarlet cloaks. This red cloak became the symbol of Spartan militarism.

In Xenophon's day the strength of the Spartan *lochos* was 144, being composed of four 36-strong *enomotiai*. All that seems to have happened is that the strength of the *enomotia* had been raised by 50 per cent so that the basic depth of the phalanx could be increased from eight to twelve. At this time there was a general tendency towards deeper formations, probably stimulated by the rise of Thebes which had adopted a much deeper phalanx. One can say with reasonable certainty that, up until the late 5th century, Sparta too retained the 'archaic *lochos*' with its standard depth of eight.

The Spartan army was organised so that every unit, no matter how small, had its own commander, and possibly rear-rank commander too. The rear-rank officers (*ouragoi*) may not have been supernumeraries in the Spartan army and the whole rear rank of the phalanx may have consisted of them. Each *enomotia* was subdivided into three files, and then again into six half files. Each file and half file had its best man as leader and its second-best man as rear ranker. The *enomotiai* were coupled into 'fifties' (*pentekostyes*), each with its own commander (*pentekonter*). Two fifties were similarly joined to form a *lochos*—the smallest tactical unit of the phalanx. The *lochos* was commanded by a *lochagos*. The whole Spartan army was composed of six divisions. Each division (*mora*) was commanded by a *polemarch* and contained four *lochoi*. In phalanx all the officers and file leaders would be in the front rank. The various officers— *enomotarchs*, *pentekonters* and *lochagoi* —would fight at the head of the right-hand file of the unit that they commanded.

Attached to each *mora* was a unit of cavalry—also called a *mora*. This was probably about 60 strong. These cavalry units only came into being during the Peloponnesian war towards the end of the 5th century.

The first *mora* contained a unit called the *hippeis*. This consisted of the 300

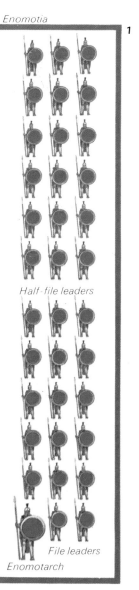

1 Enomotia

Half-file leaders

File leaders

Enomotarch

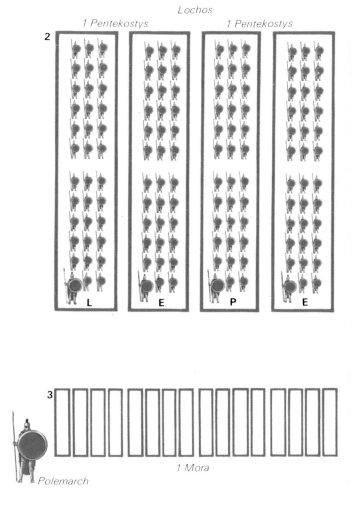

Lochos

1 Pentekostys   1 Pentekostys

L   E   P   E

3 Polemarch

1 Mora

The organisation of the Spartan army at the time of Xenophon (early 4th century).
1 The smallest unit of the Spartan army, the *enomotia*, composed of three files of twelve men or six half files each of six men. It was commanded by an *enomotarch*. The *enomotiai* were coupled to form *pentekostyes*, each commanded by a *pentekonter*.
2 A *lochos*, the basic unit of the phalanx. It was composed of two *pentekostyes* (four *enomotiae*) and was commanded by a *lochagos*.
3 A *mora* composed of four *lochoi* (576 men) and commanded by a *polemarch*. The entire Spartan army was made up of six *morae* and was commanded by the king.
L = *lochagos*   **E** = *enomotarch*
P = *pentekonter*

Spartan army = 6 morae

King

hoplites who were the cream of the army. They were selected from the men who were in the prime of life. Each year three men were chosen by the *ephors*; they were called *hippagretae*. Their job was to select 100 men each to make up the *hippeis*. These men served on the right wing of the army and made up the king's bodyguard. It is possible that only those who had sons were eligible for this unit, for the Spartans looked down on any man who had not done his duty and produced the next generation of hoplites. This would account for Herodotus' remark at the battle of Thermopylae about the Spartan troops who had sons.

Sparta in Herodotus' day

It seems likely that the Spartan army went through two reorganisations, one at the time of Xenophon at the beginning of the 4th century, and one perhaps 50 years earlier. Practically nothing is known of the army before this earlier reorganisation. However, from odd remarks about *lochoi* and the absence of the word *mora* from Herodotus' account, coupled with the constant tradition in the ancient sources that there were five *lochoi* in the Spartan army, it does not seem unreasonable to suggest that at the beginning of the 5th century the Spartan army may have been organised in five super *lochoi*. It is quite possible that the subdivisions of these super *lochoi* were also called *lochoi*—the word simply means a body of men and in no way implies a fixed number. A parallel may be quoted in the indiscriminate use of the word *taxis*, which in Xenophon's time could mean any unit of more than one *lochos*.

These super *lochoi* were probably territorial levies on the five districts or villages that made up Sparta. In prehistoric times each village may have been expected to supply one *lochos*. Gradually, as the villages expanded, so these units grew but continued to be called *lochoi*. Each of these units was commanded by a *lochagos* who was obviously much more senior than his name suggests. At Plataea in 479, each of the five *lochagoi* would have commanded about 1,000 men. This explains why the *lochagos* Amompharetus felt that he could challenge the authority of the commander-in-chief Pausanias because

under normal circumstances he would have been present at the council of war. No doubt these super *lochoi* were subdivided in a similar manner to the later army.

From the 7th century onwards the Spartan population was constantly in decline. Between the 7th and the beginning of the 5th century the army strength dropped from 9,000 to 8,000. A hundred years later it had shrunk to around 4,000, of whom only about 1,000 were Spartiates, so that manumitted *helots* and *perioeci* were having to be drafted into the army to keep it up to strength. This devastating decline in the population of the Spartan state must have been the reason for the successive reorganisations.

Recruits in Xenophon's time

Xenophon insists that there was no need to train a man in the use of his weapons, as from childhood one learns to throw up one's left arm in defence, and that striking with a spear is also natural. This is probably true. The strength of the phalanx was never based on individual prowess but on operating together in a disciplined fashion. Xenophon obviously believed that practice in the use of spear and shield was all that was necessary and certainly mock battles took place. It must also be true that every Spartan boy from the earliest age must have played at soldiers and learned his military craft this way.

Nevertheless, hoplites must have been trained in the basic movements and it has been suggested that certain positions commonly appearing in art represent these basic movements. These are shown on p. 42.

1. When at ease the hoplite stands with his spear butt on the ground and his shield resting against his thigh. Hoplites sometimes retained this position in the face of the enemy as a sign of contempt.
2. When called to attention the spear is raised to the right shoulder and the shield lifted to cover the torso.
3. From here the hoplite can come to the 'on guard' position by bringing the spear forward until his right arm is straight and the spear is parallel to the ground at waist level. This was the position for the underhand thrust—it

Above
An exquisitely modelled late 6th-century bronze statuette showing a Spartan armed for battle and swathed in his military cloak. The transverse crest may be a sign of rank. Wadsworth Athenaeum, Hartford Connecticut.

was in this stance that the hoplite advanced to battle. The underhand thrust could not be executed under normal conditions in close array as one would have to open up the wall of shields to thrust at waist level. Also there would be a risk of striking the man next in file with the pointed butt of the spear.

4. The normal striking position has to be with the spear raised above the right shoulder striking downwards at a slight angle through the dart-shaped gap between the top of one's own shield and that of one's neighbour on the right. The angle of the stroke should ensure that it passes over the head of the next in file. To take up this attitude from **2** would be impossible as it would leave the spear butt pointing forward. To do it from **3** is equally impossible with a long spear. It would be necessary to raise the spear above the right shoulder and then reverse the grip. These movements in phalanx would require considerable training. A professional soldier could always tell a badly trained army by the untidy way they performed this drill.

Training started by teaching the new recruits to march in single file following the leader. A Spartan youngster starting his basic training would have already been inured to the Spartan tradition and would only have needed to be knocked

into shape. All orders were given by word and then executed on a trumpet sound. Xenophon gives a colourful description of a *taxiarch* trying to train new recruits, obviously not Spartans, to march in single file. He lined them up behind the *lochagos* and then gave them the order to advance, at which, without waiting for the trumpet, the man behind the *lochagos* stepped forward and overtook him. With commendable patience, the *taxiarch* explained to the raw recruit that he meant all of them and not just him. He ordered the youth back into line and gave the order again. This time they all overtook the *lochagos*.

Having trained the recruits to march in line they were then taught how to deploy into ranks of various length. The *enomotia* of, say, 36 men is drawn up in single file. They are numbered off; the first man (*enomotarch*) commanded the whole file, the thirteenth commanded numbers 14 to 24, and the twenty-fifth man commanded numbers 26 to 36. On the order to form up three abreast, numbers 1 to 12 would stand fast and numbers 13 and 25 would bring up their squads on the left-hand side to form a column three abreast and 12 deep. On a second order the rear half of each squad would move up alongside its front half to form a block six wide and six deep. The files could be drawn up either in

open order with two paces between files or close order with one pace between. Since there are no markers, this drill is only practical if the leader of each squad wheels his unit to the left and paces out the distance he will need to be from the first file and then wheels to the right and leads his men forward until he is level with the *enomotarch*. Bringing up the rear half of each file is also the easiest way to form close order from open order.

When dealing with a whole *lochos* of four *enomotiai* the drill becomes considerably more complex. The diagram shows four *enomotiai* already drawn up in column three abreast forming up into a block 12 by 12. If this was done in open order then the rear half of each file could be brought up to form a close-order phalanx of six ranks each of 24.

To reform in column the phalanx did an about turn and the rear ranker

Below
A hoplite (c. 400 BC) doing weapons training. These movements are hypothetical and based on poses regularly shown on Greek vases.
1 At ease, with his shield resting against his thighs and spear butt on the ground. Sometimes this position served as a sign of contempt when facing the enemy.
2 Attention, with his spear 'sloped' and shield raised.
3 The underarm thrusting position. It was in this position that he advanced into battle.
4 The overarm thrusting position.

(*ouragos*) of the last squad, which would now be at the right end, led off and the other units followed in their correct order.

Xenophon tells us how, in order to practice this, a *taxiarch* used to march his recruits to the mess in phalanx and then have them lead off in single file with the right-hand *lochagos* leading. When they had finished their meal they had to come out in reverse order with the left-hand *ouragos* leading and form up again in phalanx facing the rear. This was the formation for retreat.

Once the new recruits had completed their basic training they were ready to take their places in the ranks. Since the Spartan army was called up by year classes, each year's recruits must have formed a separate unit. It is unthinkable that they were called up by age and then organised into units. When the mobilisation order was given, complete units must have assembled ready for action. At the time of Xenophon the army strength was about 4,000. Since the soldiers served for 40 years the turnover was about 100 a year. Allowing for losses either in battle or from natural causes, one may assume that about 50 veterans reached retirement each year and that about 200 replacements were needed. In order to make room for the new recruits one *enomotia* in each *mora*

could have been disbanded except for its officers, file leaders and *ouragoi* and the 180 best recruits drafted in to make up the numbers. The rest of the recruits would join the cavalry. The remainder of the disbanded *enomotia* could be used to bring the other *enomotiai* up to strength. The new *enomotia* would serve on the left side of the *mora* in the least honourable position. Having become part of the main army the new recruits could now take part in large-scale practice manoeuvres. They learned to use their drill in conjunction with the other three *lochoi* of their *mora*.

Once again, on a much larger scale, they would learn to deploy from column of march into phalanx. Marching in column of threes the first *lochos* would come to a halt and each succeeding *lochos* would wheel to the left. As the *lochagos*, who would be at the head of the right file, crossed the line of the left file, he would start counting out the paces that would bring him to the correct position to wheel to the right again and draw up level with the first *lochos*. The deployment of the individual *lochoi* would be as they had learned in basic training. To form up in open order 12 ranks deep the rear *lochos* would have to count off 70 paces to the left. The whole *mora* would have a front of 48 men covering a distance of 94 paces. They

must also learn to deploy from column of march to face either left or right. The exercise was basically the same except that each *lochos*, including the first, would simply have to wheel to the left or right, come to a halt and then deploy into phalanx.

They also had to learn to perform outflanking movements. These required turning the wings forward to engulf the flanks of the enemy. These movements are often mentioned in ancient battles but present a lot of problems as it would be impossible for a phalanx to wheel. Fortunately Xenophon describes the manoeuvre in his fictional battle of Thymbrara. Here the manoeuvre is carried out on both wings, though it was usually only performed on one. The army is drawn up in phalanx. On the trumpet blast the two wings turn outwards into column and begin to march away from the main part of the army. At a given distance they wheel round a marker and begin to advance towards the front in column. When all the column has wheeled on both wings the whole army begins to advance with the two wings like horns projecting in front. When the flanking columns draw level with the enemy line they turn inwards and charge. Such a manoeuvre could be very dangerous if the enemy anticipated the movement.

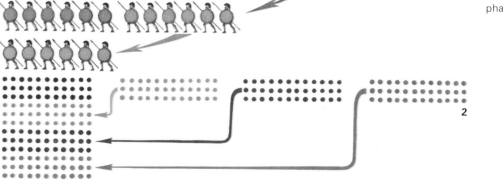

1 A Spartan *enomotia* of 36 men in single file forming up first three abreast and then six abreast.

2 A *lochos* (four *enomotiai*) drawn up three men abreast moving forwards to form a phalanx twelve wide.

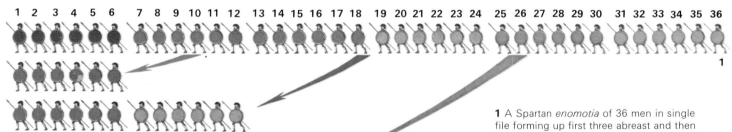

The Phalanx in the Field

Mobilisation

When the army mobilised the *ephors* announced the year classes that were to be called up, engineers and craftsmen as well as soldiers. Everything was regulated; if they were going on a campaign that was expected to last more than 15 days, each soldier had to take with him supplies for 20 days. It was forbidden to buy anything from outside traders before this time was up. Each Spartan was accompanied by a *helot* who carried his baggage. A hoplite's rations would include food for his *helot*. The basic diet was barley groats, of which he would need about 11 gallons to last the two of them 20 days. This was supplemented by cheese, onions and salted meat. When starting out on campaign hoplites were allowed to take a small amount of wine with them. This was to accustom the stomach gradually to the change-over from wine to water so that they would not become ill. Rations were carried in a haversack which proverbially stank of onions.

Spartan food was frugal—and not just on campaign; it was the same in the messes at Sparta. Everybody ate the same food. There were no special rations for officers, not even the king. When an ally once prepared a feast for the Spartan army, the king ordered all the dainties to be given to the *helots*.

When Xenophon was serving on Cyrus the Younger's abortive campaign in Asia, the Greek mercenaries were unable to afford to pay the inflated prices being charged for grain and had to live on a meat diet which, although enjoyed in small quantities, could be no substitute for their normal grain intake. This throws an interesting sidelight on the Roman general Corbulo who was compelled to do the same thing, and which has led some commentators to state erroneously that Roman soldiers did not normally eat meat. Barley was carried already ground so that hand mills would not be needed on the march. These were acquired when the army reached a place where they could forage or buy food.

The soldier also had to carry his bedding, which was kept to a minimum and sometimes strapped to his shield, and plenty of clothing. The soldiers did not carry tents but improvised, building

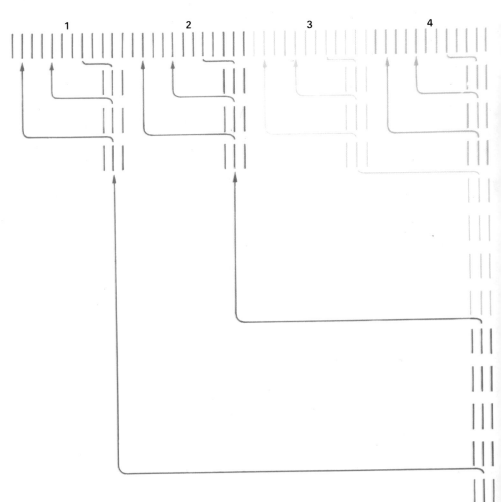

Above
Deploying a *mora* from column of threes into phalanx 12 deep. Each *lochos* wheels to the left and paces off the required distance before wheeling to the right and advancing level with the first *lochos*. The *enomotiae* deploy in the same manner as shown on the previous page.

bivouacs or huts wherever they camped.

The *ephors* also regulated the number of wagons and pack animals that were needed for the baggage train, which had its own commanding officer. Each wagon carried a shovel and a mattock, and each baggage animal an axe and a sickle. The tools were for the use of the pioneers who were made up of rejects from the light infantry. Their job was to clear the way for the wagons. Amongst the equipment taken with the army were medical supplies, spare harness straps for the men's equipment, files for sharpening weapons, spokeshaves for trimming spear shafts and spare wood for making running repairs to the wagons plus the necessary carpenter's

tools. The officers were held responsible for their men's equipment.

Amongst the craftsmen who accompanied the expedition were smiths, carpenters and leather workers of military age. Although non-combatants, they were a regular part of the army.

On the march

Before the Spartan army set out the king offered sacrifice at home. If the omens were favourable a fire bearer took the fire from the altar and carried it ahead of the army until they reached the borders of Laconia. Here the king sacrificed again and, if the omens were still favourable, took the fire from this altar and led the army on. This fire was never quenched. All the sacrificial victims that were likely to be needed on the campaign were taken with the army.

On the march the Spartan army was led by the cavalry and the *sciritae* who fanned out in a screen ahead of the column. The *sciritae* were hardy mountaineers from the northern frontier of Lacedaemon. They were light armed and used for scouting and outpost duties. Of course Xenophon is here describing the practice of his own day; at the time of the Persian wars the southern Greeks did not have cavalry and this duty would have been performed solely by the *sciritae*. Behind the

Above
A Spartan hoplite (c. 500 BC) wearing a Corinthian helmet, which he pulls down to cover his face before going into battle, linen cuirass and knee-covering greaves. He is armed with a long spear and a sword which would only normally be used if the spear is broken. In the rigidly regulated Spartan military state all men between the ages of 20 and 60 were soldiers. Although they were armed in the same way as other Greeks, Spartan hoplites wore a distinctive scarlet cloak which became the very symbol of Spartan militarism.

Below
A vase painting showing a donkey with a wood-framed pack. From Athens, c. 475 BC. Museum of Fine Arts, Boston.

Left
Bronze figurine of a pack donkey. The paniers were probably made of wicker. Origin unknown. British Museum.

Below
Two hoplites and an archer preparing to go on campaign. One hoplite is putting his Argive shield into its leather cover. The scene comes from a 5th-century vase found at the Greek colony of Paestum in southern Italy. Paestum Museum.

Below
An army marching in defensive square formation. The front and rear of the square march in phalanx and the sides in column. The individual *lochoi* march eight abreast. The baggage and non-combatants are placed in the centre.

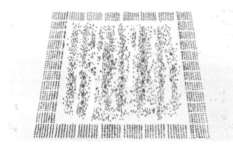

Below
When advancing through a defile the *lochoi* reduce their width to four, two or even single file according to the narrowness of the road so that they can retain their formation.

cavalry screen came the baggage train followed by the infantry, who hurried on any stragglers from the baggage train.

The army only marched a short distance the first day so that if anything had been forgotten it could be retrieved. Marching orders were given by horn and not trumpet. These orders were basically strike camp, move off and rest. However, the order to get up in the morning was given on the trumpet. If the army had to pass through a defile the infantry divided into two columns and marched on either side of the baggage train to protect it from attack. As far as possible each *mora* accompanied its own baggage so that the soldiers would work willingly to clear the way and would have everything with them when the time came to halt. If the column was attacked when passing through the defile, each *lochos* would wheel to face the threat. If the ground was broken they could continue to advance in that formation with gaps between the *lochoi* or, in open country, they could deploy into phalanx.

When Cyrus the Younger's expedition into Asia came to a sudden end, Xenophon and the 10,000 Greek mercenaries serving with him had to make a tactical retreat. This withdrawal, 1,300 km up the Tigris and over the mountains of Armenia to the Black Sea, is one of the great military adventures. It was described by Xenophon in detail in his *Anabasis*.

In order to protect themselves on all sides they formed up in an open square. This formation is often mentioned in the ancient sources. Nicias used it during his fateful retreat from Syracuse, but only Xenophon has taken the trouble to describe it.

The army is divided into four parts: two divisions marching in column form the flanks and the other two parts marching in phalanx form the front and rear of the square. All the light armed, the baggage and non-combatants are in the centre.

Each *lochos* is drawn up so that it can march either in file where the road is narrow or several abreast in open country. This shows the practical use of drill. This exercise allowed whole *lochoi* to fall back when necessary so that the square could contract or expand.

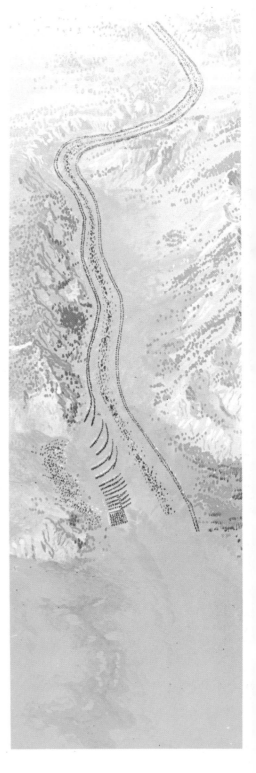

Above
An army advancing through a defile under normal conditions. The baggage train is in the centre and the phalanx in column on either side. At the bottom the column is deploying into phalanx, in readiness to meet a flank attack.

On encountering the enemy, the army would pitch camp. The Greeks were never as conscious as the Romans of the value of a fortified camp. Xenophon states that the Spartan camp was round. By this one must assume that the units of the army formed a circular perimeter and that the baggage train and non-combatants were in the middle. It is quite clear that it was not fortified even with a ditch. Often the camp was adapted to the topography and therefore Xenophon's statement should not be taken too literally. During the day cavalry outposts were set up on commanding hills. At night these outposts were taken over by the *sciritae*. No doubt before the introduction of cavalry they performed this duty in the daytime too. The reason that cavalry are used is because they can bring information more quickly. Other sentry posts were also set up at night commanding the approaches to the camp.

The only detailed account that we have of an army on the march is Xenophon's retreat of the 10,000. In this account, in which the army is basically Spartan, in spite of the constant threat of an enemy attack, no attempt was made to fortify a camp. They relied on sorties to keep the enemy at bay. It was only when a long-term occupation was intended that a ditch and palisade were constructed.

It is amusing to note that the Spartans feared a slave revolt so much that it was considered more important to guard the arms than the perimeter of the camp.

The camp had no sanitary arrangements and it was insisted only that soldiers relieve themselves at a sufficient distance so as not to offend their comrades. Each *mora* encamped as a unit with strict boundaries. Before breakfast and supper each day there was a compulsory exercise session. Soldiers were forbidden to take their exercise beyond the boundaries of their *mora*.

The king's tent was probably set up in the centre of the camp or on some commanding eminence. Around it were grouped his staff officers and those who were necessary for him to perform his military duties. They were known as 'those about the tent'. They included the *polemarchs*, diviners, doctors, and three Spartiates whose job it was to wait

upon the king. The king's bodyguard, the 300 *hippeis*, must also have been billeted fairly close to him. There were also two *pythii* who could be sent to Delphi to consult the oracle there, the flute players who were required when the king sacrificed, and the heralds whose job was to convey the generals' orders down the chain of command when contact could not be personal, for example after battle had been joined. They were also used to convey messages between warring states. As battles were often fought like duels, heralds would sometimes be sent to arrange the time and place for a battle.

Each morning the king offered sacrifice in the presence of the *polemarchs*, the *lochagoi*, the *pentekonters*, the commanders of foreign contingents and the officers of the baggage train. After this he gave his orders for the day. When battle was imminent the hoplites polished their shields, prepared their weapons and combed their long hair, which Herodotus says the Spartans always did when they were going to put their lives at risk.

The battle

The following morning the king and all the Spartiates placed garlands on their heads and the king sacrificed a nanny-goat in sight of the enemy whilst all the flautists played. The diviners, without whom no Greek general would go to war, would read the omens and advise the king whether he should attack or not. No pious general would dream of fighting if the omens were unfavourable. At Plataea the Spartan general Pausanias refused to fight even though the Persians were attacking his men, and Xenophon freely admits that he would not even move his men while the omens were unfavourable, even though they were facing starvation. Of course often the omens were falsified to suit the wishes of the general. If he then attacked and won, the diviners would have to say the omens were favourable; if he lost, then of course his impiety had called down the vengeance of the gods.

If the omens were declared to be favourable, the Spartiates would take breakfast with the garlands still on their heads and then take up their places in the phalanx, still garlanded.

Whatever orders there were for the

battle would have been decided in the war council by the king and the *polemarchs*. At the time of the Persian wars this council probably included the five *lochagoi*, which is hinted at by the action of the *lochagos* Amompharetus who refused to obey the order to retreat at the battle of Plataea. His argument with Pausanias implies that he was not consulted and that he should have been.

The king would give the final orders to the *polemarchs* and they would pass them on to their *lochagoi*. The *lochagoi* would in turn pass them on to their *pentekonters* and through them to the *enomotarchs*, and they would pass them on to the men in their files.

Each soldier would receive the message and pass it on to people whom he knew personally. When the orders had been given the officers would take up their positions in the front rank of the phalanx, each at the head of the right-hand file of his own unit, and wait for the order to advance, which would be given on the trumpet.

The king passed the watchword down the ranks, each soldier repeating it. When it reached the end of the line, it was passed back along the ranks to the king. The king then raised the customary paean, a sort of 'Land of Hope and Glory' aimed at raising the spirits of the hoplites; it was known as Castor's song. The trumpets sounded, the flutes struck up the tune, the hoplites levelled their spears and the army began to advance, keeping step to the flutes and joining their voices to the king's as he sung the paean. As they approached the enemy they stopped singing and the officers called out to the front and second ranks, shouting 'Come on friends, brave men', encouraging them to follow their leaders into battle. Those in the rear ranks responded to their officers, encouraging them to lead on boldly.

As they closed with the enemy the trumpet sounded again and the hoplites raised their spears to the attack position above their right shoulders. The phalanx would now usually break into a run and again the commander would call down the ranks: 'Who will follow? Who is a brave man? Who will be the first to strike down his man?' The soldiers hearing this repeated it like the watchword as they closed with the enemy: 'Who will follow? Who is a brave man?'

Then the two phalanxes met with a great crash as shield hit shield. The rear ranks crowded forward, each pressing against the man in front and striking at the enemy over his shoulder, trying, with his weight, to push the whole enemy phalanx off balance. And all the while the rear rankers urged them on. When a man fell his place was taken by the next in file, and so they struggled on until the enemy broke.

This description is drawn from accounts of battles, some real and some imaginary. It is of course oversimplified —this describes a set-piece battle. As often as not the circumstances of the battle were unpredictable, as at Plataea where the Spartans were attacked before they had received favourable omens. That the second and subsequent ranks, and not just the front rank, joined in the fighting is confirmed by the remark of Cyrus at Xenophon's imaginary battle of Thymbrara about the phalanx being too deep for the men to reach the enemy with their weapons.

As long as the phalanx retained its order casualties would be few, but if it broke and the hoplites turned and fled, throwing away their shields, then the slaughter started. Usually the Spartans did not pursue a defeated enemy. When the king decided that victory had been won, he gave the order and the trumpeters sounded the withdrawal. They would then collect their dead. The losing side would have to send a herald to negotiate a truce in order to recover their dead; this became the formal admission of defeat.

After the victory a trophy made up of captured arms and armour displayed in the form of a man on a tree trunk might be set up. After many victories a permanent victory monument was set up. Certain choice pieces of armour were inscribed and dedicated in the shrines at Olympia or Delphi. By Alexander's time, captured shields became the customary dedication.

Mercenaries

Greece was a poor country and from the earliest times hoplites offered their services for pay. The earliest accounts of Greek soldiers serving as mercenaries comes from Egypt in the 7th–6th centuries. They are found also serving as bodyguards to the early Greek tyrants during the same period. With the rise of Persia many Greeks found service with Persian governors, first as bodyguards and later as shock troops.

The employment of hired soldiers within Greece only really began during the war between Sparta and Athens. During this conflict both sides employed mercenaries.

At the end of this long war, many soldiers who had known no other life but soldiering offered their services for hire. Xenophon was one of the 10,000 such men who accompanied Cyrus the Younger in his attempt to usurp the Persian throne. The hiring of mercenary troops both inside and outside of Greece became common during this period.

When Alexander invaded Persia he was opposed at all three of his great battles by Greek mercenary infantry.

Auxiliary troops

The phalanx, which was originally seen as the ultimate and only weapon, gradually began to reveal its weaknesses. It was infinitely superior to what had gone before it, and for this reason it was adopted by all the Greek states. However, it could not be used over rough ground or for hill fighting and was useless against cavalry or light-armed skirmishers using guerilla tactics. Athens began employing Scythian and Cretan archers in the 6th century, but it was only the impact of the Persian wars that forced the Greek states to consider seriously the use of light-armed troops. Their response was half-hearted and, although Herodotus claims that there were 35,000 light-armed *helots* and about the same number of other light-armed troops including archers at Plataea, they had little or no effect on the Persian cavalry who seemed to be able to operate at will, charging the phalanx and cutting the Greek supply lines.

It seems incredible that in no battle of the Persian war is there mention of even a single Greek horseman. The Greeks can hardly have been unaware of the effect that the Persian cavalry must have on them. Perhaps they were relying on Thessaly and Boeotia to provide contingents of horsemen to keep the Persian cavalry busy. When these areas fell to the Persians the southern states did not try to compensate for this. When they won in spite of it, they probably convinced themselves that they did not need cavalry. Cavalry and light infantry only really came into use in the Peloponnesian war in the second half of the 5th century. This cavalry was light armed and was never used in shock action. Xenophon, in his book on the art of horsemanship, advocates the use of javelins by the cavalry rather than the traditional spear.

The light-armed soldier *par excellence* was the peltast. He was named after his wicker shield (*pelta*); according to Aristotle it was rimless and covered with goat or sheep skin. Aristotle seems to imply that it was round, but in art it is crescent shaped. It appears in Scythian art and is clearly the primeval shield of eastern central Europe. The *pelta* is being carried by the figures on the late Mycenaean Warrior Vase. The *pelta* is sometimes shown with a single hand-grip and sometimes with the double hoplite type grip; this latter is probably artistic licence. Such a grip would be a positive disadvantage to a skirmisher who had no neighbour to protect. The *pelta* also had a strap for carrying. Xenophon gives a very amusing description of peltasts climbing over fences with their shields on their backs getting caught up on the paling and hanging by their shield straps. The peltast was of Thracian origin and wore the traditional costume of his country—patterned cloak, high boots and Phrygian cap. This was a fox-skin cap with ear flaps. He wore no armour and relied on his speed to get him out of trouble. His weapon was the javelin. His tactic was to run in, throw the javelins and then run away again before the enemy could come to grips with him. The Spartans tried to deal with peltasts by ordering their youngest age groups to give chase.

For longer-range warfare archers and slingers were employed. Archers were mainly Scythians and Cretans. Both used composite bows made of wood, horn, bone and sinew. The construction of this type of bow is shown on p. 50. The Cretan bow was segment shaped and the Scythian doubly convex. Scythian bows had a range of somewhat over 150m.

Slingers were much used from the 5th century onwards. The men of Rhodes were the best; they could easily outrange the bow. Their maximum range was probably in excess of 350m. Sling shot could either be of stone, clay or lead—the last was probably the most effective. Thousands of lead sling shot have been found, including the moulds in which they were cast. Lead shot generally vary in weight between 20 and 50g, though there are isolated examples both above and below these weights. The maximum weight in use in the Near East was 185g. If Diodorus is to be believed, the famous Balearic slingers used stones weighing one *mina* (c. 350g). As Korfmann pointed out in his article on the sling, such a stone would be about 6.3cm in diameter—only slightly smaller than a tennis ball. The lead shot, which are plum shaped, could cause terrible wounds. Xenophon describes how they enter the body and the flesh closes over them.

Light-armed forces had always been treated as inferior troops used only for skirmishing. Their main purpose was to protect the all-important phalanx from enemy cavalry and skirmishers. They usually fought on the wings, but sometimes light infantry fought from behind the phalanx. From the latter position they threw missiles over the heads of the hoplites. This was only really effective on sloping ground from which they could see the enemy. In the fictional battle of Thymbrara, Cyrus lined up his peltasts behind the phalanx and the archers behind them. He then drew up his *ouragoi* behind them all to keep them in order. These light-armed specialist troops were mainly imported mercenaries. States normally produced their own cavalry though this was often supplemented by employing Thessalians. Sparta trained *helots* as light-armed troops and Athens tried to form peltast units from her poorer classes. Mercenary skirmishers were generally renowned for their unruly behaviour, but when given the right discipline and training could produce remarkable results.

In 390 BC a young Athenian general, Iphicrates, with a highly trained and disciplined group of Thracian peltasts, defeated a Spartan *mora*, killing nearly half their number. This feat completely changed the Greek attitude to peltasts and ensured Iphicrates a place in military history. In 349 Athens even sent an army against Philip of Macedon that

was composed entirely of peltasts accompanied by a small body of cavalry.

The Theban tactic
Xenophon died about 354 BC. It is a tragedy for the study of the development of Greek warfare that he never thought it worthwhile to describe Theban tactics, nor the changes that took place under Epaminondas. He tries to

49

show why the Spartans lost the battle of Leuctra but never explains why the Thebans won. It cannot be doubted that the Thebans had a great influence on the development of Macedonian warfare, but, because of the lack of evidence, it is impossible to say exactly what. We can only relate what is known and try to draw a few conclusions.

The main factor on which all the ancient sources are agreed is that the Thebans traditionally drew up their phalanx with greater depth than the other Greeks. At Delium, for example, in 424 BC the Athenians were drawn up in eight ranks, but the Thebans were 25 deep. At the battle of Leuctra where they defeated the Spartans, they were 50 deep. This 25/50 formation was almost certainly simply using the *enomotiai* or *pentekostyes* in single file.

The Theban army had an elite corps of 300 picked warriors called the Sacred Band. They are first mentioned by name at Delium in 424 BC but may be identified with the 300 first and best of the Thebans who died at Plataea. The Sacred Band appear to have originated in the heroic age. They were supposedly made up of 150 charioteers and their drivers. In classical times they fought as hoplites. They were probably organised into 12 *enomotiai*, each of 25 men as their number suggests. They were as dedicated as the Spartans and a match for them.

In 382 BC the Spartans had treacherously seized the Cadmeia, the citadel of Thebes, and put a garrison into it. This act brought about the downfall of Sparta. It generated a surge of patriotic spirit at Thebes. In 379 the Spartan garrison was thrown out and Sparta entered her last great war.

In the next few years the Theban army, mainly under the influence of Epaminondas, was converted into a first-class, disciplined fighting machine. Epaminondas must be included amongst the great tacticians. For four centuries the phalanx had dominated Greek tactics. All innovations had aimed at protecting the phalanx so that the battle could be decided in the centre. As long as this state of affairs existed Sparta must win. Epaminondas perceived a point that seemed to have escaped all other tacticians: the Spartan army, in common with the other Greek armies,

1

1 Greek view of a Scythian archer from a plate in the British Museum.
2 A vase painting from Bologna showing a hoplite stringing a Scythian bow.
3 and 4. A Cretan bow and arrow from a Greek vase in the Louvre.
5 A reconstruction of a Scythian archer.
6 The Scythian view of one of their archers from a gold cup found at Kul Oba in the Crimea. The stringing of a Scythian bow was a very complex operation.

2

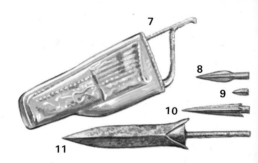

7 A small gold model of a bow and arrows case (*gorytus*) from a Scythian grave.
8–11 Various types of arrow heads found in Greece. Scale 1:2. British Museum. No. 9 is Scythian and no. 11 Cretan.

always had its crack troops on the right and from this point the rest of the army drew its encouragement. As a result of this, the strong right wing always opposed the weak left so that, during the battle, the phalanxes tended to rotate in an anticlockwise direction. This was further aggravated by individual hoplites being inclined to close up on their right-hand neighbour in order to get more protection from his shield, with the result that the right wing often overlapped the enemy's left. This happened at the battle of Mantinea.

Epaminondas believed that if he could knock out the crack Spartan troops on the right wing, the rest of the Lacedaemonian army would collapse. In order to achieve this he planned to reverse his battle order, placing his own weakest troops on the right opposite the Spartan left, lining up the phalanx *en echelon*, with the weakest troops held back, whilst at the same time massing his best troops on the left supported by the strongest cavalry and the Sacred Band.

In 371 BC, at Leuctra, Epaminondas put his new tactic to the test. The massively reinforced left wing crashed through the Spartans, annihilating the *hippeis* and killing the king. As expected the rest of the army collapsed like dominoes. The tactic was repeated at Mantinea in 362; unfortunately for Thebes Epaminondas was killed in the battle and with him fell the chances of Theban supremacy.

Of Theban armour and weapons we know nothing for certain. Bearing in mind Xenophon's comments on the depth of the phalanx it is hard to conceive what advantage the Thebans could gain using the conventional hoplite weapons. I would therefore tentatively suggest that the Thebans used a two-handed pike which would make it easier for the tremendous weight of the formation to be used. This would make much more sense of the later Macedonian phalanx, as it is hard to believe that the pike originated with the undisciplined Macedonian infantry that existed before the time of Philip II.

There is another point that ought to be mentioned: the so-called Boeotian shield. This is a sort of cross between a Dipylon and an Argive shield. It is shown on vase paintings as an Argive shield with two semi-circular slots cut

out of the rim on either side next to the handgrip. This shield has been generally condemned by scholars and dismissed as an artistic convention for a heroic shield. But is this view really justified? A few years ago, when experimenting with shield types trying to find out how a pikeman would have to hold his shield, I tried to wield a pike whilst holding an Argive shield. Because of the broad wedge-shaped rim and the angle of roughly 45° between the shield and the pike, it was impossible to grip the pike with the left hand. This could only be achieved by cutting a notch out of the shield rim, which is exactly what is shown in the paintings of Boeotian shields.

Armour and Weapons
The shield
Two main types of shield were in use in Greece during the early part of the 8th century: an oval type with a scallop cut out from either side, which is generally known as the Dipylon type after a cemetery at Athens where a large number of representations of it were found, and a round type with a central handgrip. The Dipylon shield is almost certainly a direct descendant of the Mycenaean figure-eight type which disappears from art soon after 1400 BC. The clay model illustrated (on the left) is of just such a shield and comes from the Dipylon cemetery.

It has been argued that this later form does not represent a real shield at all but is a heroic form used only in art. There are two main objections to this: first, primitive artists always drew historical

characters in contemporary costume, and second, the artist who made this clay shield knew exactly what he was making for it obviously represents a wicker shield with stretchers on the inside. It is inconceivable that such accuracy of representation could have survived for over 600 years without degenerating into a symbolic form with, for example, a small cross on the back. This has to have been copied from an actual shield. The fact that its shape differs quite considerably from the Mycenaean type reinforces its authenticity and suggests a pattern of evolution. The earlier shields must have had a reinforced rim to retain their figure-eight shape, but in the Dipylon type the stretchers have dictated the shape. There would be a natural tendency for such a shield to assume this shape as the ends of the stretchers, which had to be fitted tightly, thrust their way outwards to form four points on the rim. The consequent strain on the 'pinching' at the centre would force it into a gentle curve producing the two semi-circular indentations on either side. The implication of this argument is that at Athens, which survived the dark-age invasions and had an unbroken connection with the Mycenaean age, the figure-eight type shield survived throughout the later Mycenaean era and the dark age that succeeded it.

Below
1 A wall painting of a Mycenaean figure-eight shield from Mycenae.
2 Front, back and section of a clay model of an 8th-century Dipylon shield. British Museum. This model was clearly copied from a genuine shield.

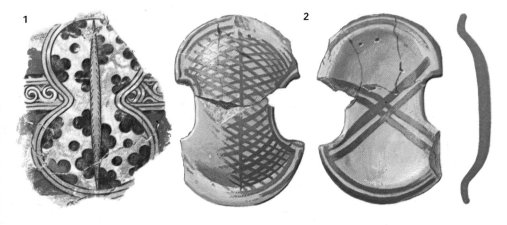

1

2

The round, central-handgrip type of shield possibly originated in central Europe like so much of the late Mycenaean weaponry. Certainly its presence in Italy as well would indicate this. It had first made its appearance in Greece in late Mycenaean times but it was probably the Dorians settling in the Peloponnesus around 1050 BC who made it the predominant type in the area. Two late examples of this type of shield dating from the first half of the 7th century have been found at Delphi. They are both made of beaten bronze but represent two distinct types: one has a very pronounced boss covering the handgrip, which would have been flush with the back of the shield, whilst the other has no boss at all and therefore the handgrip must have stood proud at the back. These two must represent the latest development of the central-handgrip type and would already have been obsolete when they were made, for a new shield had evolved in the 8th century that, in a short time, was to supersede all previous types: this was the hoplite or Argive shield.

This shield may have evolved out of the round, central-handgrip type but, at least in the form of the earliest archaeological examples, it is quite different. In fact, its only similarity is that it is round. It is much more convex than the earlier shield and has a reinforced rim. But far more important than this is the grip which has completely changed. An arm band has been fitted to the centre of the shield; the left forearm was put through this band so that the shield was fastened to the forearm. There was a handgrip in the form of a strap near the rim which was grasped with the hand to stop the shield slipping down the forearm. The earliest recognisable representations of the Argive shield come from mid-7th-century pottery such as the Chigi vase (see p. 39). This shows all the basic characteristics of the new shield which in no way resembles the earlier types. It was this shield which covered the hoplite from chin to knee, and more than anything else made the rigid phalanx formation possible. Because of the placing of the arm band in the middle, almost half the shield protruded beyond the left-hand side of the warrior and, if the man on his left moved in close, he was protected by the shield

1 An archaic type central-handgrip shield found at Delphi. Scale 1:15.
2 Hoplites with Argive shields from Greek vases in the British Museum.
3 An armband from a 6th-century Argive shield. Bari Museum. Scale 1:6.
4 An armband of unusual type from the Etruscan 'Tomb of the Warrior' at Vulci (c. 525 BC). The two 'wings' have been wrongly identified as cheek pieces. Villa Giulia, Rome. Scale 1:6.

5–8 Fragments of 6th-century Argive shields. Scale 1:3.
5 Part of the cable-patterned rim of the shield from Bari (cf. no. 3 opposite).
6 A carrying strap attachment.
7 and 8 Handgrip attachments. The section opposite shows clearly how these were fixed to the wooden core of the shield and also the thickness of the shield at this point—just about 1cm. 6, 7 and 8 are all from Olympia. Olympia Museum.
9 A reconstruction of a 6th-century Argive shield based on the finds from Olympia.

overlap which guarded his uncovered side. One of the great problems of the phalanx was this tendency to close up towards the right. After the end of the 6th century, probably as a result of the Persian invasions and the increase in the use of light-armed troops armed with missiles, a leather curtain was sometimes attached to the bottom of the shield to protect the warrior's legs from darts and arrows.

After a battle it was customary for the victorious general to dedicate an inscribed shield at one of the sanctuaries. Many such shields have been found at Olympia. They vary from 80cm to 1m in diameter. Some of these shields have a complete bronze facing, whilst others have only a bronze rim. All the non-metallic parts of these shields have disappeared but many of the interior fittings have survived. These fittings, such as the handgrip attachments, were fixed to the wooden core with nails which were bent over on the front so that they could not come loose. This not only very conveniently tells us the thickness of the shield, but also how it was made. The wooden core, probably of hardwood

such as oak, was made first. All the fittings were then nailed to the inside and the nails turned over on the front and hammered flat. When all the inside pieces were fixed in place, the front was covered with bronze or ox hide. The forearm band has two forms: either a broad band with a turned up lip (**2**), or a narrower band (**3**) which would have had a rawhide or felt backing in the shape of the first type. The broad type is generally earlier, and the narrow band later.

Several of the shields from Olympia have fittings stuck directly on to the inside of the bronze facing. These shields must have been made specially for dedications as they would have been useless in battle. It has been suggested that they were used to deflect blows but this would defeat the whole purpose of the phalanx, where each hoplite was supposed to protect his neighbour's unguarded side, not redirect missiles on to it.

There is a superb example of an Argive battle shield in the Museo Gregoriano at the Vatican. This shield, which probably comes from an Etruscan

grave, has survived sufficiently intact to permit a complete restoration with absolute certainty. The complete bronze facing has survived without distortion as well as a considerable amount of the wooden core and the thin leather with which it was lined. This shield illustrates well the technical difficulties of fitting a bronze facing to an Argive shield. Although the front of the bronze facing would have been beaten into shape before it was fitted on to the wooden core, the edge would have to be folded over afterwards. The difficulties experienced by the armourer are revealed in the cross-section where one can see how he has had to pad the rim of the shield with slivers of wood. In its original form this shield would have weighed about 7kg.

The wooden core of the Argive shield was only about 0.5cm thick in the centre and a reinforcing plate was often placed on the inside. Such plates can be clearly seen on the late 6th-century Siphnian treasury relief from Delphi and on the Chigi vase.

There is one feature of the Argive shield which only became obvious after

Left and above
The Etruscan shield with remains of the wooden core and leather lining in the Museo Gregoriano, Vatican, Rome. This shield is probably 4th century.
1 The inside of the shield showing the armband, which would have been lined with hide, the handgrip and the remains of the core. Scale 1:10.
2 Side view and section of the shield.
3 Three-quarter top view showing the armband and handgrip.
4 Reconstruction of the handgrip and rim showing the strips of wood used to fill the rim.

making a copy of the Vatican shield and trying it out. The sharp curve backwards on the inside edge of the wooden rim fits snugly over the left shoulder, which takes a lot of the weight of the shield. This means that a hoplite could march a considerable distance with his shield ready for action without feeling too much of a strain on his left arm.

The most noticeable feature of these shields as seen on vase paintings is their decorative blazons. These show an almost infinite variety—geometric designs, animals both real and imaginary, fish, crabs, birds, limbs, vases, anchors, etc. These probably identified the individual hoplite, who could not be recognised with his helmet covering his face. Later, towards the end of the 5th century, these motifs were replaced by a letter or symbol identifying a hoplite's city: the lambda, for example, for Sparta (Lacedaemon) and the club for Thebes.

Several examples of bronze blazons have been found at Olympia. These show mainly mythical beasts—gorgons, griffins, etc. They were probably made specially for dedications as they would have been defaced in the first clash of battle when, as the Spartan poet Tyrtaeus puts it, 'both sides clash, rounded shield against rounded shield'. The motifs on battle shields must have been painted.

Body armour

In 1953 an 8th-century grave was discovered at Argos in the Peloponnesus. In it were the earliest Greek helmet and cuirass yet found. Beyond this find there is a gap in our knowledge of body armour stretching back 700 years to the late 15th-century example at Dendra.

The Argos cuirass, like its forerunners, has a front and back plate. Both plates are simply decorated in the form of the anatomy of the torso, with narrow embossed ridges around the arm holes, the waist and the hips. Around the neck, the arm holes and the hips the bronze is rolled forward to strengthen the edge. The breaks in the embossed ridges show without a doubt that the front plate fitted over the edge of the back plate at the sides. On the right edge of the front plate are two tubular projections—these were fitted into corresponding slots in the back plate and held in position with two pins (3) before the cuirass was put

on. The two halves were strapped together by two loops at the bottom of the left side (one on the front and one on the back plate). Under the left arm and at the hip the rolled-over edge has been opened up to form a channel which held the front plate in position (4). The shoulders were joined in the opposite way with the back plate overlapping the front. The plates were held in position at the shoulders by two iron spikes on the front plate which passed through corresponding holes found in the back plate (5).

A semi-circular bronze plate called a *mitra* (this term is probably wrong but used for convenience) could be suspended from a belt to cover the abdomen. Although there are some Greek examples of these, most come from Crete. Examples have been found in Thrace with later versions of the bell cuirass showing that they were used together.

In the second half of the 6th century the bell cuirass declined in popularity and was superseded by the linen corselet as the basic hoplite body armour. However, the bronze cuirass continued in use and gradually evolved into the elegant muscled cuirass. Although it never enjoyed the same popularity as the bell corselet, probably because it was so expensive to make, it lasted until the end of the Roman era 1,000 years later, and became part of the uniform of senior officers. The new cuirass came in two types, either short, finishing at the waist, or long to cover the abdomen.

The muscled cuirass was usually joined at the sides, and sometimes at the shoulders, with hinges, one half of the hinge being attached to the front plate and one to the back. There were usually six of these hinges—two on each side and one on each shoulder. In order to put the cuirass on, the hinge pins were removed from one side (usually the right) and from the shoulders. The corselet was then opened out as with the previous types. When fitted the front and back plates would be drawn together and the hinge pins inserted on the right side and the shoulders. On either side of the hinge was a ring which was used to pull the front and back plates together. A fragment of a cuirass in the British Museum (9) has a clear impression of a buckle next to the ring

showing that a strap and buckle were used to pull the two sides together. Some of these corselets have no hinges and were held together with rings and straps only.

Some 4th-century cuirasses have a left-hand hinge extending from the armpit to the hip. Since it would be impossible to insert the pin in such a hinge when the cuirass was being worn, one must assume that the left side was joined before it was put on. Although the development of the muscled cuirass can be traced on Greek vases, the archaeological finds are mainly Italian.

In the 4th century the full-length muscled cuirass was adapted for cavalry

Above
A bronze shield motif from Olympia, c. 525 BC. Many of these have been found, the gorgon design being the most popular. On battle shields the motif was usually painted. Olympia Museum.

Above
An Argive shield, c. 525 BC, with a reinforcing plate to give extra protection for the arm shown on the reliefs from the Siphnian Treasury at Delphi. Delphi Museum.

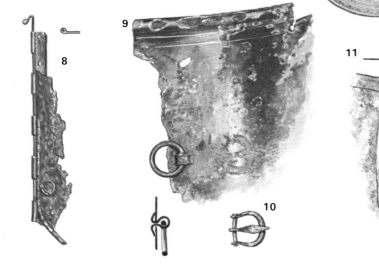

1 and 2 Front and back views of the Argos bell cuirass. Argos Museum.
3 Method of pinning the right-hand side of the cuirass. The tubular extensions on the edge of the front plate were pushed through the slots in the back plate and a pin inserted on the inside.
4 Underarm joining of the left side.
5 Method of joining the shoulders.
6 A late bell cuirass, c. 525 BC, from Olympia. Olympia Museum.

7 An abdominal plate from Crete.
8–11 Fragments illustrating the method of joining the classical muscled cuirass.
8 A full-length hinge complete with pin. Karlsruhe Museum, Germany.
9 Fragment of a cuirass with ring attachment and the imprint of a buckle (British Museum).
10 A buckle of similar type.
11 A hinge seen from the inside.
12 Method of pulling the hinge together.

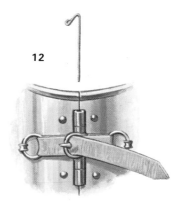

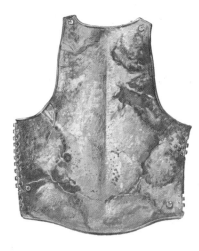

Above
Front view of a 4th-century muscled cuirass from Conversano near Bari in southern Italy. It has a full-length hinge on the left side. The muscled cuirass became part of the uniform of senior officers. Bari Museum.

Above
The back view of the same Conversano cuirass. The right side of the cuirass was joined in the normal fashion with hinges and rings. The shoulders had no hinges and were pulled together by the rings.

Above
A short muscled cuirass with ring fasteners and no hinges. This type was often used by the cavalry. Most archaeological examples of muscled cuirasses come from Italy. From Ruvo, southern Italy. British Museum.

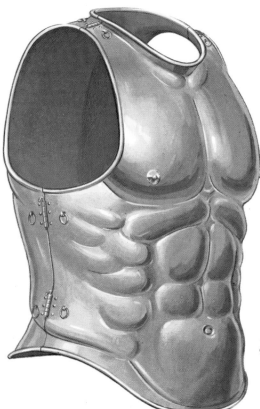

Above
A reconstruction of a full-length muscled cuirass in the British Museum. It is made of bronze and is decorated with silver inset nipples. It is joined at the shoulders and sides with hinges and rings.

Above
A hoplite wearing a muscled cuirass shown on a Greek vase, c. 460 BC. He is wearing a Thracian helmet and has a curtain hanging from his shield to protect his legs against missiles. Palermo Museum.

Above
A full-length muscled cuirass specially designed for a horseman. It is very broad in the hips to enable its wearer to sit a horse. Only three examples are known, and all come from Italy. Probably 4th century. Bari Museum.

1–4 The linen cuirass in Greek and Etruscan art.
1 Greek, c.500 BC. From Vulci. Berlin.
2 Etruscan, c.425 BC. From Todi. British Museum.

3 Greek, c.450 BC. Vatican Museum.
4 Etruscan, c. 325 BC. The Sarcophagus of the Amazons from Tarquinia. Florence Archaeological Museum.
5 Detail from the Mars of Todi in the Vatican (Museo Gregoriano) showing lamellar plates, c.350 BC.
6 A late 6th-century hoplite putting on his linen cuirass.

use. The bottom was swept outwards at the front and back so that the wearer could sit on a horse. Such a cuirass is shown clearly on the equestrian statue of Nonius Balbus the Younger found at Herculaneum, now in the Naples Museum. Three examples of this type of cuirass are known and all come from southern Italy. The evidence suggests that they were restricted to this area, but with so few examples it would be wrong to assume this.

Linen cuirasses had probably been in use since late Mycenaean times, but it was not until late in the 6th century that they became the standard armour of the hoplite. A linen cuirass was made of many layers of linen glued together to form a stiff shirt about 0.5cm thick. The corselet extended down to the hips, the lower part, below the waist, having slits to make it easier to bend forward. A second layer cut into similar strips (*pteryges*) was stuck on the inside to cover the gaps in the outer layer. The shirt, which had no shaping to the waist, was wrapped around the torso and tied together on the left side. A U-shaped piece, fixed to the back, was pulled forward to cover the shoulders. Vase paintings often show these shoulder flaps springing back when untied, illustrating the resilience of the material.

A few years ago I made a copy of one of these cuirasses. It was difficult to put on because of its stiffness, but once one had got used to it, it was quite comfortable and easy to move about in. These cuirasses were often made in several pieces and the *pteryges* were sometimes detachable.

Although the linen was considered adequate protection, these cuirasses were often reinforced with scales or plates, and Assyrian-style lamellar plates are shown on some later Etruscan examples. The great advantages of the linen cuirass were its cheapness to produce, its flexibility and its lightness. The example I made had no metal plates and weighed 3.6kg; a bell cuirass when lined would have weighed about 6kg. This type of armour remained in use until the introduction of mail in the 3rd century BC.

Shortly before Christmas 1977 it was announced that a royal grave had been found at Vergina in Macedonia. This grave, which is believed to belong to

1 A vase painting (500 BC) showing hoplites arming for battle. Vienna.
2 The cut of a linen 'stiff shirt' cuirass. This was made from layers of linen glued together.

3 and 4 Front and back views of the iron cuirass recovered from the so-called tomb of Philip II at Vergina in Macedonia. Scholars disagree about the date of this tomb. Their cuirass shows a translation into iron with gold decoration of a linen corselet. It follows the basic design in every detail. It was probably worn over a leather chiton with *pteryges* at the shoulders and hips. See the Alexander mosaic, p. 72.

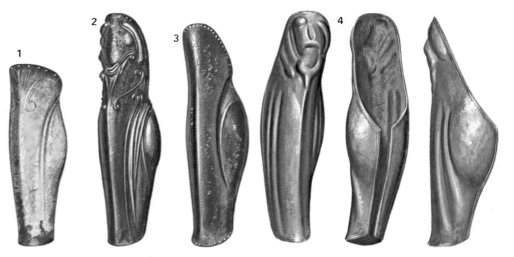

Philip II, was reported to contain an iron cuirass. Hearing this I had visions of a muscled-type cuirass made of iron. At the International Congress of Classical Archaeology held in London in September 1978, M. Andronicos, the excavator of the grave, gave the public their first view of this cuirass which, to my immense surprise, proved to be a translation into plate iron of a linen cuirass. The torso is made up of four plates, front, back and two sides, with two curved shoulder plates hinged to the back plate. The whole cuirass is decorated with embossed strips of gold. It presumably had *pteryges* of leather or some other pliant material. Unfortunately, this armour has not yet been properly published and therefore we have only the pictures to go by.

Leg and arm guards

The full-length lower leg guard or greave only came into general use in the 7th century. At first it covered the lower leg only from below the knee to the ankle, but was later extended to cover the knee. The 7th- and 6th-century greaves were often highly decorated. The later greaves, like the muscled cuirass, followed the anatomy of the leg. Many examples of these muscled greaves survive in both Greece and Italy. The musculation of the later types is generally less stylised than the late 6th-century type shown here. The Greek greave was pulled open and clipped on to the leg, but in Italy they were often strapped on to the leg. Several Italian examples have been found with rings for straps.

Many examples of ankle guards have been found which covered not just the ankles but also the heels. These are the anklets that Homer is so fond of describing. They were tied on. There are also a few examples of foot guards which were fitted to the sandals. These were made either in one piece or hinged at the toes to allow more movement. Although thigh guards are shown in sculptures, only one Greek example survives at Olympia. This is really just an extension of the greave and covers only the lower thigh. In art they are shown covering the middle of the thigh.

Guards for both the upper and lower arm have been recovered from the excavations at Olympia. Some of them are

Above
1–4 The development of the greave.
1 Late 7th-century type coming up to just below the knee.
2 Elaborate 6th-century type covering the knee. From Olympia. Olympia Museum.
3 Simple 6th-century type. Provenance uncertain. Tower of London.
4 Front, back and side view of a late archaic greave. It was found with the helmet which is displayed on p. 62. Munich Glyptotek.

5 Upper arm guard, 6th century.
6 Lower arm guard, 6th century.
7 Ankle guard, 6th century. This would have been tied on using the two prongs at the front.
8 Thigh guard, 6th century.
9 Foot guard, probably 5th century. It is hinged at the toes and would have been laced to the sandal.
5–8 From Olympia. Olympia Museum.
9 From Ruvo, southern Italy. British Museum.

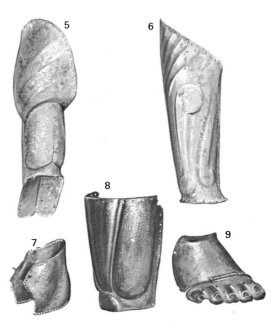

Left
Bronze figurine of a Spartan warrior, c. 525 BC. He is wearing lower arm guards and thigh guards besides bell cuirass, Corinthian helmet and greaves. National Archaeological Museum, Athens.

very elaborately decorated. The upper arm guards far outnumber the lower. In probability these arm guards were very seldom used and are certainly rarely shown in art.

All limb guards were lined with leather or fabric. Those made before the mid-6th century had the lining rolled over the edge and stitched through. The continuation of this method of fixing the lining suggests that there was a continuity in armour making between the Mycenaean and the Archaic era, and therefore we should expect to find bronze armour in use right through the dark age. All arm and leg guards except greaves went out of fashion at the end of the 6th century and the greave itself was never as popular later in the classical era as it had been earlier.

The helmet
There is much argument among scholars over the naming of various types of helmet. This controversy has nothing to add to our knowledge of the Greek military system or of its development and is therefore ignored here. Terms such as Illyrian and Attic are used here for convenience to denote a particular type of helmet and do not imply the origin of the type.

There are several forms of Greek helmet but they all seem to have evolved from two prototypes—the Kegel and the primitive Corinthian.

The Kegelhelm (1), whose name is German, meaning literally cone or skittle shaped, is the earliest Iron-Age helmet yet found in Greece. These helmets are all made in five pieces (excluding the crest holder). The example shown here is from a panoply found in a late Geometric grave at Argos. The Kegelhelm disappeared at the beginning of the 7th century. From the Kegel evolved two new types: the Insular and the Illyrian helmet. The Insular helmet (3) was popular in Crete where many miniatures of it have been found. The fragmentary example shown above, which is the only one yet found, is also from Crete. It is made in two halves (including the crest holder) which are riveted together. Each half forms one side of the helmet.

The early Illyrian helmet (4) is a clear derivation of the Kegel type, as can be seen from its general shape and the em-

bossed ridge along its lower edge. The main difference is the crest ridge across the top which became a characteristic of this type. It also shows a technical advance as, like the Insular helmet, it is made in two halves which are riveted together along the crest ridge. By the first half of the 6th century these helmets were being made in one piece (5). The type survived down into the 5th century (6 and 7).

The Corinthian helmet was by far the most successful Greek helmet. It covered the head leaving only the eyes, nose and mouth clear. It had a long life, beginning in the 8th century (2) and evolving into a very elegant helmet during the 7th and 6th centuries. The very early helmets were sometimes made in two pieces like the early Illyrian type. One of the characteristics that developed during the 7th century was an indentation in the bottom edge dividing the jawline from the neckline (8 and 10). This was continued in the late 7th- early 6th-century type. A large number of examples of this type of helmet (9) have survived, bearing witness to its popularity. It is known as the Myros type after an example that had the name Myros inscribed on it. In the early 6th century this indentation was replaced by a more positive dart which may have been derived from the Illyrian type. This remained as a characteristic of the helmet. 10 is a cross-breed between the early Illyrian and Corinthian helmets, having more than one characteristic of each. The cheek guards of the Corinthian helmet were very flexible so that it could be pulled down over the cranium

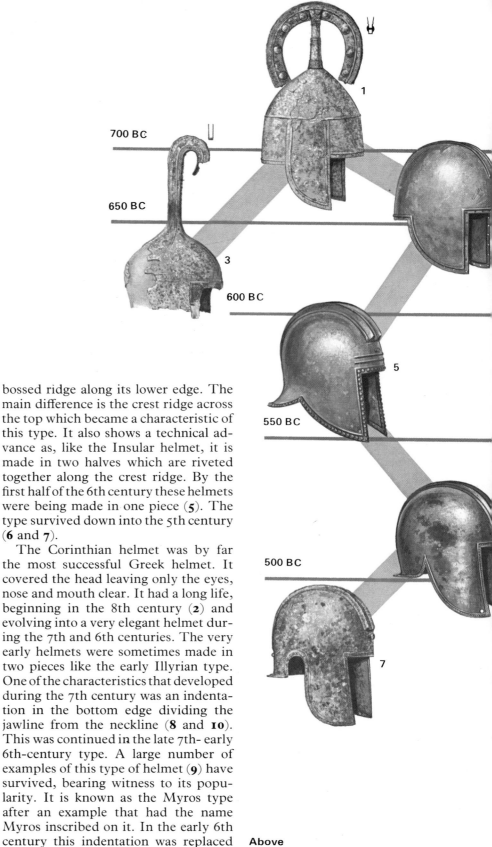

700 BC

650 BC

600 BC

550 BC

500 BC

Above
The evolution of the Greek helmet from the 8th to the 5th century. The Kegel-Illyrian group are on the left and the Corinthian-Chalcidian-Attic group are on the right. The red lines give an approximate dating, but it must be borne in mind that types evolved more slowly in some places than others.
1 From Argos. Argos Museum.
2, 4, 6, 7, 16 and 17 are all from Olympia. Olympia Museum.
12 from Corinth. Corinth Museum.

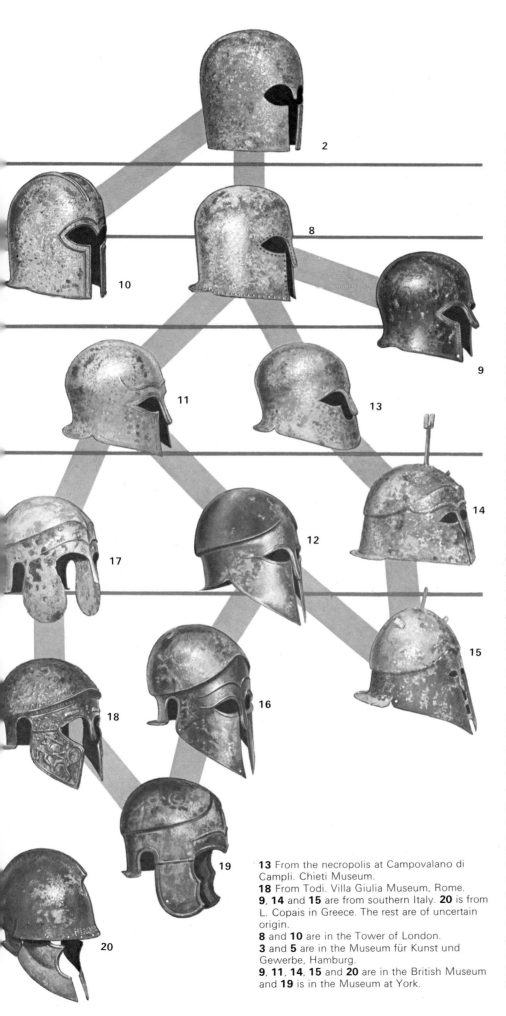

13 From the necropolis at Campovalano di Campli. Chieti Museum.
18 From Todi. Villa Giulia Museum, Rome.
9, 14 and 15 are from southern Italy. 20 is from L. Copais in Greece. The rest are of uncertain origin.
8 and 10 are in the Tower of London.
3 and 5 are in the Museum für Kunst und Gewerbe, Hamburg.
9, 11, 14, 15 and 20 are in the British Museum and 19 is in the Museum at York.

ARMOUR AND WEAPONS

and still fit snugly to the face. Because of this flexibility the helmet could be pushed up on to the top of the head, where the flexible cheek guards held it in position. This was how the hoplite wore it when not in battle. Many statues show the helmet worn this way and sometimes one can also see part of the loose undercap sticking out from under the dart in the rim of the helmet. All metal helmets require an inner cap for, although a metal helmet may give protection from the cut of a weapon, it will not break the force of it, so that padding is essential. On the earlier helmets the lining was often folded over the rim of the helmet and stitched along the edge as in the Dendra armour, but from the 6th century it was usually glued in.

The Corinthian helmet died out in Greece early in the 5th century but it lived on in Italy. The Italians during the 6th and 5th centuries gradually developed their own form of the Corinthian helmet (13, 14 and 15) which destroyed the very reason for its creation. Whilst retaining the eye holes and the nasal they turned it into a cap which was worn on top of the head as shown in Greek art (14). As time went on the eyes got smaller and closer together (15). Sometimes the holes were filled with ivory eyes. Finally they disappeared altogether, leaving only their vestiges in the incised decoration. This form of helmet, which is known as the Italo-Corinthian type, was adopted by Roman officers in the later republic and only disappeared in the 1st century AD.

Both the Corinthian and the Illyrian helmet had one great fault—they made hearing impossible. Experiments were made with perforations: several examples of this were found at Olympia. These took the form of a four-spoked wheel with the segments between the spokes cut out, or the outline of an ear similarly cut out. Finally the area around the ear was cut away altogether (16). Experiments along this line, however, had already produced a new breed of helmet, the Chalcidian. This helmet clearly evolved out of the Corinthian and appears on vase paintings from the early 6th century. This new helmet came in two types: one with fixed (17) and the other with hinged (18) cheek pieces. There was a third variant of this type which had hinged cheek pieces but

61

no nose guard (**19**); this is commonly referred to as Attic. I have no intention of arguing whether it should or should not be called that—in this book an Attic helmet means one similar to the Chalcidian but without a nose guard. There are no Greek examples of this type; practically all the survivals come from Italy where it was very popular. The Italian examples usually have feather holders and often thin bronze wings.

One final type of helmet that must be mentioned here is the Thracian (**20**). This type appears to have evolved from the Thracian cap. In some respects it is similar to the Attic helmet but it has a peak at the front which extends round the side, giving protection to both the eyes and the ears. It also commonly, though not invariably, has long cheek pieces usually cut away sharply at the eyes and mouth and curving outwards along the jaw. These cheek pieces were often highly decorated with, for example, a beard and moustache. The helmet gained increasing popularity from the 5th century onwards.

All these helmets had crests of horse hair. In most cases the crest was fixed directly on to the crown of the helmet and held in place by a pin at the front and back. It is obvious how this was done on the Illyrian type, but less clear with the majority of Corinthian types. In some examples there is an attachment at the back, in which case the front could be held by a loop over the nasal. Some of the helmets from Olympia show quite a complex system of hooks and rings which appear to be stuck on. If this is the case, then we may assume that many of the others have lost their attachments. Crests raised on a prop are a regular feature in the Archaic period (700–500 BC) in Greece and they remained popular in Italy until the 1st century AD. These crest supports were detachable and were fixed to the helmet with split pins as shown above.

Weapons

The hoplite's main weapon was the spear. An example from the dark age was found in a grave at Vergina in

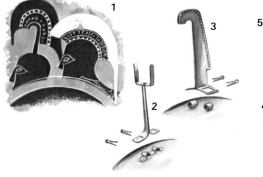

Above
1 A detail of a Greek vase painting showing the two types of crest.
2 A Greek raised crest holder. From Olympia.
3 An Italian raised crest holder. Both **2** and **3** were secured by split pins.

Right
4–7 The evolution of the Greek sword.
4 and **5** Two late Mycenaean (type II) bronze swords from Kallithea, c.1200 BC.
5a The handle of a similar sword from Italy.
6 Early Greek iron sword from Kerameikos, c.820 BC.
6a Bronze handle from a similar sword.
7 Iron sword and scabbard of Greek type with bone inlay from the Campovalano di Campli necropolis, c.500 BC. Chieti Museum.
8 Iron spearhead of Greek type from the Campovalano necropolis. Chieti Museum.
9 Bronze Greek spear butt. British Museum.

Macedonia with the iron head and butt still in position. This spear was about 2.3m long and would seem to be about the standard length—those shown on vase paintings appear to be between 2 and 3m long. By the end of the 8th century the Greeks had stopped burying their warriors with their weapons, but the practice continued in Italy. Spears varying between 1.5 and 2.5m long have been found in 6th-century graves at Campovalano di Campli near Teramo. The spears shown on Greek vases have leaf-shaped blades. Many iron spearheads of this type have been found in both Greece and Italy. These spears, which according to Tyrtaeus and Homer were made of ash, also had a metal spike, sometimes made of bronze, at the butt end. Markle, in his article on the Macedonian pike and spear, estimated that the weight of a 2.5m hoplite spear was one kilogram.

The hoplite also carried a sword. Finds from the dark age show that the late Mycenaean type II sword which was of central European origin continued in use but was being made in iron. An example from the Kerameikos has a straight-sided, double-edged blade 75cm long. By the time of the Persian wars this had evolved into a shorter sword with a leaf-shaped blade about 60cm long. Several excellent examples of these have been found at Campovalano di Campli. This sword was essentially a slashing weapon. The 6th and 5th centuries show the gradual introduction of a curved, single-edged sword (*kopis*). This weapon probably originated in Etruria. These early curved swords were vicious slashing weapons with a huge blade about 65cm long. They were later modified into the shorter cut-and-thrust weapon that became so popular in Spain and Macedon.

Macedon 360–140 BC

Introduction

The centre of development now moves from Greece to Macedon—the sleeping giant. The rise of Macedon was due almost entirely to the energy of one man, Philip II. On his accession to the throne in 359 BC he set about building up the most formidable fighting machine the world had yet seen. It was with this machine that his son, Alexander the Great, was to conquer an empire that stretched from Egypt to India. After his death Alexander's empire was divided amongst his generals. These kingdoms lasted until one by one they were swallowed up by Rome.

The prime sources for this period are Diodorus Siculus and Polybius. Diodorus wrote in the 1st century BC. His work has quite justifiably been severely criticised; it has been said of him that he is as good or as bad as his sources. For one very short period of not more than 20 years, he follows the account of the brilliant Hieronymus of Cardia, one of the most reliable historians of the ancient world. What a loss it is for the military historian that Hieronymus' history has not come down to us in its original form. After the death of Alexander in 323, he accompanied first Eumenes, until his death in 316, and then Antigonus and his son Demetrius Poliorcetes on their campaigns and gives detailed accounts of their actions. Unfortunately Diodorus' account is incomplete after 302 BC and only fragments of the subsequent books survive.

Polybius, who picks up the story about 220 BC, recounts the history of Greece down to the second half of the 2nd century BC. Unfortunately the latter part of his work has also been lost and we possess only fragments. A soldier himself, Polybius is the best of the classical military historians.

The Macedonian Wars
The rise of Macedon

Philip was brought to Thebes as a hostage in 367 BC and lodged in the house of Epaminondas. The great Theban's tactical views were not wasted on Philip. He escaped from Thebes and on the death of his brother in 360 seized the throne. He was 23 years old.

Macedon was racked with war on every side. Philip immediately set about reorganising his army and bringing it into the modern world. He then turned his attention to the invaders. In two lightning campaigns he subdued the Paeonians in the north and drove the Illyrians in the north-west back beyond

Below
Map of the northern Aegean showing the relationship of Macedonia to its neighbours. It was Philip of Macedon who transformed a war-torn kingdom into the most formidable military power of its day.

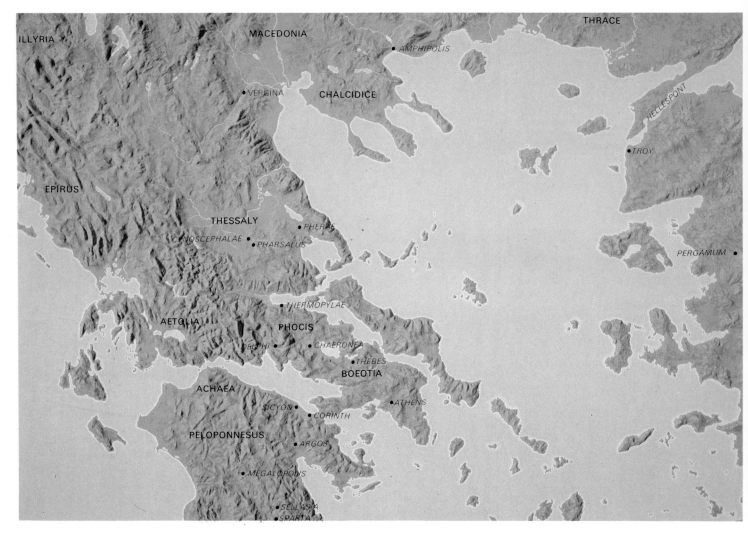

their borders. Having settled the north and west, he set about establishing routes to the east and south. Gradually he captured the towns along the coast, many of which had strong connections with the city states, and so opened the routes to Thessaly and the Hellespont. In 353 he entered Thessaly and the following year conquered most of it.

In the summer of 352 he advanced towards Thermopylae. In panic the Athenians sent a holding force to occupy the pass and Philip withdrew. Only now do the Greeks seemed to have realised the great threat that was hanging over them, but they were far too busy fighting each other to do anything about it.

Philip did not try to advance southward again for six years. In the intervening period he continued to establish his position in the east, reducing the towns of Chalcidice and the Thracian coast. In 350 he gained control of much

of Epirus on his south-west border, and by 348 the last of the Chalcidian towns had surrendered.

The Greek states were becoming ever more aware of the giant that was rising in the north, but they were not yet prepared to bury their differences and do anything about it. They needed a breathing space and in 346 signed a non-aggression treaty with Philip. This treaty, at Philip's insistence, expressly excluded Phocis which was accused of outrages against Delphi. The ink was hardly dry on the paper before Philip passed Thermopylae and overran Phocis. He was into Greece.

Having established his foothold, Philip withdrew to Macedonia to consolidate his borders in the north, west and east before embarking on the final conflict. An uneasy peace existed between Philip and the Greek states for six years. By 340 the Macedonian army

had reached the Black Sea and was besieging Perinthus and Byzantium. Both cities had strong connections with Athens, which now went to war.

In the autumn of 339 Philip took advantage of the chaos that still persisted and moved into central Greece. Athens patched up a hasty alliance with her erstwhile enemy Thebes and advanced to meet the threat. In August 338 at Chaeronea on the north-west border of Boeotia, the combined Theban/Athenian army came face to face with the war-hardened veterans of Macedonia.

In the battle that followed the Greeks were hopelessly outclassed. The Theban

Below
The beginning of the greatest career of conquest. Alexander crosses the Granicus at the head of his cavalry to attack the Persians, who had formed up on the opposite bank with their cavalry in front and phalanx behind.

Sacred Band who were opposed by the crack Macedonian troops led by Philip's young son Alexander, who was just 18, remained true to their glorious tradition and fought to the last man.

After the battle Philip offered terms that were far more lenient than Athens could have expected, and they were accepted. Philip felt no such generosity towards Thebes. Their leaders were executed or banished, the prisoners were sold into slavery and a garrison occupied the Cadmeia.

All the states of Greece, with the exception of Sparta, now came to terms with Philip. At the congress of Corinth a Greek confederacy was set up with Philip as its leader.

The Macedonian now announced his long-cherished plans to invade the Persian empire, and the necessary forces were requisitioned. Before the enterprise could be realised, however, Philip was assassinated and his 20-year-old son Alexander came to the throne.

On Philip's death the Greeks defected. Alexander's reaction was so fast that he reconquered Greece without striking a blow. Then he turned to the north and west, crushing all opposition. During these campaigns he was reported dead and Greece again revolted. Alexander turned south again and the Greeks surrendered, all that is except Thebes. Alexander took the city and rased it to the ground.

Invasion of the Persian empire

In the spring of 334 a combined Macedonian/Greek army of 30,000 infantry and 5,000 cavalry was ferried across the Dardanelles into Asia.

Whilst his army was crossing Alexander sailed for Troy. He was the new Achilles—the champion of the Greeks and, as Achilles had done 1,000 years before, he sacrificed in the temple of Athena.

The Persians were determined to stop Alexander's campaign before it started. Beyond the Granicus river the Persian cavalry were drawn up in line backed by a phalanx of Greek mercenaries. In true Theban style Alexander had strengthened one wing, which he led himself. The opening attack came from this wing; at the head of the Companion cavalry he charged across the river and smashed through the lighter-armed Persian horsemen. The Persian cavalry broke and fled, leaving the Greek mercenaries to their fate. Alexander showed them no mercy.

The following year was spent in the subjugation of Asia Minor (Turkey). The Persian king marched northwards with a large army and Alexander moved south to meet him. The two armies met at Issus on the border of Asia Minor and Syria. Again the Macedonian cavalry smashed through the Persian archers and light-armed troops. The Great King did not wait to see the outcome but raced from the battlefield in his chariot. Although at first the Persian army fought bravely, the news of the king's flight dampened their ardour and they too turned and fled.

Before advancing eastwards Alexander knew that he must secure his lines of communication by gaining control of

Below
Alexander's last and most costly battle. At the Hydaspes in 327 BC the Macedonians were confronted by an Indian army with 200 elephants. The phalanx advanced with locked shields, driving them back in confusion.

the coast and so cut off the Persians from their fleet. Only Tyre, which was situated on an island about 800m off the coast, refused to submit. The city held out for seven months. When it finally fell Alexander showed no mercy to those who had held up his grand design; he crucified many of the men and sold the women into slavery.

With their bases gone the Persian fleet defected. Alexander now advanced on Egypt which was quick to surrender, and he established the city of Alexandria on the coast closest to Greece.

The Macedonian army now returned to Syria and from here marched eastwards, crossing the Euphrates and the Tigris into the heartland of the Persian empire.

The Great King had had a year and a half to collect together a new army. At Gaugamela in 331 BC Alexander again crashed through the Persian wing and again the king fled. The Persian infantry resisted valiantly, but when subjected to a combined cavalry and infantry assault it crumbled and the Persian empire fell apart with it.

Alexander now marched on Babylon which surrendered. Susa and Persepolis also fell into his lap. Hearing that Darius was at Hamadan, Alexander hastened northwards. Once more the Persian king fled. Riding day and night Alexander pursued him. Just south-east of the Caspian Sea he caught up, but the Great King was dead—killed by his bodyguard.

All was now accomplished but Alexander's restless spirit would not let him stop. He continued his march eastwards, fighting battles and founding cities. He heard of opposition in the north and turned in this direction. He passed Samarkand and pushed on into Russia to the end of the known world. Here he established another town called Alexandria the Farthest. He now retraced his steps southwards and went into winter quarters at Balkh in what is now northern Afghanistan.

In the early summer of 327 BC the army crossed the western spur of the Himalayas known as Hindu Kush and descended into the valley of the Indus. Here it was opposed by an Indian army with 200 elephants. The Macedonians won the ensuing battle but with terrible losses. After the battle Alexander set out for the conquest of India but his army refused to go any farther. It was clear that the soldiers had had enough. Reluctantly he turned south towards the coast and from there returned to Babylon. Two years later he was dead. He was not quite 33 years old.

The struggle for power
On the death of Alexander his great empire fell to pieces as general vied with general in the quest for power. Antigonus and Eumenes fought for control of Syria. Eumenes was defeated and executed in 316 and it seemed for a time that Antigonus, with the help of his son, the brilliant Demetrius, might be able to re-establish the empire. But in 301 four other generals, Seleucus, Ptolemy, Cassander and Lysimachus, combined forces against him and he was killed.

With the death of Antigonus the south-east of the empire became reasonably settled, with most of Asia under the command of Seleucus and Egypt under the control of Ptolemy. Both these men established dynasties that lasted until the Roman conquest. The situation was different, however, in Macedon and Thrace.

After the defeat of Antigonus, Lysimachus, who already controlled Thrace, received northern and central Asia Minor also. Cassander ruled Macedon until his death in 297 when the kingdom fell to his two sons. The inevitable civil war followed. In 294 Antigonus' son Demetrius, who had been named 'Poliorcetes' (the stormer of cities) after his extraordinary exploits in the field of siege warfare, intervened and took over the throne. Having secured a power base, Demetrius immediately began assembling a vast army in order to fulfil his father's dream of once more uniting the empire.

Fifty years earlier Philip II had established his brother-in-law Alexander as king of Molossia in Epirus on the western border of Macedon. From here the new king had quickly established his authority over the whole country. By the time that Demetrius took over in Macedon, Pyrrhus, another of those extraordinary generals with which the 4th and 3rd centuries abound, had taken over as king of Epirus. Alarmed at the preparations that Demetrius was making, and seeing a chance to extend his own kingdom, Pyrrhus formed an alliance with Lysimachus and Ptolemy for the invasion of Macedonia. The Macedonians had had enough. The population was already exhausted from its many wars and, seeing Demetrius' determination to involve them in a never-ending conflict, the army mutinied and deserted to Pyrrhus, proclaiming him the new king of Macedon. But Pyrrhus' reign was equally shortlived and he in his turn was driven out by Lysimachus, who took over Macedon and Thessaly in 285 BC. Alexander's generals were by now all very old men. Ptolemy died in 282, Lysimachus was nearly 80 when he was killing fighting

Below
Map illustrating Alexander's campaigns. The red line shows the route taken by his army. After the Hydaspes Alexander's troops would go no further. He returned by way of the south coast to Babylon, where he died in 325 BC.

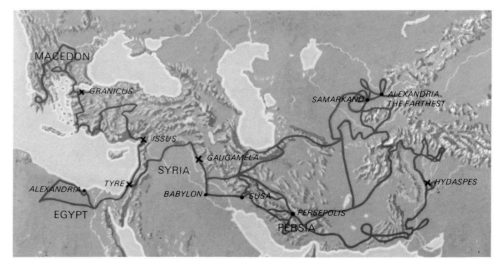

against Seleucus at the battle of Corupedium in 281, and the following year Seleucus also died.

Ptolemy Philadelphus succeeded his father as king of Egypt. His brother Ceraunus took over Lysimachus' kingdom but he lacked the strength of his predecessor and was unable to hold it together. Thrace and Macedonia were constantly threatened by barbarian invasions from the north which Lysimachus had successfully held in check.

Now the Celts and other tribes along the Danube moved into Thrace, killed Ceraunus and overran his kingdom. They pushed on southwards until they were finally defeated by the Greeks at Delphi. They then retired northwards ravaging Macedonia as they went. Antigonus Gonatas, the son of Demetrius, who had remained in control of the Macedonian possessions in Greece after the expulsion of his father, had never given up hope of regaining the kingdom. Now, during Pyrrhus' absence on his abortive campaign against the Romans in southern Italy, Antigonus marched into Macedon, defeated the Celts and seized the throne. The Celts retreated into Thrace, where they remained in control of the country for more than 60 years. Some of them crossed over into Asia Minor and finally settled in Galatia.

In Macedonia Antigonus Gonatas set about restoring order after the long anarchy. His possessions included Thessaly, Boeotia, Euboea and the towns of Corinth, Argos, Sicyon, Megalopolis and Messenia in the Peloponnesus. But peace was not so easily won. When the restless Pyrrhus returned from Italy he laid claim to much of Antigonus' realm. In 275 he invaded and conquered Thessaly and upper Macedonia and then turned to the Peloponnesus. Antigonus followed him south and Pyrrhus turned to meet him at Argos. Here the Epirot king was killed in a street fight and his army, without their leader, returned to Epirus. At last, in 272 BC, the Macedonian throne was secure and a dynasty established that was to last until the Roman conquest in 168 BC.

Eight years before the death of Pyrrhus four Achaean towns had formed a league of defence against Macedon which was to become known as the Achaean League. During the succeeding years six other towns joined and in 251

Sicyon, one of Macedonia's keys to the Peloponnesus, was liberated and joined the league. Corinth and Acrocorinth were likewise detached from the Macedonian hegemony. Finally Troezen and the other towns of the east and south joined so that the whole of the northern Peloponnesus was able to form a united front against Macedon. A second league was formed by the Aetolians in central Greece, which succeeded in extending its control over Boeotia in 245. By the time of Antigonus' death in 239 these two leagues had greatly reduced the power of Macedon in the south. Antigonus was succeeded by his son Demetrius II, who failed to restrict Illyrian piracy in the Adriatic with the result that the Romans were forced to intervene in 229, giving them a foothold in the Greek peninsula.

Conflict with Rome
Demetrius died in 229, leaving a young son who was later to become Philip V. In the meantime his half-cousin, Antigonus Doson, assumed power. In the south a rejuvenated Sparta under its king Cleomenes had begun to make inroads into the possessions of the Achaean league. Contrary to its avowed aims the league turned to Macedon for assistance and formed an alliance with Antigonus Doson against Sparta. At the battle of Sellasia the Spartans were decisively defeated and Cleomenes driven from the throne. Philip succeeded to the Macedonian throne in 221 and continued Doson's policy of co-operation with the league, but this time against their mutual enemies the Aetolians. In 215 Philip unwisely threw in his lot with Hannibal which resulted in his first war with Rome. This was an indecisive affair in which the Romans were primarily interested in keeping Philip busy while they dealt with Hannibal. The war fizzled out in 205 and a treaty was sworn, but it was only a matter of time before the conflict was resumed. Philip, looking for a new sphere of interest, turned eastwards and formed an alliance with Antiochus the Great, the king of the Seleucid realm of Syria.

During the 3rd century the small state of Pergamum had emerged in western Asia Minor. At first it had been under the suzerainty of Syria but had later thrown off the Syrian yoke and become

an independent state.

About 230 BC Attalus the king of Pergamum had won a great victory over the Celts, who had migrated to Asia Minor and virtually ruled the country, forcing its inhabitants to pay tribute to them. During succeeding years he had established a small empire over much of Asia Minor but it was soon lost to the rising power of Antiochus the Great. Now fearing the combination of Philip in the west and Antiochus in the east, Attalus appealed to Rome for help. In 200 the Romans, at last free of Hannibal and probably equally worried about the effect of the alliance between Philip and Antiochus, declared war. Late the same summer a Roman army landed in Illyria and the fate of Macedon was sealed. In 197 Philip was defeated at Cynoscephalae and forced to toe the Roman line. Antiochus, seeking to profit by the vacuum left in Greece after the fall of Macedon, invaded Europe but was driven out and defeated by the Romans, first at Thermopylae and later at Magnesia in Asia Minor. In 171 Macedon, now under the command of Philip's son Perseus, again found itself at war with Rome. The new king was defeated at Pydna in southern Macedonia in 168 and his kingdom was converted into a Roman province. A hundred years later Syria also became a Roman province, and a generation afterwards Egypt followed suit.

THE NEW MACEDONIAN ARMY
The infantry
Even before Philip's accession, the Macedonian cavalry was probably the best in Greece. It was drawn from the aristocracy and, as its name, the Companions, implies, it may have originated in a mounted royal bodyguard.

The infantry, which was raised from the peasantry, was a far different matter, lacking in discipline, training and organisation. Philip imposed an austere code of training and discipline on his army, compelling them to make regular forced route marches with full equipment and baggage to harden them against the rigours of war. He banned the use of wheeled transport and allowed only one servant to every ten men to carry the hand mills and ropes. The soldiers were forced to carry 30 days' rations on their backs when they set out on campaign. The cavalry too were restricted in the number of their servants, being allowed no more than one each. In this way Philip was able to keep the size of his baggage train and the number of his camp followers, two factors which were a constant cause of worry to any army, to a minimum.

Philip reformed his heavy infantry into a phalanx, no doubt based on the Theban model. When he took over the army it was organised in units of ten. This is confirmed by his restriction of servants to one to every ten men, and by the fact that a file in Alexander's army was called a *dekas*. At some stage he adopted the Greek system of using multiples of eight—not three times eight as in the 'archaic *lochos*', but the simpler two times eight. When this reorganisation took place is not known. However, Callisthenes, who accompanied Alexander's expedition as official historian, is quoted by Polybius as claiming that Alexander drew up his phalanx at Gaugamela in 331 BC successively 32, 16 and eight deep. Polybius, probably the best informed of all ancient historians on military matters, is sceptical that an eight-deep phalanx could have been deployed in the available space but does not query the three possibilities. So the reorganisation took place before 331. It is inconceivable that it took place earlier in Alexander's reign because of the sheer scale of his activities. One must conclude that it took place in the reign of Philip and probably well before he came into conflict with the Greeks, i.e. between 359 and 345. However, it is not until 323 BC, when Alexander was drafting Persians into his depleted Macedonian army, that we are given the first glimpse of the structure of the new phalanx.

Arrian says that each file (*dekas*) consisted of 16 men. This mixed Macedonian/Persian file was commanded by a *dekadarch* who served in the front rank. Behind him came first a man on double pay and then a 'ten stater' man; this man was getting less than double pay but more than the rank and file. Behind the three Macedonians came 12 Persians, and bringing up the rear another 'ten stater' man. These four Macedonians can be none other than the officers of the normal file. They are not receiving extra money for good service, as Arrian expressly differentiates between these men and those who are getting double pay for distinguished service. (These distinguished service order men are often mentioned.) The 'double pay' man has to be the half-file leader and the two 'ten stater' men the rear rankers (*ouragoi*).

Philip raised the dignity of his newly formed phalanx by calling them 'foot companions'. The phalanx was divided into *taxeis* after the fashion of the other non-Spartan armies. Each *taxis* was a territorial unit recruited from a specific area of Macedonia. In Alexander's time it seems likely that there were 12 of these *taxeis*, each 1,500 strong: six were left in Macedonia and six taken on the invasion of Persia.

Of the subordinate division of the *taxis* we have practically no information. The existence of a 256-strong unit called a *syntagma* (or *speira*), which was subdivided into four *tetrarchies*, in the armies of the successors suggests a common origin which has to be Alexander's army (see p. 77). If this were the case, then each *taxis* would be divided into six *syntagmata*. This is unfortunately confused by Arrian mentioning *lochoi*, which do not seem to fit anywhere into this arrangement unless he is using it to describe a file as do the later tacticians, including Arrian himself.

In the later armies the *syntagma* was the smallest independent unit of the phalanx, having its own administrative staff, and it must surely have been allotted the same position in Alexander's army.

At the battle of Gaugamela, Alexander opened gaps in his phalanx to let the Persian scythed chariots through. This could easily be done by withdrawing alternative *syntagmata* and placing each behind the *syntagma* on its right. If the phalanx was 16 deep this would leave gaps about 15m wide, and, if eight deep, gaps 30m wide.

The passage about the *dekas* in Arrian throws an interesting sidelight on the pay structure of the phalanx. In the file there were not only 'double pay' and 'ten stater' men, but there might also be men who were receiving extra as a reward for bravery. The *dekadarch* must have received triple pay. This increas-

Above
A late 4th-century hoplite painted on the Sarcophagus of the Amazons from Tarquinia. Florence Archaeological Museum. He wears a linen cuirass, greaves and a Thracian helmet.

ing rate of pay would have continued up through the officer structure. A similar system existed in the Roman imperial legions.

The *taxeis* had an order of precedence for each day so that each in turn would serve in the position of honour on the right wing.

The new phalangite was armed with a long, two-handed pike (*sarissa*). Theophrastus, a contemporary of Philip and Alexander, claims that the longest *sarissa* was 12 cubits (c. 5.4m) long. Polybius claims that, in his day, it was 14 cubits (c. 6.3m) and that it had originally been 16 cubits (c. 7.2m). Scholarly opinion favours the figure given by Theophrastus, but this is mainly because it is generally believed that the later phalanx was much heavier than the earlier version. Bearing in mind Polybius' extraordinary knowledge and deep research into these matters, the author believes that Polybius' figure has to be considered seriously.

The *sarissa* may have been made in two parts joined by an iron sleeve. This was the conclusion of Andronicos when he found an iron sleeve together with the head and butt of a *sarissa* at Vergina in Macedonia. The cornelian cherry tree was the commonest wood used in making spears, and certainly the Macedonian cavalry spears were made from it. Using this wood and the parts of a *sarissa* from Vergina, Markle, in his article on the Macedonian *sarissa*, calculated that a 12-cubit pike with a shaft just under 4cm in diameter, would weigh about 6.5kg, and Polybius' later 14 cubit one about 8kg. It is small wonder that Polybius comments on the great weight of the *sarissa*, making it difficult for the phalangite to carry palisade stakes.

It seems certain that the Macedonian phalangites were not restricted to the use of the *sarissa*, but, as occasion demanded, used other weapons. They could hardly carry on siege warfare with the pike, at least certainly not with a pike of that length. Several times both Diodorus and Arrian imply that they used javelins.

It is uncertain how the early Macedonian phalangite was armed. At the time of Polybius he probably wore greaves, a helmet and either a metal cuirass if he was a front ranker, or a linen cuirass if he served in the other ranks. He also carried a round shield about 60cm in diameter. There seems to be no real reason for supposing that he was much differently armed in the days of Philip and Alexander. Certainly Arrian refers to the lighter-armed part of Alexander's phalanx, implying that there must also be a heavier-armed part. It seems possible that those in the rear ranks, excluding the *ouragoi*, wore no body armour at all.

Several examples of 4th-century helmets have been found of which the Thracian type is the most common. One may be seen on the Alexander sarcophagus at Istanbul. Fourth-century Thracian helmets often have cheek pieces in the form of a beard and moustache. Chalcidian and Attic helmets also continued in use, and a conical type of helmet of unknown parentage was also popular at this time.

Diodorus seems to imply that equipment was supplied free. This appears to be supported by the late 3rd-century Amphipolis inscription which lists fines to be imposed for the loss of items of equipment. This could only be operable if the equipment was supplied free.

As ever-increasing territories came under Philip's control, he was able to introduce new units into his army such as the Paeonian, and later the Thessalian, cavalry. At Chaeronea in 338 he was able to muster 30,000 infantry and

2,000 cavalry. When Alexander invaded Asia five years later, his total strength had risen to 44,000 infantry and 6,500 cavalry, but this now included contingents from the Greek states.

Alexander's army

Diodorus gives a breakdown of Alexander's army: 12,000 infantry and 1,500 cavalry were left in Europe and 32,000 infantry and 5,100 cavalry transported to Asia Minor. This invasion force was made up of 12,000 Macedonian infantry reinforced by 7,000 from the allied states, 5,000 mercenaries, 7,000 infantry drawn from the frontiers of Macedon and 1,000 archers and Agrianian javelineers. These last were drawn from the mountainous northern frontier of Macedon. The 5,100 cavalry were made up of 1,800 Macedonians, 1,800 Thessalians, 600 Greeks and 900 Thracian and Paeonian scouts.

It is most regrettable that none of the prime sources for the period of Philip and Alexander have survived. The main work on Alexander is by Arrian, who lived more than 400 years after the events that he is describing.

The 12,000 Macedonian infantry accompanying Alexander were composed of the 9,000 Companions, already described, and 3,000 *hypaspists*. The 12,000 left in Europe seem likely also to have been composed of phalangites and *hypaspists* divided in the same proportion.

The *hypaspists* (literally shield-bearers) were slightly lighter infantry than the foot companions but fought alongside them in battle. They were usually drawn up between the phalanx and the cavalry. Their job was probably to protect the very vulnerable flanks of the phalanx. It seems likely that they were armed as the traditional hoplite with spear and Argive shield. Their name may well go back to a period when they formed a body of squires to the Companion cavalry. It was probably Philip who developed them as fully fledged infantry units, but they are not mentioned before the time of Alexander. The *hypaspists* were organised into battalions (*chiliarchies*) 1,000 strong. The first of these, the *agema*, was the king's bodyguard.

Towards the end of Arrian's life of Alexander, he mentions a unit in Alex-

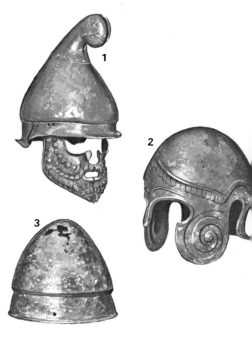

ander's army called the silver shields (*argyraspides*). He does this in such a was as to imply that they were the élite troops and that everybody knew about them. According to Justin they were a regiment of veterans formed by Alexander after his expedition into India. They are mentioned several times by Diodorus as accompanying Eumenes after the death of Alexander. In 317 they were 3,000 strong and had the same officers as the *hypaspists*. Diodorus goes on to speak of their great prestige and how not one of them was under 60 years old. Diodorus is here following Hieronymus of Cardia and, although he might be exaggerating, it is hard to believe that he is completely wrong about the age of this group, especially as he is an eyewitness. So, who were these silver shields? We shall probably never find a completely satisfactory answer. Tarn's conviction that they were just another name for the *hypaspists* is untenable if they were also veterans. There were only 3,000 *hypaspists*, so how could one get a veteran regiment of the same number, or were they 'Immortals'? The only possible conclusion is that they were drawn from the whole phalanx.

The cavalry

Alexander's Companion cavalry, which accompanied him on his expedition into

Asia, was divided into eight territorial squadrons (*ilai*). Each *ila* was commanded by an *ilarch*. The first of these squadrons, which was larger than the others, was known as the royal *ila* and was regularly commanded by Alexander.

These *ilai* fought in a wedge-shaped formation, an innovation that was introduced by Philip. It has been suggested that in total there were 15 squadrons of Companion cavalry and that seven were left in Macedonia. These were the 1,500 cavalry mentioned by Diodorus. If this is the case, then each unit should be just over 210 strong, and the royal squadron 300. This last figure is very attractive as it is the traditional size for this type of élite unit, e.g. the Spartan *hippeis* and the Theban Sacred Band. It also recommends itself as it is an exact figure from which a wedge can be formed. For units between 200 and 300 these are: 210, 231, 253, 276 and 300. The ideal figure for the other squadrons must be 210. At the end of the first year in Asia, reinforcements of 300 were received which, if one allows for losses, probably brought the seven *ilai* up to 231.

Obviously the *ilarch* could not expect to have the exact number in his squadron and would have left gaps in the rear rank. The great advantage of this wedge formation is that, having broken through, which was of course its prime function, it could then deploy or, as Marsden puts it, explode laterally.

The Companion cavalry were armed with long spears (also called *sarissae*) with shafts made from cornel wood. Markle experimented with a *sarissa* and came to the conclusion that it could be used either for the traditional overhand thrust, or couched using an undergrip, but that it would be impossible to change grip in battle as it would require two hands to do so. He is also of the opinion that, in wedge formation, the Companion cavalry could be used as shock troops against infantry. He also points out that, without stirrup or saddle, one would have to grip the horse with one's legs in order to stay on the horse when using the *sarissa* couched.

Alexander's Thessalian cavalry was also 1,800 strong. Unfortunately we do not know how many units there were nor their strength. We do know that their strengths differed and that the *ila* from Pharsalus was the largest and the

best. The Thessalians were drawn up in a rhomboid formation that was introduced by Jason of Pherae about 375 BC. This diamond-shaped formation implies that the Thessalians too could be used as shock troops. According to Polybius the charge of the Thessalian cavalry was irresistible whether in *ilai* or in mass, but they were useless for skirmishing.

The 600 Greek cavalry who accompanied Alexander should, according to Asclepiodotus, the tactical writer, have formed five *ilai* of 128 men each. They would have formed up in a square 16 wide and eight deep. Owing to the length of the horse, twice the space was needed per horse down the files as it was along the ranks, so that it was in truth a square formation.

Polybius states that eight was the maximum practical depth for cavalry drawn up in block formation. Drawn up

Below
Cavalry formations.
1 Greek. **2** Thessalian. **3** Macedonian.
A = unit commander (*ilarch*).
B = wing commander.
C = rearguard commander (*ouragos*).

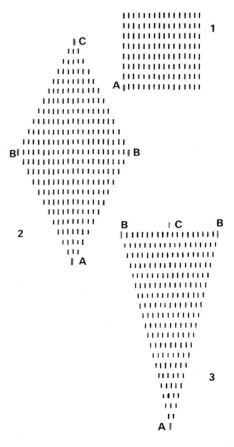

eight deep he says that 800 cavalry would occupy one *stade*. In other words two paces are allowed per horse in the ranks. The most effective depth must have been four deep.

Both the Thessalian and Greek horsemen were armed with spears. The 900 Thracian and Paeonian mounted scouts were armed with javelins. Their prime job was to scout ahead of the army to check for ambushes and to make contact with the enemy. Alexander also used them a great deal for skirmishing. Four *ilai* of Balkan lancers are also mentioned at Granicus. According to Arrian (*Ars Tactica*) they fought with spears at close quarters. Alexander also drafted 1,000 Persian mounted archers during the campaign. As more and more oriental horsemen were drafted, Alexander finally had to reorganise the cavalry. He retained the royal squadron but formed the other five *ilai* into *hipparchies*, each with one *ila* of Companions. The *hipparchy* became the standard unit of the Macedonian cavalry. Asclepiodotus divides the *hipparchy* into eight *ilai*, each commanded by an *ilarch*. His idealised army has two cavalry wings, each consisting of four *hipparchies*.

At the battle of Gaza in 312 BC, 11 years after the death of Alexander, a type of cavalry called *tarentines* are mentioned. They are drawn up in small troops about 30 strong. This may prove their Italian origin as Roman cavalry *turmae* were 30 strong. According to Arrian they were mounted javelineers.

When Alexander distributed the booty after the battle of Gaugamela, Macedonian cavalrymen received three times more than the Macedonian infantrymen, and the allied cavalry two and a half times as much. This probably reflects the comparative pay rates.

In the cavalry, as in the infantry, there was an order of precedence for each day and the first *ila* to be called out took up the position of honour.

Our main source of knowledge of cavalry equipment during the 4th century is Xenophon, who wrote some 50 years before the time of Alexander. He recommends that a cavalryman should wear a cuirass with protection for the thighs, a guard for the left arm and a Boeotian helmet with all-round vision. An excellent example of one of these helmets, maybe even belonging to one

of Alexander's troopers, was found in the Tigris. The thigh protection was probably the *pteryges*. The left arm guard, used in the absence of a shield, seems to have been in vogue only in his own day. He suggests a bronze chest plate (peytral) and face guard (chamfron) for the horse. No examples of horse armour from this period have yet been discovered. Xenophon also prefers the use of the curved *kopis* to the normal two-edged sword, and javelins rather than spears.

On the Issus mosaic found at Pompeii Alexander appears to be wearing a cuirass which is, in some respects, similar to that discovered at Vergina (see p. 58), except that only the chest and shoulder girdle seem to be made of iron. The midrift is made of scales, probably so that it was flexible, and the section above it appears to be made of linen. His horse wears a chamfron but no peytral. The Italian 4th-century muscled cavalry cuirass (see p. 56) may have been in use in Macedonia: there is unfortunately no evidence for or against it.

The army in the field

In most respects the army of Alexander carries on in much the same way as that described by Xenophon 50 years earlier. Orders are given by trumpet. The army deploys from column of march into battle line. They still do not build proper fortified camps, although Alexander sometimes constructs a ditch and palisade. In the face of the Persians at Gaugamela, Arrian says that he had no proper defences to his camp. Like the Greeks at Plataea, he camped with his army in battle order.

On the march advance scouts were sent out ahead and, since they are referred to explicitly as advance scouts, by implication there should also be flank scouts. When approaching the enemy near the Granicus, Alexander threw out a screen ahead of the army consisting of the scouts, reconnoitring parties, the Balkan lancers and 500 light-armed troops. In this respect the Macedonians were far ahead of the Greeks. Pritchett, in his article on scouts, quotes many examples where armies and fleets

Above and left
A detail from the Alexander mosaic discovered in the House of the Faun at Pompeii. Naples Museum. This shows Alexander in a composite cuirass with iron shoulder and chest pieces but scale midriff to allow easier movement.
2 Horse's head from the same mosaic showing the bridling and bit.
3 Greek bit of identical type. Archaeological Museum, Athens.

approached each other undetected because of lack of scouting or other intelligence systems. The most notable example was at Mantinea where neither the Spartans nor the Argive and allied army knew that the other was less than five kilometres away.

Scouts in the sense of intelligence seekers seem to have come into use only about the time of Xenophon, but even so they seem to have been little used in Greece. Although Alexander, and presumably Philip, made good use of these scouts, later armies seem to have fallen back into the old ways and the Roman republican armies were no better. The classic defeats of the Romans at the Caudine Forks and Lake Trasimene could both have been avoided by the simplest scouting. At Cynoscephalae in 197 BC neither the Macedonian army under Philip V nor the Romans under Flamininus had the slightest idea where the other was, in spite of the fact that both could have placed scouts on the high ground in sight of both armies. See the description on p. 205.

The army in battle

Alexander normally drew up his army with the phalanx in the centre, the strongest cavalry, including the Companions, on the right and the weakest on the left. The *hypaspists* were placed at the right end of the phalanx. The right wing was further reinforced by the archers and *agrianes*. The whole line would usually be drawn up obliquely with the right wing advanced and the left held back. The first attack would always come from the advanced right wing with Alexander himself at the head of the Companion cavalry.

This was Alexander's version of the Theban tactic. It was adapted especially for use against the fast-moving, light-armed Persian troops. See the plan of the battle of Gaugamela displayed on p. 82. Arrian is inclined to underestimate the importance of the phalanx in Alexander's battles and to treat the struggle in the centre as a sideshow. Only when the phalanx is in trouble and Alexander manages to relieve it does Arrian report its activities. This must be because he is writing a life of Alexander and wishes to concentrate on the hero of his story. In fact the cavalry is only the sledgehammer which shatters the cohesion of the Persian forces. It is the phalanx which must win the battle. Alexander may be the most successful commander of all time but he can hardly be considered the best. He left it to his generals to win the battle whilst he was off chasing the Persian cavalry. Although he had obviously read Xenophon's *Anabasis*, he learned nothing from the fate of Cyrus the Younger who was killed by a stray arrow whilst leading his cavalry. Polybius, whilst not directly criticising Alexander, says that a general who leads his troops is seen by them all but sees none of them.

For minor expeditions Alexander used only part of his army. These expeditionary forces were mainly light and fast moving. Alexander normally commanded them himself. They usually consisted of half the Companion cavalry, the *hypaspists*, the *agrianes*, the archers and one or two *taxeis* of the phalanx.

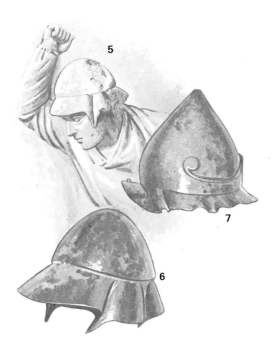

Left and above
1 A crested chamfron, lamellar peytral, masked helmet and arm guards shown on a relief from the sanctuary of Athena at Pergamon, Turkey, now at Berlin.
2 Bronze peytral. Naples Museum.
3 Bronze chamfron. Karlsruhe Museum.
2 and **3** are probably both 5th century and made in the same south Italian workshop.
4 Horses wearing blankets and a primitive saddle shown on a painting from the Kazanlak tomb in Bulgaria (ancient Thrace).

5 Horseman wearing a Boeotian helmet from the Alexander sarcophagus.
6 Boeotian helmet found in the Tigris. Ashmolean Museum, Oxford.
7 Helmet of similar type. This form of helmet is shown on many later Hellenistic monuments (see p. 80). Ashmolean Museum.

Sometimes men were selected from the whole phalanx rather than taking whole *taxeis*. On one occasion at least he chose the lightest armed of the phalanx. Marching night and day these forces could cover as much as 90km a day.

After Alexander—the elephants

The most noticeable change that took place after the death of Alexander was the introduction of elephants. At the battle of Gaugamela the Persian army was reinforced by 15 elephants. This was the first time that Europeans had come up against war elephants. In India the Macedonians had to face up to 200 elephants at the battle of the Hydaspes. They were lined up at 30m intervals in front of the whole army. Their prime object then, as it was later, was to stop the cavalry. Horses do not like the smell of elephants. The Macedonian light infantry first attacked the elephants with javelins, trying to kill the mahouts or drivers. Finally Alexander gave orders for the rear half of the phalanx to move up into the intervals between the files to form locked shields formation, presenting the elephants with a mass of spears, and in this formation drove them back.

The Europeans had been introduced to elephants and now, for better or worse, every self-respecting army had to have them. For over 100 years they were the great gimmick. Alexander brought 200 of them with him when he returned from India.

The armies of Alexander's successors used elephants almost exclusively against cavalry. Occasionally they were used in siege warfare for such jobs as tearing down palisades. When drawn up for battle, the intervals between the animals were filled with light-armed troops. At the battle of Gaza (312 BC) there was a unit of 50 javelineers, slingers and archers (of whom a third were bowmen) in each interval. Diodorus implies that this was the standard number of light armed per elephant. The elephant's main weak spot was the soles of its feet. At the siege of Megalopolis (318 BC) heavy wooden frames studded with iron spikes were laid in the path of the elephants. At the battle of Gaza spiked devices—possibly caltrops—connected by chains were thrown in front of them.

In 280 BC Alexander's kinsman Pyrrhus invaded Italy and introduced the

Romans to these living tanks. As the war was centred mainly on Lucania, elephants received the Italian nickname of Lucanian cows. All the elephants so far mentioned were Indian. However, for Ptolemy, cut off as he was in Egypt, supplies were hard to come by and it was not long before the African elephant was being used, first by the Egyptians and later by the Carthaginians.

Polybius, in his description of the battle of Raphia (217 BC) fought between the Egyptians and Syrians, mentions that the African elephant was smaller than the Indian. This has led to a storm of controversy as, of course, the reverse is true. This was often quoted as

Below
Reconstruction of an Indian war elephant as used by the Macedonians during the 3rd century BC, a time when every self-respecting army had to field a force of these living tanks. They were to fall out of favour after the time of Hannibal.

an example to show that Polybius was not as well informed as his admirers claimed. However, in recent years it has been shown that there was a species known as the forest elephant which was common in North Africa in Polybius' day but is now extinct there. This species measures about 2.35m at the shoulder, whereas the Indian measures just under 3m and the African bush type about 3.5m. During his account of the battle of Raphia, Polybius gives a vivid description of elephants fighting each other. They met head on with tusks interlocked. Each pushed with all its weight, trying to compel the other to give ground. Finally the stronger would force the weaker one's trunk to one side and then gore him in the exposed flank.

Although the Indians who opposed Alexander did not use towers on their elephants, the Indian elephant was large enough to be fitted with one. Towers seem first to have been used by Pyrrhus when he invaded Italy. The North African forest type was rather too small to carry a tower, and certainly the Carthaginians never seem to have used them. However, at Raphia Ptolemy's ele-

phants certainly carried them. This smaller elephant with its saddle back would usually have been ridden like a horse.

In 218 BC the elephant reached the height of its fame when Hannibal crossed the Alps at the head of an army which included 37 elephants. However the heyday of the elephant was past and they soon fell out of favour.

The later Macedonians seldom used elephants and certainly they played no significant part in their campaigns. This was probably because of the difficulty of obtaining them.

The Later Macedonian Army

Most of our knowledge of the phalanx and of Hellenistic warfare in general comes from the later Hellenistic period (c. 220–168 BC). Our principal source is Polybius, the most reliable of all the ancient historians on military matters. He gives many descriptions of battles in which the Macedonian type of phalanx was used, and at one point even describes the basic structure and function

of the phalanx. However, he never goes further. He wrote a separate treatise on this subject which is no longer extant, and probably for this reason did not elaborate on the subject in his history. Arrian in his *Ars Tactica* confirms the existence of this work but gives no details. It is unfortunate that Polybius never mentions the title of even one of the subordinate officers of the phalanx, which would give us a foothold when examining the writings of the later tacticians.

By the 1st century BC Hellenistic warfare was virtually dead and the study of Macedonian tactics had become a branch of philosophy. From this period comes the work of Asclepiodotus. In his treatise he gives an account of the structure, drill and tactics of an idealised phalanx. He gives a complete breakdown of a phalanx of 16,384 men, which is composed of 1,024 files, each of 16 men. The figure of 1,024 is arrived at because it is the tenth power of two. Such a phalanx as this probably never existed. Only at the battle of Pydna is a 16,000 phalanx attested. Within this framework Asclepiodotus can project a

1 Terracotta figure of an elephant with a tower attached by chains. Towers were first used by Pyrrhus against the Romans in 280 BC. It would be difficult positively to identify this as African or Indian. From Pompeii. National Archaeological Museum, Naples.

2 Painted dish from Capena, Campania, showing an Indian elephant with tower, probably from Pyrrhus' army. Villa Giulia Museum, Rome. Note the small ears and round back.
3 Indian elephant with tower shown on a silver *phalera*. The Hermitage, Leningrad.
4 A clearly depicted African elephant shown on the reverse of a Carthaginian coin. Note large ears and saddle back.

mathematical formula for the phalanx. As the files are coupled in twos, fours, eights and so on, he can record the name of every unit and officer. Arrian in his *Ars Tactica* gives an almost identical account drawn either from Asclepiodotus or from a common source.

The basic unit of Asclepiodotus' phalanx is the *syntagma* (meaning literally that which is put together). It consists of 256 men (16 files of 16) plus a rear guard officer (*ouragos*), adjutant (*hyperetes*), herald (*stratokeryx*), signaller (*semeiophoros*) and a trumpeter (*salpingktes*). These were all supernumeraries and were not part of the phalanx. The *syntagma* was commanded by a *syntagmatarch*. It was divided into two *taxeis* commanded by a *taxiarch*. Following the usual Greek practice the *syntagmatarch* would command the right half of the unit and his subordinate, the *taxiarch*, would command the left. Each *taxis* was in turn divided into two *tetrachies* commanded by *tetrarchs*. Each *tetrarchy* was divided into two *dilochiai* or double files each commanded by a *dilochites*, and each *dilochia* was subdivided into two *lochoi* or files commanded by *lochagoi*. A glance at the diagram will show that all these officers were front-rank men (*protostatai*).

Each file (*lochos*) had a half-file leader (*hemilochites*), two quarter-file leaders (*enomotarchs*) and a rear ranker (*ouragos*). It is interesting to note how the traditional Greek unit, the *lochos* and its subdivisions, has shrunk. The *pentekostyes* is now called a *hemilochion* (half *lochos*); the *enomotia* is still there but now consists of only four men. The individual ranks are called alternately front rank (*protostates*) and rear rank (*epistates*). A complete 16-man file would consist of, rank 1, *lochagos*, 2, *epistates*, 3, *protostates*, 4, *epistates*, 5, *enomotarch*, 6, *epistates*, 7, *protostates*, 8, *epistates* (who is the rear-rank officer of the half file), 9, *hemilochites*, 10, *epistates*, 11, *protostates*, 12, *epistates*, 13, *enomotarch*, 14, *epistates*, 15, *protostates*, and 16, *ouragos*. The *enomotarchs* must have been known as front and rear, as would each *epistates*, so that every man could identify his file and rank. In phalanx each man stood next to a man of similar rank on either side: officer next to officer, *epistates* next to *epistates*, and so on.

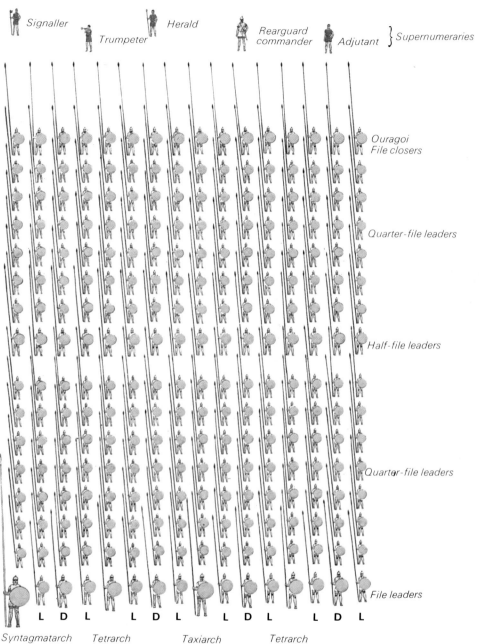

Asclepiodotus couples two *syntagmata* into a *pentekosiarchy* commanded by a *pentekosiarch*, which he similarly doubles to form a *chiliarchy* commanded by a *chiliarch*. Two *chiliarchies* formed a *merarchy* under a *merarch*. Asclepiodotus adds that this 2,048-strong unit had formerly been called a wing (*keras*) or a complement (*telos*). Consequently two of these would have made up a phalanx in an earlier period. This is reflected in the name for a double *merarchy*—a *phalangarchy* commanded by a *phalangarch* (who was originally a general—*strategos*). A double *phalang-*

Signaller · Trumpeter · Herald · Rearguard commander · Adjutant } Supernumeraries

Ouragoi File closers

Quarter-file leaders

Half-file leaders

Quarter-file leaders

File leaders

L D L L D L L D L L D L

Syntagmatarch · Tetrarch · Taxiarch · Tetrarch

Above

The composition of the *syntagma*, the basic unit of the phalanx, according to Asclepiodotus. Asclepiodotus was writing in the 1st century BC, at a time when the heyday of Hellenistic warfare was a phenomenon of the remote past and the study of Macedonian tactics had become a branch of philosophy rather than the application of practical tactical methods. He is probably basing his description on the late Egyptian or Syrian phalanx. Although the later Macedonians used the same basic unit, it was called a *speira* and was commanded by a *speirarch*. The Macedonian unit also had a simpler breakdown and was probably composed of four *tetrachies*, each consisting of four *lochoi*. The rest was probably the same.

L = Lochagos   **D** = Dilochites

archy formed a wing (*keras*) commanded by a *kerarch*, and two wings formed a phalanx commanded by a *strategos*.

It seems worth recording all this to save the reader having to refer to the original work, but there probably never was such a phalanx as this. Most of the divisions and officers above the *syntagma* are probably hypothetical, arrived at by collecting all the names that could be found and making up those that could not, to build up a rigid mathematical pattern.

The Amphipolis military code

In 1934 and 1935 a fragmentary list of Macedonian military regulations which had been found at Amphipolis was published. This inscription, which dates to the reign of Philip V (221–178 BC), lists, among other things, a series of fines to be imposed for loss of equipment and disciplinary matters such as sleeping when on guard. It also mentions several lower officers and units. The *syntagma* is never mentioned, nor is it mentioned by Polybius. The Greek historian, however, regularly mentions a unit called a *speira*. He also uses this word for the Roman *maniple*, which was the smallest tactical unit of the legion, just as the *syntagma* is the smallest tactical unit of Asclepiodotus' phalanx. The *speira*, or its commander the *speirarch*, is also mentioned several times on the Amphipolis inscription. The term *syntagma* is never used in relation to the armies of the Greek peninsula but it is mentioned in documents relating to the Hellenistic armies outside Europe. Similarly, the *speira* is never mentioned outside Europe. It therefore seems reasonable to conclude that the *speira* was the Greek version of the *syntagma*.

The Amphipolis inscription regularly mentions *tetrarchs* with *speirarchs* in such a way as to suggest that the former were the immediate subordinates of the latter. Feyal, when he published the second part of the Amphipolis code, concluded his commentary by suggesting that a *speira* was composed of four *tetrarchies* which were each made up of four *lochoi*. This seems to be reasonably certain and one must therefore hold in doubt the intermediate officers—the *taxiarch* and the *dilochites*—mentioned by Asclepiodotus.

It would seem that the structure of the Macedonian phalanx above the *speira* was also organised on a four-fold basis, i.e. four *speirai* formed a battalion (possibly called a *chiliarchy*), and four battalions formed a *strategia* commanded by a *strategos*. This has been suggested by Feyal as the code also mentions three administrative officers who seem to form a hierarchy. These are the *grammateus*, *archyperetes* and *hyperetes*. Since we know that the *hyperetes* was the administrative officer of the *syntagma/ speira*, the *archyperetes* ought to be the administrative officer of the battalion, and the *grammateus* that of the *strategia*.

The only trouble with a basic *strategia* of around 4,000 men is that we are beginning to get back to the problems posed by Asclepiodotus' formula, i.e. how do you divide into two wings a phalanx of 10,000, which was the basic strength of the phalanx of both Antigonus Doson and Philip V?

Two units appear tantalisingly in the ancient authors but, like the silver shields of Alexander's army, they are never clearly identified. Again one gets the feeling that everybody knew what they were and therefore there was no point in wasting time identifying them. The first is the brazen shields, and the other the white shields. Polybius mentions the brazen shields in his account of the battle of Sellasia (222 BC) where they appear to be part of the 10,000-strong phalanx, but he does not give their strength. Three years later they again appear, also apparently as part of the 10,000-strong phalanx. Philip takes 3,000 of them (implying that the unit was larger than this) on his winter expedition to the Peloponnesus. Plutarch mentions them again at the battle of Pydna in 168 BC, but he too adds no explanation.

The white shields turn up in Plutarch's account of the battle of Sellasia and again in his account of the battle of Pydna. On both occasions they seem to be part of the phalanx. I would therefore tentatively suggest that Philip's phalanx was made up of two 5,000-strong *strategiai* called the white and brazen shields, each consisting of five *chiliarchies*.

Armour and weapons

As has been mentioned before, the Macedonian phalangite was armed with a long pike (*sarissa*) which Polybius says in his day measured 14 cubits (c. 6.3m). This length is not quite so outrageous as some commentators would suggest. In the Middle Ages the Swiss used pikes 5.5m long, and pikes up to 5.75m in length are preserved in the New Armouries of the Tower of London.

Polybius states that the *sarissa* was weighted at the butt end (presumably this means that it had a heavy shoe). He then goes on to explain how it was held. The front hand (left) grasps the *sarissa* about 4 cubits (c. 1.8m) from the butt, with the right hand about 75cm further back. This meant that 10 cubits (c. 4.5m) of the pike projected beyond the body. In the file each man was 3ft (c. 90cm) from the man in front; therefore in a charge the pikes of the first five ranks would project beyond the front rank with, as Polybius says, 2 cubits between each line of points.

The rear 11 ranks did not level their spears but kept them slanting up in the air to break the force of missiles, whilst at the same time using their weight to add to the force of the charge. The phalanx could be drawn up either in open order with two paces per file, in close order with one pace per file, or in locked shields formation with only half a pace per man. Alexander's phalanx formed up with locked shields against Porus' elephants in India.

The pikes were carried in the upright position. Polybius says that, because of their enormous weight (c. 8kg), the Macedonians found it difficult to carry palisade stakes. By comparison, the long pikes in the Tower of London weigh about 3.5kg. When the order to attack was given, the pikes were levelled and the phalanx charged.

The Macedonian hoplite also carried a short sword which he would use only if his pike broke, or when fighting at close quarters where the phalanx formation could not be used, such as in siege warfare. Although the normal hoplite sword continued in use, the most popular sword at this period was the *kopis*, the single-edged slashing weapon with the curved blade (see p. 150). The best examples come from Spain; these have a blade about 45cm long.

The phalangite was armed with a small, round shield (*aspis*) which Asclepiodotus describes as made of bronze,

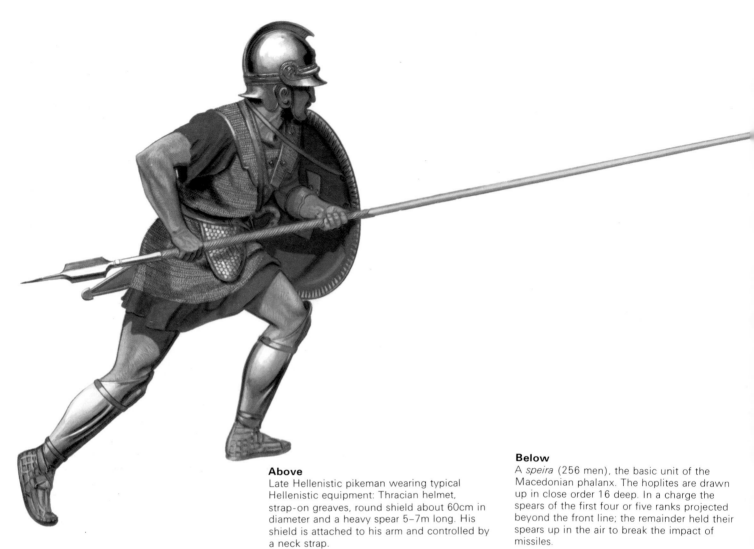

Above
Late Hellenistic pikeman wearing typical Hellenistic equipment: Thracian helmet, strap-on greaves, round shield about 60cm in diameter and a heavy spear 5–7m long. His shield is attached to his arm and controlled by a neck strap.

Below
A *speira* (256 men), the basic unit of the Macedonian phalanx. The hoplites are drawn up in close order 16 deep. In a charge the spears of the first four or five ranks projected beyond the front line; the remainder held their spears up in the air to break the impact of missiles.

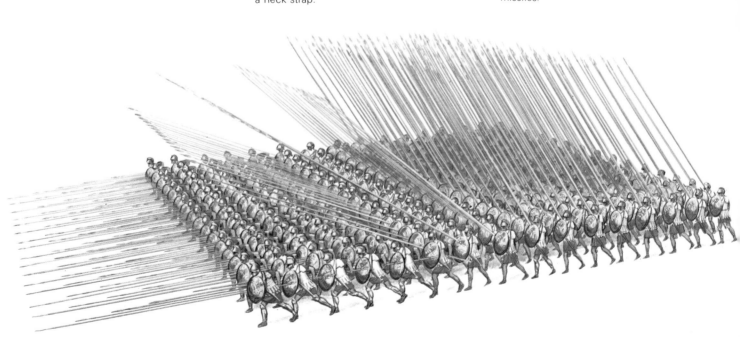

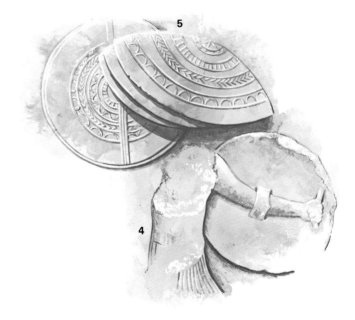

not too concave and about 8 palms (c. 60cm) in diameter. Like everything else to do with the Macedonian phalanx, the shield has caused much confusion.

Fragments of a Macedonian shield were found at Pergamum in Turkey. These consisted only of the bronze sheath (65–67cm in diameter) and small fragments of parchment that had been used as padding between the wood and bronze. Nothing remained of the grip. The sheath was attached to the wooden core by four rectangular tongues and a little over 100 darts cut along the edge of the metal which were folded over on to the inside.

Plutarch, describing the Macedonians at the battle of Pydna (168 BC), says that their shields were hung on their left shoulders, and when they advanced they brought them round to the front. This has led some commentators to suggest that the shield had no grip. Representations of the Macedonian shield show

that it was rimless, i.e. that it did not have the broad rim on the inside edge that was so characteristic of the Argive shield. This type of shield was adopted as it was impossible to hold a two-handed spear whilst using an Argive shield, as the left forearm was held against the inside of the shield by the armband and the hand could not reach the pike. This is obviously why Asclepiodotus says that the shield must not be too curved.

The Aemilius Paullus victory monument at Delphi shows the inside of such a rimless shield. It has an Argive-style armband and handgrip. A few years ago the author made a copy of this shield with a bronze facing similar to the one found at Pergamum. The shield weighed about 5kg. Experiments showed that it could be handled very efficiently using only the armband and controlling the angle with the neck strap. When an Argive shield is being carried, the inside of the rim fits comfortably over the left shoulder taking the weight off the arm. It was the absence of this ridge on the Macedonian type that made a carrying strap necessary. This strap would also

have taken much of the weight of the great pike. When used outside the phalanx without a pike, the handgrip would be used.

The representations suggest that the face of the shield was usually embossed. In the case of the silver shields brigade, the face of the shield would have been tinned just as Roman armour and weapons were. Two shields were represented on the walls of the tomb of Lyson and Callicles which was recently discovered in Macedonia. One of these is bronze or gilded and the other is painted with the royal symbol of Macedon. The bearer of this shield may have been a member of the *agema*—the brigade of *hypaspists* which served as the king's bodyguard—or a member of the royal *ila* of the Companion cavalry.

In his life of Alexander, Arrian often refers to the light-armed part of the phalanx. It is clear from the context of these remarks that he is not referring to the *hypaspists* but to the Companion infantry. This variation of equipment is also noticeable in Hannibal's phalanx, where groups of pikemen are often referred to by Polybius as light armed. As Polybius does not comment on this, one must assume that it is normal.

The Amphipolis inscription lists a scale of fines imposed on Macedonian phalangites for loss of pieces of their equipment. The cuirass for the ordinary

Below and right
1 Section of a Macedonian shield.
2 Section of an Argive shield for comparison.
3 The remains of a Macedonian shield found at Pergamum in Turkey. Scale 1:15.
4 A Macedonian phalangite shown on the victory monument of Aemilius Paullus at Delphi. This shows a rimless type of shield with an Argive grip.
5 Shields shown on the reliefs from the sanctuary of Athena at Pergamum.

rank and file is called a *cotthybos*, whereas for the front rankers or officers it is referred to as a *thorax* or *hemi-thorax*. The *cotthybos* has been plausibly identified with the linen cuirass, whilst the *thorax* and *hemi-thorax* were probably metal plated. This difference is amplified when one reads that the officers were fined twice as much as the rank and file.

The implication of this is that the front rank was more heavily armed than the succeeding ranks, and it is possible that the rear ranks wore no body armour at all. The Amphipolis relief mentions greaves, helmets and cuirasses, but this does not necessarily imply that all the ranks wore them. It certainly seems unlikely, for example, that the men behind the front five ranks would need greaves.

The sculptures and paintings of the period, both Greek and Etruscan, show the wide variety of armour in use at this time. Besides the basic linen cuirass typical of the classical era, quilted cuirasses also appear on later Etruscan sculptures. On these sculptures one also finds varieties of plated linen cuirass, covered with either scales or overlapping rectangular plates (lamellar). The most famous of these is the Mars from Todi in the Museo Gregoriano at the Vatican.

The victory frieze from the temple of Athena at Pergamum in western Turkey shows a full-length muscled cuirass, a shorter cuirass which could be the *hemi-thorax* of the Amphipolis inscription, and part of a decorated linen type cuirass. This, of course, could have been made of iron like the cuirass from Vergina. This frieze also shows a Celtic mail shirt. Polybius, in his description of the Roman army of this period, says that the wealthier Romans wore mail. As he does not explain what mail is, one must assume that the Greeks of his day also wore it.

The Thracian helmet continued to be popular and is shown on the Pergamum reliefs. Several types of high-crowned helmets are also shown. These may have been developed as a defence against the slashing swords of the Celts. This type of helmet allowed for a great deal of padding between the top of the head and the helmet. At this period, which coincides with the most aggressive period of the Celtic invasions, there was a general tendency to adopt high-crowned helmets.

The composition of the army

At a glance the composition of the later Hellenistic armies does not seem to have changed much since Alexander's day. The Macedonian army of Antigonus Doson and Philip V still had *hypaspists*, peltasts, slingers and archers supporting the phalanx. However, these do not always seem to perform the same tasks as in the earlier period. The *hypaspists* now seem to refer to a body of staff officers (who undertook special tasks) and the *agema*, the king's bodyguard. The Amphipolis code says that their tents are to be erected immediately after those of the king and his immediate entourage.

The peltasts of Philip's army appear to have completely changed. At Cynoscephalae they formed up alongside the phalanx and even doubled their depth. Walbank has suggested, and he has to be right, that these peltasts were in fact *hypaspists*. Whether they were armed with pike or spear is impossible to say as the sources are contradictory. Livy calls these peltasts *caetrati*, the word used by Caesar for the Spanish light-armed troops who, if Harmand is right, should be identified with the lightly clad troops with round shields shown on the reliefs from Osuna in Spain. In 219 BC Philip had 5,000 of these peltasts.

The most noticeable change since the time of Alexander was the switch of priority from cavalry to infantry. In Alexander's army the proportion of cavalry to infantry was about 1:6, whereas in the later Macedonian army it was around 1:20. One should not make too much of this—at the battle of Chaeronea in 338 the proportion was 1:15. The reason for the high proportion of cavalry in Alexander's army was that mobility was the key to the conquest of Persia. It was well known that Greek infantry was superior to anything Persia could produce, but the phalanx could only defeat what it could catch. It was Philip's phalanx that won the battle of Chaeronea, and yet the massive build-up of the Macedonian cavalry must be credited to Philip. There could only be one reason for this —the planned invasion of Persia with its vast cavalry resources. Although

Below
Armour shown on the reliefs from the sanctuary of Athena, Pergamum.
1 Short muscled cuirass.
2 Linen cuirass.
3 Late Thracian helmet.
4 Strap-on greaves.

Below
A relief from the temple of Artemis Leucophryene, Magnesia-ad-Meandrum, showing a senior officer, possibly of the cavalry. Late Hellenistic. Louvre Museum.

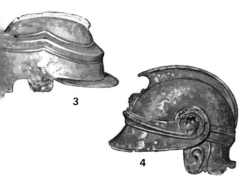

cavalry continued to play an important part in Asia for about 100 years, after the death of Alexander in Europe it quickly reverted to its subsidiary position as phalanx battled with phalanx. Epirus and all the old city states had adopted the Macedonian phalanx and, since the result of the battle depended on this, it tended to become heavier and consequently less manoeuvrable.

In Syria and Egypt the old units of Alexander's army still appear in the late 3rd and early 2nd century. Both Antiochus and Ptolemy, as would be expected, appear to have an *agema* and a royal *ila* of cavalry. *Hypaspists*, too, are mentioned by Polybius, but it would be tempting fate to suggest what they might be. Antiochus has *agrianes* who should have been raised on the northern frontiers of Macedon; no doubt they were raised locally but retained the traditional name of the earlier troops.

After the death of Alexander, the veteran silver shields regiment had come under the control of Eumenes, on whose death they passed to Antigonus. Here we lose track of them. If they were a permanent veteran unit and constantly receiving recruits from the veterans of other units, they could have survived. If not, they must have died out. A hundred years later Antiochus, the successor of Seleucus who had deposed Antigonus, had 10,000 soldiers 'armed in the Macedonian fashion', most of whom were armed with silver shields. These are distinct from his 20,000-strong phalanx and one is tempted to suggest that these were *hypaspists*. Certainly Antiochus has *hypaspists* in his army, as well as an *agema* which is mentioned at the siege of Sardis.

The army in the field
On the march in hostile territory the army was led by a regular vanguard of light-armed troops. Philip used his mercenaries for this job. They were accompanied by pioneers whose job was to clear the road. Behind these came the phalanx, with light-armed troops in parallel columns on either side to ward off attacks. If an attack was threatened from one flank, the light armed would cover this side only. Similarly, the rear guard was also made up of light-armed troops. Philip used his Cretans, whom Polybius describes as the most

effective skirmishers, as his rearguard. The baggage train was placed at the point farthest from any expected danger. If the threat was from the front, the baggage would be at the back, and when retreating it would be at the front. If an attack was expected from one flank, the baggage train would be placed alongside the phalanx on the other flank.

When looking for a camping site, ground was chosen which offered the best natural defences. Polybius criticised the Greeks for their lack of energy when camping, comparing them unfavourably with the Romans. In light of this it seems unlikely that the Romans got their ideas of camping from Pyrrhus when they captured his camp at Beneventum, as Livy and Frontinus record it. When necessary the Macedonians did entrench, especially if they intended to stay at the same site for some time. Like the Romans, they constructed a ditch and rampart with a palisade along the top. The palisade stakes were cut branches with stout shoots all round the main stem. Polybius is very critical of these, as he says that two or three attackers could together get hold of one stake and rip it out. When they had removed it, there was a gap left wide enough for them to break through.

The Macedonians may not have camped as well as the Romans, but they did post pickets along the approaches to the camp—a thing that the Romans do not seem to have done. It was the responsibility of the *tetrarchies* to provide these pickets and of the *tetrarchs* to inspect them. This duty was probably done on a rota as it was in the Roman army. The Amphipolis code stresses that, at night, inspections should be made without a light so as not to give advance warning to the guard.

The line-up for battle was still basically the same as in the previous period, with the phalanx in the centre flanked by the peltasts, the light armed and the cavalry. The difference now was that the key to the battle was in the centre and not on the wings.

At the battle of Raphia in 217 the young Antiochus III of Syria, trying no doubt to emulate Alexander, charged the Egyptian cavalry and drove them from the field. He pursued them so far, however, that by the time he returned the battle was over and he had lost.

Ptolemy, who appeared to be losing the battle, took over the phalanx who, encouraged by his presence, drove the Syrian phalanx from the field. By the time that Antiochus, confident that he had won the battle, returned, Ptolemy was in possession of the battlefield and Antiochus' infantry was scattered across the country in flight. Ptolemy stripped the enemy dead and collected and buried his own, whilst Antiochus was humiliated by being forced to retrieve his own dead under a flag of truce.

On rare occasions the phalanx was broken up into companies with other troops interspersed between them. Pyrrhus did this in Italy and Antigonus

Doson did it with his silver shields at Sellasia.

Before battle commenced the general would ride along in front of his troops with his officers and friends reminding the soldiers of their past achievements and exhorting them to fight bravely, pointing out the advantages of victory, usually concentrating on the booty to be won. In the case of Ptolemy and Antiochus, both of whom had only recently come to the throne and therefore could hardly boast of their past accomplishments, they relied more on their promises for the future.

The signal for battle, possibly a flag, was raised and the soldiers shouted their

war cry several times. At Gabiene in 316 BC, where two Macedonian armies faced each other, they raised their war cries alternately several times.

Whilst waiting for the order to prepare for battle, each phalangite stood with his pike resting on the ground and held upright with his right hand. His shield hung by its strap around his neck and over the back of his left shoulder. On the order to prepare for battle, he would swing the shield round to the front and pass his left forearm through the band. He would then raise his left hand across his chest and grasp the pike level with his head. On the order 'level pikes', his right hand would slip down

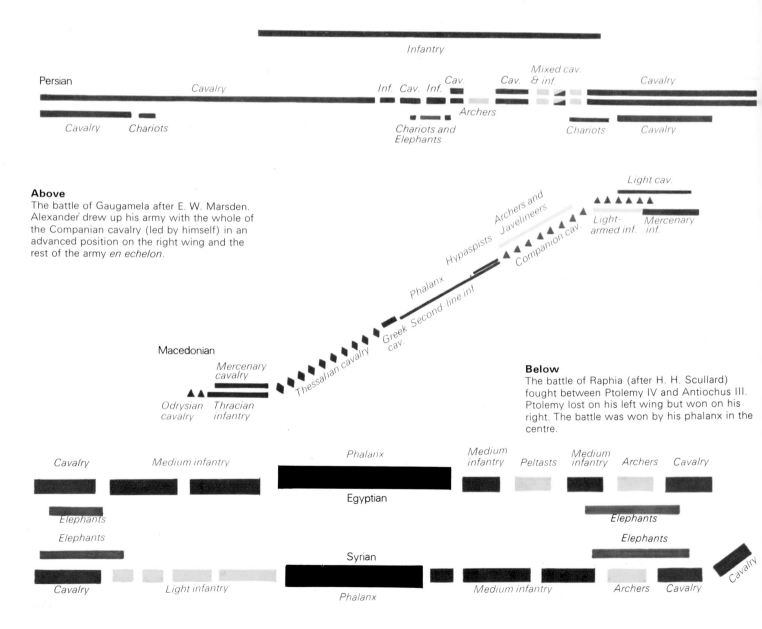

Above
The battle of Gaugamela after E. W. Marsden. Alexander drew up his army with the whole of the Companian cavalry (led by himself) in an advanced position on the right wing and the rest of the army *en echelon*.

Below
The battle of Raphia (after H. H. Scullard) fought between Ptolemy IV and Antiochus III. Ptolemy lost on his left wing but won on his right. The battle was won by his phalanx in the centre.

until the arm was straight, then he would lower his pike until it was parallel to the ground at waist level. The order to charge was given on the trumpet. If, however, the ground was very broken and the army split up as it was at Sellasia, the signal to charge was given with flags—a white one for the infantry and a red one for the cavalry—and would be relayed by the trumpeter attached to each *speira*. The battle was normally started on the wings.

When advancing in battle order, the phalanx had to be drawn up in open order and double depth. This was achieved by the alternate *lochoi* falling back and coming into line behind the file on their right. On coming into range of the enemy, the alternate *lochoi* moved up again to form close order. This was done because of the difficulty of advancing through open country in close order with no room to manoeuvre around natural obstacles.

If there was no room to deploy the whole army before reaching the battlefield, Polybius suggests that the advance should be made in either double or quadruple phalanx, and that the rear phalanxes should deploy on either wing when they reached the open ground. When the route to the battlefield was restricted, the phalanx could form up and then turn into column of march so that all the officers were on one side of the column and all the *ouragoi* on the other. Asclepiodotus mentions this formation and Polybius is certainly describing it at the third battle of Mantinea in 207 BC, and again at the battle of Cynoscephalae ten years later. At Mantinea the Spartan tyrant Machanidas wheeled his column to the right to form up in battle order, and at Cynoscephalae Philip wheeled his to the left to form up his right wing.

At Cynoscephalae, once his right wing was drawn up, Philip ordered his phalangites and peltasts to double their depth and close up towards the right. In order to do this, the alternate files would be withdrawn, each lining up behind the file on its right so that the phalanx was double depth and the files in open order. Then, with the right-hand double file standing fast, the rest of the wing turned to the right and closed up. Each successive file would take one more pace than the file in front so that they finished

up one pace apart. They then turned to face the front.

If the enemy appeared in the rear the phalanx had to turn about. This, however, would leave the *ouragoi* in the front rank and the officers at the back. This was rectified by countermarching. Any one of three methods could be used to do this. The file leaders could stand still while the rest of the file formed up in front of them, and then the whole file turned about face. This was the Macedonian method. Asclepiodotus is not very happy about this as it appears to be a retreat. He prefers the method used by the Spartans where the rear rankers stood fast and the rest of the file formed up behind them and then faced about. This appears to be an advance. There was a third possibility, the Cretan or Persian countermarch, where the file leader and the *ouragos* changed places and the intervening ranks did likewise. This involves neither an advance nor a retreat. Whichever method is used, the problem with countermarching is that the commanders finish up on the left of their units and not the right. This could be rectified by countermarching the ranks of each unit. Of course it was possible to countermarch the whole phalanx or wing in this way, but to do so in the face of the enemy would be suicidal and could only be considered as a parade ground manoeuvre. Anyway, there was no great disadvantage in having the chain of command from the left. Normally, if it was considered necessary, each *speira* would countermarch its ranks.

When drawing up a phalanx *en echelon*, in wedge or in crescent, the formation was achieved by staggering the *speirai* and not by drawing up the ranks at an angle or, even worse, on a curve.

At Sellasia Antigonus split his phalanx into its two wings and drew them up one behind the other. The attack was initiated by the front phalanx but, when this was pushed back, Antigonus ordered the Macedonians to close up 'in their peculiar formation of the double phalanx with its massed line of pikes', and in this formation drove the Lacedaemonians from their position. This can only mean that he marched the second phalanx into the spaces between the files of the first and charged with locked shields as Alexander had done at the Hydaspes river.

Polybius lists the advantages and disadvantages of the phalanx to explain to his readers why the Macedonians lost the battle of Cynoscephalae. Under ideal circumstances nothing could withstand the charge of the phalanx. But the phalanx can only operate really efficiently over even ground with no ditches, clefts, clumps of trees, ridges or water courses which break up the formation and so destroy its strength. At Pydna the flexible Roman maniples forced their way into the gaps in the phalanx and broke it up. Once this had happened the phalanx was defenceless as the *sarissa* was obviously useless for close combat and, encumbered by their long pikes, the Macedonians were unable to turn and face an attack from any other direction than the front. To signal that they wished to surrender or desert the phalangites customarily raised their *sarissae* into the upright position.

When the battle was over the troops were recalled by trumpet. The victor stripped the enemy dead and buried his own. The captured armour was hung up in the temple porticos. In thanks for the victory shields were usually inscribed and dedicated in a shrine. Polybius tells the amusing story of the dedication of the shields after the siege of Medion by the Aetolians. The siege was almost over but, as the elections were due, the Aetolian general was frightened he might be replaced before he had captured the town and so lose the credit for it. (This is a very common feature in both Greek and Roman warfare.) In order to appease the current general, but at the same time not detract from whoever might succeed him, a compromise was reached and it was determined to inscribe the shields as being won 'by the Aetolian general and the candidates for the next year's office'. Embarrassingly for the Aetolians, the siege was raised and the Medionians parodied the Aetolian resolution in amusing fashion by using exactly the same wording for their shields, changing only the 'by' of the inscription to 'from'.

ITALY AN

THE

WESTERN

MEDITER

ITALY AND THE WESTERN MEDITERRANEAN

CENOMANI

INSUBRES

VERONA
PADUA
VENETI

LIGURIA

Po

BOII

REGGIO (EMILIA)

△ SPINA

LA SPEZIA

APENNINES

△ BOLOGNA

YUGOSLAVIA

▲ ARIMINUM
(RIMINI)

PISA
Arno

SENONES

▲ SENA GALLICA
• ANCONA

ETRURIA

• AREZZO

VETULONIA

UMBRIA

CLUSIUM
(CHIUSI)
PERUGIA

GROSSETO
ORVIETO
• TODI

△ FIRMUM
• MONTEFORTINO

TELAMON

△ NARNIA

• CAMPOVALANO
△ HADRIA

COSA

• VULCI

TARQUINII

ADRIATIC SEA

SUTRIUM ▲
CAERE
VEII
FALERII
NEPET
▲ CARSEOLI
▲ CAPESTRANO

OSTIA
FIDENAE
ROME
ALBA FUCENS

LABICI
SIGNIA
ARICIA
CORA
ARDEA LATIUM
ANTIUM
SATRICUM
FREGELLAE
AESERNIA
• BOVIANUM

CIRCEII
INTERAMNA
TERRACINA
SAMNIUM
▲ LUCERA
MINTURNAE
CALES
PONTIAE ▲
SINUESSA
Volturno
BENEVENTO
• ASCULUM
CUMAE □
CAPUA
SATICULA
• CANNAE
NAPLES
CAMPANIA
CANOSA
APULIA
POMPEII △
VENUSIA
SORRENTO △
• BARI

TYRRHENIAN SEA

PAESTUM ▲

CONVERSANO

LUCANIA

CORSICA

□ ALALIA
(ALERIA)

SARDINIA

□ TARANTO

HERACLEA

LILYBAEUM

• CARTHAGE

SICILY

RHEGIUM

BRUTII

□ LOCRI

□ SYRACUSE

Introduction

The rise of Rome was not meteoric. It was a slow painstaking process fraught with many setbacks. It was this slow process, accompanied by long periods of consolidation, which was the main reason for the longevity of the subsequent Roman empire.

Italy was the first naturally bounded area of Europe to be unified. Neither Philip nor Alexander, nor any of their successors, established full control over the whole of Greece. It took Rome some 560 years to bring the whole of Italy under her control. Once that hegemony had been established, there was never any threat of it breaking up. Even the social war fought between Rome and her allies in the 1st century BC was not about secession but over the rights to citizenship of the non-Roman Italians. It took an external influence, the barbarian invasions more than half a millennium later, to shatter the unity of Italy.

The weaponry, organisation and tactics of the Roman army, unlike those of the Greeks, were not an invention of the Romans but the result of a process of adoption and adaptation. In order to understand the development of the Roman army it is necessary to examine the peoples the Romans fought and to try to isolate what they learned from each other.

The main source of our knowledge of this period is the Roman historian Titus Livius. Although Livy is a great writer, he is a poor historian. As a conservative and patriot he throws the blame for many of Rome's mistakes on to the lower classes who were struggling for recognition. He regularly covers up anything that is unfavourable to Rome, shows little appreciation of topography and military tactics and freely substitutes contemporary terms for ancient ones with complete disregard for accuracy. Worst of all, however, he often transmits accounts that he must know are false.

Dionysius of Halicarnassus has left us a very full account of the early history of Rome. Although he records much the same material as Livy, he has a marginally greater appreciation of military tactics and, because he uses Greek terms, it is often easier to visualise the items he is describing. Unfortunately his history becomes fragmentary in the early 5th century, with the result that from c. 475 to the outbreak of the first Punic war in 264 we are almost entirely at the mercy of Livy. Fortunately we have a substantial archaeological record which helps us to build up a fairly accurate picture at least of the armour and weaponry of this early period.

The Struggle for Italy

The story of Rome starts in the middle of the 8th century—traditionally 753 BC. Rome owed her foundation to the river Tiber, for she was one of a group of hilltop villages that sprang up on the left bank of the river at its lowest crossing point, probably in an attempt to levy a toll on merchants crossing the river to trade with southern Italy.

The Tiber rises in the Apennine mountains above Arrezzo. Here also another river, the Arno, rises. The Arno flows west to enter the Tyrrhenian Sea at Pisa whilst the Tiber flows south for 200km before turning south-west to flow into the sea at Ostia. Between these two rivers was Etruria. During the 8th century the population of Etruria was dispersed into a multitude of small villages. Here a high Iron Age culture (known as Villanovan) flourished.

In the 7th century a powerful ruling class emerged in Etruria. As had happened in Greece, they united the groups of villages to form such powerful city states as Veii, Caere and Tarquinii. The Etruscans were great seafarers and may well have come to Italy by sea from the east. Their sea captains soon established a mercantile empire in the western Mediterranean where they came into conflict with other contenders for this trade: the Phoenicians operating from Carthage on the north coast of Africa; and the Greeks who had colonised the southern coasts of Italy and eastern Sicily. One such Greek colony was established at Cumae west of Naples. These Greeks began to inter-fere with Etruscan ships trading with the east which had to run the gauntlet of their colonies. This trade war soon developed into a bitter conflict between the two nations.

In the closing years of the 7th century the Etruscans forced their way across the Tiber, captured the Roman villages and established a land route south through Latium. They pressed on southwards into Campania, bypassing Cumae and cutting it off from the interior. In Campania they captured several of the coastal towns, including Pompeii and Sorrento, and established a large military colony at Capua just south of the river Volturno.

An Etruscan military overlord was established at Rome. He grouped the hilltop villages into a town as had been done in Etruria, and for the next hundred years under its three Etruscan rulers Rome flourished and became the chief city in Latium.

The Etruscans reached the summit of their power when they formed an alliance with the Carthaginians against their mutual enemy the Greeks and, in a sea battle off Corsica in 535 BC, forced the Phocaean Greeks to abandon their colony at Alalia and so gained control of the island.

But the Etruscan age of glory was shortlived. Although they had isolated Cumae by their thrust southwards into Campania, they had failed to bring the Greek city to its knees. In fact in 524 they suffered a serious defeat on land at the hands of the Cumaeans. Fourteen years later, probably at the instigation of the Cumaeans, the Latins revolted and Rome expelled her Etruscan ruler Tarquin the Proud. This revolt spelt disaster for the Etruscans as the Romans now closed the river crossing to them.

With the assistance of Tarquinii and Veii, Tarquin tried to subdue the rebels. The ensuing battle was indecisive but the fact that they had survived was sufficient for the Romans to celebrate a triumph. Lars Porsena of Clusium (Chiusi) now entered the fray. Collecting together a large force of Etruscans, allies and mercenaries he made a rapid advance on Rome, hoping to catch them unawares.

The Romans had realised that an attack was imminent and had made preparations to hold the river crossing. A fort was established on the Janiculum, a hill on the Etruscan side of the river which covered the approach to the bridge, and the citizens armed themselves to withstand the attack. In spite of their preparations they were caught off guard. The Romans never seem to have come to terms with the idea of scouting. Their history is punctuated with disasters that could easily have been avoided by proper scouting. The Etruscans approached unseen, stormed the Janiculum and advanced on the bridge. In panic the Romans turned and fled. The patriotic Livy tells how Horatius and his two companions, who

curiously both have Etruscan names, heroically held back the enemy whilst their fellow citizens chopped down the bridge and so saved the city. But the more enlightened Romans felt forced to admit that the city fell.

The army of Porsena marched on into Latium, advancing on Aricia, the centre of the Latin resistance. The Greeks of Cumae, realising that this was their great opportunity, also took the field. Caught between the two forces, the Etruscan army was massacred.

With their land route cut the Etruscans were forced to maintain contact with their southern colonies by sea. In

474 they suffered yet another crushing defeat at the hands of the Greeks in a sea battle off Cumae, and as a result the towns of Campania were completely isolated. But fate had a trick to play; within 50 years both Etruscan Capua and Greek Cumae had fallen to the Samnites.

For a short while Rome, which had controlled Latium under her Etruscan rulers, fought desperately to hold on to

Below
Lars Porsena, the Etruscan king of Clusium (Chiusi), with his troops on the Janiculum overlooking Rome. The native Etruscans are armed with round Argive shields, the others are their allies from central and northern Italy.

her supremacy, but it was the Latins who had defeated the Etruscans and not the Romans. At the beginning of the 5th century, finding her position untenable, Rome was forced to sign the Cassian treaty of alliance with the other Latin towns as equal partners. The next 80 years were spent by the Latins fighting for their very existence against the eastern hill peoples, the Aequi and Volsci, who were being forced down into the plains of Latium by the expansion of the Samnites. These rugged mountain men had gradually forced their way southwards through the Apennines, driving all before them. In the middle of the 5th century they burst upon southern Italy, overrunning Campania, Apulia and Lucania.

In 431 the Aequi were defeated by the Latin League and the Volsci were driven back. By the closing years of the century the Latin League felt secure enough to turn its attention to southern Etruria. The Etruscans, meanwhile, had been searching for a new outlet for their trade. About 500 BC an Etruscan colony had been established at Bologna in the Po valley and a route opened up to Spina, a port at the head of the Adriatic. But, like the route to the south, this was also doomed. For some time the Celts of central Europe had been forcing their way through the Alps and settling in the Po valley. This migration gathered momentum as the century advanced so that by the end of it the Etruscans were under pressure from both north and south. Rome, now the dominant partner of the Latin League, launched an all-out attack on the Etruscan town of Veii which capitulated after a long siege in 396 BC. The League's pressure on southern Etruria was to have a backlash as the Etruscans, who were trying to defend two frontiers, managed to sustain neither. Less than ten years after the fall of Veii the Celts burst into Etruria and descended the Tiber valley towards Rome. At the Allia these wild men from the north crushed the legions that had been sent to oppose them and sacked the city on the hills.

It was a terrible setback for Rome and she lost her dominant position in the Latin League. Rome recovered but for the Etruscans it was the beginning of the end. The League had lost its foothold in southern Etruria and spent three years reconquering it. This reconquest brought the League into collision with Tarquinii and several other of the Etruscan cities who were becoming fearful of the growing power of the Latins. In 388 and again in 386 Tarquinii took up arms but failed to drive them back.

In 359 Tarquinii launched an invasion of Latin-controlled Etruria. Two years later Falerii joined in and the following year the rest of the Etruscan federation also took up arms. A pitiless war ensued in which both sides mercilessly massacred prisoners. Finally, in 351, the League launched an all-out offensive and brought Tarquinii and Falerii to their knees. It was difficult for the Etruscans to make a concerted effort as they were under pressure from both sides. In the north Bologna was unable to hold out and by 350 it was in Celtic hands and the Etruscan domination of the Po valley came to an end.

In the south the Volsci were still a threat to the League, which now turned and forced them into submission. The League now controlled all of western Italy from southern Etruria to northern Campania. But the question of who governed Latium—the League or Rome —remained unresolved. In 340 the final struggle began. After a bitter war lasting three years Rome emerged as undisputed master and the history of Italy now became the history of Rome.

The last war with the Volsci had brought Rome face to face with the Samnites along the Liris river. Rome had signed a treaty with them in 354 to enlist their aid against their mutual enemy the Volsci. In 343 hostilities broke out between the two nations that were to last for 50 years. The first so-called Samnite war was hardly more than a series of skirmishes as the two protagonists vied for control of Campania. The main conflict did not start for another 15 years, but it was inevitable. In 328 the Romans established a colony at Fregellae on the Samnite side of the Liris river. In retaliation the Samnites engineered a coup at Naples and detached it from its Roman alliance. Rome had been looking for an excuse and declared war.

The first years of this war were again characterised by many inconclusive skirmishes; the Samnites were reluctant to oppose the Roman infantry in the plains and the Romans were unwilling to fight these agile mountaineers in the hills. After seven years of indecisive skirmishing, the Romans decided to make a thrust into Samnium itself and embarked upon a venture that was to end in disaster and ignominy.

The two consuls for the year 321 committed their entire forces to the invasion of Samnium. This venture resulted in the capture of the combined army at the Caudine Forks. The legionaries were spared but were compelled to leave behind all their belongings and, clad only in a tunic, to 'pass under the yoke'. This was a frame made from two spears stuck in the ground and a third one tied across horizontally at a height that compelled the Romans to crouch down to pass underneath. The Romans themselves had often forced their defeated enemies to perform this humiliating exercise. It was the very symbol of defeat and kindled in every Roman breast a thirst for revenge.

For five years the Romans kept the 'Caudine peace', but by 316 they could hold back no longer and repudiated the treaty, claiming that the consuls had no right to sign it. The war was reopened on three fronts with one army operating in Campania, another further north in the Liris valley, whilst a third crossed the Apennines to the Adriatic coast and marched south to join forces with the Apulians.

The Samnites struck with breathtaking speed and completely outmanoeuvred the Romans. Keeping the Roman armies in Apulia and the Liris valley occupied, they brushed aside the Campanian army and thrust northwards. The Romans handed over power to a dictator who gathered all available forces and pressed southward. He dispatched half his troops under his deputy (the master of the horse) to cover the coast road (the later Appian Way) whilst he himself advanced along the Latin Way between the hills.

The Samnite army which had been heading for the Latin Way now changed course, crossed the hills and fell upon the master of the horse near Terracina. The Roman army was wiped out and its commander killed. Rome's southern allies now rebelled. The Samnites advanced into Latium, destroying crops and ravaging the countryside as far as Ardea within 30km of Rome.

In panic the Roman Senate recalled part of its forces from the Liris valley. The Samnites there immediately crossed the river and attacked the weakened Roman force. The Romans were on the run. To the north Rome's central Italian allies wavered. If they defected, Rome's army in Apulia would be cut off.

At this point an event happened none could have foreseen. The Greek cities of southern Italy and Sicily had often called in Greek generals to help them against their enemies. The cry for help had gone out from the Syracusans, and Acrotatus of Sparta had answered. On his way to Sicily he had briefly interfered in affairs in Illyria. He had now arrived at Taranto on his way to Sicily. For a moment the Samnites faltered, fearing that he might turn his forces against them.

Their hesitation was just enough to swing the balance. The Romans counterattacked, throwing all their available forces against the invading Samnites and routing them. They had come so near to winning, but the war was to last another ten years as it gradually wound down. In 311 several of the Etruscan cities entered the war but they were easily knocked out. How different things might have been if they had entered the war three years earlier. In 304 the Samnites sued for peace and were left hardly worse off than before.

The peace lasted only six years. In 296 BC, after two years of the usual skirmishing, the Samnites again made a dash northwards. This time a Samnite army advanced through the Apennines to join forces with the Etruscans, Umbrians and Gauls for a concerted attack on Rome. But by now the Etruscans were a failing force. In 311 they had launched an attack on the Roman fortress at Sutrium but were easily repulsed. Following this, Cortona, Perugia and Arrezzo were forced to sign treaties of alliance. Now they had the opportunity to make one last effort. This was Rome's greatest test. So far she had only had to face her enemies individually. Now for the first time she was opposed by their combined forces. But, like the Greeks, the Italians found

it almost impossible to act in unison. At Sentinum the Samnite and Gallic armies fought a long drawn out battle against the legions and lost. The failure of the Etruscans and Umbrians to turn up for the battle may have cost them all their independence. When the Samnites were defeated, the Etruscans collapsed with them. During the first half of the 3rd century the rest of the Etruscan cities were either crushed or forced into alliance with Rome. Vulci fell in 280 and Volsinii in 265. Roman colonies were planted in the heartland of Etruria and its days of greatness were over.

The battle of Sentinum not only marked the end of the Samnites but also the beginning of Rome's long purge of the Celts. Of all the peoples of the Roman empire the Celts suffered the worst during the years of expansion northwards.

In 284, as part of that general movement of the Celtic tribes which was to overthrow the kingdom of Thrace and plunge Macedonia into chaos, the Senones, the same tribe which had sacked Rome a hundred years before, moved out of their territory on the Adriatic coast north of Ancona, crossed the Apennines and raided Etruria. The Roman army which marched north to deal with the invaders suffered a crushing defeat with the loss of 13,000 men. In an act of massive retaliation the Romans crossed the mountains into the Senonic homeland and drove the entire tribe out of Italy.

The Boii, who had captured Bologna from the Etruscans and had settled in the area, now also crossed the Apennines but were defeated in central Etruria. The following year they crossed the mountains again and were once more defeated. They sued for peace. The Romans, preoccupied with the situation in central Italy, agreed to the treaty which lasted for 50 years.

With the fall of Samnium, Rome controlled almost the whole of peninsular Italy. Only the Greek cities of the south remained outside the Roman alliance. In order to consolidate her position Rome began to put pressure on these Greek states to try to force them into alliance. The immediate result was that Taranto appealed to Alexander the Great's kinsman, Pyrrhus, king of Epirus. In 280 BC he

crossed the Adriatic and landed in southern Italy with 25,000 crack troops and 20 elephants. His aim was to unite Rome's enemies in the south but the Romans anticipated him and rushed southwards with 25,000 legionaries. At Heraclea the Romans faced the dreaded Macedonian phalanx for the first time. They were defeated but although they lost nearly a third of their army they inflicted such casualties on Pyrrhus, who could not easily replace his losses, that a 'Pyrrhic victory' became the proverbial expression for an over-expensive gain.

The following year Rome despatched 40,000 troops against the invader. This time Pyrrhus was supported by the southern Italians. The second battle lasted for two days but its result was much the same as the first. Depressed by his losses, the king crossed over to Sicily to help the Greeks there against the Carthaginians. Fearing this, the Carthaginians had arranged a hasty alliance with Rome. The Epirote general almost drove the Carthaginians from the island, confining them to the port of Lilybaeum at the western tip. But faced with the prospect of a long siege, he once more lost his enthusiasm and decided to return to Italy.

Pyrrhus had been out of Italy two years. The Romans had not wasted this precious breathing space and had forced the Samnites and Lucanians into submission, so that when the Epirote general returned he was on his own. As the king crossed the straits of Messina the Carthaginian fleet attacked him and destroyed half his ships. As he marched north with the remainder of his forces he was attacked by the garrison from Rhegium, who inflicted considerable losses on him.

When, with the remnants of his battered army, Pyrrhus finally arrived at Taranto, he collected together what troops he could and advanced northwards for a final confrontation with the Romans. The two Roman armies were operating separately, covering the routes into central Italy. Ignoring the army nearest to him, he struck at the weaker of the two Roman armies stationed near Benevento. He marched through the night, hoping to gain the advantage of position before the Romans realised he was coming, but arrived too late and the

Romans managed to deploy their forces before he could attack. Once more Pyrrhus failed to gain the victory he so badly needed. Learning that the other consul was approaching, he retreated to Taranto and soon after set sail for Epirus: he had never been defeated but he had lost the war and with it two-thirds of his army.

The Pyrrhic war is the key point in Roman military history. Hannibal classed Pyrrhus as second only to Alexander in his hierarchy of generals. It is unfortunate that no first-hand report of his campaigns or his treatise on military tactics have survived. We have only the very unsatisfactory accounts of Livy, Plutarch and Dionysius.

Having survived the Pyrrhic war the Romans were now potentially the foremost among the military powers of the Mediterranean.

The Italian Military Systems

The Age of Romulus
The communities established on the hills of Rome in the 8th century would have been much the same as those of Etruria. All were influenced by the Villanovan culture which, though centred on Etruria, spread as far as the Po valley in the north and Campania in the south.

The warriors of the time of Romulus fought on foot with spears, javelins, swords, daggers and axes. Only the wealthiest wore armour, which was generally restricted to helmet and cuirass; the latter being usually only a small breastplate. A fragment of an embossed greave was found in the Grotta Gramicia at Veii, but as far as the author knows this is the only example from central Italy. Shields, which were all of the central handgrip type, varied from large body-covering types to smaller round bucklers. Chariots do not seem to have been in use in the 8th century, although the famous chariot from the Regolini-Galassi tomb at Caere shows that they were a century later. They may have been introduced into Italy from the east as part of the orientalising phase in the early 7th century. For what the story is worth Plutarch tells us that when Romulus killed Acron, king of the

Above
A group of 8th-century 'Villanovan' warriors. This is the sort of armour that Romulus might have worn. Only the wealthiest could afford helmets and breastplates, which were fashioned from beaten bronze decorated with embossing.

Ceninenses, he marched in triumph carrying the king's armour as a trophy on his right shoulder. The point to note here is that he did not ride in a chariot as was the custom of the later *triumphators*. It seems that the chariot did not come to Rome until the Etruscan conquest late in the 7th century and even then it was never used in battle but only for ceremonial purposes. The Roman foot soldier probably fought in

some loose form of phalanx.

The swords of the period vary from long slashing weapons to shorter stabbing ones. The longer weapons are generally of the antennae type named after its cast bronze handle with spiral horns. The blade, which is almost always made of bronze, although a few iron examples have survived, varies in length from 33 to 56cm. The majority of these antennae swords are cut-and-thrust weapons. Some have long points suitable only for thrusting whilst a few have a slightly curved sabre-like blade that could be used only for slashing. The antennae type swords originated in central Europe and are closely related to late Mycenaean type II swords.

The daggers may be divided roughly into three types by the shape of the blade: the majority have a leaf-shaped blade; some have a blade with straight sides which narrow about two-thirds of the way down to form a stiletto type point; and the remainder are triangular in shape. The blades, which may be either of bronze or iron, vary in length from 25 to 41cm. The handles are made of wood, bone or even stone but never bronze. The handle is capped by a T-shaped pommel clearly relating it to later Mycenaean types of dagger. This T-shaped pommel is really a description of the metal tang, which is usually all of the handle that survives. In fact the pommel normally takes the form of a bulbous disc.

Scabbards for the shorter swords and daggers are usually made of beaten bronze with a cast bronze chape. The shape of the section of these scabbards suggests that they were lined with wood in similar fashion to later Roman swords. They are sometimes elaborately engraved but a few have a punched decoration in imitation of stitched leather which was probably the commonest material used for making scabbards. An antennae sword, found at Tarquinii in Etruria (5), was still encased in a fragmentary wooden scabbard bound together with bronze wire. The chape of this scabbard was made of bronze, and indeed several other examples of bronze chapes belonging to antennae swords have been found. These wooden scabbards were probably covered with leather. The top of the scabbard of both swords and daggers is always made separately and is often missing. This must be because it was made of perishable material such as hide or wood. A few examples in bone and bronze have survived. The break in the decorative design just below the top of the scabbard on some examples (8) suggests that the baldric was tied to the scabbard at this point.

Many bronze spearheads and butts

have been found. Like the swords and daggers these could also be made of iron. Some of these have been found in position in the grave so that the length of the whole weapon can be measured: the examples are between 1.45 and 1.85m long. The size of spearheads varies enormously from huge examples more than half a metre in length (there is an example from Marino in Latium measuring 56cm) to tiny javelin heads less than 10cm long. The bronze javelin head (14) with its long thin shaft is an antecedent of the later Roman javelins, the *hasta velitaris* and the *pilum*.

All the bronze weapons were cast

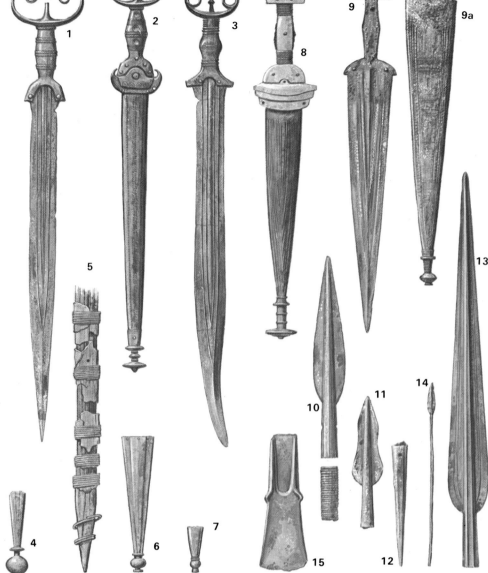

1 Bronze antennae sword from Fermo.
2 Antennae sword with bronze scabbard from Fermo.
3 Bronze antennae sabre from Bologna.
4, 6, 7 Bronze chapes from antennae swords.
5 Pieces of a wooden scabbard from an antennae sword. The scabbard is bound with bronze wire and has a bronze chape.
8 Iron dagger with bone handle and bronze scabbard with bone top from Veii.
9, 9a Bronze dagger and scabbard from Tarquinii.
10 Bronze spearhead and wire binding from the wooden shaft. From Veii.
11, 12 Bronze spearhead and butt from Tarquinii.
13 An enormous bronze spearhead from Tarquinii.
14 Bronze javelin head found in Latium.
15 Bronze axe head from Tarquinii.
Scale 1:5.

from molten metal. Iron weapons had to be beaten into shape as it was impossible to obtain sufficient temperature for the casting of iron. In fact beaten weapons are far stronger than cast ones.

Some 30 Villanovan type helmets have been discovered in Italy. More than half of these are of the metal crested type (**1**). This was an exaggerated form of a central European type. It was made in two pieces joined along the edge of the crest. This was done by making one half slightly larger than the other and folding the surplus metal over the smaller half to hold it in position. The lower edges of the cap at the front and the back also overlapped and were riveted together. The joint was reinforced by two rectangular plates which were riveted on (see exploded drawing **3**). These helmets, like all the other armour of the period, were decorated with bosses. The three long spikes projecting from the reinforcing plates at the front and back were purely decorative. The way that this helmet was worn, with the spikes at the front and back, is clearly shown on a figurine from Reggio in Emilia (**2**). The double rim at the base of the helmet on the figurine seems to show a thick undercap. Most of these helmets and the later Roman helmets are considerably oversize and it seems very likely that they all had a thick padded undercap probably made of felt. Another common form of helmet was the 'bell' type (**5**). Most examples have cast bronze crest holders which were drilled through to take a crest pin. This type is very common outside Italy, especially in France and the Balkans; one can also include a late 15th-century BC helmet from Knossos in this group. A unique example from Fermo near Ancona has a crest tube made from plate bronze (**4**).

The most common form of body armour was the small rectangular bronze pectoral (**7** and **8**). These may have been used on the back as well as the chest. Several examples have been found varying from 15 to 22cm in depth. Hundreds of round pectorals have been discovered but these seem to be of a slightly later date and are discussed under Etruscan armour. One or two cuirasses of the Alpine type are

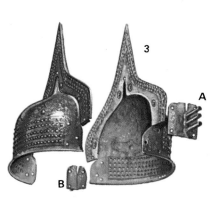

Above
1 Villanovan crested helmet, probably from Southern Etruria. Now in the British Museum.
2 Head of a figurine from Este showing how the helmet was worn.

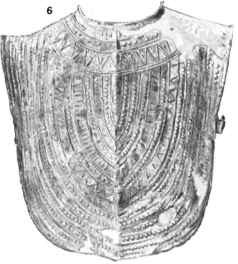

Above and below
5 A round capped helmet with cast bronze crest holder. Origin unknown. Karlsruhe Museum, Germany.
6 A Poncho type cuirass from Narce. Philadelphia University Museum.

Above and below
3 Exploded drawing of helmet no. **1** showing its construction. After the two halves are joined, plates **A** and **B** are riveted on.
4 A round capped helmet with bronze crest tube. From Fermo near Ancona.

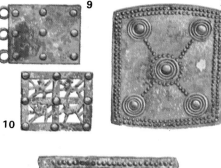

Below
7 Bronze pectoral from Tarquinii.
8 Bronze pectoral from Latium.
9 Bronze belt clasp from Terni.
10 Pierced bronze belt plate from Altri. All scale 1:5.

supposed to have been found in Italy but their provenance is uncertain. The elaborate poncho type cuirass (6) was discovered at Narce in Etruria. It was found with a crested Villanovan helmet which Henken suggests should be dated to the end of the 8th century. The cuirass consists of a front and back plate made in one piece and held in position by straps joining the front and back plates under the arms.

A few belt fastenings and plates have been found (9 and 10). The fastener consists of a rectangular plate with two or three rings riveted to the edge and a corresponding plate with hooks on the edge. These two plates were riveted to either end of a leather belt. These belt clasps evolved into the simple later Etruscan type shown on p. 98. The rest of the belt was often embellished with decorated plates.

More than 80 round bronze shields of Italian origin have been found varying between 50 and 97cm in diameter. These shields, which should be dated to the 7th century BC, are made of embossed bronze and probably spring from the same central European origin as the round central handgrip shields of dark-age Greece. In central Europe examples have been found dating back to the end of the second millennium. These shields do not have a wooden core, as might be expected, but the handgrip and strap fasteners are fixed directly to the inside of the bronze. Sometimes the bronze has been worked so thin that it has holed during manufacture. Their construction is similar to bronze Argive shields found at Olympia (p. 52) and they were clearly made for ceremonial purposes only. When asked about this type of shield an eminent British archaeologist remarked: 'Of course they were used in battle—in an emergency one might use anything, a dustbin lid for example'. Inane remarks like this, and suggestions that they might be used to deflect blows, do little to promote the understanding of ancient warfare. Such a shield would be absolutely useless in battle. Nevertheless, these shields must be based on functional examples which were probably made of wood or wicker with a rawhide facing. Rome's treaty with the Gabini was inscribed on a wooden shield covered with oxhide. Such wooden shields may have been decorated with metal studs. In fact all the armour of this period may have developed from hide or wicker covered with bronze studs, which would explain the embossing.

There was another type of shield which had probably existed since the Bronze Age. This was the large oval body shield with a spindle-shaped boss

Above
Villanovan embossed bronze shield from Bisenzio near Florence.
1 The front of the shield, showing the round central boss with three rivets above and below it to hold on the handgrip. Scale 1:6.

2 Back of the shield, showing the handgrip. The five hanging attachments were probably for carrying straps.
3 Section showing wood-filled handle.
4 Detail of the handle.

known as the *scutum* which was used by the legionaries of the later republic. A sculptural representation of a shield which in all essentials is identical to the later Roman *scutum*, was found in an 8th-century grave in the necropolis of Poggio alla Guardia at Vetulonia in Etruria. Representations of similar oval shields which lack one essential feature, the spined boss, have been found in the Po valley and in Austria. This difference is important as it establishes the origin of the *scutum* in Italy. Its continued use there is confirmed by a 5th-century boss from Malpasso in the central highlands of Italy.

The Etrusco-Roman army of the 6th century BC

As in Greece each Etruscan city had its own army. Although these cities were united in a league, they seldom operated together, which was their great weakness. Some cities might combine for a particular expedition, and the conquest of the south must have been just such a venture. However, like the Greek city states, they spent most of their energy fighting each other.

In the 7th century the Etruscans adopted the Greek method of fighting and organised their armies into phalanxes. One can say with confidence that they adopted the 'archaic *lochos*' with its 12 x 8 hoplites and four *ouragoi*.

This seems certain as the units of the Etrusco-Roman army were called centuries.

Like the later Romans the Etruscans relied heavily on troops either conquered by or in alliance with them. Those who favour an eastern origin for the Etruscans might well point to the Persian army for a parallel.

In the Roman army of this period we are probably seeing a typical Etruscan army. Under the first Etruscan king, Tarquinius Priscus, the army consisted of three parts: the Etruscans (who formed a phalanx), the Romans and the Latins. The latter fought in their freer native style with spears, axes and javelins on either wing.

Both Livy and Dionysius of Halicarnassus give an account of the reorganisation of the Etrusco–Roman army by Servius Tullius in the middle of the 6th century. Their virtually identical descriptions appear to be drawn from Fabius Pictor, who wrote a history of Rome around 200 BC. His information seems to be based on a genuine document. That some early documents or copies of them existed is attested by Polybius, who appears to have seen the first treaty agreed with Carthage c. 509 BC. He describes this as written in archaic Latin which could only be partially understood.

Servius Tullius, the second of the

Etruscan overlords, perhaps because of his Latin origin, tried to integrate the population by reorganising the army according to wealth and not race. He divided the population into six classes. The first or richest class he formed into 80 centuries or *lochoi*. The Etruscans must still have formed the majority of this class, which was armed with helmet, shield, greaves, cuirass, spear and sword. Livy uses the word *clipeus* for the shield and Dionysius describes it as an Argolic (Argive) shield. There can be no doubt that both are describing the armour and weapons of the hoplite and therefore these 80 centuries form the phalanx. Attached to the first class were two centuries of armourers and engineers (*fabri*) who were non-combatants.

The second class were formed into 20 centuries. They were armed in the same fashion as the first class except that they wore no cuirass and instead of the Argive shield they carried the *scutum*. Dionysius and Diodorus both imply that this shield was rectangular or at least four-sided. This has prompted some scholars to suggest that the rectangular *scutum* of the early empire was in use right through the republican period. Here archaeology has come to our aid in a quite remarkable way. Bologna was an Etruscan frontier town in a very similar situation to Rome but

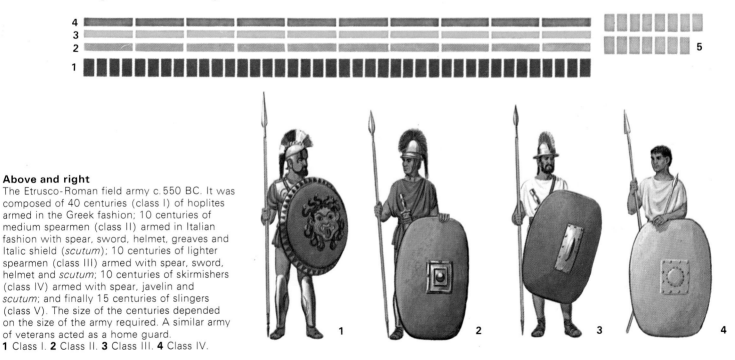

Above and right
The Etrusco-Roman field army c. 550 BC. It was composed of 40 centuries (class I) of hoplites armed in the Greek fashion; 10 centuries of medium spearmen (class II) armed in Italian fashion with spear, sword, helmet, greaves and Italic shield (*scutum*); 10 centuries of lighter spearmen (class III) armed with spear, sword, helmet and *scutum*; 10 centuries of skirmishers (class IV) armed with spear, javelin and *scutum*; and finally 15 centuries of slingers (class V). The size of the centuries depended on the size of the army required. A similar army of veterans acted as a home guard.
1 Class I. **2** Class II. **3** Class III. **4** Class IV.

on the northern frontier. The Certosa *situla*, a bronze bucket of c. 500 BC, was found here. This *situla* is embossed with warrior figures carrying round Argive shields, oval shields and four-sided shields. These figures probably represent the Etruscans and their northern allies and show that besides the traditional oval shield a four-sided shield which is probably only a variant of the oval *scutum* was in use at this time.

The third class was also divided into 20 centuries and armed as the second class but without greaves. The fourth class was similarly divided into 20 centuries. According to Livy they were armed only with spear and javelin whereas Dionysius gives them the *scutum*, spear and sword. The fifth class were formed into 30 centuries; according to Livy they were slingers, and according to Dionysius both slingers and javelineers. Dionysius adds that they fought outside the line of battle. Attached to the fifth class were two centuries of hornblowers (*cornicines*) and trumpeters (*tubicines*). The remainder of the population, the poorest citizens, were exempt from military service. The army was divided in half by age. The veterans served as a home guard, as they did in Greece, and those in the prime of life went on campaign.

This was the structure of the Etrusco-Roman army with 2 x 40 *lochoi* forming the phalanx, which was supported by 2 x 45 centuries of progressively lighter armed troops who were both armed and fought in the traditional Italian style. The differences between the two sources

are minimal and need cast no doubt on the basic accuracy of the description. Fabius Pictor wrote his history in Greek and one might be justified therefore in preferring Dionysius' account to that of Livy.

It is likely that the second, third and fourth classes fought on the wings as the allies had before the Servian reforms. However, Livy implies that they formed the second, third and fourth lines, and certainly at some point all Roman citizens must have been incorporated into the central body of troops, giving birth to the legion of the middle republic with its various types of troops fighting in successive lines. Nevertheless, it is hard to conceive how this could be done with a phalanx in the front line. The centuries of the phalanx, at least, must have been divided into four *enomotiai*. When an army was needed each century provided men in proportion to the total required: if, for example, an army of 10,000 was required, each century would supply two *enomotiai* or 50 men.

At this early period the division of the army into centuries had as great a political as a military purpose. The original structure remained in the political sphere but the army gradually adapted its structure to its needs.

When the Etruscans were driven out

Above
A hornblower engraved on the back of the Arnoaldi mirror. This must have been the type of military horn used by the Romans and Etruscans in the 6th century. Bologna, Museo Civico.

Above
1 A 7th-century bronze figurine of a warrior wearing a crested Villanovan helmet and carrying an Italian body shield.
2 Representation of a 7th-century spined *scutum* from Vetulonia in Etruria.

Below
Warrior figures shown on the Certosa *situla*, c. 500 BC. These figures prove that Argive shields, 'four-sided' and oval shields were all in use at the same time in Italy. This probably shows a typical Etruscan army of the time.

of Rome, a large proportion of the first class must have gone with them. This would have accounted for Rome's much-reduced military capability. Livy claims that the round shield (in other words the phalanx) remained in use until the introduction of pay at the end of the 5th century.

The king was replaced as commander-in-chief of the army by two praetors who commanded the two halves of the army. Around the middle of the 4th century the praetorship was superseded. The praetor who commanded the veterans may have survived in the title of Praetor Urbanus, but his job became purely legal. Certainly by the 4th century Rome had no special army for the defence of the city. The two chief magistrates were now called consuls. The name of praetor continued to be used for second rank magistrates. By the time of Polybius their number had risen to six.

Armament
The soldiers of the phalanx (the first class) were armed in Greek fashion with round Argive shield, bronze cuirass,

greaves, helmet, spear and sword. Although the Etruscans had adopted the tactics and armour of the phalanx, the native types of armour and weapons are found in Etruscan graves. These include axe heads which can hardly have been used in the phalanx. Possibly the inclusion of these weapons is traditional. On the other hand they might have been used in single combat, such as that shown on a sculpture of two hoplites from Falerii Veteres. These are armed entirely in the Greek fashion except that one wields a short curved dagger. Whatever may be the reason for the inclusion of these weapons, they certainly could not have been used in the phalanx.

The use of Italian armour, which could hardly affect the function of the phalanx, is well attested both by the grave finds and in art. A painting from Ceri shows a hoplite with Chalcidian helmet and a round Etruscan breastplate. Another example from Chiusi shows a hoplite with entirely Greek equipment but with Italian-style feathers in his helmet. The grave group from the tomb of the warrior at Vulci

(c. 525) shows a typical mixed equipment: Argive shield, Italian helmet of Negau type (see p. 98) and Graeco-Etruscan greaves.

Although Greek cuirasses were widely used, many examples of circular breastplates have been found. These all seem to come from the first part of the 7th century, possibly before the introduction of the phalanx. However their dating is very difficult as so many of them have an unknown provenance. The painting from Ceri which has already been mentioned, and which can hardly be earlier than the end of the 6th century, shows that the type remained in use long after the 7th century. These discs are shown on Assyrian bas reliefs and later examples have been found in both Spain and central Europe. Their oriental origin seems very likely. The Ceri painting shows the breastplate held on by a harness, probably of leather. On the back of these plates there are usually three loops at the top and a further one at the bottom for attaching the plate to the harness.

The commonest form of helmet in

1 Sculpture of Etruscan warriors in complete Greek panoply. From Falerii Veteres.
2 Warrior wearing complete Greek panoply but with Italian style feathers on his helmet. From Clusium (Chiusi).

ITALY AND THE WESTERN MEDITERRANEAN

Below

Helmets from Etruscan graves.
1 Greek 'Chalcidian' type. Florence Archaeological Museum. **2** Italian 'Negau' type.
2a Inside the rim of **2** showing band for stitching in lining. Villa Giulia Museum.

Below

14 Painting of a warrior with Greek helmet and Etruscan round breastplate from Ceri. **15** and **16** Front and back of a round breastplate. **17** Back of plate showing harnessing.

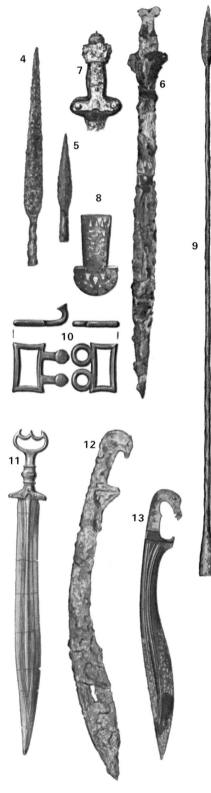

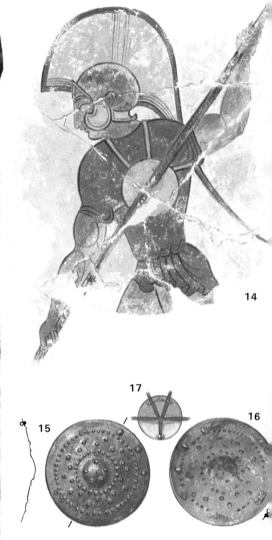

Above

3 Typical Etruscan armour and weapons. The armour is reconstructed from the mixed panoply found in the 'Tomb of the Warrior' at Vulci. It consists of an Argive shield, Graeco-Etruscan greaves and Italian Negau helmet.

Left

4 Spearhead of typical Etruscan type from Chiusi (Clusium).
5 Etruscan javelin head.
6 Etruscan sword of Greek hoplite type from Alalia in Corsica.
7 Handle of a similar sword made of wood and iron from Loreto Aprutino.
8 The chape of a similar sword, bronze with bone inlay. Römisch Germanisches Zentral Museum, Mainz.
9 Socketed *pilum* from Vulci. Museo Gregoriano, Vatican.
10 Typical Etruscan belt clasp.
11, 12, 13 The development of the curved sword.
11 Villanovan sword from Este.
12 Etruscan sword from Alalia in Corsica.
13 Spanish sword (*falcata*). British Museum.

use in Etruria at this time was the Negau type, named after a village in Yugoslavia where a large number of them were found. The most interesting example of one of these helmets was found at Olympia and is now in the British Museum. Its inscription claims that it was dedicated by Hiero, son of Deinomenes, and the Syracusans who had captured it from the Etruscans at the naval battle of Cumae in 474 BC. The earliest datable example comes from the Tomb of the Warrior at Vulci (c. 525 BC). This type remained in use unchanged right down to the 4th and possibly the 3rd century. Attached to the inside of the rim of these helmets was a flat ring of bronze with stitching holes along the inside edge to hold the inner cap; this was necessary to keep the helmet well up on the head. This helmet type evolved from a group of 6th-century helmets referred to here under the general name of pot helmets (see p. 102).

Although this type of helmet normally had a crest which followed the ridge from front to back, several examples have been found with attachments for a transverse crest (2). This was the type of crest worn by Roman centurions. Such a crest is shown on the statuette of a Spartan hoplite (p. 41) and several helmets from Olympia also have attachments for this type of crest. The significance of these crests is impossible to determine. It is unlikely that they were used by senior officers — most of the surviving helmets must have belonged to them, as only the best would be used for dedications. It is tempting to conclude that the transverse crest might have been the identifying mark of the *lochagos*; this would certainly account for its adoption by the centurions.

Several examples of Greek-style greaves have been found in Italy. The most common form is based on a 6th-century Greek style. This type has no shaping for the knee. Greaves of this form remained in use as long as the Negau helmet (i.e. down to the 4th or 3rd century) and the two are often found together.

Thigh, ankle and foot guards which were in use in Greece in the 6th century remained popular in Etruria for a much longer period. Arm guards also enjoyed

a longer life in Etruria than in Greece.

During this period the Etruscans adopted the Greek sword, and many examples have been found in Etruria. The curved sword (*kopis*) which was very popular in Greece and Spain from the 6th to the 3rd centuries may have originated in Etruria, where examples have been found dating as far back as the 7th century. The bronze sabre from Este in northern Italy may be the forerunner of this savage weapon and if so testifies to its Italian origin. The Etruscan and early Greek swords of this type were long hacking weapons with a blade 60–65cm long. The later Macedonian and Spanish examples were short pointed cut-and-thrust weapons with a blade no more than 48cm long. A variety of spearheads have been found in Etruria. The long Villanovan type remained in vogue. The long socketed head of a javelin (*pilum*) was found in a 5th-century grave at Vulci (9) showing that this type of weapon was already in use.

During the 4th and 3rd centuries Etruria seems to have continued to follow the Greek lead in armour and to have adopted the late classical styles. Fourth-century Thracian helmets appear on the Amazons sarcophagus and in the Giglioli tomb, both of which are at Tarquinii. The stiff linen cuirass was still in use but was now often covered with lamellar plates. This use of rectangular overlapping plates originated in Assyria. It is shown on wall paintings and on the famous statue of Mars from Todi. Experiments were made during the 3rd century to produce a more flexible type of cuirass made of quilted linen. This quilting was normally left bare only around the waist and hips, the chest, shoulders and back being reinforced with scales. Many of the 3rd-century sculptured funerary urns show these corselets. Often a semi-circular apron, rather like the old Greek *mitra*, is shown covering the lower stomach. These too are usually plated with scales. During the 3rd century mail shirts also appear on the funerary urns. These are cut in exactly the same style as the linen cuirass and are simply an adaptation of the old styling to the new type of armour. The plated apron is sometimes used in

conjunction with mail, which seems to have been of Celtic origin and is discussed on p. 124.

The muscled cuirass also appears frequently on Etruscan sculptures where it is usually painted grey. This need not mean that it was made of iron but rather that it was silvered or tinned, a fashion that was continued in the later Roman army. Although the sculptures show muscled cuirasses very similar in form to the south Italian examples, the specimens that have been found are quite different. The musculation on these is very stylised so that the Etruscan type is easily recognisable.

At some time during the 5th century the so-called Italo-Corinthian helmet was adopted by the Etruscans (see p. 100). This helmet was clearly derived from the Greek Corinthian type but was worn as a cap on the top of the head. The type seems to have originated in Apulia. As the 4th and 3rd centuries progressed it appeared on an ever-increasing number of monuments and ultimately became the predominant type.

From the first half of the 4th century onwards a new influence was felt: that of the Celts. The Senones who arrived in Italy about 400 BC probably brought with them the Montefortino type of helmet (see p. 120). This was quickly adopted by the Etruscans, Samnites and Romans and became the commonest form of helmet found in Italy from the 4th century BC. The reliefs in the 4th-century tomb at Cerveteri show the helmets with scalloped cheek pieces. Examples have also been found with triple disc cheek pieces. The origin of this latter type of cheek piece is discussed on p. 120. By the 3rd century this triple disc type had been completely superseded by the scalloped type which remained in use until the beginning of the 1st century AD. The large number of finds of this type of helmet compared with the predominance of the Italo-Corinthian type on the monuments implies that the latter type signified rank, and certainly it seems later to have been used mainly by officers. A very crude type of Attic helmet with a vestigial waisting probably derived from the Negau type is also commonly found at this period all over Italy.

A complete Etruscan panoply was found in the Tomb of the Seven Rooms at Orvieto near Lake Bolsena. This consists of a typical Etruscan muscled cuirass, late classical greaves, Argive shield and a Montefortino helmet with triple disc cheek pieces.

In the field of weaponry a considerable change had taken place. Although the hoplite sword remained in use, the spear was superseded by a heavy javelin. This weapon became the primary offensive weapon of the Roman legion. It consisted of a long iron point with a broad flat tang 5–6cm wide. The wooden shaft of the javelin was thickened at the top to hold the tang, which was fixed in place with two rivets. This type of javelin, known as a *pilum*, is unquestionably shown on a wall painting from the Giglioli tomb at Tarquinii. This tomb dates to the period of Rome's first conflict with Tarquinii in the middle of the 4th century. It would therefore be difficult to determine whether the origin of this weapon was Etruscan or Latin. What is certain is that it preceded Rome's contact with the Samnites and is therefore not of Samnite origin. It is clearly a development of the socketed *pilum* mentioned above which was modified to produce a heavier weapon.

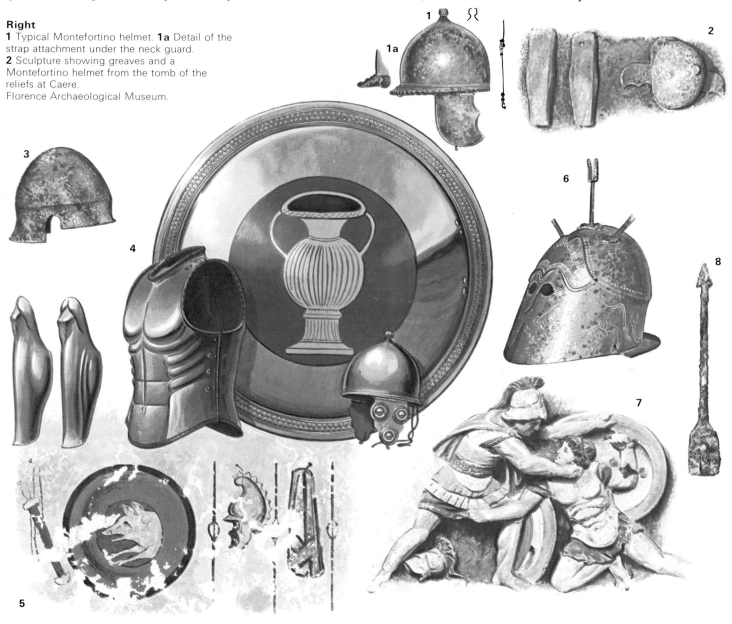

The Aequi, Volsci and related peoples

During the early years of the 5th century Rome came into violent contact with the hill peoples of central Italy: the Aequi and Volsci. These were just two of the many warlike tribes who, with the Sabines and Samnites, occupied the valleys of the Apennine mountains which form the backbone of the Italian peninsula, stretching from the Alps in the north all the way to the toe in the south. The peoples who occupied the central section of these mountains may be loosely grouped under the heading of Oscans. These peoples would have served as allies or mercenaries in the Etruscan armies. Excavations at the 6th–5th century necropolises at Alfedena 130km east of Rome and at Campovalano di Campli near Teramo on the east side of the Apennines have produced a wealth of arms and armour. These finds, when compared with the famous warrior statue found at Capestrano some 30km east of L'Aquila, enable us to draw up an exceedingly accurate picture of a warrior of the hill people.

The Capestrano warrior wears a small round pectoral and corresponding back plate joined by a broad hinged band which passes over the right

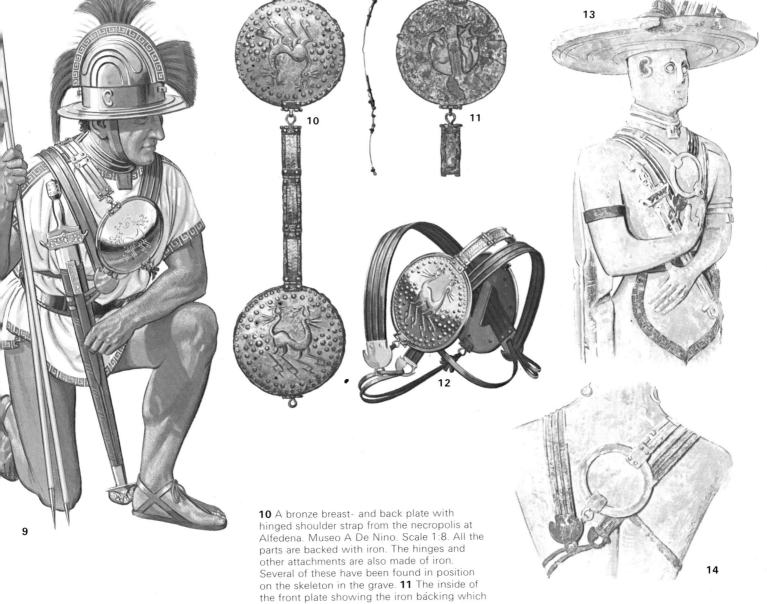

9 A reconstruction of a warrior from the central highlands. This type of armour and weapons would have been used by the Hernici, Aequi and Volsci. He wears a pot helmet, neck guard and a circular breast- and back plate. He carries two throwable spears and a Greek type sword.

10 A bronze breast- and back plate with hinged shoulder strap from the necropolis at Alfedena. Museo A De Nino. Scale 1:8. All the parts are backed with iron. The hinges and other attachments are also made of iron. Several of these have been found in position on the skeleton in the grave. **11** The inside of the front plate showing the iron backing which was wrapped over the edge of the bronze facing.
12 A reconstruction of the cuirass seen from the back. The harnessing, which was presumably of leather and never survives, is based on the warrior of Capestrano.

13 The warrior of Capestrano, showing the disc breastplate and sword. The helmet with its vast brim is probably grossly exaggerated.
14 Back of the same figure.

shoulder. On his head he has a crested helmet with an enormous brim. He is armed with two javelins which have throwing loops, an axe and a sword which he is holding close to his breast. Several examples of these disc breastplates joined by a hinged metal band have been discovered at Alfedena and Campovalano di Campli. Other examples have been found as far apart as Ancona, Caserta in Campania, and Aleria in Corsica. These are all made of bronze backed with iron. The example shown here is from the necropolis at Alfedena. The discs are 23.5cm in diameter (they are generally between 20 and 24cm wide), which is much larger than those shown on the Capestrano warrior. These discs, which are obviously derived from the earlier Etruscan examples, are usually decorated with round bosses and a mythical two-headed faun. On some examples the decoration is incised. The iron backing, which had two semi-circular pieces cut out of the centre, is rolled over the edge of the disc on to the front and hammered flat.

The broad shoulder band, which is 30cm long, is made of three plates of bronze trimmed with iron. They are joined together with iron hinges that are riveted to the plates. The band is joined to the back disc with a hinge and to the front with a hook. The cuirass was held in position by a harness composed of two broad straps, one passing over each shoulder and two smaller straps passing under each arm.

Below
A decorated breastplate of the same type as shown on the previous page. Sixth to 5th century. Ancona Museum. It shows two cavalrymen, one in a Corinthian and one in a pot helmet.

Right
1–7 Sixth-century Italian pot helmets.
1 The earliest form of Italian pot helmet. Late Villanovan. Ancona Museum. A similar helmet was found at Rome.
2 A typical four-piece helmet of the Sesto Calende type, common in northern Italy and Yugoslavia. Ancona Museum.
2a An exploded view of **2**.
2b Similar helmet on the Certosa *situla*.
3 Broad-brimmed helmet. Possibly the type worn by the warrior of Capestrano. Museo Gregoriano, Vatican.
4 Half-breed Negau/Pot helmet. Ancona.
5 Helmet of 'Cannae' type, so called after two examples that were found near Cannae in Apulia. From the Campovalano necropolis. Chieti Museum.

Left and above
5a, 5b Boss from a helmet similar to no. **5** showing lead filling.
6 Helmet made of discs and studs over a wicker frame from Yugoslavia. Ljubljana Museum.
6a Similar helmet shown on the Certosa *situla*.
6b Topknot of a disc and stud helmet.
6c Fragment of a wicker frame.
7 Conical helmet from Opeano near Verona. Archaeological Museum, Florence.
7a Similar helmet on the Bologna *situla*.

These are clearly shown on the Capestrano statue.

Many broad-brimmed helmets have been found but none with a rim as wide as that worn by the Capestrano warrior. The predominant type is the 'pot' helmet which is found all over central and northern Italy and around the head of the Adriatic in northern Yugoslavia. These pot helmets seem to bear no relation to the earlier Villanovan types. Examples of similar helmets from Austria and Czechoslovakia suggest a centre of dispersion around the head of the Adriatic. The earliest type (1, p. 102) is in the form of a round cap turned out at the brim. These helmets often have small knobs riveted on to the sides and a crest holder at the top with attachments at the front and back. The type is common in central Italy and an example was even found at Rome.

Number 2 is a type restricted to northern Italy and Yugoslavia. The most famous example was found in a warrior's grave at Sesto Calende in the foothills of the Alps. It was made in four pieces riveted together. Like the earlier helmets these have a crest holder at the top and attachments at front and back. This type is probably shown being worn by some of the figures on the Certosa *situla*.

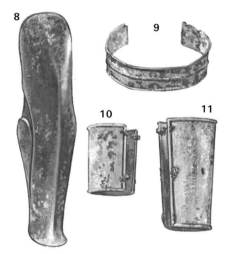

Above
8 Greave from Campovalano di Campli.
9 Throat guard from Alfedena.
10 Upper arm guard from Alfedena.
11 Lower arm guard from Alfedena.

Below
12 Warrior armed with an axe and two javelins. Văce clasp.
13 Warrior with two javelins and a spined *scutum*. Arnoaldi *situla*.
14 Iron shield boss. Yugoslavia. 1:10.

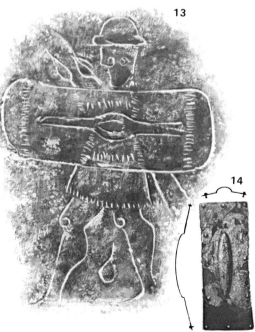

Above
15 and **22** Javelin heads from the necropolis at Campovalano di Campli.
16–21 Spearheads from the Campovalano necropolis. Triangular and quadrangular spearheads are typical of the area.
17 is Greek style and **20** echoes the Mycenaean types of some 800 years earlier.
23–25 Spear butts from Campovalano. These are often very long-pointed.
26 A mace head from Campovalano.
27, 28 Antennae dagger with iron scabbard complete with chain for attaching to the belt. From the necropolis at Campovalano.
28a Reconstruction of the dagger chain.
29 Scabbard knife found lying on top of the scabbard shown on p. 63. no. **7**.
30 Iron scabbard chape with bone inlay from Campovalano.
31, 32 Sword and scabbard, iron with bone inlay, almost identical to that shown on the warrior of Capestrano. From Alfedena.
15–32 All scale 1:10.

Number **3** is unusual—only two examples have been found. This specimen, which has no provenance, is in the Museo Gregoriano at the Vatican. It is interesting because of its broad brim, the closest yet found to the immense brim of the Capestrano statue. It has a pronounced crest channel obviously adopted from the Illyrian helmet. This is a very noticeable characteristic of the Yugoslavian pot helmets. Type **4** is common around the northern Adriatic and in the Po valley. It is clearly of the same family as the Negau type but is generally much broader in the cap.

Number **5** has received the name of 'Cannae helmet' because two examples were found in the region of the battlefield of Cannae where the Romans were defeated by Hannibal in 216 BC. These two helmets, which are in the British Museum, were long thought to come from the battle and were used to class and date other examples. Fortunately an excellent specimen was found in a grave at Campovalano which placed it firmly at the end of the 6th century. These helmets, of which about ten examples exist (half of them have no provenance) would seem to be limited to the Adriatic coast between Ancona and Bari. They are characterised by an inset crest channel at the front, a pronounced waist like the Negau type and two hemispherical bosses which are riveted to the side. These bosses are made of beaten bronze filled with lead and backed with an iron disc.

The Certosa *situla* shows a peculiar helmet made up of bosses or discs (**6a**). Examples of helmets of this type have been found in Yugoslavia (**6**). These are made of a wicker cap covered with bronze discs. The gaps between the discs are filled with bronze studs. Cuirasses made in a similar fashion have also been found in Yugoslavia. The last type (**7**), which is shown on the Bologna *situla* (**7a**), is conical in shape. It was not very popular and certainly not as effective as the brimmed types, but a few examples have been found. The one shown here is from Oppeano near Verona. It is made in two pieces riveted together and has a cast bronze topknot. There are two small bronze loops on the inside for fastening a chin strap. The other types

were also held on by a chin strap which was usually attached to the lining cap and is often visible on the *situlae*.

The warrior of Capestrano is wearing a throat guard: a very similar example was found at Alfedena. On his upper left arm he wears an armband. Such armbands have been found in position around the left *humerus* in the warrior graves at Alfedena, which brings to mind the story of Tarpeia, the Roman maiden at the time of Romulus, who betrayed the Capitol to the Sabines in return for the gold bracelets that they wore on their left arms. There is so often an underlying truth in the old legends. Even the sequel may have a grain of truth in it, for the Sabines probably spoke Oscan and they may have had difficulty in understanding what Tarpeia wanted when she pointed to what they were wearing on their left arms and offered her their shields.

The warrior of Capestrano has no shield and no shield remains have been found at the excavations. It therefore seems most likely that the non-metallic *scutum* in one of its forms was used. A decorated breast disc from the Ancona area further north shows a fallen warrior holding what must be an Argive shield. The Ancona area has produced abundant evidence that the full hoplite equipment had been adopted there, but there is no similar evidence for its adoption in the central area. Greek armour was having only the slightest influence in the central area. Of all the graves excavated at Alfedena and Campovalano only one has yielded any Greek armour: the unique Osco-Corinthian helmet (see p. 61, **13**) and a 6th-century Greek greave (see **8**, p. 103) were found together in a grave at Campovalano. This greave is exceptional, and the warrior of Capestrano certainly does not wear any. Further north, probably under the influence of the Greeks and Etruscans, greaves became commonplace and a pair were found in the famous warrior grave at Sesto Calende.

A very simple upper and lower arm guard were also found at Alfedena but these too are unique. Armour usually consisted only of a cuirass and helmet.

Suspended from the harness of his cuirass on the right side, the Capestrano warrior has an elaborately decorated

sword. An almost identical sword was found at Alfedena. This was only one of a large number of iron swords and scabbards that have been found. These swords are all of Greek hoplite type probably adopted from the Etruscans. Their blade lengths vary between 60 and 70cm. The handles and the top and bottom of the scabbards of these swords are made of bone covered with iron. This iron facing often has pierced decoration so that the bone shows through. The handles of Roman daggers of the early empire are made in exactly the same way. This and the widespread remains of hoplite swords from the Po valley to Apulia and from the Adriatic to Corsica, without counting the areas such as Bruttium, Lucania, Campania and Sicily which came directly under Greek influence, leave no doubt that this was also the primary sword used by Rome and the Latin League before the introduction of the Spanish type in the 3rd century. On the Capestrano statue a small knife is visible attached to the front of the sword scabbard. Similar knives, with a blade length of 20–25cm, have been found lying on top of the sword scabbard in the graves at Campovalano. Some of the graves contained iron daggers complete with their iron scabbards and chains for attaching them to the belt. The blades of these weapons were 25–30cm in length. Most of these daggers have four prongs projecting around the pommel, which seem to indicate a central European origin.

A wide variety of spearheads have been recovered, betraying the many influences affecting the central Italians. There are examples clearly of Mycenaean, Greek and Villanovan derivation whilst others are just as clearly from none of these sources. The most characteristic of these latter types are quadrangular and triangular shaped. Their size varies from tiny triangular javelin points less than 8cm long to a vast quadrangular spearhead over 80cm in length. All these spears and javelins have pointed iron butts. Many spearheads and butts were found in position in the grave, making it possible to establish their lengths, which vary between 1.6 and 2.6m.

Before leaving this period something must be said of the peoples of the Po valley during the time of the Etruscan expansion north of the Apennines. Although they may only have had a marginal influence on the Etruscans, they had a great effect on the invading Celts who in turn had an enormous influence on the Romans.

During the 6th and 5th centuries a vibrant culture existed just south of the Alps. This included the whole area of the Po valley and north western Yugoslavia. These people had a unique art form known to archaeologists as *situla* art. These *situlae* are bronze buckets which were elaborately decorated with embossed figures often including warriors and chariots. These representations, coupled with the weapons and armour that have been found, make it possible to draw a fairly accurate picture of the north Italian warrior of the 6th and 5th centuries. In the north, too, the pot helmet was the most common form. It was gradually superseded by the Negau type during the 5th century. Shields of all shapes and sizes are shown on the *situlae*, from round Argive types to oval and rectangular body shields. The iron shield boss (**14**, p. 103) undoubtedly comes from a body shield. Its sections show that the shield was convex. The figure from the Arnoaldi *situla* (**13**, p. 103) is often identified as an invading Celt, and indeed it is just possible that he is, but his helmet, two spears or javelins, tunic and spined shield should surely make him an Italian. However, only a short time later both this type of shield and helmet were being used by the Celts of the Po valley and were unquestionably adopted from the Italians. Metal cuirasses do not seem to have been used and the evidence of the *situlae* suggests that even the linen cuirass was rejected. Bronze studded cuirasses were in use in Yugoslavia and it is possible that they were employed in the Po valley also, though there is no evidence to support this.

Hoplite swords and four-pronged daggers are common in the Po valley but there is a strong trans-Alpine influence here, and many of the swords and spearheads show central European characteristics. The central Italian triangular and quadrangular spearheads are not common north of the Apennines. The *situla* warriors carry one or two spears and sometimes an axe. When two spears are shown one may reasonably suppose that they are throwable.

Chariots are a regular feature of warrior burials. On the *situlae* they are usually shown in a ceremonial context and it seems unlikely that they were used in battle, especially as fighting horsemen often appear on the *situlae*. The Văce clasp shows two horsemen fighting with spears and axes. One wears a pot helmet but neither have shields. A similar unshielded horseman armed with an axe appears on the Certosa *situla*. This suggests that around 500 BC cavalry did not carry shields, but the slightly later Arnoaldi *situla* shows a cavalryman still wearing a pot helmet but armed with two javelins and an Argive type shield.

The Samnites

With the defeat of the Volsci, who occupied the Lepini and Ausoni hills which hemmed in Latium to the east, the Latin League came into direct contact with the Samnites along the river Liris. Samnium was that area of the central highlands limited by the river Sangro in the north and the Ofanto in the south and it was with the people of this area that the Samnite wars were fought. However, the area occupied by tribes directly related to the Samnites was far greater. Soon after 500 BC, following the collapse of Etruscan power in the south, Samnite tribes poured down into the coastal plains. During the succeeding century they occupied the whole of the south from Campania to the toe of Italy. The Etruscan colony of Capua fell to them in 423 and two years later the Greek city of Cumae, which had played such an important part in the defeat of Lars Porsena a century earlier, was also captured. Apulia on the east coast had similarly been occupied. The Samnites mixed with the local populations and soon produced independent tribes with a mixed culture strongly influenced by the Greeks who had colonised the coastal areas before them.

In the middle of the 4th century, probably in response to the rapid expansion of the Latin League, the Samnites tried to force their kinsmen in Campania to join the Samnite federation. In 343 the Latin League, similarly nervous about the expansion of the federation, intervened to maintain the independence of Campania and so brought on the first confrontation between the two powers.

Below
Coastal Samnite warriors with standards. From Paestum in Lucania. Naples Museum. This painting is probably early 4th century. Two of the warriors have square breastplates. As here, the horsemen wore anklets.

Below
The Samnites force the Romans to pass under
the yoke after their surrender at the Caudine
Forks in 321 BC. This was Rome's most
humiliating moment, but it was a disgrace to
which she had forced many of her enemies to
submit. Rome agreed to a treaty under duress
but repudiated it five years later and the war
continued.

The long war that began in 343 is divided by the historians into three parts: the first, second and third Samnite wars. Livy's account of the first war is so unreliable that many historians have been led to believe that no such war took place. What is certain is that no gain was made on either side and in this respect the League was successful. The war lasted only three years and was immediately followed by the struggle between Rome and her allies for control of the League. The main conflict began in 328 and continued, with a break of six years, until 290. The historical record of these years may be poor, but the archaeological record, particularly in relation to armour, is far better, despite the frequent difficulty of dating the pieces. Nevertheless, it is possible to draw a reasonable picture of the Samnite warrior.

Livy gives a lengthy account of the Samnite army in which he describes them as forming two regiments, one armed with silver shields and the other with golden shields. The 'silver shields' wore white linen tunics and had silver scabbards and baldrics, whilst the 'golden shields' had multi-coloured tunics with gold scabbards and baldrics. The soldiers wore a breastplate which Livy calls a sponge (*spongia*). This could be interpreted as mail (though this would be an anachronism). They also wore a crested helmet and a single greave on the left leg. Livy goes on to describe the shield as broad and level at the top to protect the chest and shoulders but tapering towards the bottom.

This description bears no relation to the artistic or archaeological evidence and has to be rejected entirely if one is to get any sort of picture of the Samnite soldier. This entire section of Livy's history is suspect. Livy makes the ludicrous claim that the silver and gold regiments, which are reminiscent of the Macedonians, were formed specifically for the campaign of 309. Of the rest of the equipment the most charitable remark that can be made is that Livy is describing the so-called Samnite gladiators of his own day. Sculptures of these gladiators have survived and they carry what is clearly the oval *scutum* with the top cut off.

There are unfortunately no undisputed representations of Samnite warriors. Those Samnites who had migrated to the coast came into contact with the Greeks and their armour shows a strong Greek influence. There are hundreds of representations of these coastal Samnites; the difficulty is to determine which are the Greek and which the Samnite elements. These pictures nearly always show soldiers armed with the Argive shield. However, a painting from Capua shows a horseman carrying a clearly defined *scutum*, which he appears to have captured, and a fragmentary fresco from Naples shows warriors fighting with large oval shields without the out-turned rim so typical of the Argive shield. In his description of the line-up for the battle of Asculum in 279, Dionysius of Halicarnassus refers to the Samnite shield as *thureos*, which is the same word that he uses for

Above
1 A Samnite Attic helmet in the British Museum. This is the most common form. **2** Samnite Attic helmet in the Castel Sant'Angelo at Rome. **3** Feather holder. **4** Samnite triple disc cheek piece from Bovianum. Naples Archaeological Museum. The cheek piece is modelled on the characteristic Samnite triple disc cuirass, worn by the warrior above (see p. 111). **5** and **6** Paintings of Samnites armed with large shields and javelins. **7** Painting of a single-edged slashing sword (*kopis*). **5**, **6** and **7** Naples Museum. **8** A 4th-century Samnite warrior.

Below
1 Triple disc cuirass from Alfedena, scale 1:8. It originally had two shoulder plates. **1a** Detail of the side-plate hook. **1b** Detail of side-plate fastening. **1c** Hinged joint of the shoulder plate.

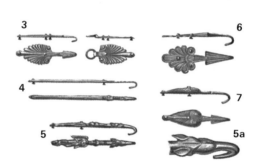

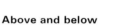

8

Above
A bronze figurine known as the 'Samnite Warrior' believed to have been found in Sicily. Louvre Museum. This is probably the only true representation of a Samnite warrior. He wears an Attic type helmet with holes in the top which originally held feathers, triple disc cuirass, broad Samnite belt and greaves. His shield and javelins are missing. The crude sculpting of this figure shows no Greek influence and marks it out as indigenous Italian workmanship. 'The Samnite Warrior' is a good example of the interplay between archaeological and artistic evidence.

Above
2 A Samnite belt from Alfedena. The belt hooks are normally riveted on.
3–7 Various types of Samnite belt hooks.
6 and **7** are the commonest forms.
5/5a is shaped like an elephant's head.

Above and below
8 Warrior wearing a triple disc cuirass from a Campanian vase in the British Museum.
9, 9a Square front and back plate decorated with stylised muscles, scale 1:8. The back plate (**9a**) has hinges for side plates. **9b** Detail of the hinge. **9c** Detail of the fastening for the shoulder plate. **10** Detail of the fresco from Paestum (p. 105) showing a square breastplate.

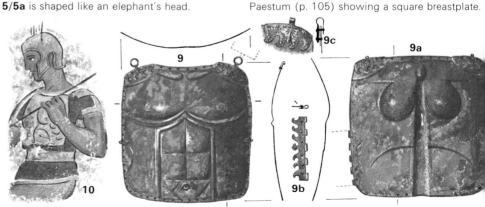

the early Roman shield which Livy calls a *scutum*. There was a tradition in the later republic quoted by Sallust that the Lucanian Samnites used shields made of osiers covered with sheep's hide. This shield seems to be a light version of the *scutum*. While it can hardly be doubted that the coastal Samnites adopted the Argive shield, what little evidence there is points towards the use of the *scutum* in Samnium itself and also in the highland territory of Lucania.

The fragmentary fresco at Naples also shows javelins with throwing loops. Warriors are most commonly shown carrying two javelins. Sometimes these are rather long and it could be argued that they are spears, but the simplest interpretation is that when there are two shown, at least one of them must be for throwing. Sometimes a single weapon that is unquestionably a spear is shown. The wall paintings confirm that all the main types of spearhead found at Alfedena and Campovalano were still in use in the 4th century, including the quadrangular and triangular types. A clear representation of the latter type is shown on a portion of a funerary painting from Naples. This also shows a *kopis*, which seems to be unique as none of the other paintings of warriors shows swords at all. All of the warriors depicted wear broad belts and helmets, usually of Attic type, topped with crest and feathers. Some wear greaves; these are even worn by the occasional horseman and a few wear a breastplate. This is usually triangular in form and embossed with three discs. The 'warriors' return' fresco shows warriors with square pectorals, but this is unique. This painting also shows flag type standards which appear on many of the vases and wall paintings and are carried by both infantry and cavalry.

There remains one small example that requires a special mention. In 1859 the Louvre museum acquired a small bronze statuette of a warrior which has all of the characteristics described above: Attic type helmet with holes for crest and feathers; triple disc cuirass; and broad belt and greaves. Unfortunately his shield and javelins are missing. This statuette, which was supposed to have been found in Sicily, is very primitive and clearly owes nothing to

the Greeks. The fact that it may have been found in Sicily is unimportant as it could have been taken there by a Samnite mercenary. Everything about it cries out for recognition and there can be little doubt that this is our only true representation of a Samnite warrior. With the archaeological evidence we are able to confirm and sometimes clarify the evidence which is drawn from paintings and sculpture.

An enormous number of broad bronze belts have been found all over central and southern Italy. Whatever else a Samnite, Campanian, Lucanian or Apulian might or might not wear, he would always have his belt which seemed to be the very symbol of his manhood. These vary from 8 to 12cm in breadth and are fastened with two hooks which were inserted into corresponding holes at the other end of the belt. There were usually three pairs of these holes so that the belt could be adjusted. The hooks are normally held to the belt by a flange in the shape of a palmette which is riveted to the belt. Although these palmettes have a variety of forms—three of which are shown in

the illustration (**3**, **6** and **7**)—the vast majority conform to this general pattern. There are a few which are long and narrow (**4**). These are normally used in a group of four or five instead of the customary two. Sometimes the flange has an anthropomorphic form and there are a few beautiful examples where the hook has been made into the form of an elephant's head and trunk. These must date to the period immediately following the Pyrrhic war. On a few occasions the holes at the other end of the belt were replaced by ring fasteners which were also held by a palmette flange (**3**). The belt was lined with leather which was stitched through in the archaic Greek style.

The triple disc cuirass which appears on many Campanian vases is well attested in archaeology. About 15 examples are known, including one from Alfedena in the central highlands and one from Paestum in Lucania, showing that they were in use both in Samnium and on the coast. The sample shown here is from Alfedena. It is complete except for one of the shoulder plates. This example is fairly representative

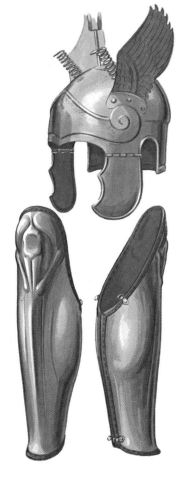

Above and right
A restored panoply from Lucania in the Tower of London, c. 375 BC. The Attic helmet has wings made of thin bronze behind which are spring feather holders. The greaves have strap attachments.

with the shoulder and side plates attached to the front and back plates by rings and hooks. The shoulder plates, wherever they survive, are hinged in the centre. (Those on the example at Karlsruhe are false as they are too short to reach the back plate.) The shoulder pieces of the two cuirasses at Naples are not only hinged in the centre but are also attached to the front and back plates by hinges. The upper edge of the front and back plate always has a reinforcing strip of bronze riveted to it. A few superbly decorated examples of this type of cuirass have been found. The finest example, which was found in a tomb at Ksour-es-Sad in Tunisia, was probably taken back to Africa by one of Hannibal's soldiers. The origin of this type of cuirass is obscure. It must somehow be related to the single disc breastplates of the 6th century. It appears on vase paintings in the middle of the 4th century and the earliest datable example, that from Alfedena, cannot be dated to earlier than the end of the 4th century. An example in the Louvre has only two discs, but this is a hoax as the right-hand disc has been removed and stitching holes have been punched along the edge of the cut to give the appearance that this was its original form. In fact one is seeing the left-hand and bottom disc with the tongue to which the side plate was attached. At the top of the left-hand disc is a fragment of the reinforcing plate that was placed along the top of all these cuirasses.

The wall painting known as 'the warriors' return' from Paestum shows men wearing square breastplates which are moulded in the form of the muscles of the torso. Several examples of these survive. The best preserved is a breast and back plate in the British Museum shown in the illustration. By comparing it to the fresco from Paestum it is possible to reconstruct it completely. It is only 29cm deep, which is far too small for the musculature to fit to the torso of a normal man. All the other examples are of a similar size. It is clear, therefore, that the navel and the pectoral muscles were never intended to fit the corresponding parts of the wearer. The two parts were only intended to cover the back and chest above the broad belt as shown on the fresco.

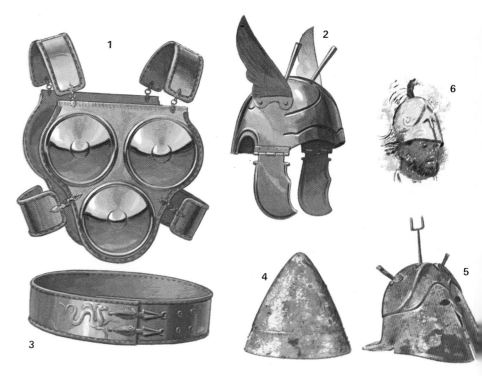

Above
1–3 A restored panoply from Paestum, Lucania, c. 300 BC. It consists of a triple disc cuirass, Attic helmet with wings and feather holders and a Samnite belt. Paestum Museum.

Above
4 A conical helmet from Apulia in the Naples Museum. **5** An Italo Corinthian helmet from Melfi in Apulia. **6** Painting of a warrior wearing an Italo-Corinthian helmet on the Amazons Sarcophagus from Tarquinia.

Below
7–10 A restored panoply from Conversano in Apulia Bari Museum. The Attic helmet has feather holders hidden behind the wings (**9a**). c. 350 BC.

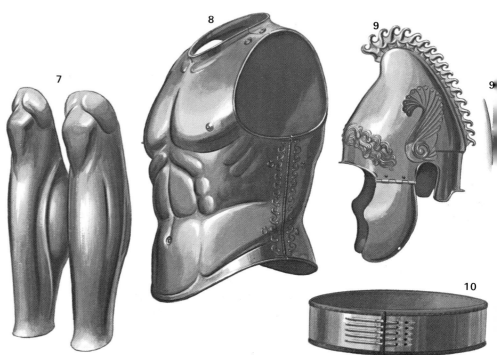

Shoulder plates, no doubt similar to those on the triple disc cuirasses, were fastened to the front and back plates with rings whilst side plates which are just visible on the fresco were attached to the back plate with hinges and no doubt hooked to the front plate. The depth of these side plates, which is determined by the depth of the hinge, is 11.5cm. Some examples have no back hinges and must therefore have had individual side plates. All the plates were lined with leather which was rolled over the front and stitched through. Traces of this are clearly visible. Because of the lack of an accurate provenance the dating of these cuirasses is very difficult. The wall painting from Paestum must date to the time of the Samnite occupation 390–273 BC. Most scholars would prefer an earlier date, so perhaps the cuirasses should be placed in the first half of the 4th century. The decoration is undoubtedly the result of Greek influence being transferred from the muscled cuirass. However, equally certainly these cuirasses in an unmuscled form must have originated in the central highlands, for this is undoubtedly a native form and Romans were still wearing them at the time of Polybius.

Two later examples, probably from the Samnite war period, are on show at Naples. At first glance these appear to be from a muscled cuirass but they are too small for this and would require shoulder and side plates. They are shown reconstructed in the illustration on p. 106.

Many Samnite helmets survive. They are easily recognisable by their feather holders. They are usually a modified form of the Greek Chalcidian helmet with hinged cheek pieces but no nose guard and will therefore be referred to as Samnite Attic (**1, 2**, p. 107). These were copied from the coastal Greeks and from there filtered inland. Most examples come from the coastal areas.

Another helmet was also making its debut. During the 4th century the Montefortino type of Celtic helmet (see p. 120) was gradually being adopted throughout Italy and several specimens have been found in the central highlands. A fine example with scalloped cheek pieces and five-pronged iron feather holder can be seen in the Louvre. It is shown in the illustration on p. 106.

The cheek piece (**4**, p. 107), which is one of several coming from Bovianum in the heartland of Samnium, is identical in design to the triple disc breastplate. This type of cheek piece is found on Celtic Montefortino type helmets except that cheek pieces from this type of helmet always have only a single loop of metal at either side to form the hinge fitting, whereas this example has a five-loop hinge which means that it must come from an Attic type helmet. The two lobes A–A that protrude from the sides of the cuirass to hold the fastenings for the side plates also appear on the cheek piece but serve no such useful purpose. It follows that the cheek piece was derived from the cuirass and not vice-versa. This is very important as this type of cheek piece has always been considered to be of Celtic origin. It is significant that these lobes were the first characteristic of the triple disc cheek piece that the Celts abandoned.

The greaves that are shown on the paintings are of classical Greek type and were obviously derived from the coastal Greeks. As in the case of the helmets they filtered inland where their use is confirmed by their appearance on the bronze statuette of the Samnite warrior in the Louvre. Examples have turned up in Lucania and Apulia, some of which have ring attachments for straps, a fashion later adopted by the Romans.

Several complete sets of armour have been found in Lucania. One of these panoplies, which is now at the Tower

Right
A beautifully decorated triple disc cuirass from a tomb at Ksour-es-Sad, Tunisia, now in the Bardo Museum, Tunis. It is undoubtedly of southern Italian manufacture. There is a very similar example at Naples.

of London, consists of a winged helmet, square breast- and back plate, greaves and belt. This is an old find and nothing is known of it except that it came from Lucania. The greaves, which appear to be of late archaic type, though they are certainly much later than this, have strap fastenings at the back. The helmet is of Attic type and has wings of thin sheet bronze, feather holders in the form of coiled snakes and a raised crest holder. It is very similar to the helmet worn by the Capuan horseman shown opposite. This panoply must be dated to the first half of the 4th century.

A second panoply, consisting of winged helmet, triple disc cuirass, and belt, was found in recent years at Paestum. Like the previous example the helmet has wings made of sheet bronze which have feather tubes behind them. Both helmet and cuirass show signs of degeneration in design and probably date to the period of the Roman conquest, c. 273 BC.

The Apulians fell much more under the influence of the Greeks than their kinsmen on the west coast of Italy. A beautiful panoply discovered at Conversano near Bari consists of a pair of late classical Greek greaves, a Greek muscled cuirass, winged helmet and, of course, a Samnite belt. The wave decoration on the side of the cuirass, which is a popular Samnite motif, is matched by the comb on the crest of the helmet which acts as a crest guide. This helmet is really a cross between the Samnite Attic and the Thracian type. Like the other examples the wings are made of plate bronze and have feather tubes tucked away behind them. This panoply can be dated to the late 4th or early 3rd century BC.

Other Greek styles were popular in Apulia. Fourth-century conical helmets have been found and are often featured on the local vase paintings. The so-called Italo-Corinthian helmet seems to have originated here in the 6th century (see p. 99). In addition to the effect of the Greeks and Samnites on this area there was also a strong Celtic influence. Whenever the Celts invaded central Italy, which they did regularly in the 4th century, they usually ended up in the corn fields of Apulia. It is possible that some may even have settled there. Several mongrel helmets

have turned up in the area and in one mid-3rd-century grave at Canosa a muscled cuirass and Celtic helmet were found together.

To summarise: the southern Italian highland warrior in the 4th century was a fairly lightly armed javelineer or spearman using a light body shield similar to the *scutum*. All soldiers probably wore helmets and belts, though metal cuirasses and greaves would have been restricted to the wealthier classes. To try to isolate the organisation and tactics of the Samnite army from the jumble of contradictory information given in Livy and Dionysius is a fruitless task. Livy calls the divisions of the Samnite army legions whereas Dionysius calls their battle line a phalanx, which is equally unenlightening. In all probability neither of them had the slightest idea of the Samnite formation and they therefore fell back on the traditional terminology. The Samnite armament suggests that they fought in a loose formation. Their ability to outmanoeuvre and outmarch the Romans confirms that they were more lightly armed and more loosely arrayed than the legions, or for that matter the Greek phalanx.

Surprising though it may seem, since their homeland was in the highlands, the Samnites produced the best horsemen in Italy. In the plains of Campania a formidable cavalry force evolved and in the 3rd and 2nd centuries the Campanians formed the backbone of the Roman cavalry. Several Campanian and northern Lucanian paintings show these horsemen. There was a fine example from Capua which was unfortunately destroyed during the Second World War. In this painting the horse wears a chamfron surmounted by feathers. On another example from Paestum the horse wears some form of peytral. Examples of both types of armour can be seen at Naples. The horsemen seem to be armed in exactly the same fashion as the infantry—some even wear greaves. One noticeable feature is the wearing of anklets but there is no sign on either the infantry or the cavalry of the earlier bracelet worn on the left upper arm.

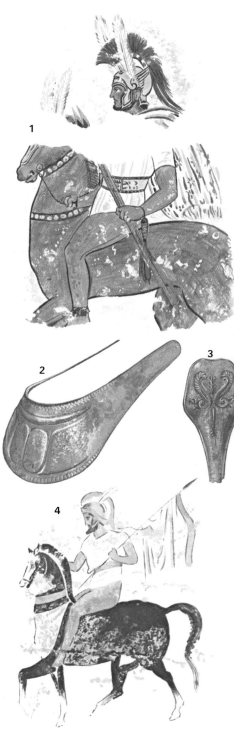

Above
1 A painting of a Campanian horseman found at Capua but destroyed during the Second World War. His helmet is almost identical to the one shown on p. 109. The horse is wearing a face guard (chamfron).
2 A peytral (chest armour for a cavalry horse) in the Naples Museum.
3 A chamfron also in the Naples Museum.
4 A painting of a horseman from Paestum. The rider is carrying a flag type standard. The horse appears to be wearing a type of peytral. Paestum Museum.

The Celts

The Celts originated in southern Germany and from there spread out over most of western Europe. By the beginning of the 5th century they had overrun Austria, Switzerland, Belgium, Luxembourg and parts of France, Spain and Britain. In the following century they forced their way through the Alps into northern Italy. The first tribe to arrive in the Po valley were the Insubres. They settled in the area of Lombardy and established their chief town at Milan. The Boii, Lingones, Cenomani and other tribes followed, conquering most of the Po valley and ultimately driving the Etruscans back across the Apennines. The last tribe to arrive was the Senones, who pressed right on down the Adriatic and finally settled in the coastal area north of Ancona. This was the tribe that sacked Rome at the beginning of the 4th century. Our name for the Celtic race as a whole comes from the Greek *Keltoi*. However, the Romans called those from the Po valley and France *Galli* (Gauls). During the 4th century the Celts began to move into the Balkans, and at the beginning of the 3rd century, taking advantage of the lack of strong government in Macedonia and Thrace, they overran both countries and spilled over into Asia Minor where they finally settled in Galatia. The latter are usually referred to as *Galatae* (Galatians).

During the 4th century the Gauls mounted a succession of plundering raids in central Italy. Usually they were deflected by the stronger groups—the Etruscans, Latins and Samnites—and were channelled into Apulia, where it is possible that they founded permanent communities.

The Romans treated the Celts as they treated no other nation. They systematically massacred them in northern Italy, Spain and France. The reconquest of the Po valley after the Hannibalic war was carried out with such brutality that in the middle of the 2nd century Polybius could say that the Celts remained only in 'a few regions under the Alps'.

Most of our knowledge of the Celts unfortunately comes to us only through their enemies, the Greeks and Romans. Diodorus, the Sicilian historian, paints a vivid picture of these warriors, describing their colourful clothes, long moustaches and hair that was washed with lime to make it stand up like a horse's mane.

Initially the Romans were terrified by these huge men who towered above them. But later, when they were able to recognise and exploit the Celtic weaknesses, they became contemptuous of the unruly barbarians. Livy's account of the Celtic wars very much reflects this view. But contemptuous though the Romans may have been, under a good general the Celts made excellent soldiers. They formed half of Hannibal's army which for 15 years dominated the Roman legions. The Romans later realised their worth and for centuries they filled the ranks of the legions.

Most primitive societies, including the early Romans and Greeks, had a warrior class. The Celts were no exception. Their warriors were drawn from a group which we would describe as the middle and upper class. This warrior class did the fighting whilst, according to Diodorus, the activities of the free poor were restricted to squiring and chariot driving.

The Celt was a warrior in the true heroic sense. Everything had to be bigger than life. He lived for war but his glorification of bravery, coupled with lack of discipline, often led him to recklessness. Diodorus in his fifth book gives an extensive and probably fairly accurate description of the Celtic warrior. But one must remember that nearly 350 years elapsed between Rome's first encounter with the Celts at the battle of the Allia and Caesar's conquest of Gaul, when Diodorus was writing. During that time many changes took place in both weaponry and tactics. A resumé of Diodorus' description, which is sometimes anachronistic, is given here before examining these changes. Diodorus' warrior was armed with a long sword suspended along his right flank by a chain. He also carried a spear or javelins. Although many warriors preferred to fight naked, some wore a mail shirt and a bronze helmet. This was often decorated with embossed figures, horns or the fronts of birds or four-footed animals. He carried a long shield as high as a man which might

Above
A Senones chieftain, c. 300 BC. The figure in the foreground is a chieftain and wears an elaborate helmet. Several of these were found at the necropolis at Montefortino, which has given its name to this type of helmet. Only chieftains would have worn such helmets. They were usually made either completely of iron or of iron and bronze, though a few have been found entirely of bronze. This chieftain's helmet here has a multiple crest holder made of iron fitted to the topknot. The ordinary warriors fought naked like the two figures in the background. It was the Senones who sacked Rome at the beginning of the 4th century and became a constant threat. A little over a century later the Romans invaded their homeland in the Marches around Aricona and drove them out of Italy.

113

be decorated with figures embossed in bronze.

Chariots were used for fighting against cavalry. When fighting from his two-horse chariot the warrior threw his javelins first and then alighted, in Homeric fashion, to fight with his sword. Before battle, warriors (here Diodorus must mean champions) would step out ahead of the line, brandishing their weapons in front of them to inspire terror, and challenge the most valiant of the enemy to single combat. If the challenge was accepted the champion, in true barbaric fashion, would break into song, extolling the deeds of his ancestors and boasting of his own accomplishments whilst at the same time pouring scorn on the challenger.

The Romans honoured several of their generals who had accepted the challenge and killed a Celtic champion in single combat. They were rewarded by being permitted to dedicate the spoils (*prima spolia*) in the temple of Jupiter Feretrius. There were also *secunda* and *tertia spolia*, which depended on the rank of the winner. Titus Manlius, in the 4th century, reputedly overcame a gigantic Celt and stripped him of his golden torque, thus receiving the cognomen of Torquatus. The most noteworthy of these heroes was Marcus Claudius Marcellus, who killed the Gallic chieftain Viridomarus in single combat in 222 BC. He went on to become Rome's most successful general against Hannibal during his campaigns in Italy.

When he had killed his enemy, the Celtic warrior cut off his head and hung it from his horse's neck. He would then strip the body and have his squire carry off the blood-spattered spoils whilst he sung a paean over them. The spoils were nailed to the wall of his house. The heads of his most distinguished enemies were embalmed in cedar oil. The head of the consul Lucius Postumius, who was killed by the Celts in the Po valley in 216, was displayed in a temple. The excavations carried out at Entremont have revealed that the severed heads were far more than mere trophies and became part of a religious ritual. At Entremont heads were displayed in niches around a ceremonial gateway.

Before moving on to a detailed examination of Celtic equipment it might be helpful to make a few comments about Celtic warfare in general. It was the general opinion of the ancient authors that the Celts showed no appreciation of tactics or strategy. Polybius accuses them of having neither a plan of campaign nor judgement in executing it, and adds that they did whatever the heat of passion com-

manded. This may give the impress[ion] that the Celts fought as a rabble, [but] the inclusion of standards and trump[ets] among the Celtic spoils shown on [the] arch of Orange suggests a fairly r[ich] organisation, and Caesar's descript[ion] of *pila* piercing the overlapping shie[lds] of the Celts must refer to a close-k[nit] phalanx which, since it cannot ha[ve] been the normal Celtic formati[on] shows that they could even change th[e] battle line. Polybius' own descripti[on] of the battle of Telamon would seem [to] support this view. Here the Celts w[ere] caught between two Roman armies a[nd] lined up back to back with two li[nes] facing each way so that the army w[as] four lines deep. Polybius is full [of] admiration for this line-up and says th[at] even in his day, 75 years later, it w[as] still a matter of debate as to whi[ch] army had the stronger position, [but] neither of the two Celtic armies cou[ld] be attacked from the rear and with [no] way of escape the Celts must fight un[til] victory or death put an end to t[he] conflict.

The Romans, on the other hand, we[re] terrified by the fine order and t[he] dreadful din of the Celts, for there we[re] innumerable hornblowers and trum[-] peters and all the Gauls were shouti[ng] their war cries at the same time. Poly[-] bius concludes by saying that the Cel[ts] were inferior to the Romans only in th[e]

arms, both their swords and their shields being less serviceable than those of the Romans.

There are many representations of the Celtic accoutrements of war: standards, horns and trumpets. The commonest form of trumpet used by the Celts was the carnyx. This was a long instrument with its mouth in the form of an animal's head at right angles to the neck of the instrument. These are shown on the Gundestrup cauldron and on the arch at Orange. A carnyx head was found at Deskford in Scotland. Originally this had a movable jaw and a wooden tongue so that when it was blown it would have emitted a raucous rattling sound. The tube of a carnyx was found at Tattershall Bridge in Lincolnshire. The use of the horn is attested by Polybius and is shown on a relief from Bormio in northern Italy. Here the hornblower is shown with a round spined shield similar to the type used by the cavalry. The same sculpture shows a standard bearer wearing a horned Negau helmet and carrying a distinctively shaped shield. A similar shield is to be seen on the tombstone of a Roman auxiliary standard bearer from Hadrian's Wall. The oddly shaped spearhead at the foot of the Bormio standard and the use of very Celtic-looking devices, which are obviously evolved from Celtic spear-

heads, as standards of *beneficiarii* in the later Roman army leads one to the conclusion that the strange spearheads, of which several were found at La Tène (**3, 4**), must be from standards. Flags similar to the Roman *vexilla*, and animal standards similar to the Roman legionary emblems, are also shown on the arch at Orange and leave little doubt that the Romans inherited them from the Celts.

There were four types of Celtic soldier: heavy infantry, light infantry, cavalry and charioteers. All four types are attested by Polybius. The heavy infantry, according to all the ancient sources, were primarily swordsmen. The light infantry were presumably javelineers.

Dionysius describes the Celts whirling their swords above their heads, slashing the air from side to side and then striking downwards at their enemies as if chopping wood. It was this use of the sword that so terrified their opponents. However, the Romans soon learned to deal with this: Polybius says that they were trained to take the first blow of the sword on the rim of the shield, which was reinforced with an iron strip. When the sword struck the reinforced rim it bent double like a *strigil*. The Celt was then forced to straighten his sword with his foot, giving the legionary the opportunity to

attack him whilst he was disarmed. The legionary also found that as the Celt slashed with his sword, he was able to break the blow with his shield and go in underneath it to thrust at the stomach.

Polybius' description of the sword bending is probably exaggerated. This may sometimes have happened but Celtic swords were generally better than this. I have seen a 2,000-year-old sword which was dredged from the lake of Neuchâtel and which is, incidentally, from the period Polybius is describing, bent almost double and then flex back. Polybius also mentions the Celtic fashion of wearing armlets in battle. However, the suggestion that heavy bracelets of the type found in Britain were worn on the right arm has to be challenged as they would never have stayed on a man's arm, particularly the upper arm, whilst he wielded his sword.

Diodorus stresses the length of the Celtic sword compared to the shorter swords (presumably of the Greeks and Romans). This exaggerated length of the sword is also reflected in the other ancient sources. However, it is not entirely true, for at the time of Celtic supremacy, c. 450–250 BC, their swords were generally comparatively short with a blade length of about 60cm, which is no longer than those used by the Etruscans and Romans of the same

Opposite
Part of the decoration of a cauldron found at Gundestrup in Denmark. It shows Celtic horsemen, foot soldiers and trumpeters. Its date is uncertain, 3rd–1st century BC.

Right
1 Sculpture from the arch at Orange in southern France showing carnyxes, flags and animal standards. These last two were introduced into the Roman army.
2 The head of a carnyx, the most common form of Celtic trumpet, from Deskford in Scotland (see Gundestrup cauldron, opposite).
3 and **4** Decorated spearheads. These are common Celtic finds and were probably used as standards. Compare to the *beneficiarius'* standard on p. 221.
5 A sculpture from Bormio in nothern Italy showing a Celtic standard bearer and a hornblower. A Roman standard bearer's tombstone of the 3rd century AD discovered at Carrawburgh on Hadrian's Wall shows a shield almost indentical to that of the Bormio standard bearer.

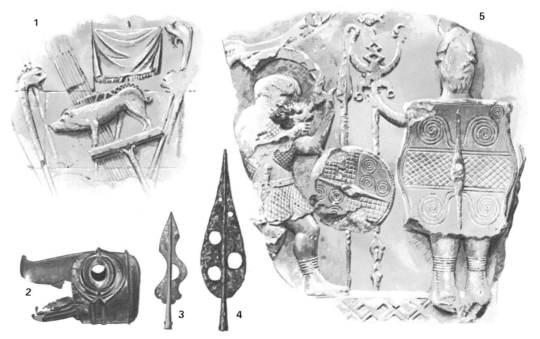

period. The longer blade did not come into fashion until the late 3rd to 1st centuries BC.

Hundreds of Celtic swords have been found of which a small sample is shown here. They are grouped by the traditional La Tène dating system—with approximate dates.

The swords from La Tène I (c. 450–250 BC) have blades that are generally between 55 and 65cm long. Number 1, which has a blade of 80cm, is exceptional. These swords are all double-edged and pointed and are of cut-and-thrust type. The most characteristic feature of these early weapons is their pronounced chape.

Daggers were also common during this period. Their blades vary from broad, almost triangular, shapes to thin stiletto types and are generally 25–30cm in length.

During the La Tène II period (c. 250–120 BC) the sword developed into a weapon used exclusively for slashing. The point became rounded and gradually increased in length until blades of 75–80cm were commonplace. Such a sword, complete with handle, would weigh about a kilogram. Although the early chape forms continued in the Balkans, in western Europe the chape was modified to follow more closely the contour of the sword. Hundreds of these swords have been dredged from the lake at La Tène in Switzerland and although there are regional differences which show mainly in the scabbard, the La Tène type may be accepted as representative of the period. The scabbards, which are usually made of iron, are constructed from two plates. The front plate, which is slightly wider than the back, is folded over it along the sides. It is reinforced by a decorated band around the top and a chape which acts as a reinforcing rim at the bottom.

During the La Tène III period (c. 120–50 BC) the length of the blade continued to increase and some examples are as long as 90cm. Although pointed swords existed, the predominant type was flat-ended. The long scabbard shown in this group is from Britain. Its scabbard shape is clearly derived from the La Tène type but its great length of nearly 84cm suggests that it should be placed in the later period.

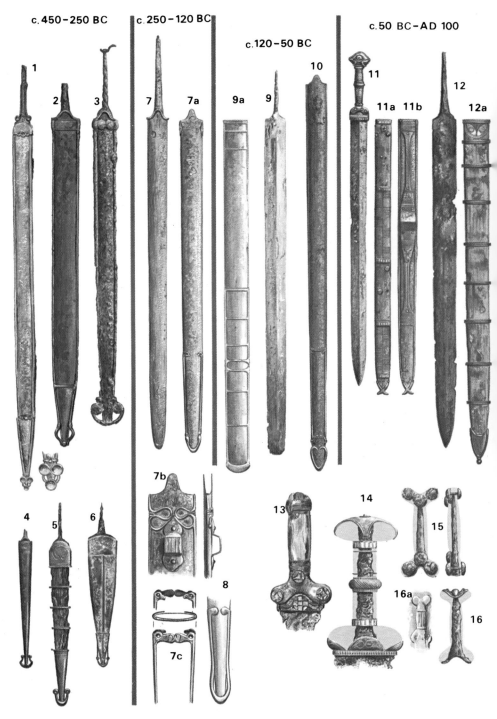

c. 450–250 BC   c. 250–120 BC   c. 120–50 BC   c. 50 BC–AD 100

Above
1–12 The development of the Celtic sword. Scale 1:8. 1, 2 and 3 Swords and scabbards from the Marne area of France. St Germain Museum.
4, 5 and 6 Daggers and scabbards from the Marne area of France. St Germain Museum.
7 and 7a Sword and scabbard from La Tène. Basel Museum, Switzerland.
7b back of 7a showing suspension loop.
7c Top of the chape of 7a.
8 Chape of a sword from France, c. 200 BC.

9 and 9a Sword and scabbard from Port.
10 Scabbard found in the Thames near London.
11, 11a and 11b Sword and front and back of scabbard from Embleton, Cumberland.
12, 12a Sword and scabbard from Yorkshire.
13–16 Sword handles.
13 From Thorpe, Bridlington, Yorkshire.
14 From Hod Hill, Dorset.
15 From the Marne valley, France.
16 From Halstatt, Austria.
16a Sculpture from Pergamum, Turkey.

The conquest of Gaul by Caesar in 55BC spelt the end of the Celtic warrior on the continent of Europe. In Britain a Celtic subculture survived for another 150 years. The sword blades from this period (La Tène IV) are generally shorter than in the previous era, varying from 55 to 75cm. The sword scabbard from Embleton in Cumberland (**11a**), with its small twin-footed chape, is typical of the period.

Sword handles, which were normally made of wood or leather or some other perishable material, have almost always disappeared. The traditional sword handle was in the form of an X, still echoing the earlier Halstatt antennae types. A handle of this type is shown on the victory frieze at Pergamum among the spoils taken from the Galatians (**16a**). A similar shape is easy to detect on the early sword from Halstatt in Austria (**16**) and on the La Tène II sword from St Maur les Fosses in the Marne valley, France (**15**). The handle of the sword from Thorpe Bridlington in Yorkshire (**13**), though late, still echoes this traditional form. Sometimes this type of handle was made in the form of a man with his arms raised. The later La Tène IV handles, such as the example from Hod Hill in Dorset (**14**), often show a strong Roman influence.

Diodorus says that the sword was suspended on the right side by chains of iron or bronze. Many pieces of such chains have been found along with scabbards. These usually take the form of a piece of chain 50–60cm long with a ring at one end and a hook at the other (see **23**). This is usually accompanied by a much shorter piece somewhat similar to a snaffle horse bit (**21, 22**). Diodorus' description is a little misleading as these are not parts of a suspension chain but of a belt from which the sword is suspended. The longer piece forms the back and left side of the belt. A strap is attached to the ring and passed through the loop on the back of the scabbard (**24**) where it is fastened to one of the rings of the shorter piece of chain to complete the belt which is fastened with the hook and remaining ring. Belts were usually made of leather, in which case two rings were fastened to the scabbard in the same fashion and a leather belt

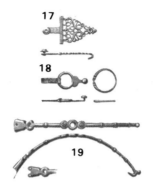

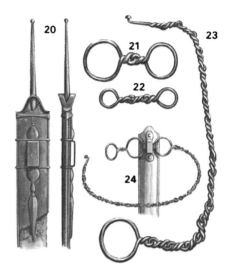

Above and right
17–19 Celtic belt clasps. They are all from leather belts.
17 From Este in northern Italy. 4th–3rd century BC. Este Museum.
18 From La Tène. 3rd–2nd century BC. Neuchâtel Museum.
19 1st-century type of hook fastener. Römisches Germanisches Zentralmuseum, Mainz.
20 Back of a scabbard from northern Italy showing the suspension loop. Milan Museum.
21, 22, 23 Parts of sword chains (or belts) from La Tène.

24 Method of attaching the sword: the longer piece of chain (**23**) is joined to one of the shorter pieces by a thong which passes through the suspension loop on the scabbard. The sword is placed on the right thigh and the longer piece of chain passes round behind the back to hook up at the front.

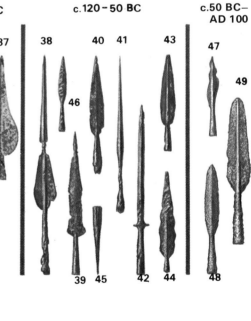

| c. 450–250 BC | c. 250–120 BC | c. 120–50 BC | c. 50 BC–AD 100 |

Above
25–49 Celtic spears and javelins. Scale 1:8.
25–29 Spearheads. **30, 31** Spear butts.
32 Javelin head. **26, 29** and **30** From the Marne area of France. St Germain Museum.
28 From northern Italy. **25, 27, 31** and **32** origin unknown. St Germain Museum. **33–36** Spearheads from La Tène. Neuchâtel Museum.
37 Spearhead from the Marne area of France.

St Germain Museum. **38–44** Spearheads excavated at the site of Caesar's siege of Vercingetorix at Alesia in central France. St Germain Museum. **45** Spear butt from Alesia. St Germain Museum. **46** Javelin head from Alesia. St Germain Museum. **47** Javelin head from southern Britain. **48, 49** Spearheads from Camelon, Scotland.

replaced the chain using a clasp. Several of these clasps, complete with part of the leather belt, have been recovered from the lake at La Tène. They are usually in the form of a hook which fastened to a ring at the other end of the belt. The early belt clasps were roughly triangular-shaped plates, often highly decorated with a tongue at one end which was riveted to the leather belt and a hook at the other (**17**). The examples from La Tène which come from the La Tène II period are much simpler, and are usually in the shape of a ring with a hook attachment (**18**). Later it evolved into a more conventional hook with an attachment plate. In the third period the hook was often very long and sometimes hinged, but in its decoration it betrays its evolution from the ring fastener of the previous period (**19**).

The Celt was renowned as a swordsman and yet Diodorus describes the spears that he used. Spear and javelin heads are also constantly present in warrior burials. This presents a considerable problem, for if he carried a spear then he was not primarily a swordsman, which is at odds with all the descriptions in the ancient sources. Some people have suggested that all the spearheads found in the graves are in fact javelin heads. Quite apart from the huge size of some of these heads, three spears complete with heads and butts were discovered at La Tène. These are nearly 2.5m long and could never be javelins. To confound matters further they all had small heads, implying that even more of the heads are from spears and not javelins. This difficulty seems to be insurmountable, for to a man who uses a spear, which is not disposable, his sword must be a secondary weapon. The only conclusion that can be drawn from this is that although the Celt may have been primarily a swordsman, he was not exclusively so.

Diodorus talks of spearheads a cubit in length (about 45cm) and even longer. This is no exaggeration; several spearheads of this proportion have been found coming from all three European periods. One enormous example from La Tène (**34**) is almost 60cm long. These spearheads come in an almost infinite variety. Those that are most typically Celtic swell out at the base and then curve concavely towards the point. Diodorus mentions a type of javelin head with an undulating edge which he says not only cuts the flesh but mangles it as well. Such spearheads (see **44**) have been found on both La Tène II and III sites.

Wherever the Celts came up against the Romans they seem to have adopted the socketed type of *pilum*. Examples of these have been found at many Celtic

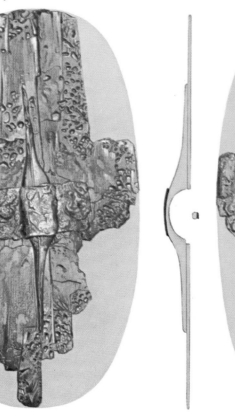

Above and right
1, 2 One of the wooden shields dredged from the lake at La Tène. Neuchâtel Museum, Switzerland.
1 The front of the oak shield showing the spine and iron strip boss, c. 250 BC. Scale 1:10.

2 The back of the La Tène shield showing the handgrip which curves outwards to make it easier to grasp. Unfortunately only the spine and boss now survive. The rest is in tiny fragments. Similar shields, covered with hide, have been found in Denmark and Ireland.

Top and above
3 Sculpted Celtic shields from the arch at Orange in southern France and from the Victory frieze at Pergamum, Turkey.
4 Celtic shields carried by foot soldiers displayed on a 4th-century scabbard.

sites in southern Europe. This might explain why Diodorus says that their javelin heads are larger than other people's swords. It is possible that the spearhead from La Tène (**34**) mentioned above is from a javelin.

When Diodorus says that the Celtic shield was as tall as a man, he is grossly exaggerating. The remains of three shields were found at La Tène. These are about 1.1m long. This would appear to be fairly representative of the shields shown in Celtic sculpture which, when resting on the ground, come up to a little above the waist.

The three examples from La Tène, which have now unfortunately fallen to pieces, were made of oak. They were approximately 1.2cm thick in the centre, tapering slightly towards the sides. Two of the shields have an Italian type spindle boss. On the third this part is missing. The centre of the spindle boss is hollowed out to allow the hand to grasp the handle. This handle is made of a separate piece of wood usually reinforced with a strip of iron which was nailed to the shield at either end. A rectangular iron plate was nailed across the front of the boss to give further protection for the hand.

Shields of this type have also been found in Denmark and Ireland. These were hide-covered and there can be little doubt that the La Tène examples were covered with hide, or possibly felt, as bare wood would have split when struck with a slashing sword. Similar bare wooden shields were also found in ship burials in Norway. This makes one wonder whether shields were made specially for burials and other ceremonials as they obviously were in primitive Greece and Italy. What is certain is that an uncovered wooden shield would be useless in battle. The Celtic shields shown on the victory frieze at Pergamum appear to have a hide facing. This would have covered both front and back of the shield and have been doubled up along the edge to reinforce the rim. An example from Clonoura Townland, Tipperary, in Ireland, has a rim of hide which is stretched through the shield. Examples of metal rims have also been found. A La Tène type shield covered with hide would weigh 6–7kg (the wood about 4kg, the hide about 2kg and the iron boss 250g). The ancients must have been well aware that oak can be hardened by baking, and no doubt the shield was given the heat treatment.

The origin of this type of shield is obscure. The similarities between the Roman *scutum* and the Celtic shield are so remarkable that they must have the same origin. The earliest evidence for the Celtic shield is provided by the

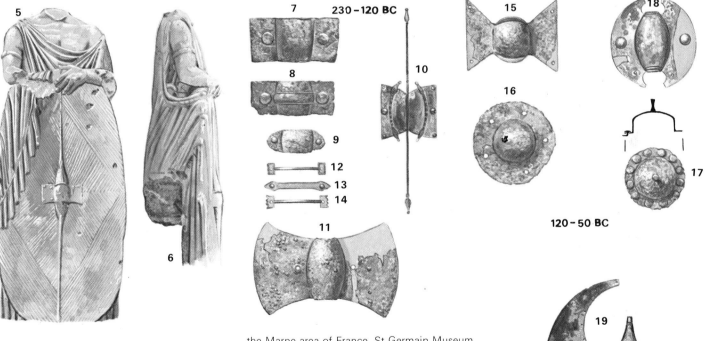

5 Sculpture of a warrior with a typical Celtic shield: From Mondragon, Vaucluse, southern France. This sculpture gives a clear idea of the great size of these shields, which should really be described as body shields.
6 The side view of the statue. Just under the right arm one can see the handle of his sword and also the belt and ring attachment.
7–19 The development of the Celtic shield boss. **7–9** Iron strip bosses from the Marne area of France. St Germain Museum.
10 Elaborate bronze strip boss with spine from the Marne area of France. St Germain Museum. **11** Iron winged boss from Formin, Yugoslavia. **12**, **13**, **14** Iron handgrip braces from La Tène. Neuchâtel Museum, Switzerland. **15** Iron winged boss from the site of Caesar's siege of Vercingetorix at Alesia in central France. St Germain Museum. **16** Round iron boss from Alesia. St Germain Museum. **17** A Germanic type of iron boss also from Alesia. St Germain Museum. **18** Iron 'butterfly' boss from Arqua Petrarca in the Italian Alps. This type is common in Yugoslavia. **19** Bronze 'butterfly' boss found at Moel Hiraddug, Flintshire, Wales. Cardiff Museum.

Above
A Celtic chief from Gaul at the time of Caesar. He wears an iron helmet and mail shirt. His long sword hangs on his right hip. Swords at this time were often as much as a metre long. Behind him stands a British Celt with lime washed hair and skin tattooed with woad. The great majority of Celts wore no armour. They lime washed their hair, combing it back from the forehead to the nape of the neck, so that it resembled a horse's mane. The style is shown on a number of coins. The attempt to make the hair stand up like that of an angry animal is exceedingly primitive and may provide the origin of horsehair crests on helmets.
The Roman attitude towards the Celts was particularly ruthless. They were systematically massacred in northern Italy, Spain and France. After the Hannibalic war the reconquest of the Po valley virtually denuded the area of Celtic tribesmen.

figures shown on the Halstatt scabbard, c. 400 BC, whereas the evidence for the *scutum* predates this by some 300 years. The only possible conclusion is that the Celts adopted the Italian shield when they invaded Italy in the 5th century and from here its use filtered back across the Alps. The Halstatt scabbard could well be an export from the Celts of northern Italy. The suggestion that the Celts did not use shields before coming to Italy is unacceptable as the Celtic style of fighting demands a shield.

The series of bosses shown above traces the development from the simple strip boss of the 3rd century BC to the elaborate butterfly bosses found in Britain in the 1st century AD. Although all the bosses shown, except **19**, were found on the continent of Europe, in most cases similar examples have been found in Britain.

The majority of Celtic shields were oval, but the archaeological examples and the representations show that they could also be rectangular, hexagonal or round. These same representations show the shields decorated with symbols, animals or geometric designs. Diodorus claims that these motifs were made of bronze, but it seems more likely that they were painted. He may be referring to the elaborate type of bronze shields that have been found in Britain, but these must have been used for some ceremonial purpose and could never have been used in battle.

Diodorus' description of Celtic helmets does not fit very well with the archaeological evidence. His helmets are of bronze with large embossed figures standing out from them, which gives the appearance of great stature to those who wear them. He goes on to explain that these are sometimes in the form of horns, which are attached to the helmet so as to form a single piece, or in the shape of the fronts of birds or four-footed animals. Helmets roughly fitting this description have been found but they do not seem to fit into the mainstream of Celtic helmet development. For convenience these mainstream helmets will be considered first.

A large number of helmets have been discovered in the region of Italy occupied by the Senones (the Adriatic coast between Ancona and Rimini). These all have a back peak to protect the neck. They are generally referred to as the Montefortino type after the burial ground where they were first found. These can clearly be traced back to a type of helmet that was in use in France and Austria during the later 5th century (**1, 2**). These were bronze helmets with an elongated topknot. This type of helmet may have been brought to Italy by the Senones.

In Italy the helmet evolved into the Montefortino type which, while retaining the topknot and back peak, had a much more rounded cap. Numbers **5**, **6** and **9** are from Senones graves and must date to the period before 282 BC, when these Celts were driven out by the Romans. They are generally dated to the late 4th or early 3rd century. The helmets from the Senones' graves are usually made either completely of iron or of iron and bronze, though a few continue to be made entirely of bronze. Several examples have a multiple crest holder made of iron fitted to the topknot (see no. **6**). This presumably held feathers at the sides and a horsehair crest at the top. The cheek pieces of these helmets are nearly always of the triple disc type (see **6**) which must have been adopted from the Italians. They are so similar to the Samnite breastplates (see p. 108) that their origin must be Italian. During the 3rd century this cheek piece degenerated into a triangular type with three bosses. The Montefortino helmet was rapidly adopted by the other Italians. An example bearing an Etruscan inscription was found at Bologna and therefore must date to the era before the evacuation of the Po valley by the Etruscans in the middle of the 4th century. Representations of these helmets also appear in the 4th-century tomb of the reliefs at Cerveteri. Both have scalloped cheek pieces. Examples of the triple disc type also turn up in Etruria, although they do not seem to have outlived the 4th century. There is also an isolated example of a scalloped cheek piece from the Montefortino cemetery (**9**) but this may be an import.

The Montefortino type spread throughout the Celtic world: **13** was found in Yugoslavia and an almost identical Galatian example is shown on the victory frieze at Pergamum.

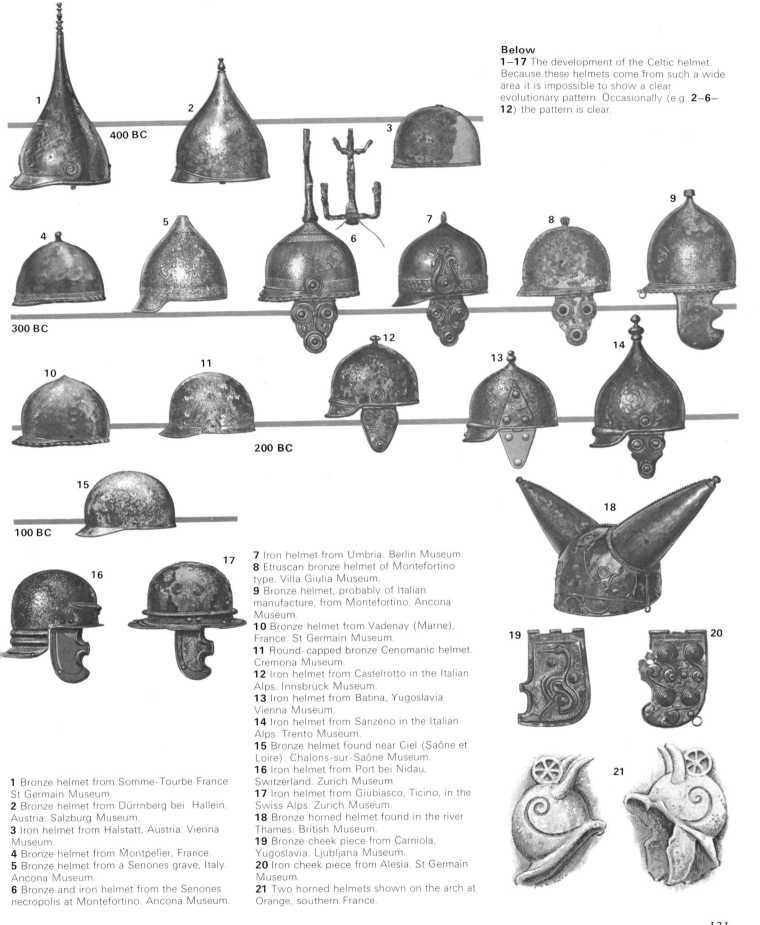

400 BC

300 BC

200 BC

100 BC

Below
1–17 The development of the Celtic helmet. Because these helmets come from such a wide area it is impossible to show a clear evolutionary pattern. Occasionally (e.g. **2–6–12**) the pattern is clear.

7 Iron helmet from Umbria. Berlin Museum.
8 Etruscan bronze helmet of Montefortino type. Villa Giulia Museum.
9 Bronze helmet, probably of Italian manufacture, from Montefortino. Ancona Museum.
10 Bronze helmet from Vadenay (Marne), France. St Germain Museum.
11 Round-capped bronze Cenomanic helmet. Cremona Museum.
12 Iron helmet from Castelrotto in the Italian Alps. Innsbruck Museum.
13 Iron helmet from Batina, Yugoslavia. Vienna Museum.
14 Iron helmet from Sanzeno in the Italian Alps. Trento Museum.
15 Bronze helmet found near Ciel (Saône et Loire). Chalons-sur-Saône Museum.
16 Iron helmet from Port bei Nidau, Switzerland. Zurich Museum.
17 Iron helmet from Giubiasco, Ticino, in the Swiss Alps. Zurich Museum.
18 Bronze horned helmet found in the river Thames. British Museum.
19 Bronze cheek piece from Carniola, Yugoslavia. Ljubljana Museum.
20 Iron cheek piece from Alesia. St Germain Museum.
21 Two horned helmets shown on the arch at Orange, southern France.

1 Bronze helmet from Somme-Tourbe France. St Germain Museum.
2 Bronze helmet from Dürrnberg bei Hallein, Austria. Salzburg Museum.
3 Iron helmet from Halstatt, Austria. Vienna Museum.
4 Bronze helmet from Montpelier, France.
5 Bronze helmet from a Senones grave, Italy. Ancona Museum.
6 Bronze and iron helmet from the Senones necropolis at Montefortino. Ancona Museum.

Although the Celts had been almost driven out of Italy by the first quarter of the 2nd century BC, the Montefortino type still turns up in the valleys of the Alps. The examples found here (**12, 14**) are exclusively made of iron and have the neck guard made separately and then riveted on. The cheek piece has degenerated considerably from its original design but **14** still retains the basic characteristics.

The Montefortino helmet was the most successful type ever designed. It won almost total acceptance in the Roman army, where it was used virtually unchanged for nearly four centuries. At a conservative estimate some three to four million of these helmets must have been made.

There was a second type of helmet that was very similar to the Montefortino type but lacked the topknot (**10, 11, 15**). This is usually referred to

as the Coolus type after a 1st-century example found in France. Although it was never as popular as the Montefortino type, its use became widespread in the 1st century BC and it appears to have been the forerunner of the early 1st-century AD Roman legionary helmet. The origin of the Coolus helmet may be as early as the Montefortino type: one was found in the Senones' graves and the example from Halstatt may be as early as 400 BC.

Some helmets have a type of wing design on the side (see **7, 13**). This seems to have originated in Italy and may have been inspired by the wings on Samnite helmets. The type became popular in the Balkans in the 3rd to 2nd centuries BC and it also appears on the victory frieze from Pergamum in Asia Minor. An example, though it could be an import, has also been found at Amfreville in northern France.

Horned helmets recalling those described by Diodorus are shown on the arch at Orange (**21**). Bearing in mind the Bormio relief (p. 115) these may be interpreted as standard bearers' helmets. Several helmets with horn-like attachments cut out of thin bronze sheet have been found in Italy. A superb example of a horned ceremonial helmet was found in the Thames at Waterloo Bridge (**18**). Helmets decorated with animals as described by Diodorus are very rare. Only one example has come to light. This was found at Ciumesti in Romania. It is a helmet of the Batina type (**13**) with a bird on top. This bird has hinged outstretched wings which must have flapped up and down as the wearer galloped into battle.

Some 4th-century Celtic graves have been discovered in northern Italy which contain Etruscan Negau type helmets.

Above
1 Bronze Celtic conical helmet from Apulia. The decoration is Celtic but the style is Apulian. Several helmets with horn-like attachments cut out of thin bronze sheet have been found in Italy. Bari Museum.
2 Horn from a similar helmet. British Museum.
3 A coin from France showing a Celt with lime-washed hair.
4 Celtic Negau type helmet from the Alps. This is almost identical to the earlier Italian type except for the crest ridge. **4a** Inside the rim of **4** showing the band which holds the internal cap.

5, 6 Front and back views of a statue of a warrior from Grèzan, near Nîmes in the south of France. This statue, which may be as early as the 4th century BC, is pre-Celtic. The warrior appears to be wearing either a square front and back plate which is strapped on, or a complete cuirass decorated in this form. Nîmes Museum.
7 Detail of the belt clasp of **5**.
8 A belt clasp of the type worn by the warrior of Grèzan. From Aleria in Corsica. This is not a Celtic type.
9, 10 Two hooded heads from Sainte-Anastasie, France. Nîmes Museum.

That the Celts adopted the Negau helmet is confirmed by the discovery of several examples of a Celtic form of Negau helmet in the central Alpine area (4, p. 122).

In the 1st century BC two new types appear. They are closely related and are generally referred to as the Agen-Port types. The Agen type (17) has a cap rather like a bowler hat with a brim. The Port type has a similar cap but a deep neck guard which is riveted on (16). Both have a new type of cheek piece which was later adopted by the Romans. The Port type was the direct ancestor of the 1st-century AD imperial Gallic legionary helmet (see p. 228). Examples of these helmets, which are made entirely of iron, have been found in northern Yugoslavia, the central Alpine region, Switzerland and central and southwestern France. The peculiar thing about their provenance is that it is along the frontiers of the Roman dominions at the beginning of the 1st century BC.

A 1st-century Celtic cheek piece from Alesia in central France (20) shows an odd mixture of the classical Italian cheek piece decorated with bosses harping back to the old triple disc type. Similar characteristics appear on the earlier cheek piece from northern Yugoslavia (19). Helmets of Greek/Italian conical type with Celtic decoration, such as 1, p. 122, have also been found. These all seem to come from the area of Apulia in southern Italy. The wheel decoration on top is almost identical to those shown on the arch of Orange.

Even in northern Italy, where helmet finds are common, the vast majority of Celts would have worn no armour. Diodorus tells us that these warriors lime-washed their hair and then combed it back from the forehead to the nape of the neck so that it looked like a horse's mane. Several coins, such as 3, p. 122, show this style. This attempt to make the hair stand up like an angered animal is exceedingly primitive and may point to the origin of horsehair crests on helmets.

Some statues from southern France west of the Rhône, show an extraordinary headgear like a hood with a crest on it (see below). These may be pre-Celtic and certainly show a great similarity to the hoods shown on the Osuna reliefs from Spain (see p. 150).

The use of body armour amongst the Celts was probably very rare. Apart from a few bronze discs which could be chest armour but are more likely to be harness decorations for horses, there is nothing from the early period (450–250 BC). The 4th–3rd century statue from Grézan in the south of France (see 5, 6, 7, p. 122) shows a warrior wearing what appears to be either a square front and

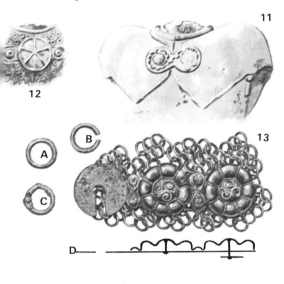

Above and right
11 Sculpture of a mail shirt with shoulder cape from Entremont in the south of France. This is a true Celtic type.
12 A clasp from a similar statue.
13 Part of a Celtic mail shirt with its clasp for holding the cape together from Ciumesti in Romania. Scale 1:2. **A, B, C** Three types of ring used in the Ciumesti mail, actual size.
D Section of the clasp.
14 Statue of a late Celtic warrior from Vachères, southern France. He wears an Italian-style mail shirt.
15 A statuette of a Celt from northern Italy wearing an Italian style mail shirt.
16 A sculpture of a mail shirt from Pergamum in Turkey.

back plate which is strapped on or a complete cuirass decorated in this form. This statue cannot be considered as typically Celtic. In fact it may not be Celtic at all. The hood type helmet, like those from Sainte-Anastasie in the same area (see p. 122) probably originated among the Iberians and not the Celts. Therefore parallels should be looked for in Spain rather than France. The claw belt fastener which is common to the whole of southern France and Corsica is a pre-Celtic type. The example shown on p. 122 is from Aleria in Corsica.

Around 300 BC mail was invented. In spite of the Celts' distaste for armour, most of the evidence points to them as the inventor of this its most successful form. Strabo refers to mail as Celtic. The earliest remains come from Celtic graves and the Celts were the great iron workers of the ancient world. Several statues of warriors from southern France which have been thought to show pigskin or leather cuirasses should be regarded as depicting mail.

The use of mail, which was very expensive to make, was probably restricted to the aristocracy.

The various statues of mailed warriors from southern France and northern Italy show two types of cuirass: the first with a cape that hangs over the shoulders (see 11, p. 123); and the second cut like a Greek linen cuirass with no overhang at the shoulders (14, 15, p. 123). The first is probably the more truly Celtic type.

Pieces of a mail shirt were discovered with the bird helmet in a 3rd-century grave at Ciumesti in Romania. There appear to be parts of two different cuirasses as one of them (p. 123) is made up of alternate rows of punched (A) and butted (B) rings whilst another piece has riveted rings instead of butted ones. This is much stronger. These rings are 8mm in diameter. It is possible that the shirt with butted rings was intended for ceremonial purposes only, which would tie in well with the extraordinary helmet. Attached to the butted mail was a bronze fastener for the shoulder pieces which is decorated with rosettes. The section (D) shows that one end was riveted to the mail of one shoulder piece, the centre rosette was purely decorative

Above and below
1 A gravestone from Padua in northern Italy showing a Celtic chariot with a double hoop side, c. 300 BC.
2 Coin from the time of Caesar showing a Celtic chariot with a double-hoop side.
3, **4** A Celtic yoke and wheel from La Tène. Neuchâtel Museum, c. 200 BC.
5–17 Metal parts of chariots from chariot burials in France. St Germain Museum.
5, **6**, **13** Articulated harness attachments.
7 Hub cap with linchpin. **9** Felloe joint.
10, **11** Bronze decorations. **12** Horse bit.
14, **17** Linchpins. **15** Terret.
8, **16** Eye bolts of uncertain purpose.

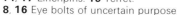

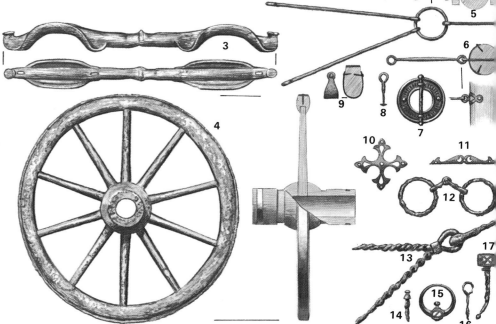

and the far end must have hooked behind a similar rosette on the other shoulder piece.

This must be from a cuirass with overhanging shoulders. The shoulder flaps of the cuirass that was made in the shape of a linen corselet fastened to the chest, but with the overhanging shoulder flaps such a fastening would restrict the movement of the arms. It was therefore essential, if one wished to raise one's arms, not to fix the fastener to the front of the shirt. This is in line with the fasteners shown on the sculptures from the south of France (see **11**, **12**, p. 123).

Before leaving the subject some comment must be made on Diodorus' statement that some of the Gauls went into battle naked. This is unquestionably true of the early period, but most of Diodorus' description refers to the later period. At the battle of Telamon in 225 BC the Gaesati, who crossed the Alps from Switzerland to fight on the Celtic side, were noteworthy to Polybius because they still fought in this fashion whereas the other Gauls did not. They wore their trousers and light cloaks.

Top and right
18 A bronze snaffle bit from the Somme-Tourbe in France. St Germain Museum, c. 400 BC.
19 A complex iron bit from Alesia in central France. St Germain Museum, c. 50 BC.
20 Bronze snaffle bit with enamel inlay from Britain. British Museum.
21 Silver harness disc from northern Italy.
22 A Celtic horseman with round spined shield, from the victory monument of Aemilius Paullus at Delphi.

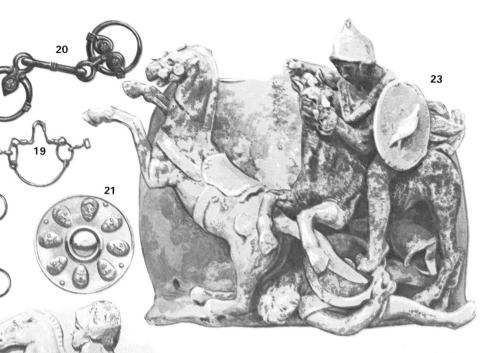

Above and below
23 A sculpture showing a Greek and Celtic horseman, c. 200 BC. Metropolitan Museum, New York. **24** Reconstruction of a Celtic chariot. The warrior stood behind the driver, which necessitated a long chariot box.

By the time of Caesar the Celts appear to fight fully dressed in shirt and trousers.

Polybius, in his account of the events leading up to the battle of Telamon, says that the Gallic army had 20,000 cavalry and chariots. This is the last reference to chariots being used in warfare on the European mainland. They are not encountered again until Caesar invades Britain in 55 BC.

Diodorus tells us that chariots were drawn by two horses and carried a driver and a warrior. In battle the warrior threw javelins from his chariot and then descended and fought on foot. Caesar's account of the British chariots is very similar. Both authors make one important point: chariots were used against cavalry. This solves a lot of problems, for one could not fight against infantry in this way except in skirmishes. Caesar expresses great admiration for the charioteers' skill. He describes warriors running along the chariot pole and standing on the yoke above the horses' shoulders.

Several chariot graves have been discovered in France. Unfortunately most of the vehicles appear to have been dismantled before burial. Many of the metal parts of chariots have been preserved in these graves. Among these are articulated harnessings (see p. 124, **5**, **6** and **13**) which can only have been used for the attachment of trace reins. The length of the bolt on these suggests that they must have been attached to the axle. This is certainly the position in which they were found in the grave. The series of rings that were found level with the horses' chests must have been fastened to the girth strap to guide these trace reins. These graves contain many other bits and pieces, including linchpins for holding on the wheels (**14**, **17**) and rein guides (terrets) which were attached to the yoke.

A very well preserved yoke (**3**) and wheel complete with iron tyre (**4**) were dredged from the lake at La Tène in Switzerland. The pieces shown here are of various dates. The aim is to try to show the sort of pieces used in the construction of a chariot. Pieces **5** and **13**, although of different date, obviously perform the same function.

Until recently one had to rely on coins to give some idea of the form of Celtic chariots. These show vehicles with what appears to be two semi-circular sides. A few years ago a gravestone was found at Padua in northern Italy which shows a chariot of a similar type carrying two men and a shield which is standing on its side in the chariot. In this relief both semi-circular side pieces are shown in front of the shield. This can only mean that these two pieces represent one side. Unlikely though this may seem, it is supported by the archaeological evidence. In the French chariot burials the space between the wheels is little over a metre, which is far less than the Cypriot chariots (which vary from 1.3 to 1.7m) where driver and warrior stood side by side. A Celtic warrior must therefore have stood behind his driver as shown on the coin of Hostilius. The long chariot box required for this accounts for the double sides and for the laying lengthways of a warrior in his chariot, as he was in the French burials.

After the conquest of Gaul, Celtic cavalry became the mainstay of the Roman army. Yet it has been suggested that the Celts had no true cavalry and that they dismounted and fought on foot. At the battle of Cannae (216 BC) the Celts, Spaniards and Romans certainly did this but it may have been necessary because of the exceedingly cramped space in which they were fighting. The comment of Hannibal at the battle of Cannae recorded by Livy seems to suggest that this was not normal practice: when he was told that Paullus had ordered his cavalry to dismount, Hannibal commented that he might as well have delivered them up in chains. This implies that dismounted cavalry were useless. In truth it is hard to conceive large numbers of cavalry dismounting to fight. If the Romans had done this, Polybius' comments about their adoption of the Greek spear which did not waver in the charge would have been meaningless. The Celtic cavalry employed by the Romans in the early empire is regularly depicted fighting from horseback. It therefore seems reasonable to conclude from this persuasive evidence that the Celts indeed produced true cavalry.

Many Celtic horsebits have been found. These are usually of the snaffle type. The sculpture on p. 125 (**22**) shows a horseman serving with the Macedonian forces at the battle of Pydna (168 BC). The round shield, which is certainly neither Roman nor Greek, must be a Celtic cavalry shield. The sculpture (**23**) on p. 125 shows a Celt riding over a fallen Greek. The riderless horse shows the type of saddle in use amongst the Greeks at this time. The Celts used the same type of saddle as the later Romans. This type of saddle, with pommels at each corner, appears on the Gundestrup cauldron and more clearly on the Julii monument at St Remi dating from the later 1st century BC. This commemorates a battle involving Romans and Celts. One of the horses has fallen and thrown its rider. The fallen rider must be a Celt as Roman triumphal monuments never depict the deaths of Roman soldiers. It follows that the four-pommelled saddle shown in this sculpture is Celtic and not Roman. The Gundestrup cauldron also shows the discs that were used to decorate Celtic horses. Some of these, made of silver, have been found in northern Italy. These *phalarae* were also adopted by the Romans.

The Roman-Latin army of the 4th century BC

The Cassian treaty of 490 BC incorporated Rome in the Latin League and for the next 160 years she shared a common military development with the other Latin states. When Rome made her bid for leadership of the League in the Latin War of 340–338, Livy assures us that the military organisation of the Latins and Romans was identical. No doubt he is right but when he says that *primus pilus* faced *primus pilus* in the battle he gets a little carried away, as they must have been at opposite ends of the legions.

But here once again Livy gives us an invaluable glimpse of the legion organisation. All legionaries now use the Italic oval shield (*scutum*). The phalanx had been abandoned and the legion was now split up into three lines. The rear line had 15 companies (*ordines*) each subdivided into three parts (*vexilla*). At the front were the cream of the veterans (*triarii*). Behind these came the younger and less distinguished men (*rorarii*) and behind these the east dependable soldiers (*accensi*). This literally means reserves. The *triarii* were armed with spears. Livy does not say what the others had.

Each of the three *vexilla* consisted of 60 men, two centurions and a standard bearer (*vexillarius*) who carried a flag-type standard, possibly resembling those of the Samnites.

The middle line was made up of 15 units (maniples) of heavy infantry (*principes*). These were the cream of the army—men in the prime of life. The front line (*hastati*) were also heavy infantry composed of young men coming up to the prime of life. They were also divided into 15 maniples. Attached to each maniple of *hastati* were 20 light-armed troops (*leves*) armed with spear and javelin. The legion strength was 5,000. Each unit of the rear line had 186 men. Each unit of *principes* and *hastati* must therefore have had a little over 60 men. These units were probably all composed of double centuries. Allowing 30 men per century, plus officers and supernumeraries such as rear-rank officers, standard bearers, trumpeters etc., we arrive at a total of about 5,000 men. Livy does not say how the *principes* and *hastati* were armed. In Polybius' day they had heavy javelins (*pila*) and swords. We know that *pila* were in use at this time and must assume that they were armed with these.

Most scholars have rejected Livy's description or revised it to conform to the pattern of the later legion. However, the Roman army was in a state of constant development and it would be very strange if it had remained unchanged between 340 and 150 BC. Livy's army is halfway between the Etruscan army (c. 550 BC) and that described by Polybius (c. 150 BC). Those who say that Livy has altered it fail to appreciate his method. He modernises. He would normally adapt his description to the usages of his own day. Here he has not done this. To the best of his ability he has passed it on as he found it. He has probably added a few embellishments but in all other respects we are left with an entirely original description. Those who try to adapt it to conform to Polybius' description of two centuries later are in fact following Livy's usual course.

In this instance Livy's description is too obscure and complicated not to be true.

Livy claims that the round shield (*clipeus*) had been abandoned about the the same time as the legionaries began to receive pay—i.e. during the siege of Veii at the beginning of the 4th century BC. He is in fact claiming that the phalanx had been abolished. The phalanx had been trampled into the ground at

Below
The units of the Roman-Latin army described by Livy. The double centuries of *accensi*, *rorarii* and *triarii* were grouped together to form one *ordo* (about 180 men). The *principes* and *hastati* each formed a maniple of about 60 men. There were 20 skirmishers (*leves*) attached to each maniple of *hastati*. Livy does not say how many centurions there were to each maniple of *hastati* and *principes*. Although Livy's account is confused and creates many problems, it would be totally wrong to suggest that he has made it up. Basically it must be correct.

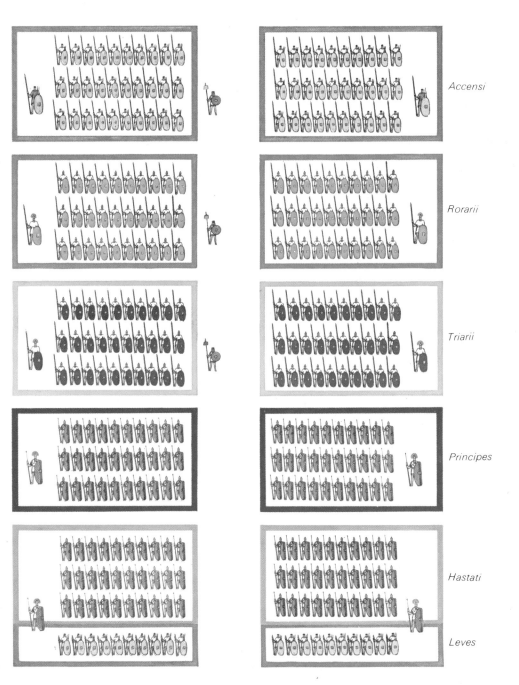

Accensi

Rorarii

Triarii

Principes

Hastati

Leves

the Allia and it was probably for this reason that it was discontinued and the whole army was armed with the larger *scutum* which was now reinforced with an iron rim.

The Servian army had consisted of two parts, each composed of 40 centuries of hoplites and 45 centuries of lightly armed troops. It can hardly be a coincidence that Livy's legion, from which the hoplites had disappeared, consists of 45 units (15 *ordines* in the rear line and 15 maniples each in the middle and front line).

Although the vestiges of the old class system still remain, classes one, two and three seem now to be grouped together and divided by age and not wealth: the youngest form the *hastati*, those in the prime of life the *principes*, and the oldest the *triarii*. The *rorarii* still seem to be the old fourth class and the *accensi* and *leves*, with their proportionately higher numbers, make up the fifth class.

The size of the centuries should not surprise one. In the earlier army the size of the centuries varied with the size of the army. The centuries of the *triarii* in Polybius' time were still only 30 strong.

In the new army the prime offensive weapon of the legionary must by now have been the heavy javelin (*pilum*). The old spearmen still existed in the *triarii*, *rorarii* and *accensi*. But now over a third of the army had been moved up to the front, probably armed with *pila* to break up the advancing enemy.

The three lines are drawn up in quincunx formation, like the black squares on a chess board. The 15 centuries of *hastati* are at the front with a gap between each. The *principes* are drawn up similarly covering the gaps. The units of the rear line similarly cover the gaps in the line of *principes*.

The battle starts with the skirmishers (*leves*) trying to break up the enemy formation with their light javelins. As the enemy advances the lightly armed troops withdraw through the gaps and the *hastati* charge, throwing their heavy javelins and then closing in with their swords. If this fails to break the enemy, they retreat into the gaps between the *principes*, who similarly charge. If both lines are beaten, they withdraw on the *triarii* and retire through the gaps in the line. The *triarii* then close the gaps and the whole army retreats. Livy's suggestion that the *triarii* also charged is probably an attempt to disguise the fact that the early Roman army sometimes lost battles. The old Roman adage, 'to have come to the *triarii*', meant that things had reached a terrible state.

Whilst the *hastati* and *principes* were fighting, the *triarii* knelt on one knee with their left leg forward. Their large oval shields rested against their left shoulders covering them from enemy missiles. Their spear butts were stuck in the ground with the spears pointing obliquely forward. Livy says, 'like a palisade'. Not unless all else had failed did they enter the battle. It is noteworthy that the standards were with the rear line, so that if the units operating out front were scattered, they knew the *ordines* on which to fall back. Livy does not tell us whether there were one or two centurions to each maniple of *principes* and *hastati*, or in fact none.

During the first 200 years of the republic Rome probably suffered many defeats. The patriotic Livy usually says that bad weather 'stopped play' to account for the Romans not gaining a victory. The greatest of these defeats was the disaster at the Allia (390 BC). These defeats, and the Allia in particu-

lar, may account for the strongly defensive character of the 4th-century legion. The more mobile formation of the *hastati principes* was probably an answer to the fast-moving armies of the Celts and Samnites. The javelineers at the front may have been particularly designed to withstand and break the force of the Celtic charge.

Top
Whilst the *hastati* and *principes* were fighting, the *triarii* knelt on their right knees with their spears sloping forwards and their shields resting against their left shoulders to protect them from missiles. Only if the *hastati* and *principes* were defeated would they enter the battle. **Below left.** A legion drawn up ready for battle with gaps between each of the units to allow the lines to interchange. If beaten, the *principes* and *hastati* would withdraw down the lanes between the *ordines* of *triarii*, *rorarii* and *accensi*. The *ordines* would then close the gaps and the army could withdraw behind a hedge of spears. **Below** How the *ordines* might close the gaps by moving up the rear centuries.

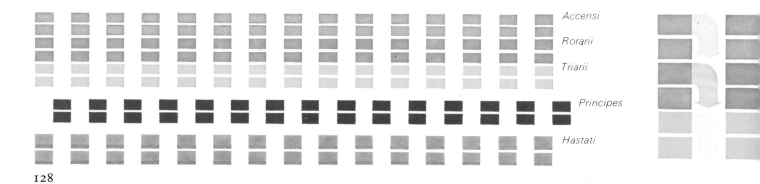

Accensi

Rorarii

Triarii

Principes

Hastati

Rome 275-140 BC

The Roman Army 160 BC

On 22 June 168 BC the Romans defeated the Macedonians at Pydna and reduced the homeland of Philip and Alexander to a Roman province.

After the battle a number of Greeks who had sided with Macedon were brought to Rome for questioning. Among these was the historian Polybius. He was placed in the custody of the Scipios, became a close friend of Scipio Aemilianus and accompanied him on his campaigns. In order that his Greek readers might understand the workings of the Roman army Polybius took the trouble to describe even the smallest details—something that our other great source, Caesar, does not do do as he assumes that his readers already know this information. The following account is taken almost entirely from Polybius.

Recruitment and organisation

At the beginning of each year two chief magistrates (consuls) were elected. Under normal circumstances each consul would have at his disposal two legions: 16–20,000 infantry and 1,500–2,500 cavalry. About half the infantry and one-quarter of the cavalry were Roman citizens. The rest were drawn from Rome's allies. In times of extreme danger the combined consular armies were put under the control of a dictator who usually held office for six months. A second-in-command (*magister equitum*) was also nominated, usually by the dictator.

After their election the consuls appointed 24 military tribunes. Ten of these were senior tribunes, with at least ten years service; the other 14 needed only to have seen five years service. The first two senior tribunes nominated were appointed to the first legion, the next three to the second, the next two to the third and the last three to the fourth. Similarly, the first four junior tribunes were appointed to the first legion, the next three to the second and so on; as a result each legion had six tribunes.

As with the Greeks, it was a privilege to serve in the army and only those who owned over a certain amount were liable for service. On an appointed day each year all citizens eligible for military service assembled on the Capitol.

Here they were divided according to property. The poorest citizens were sent to the navy. The next group (those with a census of over 400 drachmae) served in the infantry, and the richest served in the cavalry. The 1,200 men needed for the cavalry were selected by the censor before the general enrolment began. Three hundred of these were attached to each legion. A cavalryman had to serve for ten years and an infantryman for 16 years before he reached the age of 46. In time of great danger an infantryman might have to serve for 20 years.

Once those eligible for infantry service had been separated they were divided into their tribes. From each tribe four men were selected of about the same age and build and brought before the tribunes. The tribunes of the first legion had first choice, then the second and third, the fourth legion taking the one that was left. When the second group of four was brought forward the second legion had first choice and the first legion took the man that was left. So the selection continued until 4,200 had been chosen for each legion. In times of exceptional danger the legion strength was raised to 5,000.

It must be pointed out that elsewhere Polybius states that the legion strength was 4,000 infantry and 200 cavalry and that this was raised to 5,000 infantry and 300 cavalry in times of great danger. It seems unfair to say that Polybius is contradicting himself, as these figures must have varied considerably.

Once the enrolment had been completed the oath was taken. One man was selected by the tribunes to come forward and swear to obey his officers and execute their orders as far as was in his power. The others then came forward one at a time and swore that they would do the same as the first man ('*Idem in me*'). The tribunes then gave a place and date where each legion was to assemble so that the soldiers could be assigned to their units.

Whilst the levy was taking place the consuls also sent orders to the allied cities stating the numbers of troops required and the day and place of assembly. The local magistrates chose the recruits and as at Rome swore them in. They then appointed a commander and a paymaster and despatched them.

When they arrived at the rendezvous, they were once more divided into groups according to wealth and age. In each 4,200-strong legion the youngest and poorest 1,200 formed the light armed (*velites*). Of the other 3,000 the youngest 1,200 formed the first line of heavy infantry (*hastati*), those in the prime of life formed the second line (*principes*) also 1,200 strong and the oldest formed the third line (*triarii* or *pili*) 600 strong. Regardless of the size of the legion, the *triarii* were always 600 strong. The other troops were increased proportionately.

From each of these groups, with the exception of the *velites*, the tribunes elected ten centurions who in turn each nominated a partner who was also called a centurion. (These were called *prior* and *posterior*, the elected centurion being the *prior* centurion.) The first centurion elected in the legion (*primus pilus*) had a seat with the tribunes on the military council. The centurions were chosen for their steadiness. The centurions each appointed a rearguard officer (*optio*). Polybius calls them *ouragoi*, equating them with the 'rear-rankers' in the Greek armies.

The tribunes and centurions together divided each class (*hastati*, *principes* and *triarii*) into ten units (maniples). The *velites* were distributed evenly amongst these maniples. Like the four legions each maniple was given a number. The *primus pilus* commanded the first maniple of the *triarii*.

Thus we have a legion of 4,200 infantry divided into 30 maniples: ten of *hastati*, ten of *principes* and ten of *triarii*. The *hastati* and *principes* maniples had the same composition: 120 heavy infantry and 40 light-armed *velites*. The *triarii* maniples had 60 heavy infantry and 40 *velites*. Each maniple was composed of two centuries but they had no separate status. The smallest unit was the maniple. The centurions appointed two of the best and bravest men as standard bearers (*signiferi*). The Etruscan-Roman army had two centuries of trumpeters and hornblowers which allowed just about one per century. There is no mention of this group in Polybius' description but he regularly mentions trumpeters (*tubicines*) and hornblowers (*cornicines*).

It therefore seems likely that each maniple had a trumpeter and a horn-blower.

Occasionally one maniple of *hastati*, one of *principes* and one of *triarii* operated together as a unit called a cohort. Polybius uses this name several times.

How does this 2nd-century legion compare with the description that Livy gives of the legion at the time of the Latin war (340–338 BC)?

Polybius' army is divided into 30 maniples: ten *hastati*, ten *principes* and ten *triarii*. The old *rorarii* have disappeared altogether, reducing the strength of the legion from about 5,000 to 4,200, and the 1,200 light-armed *accensi* and *leves*, now called *velites*, are distributed throughout the 30 maniples. The maniples of *triarii* are still 60 strong. This should not surprise us as they are the remnants of the old phalanx. The *principes* and *hastati* have been doubled, which reflects the new aggressive spirit of the legion which is no longer fighting for its very existence but is conquering the world.

Armour and weapons

The *hastati* and *principes* were armed with a short cut-and-thrust sword (*gladius hispaniensis*) which hung from a belt on the right thigh. As its name implies, this weapon originated in Spain. It may have been seen first in the hands of Spanish mercenaries fighting with the Carthaginians in the first Punic war. No early examples of this type of sword have yet been found. The earliest specimens come from the end of the 1st century BC. These have a slightly waisted, two-edged blade, about 50cm in length with a long point. A 4th-century sword of a similar shape has been found in Spain at the cemetery of Las Cogotes (Avila). It therefore

Right
A cohort of a 4,200-strong legion as described by Polybius. His descriptions of the smallest details of Roman organisation are of great value in reconstructing the legion of his time. The unit was made up of three maniples each composed of two centuries. The maniple was the smallest independent unit of the legion. Each maniple of the *triarii* consisted of 60 veterans plus 40 skirmishers (*velites*). The maniples of *hastati* and *principes* each consisted of 120 heavy infantry plus 40 *velites*.
C = centurion. **S** = *signifer*. **O** = *Optio*.

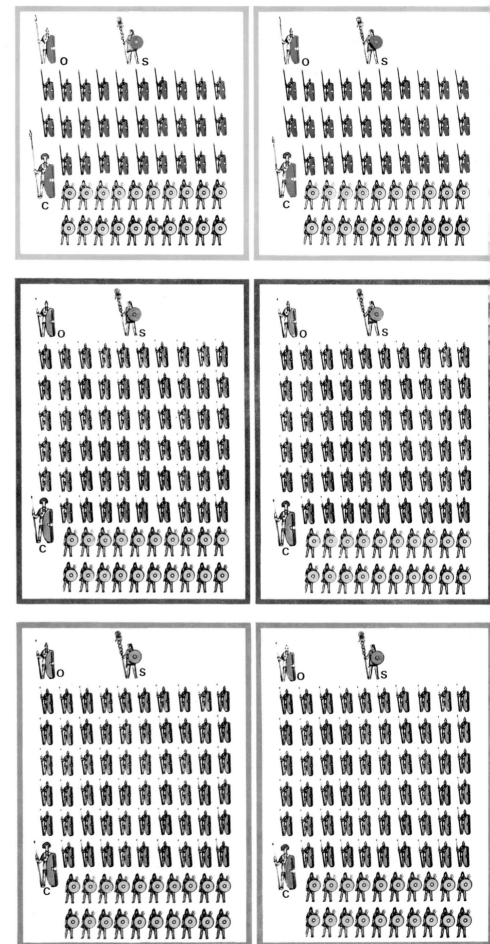

seems reasonable to assume that the 3rd–2nd-century Roman sword was of this type. Many short daggers with blades about 15cm long have also been found in Spain. These are identical to the later Roman types and it cannot be doubted that this Roman weapon also had its origins in Spain. Polybius does not mention daggers, but several examples have been found in 2nd-century Roman camps excavated around Numantia in Spain.

The *hastati* and *principes* also carried two long javelins (*pila*). Polybius' description of these weapons is slightly confusing but remains of several of them have been found at Numantia and from these one can make a reasonable reconstruction. The *pila* are of two types, thick and thin. The thin *pilum* has a long iron socketed head. Polybius says that the head is about three cubits (c. 1.35m) long, with a barbed point. Several of these have been found at Numantia. The longest is 93cm but the point is missing. Polybius has probably exaggerated the length. Examples of the thick *pilum* from Numantia have a broad flat tang 5cm wide and at least 8cm long. The iron head of both *pila* types has a long thin shaft surmounted by a pyramid-shaped barbed head. The iron shaft is about 7.5mm thick. The haft of these *pila* is, according to Polybius, about three cubits. The top of the haft of the thick *pilum* was broadened to take the flat tang. This thickening of the haft also served to protect the hand when the heavier *pilum* was being used in hand to hand fighting.

All the heavy infantry used the *scutum*, a large curved shield two and a half feet (c. 75cm) wide and four feet (c. 1.2m) long. According to Polybius it was made of two sheets of wood glued together and covered first with canvas

and then calf skin. This type of shield is shown on several monuments of the republican period. As in the earlier period it is oval with a spindle-shaped boss and a long spine. A shield of this type was found at Kasr El Harit in the Fayum in Egypt. It was identified as Celtic but is undoubtedly Roman.

This shield, which is 1.28m long and 63.5cm wide, is made of laminated birch. Nine or ten thin planks of birch wood varying from 6 to 10cm wide were laid out lengthways and sandwiched between two layers of narrower strips placed horizontally. These three layers were glued together to form the wooden core of the shield. At the rim it is slightly less than a centimetre thick, swelling to about 1.2cm in the centre. The whole shield was covered with sheep's wool felt which was doubled over along the edge and stitched through the wood. The shield has a horizontal handgrip which is held with an over-grasp. This grip is illustrated on many Roman sculptures. Polybius adds that the shield had an iron boss and an iron edging on its upper and lower rims.

Some years ago I made an exact copy

of the Fayum shield which weighed somewhat over 10kg. This weight was declared to be ridiculous on the grounds that nobody could handle a shield of this weight. Recently the remains of a shield were found at Doncaster. A reconstruction of this turned out to have a similar weight. The Roman shield of this period was essentially a body shield. It was not meant to be wielded. When the legionary charged, he generally held his shield with a straight arm and with his left shoulder resting against it. When he reached the enemy, he hit him full-on with his shield, throwing the whole weight of his body against it, and tried to knock his adversary over. He would then rest his shield on the ground and, crouching down, fight from behind it. The four-foot shield was probably the regulation size. Scipio Aemilianus severely reprimanded a soldier during the siege of Numantia for having an oversize shield.

The armour of the *principes* and *hastati* consisted of a small square breastplate about 20cm square called a heart guard (*pectorale*) and a greave. This wearing of only one greave is

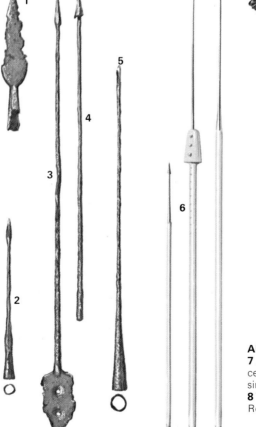

Right
Roman weapons found at Numantia. Römisch Germanisches Zentralmuseum, Mainz.
Scale 1:6.
1 Spearhead
2 Head of a javelin of the type used by the *velites* (*hasta velitaris*).
3 Heavy *pilum* head
4 Part of a heavy *pilum* head showing the barbed point.
5 The shaft of a light *pilum* head.
6 Reconstruction of a *hasta velitaris*, heavy *pilum* and light *pilum*.

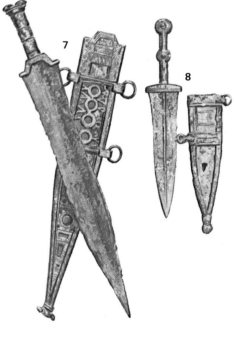

Above
7 A Spanish sword and scabbard from the cemetery at Las Cogatas (Avila). This is very similar to the later Roman type.
8 Spanish dagger. This is identical to the later Roman type.

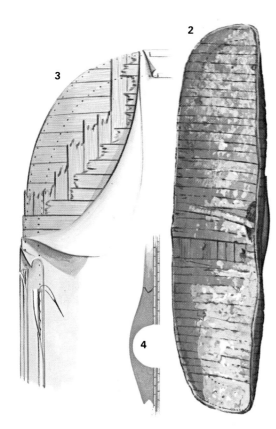

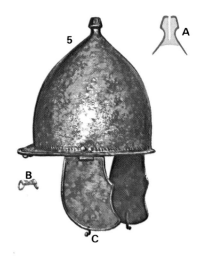

Left and above
1, **2** Front and three-quarter back view of the shield from the Fayum in Egypt. Cairo Museum. The shield, which is 1.28m long and 63.5cm wide, is made of laminated strips of birch in three layers covered with lamb's wool felt. A reconstruction made by the author weighed some 10kg. This coincides with the weight of the reconstruction of a shield found at Doncaster.
3 Reconstruction of part of the shield showing its construction and how the felt was doubled up along the rim and stitched through.
4 Section of the boss.
5 A Montefortino helmet from Canosa di Puglia, c.200 BC. Karlsruhe Museum. The topknot (**A**) was filled with lead to secure the crest pin. Under the peak at the back was a double ring (**B**) from which straps passed under the chin and fixed to the hooks on the cheek pieces (**C**).

Below
7 Figures from the monument of Aemilius Paullus at Delphi. They are wearing mail shirts cut to the shape of the Greek linen cuirass.

Above
6 Sculpture from a late-Etruscan urn from Volterra. Volterra Museum, c.150 BC. This shows an Italo-Corinthian helmet complete with crest and feathers. This type would have been in use in the Roman army at this period.

confirmed by Arrian in his *Ars Tactica* when he says, '. . . in Roman style one greave to protect the leg which was thrust forward in fighting'. This is, of course, the left leg. The *pectorale* is a descendant of the square breastplate of the 4th century. None of these have been found but remains of a circular type were found at Numantia. Wealthier legionaries wore a mail shirt. The cut of these shirts, which is similar to the linen cuirass, is shown on the victory monument of Aemilius Paullus at Delphi in Greece. This was set up after the Roman defeat of Macedonia in 168 BC. These mail shirts were exceedingly heavy, weighing about 15kg. Their immense weight is reflected in the account of the battle of Lake Trasimene where the soldiers who tried to swim to safety were drowned by the weight of their armour.

The *hastati* and *principes* wore a bronze helmet decorated with a ring of three upright black or purple feathers about 45cm high. Polybius says that this was to make every man look twice his normal height.

The commonest helmet in use at the time was the Montefortino type evolved from the Celtic helmets of the 4th and 3rd centuries. A fine example now in the Karlsruhe Museum in Germany was found at Canosa di Puglia. It was to this town that many of the legionaries fled after the disaster at Cannae in 216 BC. This helmet appears to be exactly right for the date and it is attractive to think that it belonged to one of the Cannae legionaries.

This type of helmet had a hole in the topknot. The topknot was filled with lead and a pin to hold a horsehair crest was inserted in the top. Beneath the peaked neck guard was a double ring attachment. Two straps were attached to these rings, which crossed under the chin and attached to the hooks at the bottom of the cheek pieces, holding the helmet firmly in position. The monuments show that the Italo-Corinthian helmet was still in use, and the discovery of a Samnite Attic helmet of the 1st century AD at Herculaneum shows that this type of helmet was also still in vogue. A padded cap or lining was worn under the helmet. A Celtic type of Montefortino helmet in the museum at Ljubljiana still has the remains of a felt cap inside. Felt would certainly make the most efficient form of padded lining.

The *triarii* were armed in exactly the same fashion as the *hastati* and *principes* except that instead of *pila* they carried long spears (*hastae*).

The *velites* were armed with sword, javelins and a round shield (*parma*) about 90cm in diameter. The javelins (*hastae velitaris*) are smaller versions of the thin *pilum*. They have a small head 25–30cm long. The wooden shaft is two cubits (c. 90cm) long and a finger's width in breadth. The *velites* wore no armour other than a plain helmet sometimes covered with a wolf's skin, or a similar distinguishing mark, so that the centurions could recognise them from a distance and judge how well they fought.

Cavalry and the allies
The 300 cavalry were divided into ten *turmae*, each 30 strong. Each *turma* had three decurions selected by the tribunes and three rear-rankers (*optiones*). These ten-strong units must be interpreted as files and one must therefore conclude that the cavalry lined up either ten or five deep depending on circumstances.

The first selected decurion of each *turma* commanded the unit. The horsemen were armed in the same fashion as the Greeks with cuirass and round shield (*parma equestris*). They carried a sturdy spear with a butt spike which could be used if the spear broke. Roman cavalrymen shown on the victory monument of Aemilius Paullus at Delphi (168 BC) are wearing mail shirts almost identical to those of the legionaries except for a split at the thigh to allow them to sit on a horse. The distinctive Italian cavalry shield can be seen on many monuments.

Having ordered the legionaries to arm themselves in accordance with the units in which they were serving, the tribunes dismissed them to their homes.

The allies were similarly formed into brigades 4–5,000 strong plus about 900 cavalry. One of these brigades was attached to each legion so that when one refers to a legion one means about 10,000 infantry and 1,200 cavalry. Polybius does not describe the breakdown of the allied units but they were probably similar to the Roman units.

Above
8 A Roman horseman from the monument of Aemilius Paullus at Delphi, 168 BC. He wears a mail shirt very similar to the infantry of the time but split at the thigh so that he can sit a horse.

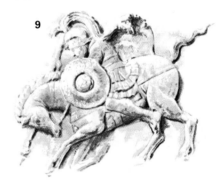

Above
9 A Roman republican horseman shown on a relief from the Lacus Curtius in the Forum at Rome. He wears a crested helmet, short muscled cuirass with *pteryges* and carries a typical Roman cavalry shield (*parma equestris*).

Above A *turma* of cavalry composed of three *decuriae*, or files, each commanded by a decurion who led his file. Each file also had a rear ranker to keep order. **D**=decurion. **R**=rear ranker.

Certainly the Latin allies had the same organisation as the Romans. In a normal two-legion army the legions fought in the centre and the two allied brigades (*alae sociorum*) fought on the wings, one being called the right wing and the other the left. Each wing was commanded by three prefects nominated by the consul. From the allies the best third of the cavalry and the best fifth of the infantry were selected to form a picked unit called the *extraordinarii*. This was a crack force used for special assignments. They also made up the covering force for the legions on the march.

Originally soldiers had served without pay but since the long drawn out siege of Veii at the beginning of the 4th century BC legionaries had been paid. A Roman infantryman in Polybius' day received two *obols* a day. A centurion received twice as much and a cavalryman six *obols* a day. The Roman foot soldier got an allowance of about 35 litres of corn a month and a horseman 100 litres of wheat and 350 litres of barley. Most of this, of course, went to feed his horse and groom. A fixed charge for this was deducted from the pay of both the infantry and the cavalry by the *quaestor*. Deductions were also made for clothing and replacement arms.

The allied infantry also received the 35 litres of corn, but the cavalryman only received 70 litres of wheat and 250 litres of barley. However, this ration was allocated free of charge to the allies.

Training

On their assembly at the place and date stipulated by the consul, the new legions were put through a rigorous training programme. Ninety per cent of them would have seen service before, but even these would have been out of practice. The new recruits must also have gone through some sort of basic training. During the empire a recruit was trained to fight 'the stake' with overweight weapons (see p. 218) and no doubt something similar took place during the republican period. Polybius gives us a good idea of the retraining of experienced soldiers. After Scipio captured New Carthage in 209 BC, he initiated a retraining programme for his army.

On the first day the soldiers had to run six kilometres in full armour. On the second they polished their armour and weapons and had arms inspection. On the third day they rested. On the fourth day they had weapons drill. Practice sword fighting was done with wooden swords covered with leather. To avoid accidents the sword had a button on the point. They also practised throwing the javelin, which similarly had a button on the point. On the fifth day there was another six-kilometre training run in full armour. On the sixth it was 'spit and polish' again. On the seventh they had another rest day, and so on.

On the march

When the retraining programme was completed the army set out to make contact with the enemy. When breaking camp everything was done in a disciplined manner. Upon the first blast of the trumpets the tents of the consul and tribunes were struck. Then the soldiers took down their own tents and packed their equipment. On a second signal the pack animals were loaded, and on a third the column set out.

In addition to his own equipment each soldier was expected to carry a bundle of palisade stakes. As Polybius says, this was not difficult as their long shields hung from their shoulders by leather straps and they only had to carry their javelins in their hands. Two, three or even four palisade stakes could be wrapped in a bundle and carried on the shoulder.

The column was usually led by the *extraordinarii*. Next came the right wing of the allies and behind them their baggage animals. They were followed by the first legion with its baggage behind. Next came the second legion followed by its baggage plus the baggage of the left wing of the allies which formed the rearguard. The consul with his bodyguard, made up of a unit of horse and foot specially selected from the *extraordinarii*, probably rode at the head of the legions. The cavalry sometimes brought up the rear of its own brigade and at other times rode on the flanks of the baggage train to keep the animals together and to screen them. If danger was expected from the rear the *extraordinarii* formed the rearguard.

One must assume that either as van or rearguard the 600 cavalry of the *extraordinarii* were dispersed and scouting. The two legions and the right and left wing of the allies exchanged positions on alternate days so that one day the right wing and the first legion led and on the next the left wing and the second legion were at the front. This manoeuvre enabled each in its turn to enjoy the advantage of the fresh water and forage.

In time of danger when the ground was open the *hastati*, *principes* and *triarii* marched in three parallel columns. If an attack was expected from the right, then the *hastati* would take up this position with the *principes* next to them so that they could turn into battle order with the *hastati* forming the front line, the *principes* the second and the *triarii* the rear (see p. 141). In this case the baggage would be on the left side of each line. If the

1

Above and below
1 A Roman military surveyor using a *groma* to lay out the camp. The *groma* enabled the surveyor to project a rectangular grid and mark out with spears the camp's grid. The example here is reconstructed from parts found in a bronzesmith's workshop at Pompeii, where it had been taken to be repaired.
2 An Etruscan horn (*cornu*). 4th–3rd century BC. Villa Giulia Museum. An almost identical horn can be seen on the sculptures from Osuna in Spain.

2

attack was threatened from the left, the *hastati* would form up on the left and baggage would be on the right. This appears to be a development of the Macedonian system. Turning into battle line could best be achieved if the maniples marched not in file but in rank—as the Macedonians did when going into battle—so that when they turned to face the enemy the front rank was in position and the files did not have to deploy. If the centuries had a ten file/six rank basic formation (see p. 141), then the soldiers would march six abreast, which is exactly what they did during the empire. The army covered an average of about 30km a day, but when necessary could march much further than this. Amongst the pioneers who accompanied the vanguard to make sure the route was clear were specialists in bridge building. Polybius mentions these when Scipio crossed the Ticino in the winter of 218 BC.

The camp
As the column approached the enemy position one of the tribunes and those of the centurions who were specifically charged with the duty of selecting the site of the encampment were sent on ahead to survey the ground and mark out the camp. They would look for a suitable stretch of open land about 800m square, preferably on raised ground. The site should not offer cover to the enemy and had to be close to water.

Having decided where the camp should be sited, they selected the spot which had the best general view of the rest of the camp and planted a white flag on top of it. This would be the site of the consul's tent (*praetorium*). This name recalls the period when the two chief magistrates were called praetors. Around this white flag an area about 30m square was measured off.

On the side of the *praetorium* best suited for watering and foraging a red flag was planted. This would be the side where the legions were to encamp. Fifteen metres from this side of the square another red flag was planted, marking the line of the tribunes' tents. These tents were pitched with their backs to the *praetorium*. A hundred feet in front of the tribunes' tents another

red flag was planted and a line was traced out parallel to the line of the tribunes' tents. Beyond this line the legions encamped. At the centre of this line the tribune set up his surveying instrument (*groma*) to measure out the rest of the camp. This instrument enabled him to draw up a rectangular grid and so mark out with spears the two main streets. The first of these (*via principalis*) ran between the line of the tribunes' tents and the line along which the legions were to be drawn up, dividing the camp laterally. The second street (*via praetoria*) ran from the point where the *groma* was placed in front of the *praetorium*, at right angles to the other street, down through the middle of the camp. Once these two roads were established he could mark out the line for the ditch and rampart.

Normally a marching camp was surrounded by a ditch about a metre deep. The earth was piled up on the inside, faced with turf and levelled off to form a low rampart. The two legions constructed the front and rear defences of the camp and the allies the lateral defences. Each maniple was allotted a section of the defences. The centurions checked that the work was done properly whilst two tribunes supervised the overall construction of each side. When encamping in the face of the enemy, far more imposing defences had to be constructed.

The baggage train was placed behind the line of the rampart (*vallum*). The *velites*, cavalry and half the heavy infantry, drawn up in battle array, were placed in front of the line. Behind this human rampart the other half of the heavy infantry set to work throwing up the defences.

The legionaries dug a trench three metres deep and four wide. The earth from the ditch was piled up on the inside and levelled off at a height of about 1.25m. The front of the rampart was faced with the turf from the ditch.

This ditch (*fossa*) and rampart (*agger*) stretched for about 700m. As the construction of the rampart proceeded the consul would withdraw the infantry maniple by maniple, but the cavalry were not brought in until the façade facing the enemy was completed.

Each soldier carried two or three stakes which he embedded in the top

of the rampart to form a fence. On a rampart with a 3,000m circuit 40–50,000 stakes would allow between 13 and 16 to a metre. These stakes were cut from trees and usually had two, three or at the most four lateral branches, all with sharpened points on one side. They were planted so that the branches intertwined in such a way that it was not easy to see which branch belonged to which stake; nor was it easy to pull out one by itself. As they were planted very close together it was difficult for more than one attacker to get hold of the same stake, and they would gash their hands trying to do so.

Once the defences were secure, the soldiers could set up the camp. The layout of the camp was always the same and every man knew exactly where to pitch his tent. The two legions encamped beyond the *via principalis* and on either side of the *via praetoria*. The cavalry were encamped *turma* by *turma*, facing the *via praetoria*, the first *turma* being nearest the *praetorium* and the tenth next to the rampart. The *triarii* were encamped back to back to the cavalry with the first maniple nearest the *praetorium*. Thus the *primus pilus* of each legion would be the nearest centurion to the general's tent.

In front of the tents of the *triarii* ran another road 15m wide along which the *principes* were drawn up facing the *triarii* and back to back with the *hastati*. Similarly, at a distance of a further 15m and facing the *hastati*, were the allied cavalry and beyond them the allied infantry. When laying out the camp a 50ft space was left between the fifth and sixth maniples/*turmae* (these were Roman feet, about 29cm). This formed another lateral road called the *via quintana*. All of these streets were marked out with spears.

The space behind the tribunes' tents on either side of the *praetorium* was used for the market (*forum*) on one side and for the office of the quaestor, who was responsible for supplies, on the other.

The select force of cavalry and infantry from the *extraordinarii* who made up the consul's bodyguard and also volunteers who were serving at the consul's request were encamped beyond the *quaestorium* and *forum* on either side. They were in constant attendance on the consul. The rest of the cavalry and infantry of the *extraordinarii* were encamped behind the *praetorium* in a similar fashion to the others with the cavalry facing the central road. On either side of the *extraordinarii*, in two rear corners of the camp, any foreign troops or allies who had come in were encamped.

For a standard-sized army of two 4,200-strong legions plus allies a space 100ft square was allotted to each maniple or *turma*. The *triarii* were allowed only 100 by 50ft. For legions which were 5,000 strong a proportionately larger space was allowed. The first tent at either end of each maniple, that is next to the road, was occupied by the centurion. If the two consuls combined forces, the two armies encamped back to back with the legions at either end of the camp.

The excavation of maniple blocks at Numantia has given us some idea of how the maniples encamped. The two centuries encamped facing inwards along either side of the square. The animals were stalled at the inside end. Many fragments of tents have been found on imperial camp sites. There is no reason to suppose that these were any different from those in use in the republic. Legionaries' tents were ten-

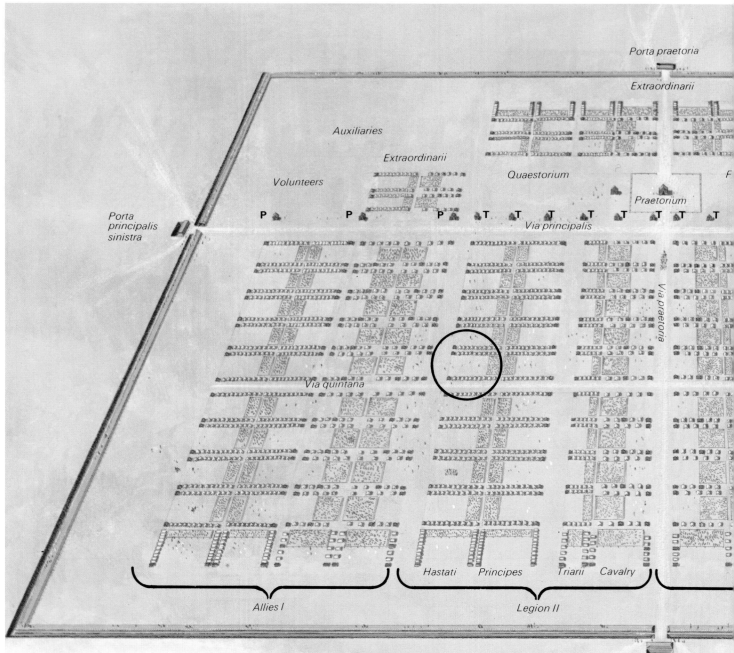

Below

A camp for two 5,000-strong legions as described by Polybius. It was about 800m square. It had three main streets (*via principalis*, *via praetoria*, and *via quintana*) and four exits (*porta decumana, porta principalis dextra, porta principalis sinistra* and *porta praetoria*). The job of guarding these exits was performed by the *velites*, who were quartered with their maniples. Other guard duties were performed by the heavy infantry. Each tent held eight men. As about a quarter of the maniple was always on duty only about 20 tents were required.

Left

1–3 The three main types of camp entrance used by the Romans. The rampart is light and the ditch dark brown. **1** Clavicular. **2** Agricolan. **3** Tutulus.

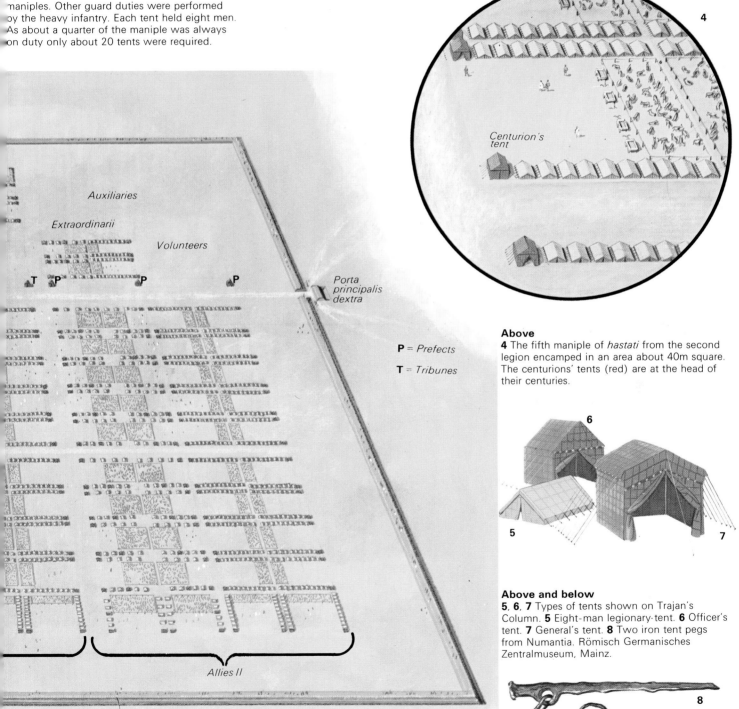

Auxiliaries

Extraordinarii

Volunteers

T   P   P   P

Porta principalis dextra

P = *Prefects*
T = *Tribunes*

Centurion's tent

Allies II

Above

4 The fifth maniple of *hastati* from the second legion encamped in an area about 40m square. The centurions' tents (red) are at the head of their centuries.

Above and below

5, 6, 7 Types of tents shown on Trajan's Column. **5** Eight-man legionary tent. **6** Officer's tent. **7** General's tent. **8** Two iron tent pegs from Numantia. Römisch Germanisches Zentralmuseum, Mainz.

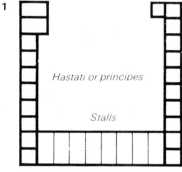

1

Hastati or principes

Stalls

2

Triarii

Stalls

3

Cavalry

Stables

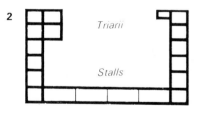

4

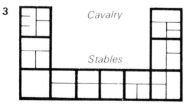

Above
The Roman army entrenching. All the *velites*, the cavalry and half the heavy infantry line up between the rampart and the enemy. The baggage train is placed behind the rampart.

1–3 Ground plans of maniple blocks from Numantia in Spain. The animals' stalls were at the back in the middle and the living accommodation down either side.
4 Reconstruction of one of the maniple blocks from Numantia in Spain. The legionaries are billeted along the sides with the centurions at the nearest end. The stalls for the baggage animals are at the back.
5–7 Three types of rampart.
5 The ordinary marching camp.
6 Marching camp in the face of the enemy.
7 A stone rampart from Numantia, Spain.

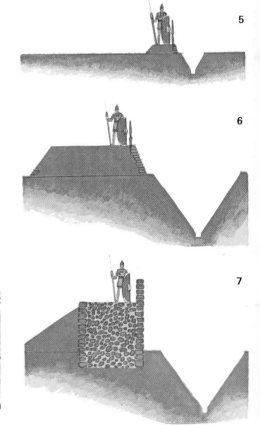

5

6

7

eet square including guy ropes. They were made of leather and held eight men and their equipment. Officers' tents as well as those of legionaries are shown on Trajan's Column.

Around the whole area marked out for the camp at a distance of 200ft from the tents the ditch and palisade were constructed.

Camp duties

After entrenching the camp the tribunes administered the oath individually to all within the camp including the slaves. Each man swore to steal nothing from the camp and to bring anything he found to the tribunes. The camp duties were divided out amongst the maniples of *principes* and *hastati*. Two maniples from each legion were responsible for keeping the *via principalis* clean, as the soldiers gathered in this 100-ft-wide thoroughfare during the day. The two maniples had to see that it was swept and watered carefully. Three of the remaining 18 maniples were assigned by lot to each of the tribunes. These maniples attended the tribune in turn on a three-day rota. They were responsible for pitching his tent and levelling the ground around it. They had to fence round any of his baggage that needed protecting and supplied guards for the front and rear of his tent where the horses were kept.

Each maniple of *triarii* had to supply a guard for the *turma* of cavalry behind it. Besides keeping a general lookout, this guard kept an eye on the horses to see that they did not injure themselves, become entangled in their tethers or get loose and cause a disturbance in the camp. Finally each maniple in turn mounted guard round the consul's tent.

The *velites*, who were free from the duties of the heavy infantry even though they were billeted with them, were responsible for guarding the rampart. The camp had four entrances at the extremities of each of the two main roads. At each entrance there was a guard of ten *velites*. Besides the guards already mentioned, at night there were usually three pickets guarding the stores at the *quaestorium* and two at the tents of each of the legates and other members of the military council. Polybius does not identify these tents, but they were presumably behind the tribunes'

tents amongst the volunteers beside the *quaestorium* and *forum*. A guard was also set over each maniple. Each guard consisted of four men, one for each of the four night watches.

At supper time each evening the hornblowers (*cornicines*) and trumpeters (*tubicines*) sounded their instruments outside the consul's tent. On this signal the guard from each maniple who was to stand the first watch was brought to the tent of the duty tribune by one of the *optiones* of his maniple. The tribune gave each guard a small tablet (*tessera*) with an individual sign on it and dismissed him to his post.

One man was selected from the tenth maniple of each class of infantry and the tenth *turma* of the cavalry, all of which were billeted at the far end of the camp under the rampart. This man was relieved of all guard duties. Each evening at sunset he too reported to the duty tribune to receive the watchword. This was inscribed on a wooden tablet. He returned to his maniple and passed the tablet in front of witnesses to the chief centurion of the next maniple. Likewise he passed it on to the next maniple until it reached the commander of the first maniple or *turma*, who returned it to the tribunes before dark.

The chief decurion of the first *turma* of cavalry in each legion had given orders early in the morning to one of his *optiones* to select four troopers to inspect the night guards. That evening the same man had to give notice to the leading decurion of the next *turma* that it was his duty to provide the guard inspectors for the next day. The four troopers drew lots for their respective watches and then went to the tribune to receive written orders from him stating what stations they were to visit and at what time. After this all four crossed the *via principalis* and waited outside the tent of either the *primus pilus* or his fellow centurion, who took it in turn to sound the night watches. At the appointed time a horn sounded the beginning of each watch.

During the first watch the trooper whose duty it was, accompanied by some friends as witnesses, made the rounds, visiting the posts mentioned in his orders and collecting the *tesserae* from each guard. If he found a man asleep or absent from his post, he

called his friends to witness it and went on with his rounds. Livy, probably following Polybius, gives a very colourful description of a legionary asleep at his post with his helmet on, his chin resting on top of his long shield, propping himself upright with his *pila*. Livy says that from this time onward (168 BC) sentries were forbidden to carry shields.

The other guard inspectors went their rounds in the other watches, visiting other posts; at daybreak they reported back to the tribune. If they had collected all the *tesserae*, they were dismissed without question. If this had not been done, the tribune could identify by the signs on them which one was missing. The tribune then summoned the centurion of the offending maniple, who brought with him the men who were on picket duty, and the trooper called his witnesses.

The tribune immediately assembled a court martial of all the tribunes, and the guard was tried. If found guilty he was condemned to suffer the *fustuarium*. He was led out and the tribune touched him with a cudgel. His comrades then beat or stoned him to death. If the failure to collect the *tessera* was the fault of the trooper he suffered the *fustuarium* instead. The same punishment could fall on the *optio* or leader of the *turma* if they had failed to give proper orders or neglected to inform the next *turma* that it was their turn to supply the patrol. Polybius remarks dryly, 'the night watches of the Roman army are most scrupulously kept'.

The *fustuarium* was also the punishment for stealing from the camp, bearing false witness, for attempting to evade duty by self-inflicted wounds, and for being convicted of the same offence three times. This punishment was also meted out for cowardice, for throwing away one's sword or shield in battle, or for lying about one's courage in battle to the tribune.

When a whole unit was found guilty of cowardice in the face of the enemy, they were subjected to decimation. The tribunes assembled the legion and led forward those who were guilty of leaving the ranks. They were lined up and ten per cent of them were selected by lot to be beaten or stoned to death. The rest were forced to eat barley instead of wheat and to pitch their tents outside the ramparts on an unprotected spot. After the battle of Cannae the survivors were all put on a ration of barley and forced to camp out all the year round. Tribunes also had the right to fine, demand sureties and flog for minor offences.

Despite this harsh discipline, not all the compulsions on a Roman to do his duty were of a negative type. Like the Macedonians the Romans had a system of rewards. For extreme gallantry they also gave gold crowns. These were awarded to the first man to mount the wall when assaulting a town (*corona muralis*) or when assaulting a camp (*corona vallaris*). After the capture of Cartagena, Scipio awarded a *corona muralis* to a legionary centurion and a marine who simultaneously reached the top of the wall. A man who saved the life of another soldier, whether citizen or ally, was crowned with an oak wreath (*corona civica*) by the man he had saved. The rescued man had to revere his saviour as he would his father for the rest of his life. Livy claims that Minucius Rufus, the *magister equitum*, did this to the dictator, Fabius Maximus, after his deliverance from Hannibal at Gerunium in 217 BC. The man who had saved an army, as Fabius had, was usually awarded the *corona obsidionalis*. This crown, made of grass, was the most coveted of all the rewards. Pliny the Elder, writing in the 1st century AD, could name only eight people who had received it.

There were also rewards given to men who had distinguished themselves by their courage in skirmishes. A man who had wounded an enemy on such an occasion was awarded a spear. An infantryman who had killed and stripped an enemy received a cup. Horse trappings were awarded to the cavalry for similar feats.

The day of battle

Every day at dawn the tribunes reported at the consul's tent. When they had received his orders for the day, they relayed them to the centurions and decurions who were waiting at the tribunes' tents. They in their turn transmitted the consul's orders down to the rank and file troops.

Like the Greek generals the consul would offer sacrifices each morning and have the omens read by the augurs who accompanied the army before offering battle. When battle had been decided on, a scarlet cloak, tied to a spear, was displayed outside the consul's tent to warn the men that battle was imminent. When the order was given, the legions assembled inside the rampart at the front of the camp and emerged by the *porta praetoria*. The allies assembled facing the two side ramparts opposite their encampments and passed out by the *porta principalis* on each side, so that each brigade would be in its correct position outside the camp with the legions in the centre. The cavalry emerged from the *porta decumana* and proceeded to deploy on the two wings.

The Roman cavalry took up their position on the right wing and the allied cavalry formed up on the left. When two consular armies were combined, all the legions must have served in the centre, as a massive blow in the centre was the basic Roman tactic. Their dismal performance against Hannibal and his enveloping movement, which was specifically designed to deal with the legions, shows that up to this point Roman generals never considered any other tactic. Even after the time of Hannibal it was not abandoned, as it required no tactical ability on the part of the general. Roman armies won battles because the legionary was the best soldier.

When drawn up for battle the *hastati* made up the first line, the *principes* the second and the *triarii* the third. As in the 4th-century legion described by Livy, gaps were left between the maniples equal to the width of a maniple so that the lines could interchange. The cavalry were similarly drawn up with spaces between the *turmae*, giving them room in which to wheel and manoeuvre.

The spaces between the maniples present the most serious difficulty in understanding the manipular formation. Did the *hastati* and *principes* really fight with gaps in their line as Polybius, by default, seems to suggest, or did they close the gaps as did the *triarii* described by Livy (see p. 128)? Some commentators have suggested that the soldiers in each maniple 'shuffled' outwards to fill the gaps. This is completely unacceptable. In the first place the ten-

dency was to close up towards the right as each man sought the protection of his neighbour's shield (centurions were chosen from men who would stand their ground to stop this happening). Secondly, the soldiers would have to disengage from the enemy and 'shuffle' back again before the lines could interchange. When looking for the answer to this problem, one should consider the method used by Polybius in explaining Roman practices. When the Romans use something entirely foreign to the Greeks, Polybius explains it in great detail: for example, their infantry shields, their camps and the boarding planks used on their ships. But when they use the Greek system, as they do for example with cavalry equipment, he does not provide any description. The explanation probably lies in the Greek system. The Greeks would have filled the gap by the simple expedient of bringing up the rear half of the unit.

Each maniple was composed of two centuries. Polybius tells us that the senior centurion served on the right. However, we know from other sources that centurions were named front (*prior*) and back (*posterior*). They could have been called right and left as were the allied brigades. The problem would certainly be solved if the centuries were lined up one behind the other, with the rear century moving up into the gap to form an unbroken line as soon as the battle began. At the battle of Cannae Polybius says that the depth of the maniples was many times their width. Such a description would be inconceivable if the centuries were drawn up side by side but quite acceptable when they are front and back.

The maniples in battle

An attempt will be made here to reconstruct a standard battle sequence.

On emerging from the camp each legion formed up in three unbroken lines with the centuries side by side. Before battle the consul would address his troops, reminding them that they were fighting for their farms and recalling their past victories. He would usually belittle the enemy, pointing out their defeats at the hands of the Romans. On a signal the *posterior* centuries turned about face and fell in behind their *prior* centuries, opening

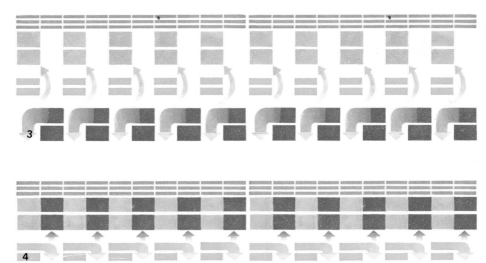

1 *Velites*

2

3

4

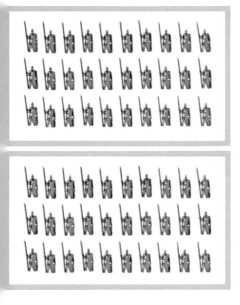

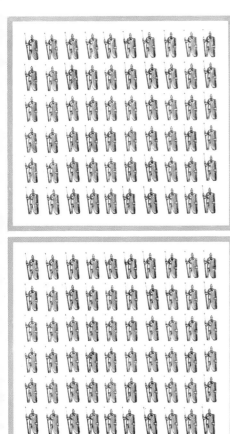

Above
A maniple of *triarii* drawn up in standard formation with a front of ten. **Below** A maniple of *hastati* drawn up in standard formation with a front of ten. A *principes* maniple would adopt the same formation.

The manipular tactic
Phase 1
The legion is drawn up in three lines with the *posterior* centuries alongside the *prior* centuries. The *hastati* are at the front and the *triarii* at the rear. On the order the *posterior* centuries withdraw and form up behind their *prior* centuries, leaving gaps in the lines. The *velites* leave their maniples and form up in front of the legion.

Phase 2
The battle is begun by the *velites*, who try to break up the enemy formation as it advances. They then retire through the gaps; the *hastati* close the gaps and charge.

Phase 3
If the *hastati* are being roughly handled, their *posterior* centuries disengage and reopen the gaps. The *hastati* then withdraw through the gaps in the *principes*, who in turn close their gaps and charge.

Phase 4
If the *principes* are also beaten, their *posterior* centuries reopen the gaps. They can now either change places with the *hastati* and let them have another go or withdraw through the gaps in the *triarii*. After this manoeuvre the *posterior* centuries of the *triarii* move into the gaps to form a solid phalanx and the whole army retreats in good order behind their spears.

up the gaps in the line. When the signal to prepare for battle was given, the *velites* left their maniples, passed through the gaps and ran forward to harass the advancing enemy, hurling a constant shower of javelins. The purpose of this was to try to break up the enemy formation in anticipation of the charge of the heavy infantry. Polybius describes this manoeuvre at the battle of Telamon. When both sides had lightly armed troops in front, this tactic was neutralised and the battle began with a skirmish. When the enemy came within range of the heavy infantry, the trumpeters sounded the recall and the *velites* retreated through the gaps. They then reformed behind the *triarii* or were dispatched to the wings to join the cavalry. Here they were customarily dispersed in the gaps between the *turmae*.

The rear centuries of the *hastati* now moved up to close the gaps and began clashing their *pila* against their shields as if impatient to get to grips with the enemy. The trumpets blared, the *hastati* raised their war cry and, cheered on by the rest of the army, rushed in hurling first their thin and then their thick *pila*. In the confusion that followed this hail of heavy javelins, the *hastati* drew their swords and charged into the enemy, throwing the whole weight of their bodies against their shields in an attempt to knock their opponents off balance. Then, allowing their long shields to rest on the ground whilst still leaning their left shoulders against them and trying to force the enemy back, they fought from behind the shield.

Sometimes this first charge was sufficient to break the enemy line. If it failed, the trumpets sounded the recall as soon as the momentum was dissipated. The *posterior* centuries disengaged and began to retreat until they were level with the rear of the *prior* centuries; then they turned to the right, presenting their shield sides to the enemy and moved across behind their *prior* centuries. Then the whole line retreated and passed through the gaps in the *principes* line. The *principes*, who were the cream of the army, now closed their gaps and on the trumpet blast charged in the same way. Usually this was sufficient to shatter the enemy, who would

turn and run. The cavalry and *velites* would then hunt down the fleeing enemy.

If, however, the *principes* were roughly handled and the battle seemed to be lost, the *hastati* would break ranks, pass through the gaps in the *triarii* and reform behind them. Now the *principes* would be given the order on the trumpet to retreat and would reopen the gaps. They would then withdraw through the *triarii*, who would move up to make the retreat easier. Once through the *triarii*, the *principes* would fill the gaps in the line of *hastati*. The *posterior* centuries of the the *triarii* would now move up to close their ranks and the whole army would retreat in good order behind a hedge of spears.

If during the battle any of the maniples became scattered, the soldiers would reform around their standards as they did at Gerunium in 217 BC.

The question of the depth of the maniples remains unanswered. With 60 heavy infantry to a century there are only three practical formations—three deep, six deep and 12 deep. These are each formed by doubling the previous formation. This 6 x 10 basic formation seems to be confirmed by the standard marching order of six abreast (see p. 135). If the standard was six deep and ten wide when the 20 *velites* were added, one arrives at the good old standard of eight men to a file, which was a sub-unit of the Roman army—a *contubernium* or a tentful. The members of a file must have shared a tent to encourage comradeship; modern military manuals call this 'small-group dynamics'. Each man had his regular place in the rank and file just as he had in the camp. Onasander confirms this when he says how wonderful it was to see the soldiers run and take up their places in the line. As he was writing in the 1st century AD, he could hardly be describing anything other than the Roman army. The man who served in the front rank, a position of honour, was probably also the senior soldier of the tent.

When the legion strength was raised to 5,000, the additional soldiers were probably used to increase the depth of the files of *hastati* and *principes* from six to eight. On the three occasions

when we know that 5,000-strong legions were used—Telamon, Cannae and Pydna—the legions either had to withstand a particularly violent charge or hoped to break through by sheer force of numbers.

The maniple could be drawn up in open order, allowing six feet per man or close order with three feet per man. The drill to form close order from open order was probably exactly the same as that of the Greeks—moving the rear half of each file into the spaces between the files. It is clear from Polybius' comparison between the phalanx and the legion that the legionary normally fought in open order with six feet per man as he says that each Roman had to face ten pikes. It follows that the Roman close order was their equivalent of the Macedonian locked shields, where there was a hoplite to every one and a half feet. Although Polybius has to be correct about the six feet per man, when the Romans went for the massed break through, as they did at the Trebbia and at Cannae, they must have formed up in close order so that they could use their weight to its maximum effect.

Something still remains to be said about the throwing of the *pila*. The suggestion that the heavy *pilum* was stuck in the ground while the lighter one was thrown, and that the legionary ran back to get it, is too ludicrous even to be discussed. He probably carried his heavy *pilum* inside his shield with the broadened part, at the junction of the metal and wood, hooked over the top of the shield. The haft could be held in place against the shield with his left thumb. I have tried this. The broadened joint seems to be designed for just this purpose. However, it must be admitted that it was very difficult to hold the haft in place with my thumb. Perhaps there was a thong on the *pilum*, or perhaps the carrying strap on the shield was wrapped round the *pilum* and grasped in the shield hand.

When the *pila* were thrown, the long thin iron shaft was expected to buckle on impact so that the enemy could not throw it back. If the *pilum* missed its mark and stuck in a shield, the barbed head prevented it from being pulled out and rendered the shield uncontrollable.

THE GREAT WARS

Rome now controlled the whole of peninsular Italy. The legions had faced up to the Macedonian phalanx under the command of one of the greatest generals of the ancient world and had shown that they were equal to anything the world could produce. In the south the Romans now gazed across the straits of Messina to Sicily. It was inevitable that Rome's expansion southwards would bring her into head-on collision with the greatest naval power of the day, Carthage, which not only controlled the African coast as far as the straits of Gibraltar, south-east Spain and Sardinia (on which she had five colonies), but also western Sicily. The east end of Sicily was controlled by the Syracusans and a band of former mercenaries, known as the Mamertines, who had seized the town of Messina a quarter of a century earlier.

The Syracusans had defeated the Mamertines and were on the point of laying siege to Messina when the Carthaginians, who were anxious to prevent the straits from falling into Syracusan hands, came to the aid of the threatened town and threw a garrison into it. At this point (264 BC) the Mamertines, not wishing to be occupied either by Syracuse or Carthage, and seeing how much freedom the town of Reggio on the opposite side of the straits enjoyed as a member of the Roman alliance, submitted to Rome.

Rome knew that to accept the submission was tantamount to declaring war on both Syracuse and Carthage, but nevertheless decided to go ahead. A military tribune accompanied by a small force was sent south by sea to garrison the town. The Carthaginians, whose fleet was patrolling the straits, were reluctant to rush into war and made only a half-hearted attempt to stop the Romans entering the town. Once the Romans had arrived the Mamertines threw out the Carthaginian garrison. Carthage retaliated by sending an army to the island, which marched along the south coast, joined forces with its erstwhile enemies the Syracusans and advanced on Messina. Meanwhile a consular army had arrived at Reggio and was ferried across the straits. The scene was now set for the longest and bitterest war in Rome's history. Over the next 120 years Rome was to wage three wars against the Carthaginians in which she lost 250,000 men and which ended in the complete destruction of Carthage and her population.

The earliest account of these wars is given by the Greek historian Polybius, who wrote about the time of the third war. Polybius had considerable military experience and a clear understanding of strategy and tactics. Unfortunately large portions of his work are missing. Livy gives an almost continuous account of events from the beginning of the second Punic war in 218 down to 167, but after that his work is also lost. As has been pointed out earlier Livy was an armchair historian with no grasp of strategy or tactics. Much of his material is drawn from Polybius, but he often supplements the Greek historian from other inferior sources and this contaminates

Below
Map showing the theatre of the first Punic war. Rome controls peninsular Italy, whilst Carthage controls North Africa, western Sicily and Sardinia. Rome's southward expansion inevitably brought on a conflict with Carthage.

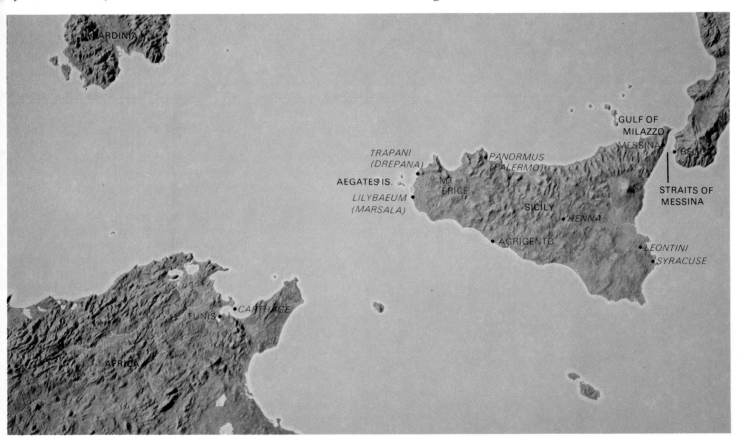

his account. There is a third source, the Alexandrian historian Appian who, in the 2nd century AD, wrote an account of Rome's wars. His work can be used to fill in the gaps left in Polybius and Livy but he is not a particularly reliable source. Only where he can be shown to be following Polybius can he be used with any confidence. In this study Polybius is practically always given precedence and often the other sources are ignored completely.

There is, however, one drawback to the use of Polybius. The Greek historian had been brought to Rome for questioning after the battle of Pydna in 168 BC. At Rome he was boarded with the Scipio family and became a close friend of Scipio Aemilianus, who was the son of Aemilius Paullus, the victor of Pydna and the grandson of the Paullus who was killed at the battle of Cannae. When his father's marriage broke up, Aemilianus was adopted by the Scipio family and his brother by the family of Fabius Maximus. Because of his involvement with these people Polybius was unable to apply his usual standards of critical analysis to their actions. His work therefore reflects the prejudices of these people and his account of the actions of the Scipio, Paullus and Maximus families must be treated with caution as he seems to have felt obliged to recount without reservation the family traditions, which are often at variance with his other sources. These he is forced to manipulate to make them fit his story.

Neither Syracusan nor Carthaginian forces felt strong enough to deal with the situation and after initial skirmishes both withdrew from Messina.

The following year (263) Rome committed both her consuls to the island and a second army crossed the straits. The two consuls decided to knock Syracuse out before dealing with the much more serious threat from the Carthaginians. They advanced on the Greek port and the Syracusans, realising that they were outclassed, submitted. The two consuls of the following year advanced along the south coast to Agrigento, where the Carthaginian forces were assembling, and laid siege to the town. The Carthaginians tried to raise the siege but suffered a serious reverse and the city fell to the Romans.

Agrigento was a Greek not a Carthaginian town, but even so the Romans sacked it and sold its inhabitants into slavery. This brutal act, though a commonplace of war, proved, as it so often has, to be counterproductive and hardened the attitude of many cities which might otherwise have proved friendly. The Romans now had to fight every inch of the way.

On the other hand the Punic fleet roamed the seas at will, ravaging the coasts of Sicily and Italy, and even regained some minor towns that had been lost.

It was clear to the Romans that if they were to compete on equal terms they must also take to the sea. During the first skirmish when the Romans were crossing to Sicily one of the Punic ships had run aground and been captured. This was now used as a model and within two months a fleet of 120 ships was launched. Realising that with inexperienced crews they stood no chance against the Carthaginian sailors, the Romans devised a boarding plank with a spike at the end which the soldiers nicknamed the raven (corvus). With this they planned to lock on to the enemy ships and board them so that they could use the invincible legionaries at sea.

With their massive fleet of unseasoned wood and men the Romans sailed south. The first 17 of their ships, and one of the consuls, fell to the Carthaginians without a blow being struck. The remainder engaged the Punic fleet in the gulf of Milazzo and against all the odds won a comprehensive victory, giving them control of the sea. This was due mainly to the use of the corvus, which took the Carthaginians completely by surprise.

The Carthaginians now realised that they would have to fight the superb Roman infantry on land and at sea and went over to the defensive. The war degenerated into a series of sieges.

By 256 the Romans had built up their fleet to 330 ships, and they decided to try to break the deadlock in Sicily by launching an invasion of Africa. The consul Regulus with 15,000 infantry and 500 cavalry landed about four days march from Carthage and immediately took the field. Twice in the following months he defeated the ill-trained

Carthaginian forces and by the end of the season was able to establish his winter quarters at Tunis within sight of the great city. During the winter the Carthaginians sued for peace but Regulus set such harsh terms that they were left with no alternative but to fight on.

In their desperation the Carthaginians handed over the drilling of the army to a Spartan officer, Xanthippus. The Carthaginians were so impressed with his performance that they handed over to him the command of the army. In the spring he marched out his troops and offered battle to the Romans lining up his phalanx with 100 elephants in front and 4,000 cavalry on the wings. The 100 elephants shattered the Roman formation and the phalanx, following up behind before they could recover, drove the legions back in confusion. Meanwhile the African cavalry stripped the Roman wings and then charged the legions from the rear. Only 2,000 escaped. The consul Regulus, with 500 men, was captured. But much worse was to come. The Roman fleet was sent to pick up the survivors. On the return journey it was caught in a storm and all but 80 ships were destroyed with a loss of perhaps 100,000 lives.

The Romans, with their usual display of stoicism, ignored this appalling disaster and built another fleet, but two years later, in similar circumstances, they lost a further 150 ships. By 251 their resources were so exhausted that they could only man 60 ships and had to surrender the control of the sea to Carthage. Meanwhile, doubting their ability ever to control the sea permanently, they decided to try to close Sicily to the Carthaginians by shutting their ports of entry. There were three of these: Panormus (Palermo) on the north coast; and Drepana (Trapani) and Lilybaeum (Marsala), both at the western end of the island. Their first step was to make a thrust along the north coast in which they captured Palermo, the most important of the Punic colonies.

In 250 the Romans made a supreme effort and managed to find the crews for 240 ships. With their new fleet they launched a combined assault by sea and land on the port of Lilybaeum and invested it.

The following year an attempt by the Romans to knock out Drepana resulted in disaster and the loss of nearly 100 warships. The consul escorting the supply fleet fell foul of the elements, losing a further 120 warships and some 800 supply vessels. Once again Rome was left without a navy. Provisions had to be hauled the length of Sicily, running the Carthaginian gauntlet, to feed the armies besieging Lilybaeum. In an attempt to rectify matters the Romans launched an attack on Mount Erice, which rises above Drepana, and captured it, thus covering their own supply route along the north coast and preventing the dreaded Carthaginian cavalry from operating freely out of the Punic port.

Both sides were exhausted and throughout 248 were content to hold their lines. But in the following year, as part of a new initiative to break the deadlock, the Carthaginians appointed the brilliant young Hamilcar Barca as commander on the island. He realised that it would be impossible to dislodge the Roman forces blockading the two western ports, but by raiding the Italian coasts he hoped to be able to draw them away from the blockade of Lilybaeum and Drepana. Failing in this he seized a hill on the north coast between Palermo and Drepana from which he could carry on the war at sea and harass the Roman supply lines. For almost three years he was able to conduct operations from this vital strategic point.

In 244 he made a daring attack on the Roman positions on Mount Erice. The Romans had built a fort on the summit and had placed another one at the foot of the mountain on the south-western side to restrict movement in and out of Drepana. Hamilcar managed to establish himself between the two forts, splitting the two forces and cutting off supplies to the garison on top of the mountain. For two years he maintained this perilous position and was only forced to vacate it when the indifference and lack of energy of his government brought the war to an end.

Right
The theatre of the second Punic war, the hardest conflict in Rome's history. Rome now controls Italy, Sicily, Sardinia and Corsica. Carthage controls North Africa, south-eastern Spain and the Balearic islands.

The lack of success in the war was having a demoralising effect at Carthage and the falling morale was reflected in the inefficient operation of the commissariat. The beleaguered garrisons soon began to feel the pinch as the expected supplies failed to arrive. In contrast Rome braced herself for the final effort and the keels for a new fleet were laid down. In the summer of 242 a new navy of 200 ships was launched and sailed south. The Carthaginian navy, unaware of Rome's new fleet, had withdrawn to Carthage to escort the long overdue supply ships, with the result that the Romans were able to seize the harbour at Drepana. When finally the supply fleet arrived off the western end of the island it was intercepted by the Roman fleet near the Aegates islands and destroyed (241 BC). This was the decisive action of the war. The starving garrisons were now at the mercy of the Romans and surrendered. Hamilcar held out for the best terms he could get but the Carthaginians were forced to make a treaty agreeing to vacate Sicily entirely and pay a large war indemnity. The losses suffered on both sides had been enormous. Polybius estimates that the Romans lost about 700 warships during the conflict and that the Carthaginians suffered losses of about 500.

After the war the Carthaginian mercenaries who had been serving in Sicily demanded their pay, and when it was not forthcoming mutinied. The Carthaginian government completely mismanaged the situation, and but for the skill of Hamilcar Barca would have been utterly defeated. Hamilcar put down the revolt with utter ruthlessness. In the confusion Rome annexed Sardinia in cynical disregard of the treaty that she had just sworn. Carthage's situation was desperate. Not only had she lost all her colonies off the Italian coast but in her efforts to retain her position in Sicily she had been compelled to divert all her resources to the island and in consequence lost her empire in Spain with its vast resources of manpower and minerals.

Hamilcar Barca, disgusted with the policies of his government which had betrayed the army in Sicily, offered his services for the reconquest of Spain. In 237 he left his native land, taking his young son Hannibal with him. He never returned, and met his death in action eight years later, after reconquering the south-east of the Iberian peninsula.

The Greek colony of Massilia (Marseilles) in southern France also had interests in Spain. The Massiliotes had been at least partially responsible for the Carthaginian losses in Spain. The colony was in alliance with Rome and there can be little doubt that Rome had

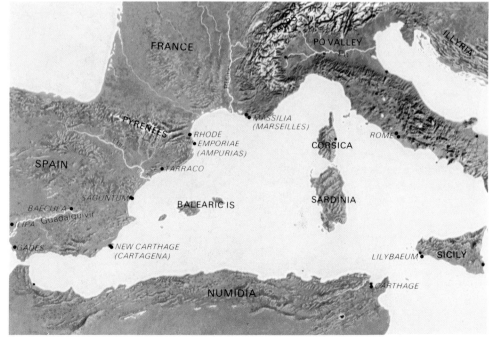

encouraged the Massiliotes in their Spanish venture. This must have had a considerable effect on the war in Sicily and may have been the cause of Carthage's inability to pay her mercenaries after the war. Now as the Punic armies thrust northwards into the Spanish hinterland, the Massiliotes found their coastal trading posts cut off from the interior. If the Carthaginians were to advance beyond the Ebro, the Massiliote colonies at Rhode and Emporiae (Ampurias) just south of the Pyrenees would be threatened. They appealed to Rome to intervene. Although the Romans were heavily committed to their preparations to meet a Celtic invasion, they sent an embassy to Spain which managed to persuade Hamilcar's successor, Hasdrubal, to accept a rather innocuous treaty agreeing not to try to extend his empire beyond the Ebro. This was a concession easily made as the Ebro flows in a southeasterly direction, leaving 95 per cent of Spain open to conquest. Five years later Hasdrubal was assassinated and Hamilcar's son Hannibal, who had come with his father to Spain as a child 16 years earlier, was elected general by the troops.

Meanwhile in Italy Rome continued her gradual expansion northwards. The legions crossed the Arno and advanced against the Ligurians, who occupied the whole of the seaboard from the Arno to the Rhône. By 230 the Romans had gained control of the coast as far as La Spezia.

On the east coast, besides the colony which had been founded at Sena Gallica (Senigallia) about 285, a second colony had been established further north at Ariminum (Rimini) in 268. During the late 230s the Romans decided to settle the area vacated by the Senones some 50 years before. Resenting this advance of the Romans towards the Po valley, the Celts began preparations for a massive invasion of the peninsula. This was held up by internal strife, but by 226 their preparations were almost complete. It was in the face of this threat that the Romans secured Hasdrubal's agreement to the Ebro treaty.

In 225 the Celts crossed the Apennines with an army of 70,000 men. It was bad timing for the Celts as the

Romans, free of any other commitment, were able to devote their entire resources to the war.

The Romans were thoroughly alarmed at the invasion but had had plenty of time to prepare. Four armies were put into the field. Each consul had a four-legion force consisting of a little over 50,000 infantry and 3,200 cavalry. One of these armies was detained in Sardinia where it had been campaigning. The other was dispatched to Rimini to cover the Flaminian route south. A third army of a similar size guarded Rome itself whilst a fourth, composed of 50,000 foot and 4,000 horse, drawn from the Sabines and Etruscans under the command of one of the praetors, covered Etruria and was probably encamped near Arezzo. Here for the first time we see the immense number of troops that Rome was capable of fielding.

The Celts did not strike at Rimini, as had been expected, but burst through the Apennines into Etruria and attacked the army there. The legions from Rimini arrived just in time to prevent a massacre and the Celts withdrew to the coast with the army from Rimini hard on their heels. On reaching the coast they started north and to their astonishment their advance foragers fell in with the army of the other consul who had crossed over from Sardinia to Pisa and was marching south towards Rome. Near Telamon, 140km north of Rome, 40,000 Celts fell fighting bravely to the end.

The threat of yet another invasion was over. The Romans vowed it would be the last. The legions now invaded the Po valley itself. In the first campaign the Boii, who lived south of the Po, were brought to their knees. The following year (223) the consul Flaminius, who was later killed by Hannibal at the battle of Lake Trasimene, crossed the Po and brought the Insubres to bay near Bergamo, wiping out their army. The Senate refused to accept the Gallic pleas for peace on any other terms than unconditional surrender. The next year 30,000 Gaesati (the ones who fought naked) crossed the Alps to assist their kinsmen in the Po valley. The Romans laid siege to the Insubrian town of Acerrae, north of the Po. In an attempt to draw off the

legions the Celts attacked the Roman supply depot at Casteggio, 50km west of Piacenza. One of the consuls, Marcus Claudius Marcellus, rushed to the relief of the town with his cavalry and light-armed troops. During the conflict the Gallic chieftain Viridomarus challenged him to single combat and although Marcellus was nearing 50 he accepted the challenge and killed Viridomarus.

Having driven off the attackers Marcellus recrossed the Po, joined forces with his colleague who had taken Acerrae and together they stormed Milan. With the fall of their principal town the Insubres surrendered unconditionally. In the following two years expeditions were sent to deal with pockets of resistance at the head of the Adriatic, but by the end of 220 all Italy except the bay of Genoa was under Roman control. The conquest was consolidated by the establishment of two colonies along the Po; one on the north bank at Cremona in the territory of the Insubres and the other on the south bank at Placentia in the territory of the Boii.

Since the annexation of Sardinia, Rome had enjoyed complete control of the Tyrrhenian Sea. With her immense navy—the legacy of her war with Carthage—it was a natural step to seek to pacify the Adriatic. The peoples of the eastern Adriatic, of whom the Illyrians were the largest, were accustomed to living by piracy and their light galleys (lemboi) were the scourge of traders in the area. During the second half of the 3rd century the power of Illyria had begun to increase and with it the arrogance of the pirates. None of the Greek states, whose sea power had declined tragically during the 3rd century, was capable of dealing with the situation. Even Macedonia, the traditional peacekeeper of the north, was both incapable and unwilling to intervene. Rome was reluctant to become involved in a situation which was no more than a minor embarrassment, but under constant pressure from Italian merchants sailing out of Brindisi, whose cargoes were being looted, she sent ambassadors to Illyria to advise restraint. When this embassy was rebuffed by the Illyrian queen Teuta, Rome invaded (229) and gained control of that part of Illyria lying opposite Brindisi which is roughly equivalent to the coast of modern Albania. This was Rome's first real overseas acquisition and opened the gates to the Greek peninsula. It was to be invaluable in years to come. In 220 trouble again flared up in Illyria which involved both the consuls and was not settled until 219. The scene was now set for the momentous events of 218 BC which plunged Rome into the greatest war in her history. The war with Hannibal is the watershed of Roman military history. Rome entered it as just another Mediterranean state but emerged 16 years later as the greatest military power in the world. It was the climax of Rome's military achievement. Never again was she put to such a test.

The preparations for the second war

Hannibal was elected commander of the Carthaginian forces in Spain in 221 BC. He was about 26 years old. For years his father Hamilcar had dreamed of continuing the war with Rome. With his three sons, Hannibal, Hasdrubal and Mago, he must have sat up late many a night around the camp fire discussing tactics and how the mighty Roman legions could be brought to their knees. In these discussions a strategy had begun to evolve. With

Hamilcar's death his plans were suspended.

His successor Hasdrubal had been a man of diplomacy but Hannibal was cast in the same mould as his father. For years 'la revanche' had been planned and now, with most of Spain secure, the time of reckoning was approaching. Doubtless if Hannibal had been in command in 225, he would have invaded Italy during the Celtic war. He knew that if the Romans invaded Spain they could expect support from many of the conquered tribes which could do great damage to the Carthaginian position. Even if the Carthaginians won they would gain little. On the other hand, if he could march a Punic army into Italy the situation would be reversed and he could expect support from Rome's traditional enemies, the Celts, Samnites and Etruscans, and so break up the federation and isolate Rome. Since that war Rome had maintained undisputed mastery of the sea. But this was of little importance as there was only one route to the Po valley, where Hannibal could expect most support, and that was by land. Before he could attempt this he had to clear the route up the coast to the Pyrenees.

About 270km north of New Carthage (Cartagena) was the lofty hill fort of Saguntum (Sagunto) which controlled

the coastal route. It presented a serious threat to the lines of communication of any army invading northern Spain, and had to be taken. It was vital to prevent the Romans from using it as a base and supplying it from the sea. In some way that none of the ancient authors explain, Saguntum, which was 140km south of the Ebro, was under the protection of Rome. It is possible that it had trading links with Marseilles and that once again it was the Massiliotes who had canvassed Roman support. Hannibal can have been in no doubt that attacking the town would precipitate the conflict with Rome. For Hannibal timing was all-important. He had to avoid being pre-empted by the Romans, who had the ability to put an army into northern Spain before he had launched his invasion.

In the meantime it was imperative to consolidate his position in Spain. He launched two campaigns into the central highlands, pushing north-west as far as the borders of modern Portugal. Returning from the second of these campaigns in the autumn of 220, Hannibal must have learned of Rome's involvement in Illyria. When both consuls for the coming year were committed to this war he knew that his opportunity had arrived and launched his assault on Saguntum. From this moment he was committed to the war. There can be little doubt that this was part of an overall strategy. Hannibal must have already planned his march on Italy; this was not something that could be done on the spur of the moment, as so many commentators have suggested, but required consummate planning. The taking of Saguntum in 219 was the first step of this plan. In the spring Hannibal launched a full-scale attack on the town and after an eight-month siege it fell.

The Romans sent an ultimatum to Carthage. It was rejected and war was declared in the spring of 218.

In the autumn of 219 Hannibal had gone into winter quarters at New Carthage. He had dismissed his Spanish

Left
A frieze showing Carthaginian arms from a triumphal monument found in Tunisia. The cuirass is probably mail. The shield on the right is North African and probably was used by the Liby-Phoenician phalanx.

forces to their own towns for the winter and prepared to hand over the government of Spain to his younger brother Hasdrubal.

He first made preparations for the defence of Carthage, sending 13,850 Spanish infantry, 1,200 cavalry and 870 slingers from the Balearic islands to Africa. For the defence of Spain he left his brother with 12,150 infantry, 500 Balearic slingers, 2,550 cavalry and 21 elephants. The accuracy of these figures, and others, is attested by Polybius who found them inscribed by Hannibal on a bronze tablet on the Lacinian promontory in southern Italy.

Hannibal had already made contact with the Celts in the Po valley. He had also made contact with the Celtic chiefs in the Alps to ensure his safe passage through the mountains. In the early spring his messengers returned to tell him that the Celts had promised help.

Hannibal now assembled a vast army of 90,000 infantry, 12,000 cavalry and about 40 elephants and prepared to bulldoze his way through northern Spain. Polybius does not give a breakdown of this army but it contained the nucleus with which Hannibal intended to invade Italy; the remainder must have been expendable. It can therefore be calculated with reasonable assurance that Hannibal's army was made up of approximately 20,000 African infantry, 70,000 Spanish infantry, 6,000 Numidian cavalry and 6,000 Spanish cavalry, the expendable elements being Spanish.

The majority of the troops fighting for the Carthaginians were foreign mercenaries. There was, however, a nucleus of both infantry and cavalry who were of half-caste Liby-Phoenician stock. This information is given by Polybius, but he does not say how many. The answer may lie in the barracks for 20,000 infantry and 4,000 cavalry which, according to Appian, was built into the walls of Carthage. In the 4th century Carthage possessed a citizen force including a Sacred Battalion which was 2,500 strong, but this was disbanded after the crushing defeat at the battle of the Crimisus river in 339 BC. From then on Carthage entrusted her defence entirely to mercenaries.

Until very recently nothing was known of Carthaginian armour, but in the past few years a monumental

building has been discovered at Chemtou in Tunisia which was decorated with a frieze of cuirasses and shields. The cuirasses, which are almost certainly mail, are of the type worn by Hellenistic officers. The shields are of two types: the oval form used by the Celts and Spaniards; and a hitherto unknown round form somewhat similar to the Argive shield but with an inset central disc and a curved rim, rather than the angled section of the rim of the Argive shield. These shields are similar to the crudely depicted Numidian shields shown on Trajan's Column and on North African gravestones and must surely be the type used by these horsemen. However, on the Chemtou monument they are shown in the form of trophies and are obviously supposed to represent captured arms. The monument is probably a *tropaeum* celebrating the victory of the Numidians and their Roman allies over the Carthaginians in 146 BC. If this is so the round shields must be those used by the Liby-Phoenicians.

The Liby-Phoenician infantry formed a Macedonian-type phalanx organised, if Polybius is to be taken literally, into *speirai*. Whether one accepts this or not, it must certainly have been composed of units of this size. The phalangite would have used the weaponry of the typical Hellenistic infantryman. On several

occasions Polybius refers to the lightly armed pikemen in Hannibal's army. These were used to perform jobs normally restricted to the lightly armed troops. On the one hand this may reflect the lighter armament of the rear ranks; on the other, the fact that it was only the heavy pike that made the phalangite cumbersome. After the battle of Trasimene (217) Hannibal armed his Africans with the best of the armour captured from the Romans—i.e. the mail shirts—and yet Polybius continues to refer to light-armed pikemen, showing that this does not imply that it was a light phalanx as so many have supposed.

On the sculpted Carthaginian galley shown on p. 270 there is a standard crowned with a disc and crescent. This symbol's frequent appearance suggests that it was the standard of Carthage. It cannot be a coincidence that these symbols appear on Roman manipular standards in the imperial period and might suggest the origin of the Roman *signum*.

The bulk of the Carthaginian army was made up of foreign mercenaries. They came from many sources: Celts, Spaniards, Balearic islanders (who were famous for their slingers), Ligurians, half-caste Greeks (mainly deserters and runaway slaves) and the largest element, the North Africans. Carthaginian discipline must have been imposed on

these troops and one would have expected them to serve under Carthaginian officers. However, it is clear from Polybius' account of the siege of Lilybaeum, in the first Punic war, that the mercenaries served under their own officers, as the superior mercenary officers tried to betray the town to the Romans. From this it would seem that the Carthagians only commanded at battalion level, much as the Romans were to do in the later republic. The remarkable success of Hannibal, whose army was 50 per cent Celtic, is a great tribute to the Carthaginian system. No attempt was made at uniformity; each native group fought in its own way and had to be used to its best advantage. Hannibal's relationship with his troops was equally remarkable. In spite of their diverse backgrounds they stuck with him for 15 years with never a whisper of a mutiny. The ignominious story told by Diodorus, that in 203 BC Hannibal massacred those mercenaries who would not cross over to Africa with him, is certainly false. Hannibal could never have shipped more than a few of his men to Africa as he had no navy. Even with a large fleet he would not have escaped attacks by the Roman navy. The Romans probably offered terms to the bulk of Hannibal's army which had been left behind and then slaughtered them.

Apart from the Liby-Phoenicians, the African troops that Carthage recruited in greatest numbers were the remarkable Numidian cavalry. Numidia roughly corresponds with modern Algeria. The camel had not yet been introduced into North Africa and the horse was ridden everywhere. In fact the nomadic tribesmen lived on horseback. They used no bridle or bit and rode bareback. Like the Indians in America they made superb light cavalry. In fact they were so good that whoever controlled them would win a North African war. Scipio Africanus' greatest achievement was to persuade the Numidians to change sides at the end of the war with Hannibal. The change was absolutely decisive.

When at the end of the 2nd century BC Rome became involved in a war with the Numidians, they proved so hard to conquer that the careers of more than one Roman general ended in humiliation because of his inability to inflict a decisive defeat on them.

Numidian cavalry were useless as shock troops, but like the Aetolians were superb in a skirmish or in the pursuit of a fleeing enemy. At the battle of Cannae they were unable to break Rome's allied cavalry, but the moment that this had been achieved by the Celts and Spaniards the pursuit was left to the Numidians.

Above A reconstruction of a Numidian horseman based on the reliefs from Trajan's Column and the description of Polybius. The horse had neither bridle nor bit. The rider controlled his mount with his legs. The Numidians, who were the best light cavalry in the ancient world, were very similar to the 19th-century American Indians. They were unsuitable as shock troops, but were superb skirmishers and relentless pursuers of a broken enemy. Although they failed to break the Roman cavalry at Cannae, they were merciless in their pursuit once this had been accomplished by the Spaniards and Celts. **Left** South Italian terracotta statuette showing a Numidian horseman in characteristic pose. Louvre Museum. 3rd century BC. **Right** Numidian horseman shown on Trajan's Column. The horses have no harnessing except a neck strap, which the figure in the top right-hand corner is clutching. Although the diminutive size of the horses is exaggerated, these animals were no bigger than ponies. The men are armed with round shields of the North African type. This is confirmed by several crude North African sculptures.

Above

Spanish weaponry. 4th–2nd centuries BC.
1 A *saunion*, a heavy iron javelin with barbed point. From Almedinilla.
2 *Pilum* type javelin head from Arcobriga.
3 Spearhead from Almedinilla.
4 *Falcata* from Almedinilla (Cordoba).
5 Straight cut-and-thrust sword (*gladius hispaniensis*) from Aguilar de Anguita.
6 Dagger from Almedinilla.
7 Spanish dagger from Numantia.
8 and **9** Spear butts.
10 Knife of the type that was fixed to the *falcata* scabbard.
All weapons scale 1:8.

The Numidians were like mounted peltasts. Their tactic was to dart in close to the enemy, throw their javelins and then retreat, making sure never to come into contact. Again and again the Carthaginians used the Numidians to draw enemies on to unfavourable ground or into an ambush.

The Numidians are portrayed on Trajan's Column in Rome where they are seen pursuing Dacians. Their horses have nothing but a neck strap. The riders have a round shield and short tunic but wear no armour. Samples of iron javelin heads and a sword with a blade approximately 60cm long have been found in a 2nd-century BC prince's grave at Es Soumâa in Algeria.

After the Africans the soldiers most valued by the Carthaginians were the Spaniards. These were drawn from south-eastern Spain and should more exactly be referred to as Celtiberians— a mixture of Spanish and Celtic stock. Spanish infantry and cavalry formed a small but important part of Hannibal's army. Of the 20,000 infantry who reached Italy, 8,000 were Spanish. There were three types of infantry

Below

12–15 Sculptures from Osuna in southern Spain. **12** Swordsman with Celtic type shield and sinew cap. **13** Cap of the same type. **14** Warrior with Spanish shield, *falcata* and sinew hood. **15** Hood of similar type. **16** Warrior shown on a vase from Liria.

grouped under the general heading o[f] Spanish in Hannibal's army: swords men, javelineers and slingers. Th[e] latter came from the Balearic island[s] off the east coast of Spain and wer[e] renowned for their skill in slingin[g] heavy stones. Polybius states that th[e] swordsmen were armed with a larg[e] shield of Celtic type and a short cut and-thrust sword. They wore shor[t] white tunics bordered with purple (b[y] this he probably means crimson) Sculptures from Osuna in souther[n] Spain show warriors who fit Polybius description well. A second type o[f] infantry who were probably javelineer[s] are mentioned by Diodorus. They ar[e] armed with round shields and appea[r] to be the same as the lightly arme[d] troops called *caetrati* by Caesar. Liv[y] uses this word to describe the peltast[s] of Philip V's army. These are als[o] shown on the Osuna reliefs. Their shields have a central boss and they wear loose tunics which come down to just above the knee.

The Spanish sword gained immortality when it was adopted by the Romans. The legionary sword, *gladius*

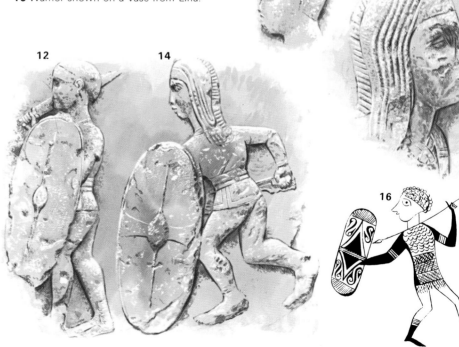

Above

11 Tombstone of a Spanish mercenary showing his shield, helmet, sword and two spears from Tunisia.

hispaniensis, was the pointed sword (**5**). However, the commonest type found in Spain was the elegant curved *falcata* (**4**). This was a cut-and-thrust weapon. The average length of a *falcata* blade was only 45cm. It is clear from a fragment of a statue (not shown here) that the sword was suspended on the left side. These swords sometimes had a short knife attached to the scabbard.

A large number of daggers have also been found (**6**, **7**). These are the forerunners of the Roman dagger. The Spanish also used a short *pilum* but the most extraordinary weapon was the *saunion* (**1**). This was a barbed javelin made entirely of iron.

Some of the soldiers on the Osuna reliefs are wearing a most striking crested headgear. The Greek geographer Strabo tells us that the Iberians wore caps of sinew. This is most likely what is shown here. The crest proves that it cannot be the soldiers' hair. These hoods are very similar to those shown on sculptures found in southwest France (see p. 122). The caps shown on **12** and **13** seem to be a simplified version of these hoods. These are

Above
17 Bronze figurine of a 3rd-century Spanish cavalryman wearing a sinew cap and armed with round shield and *falcata*. Valencia de Don Juan Museum, Madrid.
18 Front view of **17** showing round shield with central handgrip and broad belt.
19 Sculpture of a horse showing its bridling and saddle blanket. From El Cigarrelejo, 4th century BC. Sr. E Cuadrado Collection, Madrid.

Above
20 Reconstruction of a Spanish horseman of the time of Hannibal. He wears a sinew cap and a white tunic trimmed with crimson. He is armed with a round central handgrip shield, spear and *falcata*.

Above and left
21 Reconstruction of a Spanish infantryman of the time of Hannibal. Hannibal assembled some 70,000 Spanish infantry at the start of his campaign, his army's most expendable element. He wears a sinew hood with horsehair crest and a white tunic trimmed with crimson. He is armed with a Celtiberian spined oval shield, spear, *saunion* and *falcata*. He might alternatively have used the straight two-edged Spanish sword.
22 and **23** Two types of Spanish snaffle bit found at Aguila de Anguita in southern Spain.

worn by the *caetrati*. A few bronze helmets have been found, but they are very rare.

Spanish cavalry, like that of the Romans and Celts, is rather confusing to a modern reader for it is quite clear that these horsemen often dismounted and fought on foot. Sometimes a horse would carry two men and one would jump off to fight. The Spanish horseman used a small round shield with a central handgrip like that of the *caetratus* (see **17** and **18**, p. 151).

The rider is dressed like an infantryman and appears to be wearing the same type of headgear. In his right hand he holds a *falcata*.

The horse (**19**) shows the bridling and a saddle blanket held in place by a girth strap. Statues also sometimes show the Hellenistic type of saddle. Horsebits are usually of the snaffle type and come in many forms. The ring (**23**) and crescent (**22**) types are the most common.

It is clear from the many representations of elephants on Carthaginian coins that the war elephants used by the Punic armies were African. The Carthaginians hunted the forest elephant in Morocco and also on the edge of the Sahara desert at the oasis of Ghadames some 800km south of Carthage. These elephants were introduced during the first war with Rome at the time of the siege of Agrigento in 262 BC and were

used against infantry as well as cavalry. They shattered the Roman morale and for a long time the Romans would not face them. They won their laurels in 255 when they trampled Regulus' legions into the dust on the Bagradas plains. Finally, during the siege of Palermo in 250, the Romans captured some of these beasts and so regained their confidence. These elephants, like the larger African bush elephant, had a saddle back and the Carthaginians rode them like a horse.

Having subjugated the area north of the Ebro, Hannibal left Hanno there with a garrison of 10,000 foot and 1,000 horse to keep the road open. Leaving behind all the heavy baggage, including his siege equipment, he pushed on across the Pyrenees with 50,000 infantry, about 9,000 cavalry and the elephants.

The Romans also planned to fight the war overseas on two fronts, and the two consuls for 218 BC drew lots for their provinces. Tiberius Sempronius Longus drew Africa and Publius Cornelius Scipio drew Spain. Whilst enrolling their legions they gave orders for the establishment of two colonies in the Po valley at Cremona and Placentia. Each of these received about 6,000 colonists who were ordered to report there within 30 days. The two colonies had hardly been established when the Boii and Insubres, in anticipation of

Above
The reverse of a Carthanginian coin from the time of Hannibal showing an African elephant, easily identifiable by its large ears and saddle back. From Cartagena.

Below
Map illustrating the campaign of Scipio and Hannibal in the autumn of 218 BC. The Po valley had only just been conquered by the Romans, who had established two new colonies at Placentia and Cremona.

Hannibal's arrival, rose in revolt and attacked the legion that was stationed here under the command of a praetor. Polybius refers to this legion as the fourth. It can therefore only be the legion of that number from the previous year which must have been ordered to winter in the Po valley. As this is the first legion mentioned in connection with this war, for the sake of clarity it will be called the first, and all subsequent legions will be numbered consecutively in the order of their enrolment.

It is possible that Hannibal engineered the Gallic revolt to hold up Scipio's preparations. The consul was obliged to dispatch one of the legions he was enrolling (the second) to the Po valley and raise a replacement from the allies.

The Romans' manpower resources were enormous, and these were to be the decisive factor in the war. During the threat of the Gallic invasion in 226 the Senate had ordered a survey of their resources which was recorded by Polybius. This showed that Rome could draw upon a pool of 700,000 infantry and 70,000 cavalry. Of these 150,000 infantry and 26,000 cavalry came from the regions of Samnium, Lucania and Calabria, all three of which were lost to the Romans after the battle of Cannae.

It was early summer before the two armies set out. Longus, with 160 quinqueremes, sailed for Lilybaeum in Sicily with his two legions, the third and fourth, ready for the invasion of Africa. Scipio, with 60 galleys, sailed along the coast of Liguria to Marseilles and dropped anchor off the eastern mouth of the Rhône with the fifth and sixth legions.

The march to Italy
Hannibal's route from Spain to Italy is a subject of fierce contention. I have spent many years tracking down the various possible routes and have concluded that, with the exception of a considerable deviation at the beginning of his march into the Alps when he was trying to lose Scipio's army, Hannibal took the straightforward route from Spain to the Po valley: up the valley of the Durance and down the valley of the Dora Riparia to the area of Turin.

A reconstruction of this crossing is given first, with a full argument in justification at the end.

Scipio had arrived at the mouth of the Rhône while Hannibal was still fighting his way through northern Spain. Here he waited for intelligence of the situation north of the Ebro. He knew that Hannibal had crossed the river, but lacking reliable intelligence he felt unable to attempt a landing. The next information that Scipio received was that Hannibal had crossed the Pyrenees and was advancing across southern Gaul, apparently to attack Marseilles and knock out Rome's halfway house. Scipio decided to remain where he was and meet the invader in friendly territory, with Marseilles behind him and without overstretching his lines of communication with Italy.

Hannibal, meanwhile, was following the coast road towards the Rhône. This road skirted the marshy coast as far as Lunel, where it veered north-east towards Nîmes to avoid the marshes of the Rhône delta before turning due east to approach the Rhône at Beaucaire. From here the road followed the valley of the Durance into the Alps, crossed the Montgenèvre pass and descended the valley of the Dora Riparia into Italy. Hannibal's spies had informed him that Scipio was at the mouth of the Rhône, and in order to avoid encountering him while he was trying to cross the river he continued in a north-easterly direction, planning to cross near Avignon and so place the river Durance, which flowed into the eastern side of the Rhône, between himself and Scipio.

On reaching the river the Carthaginians bought up all the available craft, of which there was a great number as the natives carried on a maritime trade. In two days they had collected a vast number but by now the far bank of the river was thronged with hostile natives. Hannibal realised that he could not make the crossing in the face of such formidable opposition, and on the third night after his arrival sent off a detachment of his army with native guides to cross further upstream. These soldiers marched about 40km up the river and crossed where it divided, forming an island. Here they rested for a day. It took them a further two nights to get into position to attack the force on the east side of the river.

A little before dawn on the fifth night Hannibal embarked his men, filling the boats with his light cavalry and the canoes with his light infantry. The larger boats were placed upstream to break the current. Two men at the back of each boat held the lead reins of six or seven horses which were to swim behind.

When the barbarians saw the Carthaginians preparing to cross, they poured out of their camp and thronged the river bank. As soon as the prearranged smoke signal appeared on the opposite bank, Hannibal ordered his soldiers to pull out against the current. The rest of the army cheered on their comrades whilst the natives on the far bank screamed their war cries and pranced around brandishing their swords and bragging of their past deeds. As the boats approached the shore, part of the detachment already on the far side of the river attacked the Celts in the rear whilst the rest set fire to their deserted camp. Taken completely by surprise the barbarians fled, leaving the landing unopposed.

During the remainder of the day Hannibal managed to get the rest of his men across and pitched camp on the east bank of the river. There remained only the problem of getting the elephants across the Rhône. The following morning he dispatched 500 of his Numidian cavalry with orders to cross the Durance and check the whereabouts and numbers of the Romans.

Meanwhile some Celtic chieftains who had crossed the Alps to meet the army were introduced to the soldiers. They encouraged the troops, telling them of the welcome and the booty that awaited them beyond the Alps, and promised to lead them by an easy route across the mountains. Amid conflicting reports Scipio had sent out his cavalry to reconnoitre. When the Numidians encountered them they naturally withdrew at top speed to report to Hannibal. The Roman cavalry, interpreting this withdrawal as flight, claimed a victory and pursued the Numidians to within sight of the camp on the east side of the Rhône before returning at top speed to make a report to Scipio.

Hannibal, believing that his Numidians had fallen in with the cavalry screen advancing ahead of the legions,

Below
The elephants being towed across the Rhône.
According to Polybius several fell into the river
and waded across with their trunks above the
water. The mahouts were unfortunately
drowned.

was forced to make a quick decision. It was essential to his overall strategy that he reached Italy with his army intact. He could not afford to risk a battle in the Rhône valley. Fully aware that the Durance route was now out of the question, he also realised that it was imperative that he lose Scipio. So he ordered his infantry, with the baggage train, to press on up the Rhône at first light. He then drew out his cavalry along the north bank of the Durance with orders to stop the Romans crossing the river. With their position secured they set about getting the elephants across.

The elephants were terrified of the fast-flowing river which is between 200 and 500m wide. The sappers had built a number of very solid rafts about seven metres wide. They lashed two of these together side by side and moored them to the river bank. By adding pairs

of these rafts they built a pier about 15m wide extending out into the river. These rafts were secured by cables attached to trees on the river bank. In this way the sappers managed to build a jetty about 60m long. Two sturdy rafts were lashed securely to the jetty in such a way that they could easily be cut free. The rafts were then covered with earth so that they would appear to be a continuation of the path that led down to the river.

The elephants were lured onto the jetty by two females which were led on first. As soon as they reached the last rafts they were cut loose and towed across by rowing boats. At first the elephants were terrified and jostled around, but when they saw the water on all sides they froze with fear and huddled together in the middle of the raft. In this way most of the animals were ferried across. Some, however,

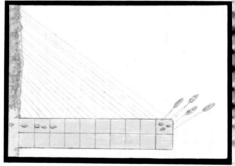

Above
The jetty made of a double line of 8m square rafts moored to the trees on the west bank of the Rhône. The elephants were lured on to the jetty by the females. When they reached the last raft they were cut loose and towed across by rowing boats.

fell trumpeting into the river halfway across, drowning their mahouts. Polybius insists, however, that the elephants managed to breathe by holding their trunks above the water and walking along the bed of the river, almost certainly impossible when one considers the depth of the river and the force of the current. Nobody seems to be willing to put Polybius to the test by throwing an elephant into the Rhône.

When all the elephants were across, Hannibal recalled his cavalry, formed them up with the elephants as a rearguard, and set off in pursuit of his infantry.

Hannibal's precautions were unnecessary as Scipio had not moved. His cavalry, which had approached the Punic camp late in the day, probably did not reach their own camp until the next day. It is impossible to say what went through Scipio's mind, but something seems to have spurred him into action. Perhaps it was the information that Hannibal had not crossed at the regular crossing place, or perhaps it was an apprehension that something was amiss. He immediately put all his baggage and unnecessary equipment aboard ship and with his men stripped down for forced marching raced north. However he did not reach the crossing place until three days after Hannibal had left and found his camp deserted. Polybius says that Scipio was 'highly astonished', and not without reason, for only at this moment does he seem to have realised that Hannibal was heading for Italy. One can imagine the consul's feelings as he raced back towards the coast. He had let Hannibal through. Italy lay wide open and virtually undefended.

On reaching the coast Scipio ordered his brother to take the army on to Spain in accordance with the dictates of the Senate while he sailed back to Italy at top speed.

The Carthaginian army marched steadily northwards for four days. At this point the scouts who had been left behind to report on Scipio's activities caught up with the army and informed Hannibal that the pressure was off. The four-day march had brought them to the junction of the Isère about 130km upstream from the junction of the

Durance. The triangular area caught between the Isère and the Rhône was known as the 'Island' because it was surrounded on two sides by the Rhône and its powerful tributary the Isère, which effectively cut it off from the south, west and north, and was hemmed in on the east by the almost impenetrable Chartreuse Massif and the Mont du Chat.

A civil war was raging on the 'Island' as two brothers contended for the throne. Hannibal intervened and drove one of the brothers out. In return the 'Islanders' supplied the army with an abundance of corn and other provisions. They replaced their worn weapons and supplied most of them with warm clothing for the Alpine crossing as it was already autumn and the nights were becoming bitter. When the army set out again the 'Islanders' provided an escort to cover the rear of the army during their passage through the territory of the Allobroges, a particularly ferocious Celtic tribe.

During the winter Hannibal had paid large sums to secure his route along the Durance valley and it was essential to return to this route now that Scipio was no longer at his heels. The 'Islanders' would have informed him that it was quite easy to get back to his original route by crossing one of the low passes that separated the upper reaches of the Drac from the valley of the Durance. This would bring him back to his original route near Chorges, cutting 150km off the distance entailed by retracking to the junction of the Durance. The new route involved following the Isère round the northern end of the Vercors and then following its tributary the Drac to its source. For ten days the army marched slowly along first the Isère and then the Drac, foraging as they went in preparation for the rigours ahead. As the Drac entered the mountains so they began to climb. Here the 'Islanders' left them, the mountains crowded in on either side and they began to climb the gentle slope towards the distant pass. While they remained on the flat ground the Allobroges—fearing both the cavalry and the 'Islanders'—had left them alone. When the Celts saw the army beginning to stretch out along the narrow track, they occupied key positions along the

route and prepared to dispute the passage. Had they only kept their positions secret they might have inflicted serious casualties on the Punic army, but being Celts they went through their ritual bragging and so gave themselves away. Hannibal called a halt, pitched camp on the flat ground at the foot of the track and sent out his Celtic guides to reconnoitre. They returned after nightfall to report that the Allobroges had abandoned their posts and retired to a local town for the night. The following day Hannibal advanced as far as he could along the road and then encamped not far from the enemy. That night he ordered all the camp fires to be kept burning and advanced with part of his army to occupy the enemy positions which had again been deserted. The next morning he began moving his army through.

At first the Allobroges accepted the *fait accompli*, but when they saw the long string of baggage animals slowly moving along the narrow path their greed overcame their caution and they attacked at several points. Here the Drac flowed through a deep ravine and the road clung perilously to the hillside above it. In the confined space the slightest jostling was sufficient to cause the animals to lose their footing and plunge into the gorge below. The barbarian attack threw the baggage train into tumult with wounded horses running amok, sending other animals hurtling over the brink. Realising that he was in danger of losing all his supplies, Hannibal took the guards who had occupied the key points during the night and managed to gain the upper ground. From there he launched a counterattack which resulted in his troops suffering heavy casualties.

The army finally managed to force its way through and capture the town from which the Allobroges had come. Here they found enough corn and cattle to last them for two or three days. They remained at the town for the rest of the day before continuing their journey. The route was now much easier, with the road running through open fields. On the second day they crossed the Col de Manse and ascended into the broad open valley of the Durance. By the fourth day after leaving the town (the sixth day of the ascent) the army had passed the Celtic strongholds at Chorges and Embrun which had been paid off the previous winter and was approaching the junction of the Guil. Here they were met by natives, from higher up the valley, carrying olive branches and wreaths as signs of friendship. These were probably willow branches, which are plentiful in this area whereas olive trees are not. The natives offered to guide the army along the next particularly difficult stretch of the route. Hannibal was suspicious but felt it best to accept their offer. As a precaution he placed the cavalry at the head of the column and the infantry at the back, with the baggage train in the centre.

For several days the army had been marching through open country, but now the mountains began to crowd in again. On the eighth day of the ascent they reached the point just north of modern l'Argentière-la-Bessée, where the Durance passes through a narrow gorge. Here the road takes to the hillsides and once more the troops were strung out along a narrow path.

The army was carrying with it an immense amount of gold to pay for the mercenaries Hannibal planned to hire in Italy. For safekeeping this was being conveyed by the African infantry. The natives had obviously got wind of this and chose this spot for an ambush. When the cavalry and much of the baggage were already through the most difficult section of the gorge, they attacked from the higher ground, throwing stones and rolling boulders down the hillside. Beyond the gorge the road again descends to the valley, but here a huge rocky spur juts out from the eastern side, leaving only a narrow passage. When the cavalry and baggage had passed this point and dusk was beginning to fall, the Celts charged down into the valley, cutting the army in half and leaving the infantry, and Hannibal with it, trapped in the defile.

The night was spent among the bare rocks. On the following morning, in fear of the cavalry, the Celts withdrew and the army dragged itself up to the broad open summit of the pass some 20km away. Here they encamped for two days to allow the stragglers to catch up. The ascent had taken the Punic army nine days.

Snow had already gathered on the summit and morale was very low. To raise their spirits Hannibal pointed down the other side of the pass toward Italy, indicating not only the direction of the Po valley, where the Celt awaited them, but also that of Rome itself. In later years, their memorie undoubtedly clouded by the trauma of their experiences, the soldiers believed that they had actually been able to see Italy and even Rome itself from the top of the pass.

The next day the Punic army broke camp and began the descent. The path was narrow and once again they had to pass along the edge of a ravine. Fresh falls of snow had covered the track and all who missed their footing were dashed headlong down the precipice. In places fresh snow had fallen on top of the snow which remained from the previous winter. Here the soldiers' feet

Below
The site of the second ambush, where the Durance passes through a narrow gorge. The rocky spur is on the left. This was where Hannibal's army was cut in two by a determined Celtic attack.

unk through the thin covering of fresh now and slid on the packed snow beneath. In contrast the hooves of the animals broke through the packed snow and they became trapped there. Further down problems multiplied as the path had been carried away by a landslip over a distance of about 300m. Hannibal tried an alternative descent, but this proved impassable and the army was forced to camp along the ridge while the road was rebuilt. The Numidians were set to work in relays and within a day they had made a path sufficiently wide to get the horses and pack animals down. These were turned out to pasture on the lower ground, which was free from snow, but it was another three days and freezing nights before the road was wide enough to get the elephants across.

From the foot of the precipice the going was comparatively easy and three days later the ragged remnants of the great army that had set out from Cartagena five months before staggered into the valley of the Po.

The climate
Before examining Hannibal's route through southern Gaul and across the Alps, one must consider the climate of the period. Recently, in order to justify taking Hannibal over a very high pass, it has been claimed that the climate was much the same as it is today. But is this claim justified?

In 1966 selected papers of the distinguished meteorologist H. H. Lamb were published under the title *The Changing Climate*. These give us a very different picture of climatic conditions in the time of Hannibal and are of particular value as the author had no interest in Hannibal's crossing of the Alps. In brief this is Lamb's picture of Europe in the pre-historic and ancient periods. Between 4000 and 2000 BC, in the wake of the retreating ice of the last glacial epoch, there was a warm dry period known as the 'post-glacial climatic optimum'. During this time the world temperature rose to 2–3 degrees Centigrade above the present norm. In the succeeding millennium, however, the climate deteriorated.

Between 900 and 500 BC the temperature fell rapidly to about 3 degrees Centigrade below its present level. This

was followed by heavy rain. The rainfall reached heights unknown since the Ice Age. In the southern Mediterranean the arid land blossomed, but what was a blessing for Greece, Italy and Spain was a disaster for the rest of Europe. The rainfall reached a climax about 400 BC. At first the lowlands became marshy, then they flooded. The prehistoric tracks became impassable and transport took to the water. The much lower temperature not only caused a lower rate of evaporation at low levels but also caused a similar decreased rate of de-icing at high levels. As a result, while the marshes advanced in the valleys the glaciers increased on the heights.

In Switzerland the enormous rainfall flooded the lakes: Bodensee rose ten metres, an almost incredible amount when it is considered that it feeds the Rhine. The lake dwellers were forced to abandon their villages and never returned. All over Europe tribes driven from their homelands began to move southwards, breaking in a succession of waves on southern Europe. The Celtic invasion of Spain and Italy was the most striking result of this movement. This migration was not halted until the conquest of Gaul by Caesar in the 1st century BC. From this period onwards there was a gradual increase in temperature which reached a climax between 800 and 1000 AD. The temperature then began to drop again, bringing on the 'Little Ice Age' which occupied the period between the 16th and 19th centuries.

It is quite meaningless to quote examples of medieval mines, or for that matter Roman ones that have been uncovered by the retreat of the glaciers after the 'Little Ice Age', as there is now no argument that the temperature during the Roman empire and later was warmer.

The situation in the 17th century was probably quite similar to that of Hannibal's time. Polybius himself supports this when he says that the passes of the Alps were snow-covered all the year round. This statement has to refer to the lowest passes as these are the ones that must have been in use. He also tells of flooded marshlands near Florence which Hannibal had to cross when he invaded central Italy in

217. All this fits in well with Lamb's description. It is against this background that one must examine Hannibal's route to Italy.

The historians
There have been many accounts of Hannibal's march from Spain to Italy. Each of these, with its own axe to grind, takes Hannibal by a different route. The quality of these accounts varies from the scholarly to the ridiculous. The commentators vary widely and include such people as Mark Twain, Napoleon and Sir Gavin de Beer, who was once Director of the Natural History Museum in London. The author has spent many years tracking down these various itineraries and feels that the time is ripe for a new approach to these studies.

Both Polybius and Livy give an account of the crossing. It is generally agreed that Livy's account is corrupt and that he is probably mixing two contradictory sources. It is impossible to reconcile Polybius and Livy. Livy's account has therefore been rejected and this study is based exclusively on Polybius.

Before beginning a study of Hannibal's march all commentators should carefully read *Polybius III*, 47, 6–12. In this passage the historian dismisses all claims that Hannibal used an unknown pass, got lost or took an extremely difficult route. He also says that he himself had inspected the passage of the Alps, 'to learn for myself and see'. Polybius further states that he can see no point in recording places with names that will mean nothing to his readers. It therefore follows that when he does name a place it was certainly well-known to the Greeks, and conversely when he does not name a place, it is for the simple reason that no well-known place was there.

The routes from Spain to Italy
At the time of Hannibal there were two main routes linking Italy and Spain. These were familiar to the ancients as the legendary routes of Hercules. One of these routes led from Tuscany along the Ligurian coast. The other crossed the Alps from the Po valley. The two routes met at the Rhône, which they crossed at Beaucaire-Tarascon, and

hen continued along the coast to Spain. The route over the Alps to Spain was superseded in about 118 BC by the Roman Via Domitia. This poses the question: were the Via Domitia and the route of Hercules one and the same?

The suggestion that the Romans cut an entirely new route through the Alps when they built the Via Domitia is clearly ludicrous. This was neither practical nor the Roman way. The easiest way would have already been established by travellers and merchants who had trodden this route for centuries. The Romans would merely have improved and paved what was already here. This road is the lowest, widest and easiest route through the Alps. It is also the shortest route to the Po valley. Travelling along the Via Domitia the distance from Nîmes, on the west side of the Rhône, to Casale Monferrato, in the Po valley where all the routes would meet, is 481km. The shortest route via the Col de Larche is approximately 500km. Travelling up the Isère valley and over the Little St Bernard, the Clapier or the Mont Cenis passes would stretch the distance to over 600km. These are all the low passes in the western Alps. These figures offer a simple explanation of the route followed by the Via Domitia.

For precisely the same reasons the route of Hercules must have followed the same course. The route from Tarascon is studded with Celto-Ligurian towns and *oppida*. Segustero (Sisteron), Caturiges (Chorges), Eburodunum (Embrun), Brigantio (Briançon) on the western side of the pass and Segusio (Susa) on the eastern side all have Celtic names and therefore must have been there before the Romans built their route. There were also *oppida* near Apt and Mont Dauphin and two more between Manosque and Sisteron. These factors make out an overwhelming case for the existence of a pre-Roman route along the Via Domitia.

The pseudo Aristotle writing in the second half of the 3rd century BC—

about the time of Hannibal—confirms this when he refers to an Alpine route on which one had to pay a toll to the Celto-Ligurian people living along it. This must be a reference to the same southern route, as the Ligurians could hardly be connected with a northern route. It may therefore be stated that there was a well-known route from Spain across the Alps to Italy which was in use at the time of Hannibal and that it followed the same route as the Roman Via Domitia.

Polybius' three check points
In his account of the journey from the Pyrenees to the Po valley Polybius gives us three checkpoints: the first is the road from the Pyrenees to the Rhône; the second is a stretch of land called the 'Island' which lies between the Rhône and one of its tributaries, and the third is the pass by which Hannibal entered Italy. Polybius gives a graphic description of the second and third checkpoints and identifies the first.

1. The road to the Rhône
When Hannibal planned his invasion of Italy there can be little doubt that he intended to use the route of Hercules across the Alps to reach the Po valley. During the winter of 219–218 BC the tribes along the route were contacted and paid off.

Very little can be said of Hannibal's march over the Pyrenees, but across southern Gaul we are on much surer ground. Polybius says that the road from Spain to the river Rhône was carefully measured by the Romans and marked off with milestones. Here he unintentionally gives us an invaluable piece of information, for he is stating that Hannibal was on the same route as that later used by the Romans. He is stating that, as usual, the Romans had merely paved and measured the prehistoric route when they built the famous Via Domitia west of the Rhône.

This measuring of the road has caused some controversy as it was built by Gnaeus Domitius Ahenobarbus in 118 BC, which is very close to the date of Polybius' death. However, many scholars believe that this passage is authentic and was probably inserted by the historian shortly before his death (cf. F. Walbank, *Commentary on*

Polybius Vol. I, p. 373 and *Vol. III*, p. 768). The route of the Roman road can be clearly traced on the western side of the Rhône between Montpellier and Nîmes. Here it follows the ridge of high ground skirting the coastal marshes about nine kilometres from the present coastline. When we take into account the climatic conditions described above, the position of the road is not surprising. Even today the coast is marshy. The coastline is constantly changing as the Rhône brings down an estimated 20,000,000 tonnes of silt a year. Most of this is carried westward, forming reefs and lagoons all the way along the coast to Spain. In prehistoric times the coast would have been much nearer the road.

Polybius gives us a set of distances for the march. Unfortunately these are very vague and are only rough approximations. They are given correct to the nearest 200 *stades*. He gives distances for each part of the route which when added up give a total distance of 8,400 *stades* from New Carthage to Italy. However, elsewhere he gives the distance as 9,000. This is probably because his breakdown figures were always an underestimate, prompting him to add a little at the end to make up for it. When describing the road from Spain to the river Rhône, Polybius comments that the Romans had measured it with a milestone every eight *stades*.

For the period 218–217 all the distances given by Polybius are in multiples of eight *stades*. The only possible conclusion is that he is using a Roman source and converting at eight *stades* to a mile, i.e. 200 *stades* = c. 37km, and not $8\frac{1}{3}$ as so many others have done. Polybius' conversion is used here.

Polybius tells us that Hannibal crossed the Rhône where it is single at a distance of about four days' march from the sea. He also refers to the large number of ferry boats that Hannibal was able to buy.

The crossing point is hotly debated. The reason for this debate is quite simple. After crossing the Rhône, Hannibal marched up the river for four days to a place called the 'Island'. So each of the contestants in the debate has to move the crossing place to suit his choice for the 'Island'.

Polybius' reference to 'about four days' march from the sea' is not helpful. It is difficult to believe that he is using this as a measurement from the mouth of the Rhône to the crossing point. It must therefore be a reference to the point where the army lost sight of the sea. This point may be located near old Lunel, for south-east of this point, about 50km from Beaucaire, the Rhône delta thrusts out into the sea.

We can also discount the suggestion that the army left the coast at Aigues Mortes. Polybius makes it quite clear that the army was on the Via Domitia. To reach Aigues Mortes it would have been necessary to march 16km south before starting back towards the Rhône.

A further problem is posed by the precise extent of a day's march. At only one point in Polybius' account is a marching pace given. Just before beginning the ascent we learn that the army marched 800 *stades* in ten days. Allowing for correction to the nearest 200 *stades*, this represents a rate of between 13 and 17km per day. However, this figure is not very helpful as the army was probably foraging before beginning the ascent. The only conclusion one can draw from this is a negative one—the river crossing could not be more than four days' march from old Lunel.

De Beer advocated a crossing at Fourques, just above Arles at the apex of the delta. Hence his choice of Aigues Mortes as the point where the army left the coast. However, this theory begs a number of important questions.
1. There was a Greek trading post here which Polybius would surely have mentioned.
2. Such a precise geographical point as the apex of the delta could hardly have failed to be recorded.
3. Seventeenth-century maps show that the area between Beaucaire and Arles was flooded. Bearing in mind the climatic conditions at the time of Hannibal, this was undoubtedly its ancient state. When the Romans built their road from Nîmes to Arles, it had to be carried across the marshes on a via-

Left
Map of the French Alps showing the two routes of Hercules—the well-trodden ancient trade routes—marked in solid black and Hannibal's route marked in a broken black line.

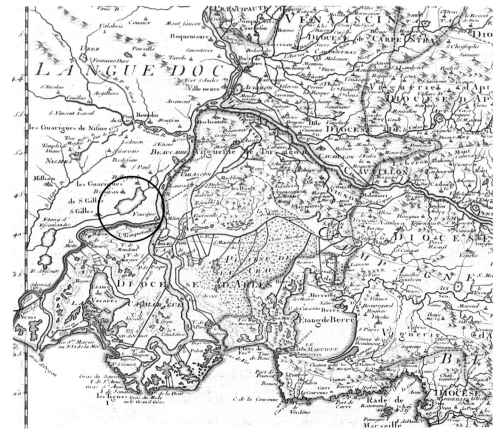

Above
A copy of an old map of the Rhône delta showing the lake that blocked the route from Nîmes to Arles. Across this marshy area the Romans built a viaduct (*pont des arcs*).

Below
Modern map of the Rhône delta showing the marshy areas (green). The ancient route to Spain (red) approached the western side of the Rhône keeping to the higher ground. Beyond the river it split in two.

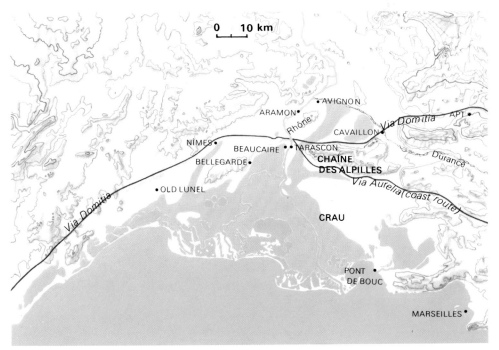

duct. No trace of this now remains but in the 18th century it was a well-known feature. The bridge was south-west of Bellegarde and is commemorated in the coat of arms of that town, where it is shown as a two-arched bridge spanning the marshes. The true length of this bridge is attested by its name 'le Pont des Arcs' (The Bridge of Arches). The number of the arches obviously impressed the local population in spite of the fact that the Pont du Gard, with its complex structure of arches, was less than 25km away. A bridge between Nîmes and Arles is referred to in the 4th-century Bordeaux or Jerusalem Itinerary under the name of Pons Aerarius.

While on the subject of de Beer's Rhône crossing, it is worth commenting on his suggestion that the river Durance, which now flows into the Rhône just south of Avignon, joined it south of Arles at the time of Hannibal. The Crau, the area south-west of Arles, is scattered with stones. This has led geologists to believe that the Durance once flowed this way and no doubt they are right. The question is, when? The ancients also noted these stones, and many explanations were put forward for their presence. It is not the explanations that are interesting but those who give them. Amongst the list are Aeschylus (525–456 BC) and Aristotle (384–322 BC), proving beyond doubt that the Durance had abandoned this course before their time.

It is certain that Hannibal did not cross the Rhône south of Beaucaire. Polybius tells us that the distance from Emporiae (Ampurias) to the Rhône was 1,600 *stades*. He also states that the Via Domitia west of the Rhône had been measured carefully by the Romans. Why, then, does he not give the accurate figure but continues to resort to approximations? Most scholars believe that the comment about careful measurement was added subsequently by either Polybius himself or a later editor. This fails to convince as Polybius did not change the figure of 1,600

Right
The Rhône just above the delta to show the possible crossing points. Before the building of the Roman viaduct (known subsequently as *le pont des arcs*) it would have been impossible to cross south of Beaucaire-Tarascon.

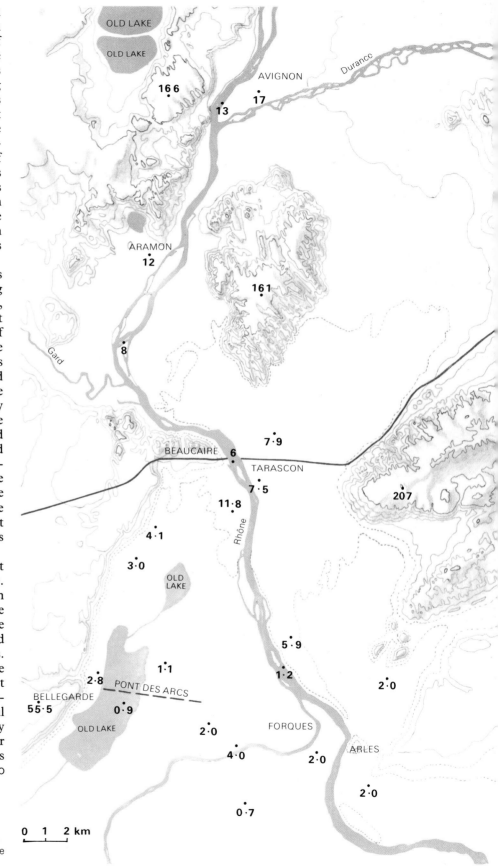

tades, nor did he state that the army crossed at the regular crossing place.

The distance from Emporiae (Ampurias) to Beaucaire can be gauged from the Roman imperial itineraries. It is 199 Roman miles or 295km. Strabo, the ancient geographer, estimates it at 194 Roman miles. At eight *tades* to a Roman mile this is 1,592 *tades*. Since Polybius' approximate figure of 1,600 *stades* allows for a variation of 99 *stades* either way, the distance could be as much as another 20km. The next possible crossing place would be Aramon, but this would seem to offer no advantage over Beaucaire. Above this is Avignon, which is 18km further than Beaucaire. This brings us to the absolute limit of Polybius' figures. It is just over 70km from Old Lunel— a reasonable four days' march. The reason for Hannibal's choice of crossing point at Avignon lies in the movement (or rather lack of movement) of Scipio. Polybius tells us that Scipio set sail in early summer and that it took him five days to sail from Pisa to the Rhône.

According to Varro, who was a contemporary of Caesar and who was familiar with both the newly introduced Julian calendar and the earlier Roman one, summer began on the 23rd day after the sun had entered the constellation of Taurus and ended 94 days later. This was officially 9 May to 11 August. Even allowing for the elasticity of the republican calendar, 'early summer' can be pushed forward no later than the end of June.

Another problem is posed by the timing of Hannibal's arrival at the Rhône. Polybius says that he reached the summit of the Alps 'close on the setting of the Pleiades'. This is another astronomical date and once again Varro gives us a dating for it. There are 57 days between the setting of the Pleiades and the winter solstice. The setting of the Pleiades must therefore be at the end of October, and Hannibal's arrival at the summit of the Alps around the middle of that month. By backtracking one can place Hannibal at the Rhône crossing around the end of August.

Polybius gives us the impression that Scipio arrived at the Rhône delta at approximately the same time as Hannibal was crossing the river. However, there is a deficit of two months.

Hannibal took five months to reach Italy from Cartagena. He therefore left Cartagena about the middle of May. There is no way he could have reached the Rhône by early July. As we discussed earlier Polybius lived in the house of Scipio Aemilianus, the adopted great grandson of this Scipio. He therefore felt that he had to toe the family line. This Scipio and Aemilianus' natural grandfather, Aemilius Paullus, were an integral part of the disaster that overtook Rome in the early years of this war. But the family traditions would not accept responsibility for these mistakes and scapegoats had to be found. At the battle of the Trebbia and at Cannae, as we shall see, the other consul was blamed. At the Rhône and at Ticinus history had to be rewritten.

According to Polybius, Hannibal did not hear of Scipio's presence at the mouth of the Rhône until after he had crossed the river. Here he is once again following the Scipionic family tradition which tries to cover Scipio's failure to stop Hannibal at the Rhône by suggesting that he only missed the Carthaginian by a hair's breadth. If Scipio reached the Rhône earlier, then Hannibal knew about it and for this reason crossed the Rhône above its confluence with the Durance to place that river between himself and the Romans.

2. The Island
When Hannibal's Numidians fell in with Scipio's cavalry Hannibal must have believed that the legions were close behind them and for this reason he abandoned his plan to follow the route of Hercules and instead turned upstream to try to throw off Scipio. Scipio arrived at his camp three days after he had left it and a day later Hannibal's scouts caught up with him and told him that Scipio had turned back to the coast.

This four-day march brought the Carthaginians to a point where the Rhône was joined by another river which Polybius calls the Skaras. The area caught between these two rivers was called the 'Island'. It was a populous district producing an abundance of corn and deriving its name from its situation. It was similar in shape and size to the Egyptian Delta, the principal difference being that its baseline was

formed by an 'almost inaccessible' range of mountains.

The 'Island', like every other aspect of Hannibal's route, has caused a mass of controversy. A quick glance at the map will show that there is one obvious candidate—the area between the Rhône and the Isère. Nevertheless, several commentators have argued that the area lay between the Eygues and the Rhône. Their main argument hinges on old names for the Eygues, among which is the name Ekaris which is very similar to Skaras. But it must be pointed out that the Latin name for the Isère was Isara, which is just as similar. Livy offers no help in this matter for he calls the river the Arar, the Latin name for the Saône. This is typical of Livy who has exchanged a name that he knows for one he does not; Professor H. H. Scullard lists a dozen or more examples of this in relation to Spain and North Africa in his book *Scipio Africanus, Soldier and Statesman*.

One can also disregard Livy's list of tribes through which Hannibal passed. Attempts have been made to locate these by comparing them to the areas of Gaul during the Roman empire. This is a pointless exercise as there was a continuous migration down the Rhône valley as each tribe pushed the next one further down. There must have also been inter-tribal wars. At the time of Hannibal we cannot even be certain that the Helvetii had occupied Switzerland with the upheaval that must have caused.

Hannibal intervened to settle a dispute in the 'Island'. This has led some commentators to reject the area between the Isère and the Rhône as during the empire this was the home of the Allobroges, and Polybius expressly states that Hannibal later had trouble with the Allobroges. But as we have seen, it is impossible say where these tribesmen were at the time of Hannibal.

So it becomes a question of description. Polybius compares the 'Island's' size to that of the Nile Delta, which in his day had an area of about 15,000 sq km. The area between the Rhône and the Isère is about 5,000 sq km and the area between the Rhône and the Aigues is only about 700 sq km. The defenders of the 'Aigues Island' argue unconvincingly that since none of the contenders for the 'Island' are as big as the Nile Delta the size can be ignored.

It is impossible to comment on the population—one can only point to the area. As for the abundance of corn, while it must be admitted that the Aigues area is more fertile, the Isère area, because of its size, produces a far greater yield and in Roman times it supported the powerful and numerous Allobroges.

The last and most important part of Polybius' description is the reference to an island. Polybius says it derived its name from its situation. The Isère is one of the three main tributaries of the Rhône; the Saône and the Durance being the other two. All the others are insignificant compared to these. The Aigues is a stream which practically dries up in the summer. One can walk across it ankle deep. As for the 'almost inaccessible' range of mountains, they do not exist in relation to the Aigues. Its defenders talk vaguely of the Baronnies but do not explain how they fit Polybius' description as they are crossed by a multitude of paths and present no sort of barrier. However, the Isère island is a virtual fortress. Most of the triangular area is surrounded by the Isère or the Rhône. The gap between the two rivers is blocked by the Chartreuse Massif and the Mont du Chat. In addition it is protected by the Lake of Bourget and its marshes which even today stretch to the banks of the Rhône.

3. The pass

Every pass from the Col de Larche to the Simplon in Switzerland has been advocated. It would be both boring and fruitless to examine all the claims. Between the years 1968 and 1973 my wife and I crossed and examined all the passes which have been suggested and all the minor passes which have been put forward as the site of the first ambush.

First we must deal with the height of the pass. Polybius says that the passes of the Alps were snow-covered all the year round. When he makes this statement he must be including the lowest passes such as the Montgenèvre and the Little St Bernard as these are the only passes in the western Alps that we know were in use at this time. This would accord well with H. H. Lamb's

view that the snow level was probably about 1,000m lower than it is today. Therefore Hannibal's pass, which still had the previous year's snow lying on it, does not have to be high.

Polybius claims that he himself crossed 'the pass'. His description of the soldiers sliding on the congealed snow corroborates this as it is too vivid to be second-hand.

From the Greek historian's account it is possible to draw several clues to the identity of the pass. The six main clues are listed below:
1. The pass should have a defile within a day's march of its summit. This must be less than 30km as all the passes to be discussed—with the exception of the Col de Larche—have a steep climb immediately before reaching the summit.
2. The top of the pass should be large enough to allow an army to pitch camp.
3. The descent should be at least partially facing north as snow and ice were encountered on the descent.
4. The pass should have a precipitous descent.
5. The far side of the pass should be three days' march (45–90km) from the flat land.
6. One should be able to see Italy from the top of the pass.

Only the seven main claimants need to be examined here.
(**A**) The Col de Larche (alt. 1,991m) fits only conditions 2 and 5. Its axis runs from north-west to south-east.
(**B**) The Col de la Traversette (alt. 2,914m). This is the only pass from which the plain of the Po can be seen. However, it fits only one other condition, no. 4. It does have a defile (Combe de Queyras), but this is about 35km from the summit and the ascent is exceedingly steep. Hannibal was marching through hostile country and would never have entered the Combe de Queyras. This is a gorge with precipitous sides stretching for 15km along the valley of the Guil. Hannibal would have had to have been a maniac to take his army this way. The strongest objection to this pass is its altitude—more than 1,000m higher than the Montgenèvre. To reach the Traversette one has to pass the much lower Col de la Croix (alt. 2,273m). At the top of the Traversette is a narrow ledge with

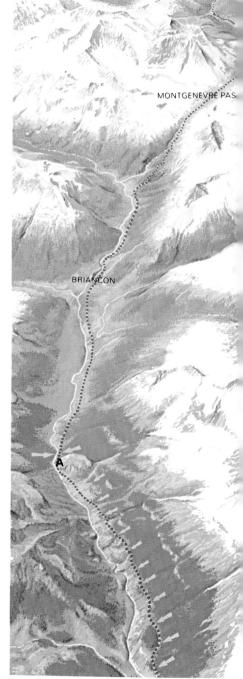

MONTGENEVRE PAS

BRIANCON

A

Above
The route from l'Argentière-la-Bessée to the Montgenèvre pass (a little over 20km). At the bottom is the Durance defile. Here the Celts attacked from the high ground whilst the army was stretched out along the hillside. Where the great rock (A) juts out and pinches the road, the army was cut in half. From here the following morning Hannibal managed to break out and reach the top of the pass where he camped for two days.

carcely room for ten people to camp et alone an army. It is also very difficult to justify a three-day march from the eastern side of the pass to the flat ground, a distance of only 20km. Even if one takes this to mean right out into the Po valley, it is still hardly more than 30km.

(C) The Montgenèvre (alt. 1,850m). This is the pass over which the Via Domitia passed. It is the second lowest of the passes. It fits all the conditions except no. **6**. It has a defile a few kilometres south of Briançon and about 20km south of the pass. This defile has steeply sloping sides along which the road runs. It is fairly easy to pass but would be very dangerous with an enemy on the slopes above. Of all the defiles discussed this best fits the description of 'rolling' down boulders on the Carthaginian army.

There is ample room to camp an army on top of the pass. Only this and the Col de l'Echelle have a south-north axis. It is actually west-south-west to east-north-east. The descent is precipitous and is followed by a permanent landslide area where the modern road has to be protected by a concrete canopy. From the far side of the pass to Susa is 37km. One could say the flat ground started a few kilometres beyond this. From Susa to the plain of the Po at Avigliana is another 30km.

(D) The Col de l'Echelle (alt. 1,766m). This is the lowest pass in the western Alps. It is an alternative to the Montgenèvre as it also joins the valleys of the Durance and the Dora Riparia. This may be the pass Pompey crossed on his way to Spain, as the ancient authors imply that he did not use the normal pass. The distance by this pass is only slightly more than by the Montgenèvre. It is just possible that the pre-Roman route went this way. It fits conditions **1**, **2**, **3**, **4** and **5**. The summit of the pass is a little over 25km from the defile mentioned in relation to the Montgenèvre. There is just about room for Hannibal to camp his army on the pass. The axis of the pass is directly south-north. It has an extremely precipitous descent.

(E) Col du Clapier (alt. 2,482m). This fits only conditions **1** and **2**. The crossing is made from the north-west to south-east. If the previous year's snow still remained on the south side of this pass, then it would have been impossible to climb the exceedingly steep north side as it would have been completely iced up. I tried to cross this pass in June 1968 before the snows had cleared but could not climb the path up the cliff face from the valley of the Ambin.

It has a steep but not precipitous descent. My wife and I lost our way descending this pass in the autumn of 1968, finally descending by the dried-up stream beds. From no point on the summit is it possible to see the Po valley. Only by trekking along the hillside to Monte Aria is this possible. One can walk from the far side of the pass to the 'flat ground' in a few hours. Even if one interprets the 'flat ground' to mean the plain of the Po, it cannot be more than 35km distant and is on the flat.

(F) The Mont Cenis (alt. 2,083m). This pass fits only no. **2**. It is adjacent to the Col du Clapier and its alignment is similar. Those who have argued that Hannibal crossed the Clapier must explain why he did not use the Mont Cenis which is both lower and easier; nor does one have to pass through a defile to reach it. Even if Hannibal had set off through the Ambin defile and had climbed up the cliff face, he would then still have found it easier to cross the Little Mont Cenis (alt. 2,182m) and descend by the Mont Cenis route which surely he would have done. Or perhaps, like myself, Hannibal wanted to go to the Clapier because he had been told there was a good view of Italy.

(G) The Little St Bernard (alt. 2,188m). This fits conditions **1**, **2** and **3**. It is about 130km from the far side of the pass to the flat ground, which is too far for a three-day march.

In the summer of 1979 an expedition of army engineers under the leadership of Lt R.A.M.S. Melvin made a survey of the Clapier – Cenis, Montgenèvre – l'Echelle and Traversette passes. Their conclusions were much the same as my own but they added that it would be virtually impossible to get elephants up the Traversette because of the scree or down the other side because of its extremely precipitous nature. They ruled out the descent from the Echelle for the same reason.

By a process of elimination, the most likely pass is therefore the Montgenèvre, the pass used by both the Roman and pre-Roman roads. That is if one assumes that the view from the top is mythical. Hannibal probably pointed vaguely in the direction of Italy during a speech of encouragement and in later years the soldiers, looking back on this, imagined perhaps that they saw more than they really did.

There is another test. According to the ancient geographer Strabo, Polybius knew of only four routes through the Alps, and he lists them:
1. The route through the Ligurians.
2. The route to the Taurini which Hannibal used.
3. The route through the Salassi.
4. The route through the territory of the Rhaeti.

All agree that these passes are listed from south to north—the first being the coastal route (i.e. the southern branch of the route of Hercules) and the third the Little St Bernard. The route that Hannibal used lies between them.

F. W. Walbank, in his monumental commentary on Polybius, claims that the route to the Taurini can only be the Mont Cenis, the Clapier or the Montgenèvre, because only these three passes lead directly to the Taurini. It is unthinkable that Polybius, the great traveller and enquirer, should be ignorant of the route of Hercules. Furthermore, he only knows of one route to the Taurini. It follows that his route to the Taurini must be the route of Hercules. As we have seen earlier, the route of Hercules could not be over either the Clapier or the Mont Cenis. Therefore route **2** which Hannibal used must be over the Montegenèvre.

Having established that the 'Island' was probably between the Isère and Rhône and that the pass was almost certainly the Montgenèvre, we are left with an apparently insurmountable problem. How did Hannibal get from one to the other? There is a fairly straightforward route from Grenoble at the eastern end of the island to Briançon at the foot of the Montgenèvre but this involves crossing the Col du Lautaret (alt. 2,058m). This is a very difficult pass and Polybius expressly states that Hannibal did not take a difficult or unknown route. There is another route which at first glance would appear unlikely for it involves turning south-east at Grenoble and crossing the low Bayard (alt. 1,248m) or Manse (alt. 1,263m) passes and so regaining the Durance valley and the route of Hercules. The approach to both these passes is across open fields. From the 'Island' at the junction of the Isère and Rhône Hannibal really had only two possible routes to Italy: first, to continue up the Isère valley and cross by the Clapier, Mont Cenis or Little St Bernard; or, secondly, to turn south and rejoin the route of Hercules and cross the Montgenèvre. He clearly chose the latter.

The only other points that remain to be identified are the sites of the two ambushes.

After leaving the 'Island' the army marched 800 *stades* (148 ± 18km) in ten days along the 'river'. Much has been made of the 'river'. Some want to make it the Rhône, others the Skaras and others a mixture of the Rhône and another river. The present writer, with no greater justification than any of the others, suggests that the army followed the Isère from its junction with the Rhône as far as Grenoble where it is joined by the Drac and then followed this river into the mountains. Since almost 700 *stades* were allowed from the Rhône crossing to the 'Island', and Polybius gives the total from the crossing to the beginning of the ascent as 1,400, it follows that the part of the journey from the 'Island' to the beginning of the ascent should not be more than 800 *stades*, or Polybius' corrected figure would be 1,600 and not 1,400. So, Hannibal advanced not more than 148km before beginning the ascent. This would bring him to the region of La Mure. Here the going gets difficult as the army is forced to march along the hillside above the gorges of the Drac. It is interesting to note how other commentators have been forced to take Hannibal over unnecessary passes in order to find a spot for the first ambush as there is no suitable site along any of the routes. Those who choose the Isère–Arc route have to claim that either the headland of the Vercors at Voreppe or the junction of the Isère and the Arc was marshy and therefore the road had to go over the hills. De

Beer takes Hannibal over the Col de Grimone in spite of the fact that if he continued along the Drôme valley he would get to the same place by a much easier, lower and shorter route.

In order to get to the Durance valley from the Isère, Hannibal had no alternative but to negotiate the difficult gorges of the Drac and it was here that the Allobroges 'occupied the key points' above the ravine. From the gorges of the Drac the army made good progress until the fourth day when they were met by ambassadors from the tribes near the top of the pass. This three to four days' march would have brought them down into the valley of the Durance, possibly near Embrun—a distance of about 90km. From La Mure to this point the marching would have been easy and mainly through open grassland.

For two days more the army marched on without trouble. This would have brought them to the Durance defile just north of l'Argentière-la-Bessée about 55km further up the valley. This site is ideal for the second ambush. The road takes to the hills and runs along the hillside above the gorge. Along this road the army would have been stretched out over 10–15km. Here the Celts attacked and rolled boulders down the hillside. Beyond the gorge the road again descends to the valley and is immediately pinched by a great mass of rock that juts out from the eastern hills. This would be the point at which the army was cut in half. It is worth climbing up the western side of the valley and sitting on the hillside there. Below is the defile and to the north one can see the Montgenèvre pass about 20km away.

Polybius gives us the distance from the beginning of the ascent to the flat ground in the Po valley—about 1,200 *stades*. He also states that the ascent began 800 *stades* after the Punic army set out from the 'Island'. Assuming, as most others do, that Hannibal encamped at the junction of the Isère and Rhône, and that it was from here that he set out again, the distance from here to the flat ground should be 2,000 *stades*, 370km plus or minus 18km.

The distance from the junction of the Rhône and Isère to Avigliana in the plain of the Po is about 386km. One

could argue that the flat ground o Polybius could be located anywhe beyond Susa as this is where the valle opens out; certainly there could b no obstacles beyond this point. Th would reduce the total by 30km. All th distances—from Emporiae to the Rhôn crossing, from the Rhône crossing t the 'Island' and from the 'Island' to th flat ground—are at the maximum o Polybius' estimates. This could ac count for the fact that Polybius' tota distance from Cartagena is 9,000 *stade* and not 8,400, which is the tota of the individual distances.

The battle for the Po valley

It took Hannibal 15 days to cross th Alps. During this time he had los nearly half his army and even more o his baggage animals. He had starte out from the Rhône with 38,000 foo and 8,000 horse. He recorded th number that reached Italy in an in scription on a column at Lacinium i the toe of Italy. There were 12,00 African and 8,000 Spanish infantr and not more than 6,000 cavalry. Thes were by no means all casualties—ther must have been many desertions.

The army was physically exhauste and morale was low. Men and animal needed rest and care. The local tribe the Taurini, seeing the miserable stat and size of the Carthaginian army, wer understandably unconvinced that Han nibal was the saviour who was going t lead them to victory against the Romans Hannibal tried to reason with then whilst he rested his men. When al persuasion failed he launched an attac on their chief town and massacred th population. It proved a salutary lesso and all the other local tribes flocked t his standard. The Carthaginian knev that the most effective propaganda fo his cause would be a quick defeat of th Roman troops in the area. With this i mind he advanced along the north ban of the Po.

Scipio, meanwhile, had sailed bacl to Pisa, crossed the Apennines and taken over command of the two legions (first and second) in the Po valley Scipio's aim was to hold Hannibal unti the arrival of his colleague, who had already been recalled from Sicily. I was decided to check the Carthaginian advance at the Ticino river. This is a powerful tributary of the Po which at this time of the year would have presented a considerable obstacle. This position is reinforced by a spur of the Apennines which juts out towards the Po on the south side at Stradella, leaving only a narrow plain between the river and the hills. In the previous year the Romans had founded two military colonies in the Po valley—one at Cremona and one at Placentia (Piacenza). Some years ago Tenney Frank put forward a well-argued case for placing the original colony of Placentia at Stradella, 30km west of modern Piacenza. The colony was besieged by Hasdrubal in 207 and destroyed by the Celts in 200. When the Romans reconquered the area a few years later the colony was re-established. Frank suggests that when it was resettled its military importance was less crucial and therefore it was refounded in the plain in the centre of the centuriated farm lands. The prehistoric route across northern Italy ran in a straight line from the Adriatic coast near Rimini to Stradella where it must have crossed the Po between the junctions of the Ticino and

Tanaro to Lomello (Roman Laumellum) and then continued along the north side of the Po to join up with the route of Hercules near Turin. The stretch of the Po between the Ticino and Tanaro is the most convenient spot for a river crossing; at any other point it would also involve having to cross either the Ticino or the Tanaro, two of the major tributaries of the Po. The obvious position to place a colony was near the river crossing to prevent the Celts sending reinforcements to their kinsmen on the south side of the Po. When the Romans built the Via Aemilia at the beginning of the 2nd century BC, the course of the old road was followed from Rimini as far as Fidenza, from which point a spur was constructed to link it to the new colony at Piacenza.

It is hard to believe that Placentia, if it were situated in the open plain where Piacenza now stands, could have withstood Hasdrubal's siege. Furthermore, the placing of Cremona at the strategic position at the junction of the Po and the Adda supposes that there should be a similar colony at the even

more strategic position at the junction of the Ticino. Whilst it must be admitted that there is no archaeological justification for a colony at Stradella, militarily the argument is very strong. A survey of some of Rome's other frontier colonies, such as Sinuessa and Luceria, suggest that she could hardly have ignored a position like Stradella. Furthermore, if Placentia was at Piacenza, Polybius' account of the subsequent battle of the Trebbia makes no sense. On this basis the author has no hesitation in placing Placentia at Stradella.

Scipio, who had moved up to Placentia, built a bridge of boats across the Po, and moved his men over to the east bank of the Ticino. With the 6,000 colonists holding the south side of the river and the main army holding the north, the Romans appeared to be in an impregnable position. If Hannibal crossed to the south bank so could

Below
The Po valley with the distribution of the Celtic tribes and the pre-Roman road skirting the Apennines all the way to the Adriatic coast at Rimini. In 225 BC the Romans fought a full-scale war with the Celts.

Scipio. To understand what happened next one must look at the character of Scipio. He had been made to look utterly incompetent at the Rhône and he was determined that it should not happen again. Scipio knew that Hannibal was advancing by the route along the north bank but his self-confidence had been so undermined by the events at the Rhône that he must now have feared that Hannibal would somehow bypass him, cross the Apennines and invade Etruria. So, instead of holding his unassailable position on the Ticino, he bridged the river and advanced up the Po. The day after crossing the Ticino the Romans learned from their scouts that the Carthaginian army was close and they pitched camp about 20–30km west of the river— probably just east of Lomello. Next morning Scipio took his cavalry and *velites* and advanced cautiously.

The scene was now set for a classic Hannibalic ambush of the type that overtook Gracchus and Marcellus later in the war. Polybius says that Hannibal was also advancing with his cavalry and that the two armies fell in with each other. Here once again Polybius is whitewashing Scipio's blunders. Polybius admits that the Romans were so surprised that the *velites* had no time to throw their javelins before the Carthaginian cavalry was on top of them and adds that the Numidians outflanked the Romans and attacked them in the rear. This suggests that in fact the Numidians were also placed in hiding. The consul was wounded and his cavalry routed. Polybius assures us that they inflicted even greater losses on the enemy! The Romans fled for the Ticino, crossed over and started to break up the bridge. Hannibal pursued them as far as the river but gave up when he found the bridge unusable.

Scipio now completely lost his nerve. He gave up his position on the Ticino, crossed the Po and camped at Placentia. Meanwhile Hannibal, who realised that it would be impossible to cross the Po in the face of Roman opposition, retreated upstream and crossed the river out of reach of the Romans.

All the local Celts now flocked to join the Carthaginian army. Two days later Hannibal appeared before Placentia and drew up his army in battle order. When Scipio refused battle the Carthaginian pitched camp about ten kilometres west of the colony.

Shortly before dawn on the following morning, the Celts serving with Scipio deserted to the enemy. In typical Celtic style, before they went they killed some of the Romans and cut off their heads to take with them. The Boii, who occupied the area south of the Po immediately behind Scipio, now threw in their lot with Hannibal. Scipio realised that his position was completely untenable. If the Boii moved up behind him he was trapped.

The following morning, just before daybreak, he broke camp and retreated to the Trebbia river just west of Piacenza. From here, if the worst happened, he could escape over the Passo Della Scoffera to Genoa and then along the coast to Tuscany.

Below
Map of the area between Lomello and Fidenza showing the strategic significance of Stradella. The pre-Roman road marked in cream probably crossed the Po between the junctions of the Tanaro and Ticino.

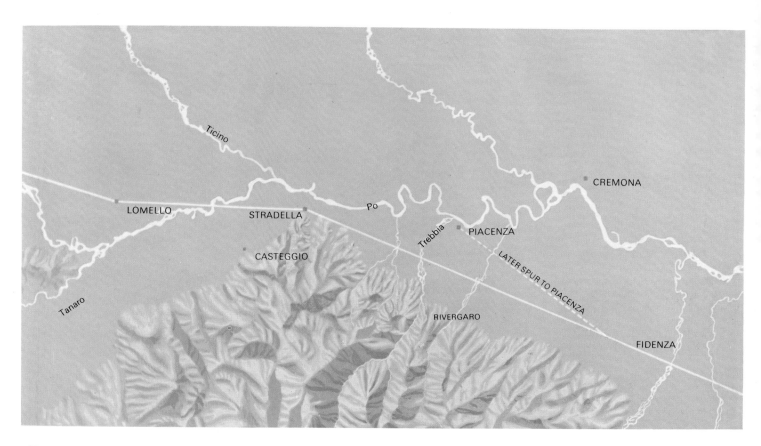

As soon as Hannibal realised what.
had happened he sent out his Numidian
cavalry in pursuit. It was fortunate for
the Romans that the Numidians stopped
to burn the deserted Roman camp
before starting their pursuit; most of the
Romans managed to cross the river
before the African horsemen caught up
with them. This retreat on the Trebbia
would be inconceivable if Placentia
were at Piacenza, for the Trebbia is
about five kilometres west of that town.
The Romans now encamped on the low
hills west of the Trebbia near modern
Rivergaro, covering their own line of
retreat. Hannibal moved up his camp
and pitched it about eight kilometres
west of the Roman position. A few
days later Sempronius, with the third
and fourth legions, reached Scipio's
camp, having covered an incredible
1,780km from Lilybaeum (Marsala)
via Rome and Rimini in 40 days, an
average of 44km per day. To achieve
this the army had been disbanded and
told to meet at Rimini by a certain date.

Some time later one of those cumula-
tive skirmishes took place in which each
side keeps on sending out reinforcements. Hannibal, realising that this
was the sort of thing that could get out
of hand, recalled his men. He wanted a
pitched battle where his supreme ability
as a tactician would decide the day.

The Romans considered the Carthaginian withdrawal an admission of
defeat and started to clamour for a
full-scale encounter. Hannibal knew
that the time was ripe and that Sempronius would respond to a little
encouragement. The space between the
camps, although flat and treeless, was
scoured by several watercourses. If he
offered battle here the Romans would
have to advance into the plain with
their left wing resting on the hills.

During the night Hannibal sent out
1,000 infantry and 1,000 cavalry under
the command of his younger brother
Mago to hide along the stream beds
where they entered the hills.

At daybreak he sent out his Numidian
cavalry to beat up the Roman camp and
then ordered his whole army to breakfast and stand by their arms. His plan
was to draw out the Romans and precipitate the full-scale battle for which
he was prepared and they were not. He
could hardly have expected his plan to

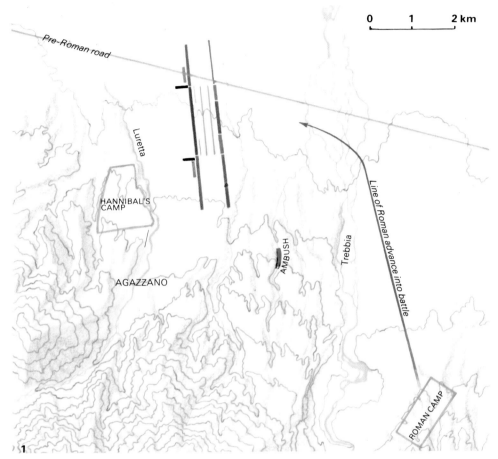

Above and below
1 Map showing the relative positions of the Carthaginians and Romans on the Trebbia. The night before the battle Hannibal placed 2,000 men in ambush, under the command of his brother Mago, between the two camps. Early the following morning he sent his Numidian cavalry to draw the Romans out.
2 The Romans were drawn up as usual with the legions in the centre and the allies on the flanks. The Roman cavalry were on the right

and the allied cavalry on the left wing. Hannibal placed his Celts and Spaniards in the centre with the elephants in front of either flank. He placed his Africans behind the cavalry on either wing.
3 The Carthaginian cavalry strip the Roman wings bare, clearing the way for the Africans to attack the allied infantry on the flanks. In spite of Mago's attack from the rear, the legions managed to break through the centre and escape.

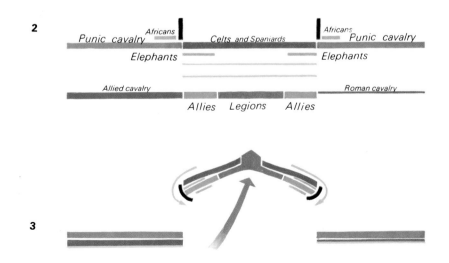

be as successful as it was.

Scipio was still incapacitated and his colleague had taken over full command. When Sempronius saw the Numidians advancing he immediately ordered out his cavalry, following up with the *velites* and finally the entire infantry. The Numidians retreated and the Romans followed. Down the legionaries plunged into the icy waters of the Trebbia which had been swollen by rain during the night. Snow was blowing in the wind as they stumbled over the shingle, the water dragging at their legs. They plunged down again and again into the troughs of the river until at last, soaked and shivering, they clambered up the far bank.

When Hannibal saw that the Romans had crossed the river he threw forward a covering force of about 8,000 pikemen and slingers and drew up the rest of his army behind this screen.

Hannibal drew up his infantry 1,500m in front of his camp. This consisted of a single line of about 20,000 Spaniards, Celts and Africans. He placed his elephants in front of either wing and the cavalry beyond

them. Although Polybius does not mention it, he must now have withdrawn his covering force. The pikemen were drawn up behind the cavalry on each wing whilst the slingers were sent to join the lightly armed troops ahead of the infantry line. The Romans meanwhile had drawn up their forces. Polybius says that they were in their usual order, that is with the four citizen legions, about 16,000 men, in the centre and the four allied 'legions' (20,000 men) on the wings. The cavalry, which had been recalled from its fruitless pursuit of the Numidians, was drawn up on the the wings. The Roman horsemen numbered about 4,000, which was a little under strength, possibly because of losses in the earlier ambush. About 25 per cent of them would have been Roman and the remainder allied.

The 1,000 Roman cavalry were drawn up on the right wing and the 3,000 allies on the left. The *velites* as usual were placed ahead of the infantry. As the Romans stood there they must have wondered what had happened to them. Only a short while ago they had been getting up. Now, soaked and

shivering and without breakfast, they were waiting to advance into battle. The trumpets sounded and the legions began to move forward at a slow step.

When the Roman cavalry were withdrawn Hannibal recalled his Numidians, placing them with his African pikemen behind the other cavalry. Then he advanced.

The light-armed troops were the first to come into contact. Although the *velites* heavily outnumbered their Carthaginian counterparts, they had used up most of their javelins in the pursuit of the Numidians and those they had left were wet and unserviceable. Seeing that the *velites* were making such a poor showing, Sempronius recalled them and they passed through the gaps between the maniples. Hannibal similarly withdrew his light troops and the heavy-armed infantry closed in. The legionaries dashed forward, hurling

Below
Map of northern Etruria and the Po valley showing the positions of the Roman forces at the two strategic points of Arezzo and Rimini. Hannibal's route through the Apennines and south to Lake Trasimene is shown in dotted line.

their *pila* into the dense mass of Celts and Spaniards.

Now the massively superior Carthaginian cavalry also charged, stripping the flanks of the legions bare. The African pikemen and the Numidians, who had been drawn up behind the cavalry, dashed past their own men and attacked the Roman flanks. Hannibal knew that his centre could not hold out long against the might of the legions. The Numidians and Africans had already taken the pressure off the wings. Now Mago's 2,000 cavalry and infantry came out of hiding and charged the Roman rear, throwing the legions into confusion. The 2,400 *triarii* would have about faced to meet the attack. The Romans managed to maintain the contest in the centre, but the allies on the wings, attacked by the elephants in front and the pikemen and Numidians in the flanks, were steadily driven back towards the river.

In the centre the Romans finally cut their way through the Spanish and Celtic infantry. Sempronius, who was in command here, thought that he had won but then found himself cut off from the rest of the army. It was raining heavily and visibility was very poor. As the Romans could see no way of getting back to their camp, especially with the victorious Carthaginian cavalry roaming the field, they retired in close order to Placentia.

Of the rest of the army most were killed by the cavalry and the elephants as they tried to recross the river. A violent storm had blown up which covered the Roman retreat, and the Carthaginians, finding the pursuit too difficult, returned to their camp to celebrate.

Polybius is rather vague about what happened after the battle. Livy, however, tells us that after nightfall Scipio and the remnants of the army recrossed the Trebbia and reached Placentia. Finding it crowded there, they crossed the Po and headed downstream to Cremona. The Romans had perhaps lost as many as 20,000 men. Although Hannibal's casualties were light, he lost all but one of his elephants in the storm.

The invasion of central Italy
The true situation in the Po valley was not immediately known at Rome as Sempronius had claimed a victory, but it soon became obvious as the two armies were shut up at Placentia and Cremona. As long as the Carthaginian cavalry could remain in the field, the two armies could not move and supplies had to be brought up the Po in ships.

In Rome feverish preparations were being made to limit the Carthaginian success. Legions were sent to Sicily (seventh and eighth) and Sardinia (ninth) to stop the Carthaginians trying to re-establish themselves there, and garrisons were rushed to Taranto and other ports of questionable loyalty in case they should defect, allowing Punic troops to be introduced into southern Italy.

At the same time the consuls for the coming year prepared for the defence of central Italy. New troops were enrolled and stores sent to Rimini and

Below
The north shore of Lake Trasimene seen from the east side. The promontory in the centre is Passignano. The site favoured by the author for the battle is behind the promontory on which the village of Passignano now stands.

Arezzo, where the two consuls were to take up their positions. Polybius says nothing more of the troops at Placentia and Cremona. Livy, if his account of the winter operations can be believed, says that the troops from Placentia crossed the Apennines into Etruria and those at Cremona made their way to Rimini. In the early spring the two consuls set out to take up their posts— Flaminius at Arezzo and Geminus at Rimini.

There were only two routes by which Hannibal could enter central Italy: by crossing the Apennines into the Arno valley; or by marching down the Po valley to Rimini, then following the Metauro valley into the Apennines and crossing the Villa Coldecanali pass (alt. 559m) into the valley of the Tiber. This was the route of the Roman Via Flaminia and was the easier but by far the longer route. There are about half a dozen possible routes from the Po to the Arno valley. The easiest and most likely is the old Etruscan route from Bologna via Marzabotto to the low-lying area between Pistoia and Florence which was probably flooded at this time. From long experience of dealing with Celtic invasions the Romans knew that they must post their armies at Rimini, covering the exit from the Po valley, and at Arezzo in the Arno valley.

Hannibal had made detailed enquiries into the possible routes to central Italy. He favoured the short route into Etruria from Bologna but was warned that the Arno valley was flooded. His guides, however, assured him that the ground beneath the water was firm and it could be crossed.

In the spring he broke winter quarters and crossed the Apennines with about 45,000 infantry and 10,000 cavalry (these figures are based on the conviction that he must have had more troops than he had at Cannae a year later). He hoped to surprise Flaminius and defeat him before his colleague could join him from Rimini.

The Punic army advanced southwards with the African and Spanish infantry at the front, the baggage train mingling with them. Behind these were placed the Celts, with the cavalry bringing up the rear. Hannibal commanded the vanguard riding the only

remaining elephant, and his brother Mago the rearguard. The Celts had been placed in the centre as they were the most unreliable troops and here the cavalry could make sure that they did not desert.

The Apennines were crossed without problems, but it took three days and nights to cross the swamps. Most of the baggage animals collapsed and died in the mud and at night the soldiers made use of these dead animals by climbing up on to their packs so that they could sleep out of the mire.

Hannibal had a severe attack of ophthalmia whilst crossing the marshes. But there was no time to stop for treatment as it was essential to get the army out of the unhealthy area as quickly as possible. As a result he lost an eye. Once across the marshes the army camped for a few days while the scouts undertook a thorough survey of the surrounding country. Hannibal used the opportunity to make careful enquiries concerning the character of the consul Flaminius. Polybius says that he found him to be a demagogue—an over-confident mob orator with no talent for the practical conduct of war. Here once again Polybius is reflecting the view of the Scipionic family. Much has been made of the rashness of Flaminius but most of it is probably fictitious. In 223 BC Flaminius had won a great victory over the Insubres. Polybius was unable to deny the victory but gave the credit to the tribunes. This battle is significant as the Romans did not use their normal tactics but opposed the Celts with a front rank of spearmen. The credit for this innovation must go to the commander as it could hardly have been carried out by the tribunes on their own initiative.

In fairness to Flaminius he was probably no better or worse than the average Roman commander of his day. The principal weakness of the Roman army throughout this war was its inefficient system of scouting.

Flaminius seems to have been encamped between Fiesole and Arezzo. Hannibal advanced up the Arno valley towards the Roman position and when the consul refused battle bypassed his camp and pushed on southwards, laying waste the countryside and burning the farms in an endeavour to draw Flam-

inius out. The consul, who had already sent word to his colleague to join him, now gave orders to break camp and follow the Carthaginian. Polybius says that Flaminius' tribunes begged him to remain where he was until his colleague arrived. A man of Polybius' experience must have known that this was nonsense. Flaminius had to remain in contact with the Carthaginian army but avoid a battle before his colleague arrived and this is clearly what he tried to do.

The Greek historian says that Hannibal was advancing along the road to Rome, with Cortona and its hills on his left and Lake Trasimene on his right. The road ran through a narrow strip of level ground with a range of hills along either side. The head of this defile was overlooked by a steep hill which was difficult to climb. Between the lake and the hillside was a narrow passage giving access to the defile and here he prepared an ambush. The first part of this description is only possible if Hannibal is on the north shore of the lake.

Recently the Italian archaeologist Giancarlo Susini made a thorough survey of the north shore. He was able to show that much of the low-lying land at the north-west corner of the lake was under water in Roman times. The level of the lake was lowered when a canal connecting the lake with the river Nestore was built in 1421. The shore-line has been further extended as a result of silting caused by the streams that flow into the north side of the lake.

When these factors are taken into consideration, the broad plain at the north-east corner of the lake assumes a quite different shape. The spur on which Tuoro stands is now in the centre of the plain but in Roman times it jutted out to the water's edge, dividing the plain in two.

I am grateful to Lt. Melvin and his team for bringing to my attention an old map covering the area from Arezzo to Lake Trasimene supposedly drawn up by Leonardo da Vinci probably towards the end of the 15th century. This not only shows Lake Trasimene covering a much larger area, but that most of the Chiana valley, which runs north to Arezzo, was also flooded. This has led some local archaeologists to suggest that the Chiana valley and

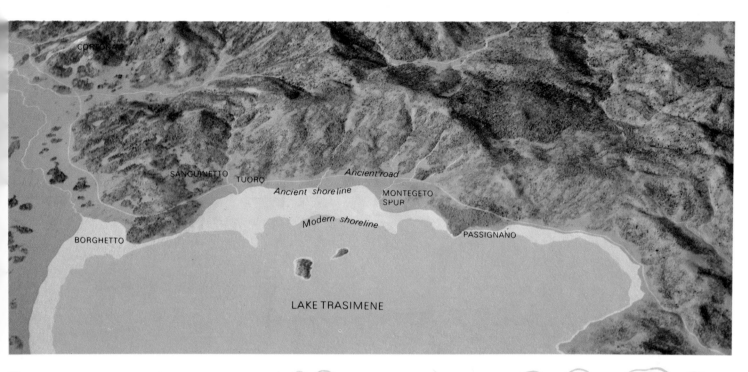

Above
A model of the north shore of Lake Trasimene and part of the plain of Cortona. The lighter blue shows the areas that were once under water. The site of the battle is between Tuoro and Passignano.

Centre
Map attributed to Leonardo da Vinci which shows Lake Trasimene overflowing into and flooding the valley of Chiana. This situation could only exist if the height of the lake was 266m instead of the present 258m, as the former is the height of the watershed at the north-east corner of the lake.

Right
The distribution of Hannibal's troops along the hillsides to the east of Tuoro. It seems unlikely that the Carthaginian would have drawn up his forces in extended line along the hills but more likely that, as shown here, he concealed them in the valleys out of sight of the Romans. He could hardly have relied on the mist that rose up from the lake in the early morning, and would never have deployed his troops at all if it had been there during the night.

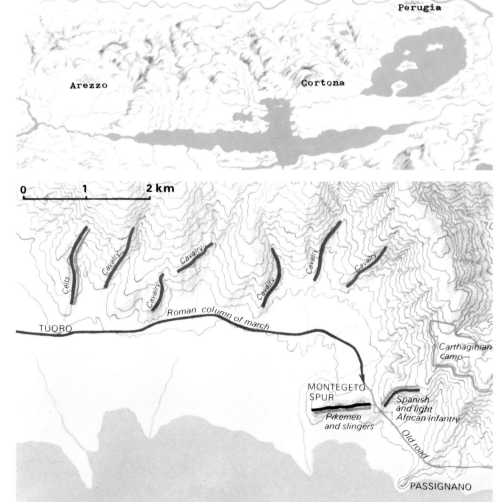

Trasimene were one vast lake. This, however, cannot be sustained as there is a watershed between the two lakes with a minimum elevation of 266m, whereas the watershed at the north end of the Val di Chiana is 248m. Therefore if both lakes were at their maximum height there would be a difference of 18m.

Lt. Melvin's expedition made a survey of the northern edge of Lake Trasimene and traced out the maximum height of the lake by establishing the 266m contour line. Their survey generally confirms Susini's projected coastline but comes in closer to the Montegeto spur just west of Passignano.

The map on p. 173 gives an idea of what the north shore must have looked like. Bearing in mind the higher water level, the road from Arezzo probably crossed over the hills where they extend right to the water's edge near Borghetto and then descended into a plain about two kilometres square. The far side of this plain was hemmed in by the spur on which Tuoro stands. Beyond this was a second plain, semi-lunate in shape, about four kilometres long and just over

a kilometre at its widest point. At the east end of this plain is a spur called Montegeto. It is about 50m high and juts out along the water's edge. The lake would have lapped the southern slope of this spur. One and a half kilometres further along, a rocky promontory projects into the lake. This is the headland on which the village of Passignano stands. When one allows for drainage and silting it seems highly unlikely that the ancient road rounded this point with its cliffs descending to the water's edge. Recently thousands of tonnes of rubble had to be tipped into the lake to make a solid base for the modern trunk road to Perugia.

Beyond Passignano there is only a narrow passageway between the hills and the lake which broadens out into a small plain on the east side of the lake. The ancient road must have taken to the hillside north of the Montegeto spur and only descended to the water's edge about 1,500m beyond Passignano.

Somewhere along this northern shore Hannibal laid an ambush. There are three possibilities for the site of this ambush: the square plain west of

Tuoro; the semi-lunate plain between Tuoro and Passignano; or the very narrow Thermopylae type pass beyond Passignano.

In spite of the fact that cremation pits and graves were found west of Tuoro, the plain here can hardly be said to fit Polybius' description. The Greek historian says that Hannibal's army was heading for Rome. This can only mean that he was heading for Perugia and Foligno to pick up the Via Flaminia. Wherever one places Hannibal's ambush, its location must be considered in relation to the road. Hannibal placed his troops on the hills on either side of the road. It follows that the site of the ambush cannot be between the Borghetto and Tuoro spurs as one cannot possibly justify a road to Rome running northwards between these hills.

The narrow pass beyond Passignano

Below
The site of Hannibal's ambush at Lake Trasimene. The picture is taken from the hillside where the cavalry were positioned. Hannibal's camp was on the hill to the left and the phalanx was drawn up along the spur.

Above
An Insubres chief from the time of Hannibal. Only chiefs would have worn helmets and mail shirts. The ordinary Celt of this period, shown behind the chieftain, fought stripped to the waist using only his shield for protection.

seems equally unlikely as the narrow plain at the east end, which would have to be Polybius' defile, could hardly be said to have Cortona and its hills on the left. This leaves the strip of land between Tuoro and Passignano. If the road did take to the hills to cross the Passignano promontory, then this could just fit Polybius' description. It also makes some sense of Flaminius' actions. When Hannibal surveyed the ground he must have realised that the best place to set an ambush lay in the narrow Thermopylae type pass beyond Passignano. But he knew that the Romans would never enter this without first scouting it thoroughly. On the other hand they would never suspect an ambush in the much more open ground before the danger spot was reached. This would account for Flaminius blundering straight into the trap laid for him, for he must have anticipated an ambush further down the road.

Hannibal pitched camp on the hill at the east end of the plain overlooking the defile. Flaminius with his forces, consisting of the tenth and eleventh legions plus the remnants of the third and fourth, about 30,000 men in all, arrived at the lake very late in the day and may well have camped on the Borghetto spur. He may even have been able to see the Carthaginian camp on the hill eight kilometres further along the north shore of the lake. Flaminius knew that his colleague was advancing down the Flaminian way and must have felt elated as he appeared to have Hannibal trapped between the two armies just as the Celts had been at Telamon eight years before. During the night Hannibal moved out of camp. It was probably a moonlit night as he felt obliged to conceal his movements. Making a detour along the far side of the hills, he placed his pikemen (c. 8,000) and his slingers (c. 2,000) in extended line along the Montegeto spur on the south side of the defile with the lake behind them. Similarly he posted his cavalry (c. 10,000) and his Celts (c. 25,000) along the hillsides facing the lake and stretching as far as the Tuoro spur. The remainder of the army, the Spanish infantry (c. 6,000) and the African light armed (c. 4,000) were drawn up in front of the camp. Because they were going to fight on a

slope the light-armed missile troops (javelineers and slingers) were probably placed behind the heavy infantry. The following morning Flaminius, wishing to keep contact in anticipation of his colleague's arrival, crossed the plain and passed the Tuoro spur. A heavy mist was rising from the lake which obscured the hillside. Hannibal could not have counted on this and therefore it could not have influenced his plan. When the Romans reached the far end of the plain and started the ascent, they found the Africans and Spaniards blocking their path. The Roman scouting system was so inefficient that the *extraordinarii* who made up the Roman vanguard came into contact with the Carthaginian forces before they realised that they were there. At first the Romans thought that they had fallen in with the Punic rearguard, but then trumpets echoed along the hills and the war cry was raised on all sides as Hannibal relayed down the line the order to charge.

The front of the Roman column was caught in an assault from three sides but somehow managed to break through. The rest of the column was at the mercy of the cavalry. They had no time to form up in battle order or probably even to throw their *pila* before the horsemen were upon them.

Livy gives more credit to Flaminius than Polybius. He says that Flaminius tried to bring order to the legions, hurrying to the points where the soldiers were hard pressed and urging his men on. Finally he was recognised by Ducarius, one of the Insubrian cavalry. The Insubres were thirsting for revenge after Flaminius' campaigns in their homelands six years earlier. Shouting to his comrades, Ducarius dashed towards the consul. The consul's armour bearer threw himself in front of Flaminius but was cut down. Then Ducarius turned on the Roman commander and ran him through. The *triarii* rallied around the dying consul to stop the Insubres despoiling the body.

The Romans held on for three hours but the Celts had cut off the line of retreat at the Tuoro spur and there was no escape.

Gradually they were driven back towards the marshes at the water's edge. Here, amidst the croaking frogs, they stumbled in the reeds and slime. The Carthaginians charged in after them cutting them down as they slithered around in the mud. Others waded farther out until only their heads were above the water and here they waited piteously for death to reach them. They held up their hands begging for mercy but found none. Some tried to swim further out into the lake but were drowned by the weight of their mail.

The Roman vanguard, about 6,000 strong, had broken through the enemy line and pushed on until they reached the crest of the hill. When the mist cleared and they were able to see the extent of the disaster, they retreated

and took shelter in an Etruscan village. On the following day they were surrounded and surrendered.

Hannibal had lost about 1,500 men, mainly Celts. About 15,000 Romans had fallen and a similar number had been taken prisoner. Hannibal released all the allied prisoners without ransom, stating that his war was with the Romans and not their allies. He had done the same after the battle at the Trebbia, hoping in this way to undermine the alliance.

After the battle Hannibal ordered a search to be made for the senior Roman officers so that he might pay them the last honours. About 30 were recovered

but there was no trace of Flaminius. Maybe the Celts had stripped the body and removed his head, or perhaps the *triarii* had dragged it into the water and there let it sink, weighed down by its armour.

When news of the disaster reached Rome the Senate were unable to conceal or soften the blow. The city praetor summoned a meeting of the people in the forum, mounted the rostrum and said simply, 'We have been defeated in a great battle'.

The crowd was all the more stunned as the Romans had not suffered such a defeat since the time of Regulus. But there was more to come.

Geminus, the other consul, was already on the march to join his colleague. He had sent ahead the 4,000 cavalry that were serving with his army as this was the arm in which Flaminius' army was weakest. Hannibal as usual had his scouts out and they brought him news that the cavalry were advancing down the Via Flaminia. Hannibal immediately sent out Maharbal with the pikemen and part of the cavalry. Polybius says no more than that they killed about half the force in the first attack and took the others prisoner the following day. Livy is even less enlightening. He says only that they fell into the hands of the Carthaginians. It sounds suspiciously like another ambush. The news of this second disaster arrived at Rome only three days after the first.

Livy tells us of the relatives waiting at the gates of the city hoping for news of their loved ones. One woman who had been told of the death of her son retired to her house to give vent to her sorrows. But as so often happens the report was wrong. When her son arrived home the strain was too much for her and she died in his arms.

The Etruscans did not flock to the Carthaginian standard as Hannibal had hoped. Their martial spirit was long dead. He had far greater hopes for southern Italy. There must have been some there who remembered the days of Pyrrhus 60 years before. From the

rasimene lake he continued his march
astwards to join the Flaminian Way
nd then advanced towards Rome.
.ivy says that he tried to take Spoleto
ut was repulsed. At Terni, 75km
orth of Rome, he turned south-east,
rossed the Sella di Corno pass over the
.pennines and arrived at the coast near
'escara. Here he rested his men and
ave much-needed attention to his
orses, which had suffered terribly
om the exertions of the previous year.
t Trebbia and Trasimene Hannibal
ad captured an enormous amount of
Roman armour and weapons. Selecting
he most suitable pieces he rearmed his
.fricans, principally with armour but

also possibly with swords.

As soon as the Punic army had re-
cuperated sufficiently they continued
their march down the coast into the
fertile plain of Apulia.

In times of extreme danger the
Romans resorted to the ancient custom
of placing total power in the hands of
one man. The man now chosen for
this onerous task was Quintus Fabius
Maximus. He was made dictator for
six months. He had seen service in the
first war with Carthage, and since then
he had been consul twice and had been
awarded a triumph for his victory over
the Ligurians. At the time of his
dictatorship he was about 60 years old.

He was a cautious man and this weighed
heavily in his appointment. The morale
of the army had reached a very low
ebb, and no doubt before he left Rome
to take up his command the Senate had
begged him not to attempt anything too
audacious before the army had had
time to recover.

Fabius was given as his second-in-
in-command (master of the cavalry)
Marcus Minucius Rufus, who had

Below
Map of northern Campania showing the main
routes and the most important towns. The
Roman and Latin colonies are marked in red.
Hannibal entered the Falernian plain by way of
Pietravairano.

served as consul in 221 BC. Fabius immediately began raising four new legions, the 14th, 15th, 16th and 17th. As soon as the Carthaginians had moved out of central Italy, Fabius ordered Geminus to march south and join him at Narni on the Via Flaminia. Geminus had with him the 12th and 13th legions plus the remnants of Scipio's first and second (c. 30,000 men). There was no cavalry; these had been lost after the battle of Trasimene.

Fabius marched north to meet him at the head of two of the hastily raised legions, the 14th and 15th. The other two remained at Rome. This is the account given by Livy, but Polybius says he took all four new legions. This contradiction between our two sources has caused much confusion for it affects not only this year but also the following one. Livy and Polybius are here drawing on two different sources but it seems possible that both these sources have a common origin. Polybius' source knew that the dictator had the nucleus of six legions in his army but failed to mention Scipio's defeated troops and therefore gave the dictator all four new legions. Livy's source, on the other hand, accounted for the remnants of Scipio's legions and therefore only had to raise two more. The only difficulty is that Livy promptly forgets Scipio's legions and talks of four legions at Gerunium where the army wintered. Fabius took over Geminus' legions, which gave him a total of around 47,000 infantry and 2,500 cavalry. He sent the consul on to Rome with orders to take over the navy and organise the defence of the coasts of southern Italy.

According to Livy, Fabius now led his army across country to Tivoli and Palestrina to join the Latin Way south of Rome. For some unexplained reason he wished to bypass Rome. Was this because a Roman commander was not allowed to enter Rome at the head of his troops and Fabius was obeying the letter of the law? He appears to have followed the Latin Way and then the Appian Way, crossing the Apennines via Benevento, and pitched camp in the foothills near Aecae (Troia) about nine kilometres from Hannibal's position. The Carthaginian immediately led out his army and offered battle but the dictator declined. It was Fabius' inten-

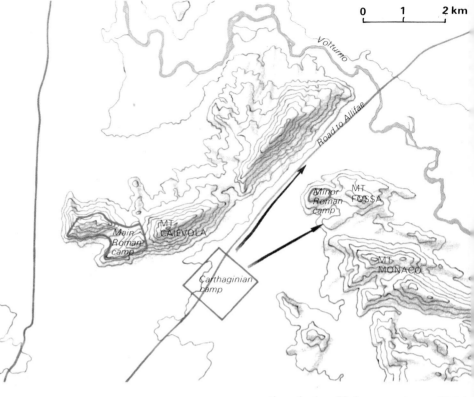

Above
Map of the pass leading from Campania to the valley of the Volturno at Pietravairano. Hannibal's feint with the oxen is shown with a brown arrow, the true thrust with a red arrow.

tion to refuse battle but to follow the Carthaginian around, burning the crops and cutting off foragers and stragglers and thus gradually wearing down the Carthaginian army whilst at the same time raising the strength and morale of his own troops, many of whom had only recently enlisted. It would be wrong to say that they were raw recruits since most of them would have seen previous service in the Celtic wars. But they would have needed training and discipline.

Hannibal ravaged the countryside around Fabius' camp. When it became clear that the dictator was not going to come out, he broke camp and tried the same tactic that he had used with so much success against Flaminius. He marched straight by Fabius and re-crossed the Apennines as far as the Roman colony at Benevento. He then followed the north bank of the Calore river as far as the town of Telesia (Telese), which he sacked in passing, and descended into the Falernian fields

north of the Volturno river. Fabius followed one or two days' march behind.

Hannibal believed that here in Campania, which was densely populated with many towns, Fabius would not be able to let him burn and pillage with impunity. He was wrong.

Fabius took up his position on the hills overlooking the plain so that the allies would not think that the Romans had entirely deserted them, but he refused to descend into the plain. Hannibal did his best to lure the dictator down and laid waste the whole of the plain north of the Volturno.

It was now autumn. Although they had collected a vast amount of booty, the orchards and vineyards of the Falernian plain could hardly sustain the Carthaginian army through the winter. It was essential that they get back to Apulia. But when they tried to return by the way they had come, they found the route blocked. Polybius says that Fabius had posted about 4,000 men blocking the route by which Hannibal had entered the plain whilst he himself encamped on a hill overlooking the pass. When Hannibal arrived he encamped on the level ground beneath the hill. He realised at once the danger of his position and gave Fabius no time to exploit it. Summoning the commander of the army servants, he ordered him to gather as many faggots as possible and assemble about 2,000 of the strongest plough oxen from the many that they had captured. Then, calling together the army servants, he pointed out a hillock between his camp and the pass telling them that when they received the order they were to drive the oxen up to the top of the hill as furiously as they could.

Hannibal ordered his soldiers to have their supper and retire early. Towards the end of the third watch (about 3 am) he ordered the servants to bind the faggots to the horns of the oxen and light them. The frightened animals were then driven up the hillside. Behind the oxen he had placed his light-armed pikemen with orders to help the servants to get the animals moving but then to run along on either side of them and keep them massed together. On reaching the high ground they were ordered to occupy the ridge in order to throw back any Roman advance. Meanwhile Hannibal himself at the head of his heavy-armed troops, made a dash for the pass. They were followed by the cavalry, then the captured cattle and finally the Spaniards and Celts.

When the Romans in the pass were awakened by their sentries, they saw the mass of torches charging up the hill and advanced to meet them. Here they were thrown into complete confusion by the pikemen and the oxen. Fabius could do no more than watch from his camp. True to his character he remained where he was until daylight. Meanwhile Hannibal, whose diversion had been more successful than even he could have hoped, forced his way through the pass getting both his army and booty through intact. The first light of dawn revealed the Romans from the pass drawn up on the hill opposite the pikemen. Hannibal immediately sent back some of his Spaniards to assist them. These attacked the Romans, killing about 1,000 of them and allowing the pikemen to withdraw.

This is the gist of Polybius' account. The problem is Polybius' vagueness about where these events took place. He implies that Hannibal left the Falernian plain by the same route he had used to enter it. Unfortunately he is very vague on this point.

He says that after leaving Samnium Hannibal traversed the pass near the hill called Eribianus and encamped beside the river Athyrnus (Volturno). Eribianus, however, is completely unknown.

Livy places the Carthaginian's route through the districts of Allifae (Alife), Calatia, and Cales (Calvi). Calatia is obviously a mistake, as it is situated on the other side of the Volturno, in central Campania. He might be referring to Caiatia (Caiazzo) or Callifae (Calvisi) or some unknown town of a similar name. As so often with Livy, we are left in the dark. The Roman historian further states that Hannibal wanted to go to Casinum (Cassino) but the guide misunderstood and led him to Casilinum (Capua). This seems highly unlikely and Polybius certainly does not mention it. The truth may be that Hannibal was trying to convince Fabius that he was marching on Rome and headed up the Volturno valley through the districts of Caiazzo and Alife towards Cassino. When Fabius refused to be drawn he turned southwest, passing through the hills just north of Monte Monaco into the Falernian plain. He then crossed the territory of Cales (Calvi) and finally camped on the north side of the Volturno. In order to solve this problem one question has to be asked. From the north side of the Calore river was it possible to enter the Falernian plain by a direct route?

Both Livy and Polybius state that Hannibal took Telesia (Telese) which is on the north side of the Calore river about seven kilometres from its junction with the Volturno. In order to advance into the Falernian plain along the north bank of the Volturno he would have first to cross the Volturno. It is doubtful that there was a road along the north side of the Volturno. A spur (Monte Raggelo) juts out from the main range of hills at the north side of the Volturno and pinches the river at the point where it enters the plain. Between here and Caiazzo there is some very low-lying ground which has now been drained. This makes it unlikely first that there was a road and second that Hannibal would have come this way. If this is so then Hannibal had no alternative but to enter the plain from the north.

Livy now goes completely haywire. He places the Romans blocking the road to Casilinum (Capua) with Capua (Santa Maria di Capua Vetere) at their backs. In other words Hannibal was trying to go southwards, but after he broke through Livy puts Hannibal in camp at Alife 32km further up the Volturno. This is very unsatisfactory, but Alife is the only checkpoint we have. After Hannibal had escaped Livy says that Fabius also went through the pass and encamped in a lofty strong position above Alife.

So we must look for this pass somewhere within about 15km of Alife. The most likely position is the gap in the hills at Pietravairano. As this is the widest and easiest route it has to be the one Fabius blocked. But there are several other routes. Why did Hannibal not use one of these? The answer may lie in the words of Polybius: 'Fabius thought that at least he would be able to capture their booty'. If Hannibal wanted to hang on to the enormous amount of loot he had amassed, then he had to take an easy route. Otherwise he might find his army stretched out and at the mercy of the Romans.

The Roman detachment of 4,000 were probably encamped on the northwest spur of Monte Fossa (Montagna di Bruno) overlooking the pass, and the main army at the west end of Monte Caievola covering the Via Latina. Hannibal must have camped on the flat below Monte Caievola and driven his diversionary oxen up the south-west spur of Monte Fossa. The Roman garrison moving round to intercept the oxen would have placed themselves between the pikemen and Hannibal's final position near Alife. To relieve his pikemen the Carthaginian sent out his Spaniards to attack the Romans from the rear.

Hannibal now recrossed the Apennines, marching past Mount Liburnon. No mountain of this name is known. However, it has been suggested that it should read Tiburnon (Latin Tifernus). Mons Tifernus (modern Montagna del Matese) rises above Alife. It is the highest mountain in this area of the Apennines. Its position and size both suggest that it is Polybius' Liburnon.

Hannibal had been told that he would find abundant corn around

Lucera and Gerunium and that the best place for collecting supplies would be Gerunium, which was about 200 *stades* (c. 35km) from Lucera. The site of Gerunium is not known. Polybius says that most of the country around the town was flat and easy to overrun. The ruins of a town have been found at Gerione, five kilometres south of Larino. But this location, in the foothills of the Apennines, could never fit Polybius' description. Gerunium is marked on the famous Tabula Peutingeriana which is a medieval copy of a Roman road map. This places the town eight Roman miles along the road to Bovianum from its junction with the coast road near Teanum. It should therefore lie four or five kilometres north of Casalnuovo Monterotaro but only about 25km from Lucera. In accordance with this Kromayer placed Gerunium on the hill known as the Colle d'Armi four kilometres north of Casalnuovo Monterotaro. In the spring of 1979 I decided to sherd the area and worked my way down the road which runs north along the crest of the spur looking at the newly ploughed fields and examining all the likely sites. In this fashion I worked my way along the crest of the hill without success until I reached the junction of the rough road to Lucera. On the west side of the spur the farmers had been raking up stones and leaving them in piles along the edge of the field. Amongst these I found masses of Roman roof tiles. The area also revealed two Roman sarcophagi which were being used as water troughs and what appeared to be a Roman well. The sherds covered an area about 300m across, forming a small spur jutting out to the west of the main ridge directly opposite the junction of the road from

Below
Model of the area around Gerunium.
1 The site of the first Roman camp.
2 The site of the second Roman camp.
3 The site of the third Roman camp.
4 The hill where the battle was fought.

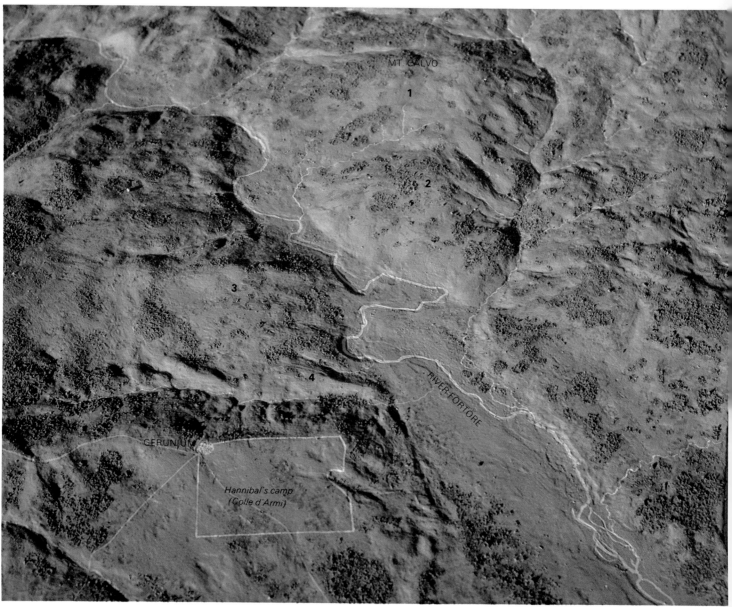

Lucera, which probably follows the track of the ancient road. This would certainly accord with Polybius' topography for the ensuing campaign. The easiest way to get here from Alife is by skirting the north side of the Monti del Matese by way of Isernia and Boiano, and then taking the road to Campobasso and descending the valleys of the Tapino and Fortore.

As usual the Romans followed, keeping to the high ground. From Campobasso they probably followed the route of the modern SS Sannitica (Route 87) along the hilltops.

Meanwhile Hannibal had encamped near Gerunium. The townspeople refused his offers of alliance, and he stormed the town putting the inhabitants to the sword. He did not destroy the town but kept its walls and houses intact so that he could use it as a corn magazine. He then established his winter quarters in front of the town, fortifying the camp with a trench and palisade. Having thoroughly defended his position he sent out two-thirds of his army to gather in the corn. The other third of the army guarded the

camp and covered the foragers. This was normal practice. Caesar did the same at Alesia.

The Romans had now arrived in the area. Fabius had been recalled to Rome to preside over some religious ceremonies and his master of the cavalry, Minucius, had taken over command.

Polybius says that when Minucius heard that Hannibal was encamped at Gerunium and foraging in the district, 'he turned and descended from the hills by a ridge that slopes down to the town. Arriving at a height in the territory of Larinum (Larino) called Calena, he encamped there . . .'. Just before the SS Sannitica reaches Casacalenda it is joined by a road which follows the crest of the hill to Bonefro (alt. 606m). About three kilometres beyond Bonefro there is a spur jutting out to the southeast. At the end of this spur is a hill called Monte Calvo (alt. 409m). This hill overlooks the Fortore river and is seven and a half kilometres from the suggested site of Gerunium.

Polybius stated that this hill was called Calena and was in the territory of Larino. In northern Campania there

was a Roman town called Cales with an adjectival form of Calenum (Livy *VIII*, 6). The name has been corrupted to the modern Calvi. It is hardly stretching the bounds of possibility to suggest that Calena has been corrupted to Calvo. It is also interesting to note that the town at the other end of this ridge is called Casacalenda. Larino is 17km from Monte Calvo. Its territory was probably bounded by the Biferno and Fortore rivers, in which case Monte Calvo would be just within its borders. The model shows the area between Monte Calvo and Colle d'Armi (Gerunium).

The manoeuvres that follow are an object lesson in tactics; a text book lesson on how to draw an opponent from an unassailable position first across a river and secondly into an ambush.

Leaving one-third of his soldiers to forage Hannibal advanced 16 *stades*

Below
View of the valley of the Fortore from the site of Gerunium. Minucius' first camp is in the distance (centre). Hannibal's second camp was established in the middle distance of the picture.

(c. 3km) from Gerunium and encamped on a hill (**3**), 'with a view to overawing the enemy and protecting his foragers'. This new position, only about four and a half kilometres from the Roman camp (**1**), made it very difficult for them to descend the Fortore valley and attack the foragers in the plain.

Between the two camps there was a hill (**2**). If Hannibal controlled this then he could effectively cut the Romans off from the plain. Accordingly under cover of night he sent out 2,000 pikemen to occupy it. At daybreak Minucius dispatched his lightly armed troops to dislodge the pikemen. In a brisk skirmish the Romans captured the hill. Because this hill controlled the access to the plain Minucius did the obvious and sensible thing—he moved his camp on to it. Round one to Hannibal. Polybius' account of what follows is seen through Roman eyes and does not reflect Hannibal's strategy. For a few days, he says, Hannibal kept all his forces in camp because of the closeness of the enemy, but after this he was compelled to put some of his animals out to pasture and send out part of his forces to forage as he was determined that his army, both men and animals, should have plenty of food during the coming winter.

Minucius was not as feeble-minded as the ancient historians would have us believe. When he saw that most of Hannibal's men were out foraging, he waited until the middle of the day and then led out his heavy infantry, drawing them up in front of the Carthaginian camp to keep Hannibal confined. At the same time he divided his cavalry and *velites* into several troops and sent them out to attack the foragers with orders not to take prisoners. This is a perfect example of the so-called Fabian tactics put into practice far more effectively than Fabius had yet done.

With the small forces left in camp Polybius states Hannibal could do nothing but endure the taunts of the legionaries and stop them breaking into his camp. When Hasdrubal with 6,000 of the harrassed foragers returned to the camp, Hannibal felt strong enough to make a sally and drive the Romans from his camp. The Romans had killed many of the enemy around the camp and in the fields. They had accomplished

their aims and retired to their camp. That night Hannibal retreated to his original encampment in front of Gerunium. The next day the Romans, seeing the Carthaginian camp deserted, crossed the river and occupied it. Round two to Hannibal: he now had the Romans on his side of the river.

The Romans were understandably elated with their success, and indeed foraging now became very difficult for Hannibal. At Rome an exaggerated account of Minucius' success was met with great rejoicing. As the mass of the people were far from satisfied with Fabius' rather indifferent performance, they now took an unprecedented step and made Minucius co-dictator. This move must have had strong support in the Senate or it could never have taken place. Fabius, who had received the nickname of 'Cunctator' (the Delayer) for the apparent lack of energy with which he had opposed Hannibal, now hastily returned to the army. Polybius tells us that he offered Minucius the choice of commanding on alternate days—a quaint Roman practice when consular armies were combined—or dividing the army. We are told Minucius opted for dividing the army. This is surely not so. It is much more likely that Fabius insisted on splitting the army for he could only continue his strategy by being permanently in command, whereas Minucius could easily practice his on alternate days. The two generals divided the army and encamped at a distance of about 12 *stades* (a little over two kilometres) apart. If Minucius remained where he was, Fabius may very well have pitched his camp in the position Minucius evacuated when he crossed the river (**2**).

Between Hannibal's camp in front of Gerunium and Minucius' camp (**3**) there was a small hillock (**4**). Knowing that if he tried to occupy it Minucius would once again attempt to dislodge him, Hannibal prepared an ambush. The ground around the hill was treeless but was pitted with hollows. During the night Hannibal sent out 5,000 mixed infantry and 500 horse in bodies of 2–300 to occupy these hollows. In order that these troops should not be discovered by Roman foraging parties as they set out in the early morning,

Hannibal did not send out his light-armed troops to occupy the hillock until daybreak so as to afford a suitable diversion.

Minucius responded with alacrity, immediately sending out his *velites* to dislodge the Carthaginians. This time, however, Hannibal had no intention of being dislodged. It is worth noting that when he occupied hill no. **1** he intended to withdraw, so he sent out his pikemen who could perform the manoeuvre in a strongly defensive formation. This time his aims were different. When the *velites* failed to take the position, Minucius dispatched his cavalry and then followed up at the head of his legions drawn up in close order. All eyes were on the battle on the hill, and the men in hiding went unnoticed. At the same time Hannibal continued to send out reinforcements to keep the fire burning. Then finally he led out the rest of his infantry and his cavalry. The Carthaginian cavalry charged, hurling back not only the Roman horsemen but also the *velites*. These retreated in disorder on the heavy infantry who appear to have already closed the gaps in the maniples and as a result the whole army was thrown into confusion. The signal was given and the ambush sprung. Troop after troop arose as if from the ground and charged the Romans in the flanks and rear. The smaller Roman force was in danger of being annihilated. The Cunctator, cautious as ever, had been watching from his camp. The legions had been put on alert and were now led out. One can well imagine Minucius' feelings when he heard the trumpeters sound the advance.

His men had been so shattered that they had broken ranks. Now when they heard Fabius coming the maniples regrouped around their standards and made an orderly retreat under the cover of the other army. Realising that the exhibition was over, Hannibal withdrew to his camp.

According to Livy, that evening Minucius' army broke camp and retreated to Fabius' position. They entered the camp of the Cunctator and advanced up the *via praetoria* to the tribunal in front of Fabius' tent. Here they planted the standards and Minucius advanced towards Fabius addressing him as 'Father' in the customary manner of a comrade saved from death, thus placing himself under Fabius' authority.

The Carthaginians meanwhile erected a stockade around the hill and dug a ditch between it and their camp. Then, placing a garrison on the hill, they finished their preparations for the winter undisturbed.

Cannae: Rome's greatest defeat

Winter had arrived. The six months of Fabius' dictatorship were over and power was returned to the consuls. The dead consul, Flaminius, had been replaced by Marcus Atilius Regulus, the son of the famous Regulus who had been defeated by the Carthaginians in the first war—an ominous choice. Two new consuls were elected for the fateful year of 216 BC, Lucius Aemilius Paullus and Gaius Terentius Varro. Paullus was the grandfather of Scipio Aemilianus and is a member of the group of people whom Polybius will not criticise. Therefore Varro becomes the scapegoat for the impending disaster. So much malice surrounds the name of Varro that it is impossible at this distance to reconstruct a real person. All one can do is to point out the rather obvious flaws in the ancient accounts. It would be pointless to comment on Livy's account of his election as it is angled to provide a suitable background to his subsequent public disgrace.

Two praetors were elected in their absence, for both men were already serving in the field. These were the famous Marcus Claudius Marcellus, who was given command of the fifth legion in Sicily, and Lucius Postumius Albinus, who was sent to the Po valley with orders to keep the Celts occupied.

The consul for the previous year, Geminus, whom the dictator had sent to command the fleet at Lilybaeum in Sicily, was recalled. He and Regulus were appointed proconsuls and placed in command of the army at Gerunium. A levy was called to raise the existing legions to their full strength and to enrol four new ones. Legions 16 and 17 which had been enrolled after Trasimene and had been undergoing training at Rome were probably posted to Gerunium to bring the number of legions there up to eight, four for each consul. Two of the

new legions (18th and 19th) were dispatched to the Po valley under the praetor Lucius Postumius Albinus and the 20th and 21st were left at Rome for the defence of the city.

This massive display of strength with 16 legions (c. 150,000) in the field can only mean that the Romans had decided to fight a pitched battle with Hannibal whenever a favourable opportunity presented itself. There can be little truth in the tradition of a conflict between Paullus and Varro, the latter wanting to fight and the former wishing to continue Fabius' tactics.

It was well into the summer when Hannibal broke camp and left Gerunium. He marched south-east about 100km to the river Aufidus (Ofanto). Here he seized the citadel of Cannae which the Romans were using as a food store, transferring the supplies to the Carthaginian camp as they required them. When they heard of this the proconsuls, who were now within a day and a half's march of Hannibal's position (c. 40–50km), sent messages to the Senate to ask for instructions. The Senate had already decided that a decisive battle must be fought; ordering the proconsuls to remain where they were, they dispatched the two consuls to join them. Polybius tells us that they had never before brought eight legions into the field. By this he means that this was the first time that two consular armies, each

of four legions, had been combined in one army. Polybius records the use of four-legion consular armies during the Gallic invasion of 225 BC.

Many commentators have criticised Polybius' figures, arguing that the Carthaginian army could never have surrounded a Roman army of 80,000 men at the battle of Cannae. But Polybius' figures are entirely consistent and no one was better equipped to estimate the comparative abilities of the Romans and Carthaginians—certainly not a modern historian. One may add that the Romans could hardly have implemented their strategy of 'crowding' Hannibal and restricting his foraging before the battle unless they outnumbered him.

Polybius adds that the legions were each raised to a strength of 5,000 and that they had 'rather more than 6,000 cavalry'. This latter figure is entirely consistent for Geminus had lost the cavalry attached to the first, second, 12th and 13th legions, a loss which would have proved difficult to repair.

Having addressed the army to put them in the right frame of mind, the

Below

A topographic map of the area between San Ferdinando and Cannae. The contours are at 5m intervals. The dykes to control the flooding of the river are marked in red. The dotted blue line marks the possible old course of the river. The line along which the Romans drew up their forces is marked with a broken black line.

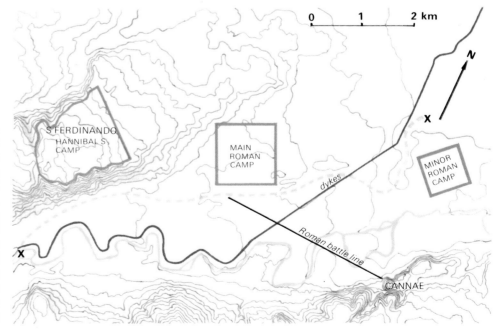

consuls broke camp and advanced on Cannae. On the second day they came in sight of Hannibal's position and encamped at a distance of about eight kilometres.

The topography of the ensuing campaign and battle depends on two factors, the siting of Hannibal's camp and the position of the river Ofanto.

A range of low hills spreads out eastwards from the Apennines at the southern end of the plain of Foggia. The river Ofanto, after leaving the Apennines, flows along the north edge of these hills. The citadel of Cannae sits upon a hillock at the northern edge of this range overlooking the river. The difficulty is encountered because Polybius quite clearly places the battle near Cannae on the south side of the river. As things are today this is impossible for the river almost laps the hills. The Ofanto has changed its course many times and it is therefore meaningless to attempt to determine the site of the battle by reference to its present course. The map on p. 183 shows the contours of the Cannae plain at five-metre invervals. These contours show several other possible river beds (marked with a broken blue line). The extent of the river's flooding is shown by the series of dykes on the north side of the river (marked in red). For the purposes of describing the battle the course marked **XX** has been selected as the most probable bed of the river. This would allow for a plain about two kilometres wide between the river and the hills.

Having surveyed the area the Romans decided to move their camp right up to the river to restrict the Punic foragers. Hannibal countered by sending out his light-armed troops and cavalry to harass the Romans as they tried to force their way up to the north bank of the river. Varro, whose day it was to command, threw forward some of his heavy infantry and later also his *velites* and cavalry to ward off the Carthaginian attacks. This appears to be the usual Roman covering force for encamping in the face of the enemy. The legions reached the river and under cover of their advanced guard dug in next to the ford.

This manoeuvre was clearly intended to crowd the Carthaginian position and make it difficult for them to forage on

the north side of the river. The following morning Paullus was in command. We are told that he had opposed Varro's advance as too dangerous but he now moved one-third of his troops across the river and they encamped east of the ford about three kilometres from the main camp and rather more from Hannibal's camp. If Hannibal were encamped south of the river, Paullus' action would appear even more desperate than Varro's and yet Polybius does not even suggest that Hannibal tried to stop them establishing a second camp. The implication of this, and the distance between the camps, suggest that Hannibal's camp lay north of the river. Certainly Polybius places it on the north side shortly before the battle and never mentions Hannibal crossing the river.

So, assuming that Hannibal was indeed on the north side of the river, where was his camp? The Carthaginian had arrived at the Ofanto weeks before the Romans and therefore would have had plenty of time to select the most advantageous position for his camp. Hannibal was a highly intelligent general, and although he was always willing to exploit his enemies' mistakes, he always tried to make sure that his own position was secure. Bearing this in mind, there is only one site on the north side of the Ofanto where he would have camped. This is the spur on which the town of San Ferdinando di Puglia now stands. This is flat-topped with steep sides on the north-west and south-east which is lapped by the river. The northeast side slopes gently down to the plain, giving easy access for his cavalry. From here he could forage with impunity. The Carthaginian could hardly have resisted such a situation, for not only is it strongly defended whilst giving easy access to the plain, but it also covered the valley of the Ofanto, his line of retreat if anything went wrong.

With Hannibal securely encamped here it is now possible to site the Roman camps (see the map). The positioning of the camp on the south bank now makes sense: it is to stop Hannibal foraging on that side of the river and is clearly part of the overall Roman strategy. This makes nonsense of the theory that the two consuls were in bitter conflict.

Hannibal was now cut off from the plain on both sides of the river and it

was only a matter of time before his provisions ran out. The time had come t fight. He assembled his army to giv them the usual encouraging speech an then moved forward his pickets and ad vance defences to secure his access t the plain. The following day the Car thaginians spent polishing their armou and preparing their weapons in antici pation of the battle. The next mornin, Hannibal led out his army and offere battle on the north bank of the river This would have allowed unlimite range to his cavalry and the Roman wisely refused.

The following morning (the ancien historians all say it was Varro's day o command) Paullus led the Romans ou of the camp on the north bank an crossed the ford. On the south bank the were joined by Varro and the rest of th army and formed up in line of battle o the narrow strip of land between th river and the hills with their right win resting on the river and their left on th hills. Here the Carthaginian cavalr would not be able to outflank them Polybius seems to corroborate thi choice of site when he says that th Romans placed their maniples close together than usual and made the dept of each maniple many times greater tha its front. The shape of a standard *hastati principes* maniple before the gaps ar closed can vary from six ranks of 20 t 24 ranks of five. It must be this las figure, 24 ranks of five, to which Poly bius is referring. If the legion strengt was 5,000, the depth of the *hastati* an *principes* maniples was probably in creased to 30 ranks. Since they wer clearly going for a breakthrough, th legionaries must have been drawn up i close order with three Roman feet pe man. A maniple would therefore b about 15ft wide and a legion, allowin for the gaps, about 300ft. The tota width of the infantry, including allies would therefore be about 4,800ft (c. 1,500m).

Since the job of the Roman horsemen was to hold the Carthaginian cavalry at all costs, they would have been drawn up to maximum depth, i.e. ten deep. According to Polybius, drawn up eight deep, there would be 800 cavalry to a *stade* or slightly under two metres per horse in the ranks. The Romans had somewhat more than 6,000 horse which,

Above
The battlefield of Cannae seen from the site of the old citadel of Cannae. The modern village of San Ferdinando, where Hannibal pitched camp, is on the low ridge in the distance to the left. The smaller Roman camp would have been off to the right and the larger camp in the distance on the right. The Romans drew up their forces between Cannae and the San Ferdinando spur with their right wing locked on the river and their left on the hills to counter the Carthaginian cavalry.

Above
The battlefield at Cannae showing the old course of the river Ofanto. Hannibal's camp is pitched on the low spur on the left where the village of San Ferdinando now stands. The main Roman camp is close to it to harass the Carthaginian foragers and watering parties on the north side of the river. The lesser Roman camp is on the south side of the river (right) to prevent Hannibal's troops foraging south of the river. Cannae is at the bottom. The Romans are on the right facing south.

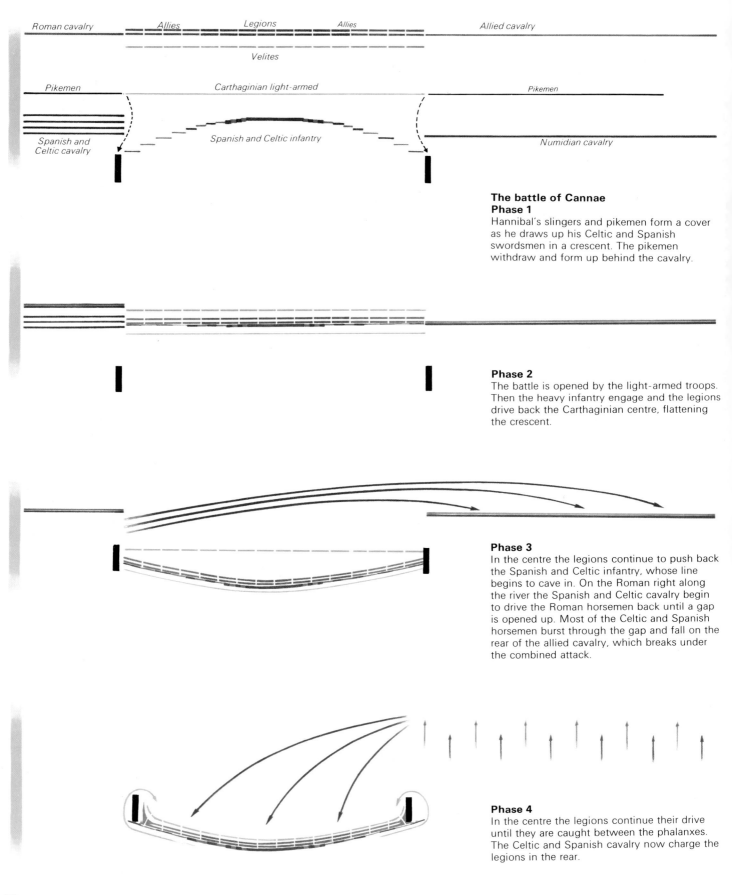

The battle of Cannae
Phase 1
Hannibal's slingers and pikemen form a cover as he draws up his Celtic and Spanish swordsmen in a crescent. The pikemen withdraw and form up behind the cavalry.

Phase 2
The battle is opened by the light-armed troops. Then the heavy infantry engage and the legions drive back the Carthaginian centre, flattening the crescent.

Phase 3
In the centre the legions continue to push back the Spanish and Celtic infantry, whose line begins to cave in. On the Roman right along the river the Spanish and Celtic cavalry begin to drive the Roman horsemen back until a gap is opened up. Most of the Celtic and Spanish horsemen burst through the gap and fall on the rear of the allied cavalry, which breaks under the combined attack.

Phase 4
In the centre the legions continue their drive until they are caught between the phalanxes. The Celtic and Spanish cavalry now charge the legions in the rear.

Roman cavalry Allies Legions Allies Allied cavalry
Velites
Pikemen Carthaginian light-armed Pikemen
Spanish and Celtic cavalry Spanish and Celtic infantry Numidian cavalry

plit in proportion of three allied to one Roman, would break down to about 1,600 Roman and 4,800 allied. Allowing for gaps between the *turmae*, the Roman cavalry would therefore have covered about 575m and the allies about 1,725m. The total Roman front would have been a little over 3,000m. The plain had a maximum width of about two kilometres. The width of the Roman front could be accommodated if the Romans lined up diagonally facing south (see map). Polybius does indeed place the Romans facing south. Ten thousand Romans were left to guard the camp with orders to attack the Carthaginian camp during the battle. The *triarii* were customarily given this job. There would be 9,600 of these in the army and this would seem to fit in well with Polybius' approximation. Contrary to popular opinion both in the ancient and the modern world, the Romans had no reason to suppose that they would lose this battle. All the other defeats had been caused by the rashness of the generals. In the present situation the Romans had selected the site of the battle, allowing Hannibal no opportunity to lay an ambush. In the other battles Hannibal had selected the site. Furthermore, in choosing this site the Romans believed that they had neutralised Hannibal's cavalry.

The division of command is most revealing. There were two positions of honour in the Roman republican army; one was at the head of the citizen cavalry and the other in charge of the legions in the centre. Since Varro was supposed to be commander-in-chief one would expect to find him in one of these two positions. As it was, Regulus and Geminus commanded the centre, Paullus the right wing and Varro the left. The only conclusion that can be drawn from this is that Paullus and not Varro was in command. It follows that it must have been Varro who declined a battle on the north side of the river the day before.

When Hannibal saw the Romans lining up he sent his slingers and pikemen across the river, drawing them up in a line across the plain. Behind this covering force he drew up the rest of his troops. On the right, under the hills and opposite the allied horse, he placed his Numidians. It is possible to make a fairly accurate estimate of their num-

bers. When he arrived in Italy, Hannibal had a total of 6,000 cavalry, part Spanish and part Numidian. Their number cannot have increased and since the Numidians were opposed to the allied cavalry numbering about 4,800 they cannot have been much less than this number. A reasonable estimate would be 4,000. The Spanish cavalry, which must therefore number about 2,000 plus the Celtic cavalry, which, since his total cavalry numbered 10,000 must have been 4,000 strong, were drawn up next to the river. Because of their number, which was four times that of the opposing Roman cavalry, they must have been drawn up in four lines. The Carthaginian infantry consisted of little more than 40,000 men of which about 12,000 were African and 8,000 Spanish, the remainder being Celts. From these must be deducted the light-armed troops who probably made up the same proportion of the whole infantry as in the legions, i.e. a little under 30 per cent. We may therefore assume that the phalanx was about 8,000 strong, the Spanish swordsmen about 5,500 and the Celtic swordsmen about 14,000.

Polybius says that Hannibal lined up his Spanish and Celtic swordsmen in alternate *speirai*. Once before Polybius mentions this type of formation where two unequal forces were lined up in alternate *speirai*. This was at the battle of Sellasia, where the Illyrians and Macedonian 'brazen shields' formed up in this fashion. One must assume that in this context *speirai* is used as a general term for company, but even so it must have a size limit. Polybius uses it to describe maniples (even of *triarii*), therefore it could be as small as 100 men. However, he could hardly use it for a unit as large as a thousand, which he would have called a *chiliarchy*. One should probably put an upward limit of about 500. If the Spanish units were put at a convenient strength of 100, the Celtic units would have to be about 250. However, Polybius may be oversimplifying. To Hannibal the Celts were the most expendable of his troops. Certainly he lost nearly three times as many Celts in the battle as his Spanish and African casualties combined. It is therefore proposed that perhaps half the Celts formed the centre of the line and that the alternate companies of Spani-

ards and Celts made up the flanks. Once he had drawn up the Celts and Spaniards, he advanced their central companies to form a crescent-shaped formation with the centre dense and the flanking companies gradually becoming thinner towards the points of the crescent. This formation had only one purpose: to break the force of the Roman charge before the crack African troops were brought into action, proving beyond a doubt that the Roman forces greatly outnumbered the Carthaginian. The African pikemen, who up till now had been drawn up with the light-armed troops ahead of the army to act as a covering force, were withdrawn and formed up in column behind the cavalry on each wing with the file leaders in each case forming the inside file so that each column could turn inwards to form a phalanx. In the light of their subsequent manoeuvres this is the only possible interpretation. Cannae only reveals one face of this unique battle formation, but it also had superb defensive qualities as the two phalanxes could turn outwards to meet a flank attack or turn inwards to trap a breakthrough in the centre, quite apart from its potential for meeting an attack from the rear. Hannibal had used the same formation at the Trebbia but had preferred to go for a quick victory on the wings rather than reinforce his centre. Hannibal himself, with his brother Mago, commanded the crucial point in the centre whilst Hasdrubal commanded the Spanish and Celtic cavalry on the left and Hanno the Numidians on the right.

The battle was begun as usual by the light-armed on both sides. During this initial conflict Paullus was struck by a heavy stone from a Balearic slinger and severely wounded. The fight was soon taken up by the Celtic and Spanish horse along the river bank. The Roman cavalry fought bravely but they were no match for the Spaniards and Celts and were pushed steadily back along the river. The Romans dragged their adversaries from their horses and struggled with them on the ground but nothing could stem the tide. On the other wing the Numidians skirmished with the allied cavalry, trying to draw them away from the legions but without success. The Romans now decided to throw in their legions before the situation on the right wing got out of hand. The trumpets sounded the recall and the *velites* began to retire. The legionaries now began to clash their *pila* against their shields whilst they waited for the order to charge. Hannibal also ordered the recall of his light-armed troops, and the Celts and Spaniards braced themselves for the onslaught. Once the *velites* had passed through the gaps, the advance was sounded and the rear centuries of the *hastati* moved up to close the gaps. The trumpets sounded the charge, both sides raised their war cry, and amidst the deafening clamour of horns, trumpets and carnyxes, the two infantry forces rushed forward. The Celts and Spaniards raised their shields and braced themselves to receive the first volley of *pila* which was quickly followed by the second. Shaking their shields to dislodge the buckled javelins the Celts and Spaniards threw themselves against the legionaries with a reverberating thud as shield hit shield. For a while the Celts and Spaniards held their formation, but borne down by the weight of the legions they gradually began to give ground.

On the river bank the Roman cavalry were being pushed relentlessly back until at last they were separated from the legions and a gap was opened. The rear formations of the Carthaginian cavalry, led by Hasdrubal, burst through the gap. Leaving their front line to complete the rout of the Romans, they galloped round behind the legions and threw themselves on the rear of the allied cavalry. Shattered by the assault the Italian horsemen broke ranks and scattered.

The legions bit deeper and deeper into the Carthaginian centre; the convex formation disappeared and the whole line was now being pushed back. The centre began at first to buckle and then, as the legionaries crowded into the salient, to cave in. Paullus, when he saw the hopeless state of his right wing, realised that all hope now lay with the legions. He rode along the back of the line and dismounting threw himself into the thick of the fight. Hannibal, too, knowing that all depended on the centre holding for just a little longer, entered the fray shouting encouragement to his men. Step by step the Celts and Spaniards were forced backwards. Hannibal had accomplished his master plan. The

legionaries had pushed his centre back so far that they had passed between the African pikemen on either wing. All that remained was to execute the coup de grâce. The pikemen now faced inwards, turning from column into phalanx, and charged the Roman flanks.

The Roman cavalry was now in flight on both wings. Leaving the Numidians to mop up the Italians, for which they were best fitted, Hasdrubal recalled his Celts and Spaniards and charged the rear of the legions. The maniples were forced to turn to meet the attack from whatever direction it came. In the centre the pressure was off and the Celts and Spaniards were able to counterattack. It was the bloodiest day in Roman history. Paullus died fighting in the ranks. The proconsuls Geminus and Regulus also fell, as did the former master of the horse, Minucius Rufus, who probably held the rank of a tribune. Besides these both the consul's quaestors and 80 senators were left on the field.

In pressing forward so far the Romans had lost contact with the ford and therefore the 10,000 men left in the larger camp on the other side of the river could do nothing to help them. The enormous casualties, which are variously reported at figures between just under 45,000 and 70,000, suggest that the legions broke and ran. It seems incredible that they could have stood their ground and fought to the bitter end as Polybius suggests. The diversity of the casualty figures reflects the disagreement about the numbers involved. According to Polybius the 10,000 left to guard the larger camp were captured the day after the battle. A further 3,500 infantry and 370 cavalry escaped to the neighbouring towns. Unfortunately the succeeding part of Polybius' account is missing so that these figures cannot be corroborated by subsequent events. Although Livy's figures are confused, they do fit in with the subsequent story. After giving conflicting accounts the Roman historian claims that about 10,000 survivors gathered at Canusium (Canosa di Puglia). This is entirely consistent as they were later formed into two legions. If Livy's account of the debate over the fate of the prisoners in the Senate is basically correct, then about 7,000 Romans fell into Hannibal's hands. One must assume that the allies which he

released without ransom made up a similar number. This would bring the total survivors up to about 25,000 and the death roll down to around 50,000, which was the traditional figure. Among those who escaped was Gaius Terentius Varro.

Polybius, in the cruellest of epitaphs, once again reflecting the family line, this time of the Paulli, says of Varro that he disgraced himself by his flight and in his tenure of office had been most unprofitable to his country. Varro's name was never cleared and he remained the scapegoat for the defeat at Cannae. And yet Livy records that the Senate went out to meet Varro when he returned to Rome and gave thanks to him for not deserting the state. Furthermore he remained in office, albeit in a secondary capacity, throughout the war.

The long struggle back

The news of the disaster shook Rome to its very foundations. Never before and never again were Romans to suffer such a defeat. In three battles Rome had lost around 100,000 of her best troops. The streets were filled with women and children crying for their lost sons, brothers, fathers and husbands. The Senate was at a loss and for several days nothing was done. At any moment they expected Hannibal to appear beneath the walls. As so often happens in these situations, the mob in its anger and fear searched for a scapegoat: two vestal virgins were accused of breaking their vows—one committed suicide and the other was buried alive. They also turned to that most abhorrent of all propitiations, human sacrifice. A Celtic man and woman and a Greek man and woman were buried alive in the cattle market.

Rome did not remain in this state for long. Gritting their teeth the senators resolved to reject all terms and fight it out to the bitter end.

A man was needed who could inspire the troops, and fate had supplied that man. The legendary Marcus Claudius Marcellus, who was the praetor in command of the fleet, was at Ostia. He was ordered to take charge of the remnants of the Cannae legions. He immediately despatched 1,500 marines to the city to help with its defence and sent a legion of marines to Teanum Sidicinum (Teano in northern Campania) to secure he Latin Way in case Hannibal should march on Rome. He then handed over he fleet to Publius Furius Philus and set out overland by forced marches to Canusium (Canosa di Puglia), where he remnants of the Cannae legions had gathered, leaving Varro free to return o the city. A dictator was named. He organised a levy of all the men over the age of 17 and two new legions were raised (22nd and 23rd).

In these dire straits the Senate decided on a measure never considered before. They enrolled two legions of volunteer slaves who were promised freedom and citizenship in return for service. Six thousand criminals were also released on the same conditions.

After his victory Hannibal immediately freed all the allied prisoners, in keeping with his policy, and offered to return the Romans for a ransom, sending representatives of the prisoners and an ambassador to Rome with this offer and terms for peace. The dictator sent out a lictor to meet the Carthaginian ambassador before he reached Rome. The message to the ambassador was the same as that given to Pyrrhus 60 years before—'Rome will not discuss terms of peace with a foreign enemy on Italian soil'. As for the captives, the Senate informed them that Rome had no use for soldiers who had surrendered and refused to accept them, even though they were prepared to pay their own ransom. Hannibal sold them to the Greek slave dealers but more than 20 years later, when Greece came under Roman influence, many of them were redeemed.

The consequences of Cannae were far more shattering than the defeat. Practically the entire southern Apennine area defected. The whole of Lucania and the Bruttii (Calabria) went over to the Carthaginian side. Most of Samnium followed suit and in Apulia the key towns of Arpi, Salapia, Aecae and Herdonea seceded. This defection reduced Rome's resources of infantry by a fifth and her cavalry by nearly a third. Rome's only course was to adopt Fabian tactics, avoiding pitched battles and trying to wear the Carthaginians out. It was said of Rome that before Cannae her armies marched out to battle but after they marched to war.

Determined to strike while the iron was hot, Hannibal marched along the borders of Samnium and Lucania following the Ofanto to its source. The mountain stronghold of Compsa (Conza) threw open its gates to him. Hannibal, appreciating the strength of its situation, left all his booty and excess baggage here. He now split his army in two, leaving one half to secure the alliance of the highlands whilst he took the other half and skirted the north side of the Picentine mountains. Descending into Campania he made a dash on Naples, hoping that the port might defect to him so that he could open communications with Carthage. The Neapolitans closed their gates on him.

In all the towns of Italy there was a constant conflict between the oligarchic ruling party (who were supported by Rome) and the commons. By fostering the democratic cause Hannibal hoped to be able to detach the towns of Campania. This explains his apparently pointless dashes around Campania as he tried to get to the right spot at the right moment.

His disappointment at Naples was mitigated by the defection of the second city of Italy, Capua, where the popular party gained the ascendancy and threw open their gates. Nola, too, seemed a likely candidate but as at Naples the oligarchic party shut the gates on him.

Meanwhile Marcellus had taken over the troops at Canosa, formed them into two legions and then crossed the Apennines into northern Campania, linking with the legion of marines that he had sent to Teano. From his position on the slopes of the extinct volcano, Monte Santa Croce, Marcellus hoped to be able to confine Hannibal to the area south of the Volturno and stop him advancing on Rome. The colony at Sinuessa (Mondragone) covered the narrow pass between Monte Massico and the sea by which the Via Appia passes on its way to Rome. If Hannibal attempted a breakthrough here, Marcellus could easily send reinforcements over the low pass between Monte Santa Croce and Monte Massico which was covered by

Below
Map of southern Italy. Virtually the whole area south of the Volturno in the west and the promontory of Gargano in the east defected after the crushing Roman defeat at the battle of Cannae.

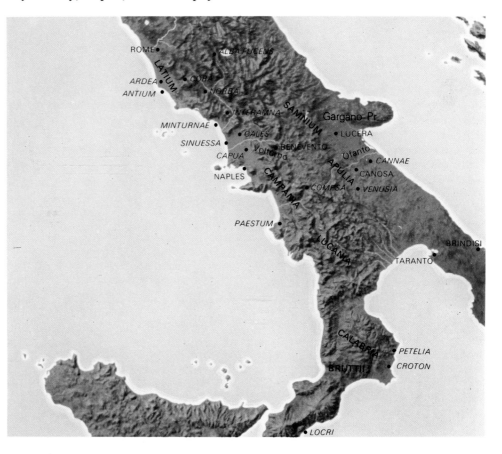

the colony at Suessa Aurunca (Sessa Aurunca). The only bridge across the Volturno was at Casilinum (modern Capua) which was held by a garrison of about 1,000 Italians. With his position secured Marcellus settled down to await the dictator's arrival.

Soon after his arrival Marcellus was approached by envoys from Nola who warned of the danger of a popular uprising which would turn the town over to Hannibal. Until the dictator arrived, however, Marcellus could do nothing.

At Rome the dictator, Marcus Junius Pera, had been frantically trying to raise sufficient forces to meet the crisis. Only the two legions raised for the defence of the city the previous spring, the 20th and 21st, were properly trained. He added to these the force of 6,000 paroled criminals, who although they were not trained could be used as they were expendable. At the head of this force of about 25,000 men he set out for Campania.

Once the dictator had arrived Marcellus was free to act. Campania had been an ally of Rome since the 4th century and the two had never been at war, with the result that no colonies had been established south of the Volturno. Several colonies covered the routes south into Campania and there was one colony at Beneventum (Benevento) in the heart of Samnium. As long as Rome had friendly towns immediately south of the river, in particular Calatia near Maddaloni 40km from Beneventum, it was possible to march into Samnium without fear of breaking vital lines of communication. A similar system of colonies and friendly towns existed in Apulia, the colonies being at Luceria (Lucera) Venusia (Venosa) and Brundisium (Brindisi). These allowed Roman armies to penetrate deep into Carthaginian-held territory without putting their supply lines at risk. This became a decisive factor in the war. As the Campanian towns of Capua and Calatia, which had followed Capua's lead, were in Carthaginian hands, the route to Benevento was broken. Thus when Marcellus set out to relieve Nola he had a twofold purpose.

Nola could not be reached by a direct route—the road south of the Volturno was in the hands of the Carthaginians who enjoyed a massive superiority in cavalry. To confuse Hannibal, Marcellus withdrew from Teano and probably taking the route which the Carthaginian had used the previous year, crossed the hills opposite Alife, descending the Volturno to Caiatia (Caiazzo). Here he crossed the river and then following the valley of the Biferchia marched behind the hills to the east of Capua, passing through the territory of Saticula and Trebula and emerging into the plain at Maddaloni. From here he crossed the Via Appia and dug in on the ridge above Cancello which overlooks the ancient Campanian town of Suessula about 12km from Nola. The Appian Way to Benevento was now reopened. This was a strategic move of paramount importance, perhaps the single most significant act of the war. This camp above Cancello, which became known as Castra Claudiana after its founder, prevented Hannibal taking over the whole of Campania and restored communications with Benevento. The camp was occupied permanently until Campania was recaptured.

With Marcellus encamped above Suessula, Hannibal realised that there was little chance of Nola defecting and so decided to make another attempt on Naples. But on approaching the port he found that the Romans had moved a garrison in by sea. The Roman control of the sea was a major factor, and in spite of the general defection in the south all the main ports remained under Roman control.

Hannibal now turned south to Nuceria (Nocera) which he sacked and burned. He then advanced on Nola again, but Marcellus anticipated him and moved into the town. Realising that the time was not right Hannibal withdrew once again from Nola and this time attacked Acerrae, about 10km west of Nola, which he also sacked and burned, almost certainly because he had insufficient troops to garrison them. Marcellus meanwhile executed the instigators of revolt at Nola and then retired to his camp above Suessula which he fortified before the onset of winter.

The two roads from Rome to southern Campania, the Via Appia and the Via Latina, converged at Cales before they crossed the Volturno at Casilinum. This was the only bridge across the Volturno and whoever held Casilinum controlled the river. The ancient town occupie[d] roughly the same position as its moder[n] counterpart, Capua, on the south ban[k] of the Volturno which nestles in a shar[p] bend in the river. The confusion o[f] names is brought about because ancien[t] Capua was destroyed by the Saracens i[n] the 9th century and its inhabitant[s] emigrated to Casilinum, taking thei[r] name with them.

Hannibal now moved up to the tow[n] and when he saw that there was n[o] chance of taking it by assault he dre[w] siege lines round it to prevent supplie[s] getting in. Then, leaving sufficien[t] forces to hold these lines, he went int[o] winter quarters at Capua four kilo[-] metres further down the road. Th[e] legend that Hannibal's troops went sof[t] during their winter in the fleshpots o[f] Capua has been debunked so man[y] times that it would be pointless to dwel[l] on it here. They never won anothe[r] great battle simply because they wer[e] never given another opportunity.

In the early spring of 215 Hanniba[l] returned to the siege of Casilinum. Th[e] blockade was beginning to have it[s] effect and the starving garrison wer[e] reaching the end of their endurance[.] The dictator had returned to Rome an[d] Tiberius Sempronius Gracchus, th[e] master of the horse, had taken over. H[e] was unwilling to risk an engagement an[d] was reduced to watching helplessly. H[e] tried floating jars of grain down th[e] river at night so that the defenders coul[d] drag them from the river as they drifte[d] past, but the Carthaginians soon caugh[t] on to this and kept watch for them. I[n] desperation the Romans tried floatin[g] down nuts, but the Carthaginians coun[-] tered by placing hurdles made fro[m] wattling in the river. At last, devoid o[f] hope, the starving garrison surrendered[.] Hannibal released them and put in [a] 700-strong garrison of his own.

Livy's account of the events of th[e] year 215 is so confused and implausibl[e] that one is tempted to believe that he ha[s] made them up. The consuls were Grac[-] chus, the master of the horse from th[e] previous year, and Lucius Postumiu[s] Albinus, who as praetor for the previou[s] year was still serving in the Po valley[.] He was elected in his absence but n[o] sooner had he been elected than he an[d] his two legions, the 18th and 19th, wer[e] wiped out in a Celtic ambush.

After a lot of manoeuvring behind the scenes, Fabius was elected as a replacement for Albinus and Marcellus the other candidate was made proconsul. The three commanders took up their positions in Campania with Marcellus at Castra Claudiana. The Senate had decided to banish the two legions made up of the survivors of Cannae and accordingly they had been sent to the Roman province of Sicily and sentenced to camp out in the open until the war in Italy was over. Their place was taken by the two legions from Sicily (7th and 8th). Gracchus took up his position covering the Appian Way at Sinuessa (Mondragone) with the two legions of volunteer slaves. Fabius the Delayer took over Pera's army and covered the Latin Way at Cales (Calvi). So far this is reasonable, but what happens next is ludicrous. In spite of the fact that the Carthaginians held the river crossing at Casilinum, Livy marches Fabius of all people across the Volturno and then under Hannibal's nose to Castra Claudiana, where he displaced Marcellus whom he ordered to garrison Nola. The story of Marcellus' victory over Hannibal beneath the walls of Nola is equally fictitious as Polybius asserts that when Hannibal left Italy he had never lost a battle. It seems that Livy has got his chronology wrong, and because he narrates his history year by year, he found himself with an empty year for 215 and had to look around for something to fill the gap. At all events the situation in Campania in the autumn of 215 had not changed since the spring.

Two events, however, did take place which were to have a momentous effect on the war. Philip V of Macedon made a treaty of alliance with Hannibal, and Hiero, the king of Syracuse, who had been Rome's faithful ally since the beginning of the first Punic war, died. Philip's ambassadors fell into the hands of the Romans with the result that they knew about the treaty before Hannibal. As a precaution the number of warships at Taranto was raised to 50 to protect the Adriatic coast.

As autumn approached Hannibal left Campania and crossed the Apennines to Arpi in Apulia. Gracchus with his two slave legions followed and went into winter quarters at the Roman colony of Luceria (Lucera).

Fabius and Marcellus were elected consuls for the following year (214). Hannibal had been held in check the previous year and it was decided to make a supreme effort to get the upper hand in the war. In accordance with Fabius' strategy it was agreed to open up the war on as many fronts as possible, knowing that Hannibal with his limited resources would not be able to protect all his allies. Six new legions were raised, bringing the total to 20, and the keels of 100 new ships laid down.

Once again both consuls were to operate in Campania. Marcellus was given the 22nd and 23rd legions and Fabius the 20th and 21st. Fabius' son, as praetor, was sent to Apulia with the 7th and 8th legions to join Gracchus who was already there with the two slave legions. This brought the number of legions in southern Italy to eight. The Po valley had been left without forces since the death of Postumius Albinus the previous year: two new legions (27th and 28th) were sent there to keep the Celts busy and stop them sending reinforcements to Hannibal. The two Cannae legions were in Sicily and a further legion (24th) had been raised the previous summer and sent to join the ninth in Sardinia which the Carthaginians were trying to recover. Varro, who had been posted to Picenum on the Adriatic side of Italy north-east of Rome, had raised a legion locally (26th). A further legion (25th) was posted to join the Adriatic fleet which was now at Brundisium (Brindisi) as a further precaution against an invasion by Philip. Two of the new legions (29th and 30th) were held in reserve at Rome.

The resources of the state were drained and no money could be found to pay for sailors to man the new ships. To meet the emergency all the wealthier citizens agreed to provide and pay sailors at their own expense.

The Capuans, alarmed at the preparations being made at Rome and convinced that they were the target of this massive build-up, sent messengers to Hannibal begging him to come to their aid. In response Hannibal recrossed the Apennines and pitched camp near Mount Tifata. Both de Sanctis and Kromayer place this camp on the hills just to the east of Mount Tifata, which seems reasonable for not only does it

give him access to the plain but it also covers the back route by which Marcellus had reached Castra Claudiana. He had taken up this same position the previous year and had severely disrupted the Roman supply lines with the result that Fabius had massed supplies at Castra Claudiana in the autumn when Hannibal had retired to Apulia.

Fabius sent word to Gracchus to hand over his position at Lucera to the younger Fabius and to move up to the Roman colony at Beneventum, thus cutting Hannibal's supply lines. Here for the first time we see the Roman strategy of containment.

Soon after arriving at Benevento this move paid off handsomely. Hanno with an army of 17,000 infantry, mainly Bruttians and Lucanians, and 1,200 North African cavalry, was advancing down the valley of the Calore, presumably to make a rendezvous with Hannibal in Campania. It was the first opportunity that the Romans had had to engage part of Hannibal's forces without their famous leader. Hanno encamped on the south bank of the Calore about 4.5km east of Benevento. Gracchus immediately moved his camp up to within 1,500m of Hanno's position and prepared for battle. He raised the morale of the slaves, promising that if they fought well freedom would be theirs.

The following morning the two armies engaged. The battle started well for the Romans but ground to a halt because the slaves, who were probably of Celtic origin, stopped fighting to cut off the heads of their fallen enemies as proof that they had killed them and then tried to continue with these gory souvenirs tucked under their right arms. When he realised what was happening, Gracchus promised them their freedom on the spot, so that they could get on with the fighting. With renewed vigour the slaves raised their war cry and threw themselves against the Carthaginians, driving them back on their camp. Finally they broke into the camp itself, killing everything that stood in their way. After the battle, in accordance with his promise, Gracchus granted freedom to them all regardless of their actions in the battle.

In Campania Hannibal made yet another effort to take Nola, but once again Marcellus, who was encamped at

Castra Claudiana, managed to frustrate him. The Carthaginian had earlier heard that he might be able to get possession of Taranto, a far greater prize, which would open his lines of communication with both Carthage and Macedon. He left Campania in the autumn and marched east towards the Greek port. With Hannibal gone the two consuls moved in on Casilinum and after a short siege regained this key position.

Meanwhile Philip was trying to open up the Illyrian coast so that he could send troops across to Italy. He had sailed into the Aegean with a fleet of 120 light galleys and reached the Bay of Aulon opposite Brindisi on the Albanian coast. This offered a large natural harbour ideally suited for transporting his men across to the heel of Italy. Here he seized the town of Oricum and then rowed up the river Aous (Vjosa) to lay siege to Apollonia. When the news reached Brindisi the praetor Marcus Valerius Laevinus embarked the 25th legion, crossed the Adriatic and threw a relief force of 2,000 into the beleaguered town. He then blockaded the mouth of the Vjosa with his galleys, cutting Philip

off from the sea. The Macedonian king was forced into the humiliating position of having to burn his fleet and retreat overland to Macedonia. The Roman fleet spent the winter at Oricum. The war had spread to Greece.

The following year the centre of the war in Italy moved to the south-east as Hannibal made repeated efforts to gain control of Taranto. The Romans had put a large garrison into the town and felt sure that they could keep the port out of Carthaginian hands.

In Sicily events had taken a turn for the worse. Hiero's 15-year-old grandson Hieronymus ascended the throne. By skilful diplomacy Hannibal managed to detach the impressionable youth from the Roman alliance and open up a new front in Sicily. This was to be Carthage's war: all support was to come from Africa, leaving Hannibal free to deal with his increasing problems in Italy. But hardly had the war begun than Hieronymus was assassinated. It was Rome's chance to reverse the situation and the Senate dispatched Marcellus with the 22nd and 23rd legions to the island. They had acted too slowly. The

Syracusans in a fit of anti-Roman fervour had elected as generals Hannibal's two agents, Hippocrates and Epicydes, and sent out 4,000 men under Hippocrates to defend the territory of Leontini (Lentini), a Syracusan town near the border of the Roman province about 30km north-west of Syracuse. Hippocrates used these forces to ravage the borders of the Roman province, deliberately trying to provoke a war that would take some of the pressure off Hannibal in Italy. Marcellus probably arrived in Sicily in the autumn of 214 and spent the winter trying to negotiate a settlement. In the spring when the Syracusans still remained obdurate, Marcellus and the praetor Appius Claudius Pulcher assaulted the town of Leontini and sacked it. Two thousand Carthaginian sympathisers who were captured when the town fell were scourged and beheaded. This act, as usual, was

Below
Map illustrating the extension of the war to Greece and Sicily. The Romans managed to keep Philip V of Macedon busy at very little cost by forming an alliance of his enemies in Greece.

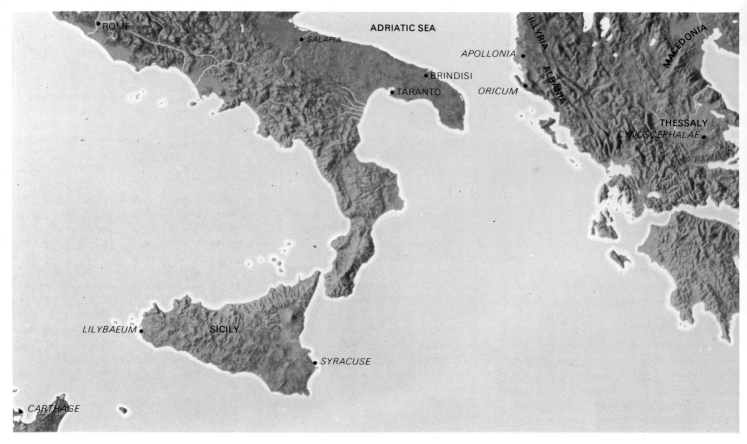

counterproductive and only served to harden attitudes. When Marcellus saw that the Syracusans were still not prepared to come to terms, he gave his men five days to prepare and then moved in on the city. He divided his forces, which were very limited as he was forbidden to bring the Cannae legions out of the Roman province, giving the command of the land operations to Pulcher whilst he took over the fleet. With only two legions a full-scale blockade was impossible so he decided to launch a simultaneous assault on the city from land and sea. Pulcher was to attack from the north whilst Marcellus came in from the sea. Their attempts were foiled by the genius of the great mathematician and engineer Archimedes, who had spent the latter years of his life improving the defences of his adopted city with the result that the walls bristled with machines that wrought havoc amongst the besiegers. A full account of this episode is given in the section on seige warfare (p. 294).

Marcellus left Pulcher to carry on the siege as best he could whilst he set out with a third of the army to recover the other towns on the island which had defected. The Cannae legions, wishing only to clear their name, approached Marcellus begging him to make use of their services. The general forwarded their request to the Senate who replied they could only be used outside Italy. Subsequently they must have been brought into action when the Carthaginians landed a force of 25,000 infantry, 3,000 cavalry and 12 elephants on the island. These were joined by 10,000 infantry and 500 cavalry from Syracuse.

The situation on the island was aggravated by yet another massacre, this time of the citizens of Henna. The atrocity drove many of the Sicilians into the Carthaginian camp.

During the winter or the following spring (213–212) Hannibal finally gained entrance to Taranto. Hostages from several of the Greek towns of the south had been held at Rome. When those from Taranto and Thurii escaped they were recaptured, scourged and then flung to their deaths from the Tarpeian rock on the Capitol. Once again Roman brutality was counterproductive and both Taranto and Thurii were betrayed to the Carthaginian. In

the case of Taranto the loss was not total as the Roman garrison there took refuge in the citadel which stood at the end of a peninsula and blocked the entrance to the harbour. Hannibal's attempts to take the citadel were frustrated as it could be supplied from the sea. Finally he threw up an earthwork surmounted by a wall across the peninsula to cut the citadel off from the rest of the town. The Tarentines were forced to drag their ships across the peninsula to get them to the sea.

The consuls for 212 were Flaccus, a contemporary of Fabius Maximus who had been consul twice before, and Pulcher who had been released from his duties in Sicily by Marcellus so that he could run for the supreme magistracy. Two new city legions (34th and 35th) were raised, bringing the total number in the field up to 25, a quarter of a million men. The two legions which had spent the previous year training at Rome were posted to Etruria in case Ligurian reinforcements tried to reach Hannibal. The resources of the state were so strained that the consuls had great difficulty obtaining the recruits to bring the existing legions up to strength, let alone form the two new legions.

The tide turns

For three years the fields of Campania had been laid waste as Roman and Carthaginian systematically destroyed the crops to deny each other forage. As a result Capua was beginning to feel the pinch and sent messengers to Hannibal begging for supplies. The Carthaginian sent Hanno north with orders to gather in supplies in the valley of the Calore near Benevento where the Campanians were to collect them. Flaccus received intelligence of this from the colonists at Benevento and marched into the Apennines. If the Campanians had showed more energy in collecting their supplies all would have been well, but before they could transfer the supplies to Campania Flaccus was on them. The consul stormed Hanno's camp, capturing the supplies and taking prisoner many of Hanno's soldiers and Campanians.

Capua, deprived of supplies, faced starvation, and the Romans were quick to exploit the situation. Pulcher joined his colleague at Benevento and with the 20th, 21st, 29th and 30th legions they

moved down into Campania intent on destroying the corn, which was now green, and investing the city in the plain.

If they were to operate in the open they would be at the mercy of Hannibal's cavalry, so messages were sent to the proconsul Gracchus, who was still campaigning in Lucania with his legions of ex-slaves, begging him to join them with all his cavalry and *velites*. Gracchus set out but on his way was ambushed and killed. The slave legions which had served him faithfully for four years felt that their obligations were fulfilled and dispersed.

As expected, without cover the legions that moved in on Capua were constantly harassed by the Carthaginian and Campanian cavalry with losses of over 1,500 men. But they persisted until Hannibal himself crossed the Apennines. True to the Fabian strategy they then withdrew, Flaccus to Cumae and Pulcher into Lucania. His object achieved, Hannibal returned to Apulia. No sooner had he left than the legions returned. The consuls sent word to the praetor Nero at Castra Claudiana, telling him to join them with his legions, and they began to dig in around the city.

The port of Puteoli (Pozzuoli) had been fortified by Fabius Maximus a few years earlier so as to ensure supplies reaching the armies operating in Campania. Now another fortified position was established at the mouth of the Volturno. With their lines of communication secured from three directions, Casilinum to the north, Puteoli to the south and the fort at the mouth of the Volturno to the west, the consuls set about the investment of Capua. Three camps were established round the town, presumably to the north, south and west on the supply routes, and joined by double lines of ditches and ramparts: the first to keep the Capuans in and the second to keep Hannibal out.

Meanwhile in Sicily the siege of Syracuse continued. The Romans were finding it difficult to prevent the Carthaginians running the blockade and there seemed no chance of assailing Archimedes' fortifications. Regular discussions took place between the Romans and the Syracusans about the exchange or ransoming of prisoners. During these meetings one of the Roman soldiers noticed that a part of the wall was not as high as it seemed and by counting the courses of the stones he was able to estimate its height, which was well within reach of the longest Roman ladders. On informing Marcellus of this a night attack was planned for the festival of Diana when most of the sentries would have been drinking. This assault was a complete success and Marcellus gained control of the Epipolae plateau. Cut off from the town, the Euryalus fortress at the west end of the plateau soon surrendered and Marcellus was free to besiege Achradina which lay to the south of the plateau. The Carthaginian army had moved up to the south side of the city, preventing the Romans from surrounding it. But plague broke out in the Punic camp, which was in the unhealthy marshy area, and the army was almost wiped out whilst the Romans on the plateau were not seriously affected. The Carthaginians made a last attempt to relieve the town and sent

a large fleet of 130 galleys and 700 supply ships, but when the Roman fleet moved up to intercept them the Carthaginian warships, whose crews seemed to be completely overawed by the Roman navy, changed course for Taranto and the transports returned to Africa. All hope of relief was now gone and soon afterwards the Syracusans opened their gates to Marcellus.

With the fall of Syracuse most of the other dissident towns sent ambassadors to Marcellus seeking peace. The area around Agrigento, where the remnants of the Carthaginian and Syracusan forces had gathered, remained in arms. Marcellus advanced into the area and defeated them near the river Himera.

The following year, 211, the army strength was again brought up to 25 legions. This required replacing the two slave legions which had deserted. It is difficult to believe Livy when he claims that the 7th and 8th legions were destroyed by Hannibal in Apulia the

previous year as this would require th levying of four more to bring the tota up to 25, an almost impossible task con sidering Rome's strained resources.

The prime objective for the year 21 was to be Capua where six legions wer concentrated. Hannibal, in an attemp to raise the siege, crossed the Apennine and reoccupied his old position behine Monte Tifata. He managed to get message into the beleaguered town tell ing them the time of his attack so tha they could co-ordinate their assault, bu by now the Romans were prepared fo him. They split their infantry in tw with one half to guard the inner line under the proconsul Pulcher whilst th consul Centumalus defended the oute lines against Hannibal. The cavalry wa

Below
The raising of the siege of Capua, which had resulted in the concentration of six legions, was Hannibal's principal objective in 211. But the Carthaginian operation proved unsuccessful.

sent out into the field: the allied to the north under the command of Nero; and the citizen cavalry to the south under Flaccus. Hannibal led his army down into the plain and launched an attack on the outer lines whilst at the same time the Capuans assailed the inner. Both attacks were thrown back. Realising that he had missed his chance, Hannibal withdrew his forces, covering their retreat with his cavalry lest the Roman horsemen in the plain should attack them.

Supplying his men with ten days' rations he ferried them across the Volturno during the night and advanced up the Latin Way towards Rome, hoping to draw off the legions that were surrounding Capua. When news of this arrived at the city there was a frantic debate in the Senate as many of the members cried out for the recall of the legions. But Fabius Maximus read the situation correctly and sent a message to the commanders at Capua telling them to hold back a sufficient force to maintain the siege and send the rest for the defence of the city. Flaccus immediately dispatched messengers to the towns along the Appian Way, telling them to have supplies ready, and then set off post haste to race Hannibal to Rome by the much longer route along the coast. But Hannibal's advance was slow as he was ravaging the countryside as he went, hoping to exasperate the allies. The Roman colonists along the way cut down the bridges to slow him down whilst Flaccus and his men raced along the coast. As the Carthaginian approached Rome he devastated the countryside, burning, slaughtering and pillaging—doing all that was in his power to force the Romans to come out and defend their people. Flaccus, meanwhile, had reached the city and pitched camp between the Esquiline and Colline gates on the east side of the town. Hannibal moved up to the river Aniene and camped about 4.5km east of the city. Livy's claim that Flaccus twice offered battle to Hannibal and on both occasions the weather prevented it is, of course, patriotic nonsense. The Carthaginian knew that his bluff had been called and returned to southern Italy, leaving Capua to its fate. In Capua the situation was desperate. The population had the choice of starvation or throwing

themselves on the mercy of the Romans who had not shown much clemency elsewhere. A meeting of the Capuan Senate was called and the majority voted for surrender. Some 28 of them who had been heavily involved in the defection committed suicide. The following day the Jupiter gate on the east side of the town was thrown open and the Roman troops entered. The remainder of the Senate were arrested. Twenty-eight of them were sent to Teano and a further 25 to Cales (Calvi), where they were publicly scourged and beheaded by the lictors. With the fall of Capua the other Campanian towns which had defected, Calatia and Atella, also surrendered. Seventeen of their senators were executed and the mass of the Campanian population either displaced or sold into slavery.

The exhilaration felt in Rome over the recapture of Campania was marred by the news from Spain that the two Scipio brothers had been killed and their armies virtually wiped out.

It will be remembered that when Scipio missed Hannibal at the Rhône he had sent his brother Gnaeus with most of the fleet and two legions on to Spain. Gnaeus landed at the Massiliote colony of Emporiae (Ampurias) just south of the Pyrenees. It is very difficult to comment on the campaigns that followed because Polybius has followed the Scipionic tradition and Livy has followed Polybius. It is clear that the Romans had some success but its extent is uncertain. It is probable that the force which Hannibal had left to hold the area north of the Ebro withdrew, but to suggest that it was decisively beaten in the autumn of 218 seems highly unlikely. After the withdrawal of the Carthaginians Scipio established a permanent base at Tarraco (Tarragona). The following summer Hasdrubal Barca crossed the Ebro with his fleet of 40 galleys, following him up the coast. Scipio seized the chance to knock out the Carthaginian fleet, launched a surprise attack and defeated them off the mouth of the Ebro, destroying six galleys and capturing 25. Later in the year, after recovering from the wound sustained at the ambush near the Ticino, Publius sailed to join his brother with 20 more galleys and 8,000 men. The story that the two Roman brothers

crossed the Ebro and during the autumn advanced as far south as Saguntum seems improbable. In any event, in 215 they are still campaigning north of the Ebro where they are supposed to have gained a great victory over Hasdrubal Barca. It is interesting to contemplate that this was the only major reverse that Hasdrubal suffered before his death at the Metaurus eight years later. Even the great Scipio Africanus was unable to defeat him decisively.

Shortly afterwards Hasdrubal was called back to Africa to put down a Numidian revolt. He was absent from Spain for three years and during this time the Scipio brothers may well have made considerable inroads into Punic Spain and recaptured Saguntum.

Hasdrubal was able to re-enter the fray in the spring of 211 and the fortunes of the Scipios changed. They had split their army to make a two-pronged thrust deep into Carthaginian territory. The two armies were engaged separately by the Punic forces, both were wiped out and their commanders killed.

Much praise has been lavished on the Scipios for preventing Hasdrubal from bringing reinforcements to his brother in Italy. But since Hannibal hardly needed reinforcements before 214, and Hasdrubal was absent from Spain from 214–212, this argument seems baseless. The remnants of the Roman force retreated to their base north of the Ebro and the positions reverted to what they had been seven years earlier.

After the fall of Capua the praetor Nero received orders from the Senate to select 6,000 infantry and 300 cavalry from the two legions under his command and take ship from Puteoli for Spain.

Affairs on the other side of the Adriatic had progressed somewhat differently. In 213 Philip again invaded Illyria and managed to fight his way to the coast where he captured the town of Lissus. Laevinus, who had been encamped on the Illyrian coast near Apollonia since he had driven Philip out two years earlier, now formed an alliance with the Aetolians, the traditional enemies of the Macedonians, with the aim of keeping Philip occupied in Greece so that he could not interfere in the war in Italy. In the late summer of 211 an agreement was sworn.

Marcus Claudius Marcellus returned to Rome at the end of 211 and was elected consul for the following year. His colleague was Marcus Valerius Laevinus, and Galba the consul for the previous year had to be sent as proconsul to Illyria to replace him.

For the first time since Hannibal had entered Italy the Romans felt sufficiently confident of final victory to discharge some of their longest-serving troops. The number of legions serving in Campania, which up to now had been the principal theatre of war, was halved. The two legions (22nd and 23rd) serving in Sicily were also discharged. Two new city legions were raised, bringing the number of legions serving in Italy and the adjacent islands to 21.

The centre of the war now moved to Apulia, which Marcellus received as his province. Laevinus, the other consul, was given the job of mopping up the last centres of resistance in Sicily. He completed the task by the end of the summer when he captured Agrigentum and brought about the surrender of the rest of Sicily.

Two armies now set about the reconquest of Apulia. Aecae and Arpi in the north had been recaptured earlier and Marcellus now retook Salapia on the Adriatic coast, 17km north-west of Cannae, before moving into Samnium where he captured two of Hannibal's supply bases. A second army of two legions (7th and 8th) under Gnaeus Fulvius Centumalus moved against Herdonea (Ordona) which, like Salapia, had defected after the battle of Cannae six years before. Hannibal, hearing that Centumalus was at Herdonea, raced up from the toe of Italy and caught the Roman unawares, wiping out the army and its general. The two legions had been in service since 217 and had spent the last six years in Apulia. The remnants of the army escaped to join Marcellus in Samnium but were later disgraced and sent to join the Cannae legions in Sicily.

Marcellus now advanced into Lucania, made contact with Hannibal and from there following him, skirmishing all the way. Livy's accounts of full-scale battles between Marcellus and Hannibal both this year and the next are false. When Hannibal moved towards Apulia, Marcellus followed. Here the Carthaginian went into winter quarters and Marcellus remained with his troops close by throughout the winter.

The two consuls for 209 were both old men. Fabius Maximus obtained the supreme magistracy for the fifth time and Flaccus, fresh from his conquest of Campania, was made consul for the fourth time. Two new legions were required to replace the seventh and eighth and accordingly quotas were demanded from the Latin and Roman colonies. For ten years a minimum of two legions plus recruits, to bring the existing legions up to strength, had been demanded annually. The state was exhausted and 12 of the 40 colonies refused to send their quota. By an enormous effort the necessary troops were raised and two new legions, the 40th and 41st to be called up during the war, went into training at Rome.

Below
The citadel of Taranto which sits in the harbour entrance. It was captured by Fabius and held by the Romans throughout the war. In Roman times it was not an island but was joined to the town on the south side.

This year it was resolved to complete the reconquest of the Adriatic coast. Marcellus kept his command and Flaccus returned to his army in Campania. These two armies were to launch a two-pronged invasion of Lucania to keep Hannibal occupied whilst Fabius laid siege to Taranto. Marcellus, following his tactics of the previous year, continued to dog Hannibal's footsteps, skirmishing with him whilst Flaccus advanced along the valley of the Tanagro taking Volcei near Buccino.

With Hannibal preoccupied Fabius advanced into the heel of Italy, taking the Carthaginian-held town of Manduria and relieving the threat to his supply lines from Brindisi. He then advanced on Taranto, which he besieged by land and sea, moving his siege weapons up to the walls of the town on ships as Marcellus had done at Syracuse. Just as Hannibal had received the town by stealth so it was betrayed to the Romans. The town was sacked and 30,000 of its population sold into slavery. Hannibal marched to the relief of the city but arrived too late. By sheer persistence the Romans had now regained half of their lost territories and Hannibal was restricted to Lucania and Bruttium.

No attempt was made to raise any legions the following year. Marcellus was elected consul for the fourth time along with Titus Quinctius Crispinus, who had served as praetor in Campania the previous year.

Marcellus returned to his old army, the 31st and 32nd legions, which had been wintering at Venusia. Crispinus took over the 27th and 28th in Campania and then crossed the Apennines and took up his position about 4km south-east of Marcellus. Livy's claim that he laid siege to Locri in the very toe of Italy before joining Marcellus seems most unlikely. However, Locri was probably the Roman aim. Whilst the two consuls occupied Hannibal in Lucania, the Roman fleet was ordered to cross over from Sicily to besiege Locri. The strong garrison from Taranto, which had been left there by Fabius, was ordered to march down the coast and attack the town from the land. Hannibal detached 3,000 cavalry and 2,000 infantry who lay in wait for the Roman column, which was advancing without scouting in characteristic fashion, and

ambushed it beneath the hill of Petelia (Strongoli), killing 2,000 and capturing 1,500; the rest were scattered in flight.

Hannibal was in north-east Lucania and the two consuls were dogging his footsteps. They were carrying out Marcellus' policy of the previous two years —crowding Hannibal by moving their camps as close as possible to his position to restrict his foragers. The Carthaginian had camped one evening and the two consuls had arrived soon after him and encamped opposite. Between the two camps was a wooded hill. From past experience Hannibal knew that the Romans were likely to try to occupy this hill as it was nearer to his camp. During the night he sent out some of his Numidians to lie in ambush near the hill. The following morning both consuls rode out from their camps to survey the ground. In incredibly slipshod fashion they took with them a tiny escort— Polybius says that it consisted of 60 cavalry and about 30 *velites* plus their 24 lictors. They rode up and over the hill to examine the part of it that was invisible from their camps. The Numidians climbed the hill obliquely to get behind the reconnaissance party and cut them off before closing in. In the attack Marcellus was killed and Crispinus severely wounded. The injured consul managed to break out and get back to his camp. During the night he retreated into more mountainous country, sending orders to Marcellus' army to withdraw to Venusia. In the confusion Hannibal tried to regain Salapia but failed. He then withdrew southwards to the relief of Locri which the Roman fleet was still besieging.

Crispinus sent word to the Senate telling them of the situation and the younger Fabius was immediately dispatched to take over the legions at Venusia and to keep an eye on Taranto in case Hannibal tried to regain the town.

Crispinus withdrew with his army to his original base in Campania where he named Titus Manlius Torquatus dictator so that elections could be held for new consuls. Shortly afterwards he died from his wounds.

The final test

Nero arrived at Tarraco (Tarragona) in Spain in the autumn of 211. He took

over command of the remnants of the Roman forces there and during the following year remained in a strictly defensive position. The Senate determined to send a general with proconsular authority to take over the war in Spain, fearing that Hasdrubal might lead a second army into Italy at a time when they were just beginning to gain the upper hand. Elections were held but none of the former consular generals in Italy seemed to be very keen on accepting the responsibility. When Publius, the 25-year-old son of Publius Cornelius Scipio, offered himself for election he was adopted unanimously. Some information relating to this extraordinary election must be missing for Scipio had held no previous position and was far too young for the job. Yet the Senate ratified his appointment and gave him two further legions and 1,000 cavalry with which to prosecute the war.

Scipio probably arrived in Spain in the autumn of 210 and spent the winter training his troops and raising their morale. On receiving the information that the three Carthaginian armies were in widely dispersed winter quarters, none within ten days march of the capital New Carthage (Cartagena), Scipio embarked on an exploit worthy of Hannibal himself. Marching out of camp early in the spring of 209 and telling no one where he was heading, he made a dash south and arrived under the walls of New Carthage before the Carthaginians realised what had happened. In one day he took the town and completely reversed Roman fortunes in Spain, for the impression that it made on the Spaniards can hardly have been less than that made on the Carthaginians. It was a brilliant stroke which raised the morale of the legions to such a pitch that they would now follow him anywhere.

During the summer Scipio launched a diplomatic offensive to win over the local Spanish tribes. When he advanced southwards again the following year he did so from a secure power base and was now supported by Spanish allies. His march probably followed the coast as far as Valencia and then cut across the heights of Chinchilla and descended into the valley of the Guadalquivir.

Hasdrubal Barca had taken up his position close to Baecula (Bailen) 12km west of Linares near the Spanish silver mines. He had been planning to join his brother and had been gathering in the mineral resources of Spain before setting out for Italy. The Punic army had taken up a strong position on a hill overlooking the river Guadiel, a tributary of the Guadalquivir. Hasdrubal was considerably outnumbered by Scipio's forces and when the Roman tried to draw him into battle by an outflanking movement with his *velites*, Hasdrubal disengaged and withdrew northward. Scipio could claim a tactical victory but the wily Carthaginian had not only escaped almost unscathed but had also outmanoeuvred Scipio, whose principal objective was to keep him tied down in Spain. Hasdrubal now headed for the central region of Spain and Scipio was in no position to follow him. There were two possibilities open to him: first, to retreat to the coast and race Hasdrubal to the Pyrenees; or, secondly, to ignore him and concentrate on breaking up the Carthaginian power base in Spain. Rightly or wrongly, Scipio elected to do the latter.

News of Hasdrubal's escape from Scipio and his march northwards must have reached Rome by the autumn of 208. There could be little doubt as to his intentions. It could hardly have happened at a worse moment for the Romans. With Fabius and Flaccus well past the age for energetic campaigning and their only successful field commanders, Marcellus and Gracchus, both dead they were hard pressed to find leaders capable of dealing with the situation. The task fell to Marcus Claudius Nero and Marcus Livius Salinator. Nero had served under Marcellus and as praetor had been involved in the siege of Capua. After the death of the Scipios he had been sent to Spain and had probably spent a little over a year there. It was obviously for this reason that he was elected, for he was the only Roman general who had had experience of Hasdrubal. His colleague Salinator, the Senate's choice, had been consul with Paullus in 219 and had been involved in the Illyrian campaign. On returning to Rome he had been accused of misappropriation of the booty. In indignation he had withdrawn to the country and refused to take any further part in public life. In 210 the consuls Marcellus and

Laevinus had insisted that he return to Rome but according to Livy he refused to shave or trim his hair and went about in tattered clothing. In exasperation the censors ordered him to shave, return to the Senate and to perform his public duty. This was the man whom the Senate chose as colleague for Nero. To make matters worse the two men hated each other but justified this by saying that they would each try to outdo the other in the service of their country. Nevertheless, the Senate tried to effect a reconciliation before they set out for their provinces.

Twenty-three legions were brought into the field for the coming campaign. The consuls had two each. There were four in Spain under Scipio; the two Cannae legions were still living out their exile in Sicily; and the 9th and 24th remained in Sardinia where they had been since 215 (in fact the 9th had been there since 217). In Italy itself there were 15: 27th and 28th in Bruttium under Flaccus, 36th and 37th near Taranto and 29th at Capua. The consul Nero was to take over the two legions, 31st and 32nd, in Lucania. This meant that there were seven legions to hold Hannibal in the south. In the north there were two in Etruria: Varro's command, the 38th and 39th, covering the route through Etruria as Flaminius had done ten years before; two in the Po valley (34th and 35th); and a further two under the consul Salinator (40th and 41st). These last two legions had had no military experience and had only been enrolled two years before, since when they had been stationed at Rome. Two new legions, 42nd and 43rd, were enrolled for the protection of the city. Livy also says that the slave volunteers were recalled to their standards, but this is sheer fiction.

News had been brought from Marseilles the previous autumn that Hasdrubal was recruiting in southern Gaul and Liguria. But the Romans were completely unprepared for the speed with which he crossed the Alps. Livy makes it quite clear that he followed the route used by Hannibal, by which he must mean up the Durance valley and over the Montgenèvre pass. The crossing was made very early in the year, possibly as early as May, which rules out any north-south pass such as the

Mont Cenis or Clapier, for these are impassable so early in the year. The Montgenèvre and the Larche are the only practicable routes at this time of the year.

On arriving in the Po valley Hasdrubal laid siege to Placentia, probably to encourage the local Celts, but failed to take the colony. He had sent four Celtic horsemen and two Numidians south with a letter for his brother arranging to meet him in Umbria. Meanwhile Hannibal had come out of winter quarters in the toe of Italy and began to advance northwards. Nero pressed south to meet him. The two armies came into contact at Grumentum (Grumento) in the valley of the Agri. Nero moved his camp to within 1,500m of Hannibal's position, covering the route north and hampering his foragers. Again Livy's accounts of full-scale battles are grossly exaggerated, but skirmishes must have taken place constantly as Hannibal tried to break through. Hannibal was obviously following the route of the later Via Herculia which ran north via Anxia (Anzi) and Potentia (Potenza) towards Apulia. The Punic general managed to elude Nero by a night march and reached Venusia before Nero caught up. From here the Carthaginian moved northeast to Canosa in the vicinity of Cannae and here awaited messengers from his brother.

The six horsemen had made their way south into Lucania, but hearing that Hannibal had already made his way north they had tried to follow him. Possibly because Nero's army was now following Hannibal, they had moved down towards the coast, where they fell in with the Roman troops near Taranto and were captured. They were immediately sent under a strong guard to Nero's camp. Nero read Hasdrubal's letter and sent it on to the Senate, advising them to recall the legion from Capua and to dispatch it with the two new city legions to Narnia (Narni) 70km north of Rome on the Flaminian Way.

Nero now embarked on a daring feat of arms. That night, selecting 6,000 crack infantry and 1,000 cavalry, telling them to take only their arms, he set out from his camp. He headed up the Ofanto valley towards Lucania, informing his troops that they were going to attack the nearest Carthaginian-held town in Lucania. When he had put sufficient distance between himself and Hannibal he told his soldiers the truth, that they were marching north to join up with the other consul at Sena Gallica (Senigallia) about 400km up the Adriatic coast. Before he set out Nero had sent messengers to the territory of Larino and of the Marrucini, Frentani and the Praetuttii along his proposed line of march telling them to bring supplies down to the roadside. The fact that Lucera was omitted from this list indicates that Nero intended to march through the Apennines and not descend to the coast until he had reached Larinum (Larino) from which point he could march down the valley of the Cigno. By this route the distance from Canosa to Senigallia is about 475km.

All along the route the people brought supplies down to the roadside so that the soldiers would not have to halt in their race northwards. Everyone realised that this was the most critical act of the war and there was immense enthusiasm for the venture. Along the route retired veterans and youngsters eager to prove their worth fell in behind the column. Nero accepted all that were fit for service. On and on they dashed. Soon the hills were behind them and they emerged on the coast. They passed under the heights of Vasto crowned by the town of Histonium and on along the endless coast road. A week after they set out they were approaching Sena Gallica where Salinator was camped with his army. Nero dispatched messengers to see whether his colleague wished him to come into camp openly or secretly. Salinator sent back telling him to come in under cover of darkness. It was arranged that each soldier should be received into the tent of a man of similar rank so that there should be no increase in the size of the camp. Already four legions were encamped there as the 34th and 35th legions had withdrawn before Hasdrubal's advance to join up with the consul. Hasdrubal himself had pressed on down the coast and was encamped only 500m away. In order not to lose the advantage that they had gained the consuls offered battle the following morning. Hasdrubal immediately guessed that something was wrong. His immense experience told him that the army had received

reinforcements. He sent out scouts to see if the Roman camp had been enlarged but with negative results. However at nightfall his scouts brought in the significant information that the call for the setting of the evening watches had been sounded once in the praetor's camp but twice in the consuls' camp. The news was out. The Romans, who were sticklers for formality, had given the game away.

Under cover of darkness Hasdrubal, who must have believed that something had happened to his brother, broke camp and started to retreat. During the march his guides deserted him and he was unable to find the ford across the Metaurus river. It must have already been well into the fourth watch and Hasdrubal ordered his men to move along the south bank of the river until daylight when they could find the road.

At first light the Romans set off after Hasdrubal. Nero raced ahead with the cavalry and must have caught up with the Carthaginians by mid-morning. Some time later the light-armed troops arrived under the command of the praetor Licinus. Realising that he could not continue his march while under constant attack from the 6,000 cavalry and the 13,000 light-armed troops, Hasdrubal tried to pitch camp on a hill overlooking the river. When Salinator turned up with the heavy infantry, probably in the early afternoon, and advanced with his forces drawn out in battle line, Hasdrubal realised that he had to fight. A fragment of Polybius records the battle but we have to rely on Livy's thoroughly unsatisfactory account of the topography for the location of the battle site. The most likely position is on the south side of the river near Montemaggiore, but this is by no means certain. Polybius says that Hasdrubal drew up his Celts and Spaniards on a very narrow front with the ten elephants in front of them. In this formation he fell upon the Roman left, determined to conquer or die. The Roman right wing which, because of the difficult character of the ground were unable to close with the Carthaginian left, circled behind Hasdrubal and attacked from the rear. The elephants, which had got out of control and were causing havoc in their own ranks, had to be killed by their mahouts who carried a mallet and chisel

specifically for this purpose. The chisel was hammered in at the base of the skull. Hasdrubal fell in the thick of the battle and with him died the last hopes of winning the war.

After the victory the Romans stormed the Carthaginian camp. Polybius says that 10,000 of the Carthaginian army were slain in the battle and 2,000 of the Romans. Livy puts the Carthaginian casualties at more than five times this number.

The following night Nero set out for Apulia. He regained his camp on the sixth day, being able to take the more direct route back. Hannibal had not even realised that he had left. At Rome the exhilaration was almost uncontrollable. For 11 years they had waited for such a victory. At first only a rumour reached the city, then more certain information. When finally news came that legates from the victorious army were coming down the Via Flaminia the entire population poured out of the city. They lined the road for nearly five kilometres as far as the Milvian bridge and mobbed the legates as they entered the city.

In Apulia Nero now stooped to an act of particular callousness. He had brought with him the severed head of Hasdrubal which he threw before the outposts of Hannibal's camp. Hannibal in despondency withdrew into Bruttium where he remained for the rest of the war.

Scipio triumphant

The centre of operations now moved from Italy. In Spain Hasdrubal Gisgo realised that any chance of winning the war depended on his defeating Scipio and supplying Hannibal with the reinforcements he needed in Italy. In the early summer he left his winter quarters at Gades (Cadiz) and moved north, recruiting as he went. He encamped at Ilipa just north of modern Seville. Scipio advanced down the valley of the Guadalquivir and encamped opposite him. The Roman army consisted of 45,000 infantry and 3,000 horse of which a little less than half were Italian. Hasdrubal Gisgo may have slightly outnumbered them.

Gisgo regularly offered battle fairly late in the day with his Libyans in the centre and his Spanish allies on the wings drawn up behind the elephants. In response Scipio brought out his troops and lined them up with his legions in the centre and his Spaniards on the wing. But he did this so late in the day that there was little chance of Gisgo accepting the challenge.

Scipio had been present at both the Trebbia and Cannae. He had studied Hannibal's battle tactics carefully and was prepared to learn. The difficulty was how to adapt these tactics to the Roman legions, which did not fight in phalanx. This was something that he would have to learn by experience. Having established a routine with Gisgo he was ready. Early in the morning, no doubt with the Trebbia in mind, he breakfasted his men, led them out of camp and drew them up in the opposite order to the previous days. This time the legions were on the wings and the Spaniards in the centre. He then sent out his cavalry and light-armed troops to beat up the enemy camp. Like Sempronius Longus 12 years earlier, Hasdrubal acted in haste, leading out his army before they had eaten and drawing them up in their usual formation. Scipio held his ground, leaving the cavalry and light-armed troops to skirmish. He was determined to make Hasdrubal pay for his impetuosity, keeping him constantly under threat of attack so that he could not change his formation. As the day advanced and the lack of nourishment began to tell on the Carthaginian troops, Scipio recalled his light-armed troops and cavalry who passed through the spaces between the maniples and reformed behind the legions with the *velites* in front and the

Below
Scipio's outflanking manoeuvre on his right wing before the battle of Ilipa.
1 The cavalry and *velites* are recalled. They pass through the gaps between the maniples and reform behind.
2 The legion turns to the right, marches outwards, wheels and advances rapidly.
3 On approaching the Carthaginians the legion deploys into line of battle. The same manoeuvre was performed in reverse on the left wing.

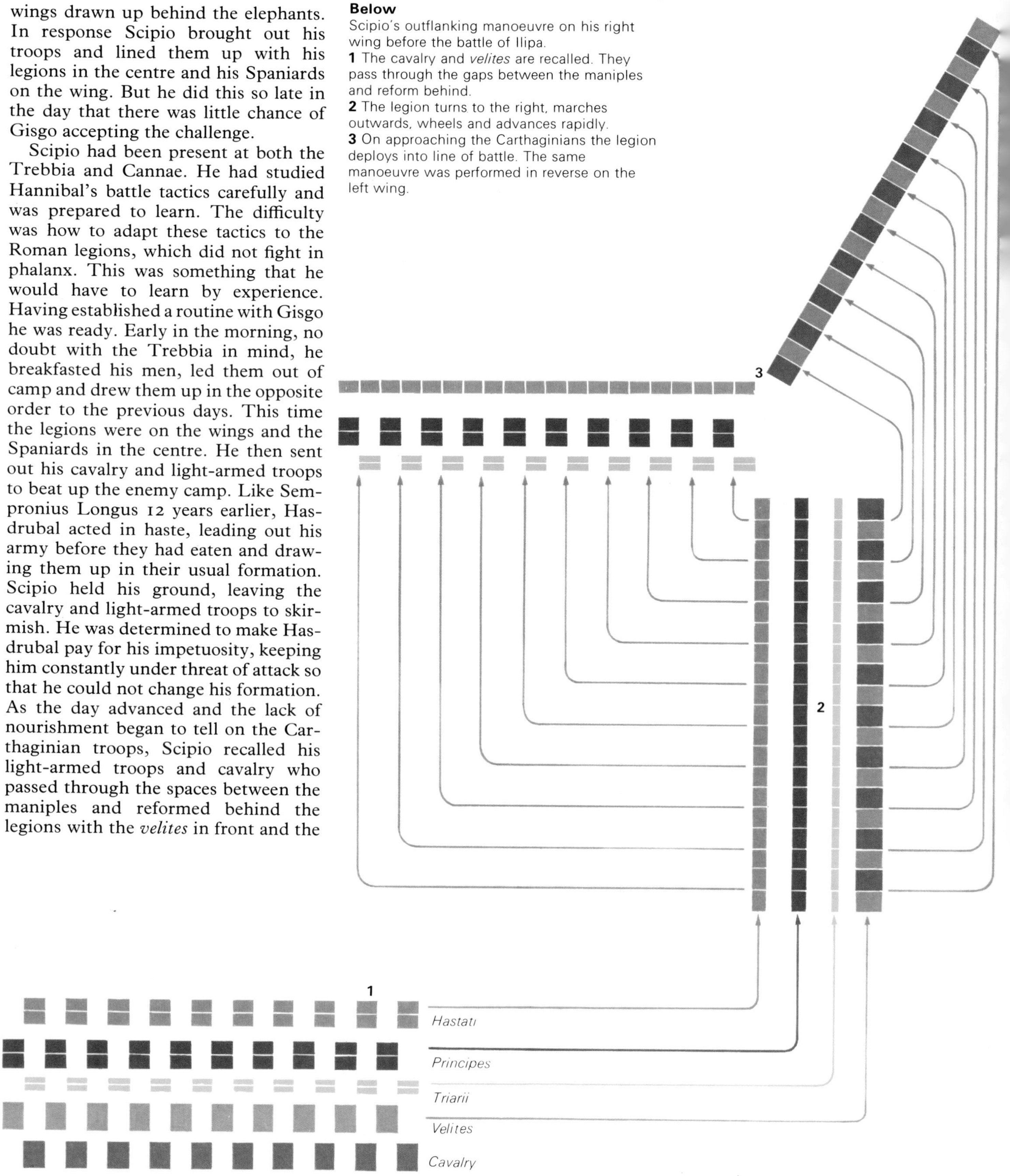

Hastati

Principes

Triarii

Velites

Cavalry

horsemen behind. At first he began to advance directly on Hasdrubal's position, but when he was about 700m from the enemy he ordered the infantry and cavalry on the wings to turn into column to right and left and move outwards from the main column and then wheel, in Spartan fashion, to outflank the enemy. So far Polybius' account makes sense, but in spite of the assurances of some commentators I fail completely to understand the purpose of the subsequent manoeuvre by the infantry which could have been achieved much more simply by advancing in line of battle. Furthermore, since this is a straightforward Greek parade ground manoeuvre why does Polybius break precedent to explain it?

According to Polybius the two columns advanced rapidly on the Carthaginian line whilst the Spaniards moved forward slowly. As the wings

approached the enemy the infantry wheeled inwards and the cavalry and *velites* outwards to outflank the Carthaginian wings. As far as the heavy infantry is concerned this would have necessitated turning the column inwards and then deploying into line through 45°, for if they simply wheeled from column into line the *triarii* would finish up at the front and the *hastati* at the back. On the other hand, if the cavalry and *velites* wheeled in column, they would finish up in their correct order; if they deployed through 45° they would finish up back to front, with their officers on the left instead of the right and with the *velites* behind them. This is exactly what happened, for Polybius says that it did not worry Scipio much that the order had been reversed. Whatever may be the real truth behind this manoeuvre, the Carthaginian forces were routed on the wings and driven back to their camp.

The problems posed by this battle are enormous. Where, for example, were the Carthaginian cavalry while this extraordinary manoeuvre was taking place on the wings? This, like all Poly-

bius' battles in which a Scipio was involved, leaves many unanswered questions, the inevitable result of the historian's persistent marriage of the Scipionic tradition with the facts.

There remained only the mopping-up operations as the Carthaginians had no army left in the field. By the end of 206 Scipio was ready to return to Italy and demand the consulship. During this time in Spain he had made contact with the Numidian king Syphax and a prince called Massinissa. Once more he wanted to emulate Hannibal. His plans were no less than to cross over to Africa and lead a Numidian revolt against Carthage.

In Italy Hannibal had remained among the Bruttii throughout the year. He had not taken the field and the Romans had been careful not to provoke him. The Lucanians, realising that the Carthaginians would no longer come to their aid, surrendered, leaving only the toe of Italy still in Carthaginian hands.

Scipio returned to Rome in the autumn. He was the darling of the people and when he let it be known that he wanted the consulship, with Africa as his province, his wish was granted. But many members of the Senate were opposed to his plans. The opposition was led by the aging Fabius Maximus and Flaccus. For too many years they had fought a defensive war and they were terrified at the prospect of a second Regulus lying dead on the sands of Africa. They could hardly stop Scipio in the face of popular demand but they could withhold the troops that he required. Believing that they were completely frustrating his plans they gave him Sicily as his province along with the forces that were in it—the two disgraced Cannae legions and 30 warships. They added sardonically that he had permission to invade Africa if he saw fit. However, they granted one concession; he could accept volunteers and receive aid from the allies. The response to his appeal was tremendous. Etruria and Umbria promised to build and man a fleet. The keels of 40 warships were immediately laid down and within 45 days the ships were launched and Scipio sailed for Sicily with 7,000 volunteers.

The Cannae legions were the ideal backbone for Scipio's army. He had been with them at Cannae and he under-

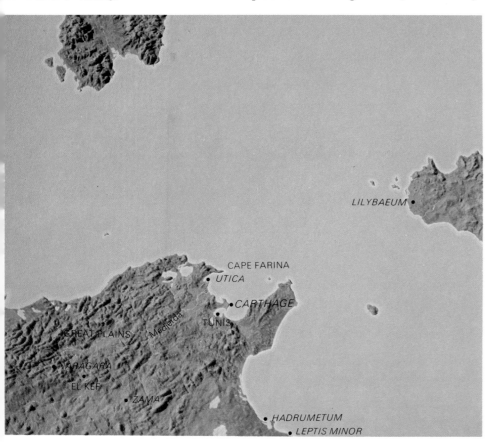

LILYBAEUM •

CAPE FARINA
• UTICA
•CARTHAGE
TUNIS
GREAT PLAINS Medjerda
NARAGARA
EL KEF
• ZAMA

• HADRUMETUM
• LEPTIS MINOR

stood their plight. For years they had begged the Senate to allow them to take a more active part in the war and now that they were to receive the chance to clear their names they responded with enthusiasm. The rest of the year was spent in preparations for the expedition.

Meanwhile Hannibal's youngest brother Mago sailed from the Balearic islands with an army of 14,000 men. He captured Genoa and tried to open a second front. The Romans, with four legions in the Po valley and two in Eturia, were content to hold their lines there for the present. Although Mago received reinforcements from Carthage, he was unable to obtain any help from the Celts who were still suffering from the crushing defeat at the Metaurus. This year also saw the end of the war against Macedonia, which Rome had only encouraged to keep Philip occupied. No longer fearing a Macedonian invasion the Romans left their allies to their fate and swore a unilateral peace treaty with Philip.

In the spring of 204 Scipio set sail from Lilybaeum. Throughout the war the Roman fleet had made raids on the African coast to keep the Carthaginians busy at home and to prevent them sending reinforcements to Hannibal. On one of these raids in 208 Laevinus had encountered and destroyed the Punic fleet. The Carthaginian naval effort during the war had been dismal and this was the final blow. When Scipio sailed to Africa with a guard of only 40 quinqueremes he was not taking an undue risk. The army landed at Cape Farina about 35km north of Carthage. Scipio's hopes that Syphax would join him had been dashed. Hasdrubal Gisgo had managed to secure an alliance with the Numidian king and sealed it with the hand of his beautiful daughter Sophonisba, the Salome of Carthage. However, Massinissa joined him with a troop of 200 cavalry.

Scipio had an initial success when he managed to lure Hanno into an ambush and killed 2,000 of his troops, but an important coup eluded him. Summer was well advanced when he laid siege to Utica both by land and sea hoping to gain a secure base for the winter. He established his camp on a promontory that jutted out into the sea just south of the town and which became known a Castra Cornelia. Here too his hope were dashed as he was forced to with draw when Hasdrubal Gisgo and Sy phax with two armies moved up from the south and encamped about 10km away. Scipio was forced to abandon the siege and retire into winter quarter without a secure base.

During the winter he made the pretence of negotiating whilst awaiting the opportunity to strike. In the spring he launched a surprise night attack on the two Carthaginian camps, setting fire to them and in the confusion wiping ou most of the two armies. Gisgo and Syphax escaped with a small body o men, and within a month the Carthaginians were assembling a new army in the Great Plains about 120km to the west. This is an open, lozenge-shaped tract of land about 30km long and 15km wide caught between the mountains or

Below
The Great Plains, looking south near Souk e Khemis. This is a broad plain surrounded by hills in the valley of the Medjerda (ancient Bagradas). Here Scipio defeated Hasdrubal Gisgo in 203 BC, in his first decisive victory

he upper reaches of the Mjerda river. As soon as he learnt of the Carthaginian concentration Scipio left part of his forces to continue the siege of Utica and set out with the rest up the Mjerda valley.

Scipio advanced into the Great Plains and drew up his forces about 1,400m from the Carthaginian position. The armies skirmished for two days before drawing up in battle array. Scipio lined up his troops in the usual fashion with the *hastati* in the front, the *triarii* at the back, his Italian cavalry on the right and the Numidians on the left. The Carthaginians placed their Celtiberians in the centre with the Numidians on the left and the Carthaginians on the right.

The Italian cavalry and their Numidian allies charged in and stripped the Carthaginian wings. Once they were clear Scipio deployed his *principes* and *triarii* on the wings, surrounded the Celtiberians and cut them to pieces in true Hannibalic style. This was Scipio's first decisive tactical triumph. Three times he had tried to duplicate Hannibal's outflanking movement, at Baecula, Ilipa and now at the Great Plains. At last he had found the answer—not to use the wings of his infantry but to deploy his *principes* and *triarii*.

After the battle Scipio decided to divide his forces yet again. Part of the army was detached to complete the defeat of Syphax, whilst Scipio, after sending his booty to Castra Cornelia, advanced on Carthage itself and took Tunis. This effectively cut Carthage's lines of communication with the interior. The same move had been made by the Syracusan Agathocles a hundred years before and also by Regulus. From Tunis Carthage could be strangled, especially as Rome controlled the sea. A concerted effort by the Romans at this moment would have brought the war to a close.

Carthage had already decided to recall Hannibal and an embassy was dispatched to him. The winter of 203–202 was spent by the Carthaginians in peace negotiations which were partly genuine and partly an attempt to buy time in anticipation of Hannibal's return. The Carthaginian general probably left Italy in the early spring of 202, hoping at this early season to avoid encountering the Roman fleet. He had been in Italy more

than 15 years and was now 45 years old. Polybius implies that he brought a large number of his veterans out of Italy but this seems highly unlikely. By now his army was probably reduced to about 20,000. Since 207 he had been confined to the Bruttii, blockaded by both land and sea. In all probability he returned to Africa with only the remnants of his African troops, perhaps 4,000 of them. at Zama his veterans, who formed the rear line, levelled their pikes to stop the Carthaginian front lines from falling back on them, proving that they were in fact his African pikemen. Subsequent events show that his Numidian cavalry were now practically non-existent. Diodorus' account of Hannibal's massacre of the mercenaries who would not cross over to Africa with him is obviously false for they had served him faithfully for more than 15 years and his other troops would never have agreed to kill their comrades. However, this story may contain a germ of truth: the Romans probably offered terms to the remainder of Hannibal's army and then massacred them. Certainly we are never told by Livy what happened to them. The troops that had been serving in Liguria under Hannibal's youngest brother Mago also sailed back to Africa. Mago, who had been wounded before he left, died on the voyage.

Hannibal landed at Leptis Minor near modern Sousse 120km south of Carthage where he was joined by a body of 2,000 Numidian cavalry. From here he moved first to Hadrumetum and then inland, camping near a place called Zama five days' journey (100–150km) west of Carthage.

Hannibal had probably moved west hoping to gather more Numidian cavalry. Scipio had also moved west to meet Massinissa who had inherited the kingdom of Syphax and was now able to supply 6,000 infantry and 4,000 cavalry. According to Polybius, after making a rendezvous with Massinissa, Scipio advanced to a town called Margaron which cannot be identified. Livy calls the place Naragara (Sidi Youssef on the border with Algeria). It may be that Polybius' name has been corrupted but it is even more likely that Livy has substituted a name he knows for one he does not. Hannibal advanced to within 6km of Scipio's camp and here after an abortive meeting between the two commanders the battle was fought.

The site of the battle is unknown. Kromayer and Scullard advocate a site 12km south-west of El Kef which fits the battle topography well. This site is shown in the photograph on p. 204 but it remains far from certain.

Early on the morning after their meeting both sides drew up their armies in the plain between their camps. According to Polybius, whose account of any Scipionic battle should be treated with caution, Hannibal drew up his army in three lines. In the front line were 12,000 Ligurian, Celtic, Balearic and Moorish mercenary infantry. These must have been mainly composed of the troops Mago was bringing back when he died. Polybius gives no details of how they were drawn up and the presence of Balearic slingers among heavy infantry seems unlikely. Somewhat over 80 elephants were placed in front of this first line. The second line was composed of

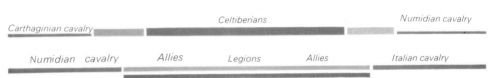

Carthaginian cavalry   Celtiberians   Numidian cavalry

Numidian cavalry   Allies   Legions   Allies   Italian cavalry

The battle of the Great Plains. The Romans used their normal formation. The Carthaginians placed their Celtiberians in the centre flanked by the other infantry and with the Carthaginian cavalry on the right.

The stronger Roman cavalry easily stripped the wings of the Carthaginian army and only the Celtiberians stood their ground. Scipio deployed his *principes* and *triarii* on the wings and surrounded them.

Liby-Phoenicans and native Cartha-ginians, no doubt forming a phalanx. At the rear, and more than 200m further back, was a third line made up of Hannibal's veterans. It is this third line which causes the greatest problem as we cannot establish whether these were the remains of Hannibal's (c. 4,000) Africans. The Carthaginian cavalry were placed on the right wing and the 2,000 Numidians on the left.

The Romans were drawn up in their normal three lines except that instead of being in quincunx formation with the middle line (*principes*) covering the gaps in the front line, the maniples were drawn up one behind the other leaving gaps through the legions. These gaps were filled with the *velites* from all three lines. Laelius with the Italian horse was placed opposite the Carthaginian cavalry; Massinissa faced the other Numidians whom he outnumbered two to one. The Roman forces probably numbered about 30,000 infantry and 6,000 cavalry.

After the Numidian horse had skirmished for some time Hannibal ordered the elephants to charge. Scipio had been waiting for this before he made any move himself and now ordered his *velites* to advance to meet them. The blast of the trumpets and horns which signalled the charge of the *velites* frightened several of the elephants who turned and scattered the Numidians who were following them. Massinissa, taking advantage of the confusion, raced in and the Carthaginian light cavalry broke leaving their left wing exposed. The rest of the elephants charged the *velites* who retired through the gaps in the legions, drawing the elephants with them. Others fleeing to the wings were met with a shower of javelins from the cavalry and fled the field in terror.

Choosing this moment of confusion the Italian cavalry charged the Carthaginian horsemen who also broke and fled. This may have been part of Hannibal's plan for he was greatly outnumbered by Scipio's cavalry which now left the field in pursuit of his horsemen. The infantry lines now moved in on each other, with the exception of Hannibal's rear line which remained where it was. When they came within range, the *hastati* in the Roman front line raised their war cry, clashed their *pila* against their shields and charged. The Roman rear ranks followed up closely cheering on the *hastati*. The first Carthaginian line held for a while and then broke and turned on their second line which had failed to support them. Since this second line must have been a phalanx the picture is a little confused. The second line charged the *hastati* but the centurions of the *principes*, seeing their comrades giving ground, added their weight and the second Carthaginian line in their turn broke and fell back on the veterans who levelled their pikes to stop them breaking up their formation and forcing them to retreat towards the wings.

Scipio recalled the *hastati* who were following up the Carthaginian flight and regrouped his men for the final assault. He removed his own wounded from the field, then, deploying his *principes* and *triarii* on either wing and clambering over the bodies which littered the

battlefield, he advanced on Hannibal's veterans. Polybius implies that Hannibal's veterans were roughly equal in number to the *hastati* who opposed them, about 5,000 strong. This could be correct but the true figure probably is much lower. The phalanx managed to hold the legions at bay until Laelius, returning with the Roman cavalry, turned the tide of the battle.

When he saw that all was lost, Hannibal fled with a few horsemen to Hadrumetum. Polybius' casualty list, 20,000 Carthaginians dead and a similar number captured, is grossly exaggerated to glorify Scipio. It is highly unlikely that there were anywhere near this number involved. Accepting the figure of 12,000 for the front line and assuming a similar number for the second line, the total Carthaginian infantry numbered less than 30,000 and their cavalry certainly numbered no more than 4,000. Polybius gives the Roman losses as more than 1,500. He offers no explanation of Hannibal's strategy. None of the genius that had won Cannae appears in his account. Could the battle have been as simple as this? Was Hannibal a spent force?

Old scores are settled
The Romans had won a great victory and the Carthaginians sued for peace. Scipio was received rapturously on his return to Rome and granted a triumph. But for his army the war was not over. The Cannae legionaries had not seen their homes for more than 14 years but they were transferred directly to Greece. Almost as soon as the war with Hannibal was over the Senate had started to interfere in Greek politics, issuing ultimata to Philip which resulted in the declaration of war. The people had not wanted another war but were finally persuaded into it in the summer of 200. In the autumn of the same year two veteran legions, made up mainly of 'volunteers' from the African army, landed on the Illyrian coast. After suffering some initial setbacks, the Roman army under Titus Quinctius Flamininus invaded Thessaly in the spring of 197. Philip advanced to meet them at Pherae 18km west of Volos. The ground was unsuitable for a battle and the two armies withdrew westwards, Flamininus to the south and Philip to the north of the Chalkodonion hills. After following parallel routes for two days Flamininus encamped probably near Pharsalus (Farsala) and Philip near Skotoussa. It had rained heavily during the night and when Philip set out again he found the going difficult owing to the mist that covered the hills. He pitched camp again, dispatching a covering force to occupy the summits of the hills which separated him from Flamininus'

army. Flamininus, meanwhile, was encamped just the other side of the ridge but both were unaware of the other's presence. During the morning the Roman dispatched 300 cavalry and about 1,000 *velites* to reconnoitre. Those reaching the top of the pass fell in with the Macedonian covering force and a fight commenced at the top of the hill. When the Romans began to be pushed back down the hill Flamininus sent out 500 horse and 2,000 foot to support them. This reversed the situation and Philip was forced to send up reinforcements. These in their turn drove the Romans back from the summit. As the mist was clearing both sides now decided to bring up the rest of their forces. The Romans were nearer to the pass and managed to deploy their forces whilst Philip was still bringing up his. Only his right wing had reached the top of the pass and since he had drawn it up in battle column all he had to do was to wheel to the left to draw it up in line. As the left wing was beginning to come up he doubled his phalanx and peltasts (these were probably spearmen and not javelineers) to the right to halve the length of the line and make room for his left wing. The cavalry and light armed who were already engaged were withdrawn and formed up on the right wing.

Flamininus placed the elephants which were with his army in front of his

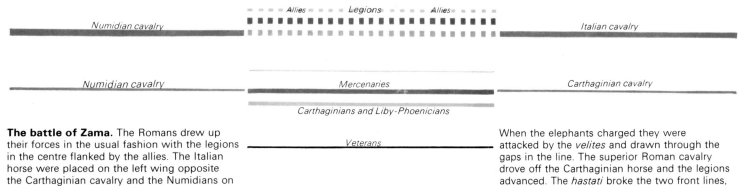

The battle of Zama. The Romans drew up their forces in the usual fashion with the legions in the centre flanked by the allies. The Italian horse were placed on the left wing opposite the Carthaginian cavalry and the Numidians on the right. The maniples were drawn up behind each other to leave gaps through the army. These were filled by the *velites*. Hannibal drew up his troops in three lines with the mercenaries in front, then the Liby-Phoenicians and Carthaginians, and finally his veterans at the rear. In front were elephants and light-armed troops.

When the elephants charged they were attacked by the *velites* and drawn through the gaps in the line. The superior Roman cavalry drove off the Carthaginian horse and the legions advanced. The *hastati* broke the two front lines, driving them back on Hannibal's veterans. These lowered their pikes to stop the fugitives from disrupting their formation, forcing them out on to the wings. Scipio now deployed his *triarii* and *principes* on the wings to outflank the Carthaginian forces. The veterans held on until taken in rear by the Roman cavalry.

right wing, told his troops there to stand fast and advanced with his left wing. Philip, realising that events had overtaken him, ordered his phalanx to lower their spears and charge. Here Livy makes one of his classic blunders. Misunderstanding Polybius he says that Philip ordered his phalanx to put down their spears and charge. Then, realising that this is rather strange, he feels obliged to explain why, going on to say that their pikes were too long to be of any use.

The charge of the phalanx drove the legionaries back down the slope. Flamininus, seeing the imminent destruction of his left wing, threw himself at the head of his right wing and charged the Macedonian left wing which was still forming up. The half-assembled Macedonian line crumbled before the onslaught of the elephants. The Roman left wing had by now been pushed some way down the hillside but the right had reached the summit. One of the tribunes, seizing the initiative, took 20 maniples of the *triarii*, faced about and charged obliquely down the hillside into the rear of the Macedonian right wing. The action was decisive; the phalanx, unable to turn, was cut to pieces. The Romans followed up their victory, cutting down the Macedonians where they stood even though they raised their pikes to surrender. Some had not even reached the summit of the pass but they were also slaughtered by the legionaries. Philip escaped from the field with a few horsemen but the greatness of Macedon was over. Polybius says that about 8,000 Macedonians were killed and at least 5,000 captured. As this battle does not involve a Scipio or a Paullus, these figures are likely to be correct. The Roman losses were about 700.

The Romans had no wish to occupy Macedonia and by 194 all the Roman troops were evacuated. But within two years Antiochus of Syria, trying to capitalise on the vacuum left by the fall of Macedonia, invaded Greece and the Romans were compelled to return. The legions drove the Syrian king from Greece and then crossed over into Asia Minor and defeated him decisively at Magnesia-under-Sipylus in 190.

In the Po valley the Romans had set about the final conquest. Hannibal's agent Hamilcar was still in northern Italy when Carthage surrendered and he refused to accept the peace of 202. In 200 he organised a Gallic revolt to coincide with the beginning of the war with Macedonia and sacked Placentia which had survived so much in the last 18 years. Rome fought a defensive war until matters were settled in Greece and then began the reconquest in earnest. In 194 the Insubres capitulated and in 191 the Boii followed suit and were driven right out of Italy to settle in Bohemia. Most of the central area of the Po valley was turned over to Roman settlers. The Ligurians were also conquered during the next decades, so that by the middle of the century the territories of Rome and Marseilles were contiguous.

Hannibal, meanwhile, had tried to lead a political life at Carthage but his social reforms gained him many enemies. In 195 his political opponents, in collusion with the Romans, drove him out. He first of all took shelter with Antiochus and was even in charge of the Syrian fleet at the battle of Magnesia. After this he fled to Crete and then to Bithynia, but the Romans hounded him wherever he went and 20 years after the

battle of Zama, rather than fall into Roman hands, he committed suicide.

In Macedon Philip V died in 179 and he was succeeded by his son Perseus who tried to throw off the Roman alliance. He was defeated by Aemilius Paullus, the son of the general at Cannae in 168, and Macedonia was broken up. Even so Macedonia made one last effort, but after the final defeat in 148 it lost its independence entirely and became a Roman province.

Carthage remained at peace with Rome for more than half a century, but in 149 at the instigation of Massinissa and the Roman censor Cato, who was an inveterate enemy of Carthage, Rome declared a completely unprovoked war on the Phoenician city. After a three-year siege it was utterly destroyed by Scipio Aemilianus, the grandson of the Paullus of Cannae. The city was ploughed into the ground and its population sold into slavery.

Although Scipio had driven the Carthaginians out of Spain, it was a further two centuries before the peninsula was finally pacified. Three wars were fought in Spain in the 2nd century culminating in the Numantine war of 143–133 BC. When the town of Numantia was taken by Scipio Aemilianus after a long siege in 133, organised resistance in Spain came to an end and the Celtiberians submitted. However, north-western Spain was not finally subdued until the time of Augustus.

The battle of Cynoscephalae.
1 The battle developed out of a skirmish with successive bodies of troops being sent up the hill by both sides. The Romans managed to deploy their whole forces whilst Philip only managed to get half his infantry up to the top of the ridge.
2 Philip formed up all his cavalry on his right, doubled up the right wing of his infantry and charged the Roman left.
3 The Macedonians forced the Roman left back down the slope. Flamininus counter-attacked the half-formed Macedonian left and it broke. One of the tribunes, seizing the initiative, took the *triarii* from the victorious Roman right wing and charged the Macedonian right from behind.

Left (top)
The view looking north from above Ambelia. Philip's camp was beyond the ridge in the distance. His pickets were on the ridge in the centre and the battle was fought on the slopes below. **Below** Map of the area.

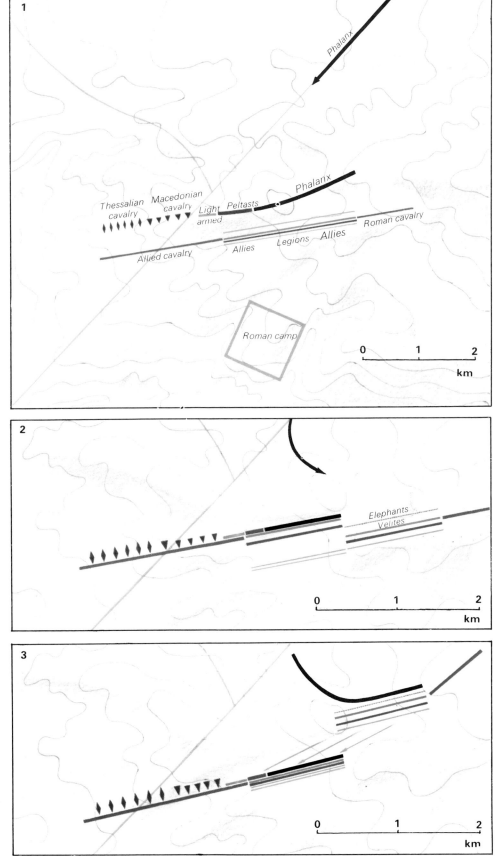

THE
ROMAN
EMPIRE

The Empire 140 BC–AD 200

Introduction

During the second half of the 2nd century BC, Rome made few territorial gains. Her grip tightened on Spain, North Africa and Greece and she conquered southern Gaul to secure the land route to Spain. A series of military reforms at the end of the 2nd century produced a new type of army composed of long-service soldiers who were loyal not to the state but to their generals. This led to an age of rapid conquest punctuated with civil wars as general fought general. Out of this chaos emerged the Roman empire, often governed by an emperor who was little more than a warlord who established a dynasty which lasted until some new general replaced it with his own.

The period from 140 BC to AD 100 is very well documented and we even have Caesar's own accounts of his campaigns. Unfortunately after the death of Caesar we have to rely on such sources as Tacitus, Josephus, a Jew who turned traitor to his own people during the Jewish revolt of AD 66–70, and Vegetius, who wrote a manual of military oddments towards the end of the 4th century AD. There is also a 'Pseudo-Hyginus', who wrote a manual on the setting out of camps probably in the 2nd century AD.

Tacitus, who wrote a history of the 1st century AD and also a book on Germany during the same period, is the most reliable source. He was son-in-law to Agricola, who was governor of Britain for seven years and completed the conquest of that country. Although he wrote a life of his father-in-law, he fails to show any clear insight into military matters and all too often falls back on vague generalisations and accepted terminology.

Josephus, who wrote an account of the Jewish revolt, is not a reliable source and greatly exaggerates, especially when describing his own exploits against the Romans before he changed sides. He does, however, make some very useful observations on aspects of Roman military practice which impressed him as a foreigner. These details are entirely lacking in the Roman sources as the Latin writers felt no need to explain the commonplace to their readers.

Vegetius is an historian with a fly-paper mind and has a lot in common with the late Hellenistic tactical writers (this is extended to include Arrian). He offers a mass of unrelated facts collected from all periods of Roman history and can therefore only be used to supply details.

Pseudo-Hyginus gives the most detailed account of castramentation since Polybius. He describes a real or imaginary force which included virtually every type of unit in the Roman army and gives a lot of information, often difficult to interpret, about the organisation of these units.

From AD 100 to AD 200 there is no adequate historical record, and even for the study of Trajan's campaigns we have to rely almost wholly on the triumphal column which he set up in Rome. The great spiral relief on the column records the emperor's campaigns against the Dacians and gives a mass of detail about the army on campaign.

The historical narrative is augmented by a wealth of archaeological evidence. Although this is sparse for Caesar's time, from the period of Augustus, when permanent camps are being established along the Rhine and the Danube, the archaeological record is superb. This evidence, which tells us so much about military installations and equipment, is supplemented by an ever-increasing fund of inscriptions which, coupled with the mass of military documents written on papyrus discovered in the Middle East, have enabled scholars to build up a very accurate picture of the organisation of the army during the empire. The sections on the organisation of the Roman imperial army have been written by two leading scholars in the field, Dr Brian Dobson and Dr Roger Tomlin.

Conquest of the World

By 146 BC Rome found herself virtually in control of the whole of the Mediterranean basin with large parts of Greece, Spain and North Africa under her direct control. This was not the result of some great plan but had come about because of the incredible success of the army in wars which at least from Rome's point of view were not of her own making.

With the destruction of Carthage in 146 BC the territory of Numidia, under the rule of the proud descendants of Massinissa, was extended, but it was only a matter of time before they came into conflict with Rome. Hostilities broke out in 111 and it was several years before they could be brought to a successful conclusion. The main interest of the war for us is that it brought to the forefront a new type of Roman general and a new type of army. This general was Gaius Marius who came from a rural background and rose to power through service in the army. Marius was a first-class general and served his country well, defeating the German tribes of the Teutones and Cimbri when they invaded southern Europe at the end of the 2nd century BC.

In 92 BC the Italians, who had for a long time been agitating for equal rights with the Romans, took up arms and the social war began. Marius was now in his mid-sixties, but nevertheless he offered his services and played a significant part in the suppression of the revolt. Although the Italians were defeated, after the war there was a general extension of Roman citizenship to all Italians south of the Po.

Marius was responsible for far-reaching reforms in the army which laid the basis for the professional standing army of the early principate. Marius's military reputation, however, is marred by his conflict with the aristocrat Sulla which resulted in the first of Rome's civil wars. He died before the end of the war and Sulla took control at Rome. In 80 BC, he retired to Campania.

The pattern had been set and Rome became the prey of her generals. Lucullus and Pompey, a young general who had served under Sulla, set out on careers of conquest in the east. Lucullus defeated Mithridates the king of Pontus (north-eastern Turkey) in 71 and the following year invaded Armenia. In 66 Pompey succeeded to Lucullus' command and completed his operations in the East, bringing Syria and Judaea under Roman control. On his return to Italy he was granted a triumph but met considerable opposition to his plans in the Senate. As a result he formed an alliance known as the first triumvirate with the rising politician Gaius Julius Caesar and the wealthy businessman Crassus. This alliance secured the consulship for Caesar in 59.

In the last quarter of the 2nd century a province had been established in uthern Gaul which had brought some egree of security to north-west Italy nd enabled Rome to establish a land ute to Spain. The Celts remained a nstant threat, however, and at the me that Caesar received his consulship ntral Gaul was again in tumult and he province was threatened. Caesar managed to secure the province of Gaul s the campaigning area for his proonsulship and early in 58 he set out on ne of the great careers of conquest. In ree campaigns he overran the whole f Gaul, and in the following years unched expeditions to Britain and ermany, both of which had a political ather than a military purpose and reulted in no permanent settlement. The auls made a concerted effort under ercingetorix to drive out the legions ut were brought to their knees at the ege of Alesia. By 51 Gaul had been reuced to the state of a province.

The relationship between Caesar and ompey had been strained for some me and now Pompey sided with the enate, which was trying to limit Caesar's ever-increasing power, preipitating a second civil war. The war entred on Illyria, where Pompey had et up his headquarters. Caesar crossed he Adriatic and laid siege to Pompey's rmy at Dyrrhachium (Durrës). When ompey broke out Caesar followed him nto Thessaly and defeated him near harsalus in 48. It took him a further wo years to complete the overthrow of he remaining Pompeian forces. Like ulla, Caesar now had complete control f the empire, but like his predecessor e was not to enjoy it for long and in 44 e was assassinated.

The murder of Caesar resulted in a ower struggle that was not fully reolved until 31, when Octavian defeated Mark Antony at Actium on the west oast of Greece and became the first Roman emperor. Four years later he eceived the title of Augustus, by which e is generally known.

Augustus inherited a vast and unwieldy empire which he set about ationalising. Although Rome had conquered territory from the Euphrates in he east to Portugal in the west and from frica in the south to Belgium in the orth, there were still enclaves of resistnce within the empire, including one within the modern boundaries of Italy

itself. The Salassi, who occupied the Val d'Aosta in the Italian Alps, were still in arms. Augustus put down these pockets of resistance, completing the conquest of Spain and securing the frontiers of southern Egypt. The vast area south of the Danube was also brought under Roman control.

Attempts were made to extend the empire beyond the Rhine as far as the Elbe, but in AD 9 the Roman general Varus with three legions was ambushed and his force wiped out in the Teutoburg forest. Augustus withdrew his troops behind the Rhine and advised his successor Tiberius not to try to extend the empire further.

During his reign Augustus reorganised the army and put it on a permanent professional basis. He died five years after the Teutoburgerwald disaster and Tiberius, true to his predecessor's request, attempted no further conquest.

The final accessions
In 41 Claudius became emperor and, feeling that he needed some military justification for his position, decided on the conquest of Britain. The limited possibilities inherent in the British venture probably convinced the cautious Claudius that the expedition would not get out of hand. In 43 Britain was invaded by four legions and a new province was established. During Claudius' reign the two client kingdoms of Thrace and Mauretania were placed under direct control, thus bringing the whole of Europe south of the Rhine-Danube line and North Africa within the empire.

Although no firm frontiers were established and further conquest was always envisaged, the legions had now come to a halt along the line of the Rhine and the Danube in the north where permanent camps had been established.

At the end of the last civil war Augustus had inherited about 60 legions. He reduced this number to 28 and subsequently lost three in the Teutoburgerwald disaster. By the end of Nero's reign (AD 68) the number had again risen to 28, of which 25 were stationed along the frontiers of the empire. In the East three (though there were normally four) legions were garrisoned near Antioch in Syria and two more were stationed in Egypt. Three legions, in-

cluding the fourth Syrian legion, were on active service in Judaea putting down the Jewish revolt. There was one further legion in North Africa. In Europe 12 legions were encamped along the Rhine-Danube frontier, poised to invade north-east Europe. A 13th was posted in Dalmatia (Yugoslavia). Of the remaining six legions three (normally four) were stationed in Britain, one garrisoned in Spain, and there were legions in Gaul (the fourth British legion) and Italy preparing for an Eastern campaign planned by Nero but which never came off. These forces were supplemented by a roughly similar number of auxiliary troops drawn from the population along the frontiers.

There was a setback in Britain about AD 60 when two of the native tribes rose in revolt under the legendary Queen Boudica and sacked several Roman towns, but the rebellion was easily suppressed. In 66 Rome had to deal with the much more serious Jewish revolt, and the emperor Nero dispatched three legions under the command of Vespasian to quell the insurrection. In 68 Nero committed suicide and another power struggle began in which the Eastern and Western legions came into conflict. The Rhine legions supported the governor of Lower Germany, Vitellius, and proclaimed him emperor on 2 January 69. Six months later the Eastern legions hailed Vespasian as emperor and gained the support of the Danube legions. The two armies met at Cremona, in northern Italy, and after a battle that lasted through the night the Eastern legions emerged victorious and Vespasian became emperor.

The new emperor and his two sons ruled until 96 but did not extend the empire. Two years later the last of the great Roman conquerors, Trajan, came to the throne. Before his accession he had been governor of southern Germany and preferred the military to the political life. In 101 he crossed the Danube into Dacia (modern Romania) which had been in conflict with Rome for some time and in five years reduced it to the status of a province. In 106 he annexed Arabia, thus completing Rome's circuit of the Mediterranean.

The East had been threatened by Parthia for nearly two centuries and Trajan decided to settle matters there.

In 115 he took Armenia, then crossed the Tigris, capturing the Parthian capital and reaching the Persian Gulf. However, he died before he could consolidate his conquests.

Frontiers established

Trajan was succeeded by Hadrian who embarked on an entirely different policy of consolidating the borders and abandoning precarious provinces such as those beyond the Euphrates. Hadrian initiated the building of the wall in northern Britain which bears his name and established a fixed frontier along the Rhine-Danube, joining the two rivers with a palisade.

Antoninus Pius succeeded to the throne in 138, but despite his extension of the British frontier up into Scotland where the Antonine Wall was built, and the putting down of revolts in various parts of the empire, no significant campaigns were undertaken. During the reign of his successor Marcus Aurelius (161–180) the Roman armies again advanced into Mesopotamia and made it a Roman protectorate, once more driving back the Parthians. But a few years later the Germans broke through the Danube frontier and invaded northern Italy. This was only the first of many such invasions that were to characterise the latter days of the empire.

The advance was halted. The emperor crossed the Danube intending to pacify central and eastern Europe, but was forced to modify his plans because of trouble in the East where a rival emperor had been proclaimed. As a compromise he formed a buffer state in the Danube area by settling semi-Romanised tribesmen there who were under obligation to defend the frontiers.

Marcus Aurelius was succeeded by his son Commodus who abandoned the problems of the empire in favour of more pleasurable pursuits and fell to the assassin's blade in 192. After his death there was a scramble for power which was only brought to an end in 197 after Septimius Severus, the governor of Upper Pannonia, marched on Rome and defeated two other claimants to the throne, the governors of Syria and Britain. Soon after his accession the Parthians again invaded the Eastern

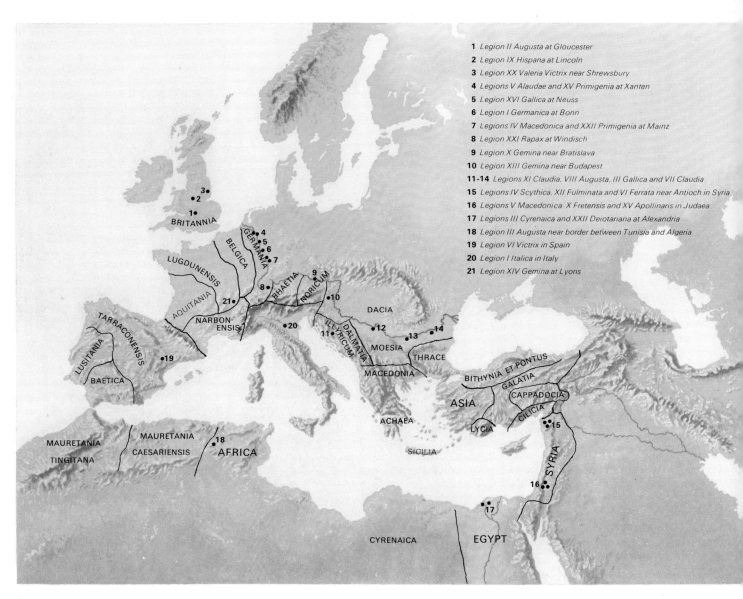

1 Legion II Augusta at Gloucester
2 Legion IX Hispana at Lincoln
3 Legion XX Valeria Victrix near Shrewsbury
4 Legions V Alaudae and XV Primigenia at Xanten
5 Legion XVI Gallica at Neuss
6 Legion I Germanica at Bonn
7 Legions IV Macedonica and XXII Primigenia at Mainz
8 Legion XXI Rapax at Windisch
9 Legion X Gemina near Bratislava
10 Legion XIII Gemina near Budapest
11-14 Legions XI Claudia, VIII Augusta, III Gallica and VII Claudia
15 Legions IV Scythica, XII Fulminata and VI Ferrata near Antioch in Syria
16 Legions V Macedonica, X Fretensis and XV Apollinaris in Judaea
17 Legions III Cyrenaica and XXII Deiotariana at Alexandria
18 Legion III Augusta near border between Tunisia and Algeria
19 Legion VI Victrix in Spain
20 Legion I Italica in Italy
21 Legion XIV Gemina at Lyons

provinces and in retaliation Mesopotamia was for the last time conquered by
the legions but again without a permanent settlement.

Army Organisation
Dr Brian Dobson
The new legions
Originally the army of Rome had simply
been its citizens, called out to fight with
the weapons and armour that they could
afford. When some order was brought
into this, a minimum property qualification was established for a legionary.

The soldier was only called up when
needed, and he was discharged as soon
as the emergency was over. He was liable for service between the ages of 17
and 46, and there was a limitation of 16
years' service in all. He was expected to
provide his own armour. Although he
was paid a small amount for his time in
service, this was more in the nature of
expenses; his main source of income
was his farm or his business interests at
home.

It is hardly surprising, therefore, that
he was not keen on long periods of service. Consequently recruiting became
increasingly difficult as the theatres of
war moved further from home and the
periods of campaigning became longer.
Those who were recruited were forever
agitating for discharge.

Towards the end of the 2nd century
BC Rome became involved in a long-
drawn-out war against the Numidians.
This war was so unattractive that it became almost impossible for Rome to
find any recruits for her legions.

Marius was the Roman consul in
charge of the war. Under these difficult
circumstances he threw the legions open
to any volunteer who could claim Roman
citizenship, regardless of whether he

Left
Map of the Roman empire in the 1st century
AD showing the provinces and the distribution
of the legions in 67 AD. Three legions under
Vespasian (two Syrian and one Egyptian) were
campaigning in Judaea, putting down a Jewish
revolt.

Right
The cohort at the time of Caesar. The *velites*
have been abolished. All legionaries are now
armed with sword and *pila*. **CT** = centurion;
O = optio; **S** = signifer; **C** = cornicen
T = tubicen.

owned property. The poor flocked to join the legions. Far from seeking an early discharge from the army, they hoped that their service would continue indefinitely. The foundations of a professional army had been laid.

Marius, however, had only taken the final step, as the property qualification had been already considerably lowered. But he did give an even greater importance to the volunteer. Already some men had made the army their career as soldier and centurion. Now the only qualification was that of citizenship. The volunteer generally followed the great generals and identified his fortunes with those of his leader. Fortunes were made of plunder, not pay, and the man who had devoted his life to the army had no farm to which to return. The veteran of the 1st century BC looked to his general to provide him with land on discharge.

Under the old system the legions were re-enrolled for every campaign and could never gain a lasting sense of identity. Marius helped to change this by providing each legion with a single pre-eminent standard, the eagle. In the 1st century BC legions might continue in existence for some time, discharging men and being made up by supplements. Although they still lacked names, Caesar's legions at least carried numbers.

Pay was still thought of as basically expenses; out of it must come the cost of food and equipment. It was probably not until Caesar doubled pay at the beginning of the civil wars that a soldier made anything from pay alone.

It was at about this time that a fundamental rethinking about the shape of the legion took place. The maniples of *triarii* were raised to the same strength as the *hastati* and *principes* and coupled with them to form cohorts. Thus the whole legion now consisted of ten cohorts instead of 30 maniples. Although the legion retained the phased commitment to battle enshrined in the old manipular tactics, there was now greater flexibility. Legions might be drawn up for battle in anything from one to four lines. This was possible because the distinctions between *hastati*, *principes* and *triarii* disappeared. All were armed alike with sword and *pilum*.

The maniple seems to have lost any significance for battle. The names lived on, nevertheless, to identify centurions

and centuries, and in camp and fortress the centuries were still paired.

After the social war all Italians living south of the river Po were granted Roman citizenship. This meant that the distinction between Roman and allied legions was abolished. From this point one legion means exactly what it says and does not imply an equal number of soldiers from the cities allied to Rome.

This tendency to eliminate differenti-

ation within the legion and between legion and *ala* (the legion of the allies was carried further by the disappear-ance of the light-armed skirmisher (*velites*) and of the legionary cavalry. The change is significant; the old legion with its cavalry and the additional cavalry of its allied complement and light infantry, artillery and engineers, had combined all arms. Now although the legion was in some ways an even mor

Above

An officer, almost certainly a tribune, from the altar of Domitius Ahenobarbus. He wears a short muscled cuirass, greaves and helmet. He is armed with spear, sword and round shield. The sash around his waist is a symbol of his rank. These young aristocratic officers held their posts to further their political careers. The generals of Caesar's era were embarrassed by the tribunes' lack of experience and placed the overall command of the legion in the hands of a *legatus*, an older man.

2–4 Trophies from a frieze found below the Capitoline Hill in Rome. The cuirass (**2**) and the helmet (**4**) are those of a general. The panoply (**3**) is possibly a centurion's. First half of 1st century BC.

efficient instrument of war in the hands of a genius such as Caesar, there were tasks for which other assistance had to be sought.

Since the time of the Hannibalic war Rome had used the standard military specialists of the Mediterranean—Cretan archers, Balearic slingers, Numidian light horse. But now large numbers of cavalry were required. Caesar used cavalry from Gaul and Germany, including a German (and Numidian) speciality, cavalry with light infantry fighting alongside them. Spain provided cavalry and infantry, both heavy and light. These were *auxilia*, non-citizen and non-allied troops.

On the march the old army had always been accompanied by a large baggage train. These baggage trains not only offered a great temptation to the enemy but also slowed down the army. Marius made the legionary carry his essential supplies on his back and because of this legionaries became known as 'Marius' mules'. Baggage trains were not eliminated, but they were reduced in size and better regulated.

The legion was still commanded by six tribunes. The office had sunk in importance, however. In earlier days it had been held by men as senior as ex-consuls, but it was now generally held by young men who hoped to enter the Senate or who simply wanted a taste of military life. There were only 20 places a year as *quaestors* (minimum age 30) for men entering the Senate. As there were many more tribunes, the rest, all equestrians (the second order of Roman aristocracy), might simply like the military life; it was possible to stay in the army as an officer for many years. Above the tribunes were the prefects, who might command cavalry (*praefectus equitum*), fleets (*praefectus classis*) or be aides to generals (*praefectus fabrum*). What they had in common was that they were appointed to single commands (not in pairs like the tribunes), generally to less permanent positions and at the will of the commander. Service as tribune and prefect formed natural stepping stones to the next stage, *legatus*.

The legate was normally a senator, which in the last century of the republic meant he must at least have held the magistracy of *quaestor*. Like so many of the posts in the Roman army it had been in existence a long time. The right to appoint men to whom powers and responsibilities might be delegated (the same word-root as legate) was normally granted to a commander. Such men derived their powers from their commander. The legates of Pompey and Caesar formed a tight group of experienced soldiers, for the most part, though sometimes, as with tribunes, less suitable people were given appointments as legates for political reasons. Caesar often gave a legate command of a legion, or numbers of legions, or of the auxiliary cavalry, or some other charge. There was no permanent relationship of legate to legion, but such men were clearly more suitable than the tribunes of Caesar's day to undertake leading the legion in war.

The consuls had succeeded the king

Below
A scene from Trajan's Column showing legionaries entrenching whilst auxiliaries stand guard. The legionaries are using wicker baskets to remove the earth from the trench. The wall is made of turf.

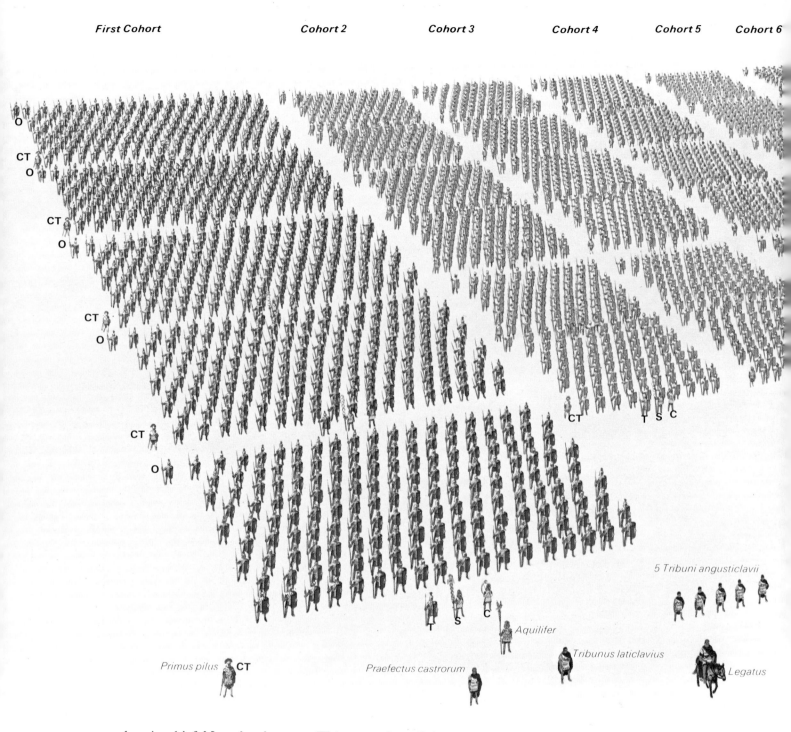

First Cohort Cohort 2 Cohort 3 Cohort 4 Cohort 5 Cohort 6

5 Tribuni angusticlavii

Aquilifer

Tribunus laticlavius

Primus pilus CT

Praefectus castrorum

Legatus

as commanders-in-chief. Note the plural—the republic did not know a single commander-in-chief, except in the direst emergency. Even in the face of Hannibal the consuls continued to change annually, but in addition to the armies they raised or took over other armies were kept in being under ex-magistrates, consuls or praetors, whose authority was extended, elevating them to the status of proconsuls, propraetors.

This extension of the powers of the senior magistrates proved the easiest way of providing governors for the provinces that Rome began to acquire after the war against Hannibal. As the theatres of war became more distant it was increasingly the proconsul who fought the battles of the republic, with no colleague to hold him in check. Caesar was such a proconsul, who held three provinces and his new conquests in

Gaul for ten years with ten legions, and then turned what had become his own army against Rome.

The legions of the early principate
The legion of the early empire was not very different from that of Caesar's time. Cohorts I to X still contained around 500 men each, organised into six centuries of about 80 men. However, at some time in the second half of the 1st

rt 7   **Cohort 8**   **Cohort 9**   **Cohort 10**

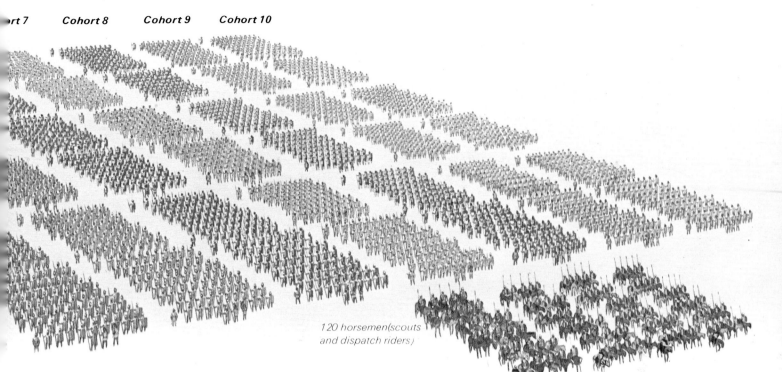

120 horsemen(scouts and dispatch riders)

century AD the first cohort was expanded to about 800 men and reorganised into five instead of six centuries. Attached to the legion were 120 horsemen who acted as scouts and dispatch riders. This brought the manpower of the legion up to about 5,500.

The legions continued to be recruited exclusively from Roman citizens. Citizenship had been granted to all Italians at the end of the republic, and was spreading slowly in the West. Spain and southern Gaul, and the old 'provincia' (Provence), made notable contributions to the legions in the Western provinces. In the East recruiting was a problem as Roman citizenship never spread there in the same way. Here it was customary for non-citizens to be recruited into the legions, being granted citizenship on enrolment.

There were about 30 of these legions which were the cream of the army. Their job was primarily offensive and they were brought into the field for further conquest, to put down a revolt or to repel an invasion.

These 30-odd legions, retained out of the many legions of the civil wars, were now to have a permanent existence. Men enlisted for a fixed period of years, and volunteers were preferred. Italians increasingly chose not to serve, or to serve in the units at Rome described below. But there was a growing number

of citizens in the provinces—sons of legionaries, auxiliaries' sons whose fathers had gained the citizenship for their children and men from the communities granted citizenship—who were prepared to join up. Italy got off lightly. New legions were to be raised there, but in practice this rarely happened.

Many of the legions originated in the rival armies spawned by the 20 years of civil war that raged between 50 and 30 BC. For this reason some legionary numbers were duplicated (there were actually three Third legions). When a legion was destroyed the number was never used again. The three Augustan legions XVII, XVIII and XIX, which were destroyed at Teutoburgerwald in AD 9, were never replaced. The numbers ran from I to XXII. Trajan added a XXX, but after Vespasian emperors tended to number new legions I to III; at one time there were five legions numbered III. Legions had names as well as numbers. These might date back to their beginnings or be given for valour in battle or loyalty to the emperor.

The life of a legionary
A legionary had to be a Roman citizen, though in the legions of the East he might have been given the citizenship on enrolment. If he had the opportunity he would be wise to bring a letter of

Above
A late 1st-century AD legion on parade. The strength at this time had risen to about 5,500 men divided into ten cohorts. The first cohort had five centuries of about 160 men each. The other cohorts had six centuries of about 80 men each. About 120 horsemen were attached to each legion.
CT = centurion **S** = *signifer* **O** = *optio*
T = *tesserarius* **C** = *cornicen* or *tubicen*.

recommendation. If accepted he received a small sum of money to cover travelling expenses to the legion. When he arrived at the fortress he took the military oath. He was then posted to a century. The oath was renewed every New Year's Day.

The new recruit would need much training and experience before he could be reckoned the equal of the veteran legionary. He must be taught to march; during his years of service he would be expected to go on a 30km route march three times a month. He was taught how to build a camp and was drilled twice a day. (The fully-trained legionary had to drill once a day.) He was given a general training in stone slinging, swimming and riding. He learned how to vault on to horseback and to mount and dismount fully armed, with shield, from either side—quite a feat before stirrups appeared.

For weapons training a stake about the height of a man was set up. The recruit was armed with a wicker shield and wooden sword, both of twice standard weight, and attacked the stake, learning to thrust and not slash with his sword. Once the fundamentals had been instilled, mock battles were arranged for which both sword and *pilum* had their points covered to avoid serious accidents.

Pay had been raised by Caesar. It was not raised again until the time of Domitian 150 years later, and then there was a further gap of a century before the next increase. The pay was about three times that of an auxiliary infantryman, although the auxiliary cavalryman's pay may have been close to that of the legionary infantryman. Large monetary awards were paid after a victory, or when a new emperor came to the throne. These rises and gifts (donatives) are often criticised by historians, but as opportunities for booty dwindled some occasional supplements to pay might well be needed to make army life attractive. Soldiers could and did save money, even though they had to pay for food, clothing, bedding, boots and arms and armour out of their pay, not to mention 'Christmas dinner' and burial club. Food and clothing were standardised payments; arms, no doubt after the initial outlay, rarely loomed large,

although soldiers adorned their armour with gold and silver. Savings were deposited with the standard bearers, who handled pay and savings in addition to their other duties. Some were compulsory—deductions which were set off against debts for food etc., or half of any donatives to be kept for the soldier against the day of retirement. An official regulation stated that soldiers were not allowed to marry, and enlistment was one form of divorce. In fact soldiers contracted marriages which were technically illegal but accepted as binding by the people most concerned. The soldier could leave his property to his 'wife' by will, which could be made orally, rather as in modern armies a simple form of will is part of a soldier's documents. Another problem was the status of the children. The legionary might well have married a non-citizen, and his children would therefore lack Roman citizenship. The legion, however, was happy to accept these disenfranchised sons of legionaries as citizens —on enrolment.

Service was for 25 or 26 years, as discharges were carried out every other year. On retirement the legionary was given a gratuity. At first this could be in money or land. Originally there was a distinction between ordinary service, fixed at 16 years, and service in the veteran reserve, undertaken by men who

stayed on with the legion for four years but had some privileges and their duties reduced. But the strain on the special treasury created to pay gratuities on discharge was such that service was extended to 20 ordinary plus five as veteran, and even then discharge was delayed. This helped to provoke the mutinies on the death of Augustus. Concessions made then were soon revoked and service became 25 or 26 years. The idea of part of this being as veterans with limited duties seems to have disappeared in time.

Grants in land tended to die out in the 2nd century AD. When these took the form of settlement of groups of soldiers in military colonies they were unpopular, as soldiers preferred to settle down close to their old bases, and land was not easily come by. In Britain two old legionary fortresses, Gloucester and Lincoln, became military colonies in the 1st century AD.

Each legion had three main types of standard. The *aquila* (eagle), which had been introduced by Marius, was the standard of the whole legion. By Caesar's time it was made of silver and gold,

Below
The training of legionary recruits in the *via quintana*. Besides marching, the recruits were taught to ride a horse fully armed, a considerable feat before the advent of stirrups, as can be seen in this illustration.

but during the empire it was made entirely of gold. The eagle never left camp unless the whole legion set out. It was guarded by the first cohort, and was the special responsibility of the senior centurion (*primus pilus*).

There were still standards for each individual century (*signa*) as there had been during the republic. The legion also carried a portrait of the emperor (*imago*) and sometimes a legion symbol, usually a sign of the zodiac. There were also special flags, called *vexilla*. One belonged to the legion, bearing its name, and others were used by detachments serving away from the legion, giving them the name of vexillations. The poles carrying the standards were pointed at the bottom so they could be stuck in the ground and also had handles with which to pull them up. In a fort the standards were kept in the shrine in the *principia*.

Religion was a powerful influence on the life of the legionary. As a Roman citizen he was expected to honour the gods of Rome, particularly the gods of the Capitol, Jupiter, Juno and Minerva. Their worship was incorporated in an official religious year for the soldiers, along with the old traditional festivals of the city of Rome. Another important element in this official religion was the worship of the standards. In modern armies colours have tremendous significance and are presented, trooped and laid up in chapels; in the Roman army the standard was a cult symbol and its loss might mean the disbanding of the unit. Finally there was homage to the emperor and worship of the god-emperors. Their birthdays, accession days and victories became so numerous that some had quietly to be dropped from the calendar. The total effect of this series of festivals would be to imprint on the soldier's mind the favour of the gods to Rome, the sanctity of his standards, that Rome was his city, and that the emperors were supermen.

But the official religion, associated with the headquarters shrine and the parade ground, only partly met a man's needs. He would have his own gods, perhaps a favourite classical god (Roman gods had been identified with the Greek gods, who were much more sharply defined). Local gods were also honoured by the soldiers, and they were clearly powers to be reckoned with on their

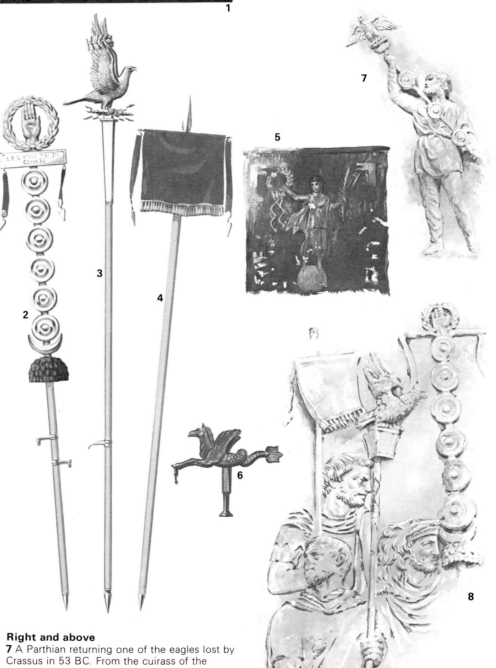

Right and above
7 A Parthian returning one of the eagles lost by Crassus in 53 BC. From the cuirass of the Prima Porta Augustus in the Vatican. **8** An *aquilifer*, *vexillarius* and *signifer* shown on Trajan's Column.

own ground. Often they were identified in the soldier's mind with gods of similar characteristics already known to him.

Some religions made the jump from local cult to empire-wide religion. Among the soldiers such were the worship of Jupiter Dolichenus, originally a Syrian god, and that of Mithras, also from the East, though modified to suit the Roman military taste. Christianity, in contrast, was slow to penetrate the army. Early Christians tended to pacifism, and in any case there was the tremendous barrier of the official military religious calendar, involving the worship of pagan gods.

A final element was underlying superstition, fear of the evil eye, of witchcraft and ill-luck. Underlying all religious belief, it shows itself characteristically in the employment of the phallic symbol, sign of fertility, to ward off the evil eye.

We do not know how much time off the legionary enjoyed. Like most armies the Roman army believed in keeping men occupied, and like most armies it became slack in peacetime. There was, however, clearly some time off during each day. After all, there were visits to be made to the wife and family living outside the fortress, and children to be begotten. There must have been time to visit the other attractions of the civil settlement, which sprang up outside every legionary fortress and which was virtually a garrison town. There was no weekend, but presumably the great festivals of the military calendar included some leisure. Leave was granted, sometimes in return for a bribe, and a blank leave pass (on pottery) has been found.

Probably the bath-house was a convenient place to gather. From the mid-1st century AD bath-houses seem to have been provided for legionary fortresses, and they also became standard for auxiliary forts. They offered steam baths and dry heat rooms. The steam baths we term 'Turkish' are descended directly from those of Rome through Constantinople. There was also provision for exercise. A later development was club rooms for junior officers' clubs. An amphitheatre was also provided outside the fortress walls, but whether this was used for drill and official occasions rather than for gladiatorial combats is not clear.

The officers

A legionary signed on for 25 years. He might hope to rise to the rank of centurion in this time. The centurions were the only officers who permanently commanded legionaries under the legionary commander. All the higher officers were staff officers. Because they rose from the ranks the centurions are often thought of as non-commissioned officers, but their responsibilities were approximately those of a captain today.

During the republic these officers at first seem to have been appointed by the tribunes, although promotion remained firmly in the hands of the army commander. The centurions were the backbone of the army. They were the only lifetime officers, and centurions often served over their obligatory 25 years as soldier and centurion. The life attracted others than legionary rankers. After completing their 16 years of service men from the Praetorian Guard might obtain legionary centurionates, and a number of men from the class immediately below senators, equites, or from the municipal councils, applied for commissions as centurions. Under the empire centurionates were in the gift of the provincial governors, though no doubt legionary commanders and tribunes could recommend men. Friends of men seeking commissions could write recommendations and the emperor could intervene.

Each legion had 59 centurions. They were still named after the old maniples, except that the alternative name of pilus was preferred to triarius. So cohorts II–X had a hastatus posterior, hastatus prior, princeps posterior, princeps prior, pilus posterior and pilus prior. The number of the cohort was placed before each name, for example decimus hastatus posterior, a traditional title which in typical Roman fashion recalls the long-dead manipular legion. Presumably the centurion with the greatest seniority commanded his cohort, though this is left obscure. A centurion might spend his whole time in the army in the same legion, but it was possible to change legions, often when bodies of men were being transferred, perhaps to make up heavy losses of trained troops, as after the Boudica rebellion in 61. Then 2,000 men were sent to bring the badly mauled ninth up to strength.

Some centurions served in a number of legions. The movement of officers was a significant factor in the spread of new religions.

A centurion could easily be recognised by his armour which was silvered. He wore greaves, which had fallen out of general use, and the crest of his helmet was turned so that it ran transversely across the helmet. His sword was worn on the left and his dagger on the right, which is the opposite to those of the legionary. This has led some people to suggest that the centurions did not use the curved scutum as it would have been extremely difficult to draw the sword from the left. This was certainly not the case in Caesar's day: at the siege of Dyrrhachium a centurion named Scaeva whilst trying to defend a redoubt received 120 holes in his shield (Caesar explicitly uses the word scutum) and is promoted from the eighth cohort to primus pilus for his gallantry.

Centurions were often brutal; many a legionary could show scars on his back from the centurion's vine cane (vitis). This reflected the centurion's disciplinary role. They were expected to be harsh disciplinarians and in mutinies they were the prime targets for the men's vengeance. On the other hand, it must be pointed out that in defeat the centurions suffered disproportionately heavy losses for they were picked as men who would stand their ground to the end.

Centurions were not above taking bribes from legionaries who wished to avoid some duty. Payment for leave made by soldiers to their centurions had become so firmly established that even the emperor felt unable to put a stop to it for fear of alienating the centurions. The emperors therefore removed the onus from the men by paying the centurions direct, thus securing the allegiance of the army.

The first cohort was divided into five double centuries commanded by five senior centurions who outranked all the other centurions of the legion and were known as primi ordines. Within the primi ordines the ascending order of superiority was as follows: hastatus posterior, princeps posterior, hastatus, princeps and primus pilus—the latter being the highest-ranking centurion in the legion.

The rank of primus pilus was the

dream of every legionary, but to many it was unattainable as the route to it through the centurionate demanded education and administrative ability as well as courage. The rank was held for one year after which the centurion either retired or moved on to better things. The minimum age was normally 50. Some men served for over 40 years as soldier and centurion without ever reaching the dizzy heights of the primipilate. Retirement brought with it a large gratuity and an honorary title—*primipilaris* (*ex-primus pilus*) just as a former consul was ever after called *consularis*. The *primipilares* formed an aristocracy of military service. Promotion might be to prefect of the camp, discussed below, or to the posts of tribunes in the cohorts in Rome, which were reserved for these most experienced and trusted of soldiers. A few went on to administrative posts as governors of provinces garrisoned by auxiliary troops alone or fleet commanders; a handful reached the peak of commander of the Praetorian Guard.

Above the centurionate was a group of semi-professional officers. The tribunes came first. There were still six of these to each legion. Technically they were all *equites*, but the senior ranking *tribunus laticlavius* wore the broad band which showed that he was accepted as a candidate for the Senate; the other five tribunes wore the narrow purple band. The *tribunus laticlavius* would be under 25, the minimum age for entering the Senate as *quaestor*. The tribunate would have been given to him by the provincial governor, who might be a relative, or possibly in response to a request from the tribune's friends or patrons—the Roman world ran on a recognised 'old-boy network'. The *tribunus laticlavius* would have no previous military experience, and would leave the army after one tour of duty (rarely more) of perhaps one or two years to begin his career in the Senate. Ten years later he might return to the army to command a legion, as we shall see.

The five other tribunes, *angusticlavii*, had a different career. By the middle of the 2nd century AD it was customary for an *angusticlavius* to have already served as prefect of an auxiliary infantry regiment. As he might well have served as senior magistrate of his hometown

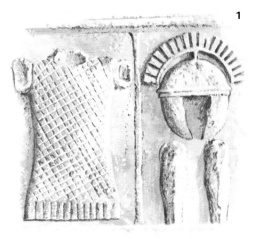

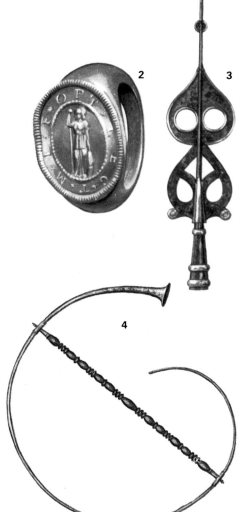

Above and right
1 The tombstone of the centurion T Calidius Severus of legion XV *Apollinaris* showing his scale cuirass, greaves, transverse crested helmet and vine cane, from Carnuntum. Kunsthistorisches Museum, Vienna. **2** An *optio*'s gold ring found at Bonn. Rheinisches Landesmuseum, Bonn.
3 The standard of a *beneficiarius* made of iron and bronze found near Strasbourg. Landesmuseum, Wiesbaden. **4** A *cornu* from Pompeii. Naples Museum.

Below
A chart showing the probable promotion ladder for the centurions of a legion. The centurions of cohorts 2–10 rose in seniority but probably did not change centuries. Promotion was to *hastatus posterior* of the first cohort and from there in four steps to *primus pilus*.

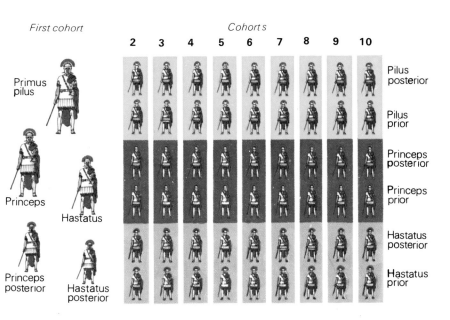

First cohort

Primus pilus

Princeps

Hastatus

Princeps posterior

Hastatus posterior

Cohorts

	2	3	4	5	6	7	8	9	10	
										Pilus posterior
										Pilus prior
										Princeps posterior
										Princeps prior
										Hastatus posterior
										Hastatus prior

before appointment (minimum age 25 or 30), he would be an older man with some military experience. In the mid-2nd century there were only 131 vacancies as legionary tribune for approximately 270 commanders of the 500-strong infantry or mixed auxiliary regiments, enabling governors to avoid appointing men who had proved to be incompetent. The best of the 270, some 30 to 40, would have been appointed by the emperor to command 1,000-strong infantry and mixed cohorts.

The future career of angusticlave tribunes will be referred to under the topic of cavalry. In the legion they had administrative responsibilities, being concerned primarily with the troops' welfare and daily routine as duty officers.

Above the tribunes was the *legatus legionis*, who was a senator appointed to his position by the emperor, not by the provincial governor. He would normally be a man in his thirties, who had probably served as laticlave tribune ten years or so earlier but had had no contact with the army since. In some provinces he might combine the command of a legion with the post of provincial governor, though in this case he would normally have already commanded a legion elsewhere. He would lean heavily on his centurions, particularly his *primus pilus*, but even more on a new officer created by the first emperor, Augustus. This

was the camp prefect, a man who had already been a *primus pilus* and had come directly from that post to be prefect. The camp prefect was concerned with the legion's equipment and transport and has often been compared to a quartermaster. He was also the senior professional officer, ranking third behind legate and *tribunus laticlavius* in the legion's hierarchy, a grizzled man in his fifties or sixties, with as many as 40 years in the legions behind him.

Below the centurionate were all the posts and trades necessary to keep a legion operating, of which over 100 are known. There were few distinctions based on pay. The first privilege a post or trade might earn was immunity from fatigues and other burdensome duties—a man became an *immunis*. Thereafter came promotion to $1\frac{1}{2}$ times normal pay (a fraction curiously dear to the Roman heart) and double pay. Dividing up the posts another way, there were those in the century, the only administrative unit below the legion, those attached to the staffs of the higher officers and those concerned with other aspects of the legion's life, such as the hospital.

The century had a standard bearer (*signifer*), who also looked after pay and

Above
A reconstruction of an auxiliary of the type most commonly depicted on Trajan's Column. He wears a mail shirt and a bronze cross-braced helmet, which is a cheap version of the current legionary type. By this time the auxiliaries' equipment had been standardised and they fought in much the same manner as the legionary. Auxiliary units were originally raised in the provinces. He is armed with spear, short sword and oval shield. Behind him is a montage of auxiliary troops from Trajan's Column including slingers, stone-throwers, and Eastern archers.

savings, and below him the *optio*, who took over if the centurion fell and was probably more concerned with training. These were both on double pay, and the trio was completed by the *tesserarius*, on $1\frac{1}{2}$ pay, whose original responsibilities were principally concerned with guard duties.

The nucleus of each officer's staff was the *beneficiarius*, literally the benefited one, as the post was thought of as a gift. A *beneficiarius* was attached to all officers, but only senior officers, down to the rank of *praefectus castrorum*, had a *cornicularius*, who headed the writing-office which dealt with the copious flow of documents characteristic of the Roman army. The Roman army generated an enormous number of documents. Many of these, written on papyrus, have been found in the Middle East. From these we can identify documents relating to the medical examination of recruits, dispatch of recruits to their units, duty rosters, daily records of watchwords, headquarters guards, departures, arrivals, and actual strength of the unit. Annual returns went in to Rome showing both permanent and temporary

accessions and losses and the number of effectives. A dossier was compiled for each man, including his pay and savings records and his absences from camp for detached duties. The writing-offices, of course, had to be staffed with clerks and book-keepers (*librarii*).

Many legionaries might be seconded to the provincial governor's office to form an additional staff there, including the *speculatores* (executioners), *quaestionarii* (torturers) and *frumentarii* (intelligence officers). Escorts (*singulares*) were also provided. The hospital (*valetudinarium*) had its own staff under the *optio valetudinarii*. These would include bandagers and medical orderlies (*capsarii* and *medici*). There were specialist officers such as doctors (also called *medici*) and *architecti*. In the Roman world the latter performed the job of surveyors, builders, engineers and artillery officers, and like the doctors there seem to have been men of differing ranks with the same title.

There was also a mass of tradesmen, workers in stone, timber, glass and tile. Though there seems to have been a generous allocation of artillery to the legion, any specialisation in its operation was not reflected in titles. Building and repairing the various engines was a task for the *architectus* and his staff. Finally, there were specialist veterinary officers to look after the legion's animals.

Originally supreme authority had rested with the king and then with the consuls. Later it was extended to cover proconsuls, praetors and propraetors. They had similar powers except that praetors and propraetors ranked below consuls and proconsuls if their armies operated in combination. They had power over citizens and non-citizens in peace and in war; purely military authority was unknown. Above the legionary legates came only the emperor with proconsular power, whose 'province' (sphere of authority) included most of the provinces (geographical divisions) containing troops. As Pompey and Caesar had once done, he controlled his province by appointing *legati*, who had the powers of propraetors (*legati Augusti pro praetore*), to take charge of the individual provinces. Each of these was the supreme military and civil authority in his province, controlling the troops stationed there but unable to leave that

province till his term of service—on average three years—came to an end. The provinces were divided broadly between those held before the consulate and those after. In the first category were provinces without legions and provinces with one legion, normally held by men in their late thirties who had already commanded legions. The provinces held after the consulate might hold two to four legions, and men reached them often in their early to middle forties. Under the empire men tended to reach high office at relatively young ages.

The auxiliary units

The term *auxilia* was applied to all units other than the legions and the old allies. It included cavalry and all types of infantry. In the early empire the infantry slowly changed from bands fighting in their own fashion, often under their own leaders, to units of similar size and organisation, commanded by equestrians (*equites*).

These units, which were called cohorts, came to be modelled on the legionary cohort, i.e. six centuries—commanded by centurions—and consisting of about 500 men. Their equipment became standardised, and on Trajan's Column the auxiliary infantry fight in much the same manner as the legionary. Archers were also formed into cohorts; slingers continued to be used, though not apparently in separate formations.

In the second half of the 1st century AD bigger versions of these units were introduced, at about the same time that the first cohort in a legion was increased in size. They were composed of ten centuries, corresponding to the five double centuries of the remodelled first legionary cohort.

The auxiliary cohorts were originally raised in the provinces. Some were posted away, but others were stationed close to home, most notably on the Rhine. A dangerous mutiny on the Rhine during the civil war of 69 led to a transfer of units away from that area, but the new ones coming in were kept up to strength by local recruiting, which was customary for the *auxilia* everywhere in the empire. Only for the specialist oriental archers were recruits sought in the lands where the units were originally raised. Unit names therefore

Above
A diploma, made of two bronze plates joined with rings, issued by Trajan granting citizenship to Marcus Spedius Corbulo on completion of 25 years service as an auxiliary.

only refer to the original area of recruitment.

Below the rank of centurion the auxiliary cohort had a similar but simpler structure to that of the legion. The centurions were drawn from the ranks and spent their lives in the same unit. This was commanded by an equestrian prefect, as the first step in a career which might lead him, via the legionary tribunate or a command of a 1000-strong auxiliary cohort, to a cavalry command. He would come to the army fresh from civilian life, possibly after holding the senior magistracy in his home town, in his twenties or thirties. The post was in the grant of the provincial governor.

The larger units were commanded by tribunes who had previously commanded one of the ordinary cohorts. They were selected for these posts by the emperor rather than by the governor and seem to have been the most promising of the infantry prefects.

The auxiliary infantryman served in the army for 25 years. On discharge he received a grant of Roman citizenship which was inscribed on a pair of bronze sheets known as a *diploma*. Hundreds of examples have been found, and they are the main source of our knowledge of the auxiliary units. The auxiliary infantryman was probably paid only about a third of the amount that a legionary received.

Like the legionaries, the auxiliary soldiers were not allowed to marry. However, they did form lasting associations which were regarded as marriages by all concerned, and the emperor accepted this by granting citizenship to their children as well as to the auxiliaries themselves. Their sons were thus entitled to enlist in the legions, though they might prefer to join their fathers' regiments. During the 2nd century the number of citizens enlisting in the *auxilia* grew steadily.

Cavalry had always been the weakest link in the Roman army and many battles were lost as a direct result of this. Hannibal's Spanish, Celtic and African cavalry were the key to his victories at Trebbia and Cannae, driving the Roman and Italian cavalry right off the field of battle and leaving the flanks open to a devastating attack by his pikemen. Although Scipio made great use of the Numidians—the key factor in his victory over Hannibal—the Romans continued to field armies with an inadequate cavalry arm. As the cavalry was part of the legion it had to be drawn, in the main, from inferior Italian sources. In the second half of the 2nd century BC the Romans made the momentous decision to abolish the legionary cavalry and employ foreign horsemen, raised in the areas of operation and led by their own chiefs or Roman commanders (*praefecti equitum*), just as the Carthaginians had done.

By the 1st century BC the practice was general and we find Caesar employing both Gallic and German cavalry units against Pompey during the civil war.

Early in the empire these cavalry units had been organised into regiments (*alae*) which were approximately 500 strong. As with the infantry, units nominally 1,000 strong appear towards the end of the 1st century AD. These *alae* were divided into 16 *turmae* (consisting of 32 officers and men) and 24 *turmae* respectively. Each *turma* was commanded by a decurion.

Under the republic command had been exercised by native princes, but under the empire commanders were soon drawn exclusively from Roman equestrian prefects. These were men who had already served as prefects of infantry auxiliary cohorts and either as tribunes in legions or tribunes of the larger-size auxiliary cohorts. There were some 90 posts as prefects of *alae* in the mid-2nd century AD. During the same period the commands of the larger cavalry units devolved on a select group of about ten consisting of the pick of the men who had already commanded the ordinary cavalry regiments. From the cavalry posts they might go on to serve in the imperial administration.

Each *ala* had its own flag (*vexillum*) and each *turma* had a standard. The officers below the rank of decurion in the *turma* have odd names: *duplicarius* (double-pay man) corresponding to the *optio* in the century; and *sesquiplicarius* ($1\frac{1}{2}$ times pay man) corresponding to the *tesserarius*. The *turma* also had an extra officer, the *curator*, whose responsibilities presumably lay with the horses. In all other respects the posts below decurion in the *ala* resemble a simpler version of those of the legion.

The decurion was normally promoted from the ranks, but direct commissions to this post were occasionally obtained, particularly in provinces where no legions were stationed and the governor had no centurionates to give away.

Caesar was very impressed by German mixed cavalry in which light-armed infantrymen ran along with the horsemen, holding on to the horse's rein in order to keep up. Similar practices were to be found in Numidia and Spain, and the Romans themselves had regularly mixed their *velites* with the cavalry. This may have been the origin of the bodies of mixed troops known as *cohortes equitatae* which are found in the empire. These were made up of the normal establishment of the auxiliary infantry cohorts, six or ten centuries, plus 120 cavalry in the '500' unit and 240 cavalry in the '1,000' unit. This cavalry is often described mistakenly as mounted infantry. Mounted infantry ride to battle and dismount to fight, but the cavalry of the *cohortes equitatae* were brigaded with the cavalry of the *alae* on the march and in battle. The Roman army had a large number of these mixed units, and they must have proved particularly valuable for frontier patrolling. The cohort troops were not as well paid or equipped as the cavalrymen in the *alae* but they were cavalrymen.

The cohorts in Rome
From earliest times a consul had 12 lictors who acted as his personal bodyguard. These men carried bundles of rods and axes as a symbol of the consul's power of life and death over the citizens. However, it was found that this was an insufficient bodyguard for the general while on active service. Thus it had become the task of the *extraordinarii* to act as guards to the consul.

During the siege of Numantia, which ended in 133 BC, Scipio Aemilianus formed a personal bodyguard of 500 men. These became known as the Praetorian Cohort, after the *praetorium*, the area of the camp where the general's tent was pitched. By the end of the republic it was usual for all generals to have a Praetorian Cohort.

The emperor Augustus used this precedent to establish an imperial bodyguard of nine Praetorian Cohorts, some 4,500 men. He kept three in Rome, billeted in private houses, and stationed he others in neighbouring towns. In 2 BC he appointed two commanders, *prae- fecti praetorio*. Under his successor Tiberius all nine cohorts were united in one camp in Rome with the three Urban Cohorts (see below) under a single com- mander, who now outranked the prefect of Egypt, originally the most prestigious of the non-senatorial (equestrian) com- manders established by Augustus.

Under a single commander the Guard might represent a threat to an emperor, and the Guard's interventions in the business of making and unmaking em- perors have been severely criticised. But such interventions came only at times of uncertainty in the succession, which were few and short in the first two cen- turies of the empire. The final word in each case lay with the legions, and Guard nominees rarely survived unless, like Claudius, they carried with them the stamp of legitimacy. In fact legions and Guard alike were loyal to emperors and the imperial families; only when there was no clear heir to the throne could they be manipulated by ambitious generals. Prefects of the Guard had little success in making emperors and they also suffered a high casualty rate at em- perors' hands.

The number of Praetorian Cohorts fluctuated in the early empire, but dur- ing the 2nd and 3rd centuries AD it stabilised at ten. It is not easy to be sure of the number of men in each cohort; for a long time it was about 500 but it rose to 1,000, and perhaps even 1,500, in the early 3rd century. The soldiers were mainly from Italy and a few neigh- bouring provinces, and as a result the cohorts were markedly different from the legions, as the latter increasingly were recruited from men of the prov- inces. There was a sharp difference in pay, which was $3\frac{1}{3}$ times that of the legionary. There was also shorter and pleasanter service; only 16 years com- pared to the legionary's 25–26, and nor- mally in Rome—relatively few emperors took the Guard on campaign.

Things changed at the end of the 2nd century. The Guard had been drawn into what was only the second major civil war, and in an unforgettable epi- sode put the empire up for auction. Again their candidate had no success, and the eventual victor, Septimius Severus, disbanded the Guard and

reconstituted it from men of his Danubian legions. Henceforth the Guard was recruited from the legions. Senators might lament the fate of the young men of Italy, left to become brig- ands, and blench at the sight of the men from the frontiers, but there was an element of logic in the change, apart from the immediate gain in security for the new emperor. The increase in the size of this and other elements in the Rome garrison emphasised that an em- peror needed to have more troops under his immediate command.

In its heyday the Guard enjoyed sig- nificant advantages beyond higher pay. It received more than its share of the donatives handed out by new emperors. The men of the Guard were well placed to catch the eye of the emperor and other important people. Their uniform and standards proclaimed their special status. Their dress uniform, like that of the royal guards of today, was of tradi- tional type, echoing the armour of the republican era. The cohort on duty at the palace wore togas. Their standards carried images of the emperor and his family, crowns and victories.

Above
A Montefortino type helmet with the inscription AVRELIVS VICTORINVS MIL COH XII VRB—Aurelius Victorinus, soldier of the 12th urban cohort. The survival of this type of helmet confirms that the city guards wore traditional republican armour. Museo Gregoriano, Vatican. **Below** Figures from the Cancelleria relief in the Vatican showing lictors (left) with their bundles of rods and axes and Praetorian Guardsmen (right) carrying the traditional oval *scuta*.

Special also were the promotion patterns in the Guard. Normally only men who had completed 16 years of service and had been retained as *evocati* came into consideration for promotion to centurion. This was not the only reason for retention as *evocati*; after 16 years service men were still relatively young and had a variety of skills that might justify their continuing in service with a special rank and pay. *Evocati* promoted to the rank of centurion might go to the legions or stay in Rome. If they stayed in Rome they would serve in turn with the *vigiles* (see below), the Urban Cohorts and the Praetorian Cohorts. Posts in Rome were guarded jealously. No centurion in Rome came from the ranks of the legions; only men from the Guard, and some directly commissioned centurions transferred to Rome from the legions, were eligible. The directly commissioned centurions were exempted

from serving with the least glamorous corps, the *vigiles*, but went to the Urban Cohorts. A few senior soldiers, who had served at the head of the clerical staff of the prefect of the Guard or other prefects in Rome, were allowed to proceed to the centurionate (but only in the legions) before completing 16 years. The Praetorian Cohorts could have no *primus pilus*, the highest ranking centurion in a legion, as they were not a

legion in name or organisation. Som centurionates, those of *trecenarius* an *princeps castrorum*, may have ranked a *primi ordines*. Men from the Guard wh had gone to legionary centurionate from the beginning, or those who ha served as centurions in Rome and ther transferred to senior legionary cen turionates, would vie with centurion who had begun in the ranks of th legions or had been directly commis

Above
A montage of soldiers from the altar of Domitius Ahenobarbus in the Louvre. This relief, probably from the first half of the 1st century BC, shows legionaries in mail shirts carrying oval *scuta*.

sioned for the coveted rank of *primus pilus*. This carried with it an enduring title of rank (*primipilaris, ex-primus pilus*) and a large gratuity, double that of the *primi ordines*. From the *primipili* were recruited the tribunes who commanded cohorts in Rome, *vigiles*, Urban and Praetorian. They were trusted men, the cream of the centurionate. This did not prevent them from becoming involved in conspiracies, though some at least would claim noble motives. But the majority played the part allotted to them. Prefects of the Guard might have begun as equestrian officers or as centurions. They came to the post, as single or joint commanders, from the prefecture of Egypt and/or the *vigiles*.

The Urban Cohorts were also stationed in Rome, but they were a sort of police force under the command of the city prefect (*praefectus urbi*). This post was reserved as an honour for distinguished senators at the end of their careers. The Urban Cohorts were formed at the same time as the Guard, and their original numbers, X–XII, followed on from the Guard cohort numbers I–IX. After a rise in numbers under Claudius they were reduced by Vespasian to four stationed in Rome, X–XII and XIV, cohort XIII, stationed in Carthage under the proconsul of Africa, and cohort I, stationed at Lugudunum (Lyons) to guard the imperial mint there. In the 2nd century these two units outside Rome changed places.

The Urban Cohorts were recruited from Italy. The number of men rose from 500 under Augustus to 1,500 under Severus, probably following the changes in the Guard. The only way to promotion for the Urban soldiers in Rome was to secure transfer to the Guard. A man applied to Hadrian for a place in the Guard, was asked his height, and was then told to go into the Urban Cohorts. If he was a good soldier, he would be transferred in his third year of service. Men in the cohorts outside Rome might have the opportunity to become centurion in their own unit. There was no *evocatio*; the Urban soldiers, however, served 20 years, between the 16 years of the Guard and the 25/26 of the legionary. Pay, like service, was intermediate between Guard and legions, half that of the Guard, $1\frac{2}{3}$ that of the legionary. Centurions and tribunes were for the most

part promoted centurions and tribunes respectively of the *vigiles*.

The *vigiles* were a semi-military force founded by Augustus primarily as a fire-fighting service, although they also performed the functions of night police. They were formed into seven cohorts, originally of 500, later of 1,000 men each, the seven being related to the 14 districts of Rome. Originally they were recruited from freed slaves. Only the head of the prefect's writing-office had hopes of promotion; from the mid-2nd century AD he could become a legionary centurion. There seem to have been two types of service: seven years for the majority, with a minority staying on to become senior soldiers and officers below centurion, and tradesmen. Centurions were drawn from ex-guardsmen who had become *evocati*; tribunes were former *primipili*. Their commander was the *praefectus vigilum*, who might have

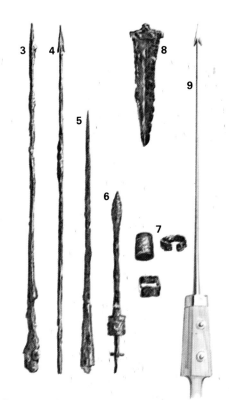

Above and below
3–9 Fragments of Roman weapons recovered from the site of Caesar's great siege at Alesia. Museum of St Germain. Scale 1:6.
3 Head of a flat-tanged *pilum*. One of the rivets is visible at the bottom.
4 Head of a *pilum* showing barbed point.
5 Part of the head of a socketed *pilum*.
6 Head of a short-tanged *pilum*. One of the rivets is still in place with a ferrule above it to hold the wood together.
7 Round and rectangular ferrules proving that both round- and square-sectioned *pila* were still in use in Caesar's day.
8 A typical Roman dagger blade.
9 Reconstruction of a tanged *pilum*.
10 Front plate of a short muscled cuirass. From southern Italy. Naples Museum.

Above
1 A late Hellenistic helmet of the type worn by officers. Hermitage Museum, Leningrad.

Below
2 A typical poor-quality mass-produced Montefortino helmet. British Museum.

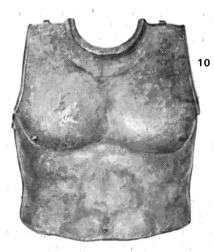

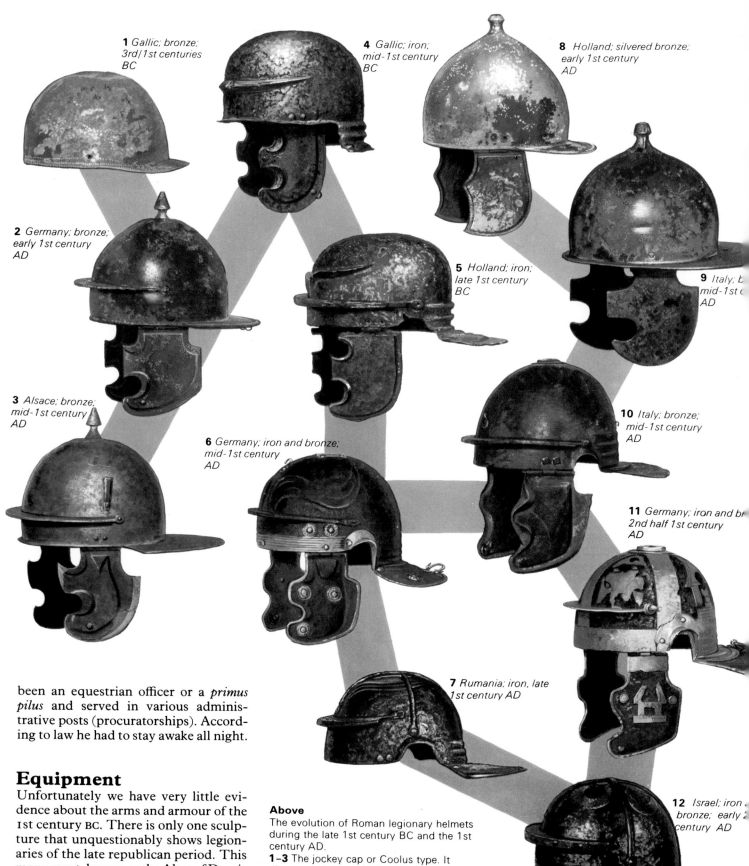

1 Gallic; bronze; 3rd/1st centuries BC

4 Gallic; iron; mid-1st century BC

8 Holland; silvered bronze; early 1st century AD

2 Germany; bronze; early 1st century AD

5 Holland; iron; late 1st century BC

9 Italy; b mid-1st c AD

3 Alsace; bronze; mid-1st century AD

6 Germany; iron and bronze; mid-1st century AD

10 Italy; bronze; mid-1st century AD

11 Germany; iron and br 2nd half 1st century AD

7 Rumania; iron, late 1st century AD

12 Israel; iron bronze; early century AD

been an equestrian officer or a *primus pilus* and served in various administrative posts (procuratorships). According to law he had to stay awake all night.

Equipment

Unfortunately we have very little evidence about the arms and armour of the 1st century BC. There is only one sculpture that unquestionably shows legionaries of the late republican period. This monument, known as the Altar of Domitius Ahenobarbus, comes from an unknown building in Rome and probably dates to the time of Marius. The sculpture, which is now in the Louvre Mu-

Above
The evolution of Roman legionary helmets during the late 1st century BC and the 1st century AD.
1–3 The jockey cap or Coolus type. It disappears in the middle of the 1st century AD.
4–7 The imperial Gallic type.
8–12 The Italian type starting with the Montefortino (**8**) and gaining characteristics from the Imperial Gallic type to produce the Imperial Italic type (**10–12**).

seum, Paris, shows a group of soldiers possibly being discharged. The group comprises four legionaries and an officer, probably a tribune. The four legionaries all wear mail shirts still cut in the form of a Greek linen cuirass and all carry the large oval *scutum*, apparently identical to that used at the time of Polybius. One wears a Montefortino type helmet and the other three Italo-Corinthian types. They all have long horsehair crests hanging from their helmets, but no feathers. None of them wears greaves.

Although no archaeological examples of body armour for this period have been found, several helmets have survived. It had been customary for soldiers to supply their own armour, and for this reason the light-armed *velites* were drawn from the poorest class. When Marius threw open the legions to all Roman citizens regardless of wealth, the army was forced to take responsibility for arming new recruits, especially as they all now required the equipment of the heavy infantry. The authorities responded by making available cheap mass-produced armour for which deductions were made from the soldiers' pay. This change of practice is well illustrated by the surviving examples of helmets from the period. These have a battered appearance, often being assymetrical. Practically all the surviving examples are of the Montefortino type,

and are very similar to those produced in the previous period except for their crudeness. Every short cut had been exploited in their manufacture; the cheek piece hinge was often held to the cap by only a single rivet instead of the customary two. There is an example of the Italo-Corinthian type in the Hermitage Museum at Leningrad which may date from this period.

The officer on the Ahenobarbus relief wears a short muscled cuirass, Italo-Corinthian helmet and greaves. He also has a round shield, spear and sword which he appears to wear on the left side. Under the muscled cuirass he wears a tunic probably made of leather with *pteryges* (strips of leather or fabric for the protection of thighs and shoulders) hanging from the waist and shoulders. This was the traditional dress of the Hellenistic officer and was worn over his military tunic. There is a sculpture in the Louvre which shows one of these leather tunics complete with its *pteryges* draped over the trunk of a tree. Around his waist the officer wears a sash which is knotted at the front with the loose ends tucked up at either side. This is the Greek symbol of high rank and can be seen worn by Alexander (p. 72). The officers shown on Trajan's Column are similarly dressed, confirming that the Romans had adopted the Greek uniform in its entirety for their senior officers.

Below
4–6 Pieces of *lorica segmentata* from Corbridge. Museum of Antiquities, Newcastle.
4 Main shoulder unit with bronze fittings.
5 Chest and upper back unit.
6 Bunch of girdle plates.

Below
1 A reconstruction of an elaborate Imperial Gallic helmet found at Mainz.
2 A pronged crest holder of the type used with this helmet.
3 The Italian type of crest holder.

Below
7 A group of legionaries wearing *lorica segmentata* shown on Trajan's Column. Recent finds have shown just how accurate these figures are. Even examples of the cross-braced helmets have been found.

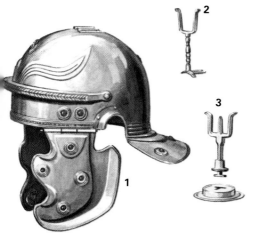

The French excavations in the 1860's at the site of Caesar's great siege at Alesia produced a wealth of assorted weapons, among which were a dagger and several *pilum* heads. Unfortunately, no Roman sword was recovered. It is almost certain that the blade was still slightly waisted and had a long point, for this type was still in use early in the empire (see below).

At the time of Marius we know that the *pilum* head was held to the wooden shaft by two rivets and therefore was of the flat-tanged type, similar to the heavy *pilum* from Numantia. Although much corroded, there is a specimen from Alesia which may be identified with this

type. Marius found that the long iron shaft of this type of *pilum* was not always bending on impact and that it was being thrown back by the enemy. He therefore removed one rivet and replaced it with a wooden dowel which splintered on impact. Caesar overcame this same problem by tempering the point, but not the shaft, of the *pilum*. Several examples of the socketed type of slim *pila* were also turned up at Alesia.

Early in the principate special workshops appear to have been set up to produce armour in the various parts of the empire. Such workshops must have existed in Gaul for there is a decidedly new Gallic influence present in the hel-

mets found along the Rhine. Although some examples of the traditional Montefortino types still come to light in the early 1st century AD, two new types turn up which are clearly derived from the helmets that were in use in Gaul in the 1st century BC. These were the round capped bronze helmet with small neck guard, usually referred to as the Coolus type, and an iron helmet with a deep neck guard which originated in the northern Alpine area. This is usually called the Port type after an example found at Port bei Nidau in Switzerland (see p. 121). The type, derived from the Coolus helmet, retained some characteristics of the Montefortino including the topknot, though this now had a slit in it to hold the crest, which was attached to a metal tongue held in place by a pin passing through the top of the knob. The Port helmet, which developed into the type known as the imperial Gallic helmet, retained most of the characteristics of its Gallic predecessor except for an enlarged neck guard which by the mid-1st century had become characteristic of all Roman infantry helmets. The most significantly Celtic feature of these helmets was the cheek pieces, which owed nothing to the earlier Roman types. Another feature was a reinforcing strip across the front of the cap which helped to protect the face from a downward sword slash. This feature also appears on late Hellenistic helmets. By the second quarter of the 1st century AD, ear guards had been added; all the features that were to characterise the Roman infantry helmet for the next two centuries had now been established.

The bronze Coolus type disappeared in the middle of the 1st century, and from then on practically all the Rhineland legionary helmets are made of iron. In the second half of the century reinforcing braces were added to the crown of the helmet. At first these were just two flat strips of bronze, but later they were replaced by two thick bands. When the chart on p. 228 was first published there was no example of an imperial Gallic helmet with these thick bands (**7**) and one was forced to make a tenuous connection between helmets **11** and **12** on the chart which come from opposite ends of the empire and are separated by about 30 years. But in the

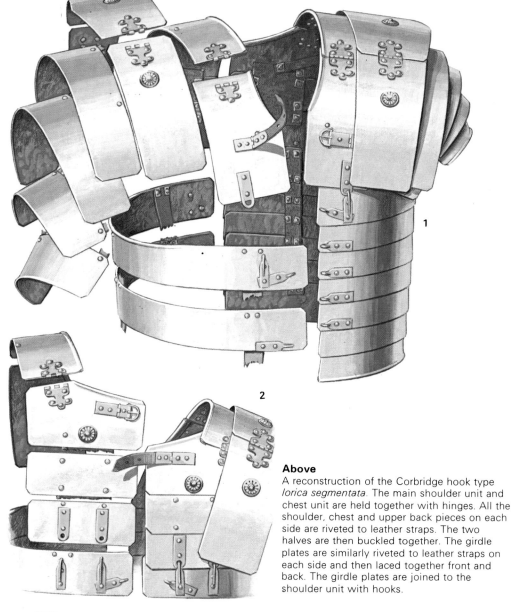

Above

A reconstruction of the Corbridge hook type *lorica segmentata*. The main shoulder unit and chest unit are held together with hinges. All the shoulder, chest and upper back pieces on each side are riveted to leather straps. The two halves are then buckled together. The girdle plates are similarly riveted to leather straps on each side and then laced together front and back. The girdle plates are joined to the shoulder unit with hooks.

ast few years several examples of the
imperial Gallic type, the same as type **6**
but with cross braces like **12**, have been
found. This was probably in response
to the book *The Armour of Imperial
Rome*, published by H. Russell Robinson in 1975, in which he postulated such
a helmet and which seems to have
prompted museums to look in their
storerooms for unpublished helmets.

Workshops in Italy continued to produce helmets which were sometimes a
compromise in bronze between the
traditional types and the new Celtic
forms. A superbly ridiculous example
of such a helmet is provided by **9**. Helmets continued to be tied on in the same
way by two straps attached to the neck
guard which crossed under the chin and
were tied to the two cheek pieces. Most
imperial Gallic types have a slot for the
insertion of a crest support which was
usually Y-shaped, the crest being fixed
between the two arms. There was
usually a hook at the front and back of
the helmet to hold it in place.

Up until the middle of the 1st century
the legionaries continued to wear the
heavy mail shirt weighing 12–15kg. In
the East it may have been worn for much
longer, but in the West the same Celtic
workshops which had developed the
new helmets began to produce an entirely new concept in body armour. This
was the first articulated plate armour,
known as *lorica segmentata* (this is not a
Roman name). The construction of
lorica segmentata has caused a great deal
of controversy amongst scholars for
centuries, but in 1964 at Corbridge near
Hadrian's Wall, two complete sets of
this armour were excavated. These still
had the remains of the leather strapping
on the inside. Reconstructions of the
two cuirasses were made by the late
H. Russell Robinson of the Tower of
London and he was able to show exactly
how they worked.

There were two methods of attaching
the chest and upper back plates to the
lower part of the armour. One type was
hooked; the other (not illustrated) was
joined with straps and buckles which
were on the outside at the front and on
the inside at the back, showing that the
armour had to be assembled before it
was put on. On both types the left and
right chest and upper back plates were
joined by straps and buckles. The seg-

Above
3 Front view of the rectangular *scutum* from
Dura Europos in Syria. Scale 1:10. The linen
and hide covering has been pulled back to
show its construction from laminated strips of
wood.

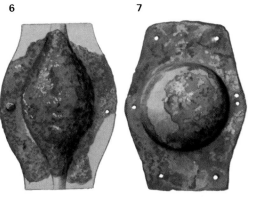

Above and top right
6–8 The development of the *scutum* boss.
6 An iron boss from an oval-spined *scutum*
found at Mainz. Late 1st century BC.
Mittelrheinisches Landesmuseum, Mainz.
7 Iron boss from a *scutum* with curved sides,
flat top and bottom but no spine found at
Mainz. Early 1st century AD. Mittelrheinisches
Landesmuseum, Mainz.

Above
8 Bronze shield boss from a rectangular *scutum*
belonging to Junius Dubitatus, who was in
Britain with a vexillation from legion VIII
Augusta in the 2nd century AD. British
Museum. Scale 1:5.

Above
4 Reconstruction of the inside of a 1st century
AD *scutum* based on the shield from Dura
Europos. The earlier shields had a metal rim (**5**)
whereas the Dura Europos example had a
rawhide rim sewn on.

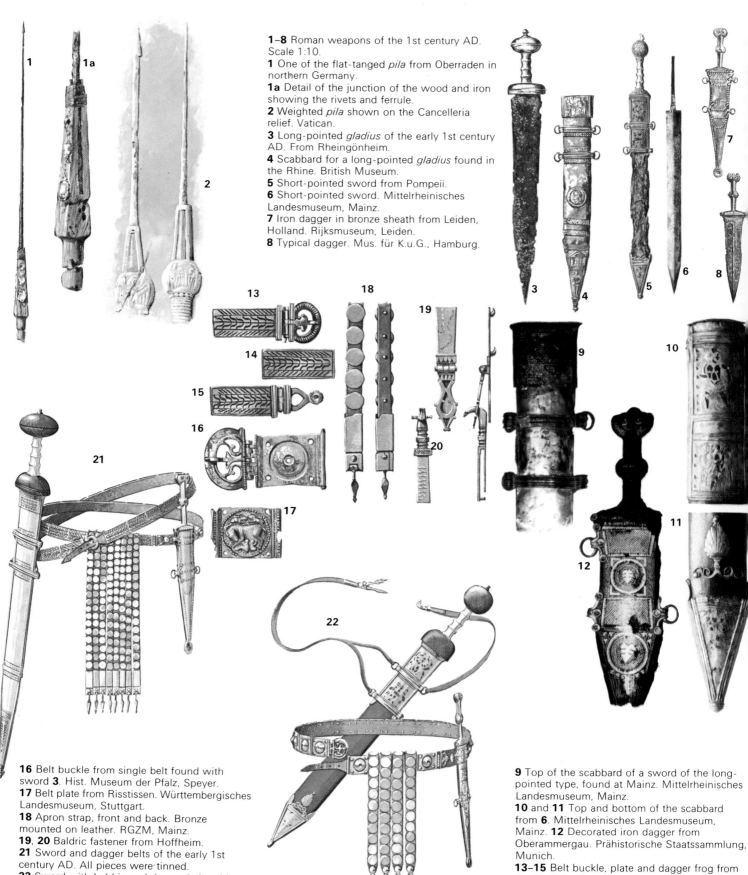

1–8 Roman weapons of the 1st century AD. Scale 1:10.
1 One of the flat-tanged *pila* from Oberraden in northern Germany.
1a Detail of the junction of the wood and iron showing the rivets and ferrule.
2 Weighted *pila* shown on the Cancelleria relief. Vatican.
3 Long-pointed *gladius* of the early 1st century AD. From Rheingönheim.
4 Scabbard for a long-pointed *gladius* found in the Rhine. British Museum.
5 Short-pointed sword from Pompeii.
6 Short-pointed sword. Mittelrheinisches Landesmuseum, Mainz.
7 Iron dagger in bronze sheath from Leiden, Holland. Rijksmuseum, Leiden.
8 Typical dagger. Mus. für K.u.G., Hamburg.

16 Belt buckle from single belt found with sword 3. Hist. Museum der Pfalz, Speyer.
17 Belt plate from Risstissen. Württembergisches Landesmuseum, Stuttgart.
18 Apron strap, front and back. Bronze mounted on leather. RGZM, Mainz.
19, 20 Baldric fastener from Hoffheim.
21 Sword and dagger belts of the early 1st century AD. All pieces were tinned.
22 Sword with baldric and dagger belt, mid- to late 1st century AD.

9 Top of the scabbard of a sword of the long-pointed type, found at Mainz. Mittelrheinisches Landesmuseum, Mainz.
10 and 11 Top and bottom of the scabbard from 6. Mittelrheinisches Landesmuseum, Mainz. 12 Decorated iron dagger from Oberammergau. Prähistorische Staatssammlung, Munich.
13–15 Belt buckle, plate and dagger frog from double belts. Found at Auerberg. Prähistorische Staatssammlung, Munich.

ments of the chest and shoulder units were held together with decorative hinges. On one example the hinge had broken and the two pieces had been riveted together, proving that the hinges were purely decorative and had no function. Fragments from Newstead of the same date (late 1st century) do not appear to have these hinges.

The narrow bands on the shoulders, waist and upper back were riveted to leather strapping and the waistbands were laced together at the front and back. The reconstructed cuirasses weigh about 9kg.

Originally this armour was believed to be from the 2nd century AD, but fragments are being found on many earlier sites. Hooks from the waistbands riveted to iron, which can hardly be interpreted as anything else, have been found in contexts that can only be dated to the first half of the 1st century. The other significant factor about this type of armour is that these finds are not confined to legionary camps, and it is becoming increasingly difficult to sustain the view that only the legionaries wore *lorica segmentata*.

Early in the 1st century AD the oval *scutum* was replaced by a shorter rectangular shield which retained the same name. At first this was just the old oval *scutum* shorn off at the top and bottom, but later the sides were also squared off. The only surviving example comes from Dura Europos in Syria and is dated to the 3rd century AD. This shield was constructed in exactly the same way as the Fayum shield, being made of three layers of thin strips of plane wood about 2mm thick glued across each other to form a curved piece of plywood. The back was strengthened with strips of wood which were also glued on. The handle was formed by thickening the central strip. The shield was encased in leather, the front was then covered with a layer of linen and the edges bound with rawhide stitched through the wood. This shield is much lighter and more flimsy than the Fayum and La Tène examples, which are about twice as thick in the centre. The elaborate decoration on this shield, and the fact that it was made at a time when the rectangular *scutum* was no longer in general use, may mean that this was some form of traditional ceremonial shield. Certainly

it had never been used in anger. There is a parallel in the Praetorian Guard, who were still using the oval *scutum* for parades at the end of the 1st century AD.

During the 1st and 2nd centuries AD the rim of the rectangular *scutum* was generally reinforced with bronze. Many pieces of this binding have been found, and they confirm that the edge of the shield was about 6mm thick. But it seems likely that, as in the earlier period, the shield was thickened to about one centimetre in the centre. Reconstructions of the rectangular *scutum*, using the Dura shield as a model and adding bronze binding and an iron boss, weigh 5.5kg. If the wood in the centre were to be thickened, the weight would rise to about 7.5kg. All examples of the *scutum* type shield, both Celtic and Roman, have a horizontal handgrip which can be seen on many monuments. It is held with an overgrip and generally used with a straight arm.

The handgrip was protected by an iron or bronze boss. The transition from the oval to the rectangular shield is well illustrated in the changing boss shape on p. 231. The face of the shield was decorated with a painted design. Tacitus, describing the second battle of Cremona in AD 69, tells how two legionaries picked up the shields of their fallen enemies and, hiding behind them, man-

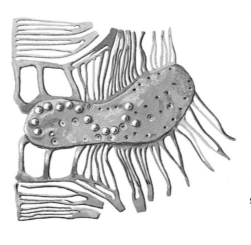

Above
The remains of a leather military sandal. The loops were laced up the foot and ankle. The sole was made of several layers of leather stuck together and shod with iron studs.

aged to infiltrate the enemy lines, where they put a catapult out of action. As this was at night with only the moonlight to see by, it suggests that the large motifs painted on the shields were a recognisable identification symbol of a unit.

The *pilum* remained in use throughout the 1st and 2nd centuries. Remains of many *pila*, both of the socketed and flat-tanged types, have been found with heads generally between 65 and 75cm long. The best-preserved examples of the flat-tanged type come from Oberraden in northern Germany. Here not only the iron but also part of the wooden shaft have survived. These are similar to the heavy *pila* of the previous periods, with the flat tang held into the wooden shaft by two rivets. However, they are much lighter in construction than the examples from Numantia, and when reconstructed weigh a little less than 2kg. The progressive lightening of the flat-tanged *pilum* during the early empire may have led to the introduction of a heavier *pilum* with a round lead weight inserted at the junction of the wood and the iron. This type is to be seen on the Cancelleria relief from Rome, in which Praetorians of the Flavian period are shown carrying them. Unfortunately we have no certain archaeological specimens of this type, though several *pila* have been found which have spiked tangs and may be from this new weapon.

There are dozens of swords from this period, including several very well preserved examples. In the first part of the 1st century AD the swords still echoed the dagger shape of the earlier Spanish prototype and had a long tapering point. The blade length of these swords varies between 50 and 56cm. Later in the century a new sword was introduced with straight parallel sides and a shorter point. It owes little to the original Spanish sword and should really no longer be referred to as *gladius hispaniensis*. The blade length of the new sword varies from 44 to 55cm. Reconstructions of these swords weigh about a kilogram, and the scabbard a little over half as much. The scabbard is usually made of wood and leather held together with bronze which is often tin-plated.

Several daggers survive from the 1st century AD which vary little in shape, although some have longer points than others. They are still very similar to

Below

1 Two horsemen, one in mail and the other in scale armour on a relief from Mantua in the Po valley. Early 1st century AD. **2, 3** Horsemen shown on Trajan's column. Note the mail shirt worn by **2** and the carrying position of the shield on **3**.

4 A late republican horseman shown on the altar of Domitius Ahenobarbus in the Louvre. **5** A detail from a Trajanic relief re-used on the Arch of Constantine at Rome. This shows clearly depicted mail and the cut of his shirt is the same as no. **2**.

their Spanish ancestors. The blade length varies from 20 to 25cm. The scabbards are made of bronze or iron and are usually highly decorated with silver inlay. About the same time as the new sword was introduced a different dagger scabbard appears. This is made from an engraved bronze front and back plate riveted to a wooden base. The dagger seems to have disappeared from legionary equipment around the end of the 1st century and is completely absent from Trajan's Column.

During the early 1st century AD the sword and dagger were suspended from two individual belts that crossed over at the back and front in cowboy fashion. From these was suspended an apron of metal discs riveted to leather straps. Later a single belt was substituted to which the dagger and apron were attached, but the sword was suspended from a baldric on the right side. These belts were covered with rectangular plates usually made of bronze plated with tin. Examples of these plates have been found on most legionary sites, including Numantia, showing that they were in use during the 2nd century BC. Examples of belt plates from the late Villanovan period (see p. 93) suggest that they were always used.

Many examples of military sandals (*caligae*) have been discovered. The upper is cut from a single piece of leather which wrapped round the foot and was sewn up at the heel. This was stitched to a heavy sole made of several layers of hide shod with iron studs. These heavy sandals weighed a little under a kilogram. Josephus gives an amusing description of a centurion during the siege of Jerusalem dashing across the paved temple courtyard, skidding on his iron studs and falling flat on his back.

Auxiliary cavalry and infantry

It has been suggested by many authors that the Romans did not employ armoured cavalry until the beginning of the 2nd century AD. This is an oversimplification, partly due to a misinterpretation of the monuments. The Romans painted their sculpture and therefore the lack of mail shown on horsemen on Trajan's Column and other monuments and tombstones is not surprising. However, legionary tombstones of the first hundred years of the empire also do not show mail, and yet there is no question that the legionaries of this period wore a coat of mail. The cavalrymen on the Aemilius Paullus monument are surely wearing cuirasses cut in exactly the same fashion as the legionaries, who are certainly wearing mail, and there is a horseman on the Ahenobarbus relief from the time of Marius who is wearing clearly depicted mail. A very detailed sculpture from Mantua in the Po valley, dating from late in the reign of Augustus, shows two cavalrymen, one in mail and one in scale armour, and there are many 1st-century cavalry tombstones from Germany showing body armour cut to the same pattern. There are also cavalrymen on the Trajanic frieze from the Arch of Constantine (c. AD 115) who are wearing mail and, incidentally, the cut of their cuirasses is exactly the same as those of the cavalrymen on Trajan's Column.

Armoured cavalry had developed in the Middle East in the 9th or 10th centuries BC. Horse armour (peytrals and chamfrons) found in both Italy and Greece, dating from the 5th–4th centuries BC, shows that partially armoured cavalry was in use throughout the classical period.

The arrival of the Roxolani, a Sarmatian tribe, along the Danube in the latter part of the 1st century AD brought Rome face to face with a new type of cavalry which had evolved in the East. These were *cataphracti*, heavily armed cavalry with both man and horse covered with armour. Rome's response was of course to begin employing these horsemen. Although some units may have existed earlier, Hadrian formed the first regular unit of *cataphracti*. These new units were armed with a heavy lance (*contus*).

At the other end of the scale the Romans employed Numidians, completely unarmoured and riding without a bridle, and also mounted archers.

Greek cavalry had worn helmets without cheek pieces or neck guards to allow all-round vision and hearing. The Roman cavalryman, however, wore a helmet that covered the whole head leaving only the eyes, nose and mouth visible, the ears being completely enclosed. In the 2nd century, like the legionary helmets, cavalry helmets were reinforced with cross braces. Towards the end of

the 1st century a reinforcing strip was also often applied to the forehead. This came to a point at the front. Body armour was either mail or scale. The mail shirts shown on cavalry tombstones of the 1st century AD are, not surprisingly, derived from the Celtic cuirass with its shoulder cape (see p. 123). This type weighed about 16kg. The cape was held to the chest by a pair of swivelling

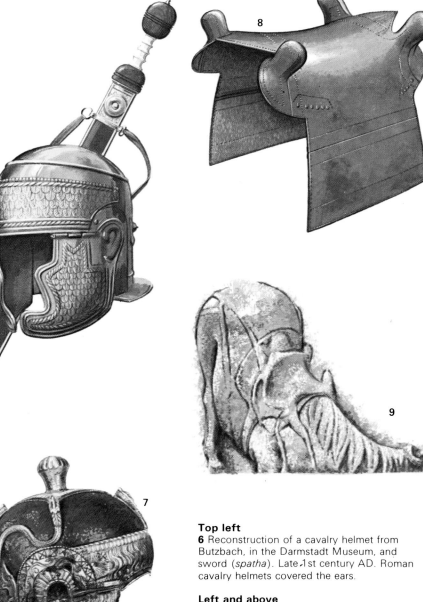

Top left
6 Reconstruction of a cavalry helmet from Butzbach, in the Darmstadt Museum, and sword (*spatha*). Late 1st century AD. Roman cavalry helmets covered the ears.

Left and above
7 2nd-century iron cavalry helmet with bronze decoration from Heddernheim. Frankfurt Museum. **8** A reconstruction of the Roman saddle found at the Valkenburg fort in Holland. After Dr W. Groenman van Waateringe. The saddle appears for the first time on Roman sculptures of the early empire and was almost certainly of Celtic origin.
9 A fallen Celtic horse shown on the Julii monument at St Remy in Provence dating from just after the death of Caesar. This horse, which has a Roman type saddle, must be Celtic as the Romans did not show their own men being defeated on their triumphal monuments.

S-shaped hooks which allowed the shoulder pieces to move easily. The shirt was split at the hips, as in the republican period, to enable the rider to sit a horse.

On Trajan's Column the cavalrymen wear a much simpler form of mail shirt with darts at the shoulders and waist. This type weighed only about 9kg. Fragments of laminated thigh guards made from strips of bronze were found at the late 1st-century fort at Newstead in Scotland.

In the early empire horses wore no armour but were decorated with pendants and discs (*phalerae*) made of tinned bronze. Many of these have been found in excavations all over the empire and are to be seen on numerous Roman sculptures and tombstones. These are also of Celtic origin and appear on the Gundestrup cauldron (see p. 114).

During the early empire, when the main source of cavalry in the West was Celtic, the Roman cavalryman used a long sword (*spatha*) with a blade length of 60 to 70cm, which is clearly derived from the Celtic long sword, and a flat oval or sometimes hexagonal shield which is equally clearly of Celtic origin. When not in use the shield was carried alongside the horse, sometimes under the saddle blanket. Josephus claims that Vespasian's Eastern cavalry carried a quiver containing three or more darts with points as large as spears: presumably this quiver was attached to the horse and not the rider.

The saddle suddenly appears for the first time on Roman sculptures of the early empire. However, it can be shown that the saddle, like most of the other equipment, was almost certainly of Celtic origin. In his commentary on the Gallic war Caesar casually remarks that the Germans scorned the use of the saddle. This was at a time when Caesar was almost exclusively employing Celtic cavalry and therefore implies that the Celts used the saddle. The Julii monument at St Remy in southern France, which dates to very shortly after the death of Caesar, commemorates an unknown battle involving Romans and Celts. One of the sculptures shows a cavalry battle in which one of the horses has fallen and thrown its rider. The horse unquestionably has a saddle of Roman type with four pommels. The fallen rider must be a Celt, for Romans did not show their own men being killed on their triumphal monuments.

Stirrups were not in use in the ancient world. Attempts to associate the introduction of the stirrup with the Sarmatians are impossible to sustain. The claim that a *cataphractus* could not ride without stirrups would involve moving back their introduction by at least three

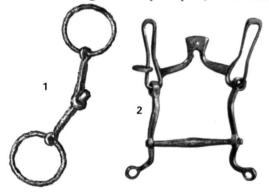

Above
1 A typical Romano-Celtic snaffle bit from Wroxeter, Shrewsbury Museum.
2 Complex Italian type of bit from Newstead. The tongued bar went in the mouth and the straight bar under the chin.

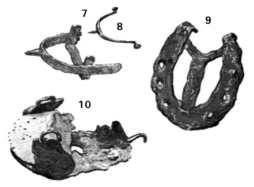

Above
7, 8 Two different types of spur from Mainz. RGZM, Mainz.
9 Horseshoe from Wiesenburg in Bavaria.
10 Hipposandal complete with horse's hoof in the museum at St Germain.

Above
3–6 Tinned bronze harness mounts discovered at Fremington Hagg, Yorkshire. Yorkshire Museum, York. Scale 1:2.
3, 3a Front and back of a *phalera*. The harness

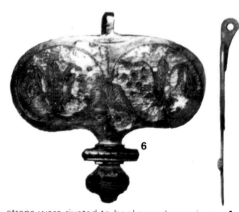

straps were riveted to hooks as shown in no. **4** which were hooked on to the back of the *phalera*. **4** A simple strap joiner.
5, 5a Pendant with stud to hold it to the harness. **6** Pendant.

Left
Cavalry helmet from Theilenhofen, c.175 AD.
Prähistorische Staatssammlung, Munich. This
tinned bronze helmet, which is the epitome of
Roman bad taste, could only have belonged to
an officer.

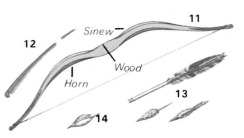

Above
11 Cross-section of a composite bow.
12 Horn nock from Scotland.
13 Part of a reed arrow and two arrow heads
from Dura Europus, c.350 AD.
14 Firebrand arrow head from Scotland.

Above
Early 2nd-century auxiliary helmet in the
Archaeological Museum at Florence. This is
the type shown on Trajan's Column. At some
time the neck guard has been cut off.

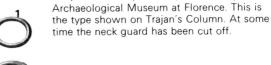

Above
Bronze scale armour. Scales are found in many
sizes varying between 1 and 5cm long. The
scales were wired together then sewn to a
fabric backing through the centre holes.
Scale 1:1.

Above
Early Celtic mail was made of alternate lines of
punched (**1**) and butted rings. During the
empire the butted rings were replaced with
much stronger riveted rings (**2**). The Celts
were great iron-workers.

Above
Bronze trumpet with curved end in the
Rheinisches Landesmuseum, Bonn. There were
several different types of Roman military
trumpet. This may be the type of cavalry
trumpet called a *lituus*.

centuries, for Antiochus the Great employed *cataphracti*. There is no Roman sculpture or painting that could possibly be interpreted as showing a stirrup. The first mention of them is in the *Strategikon* of Maurice, the Byzantine emperor (AD 582–602), and the first examples were found in 7th-century Avar graves in Dacia. The earliest evidence for stirrups comes from China in the 5th century AD. They were probably brought to the West by the Turks and Avars, perhaps arriving in Europe in the first half of the 6th century. Spurs, in contrast, were in use throughout the empire, and many examples have been discovered.

A large number of horseshoes of the traditional nailed-on type have also been found. Examples were discovered at the Belgic level at Colchester and it may be assumed that these were of late Celtic origin and adopted by the Romans.

There was also a type of detachable horseshoe known as the hippo-sandal, which was strapped to the horse's hoof. The purpose of the hippo-sandal is unclear. Both types of shoe are mainly found around civil settlements and were therefore probably used for draught animals.

There were two types of bit in use, the snaffle type with two rings to hold the reins and harness, which was o...

The Roman army on the march as described by the Jewish historian Flavius Josephus.
1 Contingents of the light-armed infantry and cavalry which scout ahead as a precaution against ambushes. **2** The vanguard composed of one legion plus a force of cavalry. As in Polybius' day, the legions drew lots daily to decide which one should form the vanguard. **3** The camp surveyors composed of ten men from each century. This must mean one man from each tent. Each man carried his own kit plus the instruments necessary for marking out the camp. **4** The pioneer corps whose job it was to clear or bridge any natural obstacles. **5** The general's personal baggage and that of his lieutenants accompanied by a strong mounted escort. **6** The general riding with his bodyguard which was drawn from the ranks of the auxiliary cavalry and infantry. **7** The combined legionary cavalry. There were 120 of these to each legion. **8** The mules carrying the dismantled siege engines—towers, rams, catapults etc. **9** The senior officers—legates, tribunes and auxiliary prefects with an escort of picked troops. **10** The legions. Each legion was headed by the *aquilifer* surrounded by the other standard bearers of the legion. It is uncertain whether the trumpeters and hornblowers preceded or followed the standard bearers as Josephus' two accounts differ on this point. They are always shown in front on Trajan's Column. Behind the trumpeters and ensigns came the legionaries marching six abreast and kept in order by their centurions. Josephus actually says one centurion, but allowing a minimum of two paces per six men each legion would be strung out over at least one and a half kilometres so that one centurion would be unable to keep order. Each legion was followed by its own baggage train controlled by the legion's servants. Those not minding the animals marched behind them. **11** The auxiliary cohorts, each presumably led by its standard bearers. **12** The rearguard composed of light and heavy infantry and a considerable body of auxiliary cavalry. The camp followers would have been found at the rear of the army, keeping close to the army for protection. These would have included prostitutes, common-law wives, slave dealers ready to buy up the prisoners of war and a collection of merchants of all kinds.

Celtic origin, and an Italian type which is far too complex to describe (see illustration on p. 236).

The auxiliary infantry varied from light-armed troops such as the slingers shown on Trajan's Column, who wore no armour at all and, if the artist is to be believed, no shoes either, to fully armed troops whose armour was identical to that of the legionaries but of inferior quality: the only difference was the use of the flat shield rather than the *scutum*. Some wore scale armour made by sewing overlapping rows of metal scales on to a linen undergarment. Scales varied in size from one to five centimetres long. The cut of the cuirass was much the same as the mail shirts. Helmets were usually cheap bronze versions of the current legionary types. The weapons of the armoured infantry were usually a sword similar to the legionary *gladius* and a short spear.

Archers, who are usually of Eastern origin, are shown on Trajan's Column wearing mail shirts which are just a longer version of the cavalry type. They used the composite bow which was much smaller than the English longbow and was made of wood strengthened on the inside of the curve with horn and on the outside with sinew. A pair of horn nocks to which the string was attached reinforced each end. Many examples of these nocks have been found on Roman military sites.

The Army in the Field
On the march

The Jewish historian Josephus in his account of the Jewish revolt (AD 66–c. 73) gives a remarkable account of the Roman army in the field. It is remarkable because it shows the extreme conservatism of the Romans. Although this account was written more than 200 years after the time of Polybius and is quite clearly not copied from his work, it is almost identical.

Each morning at daybreak the centurions still report to the tribunes' tents and then go with them to receive their

orders from the general. They then return to their centuries, who are assembled waiting to receive their work orders for the day. If it has been decided to break camp, they wait for the signal to be given by the trumpeters. On the first trumpet blast the tents are struck and the soldiers gather up their equipment. On the second the tents and other surplus baggage are loaded on to the mules; the remaining wooden structures in the camp are burnt and the soldiers assemble for the march.

Josephus' description of the legionaries' equipment very much reflects the reforms of Marius who, nearly two centuries earlier, had compelled the soldiers

to carry their equipment, from which they received the nickname of 'Marius' mules'. Each legionary had to carry a saw, basket, pickaxe (*dolabra*), sickle, leather strap, and a chain. To these should be added an entrenching tool and turf cutter, but it would be wrong to suppose that each soldier carried all of these items. Besides these he had to carry three days' rations. Legionaries on the march are shown on Trajan's Column (see below). They carry their shields on the left side, presumably suspended from a shoulder strap as in Polybius' day. The shields are shown uncovered so that the decoration can be seen, but we know from Caesar's chron-

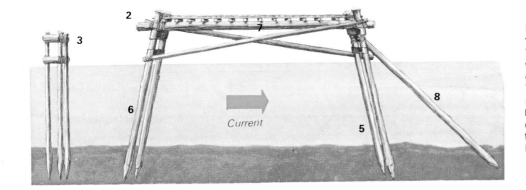

Left
1 The bridge over the Danube shown on Trajan's Column. The wooden superstructure was supported by 20 massive stone piers. **2** A cross-section of Caesar's bridge over the Rhine. The current flows from left to right. Breakwaters (**3**) were placed upstream to prevent anything being floated down against the piles. A full description is given below. **4** Iron pile point from a similar Rhine bridge. Rheinisches Landesmuseum, Bonn.

Above
Caesar's bridge across the Rhine. Working from rafts a pair of timbers (**5**) was rammed into the river bed, inclining against the current. Twelve metres upstream a second pair (**6**) was driven in inclining downstream. These were joined by a cross beam (**7**). A series of trestles made like this supported the road. The trestles were reinforced by timbers (**8**) slanting against the current.

cles that the shield had a leather cover, several examples of which have been found. These have a round hole at the front for the boss. The legionaries on the column march bareheaded with their helmets strapped to their right shoulders; otherwise they are fully armed. Over his left shoulder each legionary carries a pole with a crossbar at the top to which his baggage is tied. Amongst this luggage can be identified a mess tin (*patera*), cooking pot or bucket and a leather bag with a handle for carrying clothes and personal belongings. The sack at the top probably holds his rations which might in an emergency have to be enough for 15 days. The soldier's basic diet when on campaign was wheat baked in the form of wholemeal biscuits. This was supplemented by bacon, cheese and sour wine, all preserved types of food. When in camp the soldier's diet was much more appetising. Excavations at military sites have revealed bones from beef, mutton, pork and other meats besides poultry, eggs, fish, shellfish and a great variety of fruit and vegetables, not to mention salt, which was considered a necessity.

On the third trumpet signal the stragglers rushed to take up their positions in the ranks. Before setting out, a herald standing to his right of the general enquired three times whether the soldiers were ready for war and three times the soldiers shouted, 'We are ready'. Some, in their enthusiasm, raised their right arms in assent. The column then set out with each man holding his position in the ranks.

The auxiliary cavalry and infantry performed the jobs that in Polybius' time used to be done by the *extraordinarii*—scouting ahead of the army and acting as bodyguard for the general. It is intriguing to note the constant use of non-Romans to perform this last task. The complete breakdown of the order of march is given in the caption which accompanies the illustration on p. 238.

The army expected to cover about 30km per day under normal conditions, although forced marches of 50km per

day and more are recorded. The pioneers were equipped to deal with all obstacles. There were three methods of crossing rivers. If a river was fordable but fast-flowing, half the cavalry entered the water upstream and the other half downstream. The group upstream broke the force of the current whilst those downstream caught the men or equipment carried away by the river. If the river was too deep to ford, the bridge builders who marched with the pioneers surveyed the problem and decided whether to construct a pile bridge or a bridge of boats. When a long campaign was envisaged with the aim of bringing the area under direct and permanent

control, a more permanent structure might be built, such as that constructed by Trajan to cross the Danube at the Iron Gates. This was 1,500m long and was built of 20 massive stone piers 50m high and 20m wide supporting a wooden superstructure. The more normal bridge was constructed of wooden piles rammed into the river bed in pairs about 12m apart. These were joined by crossbeams to form a series of trestles which supported the roadway. Caesar's bridge across the Rhine, which was probably at Coblenz where the Rhine is about half a kilometre wide and up to eight metres deep, was of this type. The regular use of these bridges is attested by the

Right
A scene from Trajan's Column showing legionaries fording a river chest deep. The soldier at the front has stripped off and is carrying his helmet, cuirass, sword and clothing in his *scutum* over his head.

discovery of the supporting piles at more than one point on the Rhine. Several iron points from these piles were discovered in the Rhine at Bonn. A detailed description of the construction of Caesar's bridge is given in the caption to the illustration on p. 240.

If the current was not too strong, or if the river was too deep for a pile bridge, a pontoon bridge could be built. Arrian, in his *Anabasis of Alexander*, describes Alexander's bridge over the Indus with the comment that he does not know what method Alexander used but that he will describe the long-established Roman method which was used to bridge the Rhine, Danube, Tigris and Euphrates. Boats, he adds, are the quickest method of bridging.

At a given signal the boats were allowed to drift downstream stern first with a rowing boat controlling them against the current while they were manoeuvred into position. Pyramid-shaped wicker crates filled with stones were then lowered from the bows of each boat to moor them against the stream. As each boat was manoeuvred into position at the correct interval (probably about five metres) and anchored, timbers were laid to span the gap and secured by crossplanks to form the road. Ladders were laid along either side of the road way to make it safer for the horses and baggage animals. This type of bridge is depicted on Trajan's Column.

The great advantage of both the trestle and pontoon bridge was that they could be extended across a river without an established bridgehead on the opposite bank.

At the end of the day's march an encampment would be established, fortified with a ditch, rampart and palisade just as in Polybius' time. Many examples of stakes, five Roman feet long, pointed at either end and waisted at the centre, have been found. These have been identified as palisade stakes. They are quite different from those described by Polybius and if they are indeed for palisades they show a complete change of emphasis; they can hardly have been very effective, for when embedded in the turf of the rampart they would only have protruded about a metre. Many fragments from leather tents have been found. These tents were ten Roman feet

square, plus two feet for guy-ropes, and held eight men (a *contubernium*). The camp differs considerably from that described by Polybius. Many permanent legionary fortresses have been excavated which give an idea of the basic layout. Although the centuries are still encamped in pairs, recalling the old manipular system, and no doubt the *prior* and *posterior* centuries are still coupled, the barrack blocks generally form the perimeter of the camp. The barracks were built about 30m back from the rampart, well out of range of missiles. Each century block was composed of ten or eleven sets of double rooms which occupied about two-thirds of the block. Each double room consisted of a large bedroom about 4.5m square holding eight legionaries with a smaller room for their equipment. At the other end of the block were the century offices and the centurion's living quarters.

As in Polybius' day the camp was divided down the middle by the *via praetoria*, which led straight from the *porta praetoria*. The other end of this road, which led to the *porta decumana*, so-called because it was next to the tenth maniples in Polybius' camp, was called the *via decumana*. The camp was still divided laterally by the *via principalis*, where the soldiers had formerly assembled, but now a special building, the *principia*, which was placed on the *via principalis* facing down the *via decumana* and back to back or side by side with the *praetorium*, was provided as the operations centre of the camp. The tribunes' quarters still retained their former positions along the *via principalis*. These permanent camps were originally timber-built, but by the mid-1st century AD in Germany, and by the end of the century in Britain, they were being rebuilt in stone. This rebuilding in stone reflects their accepted permanence and not some new threat. These camps were like small towns, completely self-sufficient with hospitals, workshops, etc.

In battle

Little can be said of the basic legionary tactics of the early empire. As long as the weaponry remained the same one must assume that the legionary continued to fight in the same fashion. Although the shield had been shortened

Above
1–5 Legionaries' tools. **1** Sickle from Numantia. **2** Pickaxe (*dolabra*) from Cremona. **3** Entrenching tool from Kastell Künzing. **4** Turf cutter from Newstead. **5** Reconstruction of the digging tools.

Above
6 Leather shield cover from Hardknott. **7** Tent leather from the Antonine Wall. **8** Palisade stake from Hadrian's Wall. **9 10** Bucket and mess tin from Cremona. **11** Figure-eight chain from Numantia.

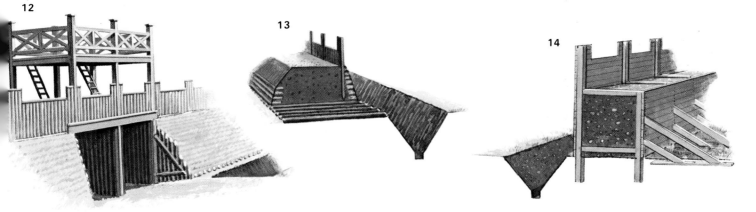

Above
12–14 The defences of timber-built camps.
12 The timber gateway of the fort at the Lunt, Bagington, Warwickshire, as reconstructed by

Brian Hobley. **13** Section of a turf-faced rampart built on a corduroy of logs to give it a stable foundation when the ground was soft. **14** A reconstruction of the section of the box

rampart excavated at the Valkenburg fort in Holland. This type of rampart was used where there was insufficient turf to face a normal rampart.

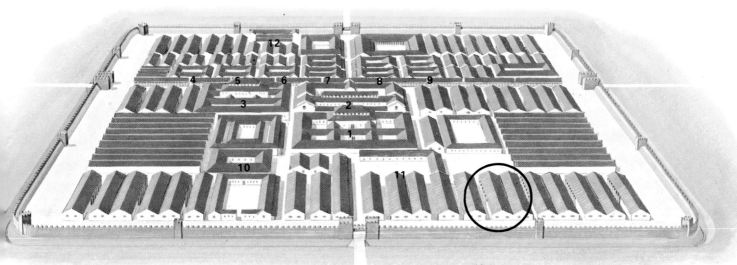

Above
The fortress of legion XVI *Gallica* at Neuss (Novaesium) on the lower Rhine. It covers an area of 450×650m.
1 The commander's house (*praetorium*).
2 Legion headquarters (*principia*).
3 Hospital. **4–9** Tribunes' houses.
10 Workshops. **11** Market place (*forum*).
12 Granaries and cookhouse.
The barracks are the long buildings built in pairs around the perimeter.

Below
The *principia* facing the *via principalis* with the commander's house (*praetorium*) behind it. The *principia* was the legionary headquarters. Here the standards were kept in a shrine.

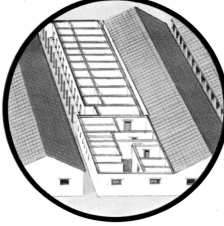

Above
The inset shows a century barrack block with double rooms for the legionaries at the far end. The centurion's quarters and century offices are at the front.

in the 1st century AD, shoulder guards had been developed to compensate. At first this was probably done by extending the mail shirt to cover the shoulders, but later it was achieved by the introduction of the *lorica segmentata* with its articulated shoulder guards.

Although the army could now fight in one or several lines, these lines still had to be able to interchange and this must have been done by the withdrawal of the *posterior* centuries. The semi-cylindrical *scutum* seems to have been specifically designed to cover both the front and side of the soldier when the gaps were opened, and it does not seem unreasonable to suppose that the abandoning of the *scutum* in the 3rd century marks the end of this method of changing lines.

During Caesar's siege of Alesia we see the *pilum* being used as a defensive weapon, which gives a deeper insight into the Roman *pilum* and sword method of fighting. Here Caesar's legionaries are trying to hold back the Gauls who are breaking through the defences. They have obviously thrown their lighter *pila* and are using the heavier ones as spears to hold the enemy at bay until reinforcements can be brought up. When this happens they throw their *pila* and close in with their swords in the usual fashion. One should not assume that this or any other of the activities of Caesar's army are innovations. This defensive method of fighting had probably been developed to compensate for the loss of the third line of spearmen (*triarii*).

One advantage of the new cohort composition of the legion was that an individual legion could be arrayed in a variety of formations. Vegetius talks of drawing it up two cohorts deep with the first to fifth at the front and the sixth to tenth at the rear. A formation that fits ideally both Roman tactics and the new ten-cohort legion is the 'breakthrough' formation known to the soldiers as the 'pig's head'. This was formed with one cohort at the front (presumably the first) with the second and third in the second line, the fourth, fifth and sixth in the third line and the other four cohorts in the rear line forming a wedge.

In general one must assume that the army continued to fight in simple formations, as they had in the republic. The system of command practised by the Romans during the early principate,

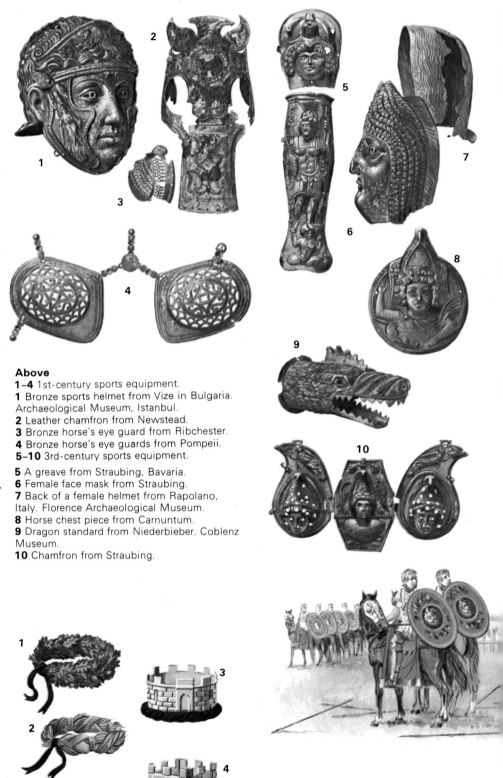

Above
1–4 1st-century sports equipment.
1 Bronze sports helmet from Vize in Bulgaria. Archaeological Museum, Istanbul.
2 Leather chamfron from Newstead.
3 Bronze horse's eye guard from Ribchester.
4 Bronze horse's eye guards from Pompeii.
5–10 3rd-century sports equipment.
5 A greave from Straubing, Bavaria.
6 Female face mask from Straubing.
7 Back of a female helmet from Rapolano, Italy. Florence Archaeological Museum.
8 Horse chest piece from Carnuntum.
9 Dragon standard from Niederbieber. Coblenz Museum.
10 Chamfron from Straubing.

1–5 Military crowns.
1 *Corona civica* made of oak leaves.
2 *Corona obsidionalis* made of grass.
3 *Corona Muralis*. **4** *Corona vallaris*.
5 *Corona navalis*. **3–5** are gold.

in which only the regular professional officers commanded at century level, precluded any possibility of imaginative tactics using large bodies of troops. Roman commanders relied heavily on tried and trusted tactics which utilised the vast experience of the centurions. Vegetius' seven tactics, which involve complicated manoeuvres, seem to be drawn rather from the exploits of generals such as Scipio and Caesar than the normal practice of the army.

After the battle

After a battle a general customarily rewarded soldiers whose performance had been exemplary. In the republic soldiers could look forward to their share of the booty quite apart from decorations for valour. During the empire this had to be modified as there were far fewer opportunities for rewards of either kind. It became customary for the emperor, in order to keep his troops happy, to give peacetime pay-outs (donatives), often the equivalent to five years' pay. Such payments were made when a new emperor came to the throne. In the turmoil following the death of Nero, when four emperors came to the throne in swift succession, the donative played a very important role. The Praetorians were offered ten years' pay to support Galba's claim to the throne. When the bribe was not forthcoming they murdered him

Above
Tombstone of the centurion Marcus Caelius of legion XVIII, showing his decorations: *corona civica, phalerae, armillae* and torques. Caelius was killed in the Varus disaster.

Above
A set of *phalerae* from Lauersfort in Germany. They are made of silver with gold inlay. Apparently of Celtic origin, they were awarded to common soldiers.

after a reign of only four months.

During the republic military decorations had been won largely on individual merit regardless of rank. During the empire certain rewards were restricted to certain ranks and the traditional reason for the award was often ignored. Thus the *corona navalis* could only be awarded to men of consular rank and no longer had any connection with the sea or ships. The *corona obsidionalis*, awarded for saving an army, was by its

Below
The *Hippica Gymnasia*. One team acted as targets, the others charged in throwing light dummy javelins. Points were scored for hits. Dragon standards with long snake-like tails added colour.

very nature awarded to a commander. It is not clear if it was awarded during the empire, though Pliny claims that Augustus was given one. The last certain recipient was Sulla. The *corona civica* retained its original significance and could still be won by anyone who saved the life of a citizen and held his ground. However, the *muralis* and *vallaris* crowns simply became decorations, completely unconnected with the town wall or rampart. These last two were made of gold during the empire and could not be won by anyone below the rank of centurion. However, common soldiers could be awarded *phalerae*, torques and armbands (*armillae*). All these would appear to be of Celtic origin. A centurion usually received these as well as the gold crowns.

Centurions of the *primi ordines* and junior tribunes could also receive a silver spear (*hasta pura*). There was also a plain gold crown (*corona aurea*) which could be awarded to centurions and above. Senior tribunes might expect two gold crowns, two silver spears and two small gold standards (*vexilla*). Legionary legates could receive three of each of these and provincial governors of consular rank, four.

In contrast to the rewards were the punishments that were meted out to those who had failed in their duty. The Romans had a great tradition of discipline, though they were not as severe as many ancient authors would pretend. Resort was seldom made to the capital punishments meted out in Polybius' day. They were usually restricted to caning, extra duties, reduction in rank

Above
A relief from the Temple of Apollo Sosianus at Rome showing a scene from a triumph, c. 20 BC. Prisoners of war are arranged around a trophy which is then carried shoulder high by eight legionaries. On the right is a *tubicen*.

Above
A scene from the triumphal arch of Titus at Rome commemorating his victory over the Jews. In the triumphal procession the legionaries are carrying the treasure from the temple at Jerusalem. In the centre can be seen the seven-pronged *candelabra*. The placards being carried in the background would have borne descriptions of the exhibits. All the soldiers are unarmed and wear laurel wreaths.

or dishonourable discharge. The greatest dishonour that could happen to a whole unit was disbandment. This happened to four of the German legions when Vespasian came to the throne after the defeat of Vitellius.

Parades and sports

The handing out of awards was performed before the whole army and took place in front of a formal parade. Josephus describes such a parade, adding that each man who received an award also obtained a rise in rank. The Jewish historian also gives an account of a four-monthly pay parade during the siege of Jerusalem. He was obviously very impressed by it: 'As was their custom, the troops took their arms from the cases in which up till now they had been stored, and advanced clad in mail to be paid. The cavalry led their horses which were richly caparisoned . . . the scene glittered far and wide with silver and gold'. The pay parade lasted four days—probably one day for each of the four legions. Josephus implies that the Romans had special parade armour. If this was so very little of it remains today. Many face-covering helmets which have come to light were once considered to be parade armour but are now known to be cavalry sports equipment. However, there is a very elaborate helmet which, if it was ever worn, could only have been used for parades. It is, incidentally, the latest surviving example of the traditional Italo-Corinthian type helmet. Some pieces of body armour from the 3rd century AD have survived. These are probably from cavalry parade armour

but might also have been worn for sports. Since most legionary helmets had crest holders, even though crests were no longer worn in battle, it seems probable that standard helmets with crests were worn for parades.

The cavalry sports (*Hippica Gymnasia*) mentioned above were highly skilled and colourful exhibitions performed by the cavalry using dummy javelins. For these exhibitions, which in some respects resembled medieval tournaments, both horse and man were elaborately armoured. A multitude of this cavalry sports equipment survives from all over the empire. The greatest find of this type of equipment comes from a 3rd-century site at Straubing in Bavaria. This site has produced several helmets, greaves and horse face pieces in a remarkable state of preservation. Helmets which have been found as far afield as Britain and Israel come in male and female types, suggesting perhaps that the contestants represented Greeks and Amazons. The drawing on p. 245 represents the *Hippica Gymnasia* in the 3rd century AD. It seems highly unlikely that this practice was of Roman origin. The appearance of a sports helmet on the victory relief at Pergamum suggests that it was either of Celtic or Eastern origin.

The triumph

During the republic a commander who had won a decisive victory could expect to be awarded a triumph. This victory celebration was enshrined in the very birth of Rome, though it owed much of its detail to the Etruscans. According to

Above
The triumphal arch of Titus at Rome. It was erected to commemorate his victory over the Jews which culminated in the sacking of Jerusalem in 70 AD.

Below
The decoration on a silver cup from Boscoreale in Campania. Louvre Museum. Beginning from the left, the scene shows the *triumphator*, possibly Tiberius, in his chariot. In his left hand he is holding a sceptre crowned with an eagle and in his right an olive branch. Behind him rides a slave holding a crown over his head. Ahead of the chariot is the sacrificial white ox being led by the priests (*victimarii*) who will perform the sacrifice. The right-hand side shows the sacrifice in front of the temple of Jupiter Capitolinus on the Capitol. The *triumphator* (with his head missing) stands in front of the tripod attended by praetorians, lictors and priests.

the famous legend, when Romulus killed Acron, king of the Ceninenses, in single combat, he stripped the dead chieftain of his armour, hung it over an oak branch to form a trophy, and then crowned with a laurel wreath raised the trophy on to his shoulder and led his men in procession singing songs of triumph. This was the origin of the triumph. The Etruscans introduced the chariot into the procession and also the basic dress of the *triumphator*. They were also responsible for the name itself and for the type of procession that evolved.

With the expansion of the empire the triumph developed in complexity and splendour. Although details might vary with different *triumphators*, a regular format was followed. At the head of the procession were the magistrates and the senators. They were followed by booty taken from the enemy, with paintings or models of the battles and the captured cities. Then came the sacrificial white oxen, followed by the prisoners, sometimes carried shoulder high on platforms amidst trophies of captured armour. Behind the prisoners rode the general in a gilded chariot drawn by four horses, clothed like a king with his face painted red. In his hands he carried a sceptre and an olive branch and behind him in the chariot rode a slave who whispered, 'Remember you are just a man'.

The chariot was followed by the soldiers wearing olive wreaths and shouting, '*Io Triumphe*'—behold the triumph.

The procession wound through the streets of Rome, passing through the two circuses before coming round the Palatine hill and up the Sacred Way to the Forum. Here the chief prisoner was normally led off to execution. Mean-

Above
The triumph of Titus over the Jews. Having wound its way through the streets of Rome the procession comes up the Sacra Via through the Forum to the foot of the Capitol. Here it begins to climb the Clivus Capitolinus.

while the procession climbed the Capitoline hill and here waited for the news that the prisoner had been executed. Then the general sacrificed the white oxen outside the Temple of Jupiter. The celebration of the triumph was restricted to generals who had won a complete victory over a foreign enemy. During the empire only the emperor and his family were allowed this honour. There was, however, a lesser form called an ovation. For this the general sacrificed on the Alban mount, several miles south of the city, and entered Rome either on horseback or on foot the following morning. Instead of an olive wreath he wore a crown of myrtle.

The Mobile Army

Dr Roger Tomlin

The Danubian wars of Marcus Aurelius exposed the weaknesses of the defensive system he had inherited. New legions had to be raised to defend Italy's northern approaches, 'field armies' had to be improvised, officers found and promoted unconventionally. Valerius Maximianus, one of the few senators to come from Pannonia, is a forerunner of the great Danubian emperors of the 3rd century: he was an experienced cavalry officer decorated by Marcus Aurelius for killing a barbarian chieftain with his own hands, who rose to be legate of six legions in turn. The first soldiers' emperor, however, Septimius Severus, had seen no active service until the Danubian legions proclaimed him in 193, but the need for military support took him on expeditions far beyond the frontiers of Syria and Britain. On his deathbed he is said to have advised his sons to 'enrich the troops and despise everyone else'. He increased soldiers' pay and supplemented it with donatives: their marriages were now legally recognised; the so-called right to wear a gold ring symbolised the opportunities now opened to them of rising into the centurionate and beyond, even into the administrative posts traditionally held by equestrians. The legionary army was increased by one-tenth, by raising three new *Parthica* legions commanded (like the Egyptian legion) by equestrian prefects who had been *primus pilus* twice. Two of them garrisoned the new province of (northern) Mesopotamia, but the Second was stationed in a fortress near Rome. The old Praetorian Guard was disbanded for having proclaimed one of Severus' opponents; it was replaced by ten new cohorts of double (milliary) strength drawn from legionaries, most of them the Danubians who seemed so uncouth to the Roman senatorial aristocracy. The new Guard and the Second *Parthica*, equivalent in numbers to three legions, formed a mobile reserve to the frontier armies—whether it was to reinforce them, or to crush an usurper.

Severus founded a precarious dynasty which lasted a quarter of a century. In these years, despite the five legions added by himself and Marcus Aurelius, the frontiers became strained to breaking-point. In Germany the existing tribes coalesced into two confederacies, both distant ancestors of modern European nations, the Franks on the lower Rhine, and the Alamanns to the east of the artificial frontier (*limes*) that linked the middle Rhine to the upper Danube. East German peoples like the Goths and Vandals moved southward from the Baltic, pressing other tribes against the Danubian frontier, and themselves threatening Dacia and the lower Danube. In the east the ramshackle Parthian empire fell to an aggressive Persian revival, which led to an invasion of Roman Mesopotamia and Syria as the first step towards the recovery of the western territories of Darius.

Alexander Severus, the grandson of the great Severus' sister-in-law, was murdered by his troops at Mainz in 235, after failing to chastise the Alamanns. His successor, Maximinus, had been a Danubian peasant. He was the first of the 'Illyrian' emperors, men of obscure origins but undoubted military genius who doggedly fought invaders and each other to restore a measure of stability—but at a fearful cost. During the period 235–84 there were almost 20 emperors who could claim to control the capital Rome, not to mention nominal colleagues and countless usurpers; but except for Decius, who fell in battle against the Goths (251), Valerian, who died in Persian hands (after 259/60), Claudius, who died of plague (270), and Carus, who was struck by a thunderbolt perhaps of legionary manufacture (283), they were all killed by their own soldiers, or someone else's. Much the longest reign was that of Gallienus (254–68), a man of some culture (he found time to patronise a philosopher who was planning an utopian city on the Bay of Naples). During these 14 years the Alamanns conquered the territory between Rhine and Danube, and the Goths Dacia; the Western provinces proclaimed their own 'Gallic' emperor; in the East, the Persians took the capital Antioch, and were only driven out by the initiative of a Roman protectorate, the caravan city of Palmyra. Gallienus controlled little more than Italy and its northern approaches, the Danubian provinces (intermittently), and Africa, but his ill-documented 'reforms' forged the weapons used by his successors in a rapid military recovery. A medieval source credits him with being the first to form cavalry units, 'the Roman army having been previously largely infantry'. This is an exaggeration: independent cavalry forces had contributed to Severus' victories in civil war. But we now hear of a cavalry army under a single commander; and gold coins were struck at Milan to honour, and no doubt repay, the 'Loyalty of the Cavalry'. These *equites* included 'Dalmatians' and 'Moors'. It can be no coincidence that units of 'Illyrian' *Equites Dalmatae* and *Equites Mauri* are systematically distributed among the 4th-century frontier armies on the Danube and further east, together with 'Illyrian' *Equites Promoti* and *Equites Scutarii*. They must derive from an 'Illyrian' cavalry army recruited from Dalmatians, Moors, *promoti* (detached legionary cavalry) and *scutarii* (apparently a reference to their use of the *scutum* shield), which was subsequently dispersed. A similar distribution is also found among units of mounted archers and *Equites Stablesiani* (perhaps the mounted legionaries posted to provincial governors' bodyguards). The infantry of the new mobile army consisted of the traditional detachments (*vexillationes*) from frontier legions, which are attested by inscriptions of Gallienus in north-west Macedonia (Second *Parthica* and Third *Augusta*) and at strategic points in Pannonia, Sirmium (the German and British legions 'with their *auxilia*') and Poetovio (the two from Dacia Ripensis, and probably the four Pannonian ones as well). The virtual independence of these detachments from their parent legions is revealed by 'silver' coins struck by Gallienus in 259/60 which honour the Praetorian Guard, the Second *Parthica*, and legions on the Rhine and Danube with the civil-war title 'Dutiful and Loyal' (*pia fidelis*). These coins, however, are not found on the frontiers—which Gallienus did not then control—but in northern Italy and its north-western approaches: they were surely paid to legionary detachments which remained loyal after their parent units proclaimed usurpers.

'Senatorial' sources are hostile to Gallienus, probably because from c. 260 he ceased to appoint the traditional legionary legates; instead, all legions are now commanded by equestrian prefects like those of Severus' three *Parthica* legions, but technically 'acting legates'. Certain senior officers, notably Praetorian tribunes and legionary prefects, but even a centurion in one of the legionary detachments, now gain the title '*protector* of the Emperor'. The title *protector* is found earlier (of legionary bodyguards), but would now develop into an important institution of the late-Roman army.

This mark of distinction for the officer corps did not save Gallienus from a conspiracy among them, which involved his successors Claudius (268–70) and Aurelian (270–75). They and their fellow 'Illyrian' Probus (276–82) restored the empire's unity by crushing defeats of the Goths and the German invaders of Gaul; Palmyra was captured, and the 'Gallic' empire terminated. In the East, Roman prestige was restored by Carus' capture of the Persian capital of Ctesiphon (283). But Aurelian, after defeating a German invasion of Italy, began to build the walls which still surround Rome—an admission that even the heart of the empire was no longer secure from sudden attack.

Political stability was restored by Diocletian (284–305), an administrative genius who turned 50 years and more of improvisation into a system. As his colleagues he chose fellow 'Illyrians' who were better generals than himself, Maximian (286–305), Constantius (293–306) and Galerius (293–311), who between them suppressed revolts and restored the traditional frontiers. The territory beyond the Rhine and Danube conquered by the Alamanns and Goths had been written off, but Diocletian was even able to make a small advance in Mesopotamia after Galerius defeated the Persian king. A hostile source accuses Diocletian of 'quadrupling' the army (an allusion to his three colleagues): the truth is that most of the 33 Severan legions survived, a total doubled by Diocletian. Most of them were posted, in the traditional pairs, to the frontier armies; with them went 'detachments' of cavalry (the term *vexillatio* is now used) apparently drawn from the army of Gallienus and his successors. These detachments and the legions were superior to the old *alae* and cohorts, in armies which increasingly

came under the command of professional soldiers, *duces*, rather than old-style provincial governors. (This tendency was complete in the reign of Constantine, who made virtually all careers exclusively military or civil.) Two new legions, however, the *Ioviani* and the *Herculiani*, named after the patron gods of Diocletian and Maximian, were not committed to frontier defence. Originally Danubian legionaries armed with the characteristic late-Roman weighted dart (*martiobarbulus*), they were attached to the *comitatus*, the imperial court which 'accompanied' the emperor. To them should be added other élite 4th-century legions, the *Solenses* and *Martenses* (named after the patron gods of Constantius and Galerius), and the *Lanciarii*, apparently picked praetorians and legionaries armed with the *lancea*. The most senior of the 4th-century cavalry units seem also to have been

Below
Late-Roman mobile armies and frontier sectors, c. 395, according to the *Notitia Dignitatum*, an illustrated manuscript of the same period whose internal chronology and purpose are still matters for dispute.

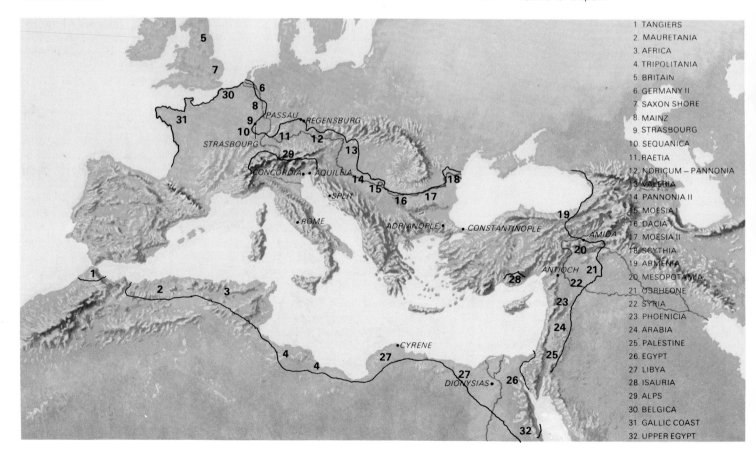

1. TANGIERS
2. MAURETANIA
3. AFRICA
4. TRIPOLITANIA
5. BRITAIN
6. GERMANY II
7. SAXON SHORE
8. MAINZ
9. STRASBOURG
10. SEQUANICA
11. RAETIA
12. NORICUM – PANNONIA
13. VALERIA
14. PANNONIA II
15. MOESIA I
16. DACIA
17. MOESIA II
18. SCYTHIA
19. ARMENIA
20. MESOPOTAMIA
21. OSRHEONE
22. SYRIA
23. PHOENICIA
24. ARABIA
25. PALESTINE
26. EGYPT
27. LIBYA
28. ISAURIA
29. ALPS
30. BELGICA
31. GALLIC COAST
32. UPPER EGYPT

aised by Diocletian and attached to the *comitatus*: these are the earliest *scholae* (mounted Guards) and the crack *Equites Promoti* and *Equites Comites*. The permanent field forces of Diocletian and his colleagues, however, were small by later standards; but they could be supplemented as required from the now-reinforced frontier armies. Thus an Egyptian papyrus of 295 records the issue of fodder not only to the *Comites*, but also to as many as ten pairs of legionary detachments, probably including the pair from Dacia Ripensis (XIII *Gemina* and V *Macedonica*). These two 'legions' are also found as the garrison of Diocletian's new Egyptian province of Herculea, and were presumably posted there by him. The implication is that Diocletian, unlike Gallienus perhaps, did not regard legionary detachments as permanent, and returned them to frontier duties when convenient.

The logistics of the army were part of reforms which lasted throughout the late-Roman period. During the 3rd century, the currency (and the related system of taxation) had collapsed; the army requisitioned labour and supplies as needed, at a 'fair' price or none at all. Diocletian regularised the system by levying the foodstuffs, raw materials and manufactured goods (clothing for example) required by the army in the form of taxation, based upon a survey of the empire's resources. The Praetorian prefect could then reckon what was needed for the coming year, and calculate what each taxable unit ought to pay; orders could then be given through the provincial governors to locally elected officials, who collected the taxation in kind and transported it to where it was wanted. The system generated a huge bureaucracy (which also had to be fed and maintained), but it worked. The army was now paid in rations, supplemented by cash payments for salary and donatives on imperial occasions like Diocletian's birthday (22 December). There is a vivid glimpse of the system in two fragments from the files of an Egyptian assistant governor at Panopolis. The first consists of copies of letters sent out by him in September 298, many of them relating to preparations for 'the auspiciously impending visit of Our Lord the Emperor Diocletian', but others

authorising the issue of military rations. Thus officials are ordered to pay a garrison, which can be identified as the *ala I Hiberorum*, two months' rations of barley and wheat: the totals are given, and suggest that the *ala* numbered only 116 men and their horses. The second fragment consists of letters received from the *procurator* of the Lower Thebaid, many of them authorising cash payments to military units in early 300: thus on 30 January the *procurator* wrote to the *strategus* (who received his letter on 9 February), ordering him to pay the *ala I Hiberorum* 73,500 *denarii* (pay) and 23,600 *denarii* (in lieu of rations) due on 1 January for the last four months of 299. The mills ground slow, but exceeding fine: the *strategus* even acknowledges a requisition for hides to repair a cavalry fort's gates, and informs the bearer that it has been 'nibbled by mice and mutilated'.

Diocletian had dominated his colleagues. When he abdicated in 305, and retired to a fortress palace on the Dalmatian coast, a series of civil wars followed, from which Constantine (306–37), the son of Constantius, emerged in 324 as sole emperor. A lightning campaign (312) eliminated Maxentius, the son of Maximian, who had held Italy even against Galerius. Constantine, who had used only a fraction of his available forces, gave the credit to the Christian God. More prosaically, he monopolised a new infantry unit, the *auxilium*, which was to provide the shock troops of the late-Roman army. The first *auxilia* were probably raised by Constantius or Maximian: they were the *Cornuti*, the 'horned men' who are apparently depicted on the Arch of Constantine, and the 'armlet-wearers', the *Bracchiati*. Later we find them, and another crack *auxilium* pair, the *Iovii* and *Victores*, raising a German war cry before they charge. There is good reason to suppose that the formidable *auxilia* were raised and recruited from Rhine-Germans, whether volunteers or prisoners of war, or the young men of *laeti* settlements of submissive Germans established by Diocletian and his colleagues on derelict land in Gaul.

Constantine also raised new legions, but a more important source of new 'mobile' units were the existing frontier legions and the garrisons of other

strategic points. Legionary detachments were withdrawn for good: some of them kept their old name, like the *Quinta Macedonica*, the longest-lived of all legions (it was part of Justinian's army in the 6th century); others took numerical names, like *Primani* or *Undecimani*, or names from a previous station, like the *Divitenses*, which had been a detachment of Second *Italica* stationed at the Cologne bridgehead of Divitia. 'Paired' with the *Divitenses* are the *Tungrecani*, which had presumably been the garrison of Tongres (Tungri). The old Praetorian Guard was disbanded, no doubt because it had fought for Maxentius, but also because it was now obsolete: there was a new mobile army. The role of imperial guards was now filled by the *scholae*, crack cavalry units 500-strong (at least in the 6th century), of which there were a dozen by the end of the 4th century. They were followed by cavalry *vexillationes* like the élite *Comites* and *Promoti*, units drawn from the same sources as the *auxilia* (*Equites Cornuti* etc.), and many units with titles also found in the frontier armies (*Dalmatae*, *Stablesiani* etc.) which recall the cavalry army of Gallienus. Some of the latter belong to numbered sequences, like the well-paid trooper of *VI Stablesiani* who disappeared with his splendid helmet into a swamp in c. 320, or have titles which recall a time in garrison (*Equites Dalmatae Passerentiaci*). The most likely explanation is that these are frontier units drawn from Gallienus' cavalry army, which were withdrawn once more by Constantine to swell his mobile army.

A hostile critic of Constantine accuses him of reversing the strategy of Diocletian, which had made the frontiers impregnable: most of the army was withdrawn from the frontiers and posted in cities which did not need a garrison, a burden for the cities concerned, and demoralising for the troops. This criticism misrepresents the new strategy, which was also essentially that of Constantine's successors. It was impossible to hold the frontier line against all attack, since external enemies retained the initiative and could always concentrate superior forces locally. Instead, the screen of garrisons in the frontier zone would—in theory at least—check minor incursions, and hinder major invasions by holding fortified towns and supply-bases, and strongpoints of all kinds along the lines of communication. This would protect the civil population, deny food to the enemy, and gain time to concentrate mobile forces for counter-attack. The invaders would either be forced to disperse over the countryside to forage, where they could be hunted down piecemeal by small mobile detachments; or if they massed together, they could be brought to battle, when the Roman mobile army, better armed and disciplined and regularly provisioned, had a good chance of winning against numerical odds. Once defeated in the field, invaders could be pursued into their homeland, and reprisals would follow until they made peace. For the emperor himself, this strategy had an important side-effect: he could retain personal control of the empire's best troops and insure himself against usurpers. The drawbacks were the danger that inactive troops, whether on the frontiers or in reserve, would deteriorate; and the slowness of communications. No army, however 'mobile', could move faster than its infantry could march (approximately 15–20 miles a day). Inevitably, mobile armies multiplied during the 4th century: this shortened the empire's reaction time, but divided its strength and increased the risk of an usurpation.

Constantine was succeeded by his sons, Constantine II (337–40) in the West, Constans (337–50) in Italy, and Constantius II (337–61) in the East. Constans soon eliminated Constantine II, only to succumb to one of his own generals, the commanding officer of the *Ioviani* and *Herculiani*, whom Constantius defeated after a very bloody civil war. Thousands of *comitatenses* were killed, and the Franks and Alamanns seized the chance to invade Gaul *en masse*. Constantius II, a conscientious but ungifted general with an unfortunate reputation for winning civil wars and losing foreign ones, appointed his cousin Julian as his junior colleague in Gaul (355) while he pursued the Persian war he had inherited from his father. Julian, a would-be philosopher whose studies made him reject his family's Christian beliefs, turned out to be an inspiring general: after defeating an Alamann army near Strasbourg

(357), he successfully invaded its home territory, before rebelling against his cousin (360). When Constantius died of natural causes, Julian found himself sole emperor (361–3). Instead of solving outstanding problems on the Rhine and Danube, Julian decided to teach the Persians a lesson by attacking Ctesiphon: the expedition was a disaster, and Julian lost his life in a skirmish during the retreat. The new emperor, Jovian, extricated the army by making concessions to Persia, but died a few months later. The army replaced him with a dour frontier emperor in the tradition of the 3rd-century 'Illyrians', Valentinian I (364–75), who co-opted his younger brother Valens (364–78) as Eastern emperor. While Valens made a demonstration against the Visigoths on the lower Danube and checked Persian intervention in Armenia, Valentinian and his generals campaigned in Britain and on the Rhine and middle Danube. Valentinian's abrupt death—he died of apoplexy brought on by berating a barbarian delegation—allowed Valens to bungle the greatest military crisis of the century. In 376 the Huns drove a stream of refugees towards the lower Danube, among them Ostrogoths from the Ukraine and Visigoths. Valens gave the Visigoths refuge, and in the confusion the Ostrogoths crossed as well. Roman maltreatment soon made the Goths rebel. After limited offensives had failed to contain them, Valens decided to mobilise his full force and assume active command. The ensuing disaster, the battle of Adrianople (9 August 378), crippled the mobile army and halted the military recovery we have been studying.

Sources, 4th century AD

Our knowledge of the army of Constantine and his successors depends on two sources, the surviving books (they cover 353–78) of the *History* of Ammianus Marcellinus, and the enigma which calls itself the *Notitia Dignitatum*. Ammianus was a Greek-speaking officer in the army during the decade 353–63, in which he saw active service from the Rhine to the Tigris. In retirement at Rome in the 390's, he began to publish a detailed history in florid 'Ciceronian' Latin, on a scale unequalled by any Roman writer since Tacitus. He is more fair-minded than Tacitus—or perhaps less skilful at

concealing his prejudices—and a military historian of more experience. Unfortunately he saw himself as a 'classical' historian, which is why his battle scenes are full of blood and clouds of missiles in the style of Livy, and why he avoids contemporary terminology: he uses 'legions' and 'cohorts' of late-Roman *auxilia* and (cavalry) *vexillationes*, for example, and *turmae* indifferently of cavalry and infantry. The *Notitia* is a 'list of high offices', an illustrated manuscript of c. 395 which survives in several (indirect) copies, whose internal chronology and purpose are still matters for dispute. It is arranged by chapters, each one devoted to a major official, with a schematic picture of his responsibilities: thus the Master of the Offices, who was responsible for the *scholae* and the arms factories, is represented by spears, shields, helmets, mail coats and other armour. Within these chapters the *Notitia* lists offices in both halves of the empire, including the commanders-in-chief of the mobile armies with lists of their regiments (arranged more or less by seniority and type of unit), and the frontier generals with lists of their regiments (and where they are stationed). Both Eastern and Western chapters contain a great deal that is earlier than 395 (when the empire was divided in this way), but only the Western lists have been 'updated' thereafter, during the supremacy (395–408) of the generalissimo Stilicho, and even later. The Western chapters include an unique feature, a breakdown by army of all mobile units. These points suggest that our copy of the *Notitia* might have come from the files of the Western commander-in-chief: his staff issued officers with their commissions, for which they received a fee, and would have needed a list of appointments. The final draft survives of a petition to the emperor by Abinnaeus, the newly-appointed prefect of an *ala* in the Egyptian Fayum. He complains to Constantius II (337–61) that, although he had been appointed by the emperor himself, when he presented the 'sacred letter' to his immediate superior, he was told that other men had already presented similar letters of appointment to the same command. They had been obtained illicitly from the central bureaucracy. Abinnaeus was confirmed in his appointment (c. 342), ortunately for us, since he kept the etters he subsequently received. The rown of his career, only achieved after 6 years' service, occupies one line in he Eastern *Notitia: Or.* 28.34, *Ala Quinta Praelectorum, Dionisiada*.

The 'official' view is supplemented by coins, a few building-inscriptions, and above all by the Theodosian Code, a great compilation of extracts from imperial legislation (Constantine to Theodosius II) arranged chronologically by topics in 16 books. Book VII is devoted o legislation affecting the army, and is a treasury of minute regulations and good intentions. A single chapter, for example, contains 17 extracts relating to deserters and those who harbour them'. Ammianus is supplemented by a number of inferior historians, including his contemporary Eunapius' Greek account of the 4th century, which partly survives at second-hand. Panegyrics, a favourite late-Roman literary genre, are sometimes helpful: thus Libanius' obituary of the emperor Julian (355–63) uses eye-witness accounts of his last campaign, and Stilicho's publicist, the poet Claudian, succeeds in versifying the names of seven mobile regiments which suppressed a revolt in 398. Important details turn up in unlikely places: a complete list of non-commissioned ranks in a cavalry *vexillatio* is given by Saint Jerome in his invective against the Bishop of Jerusalem.

The late-Roman army, AD 337-78

Constantine, as we have seen, divided the army into mobile forces (*comitatenses*) and frontier troops (*limitanei*). The latter, with the help of inferior troops in the ubiquitous small strongpoints (*burgi*), garrisoned forts and fortified towns in the frontier zones. With a few exceptions, they consisted of new-style units of *equites* (sometimes reduced to *cunei* on the Danube) and *auxilia*, or old-style legions, *alae* and cohorts. Archaeologically there is growing evidence that late Roman forts, or at least their garrisons, were often smaller than their counterparts of the early empire. The Diocletianic *ala* which apparently numbered 116 (or 118) men has already been mentioned; the same source suggests that there were 77 troopers in a legion's *Equites Promoti*, 121 in an unit of *Equites Sagittarii*, 164 men in the *Cohors XI*

Chamavorum, and about 1,000 in each of two legions. These 4th-century *limitanei* were grouped into armies covering one or more provinces, under the command of a duke (*dux*), except in most of Africa, where the 'frontier' (mountain massifs or semi-desert tracts) was divided into sectors under *praepositi limitis* supervised by a count (*comes*) with a powerful mobile army. The lists which survive in the *Notitia* are full of chronological problems: thus the garrison of Hadrian's Wall seems to have survived virtually intact from the early 3rd century, whereas the garrisons of the Mainz sector cannot be earlier than *c.* 368.

The letters saved by Abinnaeus contain vivid glimpses of the duties of an officer of *limitanei* in the 340's, not that we can assume the 'internal security' problems of the Fayum were typical of the empire as a whole. 'Your valiance, my lord *praepositus*, is wont to restrain the robberies and usurpations committed in the localities by the more influential men', writes a petitioner. (Abinnaeus, a soldier of some 40 years' experience, was also a man of property with house rents in Alexandria and farm stock of his own, and is clearly one of the ubiquitous 'patrons' of late-Roman society.) He receives appeals from the victims of burglaries, from people who have had sheep or pigs stolen. One of his own men is alleged to have been drunken and violent; another to have led a gang which stole the wool off 11 sheep's backs and drove off six pigs. A clergyman intercedes for a soldier of the same name who has deserted: Abinnaeus should exercise his Christian duty of forgiveness. Another clergyman asks for a loan of the nets kept at headquarters, to catch gazelles which have been eating the crops. Official letters require Abinnaeus to provide escorts for tax collectors, to look after two craftsmen cutting timber for a cavalry *vexillatio*, to help control the illicit traffic in soda. These intriguing documents should not be used, however, to support the old-fashioned idea of the 4th-century *limitanei* as an hereditary 'peasant militia'. Gallic garrisons, it is true, collapsed during the early 350's, but the frontier legions trapped in Amida on the Tigris in 359 fought with skill and determination against the Persians. *Limitanei* from the neighbouring province of Osrhoene took part in

Above
Tombstone of M. Aurelius Lucianus. Note the double-weighted *pilum* and the broad baldric.
Below Tombstone of an unknown soldier from Istanbul. c. AD 214.

253

the Persian expedition (363), and shortly afterwards units made redundant by Jovian's surrender of territory to Persia were added to the mobile army of the East under the cumbersome title of *legiones pseudocomitatenses*. As late as the 5th century, some 30 garrison units from Gaul, most of them survivors of the collapse of the Rhine frontier in 406/7, also gained this title, but this must have been by now a desperate expedient.

Comitatenses, though they might well have families, did not have fixed stations like the *limitanei*. Unless they were on campaign, they were billeted in towns, where they were entitled to one-third of the available accommodation—a system that caused friction with their civilian 'hosts'. Constantine created two commanders-in-chief, the Master of Cavalry (*magister equitum*) and Master of Infantry (*magister peditum*), who absorbed the Praetorian prefect's military functions, although the prefect remained responsible for provision and supply. In practice it was not possible to keep all mobile troops at the emperor's immediate disposal: we soon find 'regional' armies, the most important being those of Gaul, Illyricum (the Danubian provinces), and the East (based on Antioch), commanded by a Master of Cavalry in the absence of the emperor. Smaller mobile forces were detached as required, usually under the command of a count (*comes*), like the four units sent to Britain in the emergency of 367. Africa acquired a mobile army of its own, and by the time of the *Notitia* there were others in Britain, Spain and Thrace. Theodosius I (379–95) grouped the Eastern forces into five armies, two of them at his immediate disposal, all of them commanded by a Master of Soldiers (*magister militum*). His purpose may have been political, to avoid having a single commander-in-chief, of the sort that developed in the West, where Stilicho (as Master of Infantry) made himself the master of the whole military hierarchy. The various mobile armies in the time of the *Notitia*, that is, c. 395 in the East, and 395–408 in the West, are tabulated on the chart.

In the Eastern armies, cavalry precedes infantry; in the West they are listed separately. The title 'palatine', applied to all new-style mobile *auxilia* and some legions and *vexillationes*, seems to be an honorific rather than of strategic significance. Since the lists contain many units of recent date, it is possible to estimate earlier army strengths, although unit strengths need not have been constant. Ignoring *pseudocomitatenses* and African units, Valentinian I may have found about 150 units at his accession (364). Some check is possible on the *Notitia* lists. Many units are otherwise known; and we happen to know that Stilicho mustered at least 30 units in north Italy in 405. His apparent weakness in cavalry, however, and its absence from the upper Danube, is puzzling: he may have mobilised units of *equites* from the frontier armies, as seems to have been done earlier, when required. The powerful Spanish army is also puzzling: we hear nothing of it when there was fighting here in 407 and later. Worst of all, we know little about unit strengths. The only certain figure is that a 6th-century *schola* numbered 500 men. But two Danubian cavalry units in Mesopotamia in 359 totalled only 700 men; and a mobile cavalry unit of 'Unnigardae' in Libya in the early 5th century numbered only 40. These figures should be compared with the Diocletianic ones from Egypt: *Equites Promoti* of about 80, *Equites Sagittarii* and an *ala* of about 120. Infantry units were evidently larger. The same source suggests 1,000 for a provincial legion, 500 for a detachment. At Amida in 359, Ammianus (who was there) estimates the besieged as 20,000 in number, including seven legions. The old legions, already weakened in the course of the 3rd century, by the time of the *Notitia* have been broken up into numerous detachments: Third *Italica*, for example garrisons four forts as well as its old base at Regensburg, in addition to providing a 'legion' for the nearest mobile army. Ammianus twice mentions detachments of 300 men from (unspecified) mobile units, once 500 from 'legions'. The emperor Honorius (395-423) is said to have withdrawn five units from Dalmatia which totalled 6,000 men; six units of infantry, however, sent to his aid from the Eastern empire shortly afterwards, totalled only 4,000. The impression one receives is that mobile infantry units may have been between 500 and 1,000 men strong, and cavalry units well below 500, with the exception perhaps of the *scholae*. This impression is reinforced by Julian's self-congratulation at taking 1,000 German prisoners 'in two battles and a siege'; in the siege 600 Franks were painstakingly starved out of their refuge in two derelict forts, and sent to Constantius for service in the Eastern army. Elite units were small and precious. Julian's army at Strasbourg (357) numbered only 13,000 men; in 363, with the whole empire to draw upon, and no other commitments, his two armies for the invasion of Persia totalled only 65,000. These figures for first-rate troops are of course only a fraction of the empire's paper strength.

Below
Unit strengths of the late-Roman armies c. 395, according to the *Notitia Dignitatum*, which contains a breakdown of all the mobile units in the West. Possibly our copy is from the files of the Western C-in-C.

ARMY	CAVALRY vexillationes	INFANTRY legiones	auxilia	leg.pseudocomit.
(I) Eastern Armies				
Court (I)	12	6	18	
Court (II)	12 + 7 scholae	6	17	1
The East	10	9	2	10
Thrace	7	21		
Lower Danube	2	7	8	9
	50	49	45	20
(II) Western Armies				
Italy	7 + 5 scholae	13	21	2
Gaul	12	5	19	27
Upper Danube		6	12	6
Africa	20	11	1	
Tangiers	3	2	2	
Spain		5	11	
Britain	5	2	1	
	52	44	67	35

We have a 6th-century figure for the army of Diocletian's reign (date unspecified) of 389,704. The 4th-century maximum is likely to have been in the region of another 6th-century estimate for 'the old empire', 645,000.

Sons had followed their fathers into the army since the early empire: Diocletian made hereditary military service obligatory, and in addition levied recruits from landowners as a kind of tax. The difficulty of finding recruits made Valentinian reduce the height qualification from 5'10" (Roman) to 5'7"; he found his own soldiers were harbouring men liable to military service under the guise of 'relatives' or 'servants'. Among Abinnaeus' correspondence is a clergyman's plea for his brother-in-law, the son of a soldier now deceased and the sole support of his widowed mother, who has been called up. Release him, or, failing that, 'please safeguard him from going abroad with the draft for the *comitatus*, and may God reward you for your charity'. The army also recruited non-Romans, mostly Germans. Some of them were prisoners of war like Julian's 600 Franks, but many were volunteers attracted by a much higher standard of living. Some of them rose to high rank, to the command of regiments and armies: one of Valens' generals was an Alamann king who had been kidnapped at a dinner party by order of Julian; the great Stilicho himself was the son of a Vandal cavalry officer. Frankish officers at the court of Constantius II in 355 protested that they were 'men devoted to the empire', and it is strange but true that we almost never hear of treachery by German-born soldiers. This changed after Adrianople (378), when a desperate shortage of trained soldiers forced the Roman government to enlist barbarian contingents (*federati*) under their own chieftains. These did not have the same feeling of 'belonging', and after 395 became increasingly conscious of their political and military power, which they used to extort food and land from their reluctant hosts.

Late-Roman soldiers did not have to pay for their arms and equipment and uniforms, which were issued to them. They were also issued with rations which increased as they rose in rank. It was suggested to Valentinian and Valens

that it might be worth retiring men who had achieved quintuple rations, to save expense and encourage recruitment. This payment in kind was supplemented by the regular salary (*stipendium*) paid in the bronze small change minted in vast quantities during the 4th century, and by donatives paid by the emperor on accession and five-year anniversaries. The accession donative became standardised in 360 as a pound of silver and five *solidi* (the late-Roman gold coin five-sixths the weight of the old *aureus*), and five *solidi* thereafter. Imperial gifts to officers were also manufactured: inscribed silver plate, gold and silver 'medallions', gold and silver belt-fittings and brooches as marks of rank—and special silver coins probably for *comitatenses*.

Saint Jerome uses all the non-commissioned ranks as a metaphor of the distance between a demon and an angel: recruit, trooper (*eques*), *circitor*, *biarchus*, *centenarius*, *ducenarius*, *senator*, *primicerius*, commanding officer (*tribunus*). The recruit rose slowly, by seniority within the unit. A late-Roman cemetery at Concordia in north-east Italy contained the stone coffins of about 30 mobile army non-commissioned officers and privates: they include a *biarchus* of 20 years' service, a *centenarius* (22), two *ducenarii* (20, 23), two *senatores* aged 40 and 60, and the drill instructor (*campidoctor*) of the *Batavi seniores*, who died after 35 years' service at the age of 60. Abinnaeus was a *ducenarius* of 33 years' service in a cavalry *vexillatio* before a special mission took him to court, where he 'adored the sacred purple'. By kissing the hem of Constantius' garment, he automatically became a *protector domesticus*: the *protectores* from the reign of Diocletian became a kind of staff college in which senior NCOs prepared for regimental commands. After three years Abinnaeus became the prefect of an *ala*—when he found that his competitors had used influence to take a short-cut. Thus the senior member (*primicerius*) of the *protectores* in 363 was the future emperor Jovian, at the age of 32—it can be no coincidence that his father had just retired as their commanding officer, the *Comes Domesticorum*. Ammianus himself, who was a *protector* in his early 20s, must have had connections. The same

is true of higher commands. Flavius Memorius, the *comes* of the Tangiers army, had served 28 years in the *Ioviani* before he became a *protector*. The future emperor Valentinian, however, was already commanding a cavalry *vexillatio* at the age of 36, and the future emperor Theodosius was a *dux* at the age of about 28. Both were the sons of generals: Valentinian's father Gratian, like Memorius, is one of the few privates to achieve the rank of *comes*.

Officers could make their fortune (Gratian, a peasant when he enlisted, became a landowner), but most recruits, if they survived 20–25 years' service, would retire with a modest competence as veterans. Veterans were encouraged to cultivate derelict land, for which they received a small grant. They also received some tax concessions, including a limited exemption from the five-yearly tax on commerce which was used to pay the donatives of their old comrades-in-arms. A number of letters received by Abinnaeus show veterans to be men of substance: there are two requests, one from a 'landowner', that he arrest local officials to make them produce persons guilty of housebreaking; a veteran's daughter, another 'landowner', requests action against a debtor who has beaten her up with the help of the village policeman when she demanded the money he owed her; a veteran promises to reimburse Abinnaeus for any money he may have to spend at court to secure the promotion of his son within the local *ala*.

The army in action

The army was the ultimate, though not the only, source of political power and public security. This was symbolised in the accession ceremonies described by Ammianus. Valentinian, who had been chosen in conclave by senior officers and civil servants, was presented to the army on parade: he was acclaimed *Augustus*, clothed in purple and crowned with a diadem, before making a speech and leaving for the palace, 'hedged in by eagles and standards, already an object of fear'. There is a splendid picture of Constantius II making a state entry into Rome. He rode by himself in a golden carriage glittering with jewels, with purple silk dragon standards hissing in the breeze overhead. Armoured infantry and *clibanarii*, cavalry that looked like moving statues, marched either side. Amidst a storm of applause Constantius gazed fixedly in front of him, moving his head only to bow as the carriage passed under an arch. The emperor in his full robes or battledress, flanked by his guards, is a favourite motif in late-Roman art, on silver dishes, reliefs and mosaics and illuminated books. More than 80 years before Constantius' entry into Rome, Aurelian overawed a German delegation by receiving it on a platform with his army drawn up in a crescent on either side; his generals were on their horses, and behind were the imperial standards, 'gold eagles, pictures of the emperor, the names of regiments picked out in gold letters, all of them on silver-plated lances'.

Intelligent emperors advertised their closeness to their men. Julian ate porridge 'even a common soldier would have despised'. Stories were told of both Constantius II and Theodosius begging a crust of bread in a moment of crisis; Valentinian, leading a flying column somewhere near modern Frankfurt, slept in the open under a blanket. The latter's son Gratian (375–83) lost touch with his army by a passion for hunting, and favouritism for a particular regiment of Alans: his army abandoned him for Maximus, the commander of the army in Britain, whose first coins (struck at London to pay his first supporters) pointedly imitated the coin portrait of Valentinian. The survival of the sons of Theodosius, Arcadius (395–408) and Honorius (395–423), is all the more surprising, therefore, since they reigned as figureheads without military ability or interest; a critic compares Arcadius in the eunuch-haunted depths of his palace to a deep-sea mollusc.

On campaign, the 4th-century army tried to live up to the standards of the early empire. Ammianus makes rhetorical complaints about its indiscipline—Valentinian's flying column gave the game away by looting and raising fires—but on the whole this is belied by his narrative. The *comitatenses*, given good leadership, would fight tenaciously and usually with success against odds. What we hear of the maintenance of discipline may not be typical. The antiquarian-minded Julian distributed crowns and wreaths (*corona navalis*, *civica*, *castrensis*) after a victory at the

the gates of Ctesiphon; he also 'decimated' a cavalry unit, a punishment he may have misunderstood, since he selected ten victims, not a tenth. Valentinian revived another ancient punishment, according to an unreliable source, by making the *Batavi* encamp outside. His general Theodosius (the father of the emperor) treated African units very harshly for political disloyalty; cavalry officers had their hands lopped off, the survivors of a legion were clubbed to death 'in the ancient fashion', deserters were burnt alive or lost their hands. Ammianus, who normally condemns 'inclemency' when he finds it, seems embarrassed at having to defend this 'salutary vigour', and quotes a criticism of these 'savage innovations'. Late-Roman legislation is full of such threats; but as a rule, trained *comitatenses* were too valuable to be treated with indiscriminate brutality. They still entrenched themselves in marching camps with palisades and built permanent forts in stone. They were expected to carry 20 days' rations. They bridged the Rhine, Danube and Euphrates by pontoon bridges, and handled small boats skilfully enough to make a night-landing in Alamannia or to hunt down Sarmatians in the marshes at the Danube-Theiss confluence. Julian mustered 500 men 'who from early childhood were taught in their native lands to cross the greatest of all rivers', like the Batavians of the early empire; after they had secured a bridgehead across the Tigris, the rest of the army followed on rafts, or used the local method of inflated skins.

If the 4th-century *comitatenses* were at least comparable with the auxiliaries of the early empire, why then was the Persian expedition (363) such a failure? After convincing the Persians that he was coming down the Tigris, Julian led his army down the Euphrates in good order, with a cavalry screen in front and on his open flank. A river fleet of more than a thousand boats accompanied him, carrying provisions and the siege train which enabled him to reduce a series of fortified towns on the way. Despite delays due to flooding, the army reached Ctesiphon intact. The main Persian forces were still somewhere up the Tigris. Yet Julian decided not to assault Ctesiphon as Carus had done, even though he had brought a siege train for

Above
Tombstone of Aurelius Sudecentius of legion XI *Claudia*. From Aquileia. **Below** The tombstone of Lepontius from Strasbourg. Behind him appears to be a standard surmounted by a cockerel.

the purpose. Instead he burnt his boats (literally), and tried to penetrate further east. These decisions were so extraordinary that legends were soon invented to explain them. It is true that it would have been hard for the fleet to negotiate the Tigris against the current, but its cargo proved indispensable, for the Persians now adopted scorched earth tactics, which is precisely the tactic adopted by Romans in northern Mesopotamia to deny fodder to invading Persian cavalry. Julian was forced to retreat up the Tigris, harassed by the main Persian army (which had now appeared), until a lance-thrust from an Arab irregular in the Persian service put an end to him. In the retreat the Roman infantry gained an ascendancy over the Persians, but it was starving. One cannot acquit Julian of strategic miscalculations and lack of anticipation. Did he remember the campaign against the Franks in 358, when his army ran out of biscuit—only to find it was too early in the year for them to be able to live off the country?

The poor performance of the cavalry is a marked feature of the Persian expedition. In the advance to Ctesiphon, Julian twice punished cavalry units which had broken when caught by surprise, the first by 'decimation', the second by reducing them to infantry, 'which is more laborious and lower in rank'. Shortly afterwards the infantry actually complained of the *Tertiaci*, which had given way as the infantry was penetrating the Persian line: they were made to march with the camp followers, and four other cavalry tribunes were cashiered. This is surprising, since the *Notitia* and other sources make it clear that cavalry was regarded as the senior service. In 355 the Alamanns attacking a marching camp drove back a sortie by the *Scutarii*, only to be decisively repulsed when it was reinforced by a second *schola* and the crack *Equites Comites* and *Promoti*. In 370 an ambush of a Saxon raiding band would have turned to disaster, if a unit of light-armoured cavalry (*cataphracti*) had not unexpectedly intervened. In 359, on the other hand, a Master of Cavalry and his staff (Ammianus included) nearly fell into Persian hands because the two Danubian cavalry units already mentioned had deserted their post; the

'cowards' let through a Persian army unobserved. In 357 Julian, with an army of 13,000 men, confronted an Alamann host of 35,000 near Strasbourg, but his men and their generals were confident of winning. The Roman cavalry was massed on the right wing, opposed by Alamann cavalry stiffened by light infantry, a tactic which Caesar had learned from their ancestors the Suebi. When the armies met, the tribune of the *cataphracti* was wounded, and the Roman cavalry fell back upon the infantry in confusion. (After the battle Julian is said to have humiliated the unit concerned by parading it in female clothing.) The Alamann infantry now made a series of charges, culminating in one by 'a fiery band of tribal nobility, kings included', which cut its way to the *Primani*. This legion, however, stood its ground like the infantry 'wall' later recommended by the writer Vegetius, and the Alamanns faltered and gave way. In their retreat to the Rhine they suffered severely.

Strasbourg was an infantry victory. The Alamanns were bigger, Ammianus comments, but the Romans were better disciplined. Late-Roman infantry was still steady but adaptable—whether mopping up Isaurian brigands on level ground, storming hilltops in Alamannia, or charging the Persian archers before they had time to shoot. The famous heavy-armoured cavalry (*clibanarii*), on the other hand, seems to have been ineffective and expensive—the *Notitia* lists four factories which manufactured their plate armour. *Clibanarii*—derived from a word for oven, referring to their appearance or what it felt like to wear one of their suits—were first used in Italy in 312 against Constantine; his army simply opened ranks when they charged, then surrounded them and knocked them to the ground with clubs. The unit was annihilated. Constantius II is said by several sources to have taken a personal interest in them: Libanius maliciously contrasts his eagerness to outdo the Persians in their own armoured cavalry with the failure of his counter-offensives. There is in fact no good evidence that *clibanarii* were effective against disciplined opposition; as parade-troops, however, they made a deep impression upon Ammianus and the poet Claudian. Without stirrups and

under-horsed, they are a feeble anticipation of medieval chivalry.

The battle of Adrianople has been seen as a victory of cavalry over infantry and a revolution in warfare. Unfortunately Ammianus' narrative ekes out some vital facts with masses of 'colour', and it is difficult to see what really happened. First Valens made the mistake of deciding to fight before his nephew Gratian arrived with the Western army. Faulty intelligence may have underestimated Gothic numbers—Valens is said to have been jealous of his nephew. As at Strasbourg, the Roman army made a long march in the heat of the day and arrived, hungry and thirsty, within sight of the Gothic wagon circle. There was a delay while the Goths renewed previous negotiations, if only to gain time for the return of their cavalry (Ostrogoths and Alans) which was out foraging. Meanwhile the Roman army advanced in column, its right wing almost engaged, the left wing still coming up as fast as it could. A truce was being negotiated, when some Roman cavalry (presumably on the right wing) made an insubordinate attack which collapsed. Fighting became general, and at this moment the Gothic cavalry arrived. Ammianus unfortunately does not say where its first blow fell, only that the Roman left wing had now reached the wagons, when 'it was deserted by the rest of the cavalry, overwhelmed by weight of numbers like a collapsing rampart, and thrown back, leaving the infantry exposed'. Thus outflanked, the Roman infantry was enveloped ('they looked round and saw no means of escape'), its line was broken in a bloody melée, and the survivors were pursued until darkness fell. Two-thirds of the army were killed. The losses were equalled only by Cannae, Ammianus comments. Here too the Roman cavalry had been driven from the field, and the legions enveloped and crushed. The prime cause of disaster at Adrianople would seem to have been the decision to assault a field fortification (which is what the wagon circle virtually was) while the enemy's powerful cavalry was uncommitted. This 'decision' was forced upon Valens by the undisciplined and incompetent cavalry on his right wing. The left wing, advancing hastily, was caught unprepared by a devastating charge on its flank or even from behind, leaving the infantry, already deployed in a crescent round the wagon circle and fighting hand-to-hand, trapped. We know from Libanius that there were post mortems after the disaster, and that cowardice or lack of training was held responsible. This would seem to be a fair comment—on the Roman cavalry which lost the battle.

The decline of the Roman army, AD 378–476

The trained infantry lost at Adrianople could not be replaced. The new emperor Theodosius I (379–95), whose descendants were figurehead emperors in East and West until the mid-5th century, allowed the Goths to settle in the Danubian provinces under their own chieftains. When Theodosius died, they were on the move again—westward, against an empire which was weakened by the civil wars that followed the deaths of Valentinian's sons Gratian (375–83) and Valentinian II (375–92). For a time Stilicho, one of Theodosius' generals and the guardian of his son Honorius the new Western emperor (395–423), kept them in check, but he was fatally discredited by the collapse of the Rhine frontier at the end of 406, when east German peoples, followed by the Alamanns and Franks, flooded across Gaul and Spain. The Visigoths invaded Italy; when their demands were ignored by Honorius, they sacked Rome (410). Effective power was in the hands of the Western commanders-in-chief, notably Constantius (411–21), Aetius (430–54) and Ricimer (456–72), who tried to keep Italy and footholds elsewhere by playing one barbarian people off against another, but the last real hope of recovery disappeared in 429, when the Vandals crossed the Straits of Gibraltar, to pursue an orgy of conquest across the last intact provinces of the Western empire. In 444 Valentinian III (425–55), the grandson of Theodosius, admitted economic and military bankruptcy: 'Neither for recruits nor for the veteran army can those supplies suffice that are delivered with the greatest difficulty by the exhausted taxpayers, and it seems that from that source the supplies that are necessary for food and clothing cannot be furnished. Unless the soldiers should be supported by trading, which is un-

worthy and shameful for an armed man, they can scarcely be vindicated from the peril of hunger or from the destruction of cold . . . (yet) if we require these expenses from the landowner, in addition to the expenses which he furnishes, such an exaction of taxes would extinguish his last tenuous resources'. When Valentinian was murdered in 455, the Vandals descended on Rome and sacked it again. The Eastern empire survived the crisis of the 5th century: it was economically stronger, and its territory except in Europe was virtually free of invasion. It even intervened from time to time in the West, but without lasting effect. The Western empire was bleeding to death as

it lost the territory which alone could support a regular army, and was forced to rely more and more upon barbarian *federati*. The last years were very confused. Not long before the now-barbarian army of Italy deposed the last Western emperor, Romulus 'Augustulus' (475–6), we catch a glimpse of the last *limitanei* on the upper Danube. The *Cohors IX Batavorum*, the garrison of Passau, sent some men back to Italy to draw back-pay for the unit. No more was heard of them, until their bodies came floating down the river. The unit disappeared. 'While the Roman empire still stood, soldiers were maintained with public pay in many towns for the

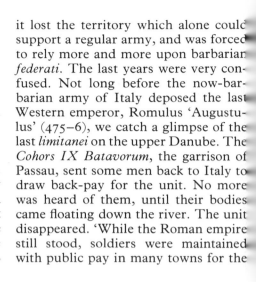

Left
One of the scale trappers found at Dura Europus, mid-3rd century AD. This is part of the armour of a cataphract or *clibanarius*. It is made of metal scales sewn onto a fabric and leather base. It fitted over the horse's back like a saddle blanket. The hole in the middle was for the saddle. **Below** A graffito of a *clibanarius* from Dura Europus. The rider was covered in plate armour. The cataphract wore scale.

Right
Cataphracts wearing long-sleeved scale coats shown in a wall painting from the synagogue at Dura Europus. The figure on the left wears a scale hood. Both carry hexagonal curved shields.

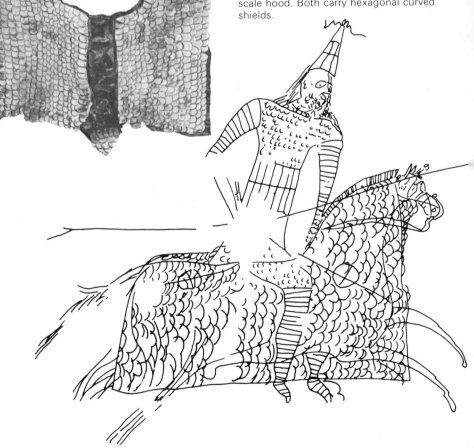

defence of the frontier, but when that custom lapsed the military units were abolished with the frontier'.

Equipment

From the time of Polybius to the reign of Septimius Severus it is possible to trace a continuous evolution of Roman military equipment. The Arch of Septimius Severus at Rome is the latest monument showing *lorica segmentata*, and it marks the end of an era in Roman military history. From the middle of the 2nd century the arms so long associated with the legionary begin to disappear. Piece by piece the old weapons and

armour were abandoned. The semi-cylindrical *scutum* began to be phased out during the 2nd century and by the middle of the 3rd it had disappeared altogether to be replaced by the oval auxiliary shield. At the same time as this change was taking place and almost certainly connected with it, the position of the sword scabbard was moved from the right to the left side.

Round shields appear on several of the monuments. These are sometimes associated with standard bearers, such as on the tombstone of Lepontius, and were the traditional shield of ensigns. Hexagonal shields are shown on the synagogue paintings from Dura Europos in Syria. These are exceptional and may be part of the equipment of the *cataphractus*. Five oval shields varying between 1.07 and 1.18 metres in length were found at Dura. These are generally flat but one is dished with a concavity of about 9cm in the centre. The *scutum* discovered at Dura (p. 231) is the latest example of this type and may have been intended for ceremonial purposes. All the shields discovered at this site have

Above
A bronze legionary helmet from Niedermörmter. Rheinisches Landesmuseum, Bonn. This late 2nd- or early 3rd-century helmet is the latest example of the Roman imperial helmets and is clearly derived from the 1st-century imperial Italic helmets. Russell Robinson classes this as imperial Italic H. Infantry helmets are not found again until the 4th century. These bear no relationship to the earlier types.

Left
One of the painted flat oval shields found at Dura Europus. Scale 1:14. These shields had a rawhide rim stitched on. The bronze shield boss which is from the same type of shield was found at Mainz. Städtisches Museum, Wiesbaden.

a rim reinforced with hide and not the customary bronze. This was stitched on in the manner of the Fayum shield.

From the 3rd century the use of body armour declined. This may have been a result of the slackening of discipline that accompanied the near anarchy of much of the century. The complaints of Vegetius that the soldiers of his day had become too soft to bear the weight of their armour may well have been equally true of the 3rd century.

Body armour seems to have become restricted to the heavy cavalry who continued to wear mail and scale shirts: long-sleeved knee-length examples can be seen on the wall paintings from the synagogue at Dura. Some of these are hooded and clearly represent the armour of the *cataphractus*. Similar hooded cuirasses are to be seen in a 5th-century copy of Vergil's *Aeneid*. Cataphracts in scale shirts are also shown on the Arch of Constantine at Rome, where they are the only soldiers with the exception of officers wearing body armour, and on the Arch of Galerius at Saloniki. Scale or mail shirts of knee length would have to be split at the front or sides in order to sit a horse. Cuirasses split up the front can be seen amongst the armour shown on the Master of the Offices illustration from the *Notitia Dignitatum*. These hooded cuirasses, which were very similar to those worn by the Norman knights, must have weighed 25 to 30kg. The *cataphractus* should be differentiated from the *clibanarius* or 'oven man' who was far more heavily armed, being covered from head to foot in a combination of plate and scale armour.

Three scale trappers from either *cataphracti* or *clibanarii* were found in tower 19 at Dura. These were made in two main pieces consisting of bronze or iron scales wired together and stitched to a linen backing. These two pieces covered the sides of the horse and were laced to a central leather strip which ran along the back of the horse, leaving a hole for the saddle.

Similar pieces must have covered the horse's neck and head. The *cataphracti* shown in a very imaginative way on Trajan's Column wear perforated eye guards. Since these were used by the Roman cavalry for their sports armour, it seems likely that they were also used by the *cataphracti* and *clibanarii*.

The archaeological evidence for infantry helmets during the 3rd century is very sparse. When in the succeeding century helmets regularly appear again, they are of an entirely different type and are clearly unrelated to the earlier forms. The last type of legionary helmet which retains the original form is Robinson's imperial Italic type H (see p. 259). This is a clear derivative of the imperial Gallic and Italic forms, except that the neck guard has been deepened, making it similar to the 2nd-century cavalry helmets. The next infantry helmets come from more than a hundred years later. These may be grouped under the heading of the Intercisa type, after a site in Hungary where no less than four of them were found. These helmets bear no resemblance to the earlier legionary helmets. They are made of iron and are of very crude construction, the cap being made in two pieces joined along the crest. They have a small neck guard which is made as a separate piece usually stitched to the lining and not directly attached to the helmet. The cheek pieces, which are similarly attached to the lining, come down directly over the ears and have a semi-circular piece cut out so that the wearer can hear. These helmets may have been introduced into the army by mercenaries of north-eastern origin entering the empire from the Danube region. Many of the monuments show what at first glance appear to be helmets similar to late-classical and Hellenistic types which curved forward at the top in the form of a Phrygian cap. Vegetius mentions the Pannonian leather caps worn by the soldiers, and this is obviously what is being shown in such scenes as the Red Sea crossing from the catacombs on the Via Latina and in the church of Santa Maria Maggiore at Rome.

Several very elaborate examples of the Intercisa type of helmet have been found. These have cheek pieces which completely cover the ears and are clearly all cavalry helmets. They illustrate well the reversal of status between the legions and the cavalry. It seems most likely that this type of helmet was originally adopted by the cavalry and was later adapted to the crude form used by the infantry. These helmets are basically of the same construction as the infantry form: the cap is made in two pieces

joined along the crest. The neck guard is attached to the cap by straps and buckles—the buckle always being on the neck guard. By the beginning of the 5th century the caps of these helmets were being made in four segments riveted to a frame, showing a clear evolutionary line to the *Spangenhelm* of the early medieval period. Both the infantry and cavalry types usually have a slit along the crown of the cap to hold a crest.

During the late 2nd and early 3rd centuries the *gladius* was gradually superseded by the *spatha*. According to Vegetius, by the time of Diocletian at the end of the 3rd century all legionaries used the *spatha*. There is a fine 4th-century example from Cologne at the Landesmuseum in Bonn with a blade length of 70.5cm. This is a fairly standard length, although there is an example from Carnuntum with a blade length of 85cm. The scabbard of this sword is not of the Roman type but is based on the current Germanic type with a Celtic loop rather than the Roman ring fasteners. The dagger, which disappeared at the beginning of the 2nd century, reappears in a much cruder form as part of the equipment of the auxiliaries.

During the 3rd century the *cingulum* (the military belt), the very symbol of the soldier, was also discarded to be re-

Above
1 One of the crude iron infantry helmets found at Intercisa, Hungary. It bears no relationship to the earlier helmets. **2** The elaborate bronze cavalry helmet found in a bog at Deurne in Holland.

Above
The head of a figure from the 4th-century Lion Hunt sarcophagus in the Museum of San Sebastiano, Rome. This shows the Pannonian cap which was worn by soldiers in Vegetius' day.

Above
A silver-plated cavalry helmet from Concesti in Rumania. This early 5th-century helmet is clearly related to the early medieval *Spangenhelm*, being made of several segments riveted to a frame.

placed with a leather belt often worn around the hips rather than the waist. The sword was suspended from a broad baldric about 5cm wide. In the 4th century, influenced by the massive influx of barbarian mercenaries, both belt and baldric were abandoned in favour of the Germanic belt.

Decay appears in other areas; the infantry of Vegetius' day were still armed with throwing weapons, the *spiculum*, *verutum* and *plumbata*, all three of which were possibly derived from the *pilum*. The *spiculum* had an iron head with triangular section nine Roman inches (22cm) long and a wooden shaft 5.5ft (c. 1.6m) long. This is possibly the weapon which is shown on several tombstones of the 3rd century. Although roughly fitting Vegetius' description, it has an ovoid weight, presumably of lead, between the wooden shaft and the short iron head.

The *verutum*, which was originally called a *vericulum*, had a head 12cm long and a wooden shaft which measured just over a metre. Vegetius unfortunately does not describe the third weapon, the *plumbata*. He does, however, tell of two Illyrian legions who under Diocletian and Maximian gained the title of *Martiobarbuli* because of their skill with this weapon. The two names imply that it was a barbed weapon weighted with lead, and therefore with much justification it has been identified with the short barbed weapon with a lead weight which has been found on many 3rd- and 4th-century sites. An example from Wroxeter is complete with barbed iron head, lead weight and part of the wooden shaft which is about one centimetre thick. Neutron radiographs show the head was split socketed. Examples have also been found with spiked tangs. Vegetius says that each soldier carried five of these in the hollow of his shield. Reconstructions were made by the late Russell Robinson, and experiments showed that the weapon handled most efficiently with a fleched shaft 94cm long. It was also found that the range could be greatly increased by the use of a thong.

Vegetius may be right in his description of the *verutum* and *spiculum*, which were in use in his day, but in regretting the loss of the *pilum* he talks of it having a head 27–29cm long. This is clearly not the *pilum* of the earlier empire.

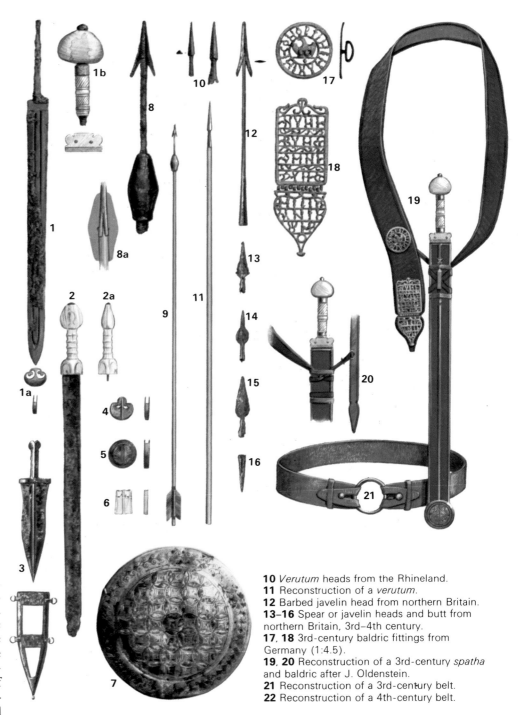

Above and right
1–16 Late Roman weapons. All except **7** and **8** scale 1:10.
1, 1a 3rd-century *spatha* and chape from Kent.
1b Parts of a 3rd-century sword handle.
2, 2a 4th-century *spatha* from Cologne.
3 3rd-century dagger from Kastell Künzing.
4, 5, 6 3rd-century chapes from various sites.
7 4th-century chape from Cologne (1:2.5).
8 *Plumbata* head from Wroxeter (1:2.2).
8a Section of the lead weight.
9 Reconstruction of a *plumbata*.

10 *Verutum* heads from the Rhineland.
11 Reconstruction of a *verutum*.
12 Barbed javelin head from northern Britain.
13–16 Spear or javelin heads and butt from northern Britain, 3rd–4th century.
17, 18 3rd-century baldric fittings from Germany (1:4.5).
19, 20 Reconstruction of a 3rd-century *spatha* and baldric after J. Oldenstein.
21 Reconstruction of a 3rd-century belt.
22 Reconstruction of a 4th-century belt.

War at Sea

Naval warfare played a very important part in the military history of Greece and, at least in the crucial 3rd century BC, of Rome. Without her navy Athens would never have been able to form her overseas empire.

The ships described by Homer in the *Odyssey* are almost certainly those of his own day, the 8th century BC. These ships are of two types: light, fast ships of 20 oars and heavier warships with 50 oars (*pentekonters*). These are unquestionably galleys and not canoes as thole pins with leather loops for holding the oars are often mentioned. They have benches for the oarsmen; Odysseus drags one of his drunken comrades aboard and leaves him 'beneath the benches'.

Odysseus makes his boat from pinewood and his oars from polished spruce. When at sea the boat could be anchored with a large stone tied to a rope. Stone anchors, which were usually just a simple cut stone with a hole in it for attaching the cable, had existed since the Bronze Age. An example from Cyprus has a large hole for the hawser and two smaller holes which were fitted with sharpened stakes. These would dig into the sea bed and so give the ship a secure mooring. The much more efficient admiralty anchor was introduced about 600 BC but did not completely oust the stone type which continued in use right down until the Hellenistic age.

At night, whenever possible, ships would be dragged up the beach stern first. Here they were propped up with stones or poles. Like all galleys Homer's ships had masts and square sails which could only be used when the wind was in the right direction. The mast, which was made of spruce, was slotted into a box fitted to the keel of the ship. The mast and sail were always taken down before going into battle. When the ship was not in use the mast and rigging were taken from the ship and stored ashore. Like the ships from Thera, Homer's ships were steered by one or two stern oars and had a ram at the front. The ships in the *Odyssey* are most frequently described as black but, on the other hand, the poet sometimes refers to them as red- or blue-painted. The black probably refers to the tarring of the keel, whereas the other colours may describe the parts of the ship above the water level. One must not forget that the early Greeks were more accustomed to seeing their ships drawn up on the shore than at sea and would therefore be more familiar with the part below the waterline than we are.

The very stylised vase paintings of the 8th century often depict ships. Not a great deal can be learned from them, but they invariably show a curved stern like a scorpion's tail, a ram at the front and above the prow a great S-shaped horn. Homer describes Achilles' ships as having these upright horns. These same characteristics also appear on a fire dog made in the form of a galley from the 8th-century warrior's grave at Argos. This fire dog adds one small piece of information; it shows that the prow horn was single and not double as had previously been supposed. The ships shown on geometric pottery are certainly galleys rowed by men who face the rear of the ship. Often thole pins can be seen in the paintings.

The interpretation of the geometric pottery ships is very difficult. It seems most likely that the artist is trying to show both sides of the ship at once. The confusion is even greater when he apparently shows rowers at two levels. This should probably be interpreted as one level of rowers at each side of the ship. In other words, the artist is depicting a galley with a single bank of oars and not a bireme. The situation is aggravated by the fact that probably late in the 8th century the bireme was invented. This galley with two banks of oars was almost certainly developed by the Phoenicians and later adopted by the Greeks. There is no reason to believe that the Greeks at this primitive stage in their development invented the bireme. This improvement involved inserting a second row of oars operated by rowers at a slightly higher level. Because of the lack of evidence the details of this system are impossible to work out. It may have been just the same as the later trireme but with one less bank. The largest Greek galley at this period still had only 50 oars, so the aim may have been to produce a shorter more manoeuvrable craft.

After the collapse of the Mycenaean civilisation the Phoenicians became the major Mediterranean sea power, and later their fleets became the mainstay of the Persian navy. The Phoenicians were always the principal enemies of the Greeks at sea and their maritime colonies were constantly at war over trade along the whole length of the

Below
A reconstruction of an 8th-century 50-oared galley. It has a bronze-plated ram and a forecastle which is similar to the earlier Mycenaean galleys. This was the type of ship described by Homer.

Mediterranean. Peace between the two races was established only after they both fell under Roman rule. After the first Persian invasion of Greece in 490 BC Athens became involved in a naval war with the island of Aegina in which she came off worst. This insult to Athenian pride prompted her to divert her resources to the building of a modern fleet. When the Persians invaded again in 480, although she could not match the skill and experience of the Phoenician seamen, Athens could put to sea a navy of 200 of the latest-style triremes. This was more than all the other Greek states combined. Without the Athenian fleet the Persian navy could not have been withstood and with Persia in control of the sea nothing could have stopped them invading the Peloponnesus.

After the defeat of the Persians Athens formed a league with the maritime states of the Aegean known as the Confederacy of Delos. Each member of this league contributed ships, or, more often, money to continue the war against Persia. The result was that Athens built up a vast fleet at the expense of the other members of the confederacy. By 420 BC the strength of her fleet had reached 350.

The quantities of timber needed for the building and maintenance of this fleet probably caused the deforestation of central Greece, and the soil erosion which is the perennial curse of the modern Greek farmer was noticeable as early as the time of Plato.

Athens' control of the sea lasted for 75 years and the renown of her sailors rose to equal that of the Phoenicians.

1 Galleys shown on early vase paintings. These are probably both the same type of galley with rowers at one level only.
2 Fragments of an early vase painting showing thole pins with straps.

3 8th-century fire dog, in the form of a galley, from Argos.
4 Stone anchor from Piraeus.
5 Lead anchor stock from Syracuse.
6 6th-century painting of a hook anchor.

Above
A bireme in rough sea from a 6th-century vase painting. It has a ram in the shape of a boar's head. The crew are furling the sail.

When compelled to raise the siege of Syracuse in 415 she had to abandon half her navy. The final humiliating defeat came ten years later at Aegospotamoi. This defeat was not caused by any lack of skill but sheer carelessness. When Athens finally fell the Spartans confiscated all except 12 of her triremes.

The trireme

At some time during the 6th century a third bank of rowers had been added to the bireme to produce the famous trireme. By the end of the century the trireme had become the standard warship of the Mediterranean.

There is still a great deal of controversy surrounding the trireme but certain factors are clear. It was rowed at three levels with one man to each oar. From the pictorial evidence alone it is abundantly clear that the trireme was rowed at three levels and a chance remark by Thucydides—'It was decided that each sailor taking his oar, cushion and oar-strap . . .'—proves that there was one man to an oar. We learn from Athenian naval records that these oars were between four and 4.5m long. Ship sheds at the Athenian harbour of Piraeus have been excavated and these give maximum dimensions for the ships, 37m long and 3m wide at bottom, increasing to a width of about 6m at outrigger level.

According to Athenian records there were 27 rowers (*thalamites*) each side at the lowest level. These rowers worked their oars through ports. Although these were not far above water level they must have been at a sufficient height above the waterline for light rowing boats to slip underneath them. This is the tactic the Syracusans employed to attack the Athenian rowers at their benches during the siege of Syracuse. The second bank of rowers (*zygites*) were also 27 in number. The top bank of oarsmen (*thranites*) rowed through an out-rigger. This was an extension beyond the side of the ship which gave greater leverage to the oars. There were 31 *thranite* rowers on each side. As in the previous eras the ships were steered by broad oars at the rear. Each galley had two anchors, which hung from the catheads on either bow, and two landing ladders which can often be seen at the rear of the ship.

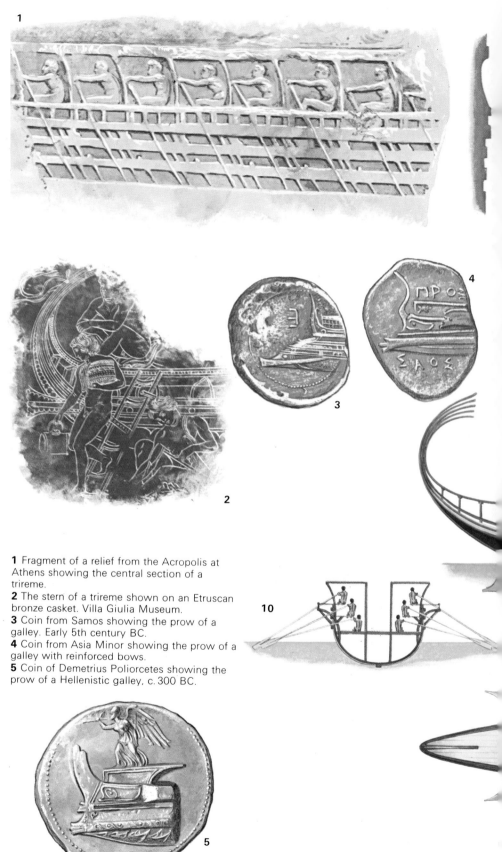

1 Fragment of a relief from the Acropolis at Athens showing the central section of a trireme.
2 The stern of a trireme shown on an Etruscan bronze casket. Villa Giulia Museum.
3 Coin from Samos showing the prow of a galley. Early 5th century BC.
4 Coin from Asia Minor showing the prow of a galley with reinforced bows.
5 Coin of Demetrius Poliorcetes showing the prow of a Hellenistic galley, c. 300 BC.

There were 200 men in a trireme's crew of whom 170 were rowers. These were drawn from the poorer classes but they were not slaves. At the battle of Salamis each ship had 10 marines and four archers. The crew also included a flautist, who piped time for the rowers, and 15 deck hands. The ship was commanded by a *trierach* who was appointed by the admiral.

Over long distances and under favourable conditions a trireme could hope to average nine kilometres an hour. There are numerous examples of long distances being covered at better than eight kilometres per hour. Aeneas the Tactician, writing in the 4th century, recommends ships as the quickest method of moving troops. It is impossible to estimate a trireme's top speed but it is possible to bracket it. The record speed for a rowing eight over 2,000m is a little over 20km per hour. A trireme's top speed must have been well below this, perhaps 12–15km per hour.

The main weapon of the trireme was its bronze-plated ram, but to use this required great skill. During the Peloponnesian war the Corinthians, like the

6 **6a**

7

Below and opposite
8–10 Reconstruction of an early 5th-century trireme. Scale 1:160. **8** Side view. **9** Plan view. **10** Section showing positions of rowers.

Above
6, **6a** Side and rear views of a galley from Sperlonga, Italy, showing the housing of the steering oar.
7 Rear of a light galley from Lindos, Rhodes, c. 200 BC.

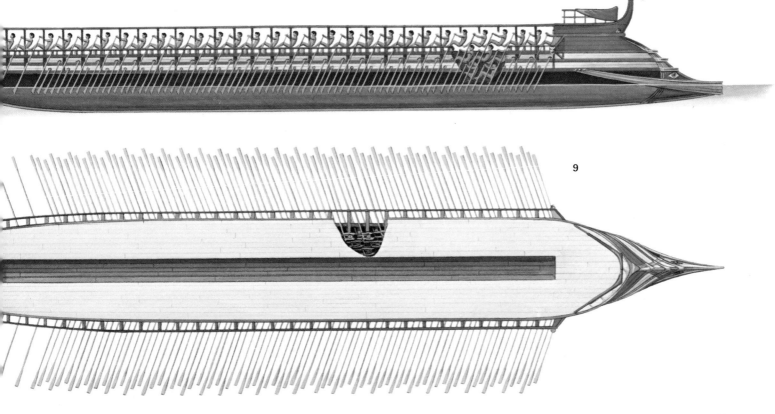

8

9

later Romans, found a way of neutralising the superior seamanship of the Athenians. They reinforced the bows of their galleys and crashed them into the lighter Athenian ships, replacing skill with brute force.

The Greek ships that fought at Salamis in 480 were almost totally unprotected. They were only partially decked and, if the representations are not misleading, the rowing benches of at least the upper bank were completely open, protected only by the decking above. There was no railing along the sides of the deck—this may have been to make boarding easier. By the end of the 5th century, rowers must have had more

protection as the Syracusans had to get under the oars to attack the Athenian rowers through the oar holes.

The juggernauts
In the Hellenistic period the function of galleys changed; ships were increasingly designed as heavily armoured floating platforms to carry catapults and marines. These ships were fully decked and their sides completely blocked in.

About 400 BC we first hear of galleys with greater rowing capacity than the trireme. According to Diodorus the development of these larger galleys was pioneered in the scientific warfare establishments of Dionysius I at Syracuse.

The Greek word for a three-banked galley was *trieres*. Now there appeared a *tetreres* and a *penteres*, i.e. four- and five-banked craft. 'Sixes' make an appearance about 350 BC and by the end of the century the number of banks had risen progressively to 13. Early in the 3rd century we encounter a 'sixteen' and by the end of that century a 'forty'. This multiplication of banks of oars has mystified scholars for centuries and will no doubt continue to do so. There is certainly no difficulty in reconstructing them on paper. In 1864 Graser published his *De Veterum Re Navali* in which he illustrated how all these galleys could be rowed. He multiplied

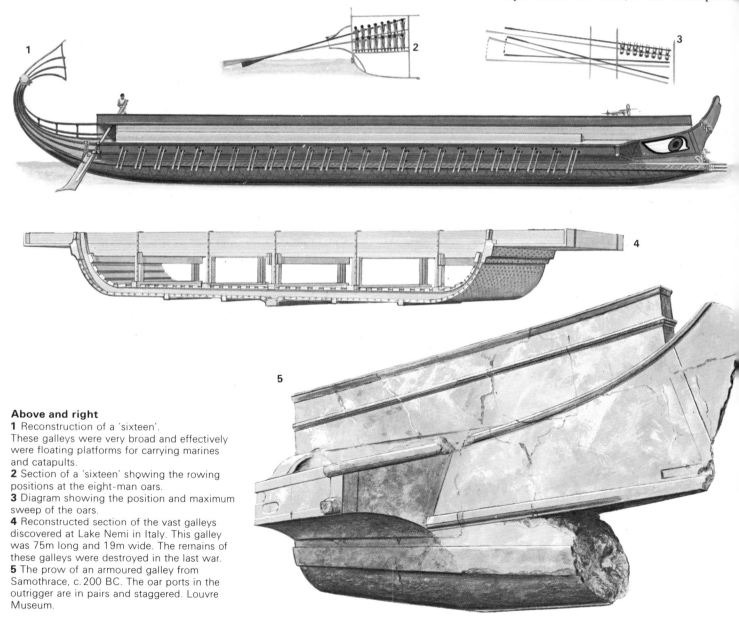

Above and right
1 Reconstruction of a 'sixteen'.
These galleys were very broad and effectively were floating platforms for carrying marines and catapults.
2 Section of a 'sixteen' showing the rowing positions at the eight-man oars.
3 Diagram showing the position and maximum sweep of the oars.
4 Reconstructed section of the vast galleys discovered at Lake Nemi in Italy. This galley was 75m long and 19m wide. The remains of these galleys were destroyed in the last war.
5 The prow of an armoured galley from Samothrace, c. 200 BC. The oar ports in the outrigger are in pairs and staggered. Louvre Museum.

the basic principle of the trireme so that in his 40-banker his top rowers sat about 15m above water level and wielded oars about 75m long. Laughable though Graser's theories may be, the alternative advanced by his critics is equally ludicrous. They suggested that none of these galleys ever had more than one level of rowers and that the 'remes' or 'reis' refers to the number of men who pulled each oar. This is fine for anything up to eight but becomes totally ridiculous at figures at or beyond 16.

The answer to the problem has to lie somewhere between the two solutions. Sculptures of Roman galleys show clearly that they were rowed at more than one level but they never show more than three banks of oars. Here may lie the key. These ships are just larger versions of the bireme and trireme. It is probable that no ship ever had more than three banks. The numbers refer to the total number of men rowing each vertical group of oars: for example, a 'six' could be rowed in the same fashion as a trireme, with two men per oar, or as a bireme with three men per oar. In the 17th and 18th centuries it was found that eight was a maximum number of men who could handle a single oar efficiently. On the trireme principle a 'twenty-four' is therefore conceivable though admittedly unlikely. The most frequently mentioned of these giants is the 'sixteen'. Perseus, the last king of Macedon, had just such a galley as the flagship of his navy. This type is most acceptable as a bireme with eight-man oars. Such a galley would have to be at least 12m wide, excluding the outrigger. The galleys discovered in Lake Nemi in Italy are twice this width and may well have been these juggernauts. The galley reconstruction shown here is based on two banks of eight-man oars. Obviously a forty requires some further reorganisation. Casson has made the suggestion that it had two hulls and as a result is therefore a double 'twenty'.

Several representations from the Hellenistic period show galleys with two banks of oars, both coming from the outrigger. The most famous of these is the base of the Victory of Samothrace. This has an outrigger with oar holes grouped in staggered pairs—one up, one down. This was probably the arrangement for heavy galleys.

Naval tactics

The battle tactics of the Greek fleets were comparatively simple. Victory usually depended on the ability of individual ships. Herodotus has very little grasp of the principles of naval warfare and his account of the battle of Salamis lacks insight. However, 173 years later a battle with exactly the same name was fought off the town of Salamis in Cyprus. This battle, which was recorded by Hieronymus of Cardia, and the battle of Chios in 201 for which we have Polybius' account, give us a considerable insight into galley warfare. Unfortunately Hieronymus' account of the battle has only come down to us via Diodorus.

In 307 BC Demetrius Poliorcetes was laying siege to Salamis in Cyprus when Ptolemy, king of Egypt, approached with a fleet of some 140 galleys and 200 transports carrying more than 10,000 soldiers in an attempt to raise the siege. All Ptolemy's galleys were either quadriremes or quinqueremes. Demetrius with about 190 ships launched his fleet and prepared to meet the attack. The majority of his vessels would appear to have been triremes or smaller galleys but he also had a fair number of larger ships. Before putting to sea all the rigging was removed and masts lowered. On the bows of his ships Demetrius mounted bolt-shooting catapults capable of discharging arrows 55cm in length. He also put several stone-throwers aboard and a supply of missiles. Then, leaving ten of his quinqueremes to blockade the narrow entrance to Salamis harbour so that the 60 galleys in there could not join the battle, he put to sea. Diodorus gives details only of Demetrius' left wing which was made up of two lines with 30 Athenian quadriremes and seven Phoenician 'sevens' at the front and ten quinqueremes and ten 'sixes' behind. Demetrius commanded this wing in one of the 'sevens'. The lighter ships formed the centre and the rest of the heavy galleys made up the right wing.

Presuming that there were around 50 ships on the right wing, one may estimate the lighter centre to consist of about 75 triremes and lighter galleys.

Ptolemy placed his transports in the rear, took down his rigging and lowered his masts. He placed all his quinqueremes on his left, where he commanded, leaving his quadriremes to face the centre and Demetrius' much heavier left wing. When the fleets were drawn up in battle order both sides offered prayers to the gods beseeching their help in the coming battle, the signalmen leading the prayers and the crews joining in the responses. When the prayers were over the two fleets began to advance with the signalmen sounding out the stroke to the rowers. When about 500m separated the fleets Demetrius ordered the pre-arranged signal to prepare for battle—a gilded shield to be raised on his flagship. The signal was repeated down the line in relays. A similar signal was raised by Ptolemy and the two fleets closed. As they approached the trumpets sounded the charge, both sides raised their war cries and the two fleets dashed upon each other. The artillery and the archers opened the battle and, as they came into range, the javelineers also discharged their missiles. The soldiers on the deck crouched down and braced themselves for the shock of the collision whilst, urged on by the signalmen, the rowers strained desperately at their oars. Some of the ships met prow to prow and were forced to back water so that they could charge again. At close quarters the marines were able to rake the decks of the enemy ship with their missiles. When a galley managed to ram an opponent amidships and the ram had become firmly lodged, the marines leapt aboard the stricken ship to fight it out hand to hand. Sometimes the marines of such a stricken ship managed to board their attacker and capture it. Jumping from one ship to the other was not without its perils and many a marine misjudged as he leapt towards the approaching enemy ship and failed to get a firm grip on the rail. Those who missed the rail or lost their footing on the slippery foam-soaked decks plunged into the sea where they were dispatched by the spears of those on the ship above them. Some ships, avoiding the head-on charge of the enemy, managed to swing their sterns around and sweep off the oars of the opposing galley, leaving it powerless. Demetrius soon got the upper hand and broke the Egyptian right wing. When Ptolemy saw his right wing beaten by Demetrius' heavy galleys he gave up hope of winning the battle and withdrew. Demetrius decked out his victorious galleys with bow and stern ornaments and towing the captured Egyptian galleys returned in triumph to his camp.

The battle of Chios, fought 106 years later between Philip V of Macedon and Attalus I of Pergamon, adds some further details. The two fleets included 'tens', 'nines', 'eights', 'sevens' and 'sixes' as well as the more conventional quinqueremes and a host of lighter ships. Although Polybius gives no details of the line-up or of the preliminaries to the battle, and even the result is in doubt, there are some very enlightening descriptions in his account. The most noteworthy performance was given by the Rhodians who were the ablest sailors of their day. They had perfected the manoeuvre of breaking the line. To do this they would charge head on and at the last moment veer away, passing along one side of the enemy galley and if possible sweeping off its oars. This manoeuvre necessitated shipping their oars. As they came out behind the line they would rely on their greater seamanship to enable them to turn their galley faster than their opponents so that they could ram them whilst they were still turning, catching them with a shattering blow in the unarmoured flank or even in the stern.

The Rhodians had also developed a technique which enabled them to dip their prows, and they used this technique when charging head on. Unfortunately Polybius does not explain how this manoeuvre was performed. One can only assume that just before impact they must have plunged in their front sets of oars as if for a back stroke so that the stern of the galley lifted and the front plunged down under the ram of the opposing ship with the result that any damage to the Rhodian ship was above the waterline whilst the enemy ship suffered its damage along the bottom of the keel. These two techniques combined must have had a devastating effect as their opponents did not know which one to expect.

During the battle Philip's flagship, a vast 'ten', charged a *trihemiolia* which was in its path. These ships were a sort of light undecked trireme. The huge galley rammed the lighter vessel with great force in the flank. Usually such a light galley would have been shattered by the impact and probably broken in two, but on this occasion the prow of the 'ten' stuck fast under the outrigger that supported the top bank of oars of the smaller ship. Disabled in this way she was attacked by two triremes and sunk.

Things were evened up when one of the opposing admirals charged an enemy at full speed but badly misjudged his collision course. He missed his target by the narrowest margin and as he swept past caught his right-side oars on the stern of his intended victim losing not only all his oars but his turrets too. Another galley suffered the indignity of losing its ram when it charged, leaving a gaping hole in the prow. Such damage was of course fatal and it could only be a matter of minutes before the crippled ship sank. These two accounts give a considerable insight into ancient naval warfare.

Above
Aerial view of the harbour area at Carthage showing the horseshoe and lozenge-shaped ponds. The areas where the outside quays and sea wall have sunk can be seen in dark blue. Much of this area has been surveyed and excavated and has vindicated the description of the Greek historian Appian.

Below
A reconstructed plan of the island in the military harbour after Dr Hurst's excavations. In the middle are the admiral's headquarters. The dotted lines are ship sheds. The actual remains are shown in black.

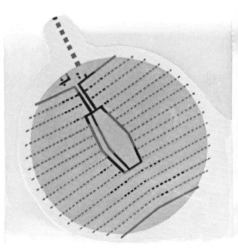

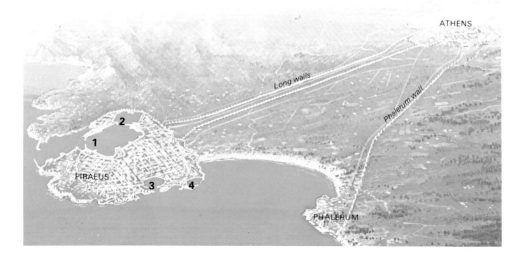

Left
Reconstructed aerial view showing Athens and her harbours, c. 450 BC.
1 Main harbour (Kantharos).
2 Inner harbour. **3** Zea harbour.
4 Munychia harbour.

Harbours

Enclosed harbours appear to have developed in the Mediterranean during the 6th century BC. Herodotus mentions the harbour at Samos which was enclosed by a mole about 400m long extending out into water 30m deep.

During the 6th century the Athenians beached their ships in the open bay of Phalerum just south of the Piraeus but early in the 5th, at the instigation of Themistocles, the harbour was moved to the Piraeus. On the north side of this rocky promontory is a large inlet which became the commercial harbour Cantharus and on the south side there are two much smaller inlets, Zea and Munichia, which became the military harbours. The whole area was surrounded by walls of heavy limestone blocks. The harbour entrances were narrowed with moles so that they could be closed with chains. The moles were surmounted by walls with towers at the end. The entrance to the Zea harbour was reduced to only 35m. Ship sheds, which were really covered slipways, were built in the two military harbours. These sheds were grouped in fours or eights. They

were just under 6m wide and about 40m long and were separated by a row of columns. Each pair was covered by a single roof. The sheds sloped down to the water's edge with the slipways extending some distance into the water. The galleys were dragged up the slipway into the shed, probably stern first. There were nearly 400 of these sheds at the Piraeus in the 4th century. The main military harbour was at Zea where the naval stores were kept. To complete the fortifications long walls were constructed joining the Piraeus to Athens.

The great harbour of the 3rd century BC was that of Carthage. This double harbour, one part commercial and the other military, is described by the Greek historian Appian who is probably drawing on a lost part of Polybius' history. The two harbours were placed one behind the other, separated by a double wall. The front port was for commercial shipping. It had an entrance about 20m wide which could be closed with iron chains. Behind the commercial port was the military harbour which had access to the sea through the mercantile port.

In the centre of the military harbour was an island on which stood the admiral's headquarters, rising high above the surrounding buildings and fortifications and enabling the naval commander to see what was going on out at sea. Both the island and the harbour itself were lined with ship sheds and stores sufficient for 200 galleys. Two columns stood at the entrance to each shed which gave the appearance of a

Above
A cut-away section of a reconstructed ship shed at Carthage. **Below** A reconstruction of the military harbour at Carthage based on the drawings of Dr H. R. Hurst and S. C. Gibson.

continuous portico to both the harbour and the island.

There are two ponds, one horseshoe- and the other lozenge-shaped at the south-east corner of the site of Carthage. These have long been thought to mark the site of the ancient harbours. But in recent years much doubt has been cast on this. As recently as 1976 the late French expert on Carthage, Pierre Cintas, published the second volume of his *Manuel d'Archéologie Punique* in which he poured scorn on Appian's description and also on the suggestion that the two ponds marked the site of the ancient harbours. But even before the book went to press a British archaeo-

Above and right
The prow of a galley shown on a Carthaginian coin from Spain, c.225 BC. Carving from Carthage showing the front of a galley. Note the disc and crescent standard on the prow.

Above
1 Part of the hull of the first of two Carthaginian warships discovered near Lilybaeum in Sicily. 2 Part of the ram of the second ship. A Method of joining planks together with tenons and dowels. B Method of nailing planks to ribs. C and D Sections of keel. E Section of rearmost rib. F Section of fifth rib showing planking nailed to both rib and keel. G and H Sections of the ram.

Below and opposite
3 Side view of a reconstructed quinquereme without lead sheathing on the hull or bronze on the ram. 4 Front view of the fully-clad ship. 5, 6 Sections showing rowing positions.

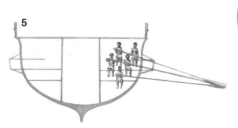
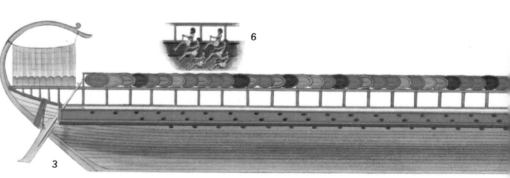

ogical team under the leadership of Dr Henry Hurst was beginning excavations in the centre of the horseshoe. Pierre Cintas died in July 1974 before seeing even the earliest results of these excavations which established that the military harbour was indeed there and vindicated the description of Appian. In the centre of the horseshoe Dr Hurst uncovered the foundations of a large building with rows of rectangular stone blocks radiating from it. These rows, which are 5.9m apart, can only be the foundations of ship sheds and the large building is the admiral's HQ.

Over a hundred years ago the French archaeologist Beulé found similar rows of blocks on the north side of the pond. The north edge of the later Roman harbour has also been found. If this coincided with the earlier quayside then the harbour would have had a circuit of over 1,100m, sufficient for about 160 ship sheds. As there are 30 on the island it supports Appian's claim that there were sheds for 200 galleys.

The fleets of Carthage

Carthage's powerful fleet gave her control of the western Mediterranean. We know from Polybius that the principal fighting ship of the Carthaginian navy in the 3rd century was the quinquereme, though the Carthaginians also used some triremes and quadriremes. One of her fleets had a 'seven', which had been captured from Pyrrhus during his invasion of Sicily, as flagship.

The military harbour at Carthage had sufficient housing for 200 ships but during the first Punic war the Carthaginian navy was often well over this strength. In 256 Carthage was able to put to sea a fleet of 350 decked warships. There were probably subsidiary fleets permanently stationed at such places as Palermo and Lilybaeum. Certainly a military habour has been excavated at the early Carthaginian colony of Motya, off the west coast of Sicily, which was destroyed by Dionysius I in 397 BC.

One of the most remarkable features of the fleets of Carthage and Rome in the 3rd century BC was the enormous speed at which they could be constructed. In 261 BC the Romans built their first fleet of 120 ships in two months. Seven years later they built a second fleet of 200 in three months. In 1971 the hull of a Carthaginian galley was discovered in the shallow water just north of the port of Lilybaeum. This ship, and another which was discovered nearby, have been carbon dated to the period of the first Punic war. The many shipwright's markings on the timbers which are still visible imply that the pieces were mass produced, offering an explanation of the speed with which fleets could be assembled.

Some of the pieces of the two ships from Lilybaeum are shown here. The large piece (1) is the stern of the first ship discovered, the other piece (2) is part of the ram of the second. The keel is of maple, the ribs of oak and the planking and tusk-like pieces of the ram are of pine. The ships were carvel built, i.e. the outside planking was assembled first and the ribs inserted afterwards. The planks were joined together with flat wooden tenons which were held in place with wooden dowels. All the Mediterranean ships so far found were assembled in this way. The planking was nailed to the ribs from the outside and the nail bent over on the inside. The joints were caulked with a putty-like substance and then the hull was covered with lead sheeting and the ram encased in bronze. The excavator Honor Frost believes that both these galleys were *liburnae*, the type of fast light ships used by the Illyrians. This type appears to have been adopted by Philip V during the second Punic war. There is, however, no literary evidence which indicates that Carthage used these types in the 3rd century. The fast light vessel belonging to Hannibal, the 'Rhodian' which constantly ran the Roman blockade of Lilybaeum, was a quinquereme. We can deduce this from the fact that the Romans constructed a fleet of quinqueremes using the 'Rhodian's' vessel as a model. Quite apart from this the estimated size of the Lilybaeum ship— approximately 35m long and 5m wide without the outrigger—is very large. The ship sheds at Carthage which must have held quinqueremes were only 5.9m wide.

The main interest of the Lilybaeum ships, of which only the keels survive, is their structure. This has been used for the reconstruction of a quinquereme shown below. The superstructure is based on a Carthaginian coin from Spain and a carving from Carthage, both shown here. These show unmistakably an outrigger just behind the eye with a deck above it. The coin shows oval shields, no doubt Celtiberian, strapped along the railing. The ram shown on both these representations is the Greek type which was attached to the bilge stringers. The type used on the Lilybaeum wreck more closely resembles those shown on Trajan's Column, which probably accounts for the assumption that the ship is a *liburna*.

Polybius implies that Carthaginian ships carried the same number of crewmen as the Roman ships of the same period—300 seamen and 120 marines—

Below
Relief of a galley with three banks of oars from Ostia, c. 30 BC. It could be a quinquereme, or bigger, as all the oars come from the outrigger.

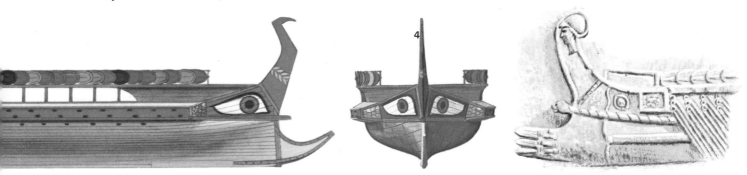

when he says that their fleet of 350 galleys had a crew of 150,000. The method of rowing a Carthaginian/ Roman quinquereme has caused enormous controversy. It was certainly not rowed at one level with five men to an oar as Tarn advocates; equally certainly it was not rowed at five levels. There are several representations from the Roman republican period which show galleys rowed at two or three levels.

The trireme had 170 oars with 62 rowers at the highest level and 54 at each of the lower levels. It is known from the excavations of ship sheds that quadriremes and quinqueremes were much the same size as triremes. It therefore comes as some surprise to find out that the oars for a quadrireme cost less than those for a trireme. This was pointed out by Morrison and Williams in their book *Greek Oared Ships*. The only conclusion that they could draw was that a quadrireme had less oars than a trireme. From this one must deduce that it was rowed at only two levels with two men per oar. The natural progression from this is to suggest that a quinquereme was rowed at three levels with two men

each to the oars of the upper banks, where the boat was widest, and one per oar at the lower level.

Since a trireme had a crew of 200 of which 170 were rowers, one would expect 270 of the 300 crew members of a quinquereme to be rowers. The reconstruction shown on p. 270 has 112 two-man oars (58 at the highest level and 54 in the second bank), and 46 one-man oars at the lowest level, giving a total of 270 rowers.

The early Roman fleets

Within three years of the start of the first war with Carthage it became obvious to the Romans that they would have to build a fleet. Up until then they had made use of ships belonging to the allied states of Magna Graecia and Etruria. But none of these states was using quinqueremes. The Romans modelled their galleys on a Carthaginian ship that was stranded on a reef and captured at the very outset of the war. So the first Roman fleet of 100 quinqueremes and 20 triremes was built. The crews were taught to row on land whilst the ships were being built.

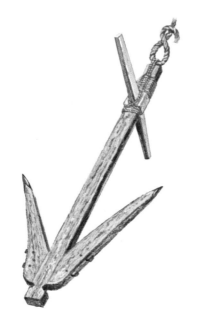

Above
A Roman anchor complete with wood frame, lead stock and rope from a galley excavated at Lake Nemi. It is over 5.5m long excluding rope.

Below
Bas relief of a war galley, late 1st century BC, found at Praeneste. It probably commemorates Augustus' victory over Antony and Cleopatra. If the decoration along the outrigger represents shipped oars, it could be Augustus' flagship with three banks of two-man oars.

These first ships were slow and clumsy and the Romans realised that they would be no match for the Punic seamen. So they compensated by developing a boarding plank with a long iron spike at the end which swivelled on a pole mounted on the prow of the ship. The sailors nicknamed this the 'raven' (*corvus*) because of its beak.

The boarding plank was about 1.2m wide and 11m long whilst the pole around which it swivelled was about 7m high and 20cm thick. The 'plank' had a knee-high fence running along each side, and was raised by a pulley attached to the top of the pole. As the galley came close to an enemy ship the 'plank' was swivelled round and dropped on to the opposing ship where the spike stuck in the deck and locked the two ships together. The marines then mounted the plank, resting the rims of their shields on the knee-high fencing so that they were completely protected. This device turned a naval battle into a fight between marines which the superb Roman infantry were bound to win.

Although the *corvus* won Rome's early naval battles, it made the ships even less seaworthy than before and may have been the cause of the disastrous losses which Rome suffered from the elements. Certainly the *corvus* is not mentioned after the first war with Carthage and never again did she suffer such appalling losses.

Besides the quinqueremes the Romans also built two 'sixes' which they used as flagships. These were probably outsize quinqueremes with two rowers at each of the three levels.

When they embarked on the invasion of Africa in 256, the Romans drew up their ships in four lines, calling them the first, second, third and fourth legions. Two of these lines, each led by a 'six', formed a dart with a slight gap at the front. The third line formed the base of the triangle. Behind the third line were placed the horse transports and behind these was the fourth line of galleys which overlapped either end. The Romans quaintly called this fourth line the *triarii*. When ancient fleets set out they were always preceded by light craft which acted as scouts. Each galley had a jolly boat which was towed astern.

This fleet of 330 decked warships was the largest that the Romans ever put to

sea. Although Rome lost fleet after fleet to the elements, she carried on doggedly until she finally wrested control of the sea from the Carthaginians. The Carthaginian navy were so humiliated by the Romans during the first war that they never regained their confidence. In the Hannibalic war the Carthaginian navy tried to avoid coming into conflict with the Roman fleet even when they enjoyed numerical superiority. Philip's behaviour was similar. He sailed into the Adriatic with 100 *liburnae* in the early summer of 216 but turned and fled in disorder when the Romans dispatched ten quinqueremes against him.

Rome started the second war with Carthage with 220 ships and never stood in the slightest danger of losing control of the sea. For the first half of the 2nd century BC the Romans retained a substantial navy, but after the destruction of the naval power of Rhodes and Syria they saw no point in maintaining a fleet as the Mediterranean was at peace. From this point she began to rely almost entirely on the Greek states of the east to supply both ships and crews as she needed them. This general decline in naval strength encouraged the rise of piracy. By the first half of the 1st century BC the east was terrorised by Cilician pirates and in 70–68 they ravaged the coasts of Italy, sinking a consular fleet at Ostia and capturing two praetors with their lictors. This resulted in a purge of the pirates by Pompey which restored peace to the Mediterranean. The 200 galleys with which Pompey performed this task must have been supplied by the Greek states. During the civil wars the fleets, like the legions, multiplied so that after the battle of Actium in 31 BC Augustus was left with about 700 ships. Although Antony had had galleys up to a 'ten' in size, Augustus wisely kept nothing larger than a 'six' which became his flagship. This may well be the ship that is shown on the Praenestine relief.

The Roman imperial navy

Octavius used these ships as the basis of a standing navy which, because of its origin, was Greek in character. If such a standing navy had been formed 200 years earlier, it would have been Carthaginian in character. Captains were called *trierachs*, after the commanders

of Greek triremes. Because the fleets were of foreign origin they were not organised as legions but as auxiliary units and for this reason remained an inferior 'service'.

Augustus established three permanent naval bases, one at Forum Julii (Fréjus) near Marseilles to control the coasts of Gaul and Spain, another at Misenum at the northern end of the Bay of Naples to cover the south-west and a third at Ravenna to cover the Adriatic. The Italian fleets soon superseded the fleet at Forum Julii which was gradually run down.

These fleets were commanded by prefects (*praefecti*) who received their orders from the emperor and not from the Senate. There is no evidence that slave labour was used in the galleys, either in the republic or the empire. Seamen were also soldiers and proud of it. The fleets were organised in much the same fashion as the auxiliaries. The sailors served for 26 years and received a grant of Roman citizenship on discharge. Marines, who were also auxiliaries, were commanded in the same fashion as legionaries and were divided into centuries commanded by centurions and *optiones*. Early in the empire provincial flotillas were established off Syria and Egypt. There were also subsidiary fleets in the Black Sea, the English Channel and on the Rhine and Danube.

Individual ships were commanded by *trierarchs*; squadrons were commanded by *navarchs*. This name had originally meant a captain of a Greek ship but by the time of Polybius it was used generally for a squadron commander and as such the term was inherited by the Romans.

Quinqueremes fell out of favour in the imperial fleets, although they continued in use. The quadrireme became more common but during this period the most popular ship was the trireme. The role of *liburnae*, or light galleys, in the Roman fleets is unclear as the word became synonymous with galley and it is impossible to distinguish between its restricted or general meaning. One would expect to find *liburnae* in the Rhine and Danube fleets; some of the galleys from the Danube fleet shown on Trajan's Column are in all probability *liburnae*.

APPENDIX 1
Fortifications and Siege Warfare

The city states

Fortifications and siege warfare are inextricably combined. The development of one inevitably stimulates changes in the other, and therefore the two are treated together here.

Early Greek fortifications are clearly derived from their Bronze Age predecessors and it is necessary to go back to the citadels of the Mycenaean era. These citadels were normally built on hilltops and surrounded by walls which followed the contours of the hill. Mycenae itself has walls which are typical of the age. They are on average five metres thick and built of massive stones sometimes weighing as much as ten tonnes. The walls are pierced by two gates, both built at right angles to the wall so that the enemy would come under attack from the wall before the gate could be reached. A bastion was built out from the far side of the gate so that the defenders could bombard the enemy's unshielded side. The walls are also pierced by two narrow sally ports from which attacks could be made on the enemy without opening the main gates. The walls of Tiryns have galleries with vaulted roofs built into the walls which also show evidence of mud brick battlements topping them.

Without the stimulus of mature siege warfare the system of fortifications showed no developments in the 600 years that followed the fall of Mycenae.

The focal point of town defences was still the citadel or acropolis. The 7th-century walls of Emporio on the island of Chios are almost identical in concept to those of the Bronze Age but in the strength of the fortifications are inferior.

Only in the 6th century were serious attempts made to fortify whole towns. Under pressure first from Lydia and then Persia, the Ionian Greeks were compelled to improve their fortifications.

When tracing out the walls to encompass a town there was a tendency to try to make use of natural defences such as cliffs or steep slopes. This often meant increasing the area of the town. These walls were usually pierced with narrow sally ports enabling the defenders to launch attacks on the besiegers.

Earlier walls were constructed of rubble masonry or even mud, but by the 6th century carefully cut rectangular or polygonal blocks of stone were being used, although mud brick probably remained in use for battlements.

The principal innovation was the introduction of projecting towers. Although bastions had been in use in the Mycenaean era, the earliest archaeological evidence for the use of towers comes from the late 6th-century site at Burunkuk on the western coast of Asia Minor. At first towers were only used at weak points and at gateways but by the 5th century regularly spaced two-storey towers were the norm. These towers enabled the defenders to pour down a greater concentration of missiles on their attackers.

After the retreat of the Persians, Athens set about rebuilding her walls. It was essential to Athens that she secured communications with her new harbour at Piraeus. To accomplish this the Athenians built a massive wall round the Piraeus and linked the harbour with the town by two long walls fortified at intervals by two-storey towers. These long walls enclosed a corridor about 100m wide and 6,500m long.

Other Greek maritime states such as Corinth followed the Athenian lead, but although this type of defence might be effective against Sparta, it could hardly have withstood a concentrated Persian siege.

During the late 5th and early 4th centuries Athens built a series of frontier fortresses to secure her communications and as a first line of defence against attack.

The fortress at Eleutherae (Gyphtocastro) is typical of such forts. It is built to crown a steep-sided hillock on the south side of the pass between Mount Cithaeron and Mount Pastra, guarding the road from Thebes to Athens. Its walls, which are two metres thick, are faced with rectangular blocks of grey stone and filled with rubble. A series of two-storey towers project inwards and outwards from the walls. These are concentrated mainly on the north side where the approach was easiest. The towers were entered from the inside of the fort by a door at the street level. Two doors at first-floor level led out on to the battlements at either side. The sentry walk could also be reached by steps directly from street level. In the early 4th century the towers would have had

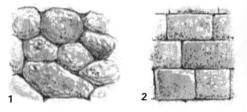

Above
The two main types of Mycenaean masonry. The stones were set in clay. The core of the wall was of rubble.
1 Rough-cut polygonal stones.
2 Carefully cut rectangular stones.

Above
A section through the walls at Tiryns showing the galleries and mud brick battlements. This is the most sophisticated of the Mycenaean fortifications.

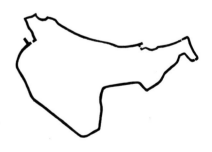

Above
Plan of the fortifications at Mycenae. The Lion Gate is on the left side. **Below** Plan of the 7th-century fortifications at Emporio on Chios.

flat platforms with crenellations at the top. The tower marked **X** on the plan faces directly up the pass and has a loophole in the north wall giving a perfect view of the head of the pass. The foundations of two watch towers have been found just to the west of the road at the summit of the pass. These would have given an excellent panoramic view of the plain of the Asopus; any troop movements could have been signalled back to the fort and from there transmitted to Athens.

Signalling by fire or smoke had been used from the earliest times. Originally fire signals had been restricted to a simple beacon which announced that some expected event had happened. Aeneas, the 4th-century writer on tactics, had suggested a system by which several different messages could be transmitted.

This method could only be used for signalling from a fixed lookout post and was based on a time delay system. Two large earthenware jars of exactly the same size were prepared. Each had a hole in the bottom which allowed water to flow out at a given speed. A cork float

with a rod stuck in it which was marked off in sections about 3cm wide was floated on top of the water. Each of these sections referred to one of the possible messages that could be sent. One of the jars with its rod and float was placed at the observation post and the other at the receiving point.

To send a message, the lookout raised a lighted torch and waited for the receiver to raise his torch to show that he was ready with his jar. Then the signaller lowered his torch and they both let the water run out of the jars. When the appropriate mark on the rod sank to the level of the rim of the jar, the signaller raised his torch again and the receiver read off the message from the sinking rod in his jar, which should be in exactly the same position.

The 2nd-century historian Polybius was not very impressed with this system and describes a method devised by a certain couple called Cleoxenus and Democleitus which, he says, he had perfected. If this is true, it was probably used by the Roman army. The system requires five boards, each containing five letters of the alphabet. The

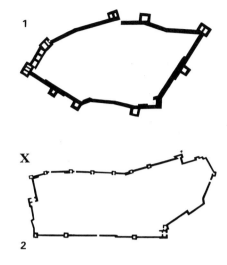

Above.
1 Plan of the 6th-century fortifications with projecting towers at Buruncuk-Larisa. **2** Plan of the 4th-century Athenian frontier fort at Gyphtocastro.

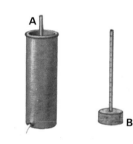

Below
A reconstruction of part of the walls and one of the towers at Gyphtocastro. Next to the tower is a sally port. The sentry walk could be mounted either from the tower or the ground.

Right
Time-delay signalling. The pot (**A**) is filled with water and the float (**B**) placed in it. On a signal the water is let out and at a second signal stopped. The message is read off the rod.

Below
Bar and lock from the Lion Gate at Miletos. The bar (**A**) is pulled across from its channel in the opposite wall (**B**) and slotted into hole (**C**). The locking bar (**D**) is fitted over (**A**) and slotted into hole (**E**). The lock pin (**F**) is pushed down, locking the two bars together.

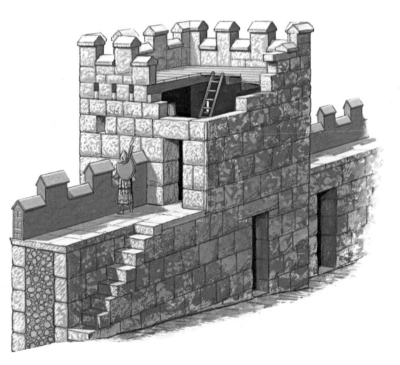

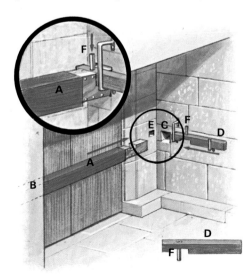

signaller in this case uses five torches, which he raised in groups alternately on the left and right to show first which board and second which letter on that board he is transmitting. If, for example, he wishes to signal the letter gamma he raises one torch on the left to show that it is on the first board and then three on the right to show it is the third letter.

For long-distance signalling Polybius recommends the use of two tubes through which the receiver can look. These limited the area of vision and prevented the receiver confusing the left- and right-hand signal. Of course, these methods could not be used by an army on the move, but might be utilised by the pickets of an encamped army to warn of enemy movements.

Very little advance was made in gateway design before the 4th century. The old Mycenaean types with modifications remained in use, such as the overlap type often defended with a tower at the end of the outside wall. This form was usually designed to expose the enemy's unshielded right side. When gates were cut straight through the walls they were usually defended by one or two towers or bastions.

The gates were made of heavy timber and closed by a bar locked in place by a cylindrical pin which was dropped into a hole in the bar locking it to the jamb. The pin disappeared below the top of the bar and could not be removed without a key.

Aeneas, the tactician writing in the 4th century BC, warns of the methods used by traitors to withdraw the pin and insists that a commander must insert the pin himself as people had been known to file a notch in the pin and tie a thread around it so they could pull it out later. Others had sprinkled fine sand into the cracks around the pin and then, by shaking the bar noiselessly, the sand had worked its way down so that the pin rose. Another method was to hit the underside of the bar with a mallet to make the pin jump up. On many occasions one reads of the bar being sawn through to let in a hostile force.

Siege tactics: the city states

The complexity and size of the Mycenaean fortifications suggest an equally sophisticated siege method. Unfortu-

nately no trace of this remains and only a vague hint of sophisticated tactics appears in Homer.

It has been suggested that the wooden horse by which the Greeks gained access to Troy was a battering ram. It is significant that part of the wall had to be knocked down to get the horse through. Picture a primitive battering ram: a long beam with a reinforced head suspended within a wooden frame with four sturdy legs, the head of the ram projecting from the front and the ropes by which the ram was pulled back trailing out of the rear. It is hardly surprising that it was called a horse. In later times all siege weapons were given such names.

The battering ram first appears on the Assyrian reliefs from the palace of Assurnasirpal in the first half of the 9th century BC. This shows a very complex box-shaped structure topped by a tower. This scene shows that by the 9th century siege warfare had become quite sophisticated. In Greece, however, whatever knowledge had existed was lost when the dark age engulfed the glittering civilisation of Mycenae. There is no further evidence of siege tactics in

Below
Types of gateway used in the classical period.
1 Gate guarded by one tower.
2 Gate flanked by towers.
3 Overlap gate with tower.

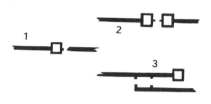

Below
A 9th-century Assyrian bas relief showing Middle Eastern siege techniques of the period. The besiegers have moved a covered battering ram up to the walls under cover of archers in a tower who keep the defenders away from the battlements. The defenders retaliate by dropping what appear to be pots of fire on to the ram. Other defenders have managed to catch hold of the ram with chains and are pulling it up whilst two attackers try to pull it down again. Meanwhile two more soldiers are undermining the walls. These methods were completely unknown in Greece at the time and only came into use in the 4th century. They may, however, have been known to the late Mycenaeans.

Greece until the mid-5th century. In the east the Assyrian traditions were continued by the Persians. Their mounds and mines are mentioned several times by Herodotus.

In Greece there was no sign of either of these tactics before the second half of the 5th century. Even then the main siege tactic of the Greeks was the blockade.

The first evidence of Greek siege tactics comes during the Peloponnesian war when the Spartans laid siege to Athens' ancient ally Plataea in 429 BC. Thucydides gives a vivid description of the siege in which the methods applied were entirely Persian. Initially the Spartans erected a stockade around the town so that no one could escape; then they began to raise a huge mound of earth against the wall. First two containing walls of timbers laid like lattice work were constructed to contain the mound. This type of timber wall can be seen on Trajan's Column. Next the space between the timber walls was filled with earth, rubble and wood. The construction of this mound, from which the Spartans hoped to storm the battlements, took the Spartans 70 days and nights.

The Plataeans countered by heightening the fortifications with a wooden framework within which they erected a wall using bricks from the nearest houses. The structure was covered with hides to protect the workmen and to stop fire arrows reaching the woodwork. They also tried to hinder the building of the mound by knocking a hole through the bottom of the wall where the mound touched it and drawing the earth into the town. When the Spartans discovered this and blocked the hole, they dug a tunnel under the wall and began removing earth from the bottom of the mound. Fearing that this would not stop the besiegers they constructed a crescent-shaped emergency wall behind the area that was under attack. The building of a second wall became one of the standard features of counter-siege operations.

The Spartans now brought up battering rams which shook down the superstructure that the Plataeans had erected on top of the wall. The defenders countered by lowering nooses over the battlements and pulling up the rams. There

was nothing novel in this tactic—the defenders are doing exactly the same thing in the 9th-century Assyrian bas relief shown opposite. The defenders also hung great beams over the battlements suspended from poles by chains. These were dropped on the rams in an attempt to break off their heads.

In desperation the Spartans now tried to fire the town by lobbing bundles of brushwood from the mound over the walls and then throwing in sulphur and pitch before setting them on fire. The wind carried the fire through the town and the Plataeans were only saved by an opportune thunderstorm.

When their attempts to fire the city failed, the Spartans gave up all hope of taking it by storm and reverted to the usual Greek and Roman tactic of building a wall around the town to starve it out. They dismissed the larger part of their army and began digging the trenches. First two ditches were dug about eight metres apart. On the inner side of each ditch a wall was built of mud bricks made from the earth excavated from the ditches. The space between the two walls was roofed over to form a sentry walk above and living quarters below. The sentry walk was fortified with battlements on either side and two-storey towers were constructed at 15m intervals. Most of the Plataeans had escaped before the siege began and

Below
A suggested reconstruction of the wooden horse of Troy as a battering ram with a covered housing. Part of the wall had to be broken down to get the wooden horse into Troy.

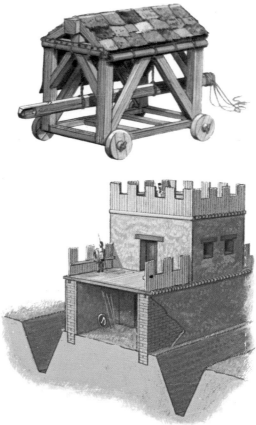

Above
Cross-section of the siege works the Spartans built round Plataea to keep the defenders in and help out. It consisted of two walls which were roofed over. **Below 1** The Spartan siege mound at Plataea. As a countermeasure the Plataeans heighten their walls using bricks (from demolished houses) inside a wooden framework. **2** Timbers laid like 'lattice work' form the containing walls of the mound to prevent the earth from spreading.

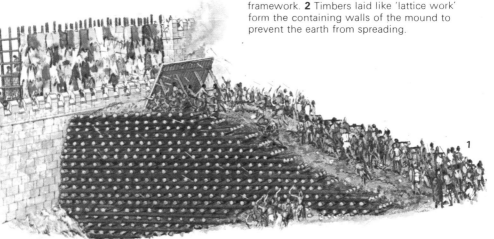

only a garrison of 480 men, and 110 women to prepare the food, remained in the town. They held out for two years. Half the garrison managed to escape in the later months of the siege by climbing over the Spartan siege walls one dark rainy night, but the remainder held out in the pathetic belief that the Athenians would relieve them. In the end, faced with starvation, they surrendered. Under pressure from the Thebans, the Spartans executed all 225 survivors and sold the women, who along with the men had borne all the rigours of the long siege, into slavery.

Eleven years after the fall of Plataea, Athens decided to annexe Sicily. The expedition culminated in the siege of Syracuse which should have been easily accomplished but, owing to the superstition, incompetence and indecision of the Athenian general Nicias, turned into an unmitigated disaster.

The Athenian armada beached at Catania and prepared for an assault on Syracuse, 50km to the south. At first the people of Syracuse did not believe that their city was the Athenians' principal objective and therefore took no precautions.

The Athenians made a brilliant start, drawing the Syracusan cavalry northwards while they sailed southwards for a seaborne invasion. But in spite of a victory in the battle that followed, Nicias failed to exploit his success and withdrew.

It was not until the following summer that Nicias again approached Syracuse. Anticipating an Athenian assault the Syracusans arranged a review of their troops in the plain south of the Epipolae plateau. Nicias heard of the review and the night before it was due to take place he embarked his troops and sailed southwards.

Once again the Athenians made a brilliant start. They landed their army just north of the plateau and while the parade was taking place to the south stormed the hill.

Once established on the plateau, the Athenians set about securing the north and south ascents. They built two forts, the Labdalum and the round fort. From the latter the Athenians began to construct double lines of ditches and walls, like those at Plataea, from sea to sea in order to cut off the city from any help

from the interior. The wall was planned to extend north and east from the round fort across the Epipolae plateau to the Trogilus harbour and south across the marshes to the Great Harbour. Here the Syracusans tried to impede the work with their cavalry, but when this failed they constructed a counter wall across the line of the Athenian walls (**X–X** on map). The Athenians mounted a surprise attack and, catching the Syracusans off guard, captured the counter wall. This they dismantled, using the materials to continue their own wall southwards. Again the Syracusans tried to hinder them, this time with a ditch and palisade (**Y–Y**) across the marshes at the edge of the Great Harbour. The Athenians again attacked, carrying doors and planks to help them as they crossed the marshes to the palisade. Once more the Athenians were successful and the Syracusans retired within the walls of the city, leaving the besiegers to complete their lines undisturbed. At the southern end the two walls diverged to contain the Athenian naval base on the edge of the Great Harbour. Piles were driven into the harbour bed to protect the ships against attack from the sea.

Now that the Athenians were in control of the sea and had isolated Syracuse from the interior, the city's fate was sealed. But Nicias, in an act of incredible stupidity, let the Syracusans off the hook. Convinced that the city would surrender, he failed to complete the wall across the Epipolae plateau. Syracuse appealed to Sparta which refused to send an army but did send a general, Gylippus. He landed in northern Sicily, managed to gather about 3,000 irregular troops and advanced on the beleaguered city. He was prepared to fight but to his astonishment he was not opposed. Under cover of night he climbed the Epipolae hill and entered Syracuse.

From this point everything went wrong for the Athenians. The Spartan immediately took over command of the Syracusan forces. Accepting that the Athenian southern lines were impregnable, he concentrated on the unfinished walls across the Epipolae plateau and launched a surprise attack on the hill, capturing the Labdalum fort. He then constructed a wall (**Z–Z** on the sketch) across the hilltop, making it impossible

for the Athenians to complete their wall. The Athenians should now have packed up and gone home but they decided to see it through to the bitter end.

In spite of receiving reinforcements the Athenians failed to retrieve their position. They were defeated by the Syracusans both on land and in a sea battle inside the Great Harbour. The Syracusans captured the Athenian store bases (**N, N, N**) on the south side of the Great Harbour and sealed it off by chaining a line of ships across the entrance. Now the Athenians were under siege. In desperation the Athenian fleet tried to break out but lost nearly half their ships in the attempt. The decision was made to abandon the fleet and retreat by land. The army set out in a westerly direction, marching in a hollow square. They were under continuous attack by the Syracusan cavalry and light-armed troops. Finding the route impassable they turned south, marching through the night. The next morning the Syracusan cavalry caught up with them again and they surrendered. Of the 50,000 men who had set out on the expedition only 7,000 remained. The Syracusans

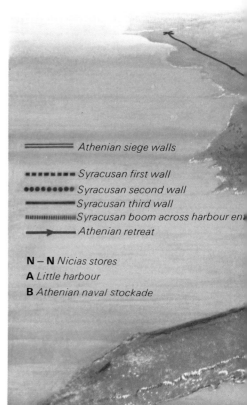

══════	Athenian siege walls
▪▪▪▪▪▪▪	Syracusan first wall
●●●●●●●	Syracusan second wall
───────	Syracusan third wall
▥▥▥▥▥▥▥	Syracusan boom across harbour en
──────▶	Athenian retreat
N – N	Nicias stores
A	Little harbour
B	Athenian naval stockade

executed the generals and the rest of the army was shut up in the quarries, where many died in appalling conditions. The survivors were later sold into slavery. These two sieges are excellent illustrations of the state of Greek siege warfare in the late 5th century.

By the beginning of the 4th century the first real improvements were made in siege techniques. The new advances took place not in Persia or Greece but in Sicily.

When the Persians invaded Greece in 480 BC the Carthaginians had launched a simultaneous and equally vain attack on Sicily. Soon after the destruction of the Athenian army at Syracuse the Carthaginians again attempted to take over the island. They had revived and improved ancient siegecraft, building huge movable towers which overtopped the walls of the towns they besieged. From these they raked the battlements with missiles to clear them of defenders so that the rams could be brought up against the walls. These new methods made the countermeasures which had been used at Plataea impossible.

Seven years after the defeat of the Athenians the Syracusans elected Dionysius I *strategos* on a permanent basis. This man was to revolutionise Greek siege tactics.

Dionysius established scientific warfare laboratories at Syracuse, offering large rewards for new inventions. The result was that when he laid siege to the Carthaginian port of Motya in 397 he was armed with the most sophisticated siege weapons of the day. Motya lay on an island about a kilometre off the west coast of Sicily and was linked to the mainland by a narrow causeway which the Carthaginians broke up on the approach of the Syracusan army. Dionysius repaired and widened the causeway in order to bring up his engines. These consisted of huge towers six storeys tall which moved on wheels, and the latest invention, bolt-shooting catapults. The catapult was not entirely new: it was probably used by the Assyrians and may have been introduced into Sicily by the Carthaginians. The bow of the day was of composite construction made of wood reinforced by sinew and horn. Because of their con-

struction these bows could be made to exert enormous power. Their only failing was that no one was strong enough to draw them. In its earliest form the catapult was simply a crossbow (*gastraphetes*, literally a belly bow). It acquired this name because the stock was placed against the stomach and the weight of the body was used to force back the slider.

The maximum range of the composite hand bow using a heavy war arrow was probably in the region of 150–200m, although it was. claimed that more than twice this range was achieved with special light arrows. E. W. Marsden, in his *Greek and Roman Artillery*, suggests that the *gastraphetes* had a range of about 250m, just sufficient to outrange the hand bows of the enemy. The invention of the *gastraphetes* opened up enormous possibilities. Using a stand and a winch to draw the string, the

Below
The Athenian siege of Syracuse. The Athenians tried to blockade the city with a double wall. The Syracusans tried to stop them with cross walls at **X–X**, **Y–Y** and finally succeeded with **Z–Z**.

power of the bow could be increased massively. Although there is no direct supporting evidence, it is possible that these latter were Dionysius' new weapons.

As the Syracusans widened the causeway they brought up their towers, presumably with the catapults in them (although Diodorus does not say so) and kept up a constant barrage against the defenders on the battlements to cover the workers on the mole. As the Syracusans drew nearer, the Motyans erected masts on the walls with yard-arms that swung outwards high above the towers. At the end of these beams were housings from which the defenders could hurl on to the towers lighted fire-brands and burning tow with pitch.

When they reached the island the Syracusans brought up their rams and under cover of the towers managed to breach the walls. The defenders retreated to the houses and the Syracusans moved their siege towers right into the town. Wooden boarding bridges were run out from the towers, which were about the same height as the houses, so that the soldiers could get on to the buildings. Motya fell with the usual slaughter and only those who sought sanctuary in the temples survived to be sold into slavery. Any Greeks found in the town were crucified.

It is rather surprising that the new technology did not spread more quickly. It seems to have gained impetus only under Philip II of Macedon. When the Macedonians besieged Perinthus in 340 BC, they constructed towers 80 cubits (c.35m) high which rose above the towers on the town walls. The walls were brought down by a combination of battering rams and undermining. However, for all his use of the latest techniques Philip's favourite weapon was bribery. When faced with impregnable fortifications, Philip asked if gold could scale its walls. In this way Olynthus fell.

The most important development in siege warfare was the use of artillery for defence as well as offence. The Perinthians had no artillery of their own but borrowed pieces from Byzantium. By now a new type of catapult had evolved powered not by a bow but by springs of twisted sinew or hair. There was almost no limit to the size of these torsion machines and the same principle could be used to shoot either bolts or stones. Torsion stone-throwers make their first appearance during Alexander's siege of Halicarnassus in 334. The main purpose of the catapults was to keep the defenders off the battlements. When two years later Alexander laid siege to Tyre he was faced by very similar problems to those encountered by Dionysius at Motya. Tyre was situated on an island off the coast and Alexander, who did not control the sea, was forced to build a mole to get out to it.

The Tyrians, who had withstood an Assyrian siege lasting 13 years, believed that Alexander stood no chance of capturing the city, which had catapults ranged along the entire circuit of the walls.

As Alexander's mole came within range of the walls he built two towers armed with catapults at the end of it and kept up a constant barrage against the battlements as Dionysius had done at Motya. He also brought up his stone-throwers and used these to shake the walls. To counter this the defenders erected multi-spoked wheels on the walls which rotated mechanically. These spinning wheels destroyed, deflected or broke the force of the bolts from the catapults. They also placed padding on the walls to soften the effect of the stones. Not content with defence, their catapult-armed ships attacked the workers on the mole and Alexander was forced to erect palisades to protect them. When the mole continued to advance the Tyrians prepared a fire ship using a cavalry transporter fitted with two masts at the front. A double yardarm was attached to each mast from which were hung cauldrons filled with anything that would increase the fire. The sides of the ship were built up and the hull filled with dry branches, wood shavings, pitch and sulphur. The stern of the ship was weighted down so as to raise the bows. When the wind was blowing in the right direction they towed it out and ran it aground on the end of the mole. The crew of the fire ship, having set it alight, swam to safety. As the yards burned the cauldrons collapsed into the fire, increasing the blaze. Assaulted by a constant hail of missiles from the Tyrian warships Alexander was forced to withdraw and watch his siege towers burn.

Just when his hopes of taking Tyre seemed at their lowest ebb, Alexander had an almost unbelievable stroke of luck. The Persian fleet was composed mainly of Phoenician ships; when the crews heard that most of Phoenicia had surrendered, the fleet disintegrated and the Phoenician and Cypriot squadrons offered their services to Alexander.

Now that he controlled the sea Alexander set about widening the mole so that it would hold more towers and engines. The engines were constructed on the spot, some of them being placed on transport ships and the remainder on the heavier triremes. When all was ready the engines were brought up to the end of the widened mole and the attack began again.

The Tyrians in the meantime had constructed wooden towers on the battlements facing the mole and dropped boulders into the shallow water near the foot of the walls to stop the ships coming in close. The boats trying to clear these rocks, which had to be anchored under the walls, came under attack from both the town and from specially prepared armoured galleys which broke through their cables, making it impossible for them to lie close under the walls. Alexander responded by covering several of his 30 oared galleys with protective armour and placed them in front of the ships that were retrieving the rocks. The Tyrians countered by sending down divers to cut the mooring cables, forcing the Macedonians to replace them with chains. Finally Alexander's men managed to secure nooses around the rocks and drag them on to the mole, where the catapults were used to fling them out to sea. With the way clear the Macedonians brought up ships with rams mounted on them to test the walls. At first they made little impression, but finally they managed to bring down the wall on the south side of the town. When the breach was wide enough the ships with the rams were withdrawn and two others carrying drawbridges were moved up. One of these was manned by *hypaspists* and the other by a *taxis* of the phalanx. Here is an example where the phalangites could not have been armed with the *sarissa*.

The other ships were ordered to launch a concerted attack against other points on the wall to disperse the

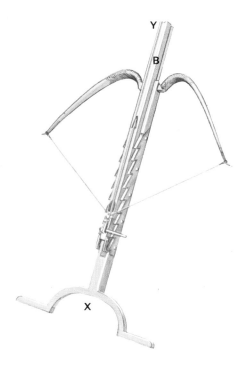

Above
The earliest catapult—the belly bow (*gastraphetes*). The bow was drawn by placing **X** round the belly, **Y** on the ground and using the weight of the body to force back the slider **B**—hence its name. After E. W. Marsden.

Below
This development of the *gastraphetes* shot two arrows together. The bow was too strong for a man to draw, so the slider had to be winched back. After E. W. Marsden.

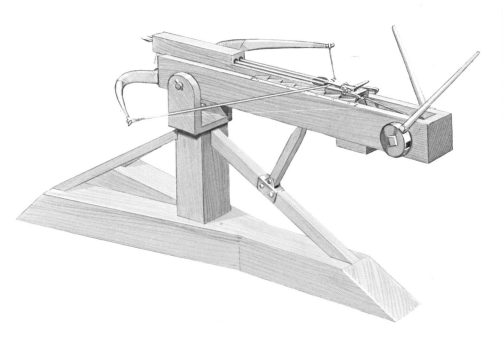

defenders, the drawbridges lowered into the breach and the Macedonians gained a foothold in the city. The Tyrians suffered the usual atrocities in the aftermath of the siege. Arrian says that the 30,000 survivors were sold into slavery whilst Diodorus claims that all the men of military age were crucified and the rest sold into slavery.

This siege provides a good illustration of the use of catapults: arrow-shooters on the towers to keep the defenders from the battlements and stone-throwers being used from the ground to shake the walls. Catapults and battering rams were also mounted on ships, an innovation forced by the problems of besieging an island fortress.

The Hellenistic period
After the death of Alexander, as the generals fought for supremacy, great advances were made in the construction of siege machines. When Demetrius Poliorcetes (The Besieger) laid siege to Salamis in Cyprus he built a tower 90 cubits (about 40m) high with nine storeys. The base of the tower was 45 cubits (c. 20m) square and it moved on four solid wheels eight cubits (c. 3.5m) high. This vast tower was nicknamed *Helepolis* (the city destroyer). The tower was filled with catapults: heavy stone-throwers capable of throwing stones weighing three talents (c. 80kg) were

placed on the lowest floors; heavy bolt-shooters in the middle storeys; and light arrow-shooters and stone-throwers at the top. The tower required 200 men just to operate the machines. The heavy stone-throwers tore away the battlements, leaving the sentry walk fully exposed to fire.

Possibly the most interesting and best-described siege in the ancient world was Demetrius' attempt to take Rhodes in 305–04. An account of both the siege of Salamis and Rhodes is given by Diodorus following the eyewitness account of Hieronymous of Cardia.

For the siege of Rhodes Demetrius prepared two penthouses, one for his stone-throwers and the other for his bolt-shooting catapults. Each of these was mounted on two cargo vessels fastened together. He also built two four-storey towers which overtopped the towers of the harbour and similarly mounted these on pairs of boats. A floating boom was constructed of squared logs studded with spikes to prevent the enemy ships from ramming those carrying the siege machines. Demetrius' aim was to capture the harbour and cut the Rhodians off from their corn supplies coming in by sea.

In anticipation of the siege the Rhodians had begun heightening the walls along the harbour. They placed two penthouses on the mole and three upon cargo ships near the boom of the small harbour, filling them with bolt- and stone-throwers of all sizes. They also placed platforms on cargo ships in the harbour so that catapults could be mounted on them.

During the night Demetrius managed to seize the end of the mole about 150m from the city wall. Here he established an artillery battery with 400 men and catapults of all types. At daybreak under cover of the battery on the mole he brought his seaborne engines into the harbour. From these he used his light bolt-shooters, which had the greatest range, to drive off the workers who were heightening the walls. Then, using his stone-throwers, he destroyed the enemy machines and the wall that they were building across the mole.

The first attempt to take the harbour proved unsuccessful and one of the floating engines was destroyed by fire. Demetrius was forced to withdraw to repair his machines. When he returned to the attack, and it seemed that he might take the harbour, the Rhodians launched a desperate assault against his three remaining floating engines with their three strongest galleys. Showered with missiles they crashed through the spiked booms, and by repeatedly ramming the floating engines managed to sink two of them. The floating machines were manoeuvred within the harbour by ropes and the besiegers succeeded in pulling back the third one. When the Rhodians pushed on in an effort to sink it, one of their ships was captured but the other two, although severely damaged, managed to escape.

Diodorus tells us that Demetrius now built an enormous floating battery three times as tall and three times as wide as the previous ones, but it was wrecked by a storm as he was trying to bring it into the harbour. During the storm, knowing that Demetrius would be unable to send in reinforcements, the Rhodians launched an attack on the battery at the end of the mole and captured it, thus regaining control of the harbour.

Demetrius now gave up his attempts to take the city from the sea and concentrated on the more conventional land assault. The word 'conventional' is used with reservation as one could hardly refer to anything that Demetrius did as ordinary. He now constructed another *Helepolis* even larger than the one he had used at Salamis. Its base was almost 50 cubits (c. 22m) square. The frame was constructed of squared timbers and bound with iron. Bars were placed across the centre at one cubit intervals to allow space for the men who were to push the tower forward. It was mounted on eight solid wheels, each nearly a metre thick, which were covered with iron plates. The wheels were on pivots so that the machine could move in any direction. The framework of the tower was made of four upright timbers nearly 100 cubits (c. 45m) long placed at each corner of the base and sloping inwards so that the tower tapered to about 20 cubits (9m) square at the top. It was divided into nine storeys. The front and sides were covered with iron plates nailed on to protect the tower from fire missiles. There were ports at the front at each level covered by shutters which were raised mechanically. These shut-

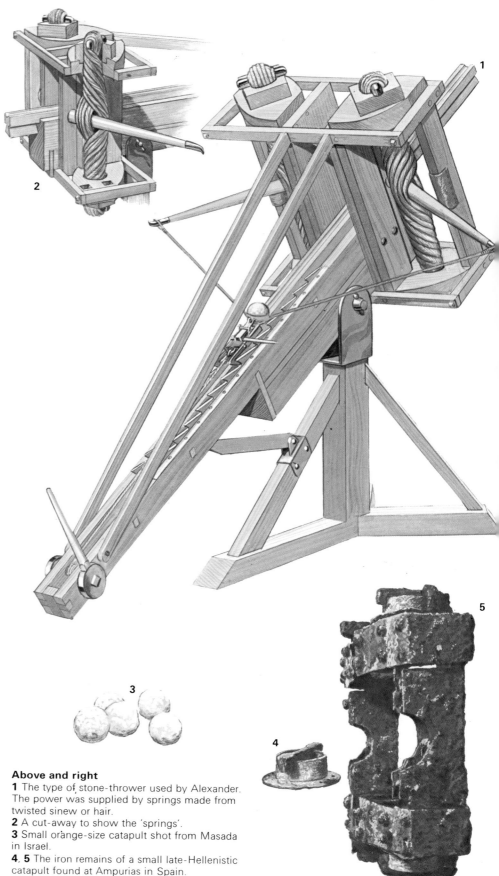

Above and right
1 The type of stone-thrower used by Alexander. The power was supplied by springs made from twisted sinew or hair.
2 A cut-away to show the 'springs'.
3 Small orange-size catapult shot from Masada in Israel.
4, 5 The iron remains of a small late-Hellenistic catapult found at Ampurias in Spain.

ters were made from hides stitched together and stuffed with wool to provide excellent protection against stone missiles. Each storey had two wide stairways—one up and one down. The tower was moved by 3,400 men, some inside and others pushing at the back. Allowing 15cm each for the thickness of the bars across the base, which were one cubit apart, it would be possible to squeeze a little over 30 rows of men inside the base of the tower, and at 60cm per man one would similarly get just over 30 men to a row. Therefore the total number of men pushing inside the machine could hardly exceed 1,000. Either Diodorus' figures are wrong or this represents three shifts.

According to the Roman engineer Vitruvius this tower was designed by Epimachus, an Athenian architect. Unfortunately he gives a different description of the tower, saying that it was 125ft tall and 60ft wide, weighing about 120 tonnes. He adds that it was covered with goatskin and undressed hide so that it could withstand the blows of catapult stones up to 360lb (118kg). Vitruvius has obviously got hold of the wrong

description. This would far better fit the Salamis *Helepolis*. Perhaps the Roman engineer did not realise that there were two different machines.

Vitruvius, quoting from a lost work by the engineer Diades who accompanied Alexander on his campaigns, gives the ideal dimensions of siege towers. The smallest tower, which has ten storeys, should be 60 cubits (c. 27m) high and 17 cubits (c. 7.5m) wide at the base. The top should be 20 per cent narrower than the base (c. 6m). The upright timbers that form the frame of the tower should be about 22cm thick at the base, tapering to 15cm at the top. His largest tower is twice this height, with 20 storeys, and has a base 23.5 cubits wide with a similar contraction of 20 per cent at the top. The uprights have to be 30cm at the bottom, again contracting to 15cm at the top. This 20-storey tower, with its base less than one-fifth of its height, would be very unstable. Demetrius' tower, with its base half its height, seems far more realistic. Diades' towers, which were covered with rawhide, had balconies around each storey. He adds an interesting detail in that these towers

were collapsible and could be taken on campaigns.

Demetrius also prepared penthouses to protect the men while they filled the ditches, and to cover the rams. Covered passages were constructed in movable sections ready for the assault on the walls. Vegetius, writing in the 4th century AD, says that these covered galleries were built in sections 5m long, 2.5m high and just over 2m wide, and there is no reason to suppose that they would be different at the end of the 4th century BC. When everything was ready the besiegers cleared an area about 600m wide leading up to the walls, exposing seven towers and the intervening sections of wall. They then began moving up the engines, placing the *Helepolis* in the centre with four penthouses on either side connecting them with the covered passages so that the soldiers could get to their posts in safety. They also brought up two enormous penthouses in which the battering rams were mounted. Once again Demetrius had built the biggest and the best. Each of the rams was 120 cubits (c. 54m) long and sheathed with iron (Diodorus com-

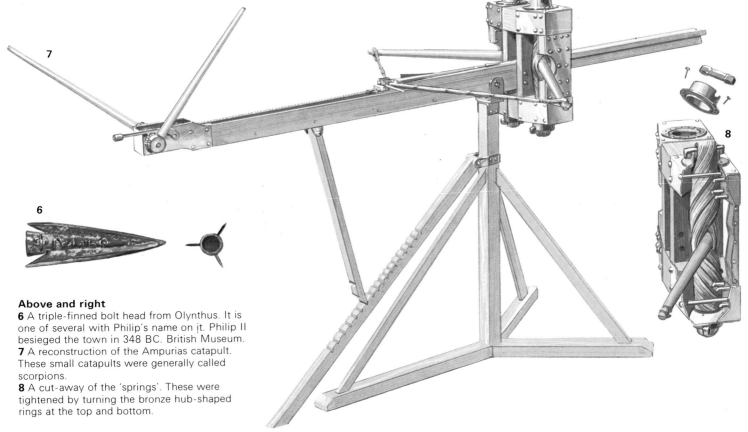

Above and right
6 A triple-finned bolt head from Olynthus. It is one of several with Philip's name on it. Philip II besieged the town in 348 BC. British Museum.
7 A reconstruction of the Ampurias catapult. These small catapults were generally called scorpions.
8 A cut-away of the 'springs'. These were tightened by turning the bronze hub-shaped rings at the top and bottom.

pares its blow to that of a ship's ram). The ram was mounted on rollers and powered by 1,000 men. This description has met with considerable scepticism, but what the critics have not taken into consideration is that the ram moved on rollers and the prime purpose of its length was to increase its momentum. As it was not suspended there was little chance of it buckling.

A description of a ram of this sort moving on rollers, also drawn from the writings of Alexander's engineer Diades, is given by Vitruvius. This ram had a housing 32 cubits (c. 14.5m) long and about 8m high with a low pitch roof which was surmounted by a tower about 2m square and 8–10m high with three storeys. The lower two storeys held pots of water for extinguishing fires while the top floor contained a small catapult.

Inside the housing the ram itself, which was pulled backwards and forwards by ropes, moved on rollers. Earlier rams would have been suspended by ropes or chains from the roof of the housing and operated like a pendulum. These primitive rams had a limited stroke with a decreasing momentum at the point of impact. Roller rams had a constant momentum and much greater penetration. The housings of these machines, which were called tortoises, were covered with planks of oak or some other low-combustion wood overlaid with a layer of green wattle. The housing was covered with seaweed or straw soaked in vinegar and sandwiched between two layers of oxhide.

Vitruvius also includes a description of a massive tortoise ram built by Hagetor of Byzantium. It was 18m long, 4m wide, 11m high and moved on eight wheels each 2m high and 1m thick. The ram, which operated like a pendulum, was suspended from a frame 12.5m high and operated by ropes. It was over 31m long and made from a squared timber 30cm wide and 22.5cm deep at the front, increasing to 37.5 by 30cm at the butt. The head was covered by a beak of hardened iron and the 4.5m behind the beak were sheathed with iron plates. Three ropes 15cm thick bound the ram from head to butt and these were bound to the ram by other ropes. The whole ram was then wrapped in rawhide.

Below
The *Helepolis*, the great iron-clad siege tower of Demetrius Poliorcetes. It was more than 40m high and had a base 22m square. It was divided into nine storeys crammed with catapults.

Diades' siege engines also included borers which were used to knock holes through the walls as opposed to rams which shook the walls down. Diades' borer was housed in a tortoise about 22m long. The borer itself, which was a long beam presumably with an iron point, moved on rollers along a wooden trough and was operated by a windlass and pulleys.

When the Rhodians saw which part of the wall was to come under attack, they immediately began building the customary internal wall. The besiegers commenced undermining the outer wall and the Rhodians responded by digging down on the inside and breaking into the mines, preventing the sappers from doing any further damage. But the force of Demetrius' machines was irresistible, and under remorseless pressure from the engines the walls began to crumble. The mass of bolt-shooting catapults in the *Helepolis* drove the defenders back from the battlements and, as at Salamis, the heavy catapults in the lower storeys of the tower stripped the crenellations from the wall. The largest of the seven wall towers that had come under attack was brought down and with it a whole stretch of the curtain wall so that the defenders could no longer move along the sentry walk from one part of the wall to another. The Rhodians launched an all-out attack on the *Helepolis* one moonless night, but failed to set fire to it. Demetrius, fearing for the safety of his monstrous offspring, pulled it back out of range. But as soon as it was repaired he returned to the assault. While he was preparing to continue the assault the Rhodians built a third crescent wall to back up all the parts of the outer wall that were in a dangerous condition and dug a deep ditch behind the part of the wall that had collapsed to stop the engines being brought into the town. Once again, when the *Helepolis* approached the walls, the catapults cleared the ramparts of defenders and the rams overthrew two more consecutive stretches of the curtain wall, isolating one of the towers. The Rhodians fought desperately in the tower and in spite of sustaining terrible losses foiled all Demetrius' attempts to take it.

Demetrius attempted one last assault on the town: a unit of 1,500 picked men burst into the town through the breach in the wall during the night, but although a desperate attempt was made to take the city both by sea and land, the following morning it was beaten back and Demetrius' commandos driven out again. Demetrius had shot his bolt and under pressure from the other Greek states came to terms with the Rhodians.

Vitruvius adds something to this story, though it may well be apocryphal. According to his account Diognetus, who had once been the town architect of Rhodes, was begged by the inhabitants to devise a method of capturing the *Helepolis*. He knocked a hole through the town wall at the point where the *Helepolis* was expected to attack. He then ordered the Rhodians to collect a great quantity of sewage, water and mud and channelled it out through the hole in the wall during the night so that when the tower was moved up it became stuck fast in the mire.

Below
1 The giant tortoise ram described by Vitruvius. The ram itself moved on rollers and was operated by two teams of men. The housing was made of hide padded with seaweed.
2 A bronze ram head from Olympia.

Above
A battering ram as described by Vitruvius. The timber was squared off, bound with ropes and covered with rawhide. The end was plated with iron and capped with an iron ram-shaped head.

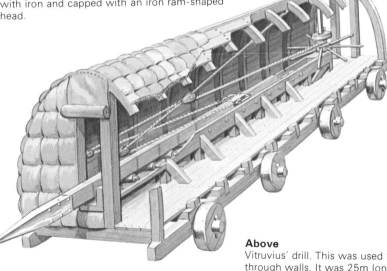

Above
Vitruvius' drill. This was used to pierce holes through walls. It was 25m long and was operated by a winch.

After the siege the Rhodians outdid Demetrius by selling his engines and using the money to erect one of the Seven Wonders of the World, the Colossus of Rhodes. This enormous bronze statue of Apollo, which was over 30m high and took 12 years to erect, stood at the entrance to the harbour which Demetrius had tried so hard to capture. It remained standing for only 56 years before it was shaken down by an earthquake. The statue lay in fragments for nearly a thousand years before the Arabs captured the island and sold it off for scrap in 672 AD. Tradition has it that it was sold to a Jew from Emesa who then carried the pieces away on the backs of 900 camels.

The siege of Rhodes marks the end of an era. Never again were such enormous machines used. Ninety years later Philip V preferred stealth and the more conventional forms of siege warfare. He generally circumvallated a town with a ditch and palisade before commencing the siege. When he laid siege to Thebes in Phthiotis (217 BC), he divided his army in three and joined the three camps with a trench and double palisade reinforced with wooden towers every 30m. At Abydus 17 years later he succeeded in cutting the town off from the sea by driving piles into the harbour entrance.

Once a town was surrounded Philip used his catapults and stone-throwers to hold back the defenders whilst he moved up his siege equipment. At Echinus (211 BC), having elected to make his assault opposite two towers, he set up a ram complete with a shelter in front of each tower and erected a gallery from one ram to the other running parallel to the wall; this enabled his men to move from one post to the other without coming under fire from the walls. These works looked very similar to the wall as there were wickerwork towers above the ram sheds and also wicker battlements along the top of the gallery. From the ground floor of the ram sheds men levelled the ground so that the rams could be moved forward. On the floor above, in addition to water jars and other fire-fighting equipment, there were catapults. At the top, level with the town towers, soldiers were posted to prevent the defenders interfering with the ram. The whole structure was defended by three catapult

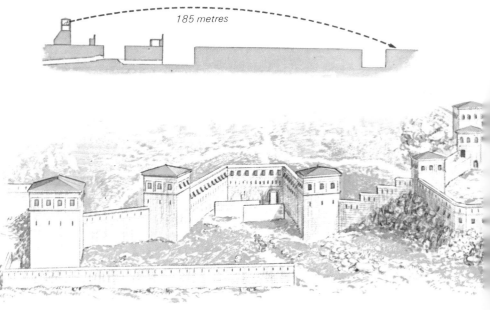

185 metres

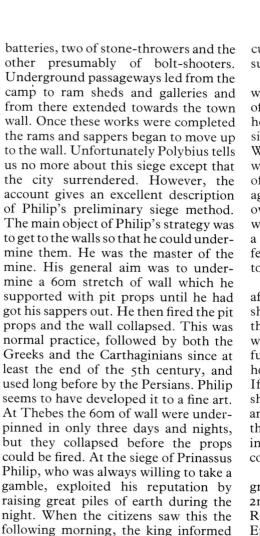

batteries, two of stone-throwers and the other presumably of bolt-shooters. Underground passageways led from the camp to ram sheds and galleries and from there extended towards the town wall. Once these works were completed the rams and sappers began to move up to the wall. Unfortunately Polybius tells us no more about this siege except that the city surrendered. However, the account gives an excellent description of Philip's preliminary siege method. The main object of Philip's strategy was to get to the walls so that he could undermine them. He was the master of the mine. His general aim was to undermine a 60m stretch of wall which he supported with pit props until he had got his sappers out. He then fired the pit props and the wall collapsed. This was normal practice, followed by both the Greeks and the Carthaginians since at least the end of the 5th century, and used long before by the Persians. Philip seems to have developed it to a fine art. At Thebes the 60m of wall were underpinned in only three days and nights, but they collapsed before the props could be fired. At the siege of Prinassus Philip, who was always willing to take a gamble, exploited his reputation by raising great piles of earth during the night. When the citizens saw this the following morning, the king informed them that he had undermined the

customary 60m of their walls and they surrendered.

The ancient authors tell us of many ways of dealing with mines. The earliest of these comes from Herodotus when he is describing the siege by the Persians of Barca in Egypt around 600 BC. While the Persians undermined the walls a smith was sent around the inside of the wall clapping a bronze shield against the ground. It struck a dull thud over solid earth, but over the place where the mines were being dug it rang a higher note. At this point the defenders dug a countermine and managed to drive out the sappers.

Aeneas, the tactician writing shortly after 360 BC, suggests that a deep trench should be dug in front of the walls so that the sappers could not get to the wall without revealing their position. He further advocates that a wall built of heavy masonry be erected in the ditch. If this last cannot be done the defenders should collect together a supply of logs and rubbish. When the mines appear in the ditch the rubbish should be thrown into the trench, set alight and then covered over to smoke out the sappers.

These countermeasures had been greatly refined by the beginning of the 2nd century. When in 189 BC the Romans laid siege to Ambracia in Epirus and tried to undermine the walls, at first they removed the earth in secret

Left
The Euryalus defences as they were originally planned. The huge catapults, from their elevated position at the top of the battery, could outrange the enemy and assault them as they tried to cross the outermost ditch. **Below** The great battery at Euryalus with the Epipolae gate in the background. An underground passageway ran from the left side of the gate to the battery and the inside ditches.

by an underground passageway, but finally they could no longer disguise the rising mound of earth from the town's inhabitants. The defenders immediately dug a trench along the inside of the wall and lined the side nearest to the wall with very thin plates of bronze; by placing their ears against the plates they were able to hear the miners. They then dug a tunnel under the wall and broke into the mines. When they were unable to drive the sappers out they jammed a large corn jar lying on its side into the tunnel under the wall. Jars of this size, over 1.5m in diameter, may be seen at Pompeii. This jar had been prepared with a hole in the bottom and an iron lid with holes in it over the top. The jar was filled with fine feathers and pieces of burning charcoal. The defenders then filled in the space around the jar, leaving only two holes through which pikes were thrust to stop the Romans getting near. An iron tube was fitted into the hole in the bottom end of the jar and a bellows attached. With this the defenders pumped pungent smoke through the perforated iron lid into the mine and managed to drive out the besiegers.

Aeneas also suggests many methods of dealing with siege engines. Besides the long-established ploy of catching the ram in a noose and drawing it up, he also suggests suspending over the walls huge boulders attached to beams by grappling hooks. These were to be aimed with long plumb lines also attached to the beams and were only to be released when the plumb line touched the top of the ram housing. He also suggests using a ram on the inside of the wall to counteract the enemy ram. Towers should be undermined so that they sink into the ground and become immovable. He also gives the recipe for preparing incendiary bombs: pitch, sulphur, tow, granulated frankincense and pine sawdust packed into sacks. The fire to ignite these would be carried in pots. During the siege of Lilybaeum the Carthaginians made particularly effective use of pine brands and tow to fire the Roman siege engines.

It would be impossible to storm a town without the most primitive of all siege weapons—ladders—but these are not as simple as they may seem. They must be exactly the right length for a particular wall. If they are too long the defenders can push them over backwards with a forked stick. The ladders must rest against the wall at such an angle that they will neither overbalance on the one hand nor break under the weight of the climbers on the other. They must also be sufficiently strong in relation to their length. At the siege of Cartagena the ladders were so long that they broke under the weight of the climbers. There are many instances of soldiers counting the courses of stones in a wall to work out the height. Polybius points out that the height of a wall can be worked out with the use of trigonometry and that once having established the height of the wall the ladders should be made 20 per cent longer. So, if a wall is ten cubits high the ladder should be 12 cubits to allow for the angle of incline. The Greek historian tells how the brilliant but erratic Philip V was offered the chance of capturing Melitaea by treachery. He planned to launch a surprise attack about midnight but started his march too early and arrived before the inhabitants had gone to bed. Realising that if he were to retain the element of surprise he would have to attack immediately, he ordered his ladder bearers forward only to find to his exasperation that the ladders were too short.

Hellenistic fortifications

There was only one real answer to the new siege techniques and this was to keep the enemy away from the walls; once he was up to the walls defence was hopeless. The improvements that took place in the 4th and 3rd centuries BC were mainly concerned with keeping the enemy at a distance.

Catapults could be used for defence as well as offence, and from the middle of the 4th century walls and towers were designed to hold artillery. Both were pierced with loopholes and artillery ports. The towers were often as many as four or five storeys high with heavy artillery at second-floor level and lighter pieces at the top. The higher the artillery could be raised the greater was its range. A pitched roof now replaced the old crenellations at the top of the towers, primarily to protect the defenders from the stone-throwers. The towers had postern gates through which sallies could be made to keep the enemy away from the walls. A large ditch (or series of ditches) was dug in front of the walls not just as a precaution against sappers but also to make it difficult to bring up siege engines. The outer ditches were usually fronted with palisades or thorn hedges. The inner one was protected by stone outworks behind which were artillery emplacements. Beyond the trenches were covered holes and artificial marshes to trap the machines.

The city walls were thickened and heightened. The old crenellated battlements were replaced by screen walls with shuttered artillery ports and loopholes. Vaulted rooms reminiscent of

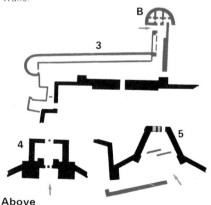

Above
A reconstruction of part of the walls and a tower at Paestum (after Krischen). The tower had shuttered windows and loopholes for catapults, but no crenellations on the tower or walls.

Above
Vaulted wall compartments with loopholes at Perge. Archimedes' catapults which shot from ground level at Syracuse must have been housed like this. The inset shows a section of a loophole.

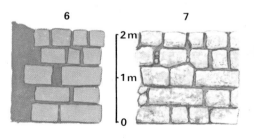

Above
The north gate at Selinus with complex outworks (**B** = artillery battery).
4 An enclosed courtyard gate at Athens.
5 The Epipolae gate at Syracuse. Outworks are marked in red.

6 Section of the Etruscan terrace walls at Veii in Etruria. The walls are 1.58–2.08m thick.
7 The face of the terrace walls at Veii.

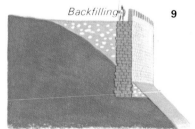

8 Earth and rubble

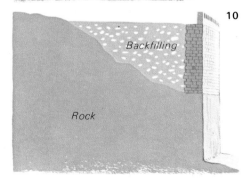

Backfilling **9**

Rock

Backfilling **10**

Above
A reconstructed aerial view of the Etruscan town of Veii at the time of the Roman siege, c. 400 BC. The main town is in the background and the citadel in the foreground.

Left
8 9 and **10** Reconstructed sections of the three types of terrace walls at Veii.
8 The type used on level ground. The wall is set into a rampart of earth.
9 The type used on sloping ground.
10 The type used on cliffs. The cliff face is cut away and the wall built on top. The space behind the wall is filled with rubble and earth.
Right Plans of Veii and Rome. Walls are black, ramparts brown and roads red.

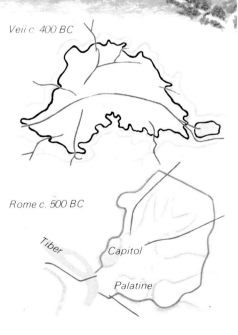

Veii c. 400 BC

Rome c. 500 BC

Tiber   Capitol

Palatine

289

Tiryns were built into the walls for the troops' quarters, and at Carthage even elephants were stabled in the walls.

The gates were massively reinforced. The north gate at Selinus in Sicily has a complex system of outworks forcing a would-be attacker to run the gauntlet before reaching the gates. The entrance to these outworks was defended by an artillery battery. The most common form of gate was the courtyard type which involved indenting the line of the walls to form a courtyard in front of the gate. This was often enclosed by a second gate at the outer end. A fine example of a closed courtyard gate defended by two towers is found on the Pnyx-Mouseion saddle at Athens. When Dionysius I became tyrant of Syracuse he constructed a long wall surrounding the Epipolae plateau so that it could never again be used against the city as it had been by the Athenians. The west gate of the plateau was a simple wedge-shaped courtyard type gate with an open outer end. Later, under pressure from the Carthaginians, it had been strengthened with outer cross walls so that it could not be approached directly.

Originally it had a triple portal, but one or two of these were later blocked off. A similar blocking of gates appears in the forts along Hadrian's Wall. The Epipolae gate was the weakest point of the Syracusan defences and was reinforced by a fortress, the Euryalus, built on a spur jutting out from the plateau just south of the gate. The outworks in front of the Epipolae gate forced the attackers over towards the Euryalus fort, bringing them under fire from the artillery batteries there.

Like the gate, this fortress went through several stages of development. The last is probably the work of Archimedes, the greatest engineer of the ancient world. The famous scientist had been given the job of improving the fortifications of his town and covered the wall with a wide range of ingenious machines which will be discussed when dealing with the Roman siege of Syracuse. Archimedes' greatest military achievement is probably the Euryalus fortress. The centrepiece of the fort is a massive catapult battery raised on five solid stone pylons 11m high. On top of these were mounted huge stone-throw-ing catapults which, because of their elevated position, could outrange anything that the enemy brought up. These faced westwards along the spur by which an enemy would have to advance in order to attack the fortress. The system was not completed when the Romans captured the town in 211 BC. Even so, it is noteworthy that they never made any attempt to capture the fortress or the Epipolae gate.

In front of the great battery were three rock-cut trenches, the furthest being about 185m from the battery. This was probably at the maximum range of the catapults so that an enemy would have to cross this under fire but out of his own artillery's range. From this point he would have to cross two more ditches and walls, each defended by catapults, before reaching the main battery. Tunnels were dug connecting the Epipolae gate with the forward defences so that the defenders could withdraw to the fort or the town if the outer defences were taken.

Early fortifications in Italy
Most of the villages of 8th-century Italy were sited on hilltops just as they were in the rest of Europe. These villages could usually rely on steep slopes for their defence, and this was often reinforced with palisades and ditches. Hundreds of such villages crowned the hills of Etruria. With the rise of the Etruscan ruling class in the 7th century, groups of villages were united into formidable towns and the ramparts of the earlier period were gradually replaced by terrace walls.

Excavations at Veii, 12km north of Rome, have revealed several stretches

Above
Etrusco-Roman arched gate, at Santa Maria di Falleri. **Below** Wall of polygonal masonry, Segni. When this masonry was used, gateways often had sloping sides and were either pointed at the top or had a long lintel across.

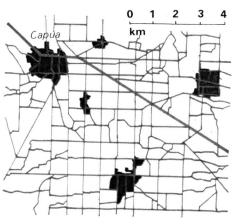

Above
Capua, c. 300 BC, which was very large, covering two square kilometres. **Below** Map of ancient Capua showing the roads and paths that still follow the Roman centuriation grid.

Above
Diagram of the fortress town of Minturnae, a typical Roman colony. **Opposite** Caesar's blockade lines around Alesia; see p. 293 for a complete description of the techniques of bicircumvallation.

of the terrace walls, a unique form of walling common to many Etruscan towns. Like many other Etruscan towns, Veii was built on a plateau defended by steep slopes at all but a few points.

Walls varying from 1.58–2.08m thick have been uncovered at several points along the rim of the plateau. These date to the end of the 5th century, just before the final Roman siege. They are constructed of rectangular blocks of stone about 45 x 45cm in section and up to 1.38m long. Where the approach was flat, walls just under 8m high, excluding battlements, were constructed with a steep ramp at the front to make it difficult for rams to be brought up and a massive mound at the back making it unbreachable. Where there was a steep slope the wall was constructed a little distance down the hillside and then backfilled to level it off with the summit of the plateau. On the other hand, if there was a cliff face the rock was cut back to make it sheer and the wall was built on top. It was then backfilled as before. Some Etruscan defences were strengthened with ditches in front which sometimes had to be cut out of the rock.

No traces of towers have yet been found at Veii, but at Luni a mound was erected crowned with a tower where the natural defences were weak.

Like the Etruscan cities Rome also grew out of a group of hilltop villages. The original site of Rome was the Palatine hill which rose out of the marshes on the left bank of the Tiber, but the other hills in the area were also occupied and these were gradually united to form the city.

According to Dionysius the Palatine, Aventine and Capitoline hills were fortified with palisades and ditches in the time of Romulus in the second half of the 8th century. It was probably the Etruscans who first gave the town one continuous line of defences, and the Capitoline hill then became the citadel: it was the only part of the city that did not fall to the Celts in 390 BC. The Etruscans probably erected the massive rampart fronted with a ditch which stretched across the eastern side of the old city.

The ramparts of Rome may have been replaced by stone walls but these proved no protection against the Celts and in

378 BC the Romans began to build a wall which at the time was probably the finest in Italy. This was the famous 'Servian Wall' which was constructed of rectangular blocks of tufa 60cm high by 45–65cm thick and between 74 and 210cm long. Across the weakly defended eastern side of the city a massive terrace wall was erected; it was 3.6m wide at the base, backed by an enormous rampart 10m high and levelled off to form an artificial ridge. This was fronted by a ditch 10m deep and 30m wide.

Rectangular blocks were the most common form of masonry used in Etruria and Latium. However, amongst the peoples of the Apennines we find that the more primitive polygonal masonry, recalling Mycenaean times, was still in use.

In Etruria and Latium the arched gate became almost universal, but where polygonal masonry was used gateways often had sloping sides and were either pointed at the top or topped by a heavy lintel.

Colonies
The Etruscans established colonies in

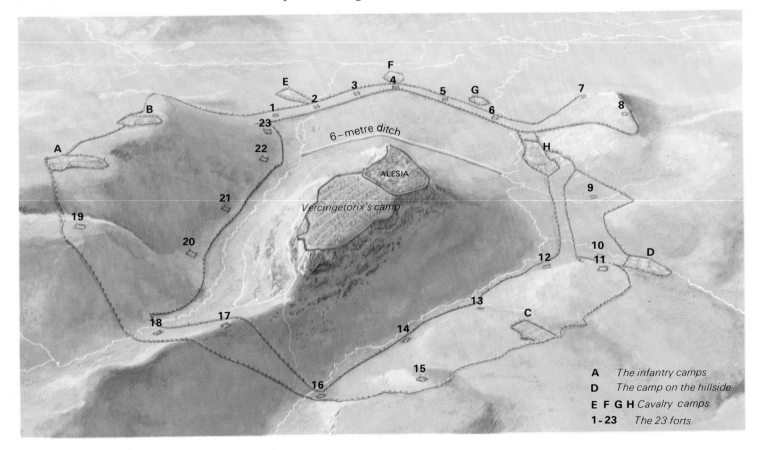

6–metre ditch

ALESIA

Vercingetorix's camp

A	The infantry camps
D	The camp on the hillside
E F G H	Cavalry camps
1–23	The 23 forts

the lands they conquered which served as both military and trading outposts. The Latins and Romans followed this practice but the prime objective of their colonies was military—to keep a foothold in enemy territory. The largest and most famous of the Etruscan colonies was Capua in Campania. Like other Etruscan and Roman colonies, Capua was built on a rectangular grid. It was exceedingly large, covering two square kilometres. It is inconceivable that the original settlement was so large: it is 80 times the size of typical Roman colonies such as Minturnae and Ostia.

Latin and Roman colonies were usually placed at strategic points in conquered territory, often covering routes into the area. Although Livy lists 40 colonies in Italy at the time of the second Punic war, they were not placed systematically; after the war many new colonies were established, especially along the coast, giving Rome quick access to any part of Italy. During the second Punic war Rome's colonies were one of the most significant strategic factors for they enabled Roman armies to operate deep in Carthaginian-held territory without breaking their lines of communication and provided strongholds and storebases on which the armies could fall back. However, colonies had only been established in conquered territory with the result that at the time

of Hannibal there were none in Campania which up to that time had not been at war with Rome. This caused serious complications for the Romans when Campania defected to the Carthaginians after the battle of Cannae in 216 as they had no 'safe house' in the area.

During the republic when every eligible citizen was a soldier, the colonies were established from those on the military roll but later they were formed from retired veterans, and the distribution of conquered land among the soldiers was one of the rewards of service. The colonies of the imperial period had the added purpose of Romanising the area. When a colony was formed the land was divided up into lots about 700m square (a *centuria*) which was farmed by four families. This 'centuriation' of the land was practised over the whole of the Roman world. Even today the system of square plots shows up on aerial photographs and may sometimes be seen clearly in the road systems on maps. It can be seen very distinctly around Capua, which was colonised after it was recaptured by the Romans in 211.

Early Roman siege techniques
We know practically nothing of Latin and Roman siege warfare before the 3rd century BC when Polybius takes up the story, but it was probably very similar to the Greek method. There was a

tradition that the siege of Veii, like that of Troy, took ten years and the Romans are supposed to have only finally captured the town by digging a tunnel under the walls. There may be a grain of truth in this story for the walls of Veii were undermined by many drainage tunnels (*cuniculi*) which the Etruscans themselves had built and blocked off when they constructed the terrace walls. It is quite possible that the Romans got in through one of these.

The earliest siege for which we have any accurate details is that of Agrigentum (Agrigento) in Sicily at the beginning of the first Punic war in 262 BC. In this siege the basic Roman method of blockading can be seen already fully developed. This was the technique of bicircumvallation, which was a development of the technique used by the Greeks during the Peloponnesian war. Several camps would be established around the besieged town at some dis-

Above
1 An iron spike from Alesia. These were hammered into short logs and buried in the ground so that only the point protruded. **2** A caltrop from Britain. This had a similar purpose.

Below
Caesar's lines of bicircumvallation around Alesia. The vast number of obstacles in front of the rampart enables it to be held by comparatively few men.

tance from it. These would be joined by lines of trenches and ramparts cutting the town off from the surrounding country and preventing anyone from escaping. If there was no enemy army in the field this would be sufficient, but if there was any possibility of relief from the outside a second line of ramparts and ditches would be established facing outwards. Between the two lines there was a broad thoroughfare, often several hundred metres wide, facilitating rapid troop movements to any part of the fortifications. Forts and picket posts were placed at intervals along the whole circuit so that every point of the lines was watched. The Romans were keenly aware that it was as important to bottle up the whole population within a besieged town as it was to prevent help from reaching them. The more people there were within the town the quicker the pangs of hunger would begin to tell. This puts into perspective Caesar's refusal to allow the old men, women and children to leave Alesia, for this could only lengthen the siege.

Bicircumvallation became the standard Roman system. It admirably suited the dogged Roman character and was used at the great sieges of Lilybaeum, Capua, Numantia and Alesia. Usually an attempt was made to take the town by storm first and when this failed it was starved out. Unless he wanted a quick result a Roman commander preferred the latter technique; if the town surrendered the booty fell into his hands, whereas if it was stormed the soldiers plundered it.

When besieging a port such as Lilybaeum or Carthage it was impossible to close the lines. At Lilybaeum the Romans tried to fill up the harbour entrance with earth but it was carried away by the current. When Scipio Aemilianus laid siege to Carthage in 147 he constructed his lines of vallation across the isthmus which joins the city to the mainland and then tried to construct a mole across the harbour entrance. The Carthaginians countered this by opening a new entrance to the harbour on the east side.

The only complete description that we have of bicircumvallation comes from Caesar's siege of Alesia in central Gaul in 52 BC. Alesia was situated on a lozenge-shaped plateau 1,500m long,

1,000m wide and 150m high. The town itself covered only the western end of the plateau, the other half being occupied by Vercingetorix's army of about 80,000 men which had recently broken out of Gergovia and retired to the apparently impregnable position at Alesia. When Caesar arrived he realised that the position was unassailable and decided on a blockade.

The hill of Alesia is part of a much larger plateau which has been eroded by two streams flowing to the north and south of the town. These have left two deep valleys which separate the town from the surrounding hills. To the west of the town the two valleys merge into a broad plain. Caesar encamped his legions around the town and traced out the line of his siege works. The inner lines were drawn along the foot of the hills to the north and the south of the town and then across the plain at the west end about 1.5km from the town. The outer lines extended along the top of the hills to the north and south and across the plain about 200m beyond the inner lines, leaving ample room for troop movements. Along these lines Caesar first constructed 23 forts to cover his workers before giving orders to begin digging the trenches. The legionaries first dug a vertical-sided trench about six metres wide across the plain at the foot of the plateau. This was to prevent any attack on the soldiers whilst they were erecting the main works in the plain. Four hundred metres behind this trench the legionaries dug two ditches five metres wide and where possible filled the inner one with water. These two trenches were extended all the way along the foot of the hills that surrounded the town until they formed a complete circuit 16km long. The earth from these ditches was piled up beyond the outer trench to form a rampart which was crowned with a palisade fortified by towers every 25m. Pointed stakes were embedded in the top of the rampart so that they projected horizontally to prevent any attempt by the enemy to scale it. In order to free the majority of his troops from the job of guarding the lines so that they could collect forage and timber, Caesar constructed a series of booby traps ahead of the lines. They dug trenches 1.5m deep in which were set sharpened branches

to form a hedge of spikes. In front of these they dug eight rows of circular pits with pointed stakes embedded in them. The soldiers nicknamed these 'lilies' because of their similarity to the flowers. These were then covered with brushwood to hide them from the attackers. Similar pits have been discovered in front of the Antonine Wall in Scotland. Finally, in front of the 'lilies' the soldiers planted small logs about 30cm long which bristled with barbed spikes. These were buried so that only the spike protruded from the ground. The outer lines which were constructed in a similar fashion stretched for over 28km and were similarly booby-trapped.

The Romans' unparalleled success in this form of siege warfare was due mainly to their perseverance. Because they never gave up a siege once it had been started, the besieged knew that they stood no chance of winning and were usually quick to submit. The story goes that a Roman commander, when informed by the ambassadors from a town he was about to besiege that they had food enough for ten years, replied casually that he would take it in the 11th year. As a result of this remark the town capitulated immediately. This attitude was the single most important factor in Rome's success in the field of siege warfare.

An interesting variation of the technique of bicircumvallation is seen in Caesar's attempt to enclose Pompey's army at Dyrrachium. Pompey was encamped on the hills along the coast near Dyrrachium (Durrës) in Albania. Here there was no question of Caesar cutting off his opponent's supplies as Pompey was being supplied daily from the sea which he controlled. Pompey's army was superior in cavalry and this was making it difficult for Caesar's troops to forage. Caesar decided to circumvallate his position. He began by constructing forts on the hills around Pompey's position which would be joined with ramparts and ditches. When Pompey realised what Caesar was doing he established 24 redoubts at as great a distance as possible from his camp to form a circuit of about 23km, knowing that Caesar would have to include these within his lines. Pompey's aim was twofold. First it gave him a small area in which to forage, and secondly it forced Caesar to over-extend his lines. As Caesar's troops dug their ramparts so Pompey began constructing inner lines, trying to occupy as many hills as possible and forcing Caesar once again to extend his lines. The result of this manoeuvring and countermanoeuvring by two vastly experienced generals was that Caesar built the external lines and Pompey the internal lines of bicircumvallation. Pompey's attempts to make Caesar overstretch his lines paid off and he was ultimately able to break out.

In the scientific techniques of aggressive siege warfare the Romans fell well short of the standards reached by the early Hellenistic monarchies. The Romans only adopted Hellenistic machinery when they were operating with Greek allies, as at Ambracia where they used mechanically operated grappling hooks to try to pull down the battlements; but they made little effort to understand or develop these techniques. They preferred methods which exploited the boundless energy of the legionary—undermining and the building of ramps—and in this area they far excelled the Greeks.

The Romans probably came into contact with scientific techniques for the first time when they invaded Sicily and must have learned much from the Greeks and Carthaginians during the first Punic war. They used rams when storming Panormus (Palermo), and both towers and rams were used in the siege of Lilybaeum. The Romans experienced their greatest problems when besieging ports such as Lilybaeum and Syracuse where, with their inferior technical knowledge, they found it impossible to close the harbour entrance. Their only successes against such towns in both the first and second Punic wars were when the town was either surprised by a sudden assault, such as at Panormus and New Carthage, or was in some way betrayed either by laxity of the guards or by straightforward treachery. It was only in the 2nd century that their techniques were sufficiently advanced to enable them to close a harbour with a mole.

The Romans' rather unsuccessful attempts at scientific warfare are well illustrated at the siege of Syracuse in 213. The example is perhaps a little un-

fair as they were trying to compete with the greatest scientific brain of the era, Archimedes. Dionysius I had walled in the Epipolae plateau at the beginning of the 4th century, but the defences had been brought up to date by Archimedes who had placed a host of engines on and within the walls.

The Romans, now in complete control of the sea, had decided on a simultaneous two-pronged attack by sea and land. Marcellus attacked from the sea with 50 quinqueremes packed with archers, slingers and javelineers whose job was to clear the battlements. The most noticeable feature here is Rome's lack of artillery. Eight of the quinqueremes had been lashed together in pairs, side by side with the oars removed from the sides that were in contact. On each of these pairs was a ladder about 1.2m wide which, when erected, was the same height as the wall. A breastwork was fitted along either side of the ladder and a platform placed at the top protected at the front and sides by wicker screens with room for four soldiers whose job was to drive away the defenders while the ladder was being placed in position against the wall. The ladder was laid horizontally along the double galley so that it protruded beyond the prow. Ropes were attached to the forward end of the ladder and it was raised into position by pulleys attached to the top of the two masts. Once the ladder was erected the double galley was moved up to the walls by the rowers on either side. This device was nicknamed a *sambuca* by the sailors because of its similarity to the harp-like musical

instrument of that name. As soon as it was moved into position the soldiers pulled down the wicker screens on the sides of the platform and mounted the walls whilst the rest of the troops followed them through the *sambuca*.

The Romans had not allowed for Archimedes, for as they approached the walls they were deluged with missiles from the catapults that the great scientist had placed on the walls. These machines threw stones at fixed ranges, some long and some short, subjecting the Romans to a constant bombardment as they advanced. These brought the Roman advance to a halt, forcing Marcellus to bring his ships up under cover of darkness. In this way he managed to get inside the fixed range of the heavy artillery at the top of the walls, but Archimedes had allowed for this too and had pierced the walls with loopholes at the level of the attackers. These were manned by archers and small bolt-shooting catapults nicknamed 'scorpions'.

In spite of the continual barrage of missiles Marcellus tried to raise his *sambucae*. Now cranes which hitherto had been out of sight reared up above the walls and swinging out their armlike beams dropped huge stones and lumps of lead on to the *sambucae*. The beams were swung round on a pivot and the weights lowered by pulleys at the end

Below
A section through *murus gallicus* showing the stone facing and timbers fastened together with nails. Caesar says that this type of wall was impervious to battering rams.

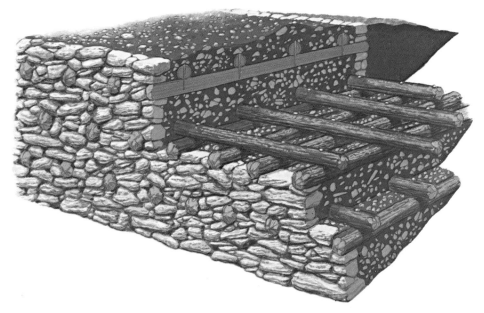

of the beams. These could be man-oeuvred to hit the *sambucae* wherever the Romans tried to raise them. Other engines hurled stones large enough to drive the soldiers back from the prow of the ship and then lowered giant grappling hooks attached to chains. These took a firm grip on the ships, which were then upended by counterbalances. The grappling hooks were then released so that the ships fell sideways, either capsizing or filling with water. Marcellus was completely outclassed but made light of the situation saying, 'Archimedes uses my ships to ladle sea water into his wine cups, but my *sambuca* band is flogged out of the banquet in disgrace'.

The Romans were forced to abandon their attempts to take the town by assault and in the end they gained access to the town by stealth.

Scipio's assault on New Carthage (Cartagena) three years later is particularly interesting, not because of any new technique but because it provides the first clear picture of Roman methods after a town had been taken. Polybius makes it quite clear that the Romans followed normal practice at Cartagena. When the soldiers broke into the town they killed every living thing; not only humans but dogs and other domestic animals were cut in half and dismembered. While the massacre was at its

height, pillaging was forbidden. When the general considered that there had been sufficient slaughter, the trumpets sounded the recall. Soldiers were selected from each maniple (sometimes whole maniples were chosen) to carry out the pillaging. Never more than half the army were permitted to take part. The rest stood guard in case there was a counterattack. All the booty was collected together, sold off and the proceeds distributed evenly amongst the soldiers. This controlled pillaging provides a graphic illustration of Roman discipline and underlines the superiority of their system. So many other armies would have been caught off balance by a counterattack when they were pillaging.

This reign of terror after the soldiers had broken into the town is also seen in the storming of Carthage in 146. The Romans broke into the city through the harbours and captured the forum area. From here they launched an attack on the citadel (Byrsa). There were three narrow streets lined with six-storey buildings leading from the forum to the Byrsa. To reach the citadel the legionaries were forced to capture each building as they went. The soldiers fought from house to house using planks to cross from roof to roof high above the narrow alleyways. Once they reached the Byrsa they set fire to all the houses

along the three streets. The fire spread and the soldiers pulled down the houses where many of the old people and children had taken refuge. Some were burned and others fell into the streets and were buried under the rubble. The streets had to be cleared so that the troops could move freely and the wounded were slung into pits together with the dead.

For six days and nights these scenes of terror continued with the legionaries fighting in shifts. When the Byrsa was finally taken many of the remaining Carthaginians burned themselves alive in the temple of Aesculapius. The rest were sold into slavery. The whole town was destroyed and ploughed into the ground, and salt was sown so as to make the ground uncultivable. This punishment was also meted out to Numantia 13 years later, and to Jerusalem in AD 70.

The laws of siege warfare changed little throughout history. A failure to surrender before the battering ram touched the wall left a town completely at the mercy of the besiegers. No one in the town was in any doubt as to the con-

Below
A reconstruction of a part of Hadrian's Wall in northern Britain showing turret 41a and mile castle 41, which is on the hillside in the middle distance. This wall stretched for nearly 120km.

sequences of their refusal to surrender. Rome's record in these sieges does not differ from that of other nations. Wellington's troops in Spain were notorious. The atrocities that accompanied the break-in were all part of the psychological method employed to discourage resistance, and anyway it would have been practically impossible to restrain the troops.

In 49 BC, during the civil war, Caesar laid siege to Marseilles. This was the last of the great Hellenistic sieges. The Massiliotes had the most modern countersiege engines, including enormous catapults capable of shooting bolts 3.5m in length. These bolts could pierce four layers of hurdles, and penthouses made of the normal woven osiers were no protection against them. So the roofs of the penthouses had to be reinforced with timbers 30cm square which were clamped together with iron, and a tortoise 18m high had to be constructed to cover the men clearing and levelling the ground. The most interesting detail of this siege was the building by the legionaries of a brick tower close beneath the walls of the town. The initial purpose of this tower, which was nine metres square with walls 1.5m thick, was to protect the soldiers operating close to the wall, giving them a refuge when they came under heavy attack. Later it was decided to increase the tower's height and a floor was put in at first-storey height with the beams fitted into the wall so that they were not exposed on the outside and could not be fired. Then the building was continued until the second-floor level was reached. Up to this height the soldiers had been covered by a shed and penthouses, but beyond this it would be too high to protect. So they built a roof resting on top of the tower with beams that extended beyond the walls. From these beams they hung screens to protect them as they worked. As the height of the tower increased they levered up the roof until they had a tower six storeys high. A covered gallery was then constructed from timbers 60cm square through which they could reach the enemy's tower and wall somewhat less than 20m away. To construct this gallery two beams of equal length were laid on the ground about 1.2m apart. These had upright posts 1.5m high fitted to them.

These were connected to rafters on to which the boarding for the roof was fixed. Over this were laid 60cm beams which were held in place with plates and bolts. This was covered with shingles 7cm square on top of which was constructed a tilt roof of bricks, tiles and clay. Hides were drawn over the bricks, which had not been fired to protect them from water, and finally patchwork padding was stretched over the hides to shield them from fire and stones. The gallery, which had been constructed out of range of the enemy, was finally lifted on to rollers and moved up against one of the wall towers under covering fire from slingers, archers and catapults in the brick tower. In spite of the hail of missiles the Massiliotes managed to bring up cranes which dropped heavy rocks and fire barrels on the gallery but they failed to break through it and the legionaries managed to prise

Below
Plan of the auxiliary fort at Utrecht in Holland. The internal corner towers and partially protruding gate towers are typical of the 1st to 2nd centuries AD.

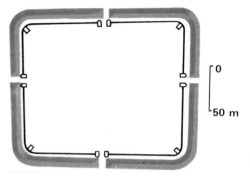

Below
A reconstruction of the Porta Nigra at Trier in Germany. It has been cut away to show the portcullis. This novel method of closing gates is first mentioned in the second Punic war.

loose the foundations of the tower and bring it down.

By the middle of the 1st century BC most of the civilised world had fallen to Rome. In Europe the only enemies remaining in arms were the barbarians of the north, with the result that most of the sieges over the next century were against hillforts.

Caesar gives a full account of the techniques he used to besiege one of the hillforts of central Gaul. This was Avaricum (Bourges), which was situated on a spur jutting out into the marshes. This spur first slopes down towards the marshes and then rises to a hillock at its end. The town itself, surrounded by what Caesar calls a Gallic wall (*murus Gallicus*), was on this hillock. Gallic wall was built with a stone facing at the front and back but with the centre filled with soil or rubble and laced with timbers which were built into the stonework at the front and back. The soft filling and timber lacing made it virtually impervious to battering rams. The inhabitants, believing that the town was unassailable, were prepared to defy Caesar, but they had not taken into consideration the energy of the legionary. Caesar's troops attacked along the spur, filling up the dip between the hill and the town with a vast ramp. Two siege towers were constructed on the spot and moved up as the mound approached the walls. The Gauls followed the usual procedure and tried to undermine the ramp while at the same time erecting wooden turrets covered with hides on the walls opposite. They also launched frequent night attacks in which they tried to fire the timber containing wall of the ramp. The amount of wood required for building these ramps and other siege equipment was enormous. The Jewish historian Josephus remarked that when the Romans besieged Jerusalem not a single tree was left standing within a radius of 18km.

In 25 days the legionaries had constructed an enormous artificial platform 100m wide and 25m high, filling the dip between the hill and the town. From this they stormed the town and slaughtered every man, woman and child in it.

The early empire
Without the spur of sophisticated siege warfare, fortifications in the West began to decline from the middle of the 2nd century BC and little advance was made until the barbarian invasions of the later empire. In the 1st and 2nd centuries AD the defences of both towns and camps usually consisted of a wall or rampart fronted by a ditch. The gates were defended by towers which were normally rectangular and did not protrude beyond the line of the walls. The defences were often strengthened by corner towers, and sometimes interval towers, which were always built inside the line of the walls.

There was, however, one significant advance made during the later republic and early empire. This was the introduction of the portcullis. The channels for these gates can be seen clearly on many Roman sites, at Nîmes, Aosta and Trier, for example. The origin of this very clever innovation is unknown. It is first mentioned during the second Punic war when some Carthaginian soldiers who were trying to recapture Salapia in Apulia after it had fallen to the Romans were trapped by the portcullis and their escape cut off.

From the time of Hadrian the Romans began to think more in defensive terms, but even so the fortifications of the period are more impressive for their scale than their strength. From this period come Hadrian's Wall and the vast chain of camps and forts along the Rhine-Danube line. Hadrian's Wall shows no advance in defensive thinking over the 5th century BC, but it was adequate for the purpose for which it was built. The thickness of this wall, which stretched for nearly 120km, varied between just under two and just over three metres; it must originally have been about five metres high. It was defended by 80 small mile-castles about 1,500m apart and about 160 turrets. Two of these were placed between each mile-castle about 500m apart. Along the front of the wall there was a broad berm and a ditch eight metres wide and about three deep. Behind the wall was a space about 35m wide bounded by a ditch about 6.5m deep known as the *vallum*. This ditch has no military significance and must have been dug to stop civilians approaching the wall and force them to use the authorised approaches. The wall was further strengthened by forts, generally built astride the wall at approximately 10km intervals.

Along the Rhine a string of forts was constructed to defend the west bank. These were integrated with the legion-

Above right
A tortoise (*testudo*) formed by 27 legionaries. The four ranks are shown in different colours. This formation is first mentioned by Polybius who compares it to a tiled roof.

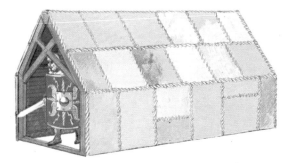

Above
A hide-covered gallery as described by Vegetius. It was 5m long, 2.5m high and just over 2m wide. These galleries were used to get up to the walls during a siege.

ary fortresses along the west side of the river. Watch and signal towers were also established so that the whole river from Bonn to the sea could be supervised. The river Danube was similarly fortified from Regensburg to the Black Sea. A ditch and palisade were constructed from a point just south of Bonn to one near Regensburg to join the two rivers. These fortifications stretched for about 450km and like Hadrian's Wall were reinforced by a fort every eight to ten kilometres. In places, as it approached the Danube, the palisade was replaced by a wall with turrets similar to the British wall.

The early principate

Roman siege technique in the early principate is best illustrated by the sieges of Vespasian and Titus during the Jewish revolt of AD 66–c. 73. Three of these, Jotapata, Jerusalem and Masada, are described in considerable detail by Josephus. Apart from the use of artillery, in all three sieges the Romans reverted to the age-old method of mound building. Josephus, who commanded the Jewish forces at Jotapata, comments on the deforestation of the area to provide timber for these earthworks.

Jotapata was a mountain fortress in Gallilee which underwent a 50-day siege. The siege was undertaken by three legions, V *Macedonica*, X *Fretensis* and XV *Apollinaris*, supported by various auxiliary regiments. According to the Jewish historian the Romans had 160 catapults varying from rapid bolt-shooting machines to one-talent (c. 40kg) stone-throwers. The Romans referred to bolt-shooting machines as *catapultae* and to stone-throwers as *ballistae*. However, during the empire the meaning of these names was reversed, so for clarity they will be referred to as bolt-shooters and stone-throwers. Vegetius says that in his day each legion had 55 pieces of artillery. This approximates very closely to Josephus' 160 pieces for three legions. Vespasian moved up his artillery first to keep the defenders off the battlements whilst the mound was being built because the Jews were dropping boulders on the screens (*plutei*) under which the mound builders were working. These screens were made of wicker probably covered with hide. He

later used the artillery in the same way to protect his ram which was of the primitive suspension type. Josephus is keen to describe the effect of the stone-throwers which carried away the battlements and broke away the angles of the towers. A man standing on the walls had his head knocked off and the force carried it a distance of three *stades* (c. 550m). A pregnant woman was hit in the stomach and the baby was flung half a *stade*. Thackeray, the translator of the Loeb edition, saw fit to add a footnote: 'Josephus is prone to exaggeration'.

The defenders used the well-tried methods of countering the Roman assaults: the walls were heightened, with the masons working behind palisades covered with fresh hides, and sacks of chaff were lowered over the wall to break the force of the ram. Characteristically, Josephus claims that these countermeasures were invented by himself to meet the emergency.

The ram was protected by hurdles and would have been approached in the normal fashion through galleries

(*vineae*). A breach was finally opened in the wall and gangways were moved up into the gap just as Alexander had done at Tyre. Vespasian ordered a general attack to be made on the walls to draw some of the defenders away from the breach and then moved up his men in tortoise formation (*testudo*). This formation, which was first described by Polybius who aptly compared it to a roof of tiles, is illustrated on Trajan's Column. It is shown on p.297 formed by 27 men in four rows. The front row of six men crouch down behind the shields of the middle four men, which are held rim to rim, and the two men at the end turn their shields outwards. The second, third and fourth rows of seven men each close up in a similar way, but the middle five men in each rank hold their shields above their heads. This formation can

Below
Diagram showing the siege of Jerusalem in AD 70. During the Jewish revolt the energy of the legionary and the doggedness of Roman siege technique were shown at their irresistible best.

A *The Temple*
B *The fortress of Antonia*
C *The middle town*
D,E *2nd camps of Legions V. XII and XV*
1–6 *Successive Roman thrusts*

be formed up by any number of men as long as there is one less in the front rank than the subsequent ranks. There are stories of chariots being run across these formations to test their strength.

The defenders poured boiling oil over the tortoise to break it up and tipped boiled fenugreek (*foenum graecum*) over the gangway, rendering it too slippery to negotiate.

After the fall of Jotapata and Josephus' desertion to the Romans, Vespasian withdrew from the war to devote himself to the struggle for the throne and placed his son Titus in charge of the war. With his army reinforced by an extra legion, XII *Fulminata*, Titus advanced on Jerusalem. So many conflicts raged in Jerusalem that there was hardly time to fight the Romans. Groups of religious fanatics had entered the town and were fighting with each other over how the war should be waged. During these quarrels parts of the city were burned. The flames engulfed the granaries and vast hoards of food were destroyed. It was only when Titus began the assault that any attempt was made to unite the Jewish forces.

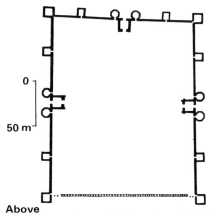

Above
Diocletian's palace at Split: outer wall with three gates and projecting towers. **Below** Abinaeus' fort of Dionysias (Quasr Quarum), Egypt, built by Diocletian.

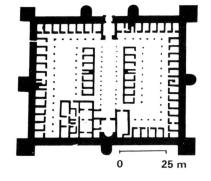

0   25 m

The city was composed of five parts, each with its own wall. The first of these parts was the old town, which was built on a spur with steep cliffs to the east and south. Above this to the west was the upper town where Herod the Great had built his palace. To the north of the old town was the massively walled temple enclosure, and adjoining both the temple and the upper town was the middle town. Beyond this sprawled the new town. Titus moved the camp of the 5th, 12th and 15th legions up to the walls of the new town and here launched his attack. Weakened by internal squabbles among the defenders, this sector soon fell into his hands. The main camp was then moved within the walls of the new town. Five days later the middle town also fell. Titus now divided his forces, with two legions to attack the old town and two the temple. At the point where the middle town wall joined the temple, Herod the Great had erected a fortress which he had named Antonia in honour of his benefactor Mark Antony.

At first the Romans tried to construct earthworks in order to get the siege machines up to the level of the fortress but the defenders undermined them and they collapsed.

Titus now surrounded the city with a rampart and palisade; once he had secured the whole circuit, he began to re-erect the earthworks against the Antonia fortress. The defenders failed in an attempt to fire the earthworks and the battering rams were brought to bear on the walls. That night the wall came down as a result of the constant battering and the network of tunnels that the defenders had driven under their own fortifications in an attempt to collapse the earthworks. Forseeing that the wall might be breached the defenders had taken the normal precaution of erecting an inner one. For two days the legionaries struggled in vain to take this wall which defied direct assault and the bringing to bear of rams. On the second night a small party of legionaries, including trumpeters, scaled the walls; they disposed of the sentries and sounded their trumpets, giving the signal for Titus to lead an attack on the wall. The defenders, believing that the wall had already been taken, left their posts and retreated to the temple. Most

of the fortress was now destroyed so that a ramp could be pushed straight up to the temple platform and the towers and rams brought up. For five weeks the temple held out. Titus endeavoured to spare it but when all attempts to obtain a surrender had failed and the battering rams had proved impotent, he gave orders for the gates of the temple enclosure to be fired. The fire spread to the porticoes and much of the outer enclosure was destroyed. Two days later, after vicious hand-to-hand fighting around the outer court of the temple, the Romans burst into the inner court. During the fighting a Roman soldier threw a firebrand into the temple, igniting the furniture and drapes within the shrine, and the whole building was reduced to ashes. From here the Romans were able to assist the two legions besieging the old town and it too was captured. Only the massively defended upper city remained in the hands of the insurgents. The legionaries raised earthworks on the west side whilst the auxiliaries conducted a similar assault from the east. In 18 days the works were complete, the engines were brought up and the town stormed. The siege had lasted five months and the population had experienced all the rigours of starvation. In the last days mothers are said by Josephus to have eaten their own children.

The city was turned over to the soldiers and when they had wearied of their killing and pillaging it was set on fire. Titus then ordered the remains to be razed, leaving only the three highest towers and part of the wall. The wall was for the encampment of the garrison and the towers to remind the people of the stature of the city that had once stood there.

After the fall of Jerusalem, Titus returned to Rome leaving to successive Roman governors the task of mopping up the remaining centres of resistance. The last of these was the fort of Masada, perched on a column of rock rising 400m above the western shore of the Dead Sea. The job of reducing this mountain fastness was given to legion X *Fretensis*, which was reinforced with about 4,000 auxiliaries. The Roman legate Silva first surrounded the hill in the normal Roman fashion with a wall nearly two metres thick fortified with towers every

25–30m. His forces were dispersed in eight camps around the base of the hill. They then set about the task of constructing an enormous ramp on the west side of the hill up which they winched their siege engines. The defenders, rather than be captured by the Romans, committed suicide. This siege, though very minor in scale, has left behind the clearest evidence in the whole field of ancient siege warfare: although unexcavated, the lines of circumvallation, the camps and the remains of the ramp are there for all to see.

Fortifications, AD 284–378 (Roger Tomlin)

When the emperor Diocletian abdicated in 305, he retired to what our sources call a 'villa' on the Dalmatian coast. His colleagues also built palaces at their birthplaces, and other late-Roman fortified villas are known, but Diocletian's at Split is the grandest of them all: a rectangular complex 2.9 hectares in area —almost the size of the contemporary legionary fortress of Kaiseraugst near Basle—enclosed by a towered wall of limestone ashlar 17m high. One can still walk through the north gate with its arcaded gallery and remains of octagonal towers, down the *via praetoria* to a colonnaded piazza. On the right is Diocletian's chapel, on the left a mausoleum which is now the cathedral; in front is the pedimented entrance to the imperial apartments which stretched the entire length of the south side, raised above the sea on their vaulted platform like a cliff. This was a fitting retreat for the self-styled Father of a Golden Age who had filled the frontier zones with miniature versions of his fortress palace. Massive rectangular forts, with stone walls at least three metres thick, projecting towers and heavily defended gates, sometimes explicitly dated to Diocletian by an inscription or a literary reference, can be found in North Africa, Switzerland, and on Diocletian's Road in Syria, which linked Damascus and Palmyra with the Euphrates. The fort of Dionysias in the Egyptian Fayum, where Abinnaeus was commandant in the 340's, is Diocletianic: it had a single gate, and towers projected at the corners and at intervals along a stone wall nearly four metres thick and at least seven metres high. Considering the absence of

any real external threat, and the peaceful nature of Abinnaeus' routine, the strength of the defences is remarkable: it is an index not of internal unrest but of how widely general principles were applied by Diocletian, and the defensive mentality of late-Roman strategy.

This strategy has been summarised already. Diocletian and his colleagues restored the old frontiers, except for retrenchment beyond the Rhine and Danube, in southern Egypt and in western Mauretania. To hold a line of 4,000 miles and more against what a 4th-century strategist calls 'the frenzy of the native peoples howling around the Roman empire', Diocletian and his successors to Valentinian I (364–78) embarked on an enormous programme of building and reconstruction. Diocletian envisaged powerful frontier armies of new cavalry units, legions, and increased numbers of *alae* and cohorts, all of which needed fortified bases. Constantine weakened these armies in order to strengthen the mobile reserve, the *comitatenses*, but his strategy still required the same kind of frontier zone: a defence in depth consisting of chains of strongpoints along the frontier, and down the lines of communication in the hinterland, that would protect foodstuffs and military stores (and taxpaying civilians) during invasion and speed the mobile army's response. Late-Roman fortification is emphatically defensive. This is not a truism, because the fortified towns of the early empire often made their walls as extensive as possible, and built gates that were public monuments, to advertise their prosperity. The forts were also sited aggressively, to control movement, with towers that projected above their ramparts for observation, not beyond them for enfilading fire. The army of the early empire trained to meet its opponents in the field; in the late empire this role was reserved for the *comitatenses*, which is why fortifications were now intended for prolonged defence. There are, of course, variations in technique directed to the same end: thus towers almost invariably project from the curtain, but they may be round, semi-circular, D-shaped, fan-shaped, polygonal, or rectangular. Some changes in outline or internal layout may be significant for dating, though it would be unwise to press them: it seems to be

the usual practice after the reign of Constantine to set internal buildings against the perimeter wall, in the manner of a medieval castle's bailey.

Just as the frontier strategy envisaged a defence in depth, so was it the tactic of individual strongpoints to keep assailants as far away as possible. New forts were sited on elevated ground, preferably a plateau, even if its irregular outline imposed the same outline on the

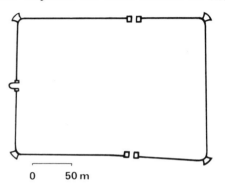

0   50 m

Above
Fort of Intercisa, Dunapentle, Hungary, with fan-shaped towers and west gate later converted into a tower built by Constantine.

0

50 m

Above
Fort of Alta Ripa (Altrip, near Ludwigshafen, West Germany) built by Valentinian in 368.
Below
Contemporary tower within outer breastwork, built on the Yorkshire coast at Goldsborough.

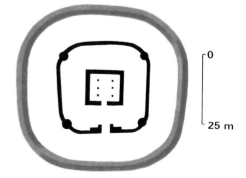

0

25 m

defences. The narrow V-section ditches of the early empire were superseded by wide flat-bottomed ditches, flooded if possible, set further from the wall so as to create a 'killing zone' like the lists of a medieval castle. In the Byzantine period one finds double walls—the 5th-century Land Walls that made Constantinople impregnable for so many centuries are the most famous—and even a breastwork on the inner face of the ditch. An early instance occurs at the siege of Aquileia in 361, where the defenders defeated an attempt to cross the ditch by making a sortie under cover of 'a turf rampart in front of the walls'. Late-Roman walls also required a wider berm for stability: they were not the revetted embankments of the early empire, but thick curtain walls of concrete rubble faced with masonry, again like a medieval castle. There is a wide variety of building techniques: brick facing, like Aurelian's walls at Rome; small ashlar with bonding-courses of brick, seen at its most regular in the Diocletianic walls of York; and often masonry that is frankly irregular. The use of salvaged material is common, including monumental sculptures and tombstones. City walls in particular betray improvisation and haste, by covering drastically reduced circuits, sometimes no more than a 'citadel', or by incorporating earlier buildings, like the walls of Rome. Some Gallic perimeters incorporate the amphitheatre as a kind of bastion, a feature which is already found at Trier, where the large enceinte was built at leisure in the late 2nd century. This amphitheatre saw the rise and fall of the Gallic mobile army: here in 306, while Trier was his first capital, Constantine threw two Frankish kings to the wild beasts; a century later, in the invasion of 406–07, it was the last refuge of the population. Different techniques are found within the same circuit. At the Saxon shore fort of Richborough, Diocletianic in style but dating perhaps to the reign of Probus, one can see changes of pattern in the masonry between the work of one building gang and the next. In the main walls of Nicaea (Iznik), of about the same date, one can see some D-shaped towers of timber-laced concrete faced with bricks on a foundation of column drums, others that are rectangular, because they were

built of magnificent ashlar taken from a public building, perhaps the theatre.

The projecting bastions which dominate so many late-Roman enceintes, sometimes a 'modernisation' added (as in Britain) to an existing wall, provided enfilading fire and advanced positions for artillery. When Julian rebuilt a Trajanic outpost in Alamann territory in 357, he was careful to install 'artillery for the walls'. There were two kinds, the *ballista* and the 'scorpion'. The *ballista*, metal parts of which have been found in two late-Roman outposts across the Danube, was the same as the 'field artillery' of Trajan's Column, a two-armed torsion engine that fired bolts; the stone-firing *ballista* seems to have been obsolete in the late-Roman period, though parts of one dating from the first half of the 3rd century have been found on the Mesopotamian frontier at Hatra. There is a long story in a Greek source of a gunner in the reign of Probus who shot a man peering out of a postern gate. Anecdotes of near misses in Ammianus confirm that the *ballista* was an effective weapon: a bolt aimed at Julian killed a soldier by his side; a client king of the Persians lost his son in the same way at the siege of Amida. At the same siege, by moving five 'light' *ballistae*, the Romans were able to gun down 70 Persian archers who had seized one of the towers. The identity of the gunners remains a problem: there are several late-Roman units of *balistarii*, but we only hear of them as an infantry escort of Julian on a hazardous cross-country journey, and on a fragmentary building inscription from the Crimea. The other catapult found in late-Roman sieges is an innovation: the 'scorpion' (or 'onager') was a one-armed torsion engine that hurled a large stone ball, like the medieval mangonel. Ammianus has a gruesome story of an engineer who stood behind one when it backfired, and was smashed to an unrecognisable pulp. The 'scorpion' was crucial at the siege of Amida because it reduced several Persian towers, but its drawback was the vibration, which meant it had to be fired on a solid, resilient platform.

Many forts and fortresses were simply 'brought up to date' by repairing the existing defences and perhaps modernising them. Thus almost all the old forts on the Pannonian frontier received

a new type of angle tower in the reign of Constantine which was standard to new forts, the fan-shaped tower (it looks more like an axehead) that projected far enough to provide enfilading fire down both sides. There is archaeological evidence of many new forts being built, and occasionally an eye-witness account. The emperor Valens in c. 368 decided to plug a gap in the lower Danube frontier, where it was possible for raiders to evade the *limitanei* by slipping across a lagoon. He succeeded in fortifying a headland, which had defeated one of his predecessors because of the difficulty of transporting stone, brick and lime; his panegyrist, who was there, claims to have seen chamberlains and guardsmen bringing their quota of crushed tile (a constituent of the hydraulic cement that would set under water). In the same year, his brother Valentinian was fortifying a new site on the middle Rhine, at Altrip; Ammianus, or more likely his informant, saw 'the disciplined soldiers often working up to their necks in water' to revet the fort with oak beams and piles.

We hear of fortified depots, like one besieged by Isaurian brigands, 'a walled enclosure by the sea, where supplies are still stored for distribution to the soldiers defending the whole Isaurian sector'. It must have been like Veldidena near Innsbruck, a quadrangle 70m square with projecting towers and a single fortified gate, enclosing a courtyard with a large granary on either side. Perhaps the most characteristic feature of a late-Roman frontier is the *burgus*, a free-standing tower, chains of which have been excavated along the Swiss Rhine, the Danube bend north of Aquincum, and the Iron Gates sector. They fill the gaps between forts, each one in sight of the next, like the watchtowers on an Iron Curtain frontier. They are small square structures, solidly built, and more than one storey high, since they often contain the bases for floor-supports. One of the largest, which happens to be mentioned by Ammianus, is *Robur* ('Strength') on the enemy bank opposite Basle: it was 13m square with turrets at the corners and walls 4m thick, built on a 'raft' of concrete and beams, and must have looked like a medieval castle keep. Some *burgi* are protected by an outer breastwork like a medieval 'shell' keep, for example the towers on the North York coast. Of course the *burgus* was not a late-Roman invention. Its rationale emerges from inscriptions of the Danube sector south of Aquincum; Commodus in 185 'fortified the whole bank with entirely new *burgi* and strongpoints in suitable places, to prevent clandestine crossings by raiders'. It was an essential element of border control, which had the merit of being fairly cheap: in 371 the *burgus* 'Commerce' ('which is why it was built') took a working party from the First *Martia* legion 48 days to build. A special kind of *burgus* sometimes found on the enemy bank of the Rhine and Danube consists of a central tower with two wing-walls ending in turrets, which project into the river. It seems to have been intended as a landing place, presumably for the patrol boats mentioned by Ammianus and other sources. There is an eye-witness account of one being built opposite the fort at Altrip: 'with battlements surrounding it . . . and frequent openings from which arrows can be fired under cover. The top of the tower is gilded . . . it has a sloping roof of lead plates like armour'. This sombre tower, like 'Commerce' and *Robur* the work of Valentinian, was one of the last fortifications to be added to the frontiers of the Western empire.

Siege warfare, 4th century (Roger Tomlin)

In spite of annihilating the East Roman mobile army near Adrianople (378), the Goths were not able to storm the city next day. After a futile attempt to infiltrate the defences with deserters from the Roman army, they resorted to massed attacks against the gates, from which stones and other missiles were hurled upon them. There was a panic when a Roman 'scorpion' discharged a stone ball, even though no one was hit. After two days they gave up, regretting they had not followed their leader's advice to 'keep at peace with walls'. This episode is typical of barbarians' inability to take fortified towns by siege: they lacked the technology (the Goths had been reduced to firing back Roman arrows) and they lacked the technique. Ammianus Marcellinus, our principal source, takes this for granted. In winter 356/7 Julian was trapped in Sens with

a weak garrison, but rallied it against Alamann attack; after a month the Germans gave up, 'muttering they were fools to have thought of besieging a town'. The Danubian capital of Sirmium was only weakly defended in 374, when the Quadi and Sarmatians overran Pannonia, but the governor cleared out the ditches and repaired the walls, and the invaders, 'who had little skill in these refinements of warfare', turned aside. Valentinian's principal opponent, the Alamann king Macrian, was particularly formidable because 'he would even attempt walled towns'.

Yet when Julian was appointed Caesar in November 355, the news broke that Cologne had fallen to the Franks 'after a stubborn siege'. (Conversely, a raiding band of 600 Franks held out in two derelict Roman forts for two months in midwinter 357/8, before starvation forced them to surrender.) When Julian arrived in Gaul, some 45 Gallic towns, as well as minor forts and towers, had fallen to the invaders: compare this with the 70 towns restored by Probus, again according to Julian, presumably after the great invasion of 275. We are not

told why the Germans were so successful. Some towns were strong enough to resist outright attack, according to Julian's panegyrist Libanius, but their inhabitants could not venture outside the walls, inside which they were even forced to grow corn. At Autun the Germans followed their 'usual method' of trying to scale the wall near an unguarded gate; the regular garrison was 'paralytic', according to Ammianus, but local veterans rallied to the town's defence and held it until Julian arrived with a relieving force. In 368, on the eve of Valentinian's offensive, Alamann raiders were able to break into Mainz during a Christian festival because there happened to be no garrison. It seems,

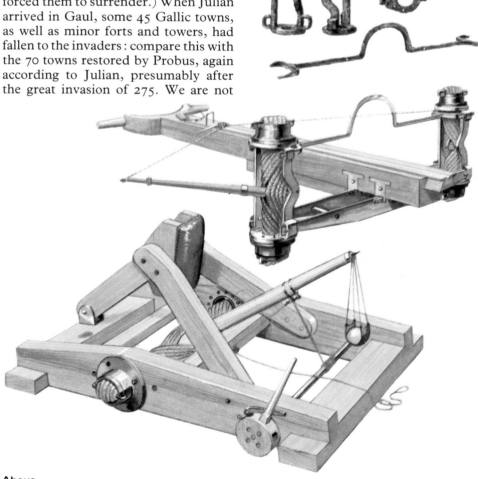

Above

Field-frame, front, side and top view and an arched strut from a Cheiroballistra found at Orsova in Rumania. A reconstruction of the Orsova *Cheiroballista* after Dietwulf Baatz

(centre). Reconstruction of an onager after E. W. Marsden (bottom). This primitive weapon was introduced in the later empire. It had only one arm and 'lobbed' stones rather like a mortar.

therefore, that the barbarian invaders lacked sophisticated siege techniques, and were forced to rely upon surprise, blockade, and the demoralisation of second-rate garrisons.

The Western provinces only saw real sieges during civil war, like that of Aquileia in 361. This key city, whose resistance in 238 had brought down the emperor Maximinus, was held against the usurper Julian by soldiers loyal to Constantius II. Its surviving defences are no more impressive than those of a legionary fortress of the early empire, and it is difficult to appreciate the difficulty the besiegers found in approaching the walls. They tried instead to attack the riverfront, by building wooden siege towers on three boats lashed together; but the defenders fired incendiaries which set the towers on fire, and they fell over. After further resistance, Aquileia surrendered only when its defenders had been convinced that Constantius was dead.

Almost all the sieges described by Ammianus occur in Mesopotamia, where both Rome and Persia were the heirs to centuries of experience. The frontier was roughly midway between the two capitals Antioch and Ctesiphon, reflecting the difficulty both sides experienced in advancing from their bases into the opposing network of fortified towns and military strongpoints. A campaign like the Persian offensives of 359–60, or Julian's offensive of 363, entailed siege warfare. The methods were all well-tried, with no great margin of superiority on either side. The Persians used elephants, with great moral effect. Ammianus always refers to these 'walking hills' with disgust, but they were of little real use; at the siege of Amida they were driven off with firebrands. The Romans may have had the edge in artillery; the Persians at Amida were using *ballistae* they had captured from the Romans 11 years before, and do not seem to have had the 'scorpion'. But the use of these weapons was subordinated to the prime object of getting close enough to storm over, or break through, the enemy's walls. There were four primary weapons—all of great antiquity, with appropriate countermeasures—which could take a walled town. They were battering rams, siege mounds, siege towers, and mining. Ideally they

were used in conjunction, the ram being perhaps the most effective. The problem was to bring it safely to the angle of a projecting tower. At the Persian siege of Bezabde (360), a Roman barrage which included iron baskets of burning pitch hurled by 'scorpions' made this almost impossible. At last the Persians got a ram into position by fire-proofing it with wet bullhide, demolished the tower and broke in. The Romans in their attempt to recapture Bezabde the same year used a huge ram which had been employed by the Persians a century before to destroy Antioch, and abandoned during their retreat. It was elaborately fire-proofed with wet hides and material, and by smearing the timbers with alum, but the defenders neutralised it by lassooing the iron head. A successful sortie set the other siege engines on fire. So the Romans concentrated on raising siege mounds: the two *ballistae* mounted on each had given them a decisive superiority in firepower when the Persians made another sortie and succeeded in setting the mounds alight by stuffing burning coals into the branches and reed bundles they contained. Siege towers could be used in much the same way: the Persians at Amida mounted a *ballista* on top of each. In Julian's siege of Pirisabora (363) preparations for building a siege tower reduced the garrison to surrender. Certain features in Western fortifications—the use of pile foundations and the raising of floors in towers—have been seen as precautions against mining, but it is doubtful whether German invaders had the necessary expertise. The Persians, however, had used the technique at the siege of Dura in the mid-3rd century. A Roman mine was successful at the siege of Maiozamalcha (363) in the advance to Ctesiphon; when the sappers had reached the foundations of the walls, a diversionary attack was launched above ground, enabling them to break into a room and kill the sentries on the wall.

The great siege of Amida (359), which has been mentioned already, illustrates most of the siege techniques practised in the mid-4th century. The detailed narrative of Ammianus, an involuntary participant, becomes even more vivid when one sees the basalt walls which still surround modern Diyarbakir. This dusky enceinte has been enlarged and

repaired since 359, but the impregnable east face, 'beneath which yawned rocks so precipitous that one could not look down without vertigo', substantially remains the work of Constantius. In 359 the Persians were attempting a new strategy, suggested by a Roman defector, of bypassing the frontier fortress of Nisibis and advancing up the Tigris to descend on Syria from the north-east. The Romans were deceived; but unfortunately for the Persian strategy—and for Amida—a Roman gunner aimed his *ballista* at a client king and killed his son who rode by his side. The Persian army was bound by its code of honour to avenge his death—at the cost of 30,000 dead and 74 days delay, which saved Syria. Amida was strongly held, by its regular garrison of the Fifth *Parthica*, four other frontier legions, and a pair of *auxilia* which had been drafted from Gaul for supporting the usurper Magnentius. The latter played no real part in the siege (Ammianus' description of them as 'legions' is a literary archaism): their sorties were as destructive to themselves as to the Persians. The five legions, however, fought tenaciously and skilfully, and might have saved Amida but for bad luck.

At first the Persians tried to storm the walls with the help of elephants, 'hideous with their wrinkled bodies, most gruesome of sights'. They began to raise siege mounds and iron-plated towers with a *ballista* on top. Then a Roman deserter betrayed an underground passage which led down to the Tigris from one of the towers on the east side. A force of 70 Persian archers crept into the tower at night through the passage; next day they opened fire, covering an attempt to storm the walls, but were driven off by *ballista* fire. The Romans achieved another success when the fire from their 'scorpions' brought down the Persian siege towers. But disaster struck when a mound raised inside their walls—to counter the Persian mounds—collapsed, bridging the gap between the wall and the Persian mound. The Persians threw in all their troops and stormed into Amida. Street fighting continued all day, but Ammianus prudently lay low until nightfall, when he slipped out of an unguarded postern and 'returned beyond all hope to Antioch'.

Roman Military Costume

This series of paintings, to illustrate the development of Roman military costume from the 1st century BC to the 3rd century AD, were painted by the author with the help of H. Russell Robinson for the Romisch-Germanisches Zentralmuseum at Mainz and are on display there. Numbers **18** and **19** have been added to take the series through to the beginning of the 5th century. Numbers **1–17** are published here by the kind permission of the Römisch-Germanisches Zentralmuseum, Mainz.

Where possible the reconstructions are based on archaeological evidence and confirmed by sculptural or other artistic evidence. The archaeological evidence increases in quality and quantity up until the second half of the 1st century and then declines rapidly so that for the best period we know every detail of the equipment including belts, baldrics and sandals, whereas for the 3rd century the evidence is very sparse indeed. After the middle of the 3rd century very little body armour was worn, so it did not seem worthwhile reconstructing an infantryman from this period.

A centurion of the early empire always wears his sword on the left and dagger on the right, whereas the legionary wears them the other way round. With the *aquilifer* it seems to be optional which way round he wears them. Other standard bearers wear them on the right. The animal skins worn by standard bearers seem to vary according to rank: *aquilifers* wear lion skins and others wear bear skins. However Praetorian standard bearers wear lion skins. Standard bearers carry round shields. One can be seen slung across the back of the *aquilifer*.

Several items of equipment shown here are not included in the main body of the book. The helmet worn by the cavalryman (**6**) is reconstructed from pieces found at Koblenz-Bubenheim in Germany. The helmet worn by the archer (**12**) is from Bryastovets (Karaagach) in Bulgaria. The cuirass worn by the legionary (**14**) is reconstructed from fragments found at Newstead, Scotland. The belt fittings on the cavalry officer (**19**) come from Ténès in N Africa.

Right
Caesarian legionary armed with oval *scutum*, crude Montefortino helmet, mail shirt, two *pila* and sword. The archaeological evidence is lacking only for the sword.

2

Left
Legionary of the first half of the 1st century AD armed with oval *scutum* squared off at top and bottom. Coolus type helmet, mail shirt, sword, dagger and *pilum*.

Right
A centurion of the mid-1st century AD wearing his decorations on a harness over a scale shirt. He also wears greaves and a transverse crested helmet as a sign of his rank.

3

Left
An *imaginifer* of the mid-1st century AD. He carries an image of the emperor or one of his family. The reconstruction is based on the tombstone of the *imaginifer Cenialis*.

Right
An *aquilifer* of the mid-1st century AD based on the tombstone of L. Sertorius. He wears his sword on the left as centurions do, but the *aquilifer* Gnaeus Musius wears his on the right.

Opposite
An auxiliary cavalry- and infantryman of the mid-1st century AD. The cavalryman is based on the tombstone of Flavius Bassus and the infantryman on the tombstone of Firmus.

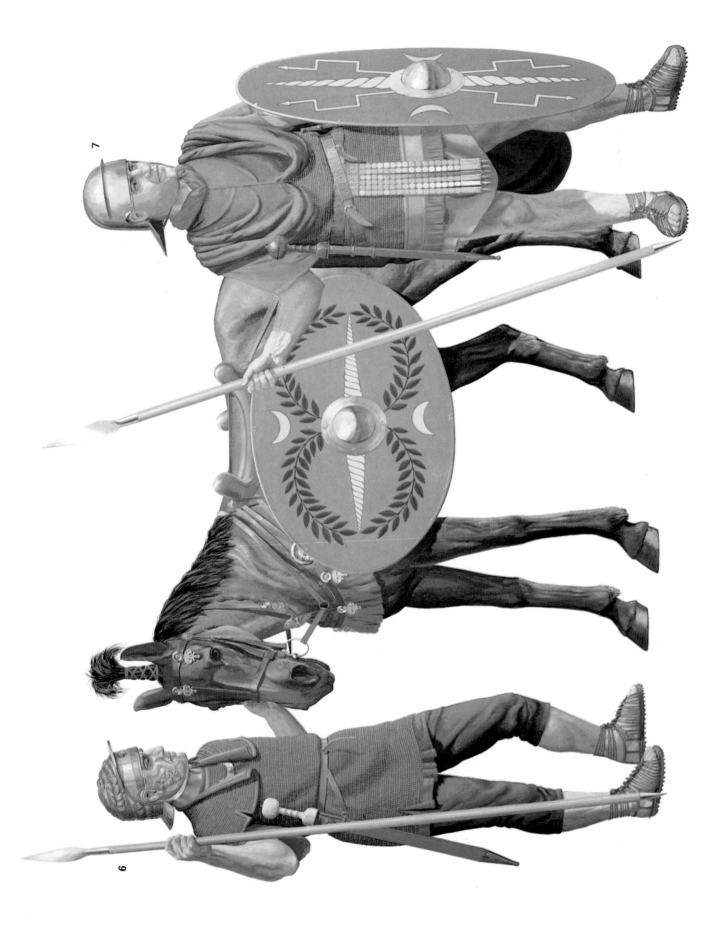

8

Left
A legionary of the second half of the 1st century AD. There is more archaeological evidence for this period than any other. Every item except his shield and *pilum* is based on contemporary evidence.

Right
A provincial legate of the 1st–2nd century AD based on imperial sculptures. He wears a short decorated muscled cuirass with a tie belt as the symbol of his rank.

9

Three types of auxiliary soldiers: slinger,
archer and clubman of the early 2nd century,
based on Trajan's column.

13

14

A *cornicen* and legionary of the early 2nd century based on Trajan's Column. The legionary is shown on the march with all his personal belongings and his food on a pole over his shoulder

15

Left
A Praetorian guardsman of the 2nd century based on a bas relief in the Louvre Museum. There is no archaeological evidence for his shield or helmet and his sword and belt are of legionary type.

Right
A legionary of c. 200 AD By now the rectangular *scutum* was being replaced with the flat oval shield and the sword moved to the left side. The evidence for his cuirass is very fragmentary

16

17

A cavalryman of the mid-3rd century dressed in sports armour. Most of the equipment shown comes from Straubing. His shield is one of the flat oval examples from Dura Europus.

Below
A cataphract of the mid-3rd century based on
the paintings from Dura Europus. **Right** A
cavalry officer c. 400 AD based on the diptych
of Stilicho.

Acknowledgments

The author would like to thank
Professor F. W. Walbank, Dr B.
Dobson and Professor A. M. Snodgrass
for reading through the text and for
their many suggestions. The author
would also like to thank the following
for their assistance and much-valued
advice:

Professor H. H. Scullard
The late Mr H. Russell Robinson of the Tower of London
Dr G. Ritchie
Dr H. Hurst of the British Carthage Expedition
Dr U. Schaaff of the Römisch Germanisches Zentralmuseum, Mainz
Dr I. Stead of the Romano-British Department of the British Museum
Dr V. Maxfield of the University of Exeter
Dr D. J. Breeze
Dr E. Künzl of the Romisch Germanisches Zentralmuseum, Mainz
Dr H. G. Horn of the Rheinisches Landesmuseum, Bonn
Dr K. V. Decker of the Mittelrheinisches Landesmuseum, Mainz
Mr M. Hassall of the Institute of Archaeology
Dr M. Roxam of the Institute of Archaeology
Mr M. Macdona
The Greek and Roman department of the British Museum
The Society for the Promotion of Hellenic Studies
The Society for the Promotion of Roman Studies
Lieutenant R. A. M. S. Melvin and the members
of Expedition Alpine Elephant

All photographs are by Peter Connolly
except the following:

13TL	Snark International
41	Wadsworth Athenaeum, Hartford, Connecticut
62	Staatliche Antikensammlungen und Glyptotek, Munich
72	Scala
111	Musee du Bardo, Tunis, photo William Graham
147, 148, 150BL	Rheinisches Landesmuseum
161TR	Macdonald Educational/ Bayntun Williams
196	Servizio Editoriale Fotografico
276B	Michael Holford/British Museum

Bibliography

General

W. Kendrick Pritchett
Studies in Ancient Greek Topography. *University of California Press 1965, 1969.*
New light on Thermopylae. *American Journal of Archaeology (62) 1958.*
The Greek State at War. *University of California Press 1971, 1974.*

A. R. Burn
Persia and the Greeks. *A. & C. Black 1962.*

N. G. L. Hammond
Battle of Salamis. *Journal of Hellenic Studies 1956.*

J. K. Anderson
Military Theory and Practice in the Age of Xenophon. *University of California Press 1970.*

M. Korfmann
The Sling as a Weapon. *Scientific American vol. 229 no. 4.*

A. M. Snodgrass
Early Greek Armour and Weapons. *Edinburgh University Press 1964.*
Arms and Armour of the Greeks. *Thames and Hudson 1967.*

E. Kunze
Bericht über die Ausgrabungen in Olympia. *Deutsches Archäologisches Institut.*

P. Roussel, M. Feyel
Le Règlement Militaire Trouvé a Amphipolis. *Revue Archéologique 1934, 1935.*

F. W. Walbank
A Historical Commentary on Polybius. *Oxford University Press 1957, 1967, 1979.*
Philip V of Macedon. *Cambridge 1940.*

M. M. Markle
The Macedonian Sarissa, Spear and Related Armor. *American Journal of Archaeology (81) 1977.*

V. Bianco Peroni
Die Schwerter in Italien (Prähistorische Bronzerunde). *Munich 1970.*

H. Henken
The Earliest European Helmets. *Peabody Museum, Harvard University 1971.*

V. Cianfarani
Antiche Civilta d'Abruzzo. *De Luca, Rome 1969.*

H. H. Scullard
The Etruscan Cities and Rome. *Thames and Hudson.*
Scipio Africanus: Soldier and

Politician. *Thames and Hudson 1970.*
The Elephant in the Greek and Roman
World. *Thames and Hudson 1974.*
E. T. Salmon
Samnium and the Samnites. *Cambridge
1967.*
Roman Colonisation under the
Republic. *Thames and Hudson 1969.*
U. Schaaff
Frülatenezeitliche Grabfunde mit
Helmen vom Typ Berru. and Keltische
Eisenhelme aus vorrömischer Zeit.
*Jahrbuch des Römisch Germanisches
Zentralmuseum, Mainz 1973, 1974.*
H. G. Horn, C. B. Rüger
Die Numider. *Rheinisches
Landesmuseum, Bonn 1980.*
H. Sandars
Weapons of the Iberians. *Archaeologia
(64) 1913.*
A. Schulten
Numantia. *Munich 1914–31.*
J. Kromayer and G. Veith
Schlachten-atlas zur antiken
Kriegsgeschichte. *Gotha 1922–*
T. Frank
Placentia and the Battle of the Trebbia.
Journal of Roman Studies 1919.
J. Harmand
L'armée et le Soldat à Rome de 107 à
50 avant notre ère. *A. & J. Picard
1967*
**B. Dobson (with contributions by
D. J. Breeze and V. A. Maxfield)**
Officers and Men of the Roman Army.
Croom Helm (in press).
D. J. Breeze and B. Dobson
Hadrian's Wall. *Allen Lane, Penguin
Books 1978. Chapters 5 and 6 with
bibliography*
G. R. Watson
The Roman Soldier. *Thames and
Hudson 1969.*
H. D. M. Parker
The Roman Legions. *Oxford 1928.*
G. L. Cheesman
The Auxilia of the Roman Imperial
Army. *Oxford 1914.*
H. Russell Robinson
The Armour of Imperial Rome. *Arms
and Armour Press 1975.*
M. I. Rostovtzeff
The excavation at Dura Europos.
6th season, 1936.
J. Oldenstein
Zur Ausrüstung römischer
Auxiliareinheiten. *Bericht der
Romisch-Germanischen Kommission
(57) 1976.*

H. Klumbach
Spätrömische Gardhelme. *Munich
1973.*
J. S. Morrison and R. T. Williams
Greek Oared Ships: 900–322 BC.
Cambridge 1968.
L. Casson
Ships and Seamanship in the Ancient
World. *Princetown 1971.*
H. Frost
The Punic Wreck in Sicily.
*International Journal of Nautical
Archaeology Vol. 2 no. 1 and Vol. 3
no. 1.*
G. Ucelli
Le Navi di Nemi. *Rome 1950.*
H. Hurst
The excavations at Carthage (The
Military Port). *The Antiquaries
Journal 1976 part II.*
F. E. Winter
Greek Fortifications. *Routledge and
Kegan Paul 1971.*
E. W. Marsden
Greek and Roman Artillery. *Oxford
1969.*
The Campaign of Gaugamela.
Liverpool University Press 1964.
J. B. Ward Perkins
Veii, the Historical Topography of the
Ancient City. *Papers of the British
School at Rome (29) 1961.*
M. J. Jones
Roman Fort-Defences to AD 117.
*British Archaeological Reports (21)
1975.*
D. Baatz
Recent Finds of Ancient Artillery.
Britannia (9) 1978.

The Late-Roman Army
A. H. M. Jones
The Later Roman Empire 284–602.
(1964), esp. ch. 17.
D. Hoffmann
Das spätrömische Bewegungsheer.
(1969/70).
H. I. Bell (and others)
The Abinnaeus Archive. *(1962).*
T. C. Skeat (ed.)
Papyri from Panopolis. *(1964), with
analysis by* **R. P. Duncan-Jones** *in
Chiron. 1978.*
**R. Goodburn and P. Bartholomew
(eds.)**
Aspects of the Notitia Dignitatum.
(1976).
E. N. Luttwak
The Grand Strategy of the Roman
Empire. *(1976).*
R. MacMullen
Soldier and Civilian in the Later
Roman Empire. *(1963).*
C. Pharr (trans.)
The Theodosian Code. *(1952).*
O. Seeck (ed.)
Notitia Dignitatum. *(1876).*

Ammianus Marcellinus, Julian and
Libanius are translated in the Loeb
Classical Library

Artillery

E. W. Marsden
Greek and Roman Artillery: Historical
Development. *(1969).*
D. Baatz
'Recent finds of ancient artillery'.
Britannia 9 (1978).

Fortifications

M. Todd
The Walls of Rome. *(1978).*
S. Johnson
The Roman Forts of the Saxon Shore.
(1976).

Congress of Roman Frontier's Studies.
Collected Papers.
H. von Petrikovits
'Fortifications in the north-western
Roman empire from the 3rd to the 5th
centuries AD'. *JRS 61 (1971).*

Index